AMERICAN GOVERNMENT
Readings and Cases

NINTH EDITION

PETER WOLL
Brandeis University

LITTLE, BROWN AND COMPANY

Boston   Toronto

Library of Congress Cataloging-in-Publication Data

American government.

Includes bibliographical references.
1. United States—Politics and government—
Collected works.   I. Woll, Peter, 1933–
JK21.A445   1987   320.973   86-20910
ISBN 0-316-95175-7

Library of Congress Catalog Card No. 86-20910

ISBN 0-316-95175-7

9 8 7 6 5 4 3 2 1

MV

Published simultaneously in Canada by Little, Brown & Company (Canada) Limited

Printed in the United States of America

This book is dedicated to
my mother,
RUTH C. WOLL,
and
to the memory of my father,
JOHN W. WOLL

Preface

Providing key classic and contemporary readings and cases that introduce students to the underpinnings and current practices of American government, this sourcebook complements regular texts by illustrating and amplifying important issues and concepts. At the same time, the organization and design of the book make it suitable for use as a core text. Extensive notes are included that prepare the ground for, connect, and comment upon the selections within the broader context of American government.

The new edition contains up-to-date and relevant material designed to stimulate student interest and discussion and at the same time to show how our government functions. As in previous editions, a balance is maintained among classical selections, important historical and current constitutional law cases, and contemporary readings that pinpoint and analyze evolving political trends.

The basic areas covered in this edition include the nature and origins of constitutional theory and practice; federalism and intergovernmental relations; civil liberties and civil rights; the organization and functions of political parties; elections and electoral behavior; political campaigning; the media and political consultants; the nature and functions of interest groups; the powers, responsibilities, and limitations of the presidency; the presidential establishment; presidential character and style; the president and the press; the scope of executive privilege; the rise of the bureaucracy and the implications of the administrative state to constitutional democracy; the role, powers, and functions of Congress; Congress and congressional staffers as part of the Washington political establishment; Congress and the electoral connection; the re-election incentive and differences between legislators' home styles and their Washington careers; the Supreme Court and the role of the judiciary, focusing upon and illustrating the ebb and flow of judicial activism and self-restraint.

The selections for the new edition were chosen not only to present students with important readings and cases that give them an understanding of American political institutions and processes, but also to heighten their interest and appreciation of the richness and excitement of politics.

The new edition continues to give students an appreciation of their rich political heritage through classic readings from *The Federalist*. Particularly emphasized are Federalist Papers 47, 48, and 51 (separation of powers and checks and balances); 10 (parties and interest groups); 39 (federalism); 70 (presidency); and 78 (judicial review).

Following the precedent of previous editions the text continues to present major Supreme Court cases, including *Marbury* v. *Madison* (1803), *McCulloch* v. *Maryland* (1819), and the key cases that have set the tone of contemporary constitutional law. The Supreme Court and the judiciary continue to be uniquely powerful in our political system, and the new edition has added the Court's precedent-setting school prayer (*Engel* v. *Vitale,* 1962) and abortion (*Roe* v. *Wade,* 1973) decisions to illustrate, along with the *Bakke* (1978) affirmative action decision, the sources of three major and continuing controversies over civil liberties and civil rights.

Throughout the text, students sample classic readings along with lively accounts of government and politics in action. The new edition strengthens the worthy cast of authors by adding Morton Grodzins's seminal discussion of the federal system; Samuel J. Eldersveld's provocative analysis of whether or not the party declined thesis is fact or fiction; Brookings Institution scholar Stephen Hess's depiction of the role of Washington reporters; Austin Ranney on the president and his party; Michael Nelson's defense of the current presidential nominating process; James David Barber's special focus on the Reagan presidency within the framework of his discussion of presidential character; James Q. Wilson on the rise of the bureaucratic state; Morris P. Fiorina's thesis that Congress is the keystone of the Washington establishment; and James Sundquist's discussion of representation and the will to govern within the context of congressional decline and resurgence.

Also new in the ninth edition are a number of articles by top-flight journalists that bring politics alive and rivet the reader's attention to the page. Ron Suskind focuses upon politics in the 1980s as he discusses the growing power of the political consultants who shape candidates' images and issues at all governmental levels. *Time* writer Evan Thomas complements a cover story by one of his colleagues on running with the PACs with a new account of influence peddling in Washington. *Washington Post* columnist and reporter David Broder addresses the question of who took the fun out of Congress in a fresh look at the increasingly complex and high pressured political environment of Capitol Hill. And Judge Irving R. Kaufman adds his views to the debate over "strict" versus "loose" constitutional construction.

As in previous editions, an extensive *Instructors Manual* accompanies the text. It provides a comprehensive guide to the selections, background material, and multiple-choice questions. Of course at the instructor's discretion any part of the manual may be reproduced for students as an instructional aid.

Over the years numerous individuals have generously given their time, energy, and ideas to help the author make this work a major American government source book. For his valuable ideas and suggestions, I would especially like to thank Neil Sullivan.

Finally, I would like to thank John Covell, whose editorial judgment was invaluable in shaping the final manuscript. Virginia Shine and Lilliane M. Chouinard skillfully guided the book's production. Elaine Herrmann and Lisa Carisella word-processed my notes and comments with an accurate touch.

P. W.

Contents

The Constitution was largely the result of political trade-offs among
the state delegations, and not a conspiracy of the elite or the result
of theoretical considerations.

The framers of the Constitution "represented the solid, conservative,
commercial and financial interests of the country...." They were
largely an economic elite seeking to preserve their property. They
were distrustful of majority rule and sought by every device possible
to structure the government in a way that would prevent the excesses
of democracy and safeguard the interests of the propertied class.

The Federalist will discuss, in a series of articles, why citizens should
support the proposed Constitution.

The Constitution provides for a system of separation of powers and
checks and balances designed to prevent the arbitrary exercise of gov-

federalism is symbolized by a three-layer cake, representing national, state, and local governmental levels. However, a more accurate image is a marble cake that mixes and often inseparably mingles colors. Shared rather than divided governmental functions characterize American federalism.

THE JUDICIAL SOURCES OF THREE MAJOR POLITICAL CONTROVERSIES OVER CIVIL LIBERTIES AND RIGHTS

The First Amendment's Establishment Clause prohibits, as part of its ban on government-sponsored religions, state-sponsored prayers in public schools. A New York state law requiring public school pupils to recite a short non-denominational prayer each day before their teachers violates the constitutional separation of church and state.

The constitutional right to privacy grants women the absolute right to have abortions during the first trimester of their pregnancies. Thereafter states have the authority to regulate abortions to preserve the life of the mother and human life, the extent of their regulatory powers being determined by the maturity of the pregnancy.

The use of quotas by a university to give preference to racial groups in an admissions program is a violation of the Equal Protection Clause of the Fourteenth Amendment. However, an applicant's race can be considered as one factor in the admissions process.

CONSTITUTIONAL BACKGROUND

Factions are groups that unite to serve selfish goals, not the national interest. It is necessary to control factions through constitutional means, one of which is the creation of a large republic that helps to disperse factions and reduces their influence on the national legislature.

Interest groups are controlled by a variety of constitutional provisions, including the separation of powers and checks and balances. Moreover, groups are checked because of their inability to claim the total loyalty of their members.

FUNCTIONS AND TYPES OF ELECTIONS

Critical elections are those in which voting patterns suggest that there has been a permanent realignment of the electorate between parties.

The group theory of politics is inadequate because of its failure to
recognize the need to develop standards of law that will be above the
selfish interests of pressure groups.

Interest groups interact with government primarily through the voices
of their leadership, which often do not reflect the involvement of the
membership of the groups.

CASE STUDIES IN PRESSURE GROUP POLITICS

Political Action Committees win friends and influence elections by
supplying the most important grist for the electoral mill—money.

An ever-present force in the nation's capital, lobbyists have almost
become a separate branch of the government in themselves. Often
former congressmen, staffers, and administration officials who use
their prior contacts to boost their influence, lobbyists represent a
wide array of clients as they prowl Washington's corridors of power
seeking to protect and advance special interests. Their styles and
techniques vary, the most influential lobbyists effectively employing
a mixture of public relations, expert advice, and one-on-one pressure
to achieve their ends.

THE MEDIA AS THE FOURTH ESTATE

"PAC journalism" often characterizes the Washington press corps,
which is a unique kind of interest group, a "fourth estate" that
derives its power from control over information. The relative autonomy of Washington reporters within their news organizations, combined with their collective inside-the-beltway tunnel vision, importantly
shapes and sometimes distorts the political information conveyed to
the public.

expertise, courtesy, and respect for the institution continue to characterize those senators who seek power and status in the body.

Numerous political obstacles confronted the Supreme Court as it decided the two *Brown* cases in 1954 and 1955. One surprising occurrence while the first *Brown* case was pending was an expression of sympathy for the Southern cause by President Eisenhower to Chief Justice Warren at a White House dinner where the attorney for the Southern states was present.

Appendices

AMERICAN GOVERNMENT

PART ONE

The Setting of the American System

CHAPTER 1

Constitutional Government

A remarkable fact about the United States government is that it has operated for almost 200 years on the basis of a written Constitution. Does this suggest unusual sagacity on the part of the Founding Fathers, or exceptional luck? What was involved in framing the Constitution?

Framing the Constitution: Elitist or Democratic Process?

In the following selection John P. Roche suggests that the framing of the Constitution was essentially a democratic process involving the reconciliation of a variety of state, political, and economic interests. Roche writes that "The Philadelphia Convention was not a College of Cardinals or a council of Platonic guardians working in a manipulative, predemocratic framework; it was a *nationalist* reform caucus that had to operate with great delicacy and skill in a political cosmos full of enemies to achieve one definitive goal—popular approbation." Roche recognizes that the framers, collectively, were an elite, but he is careful to point out that they were a political elite dedicated for the most part to establishing an effective and at the same time controlled national government that would be able to overcome the weaknesses of the Articles of Confederation. The framers were not, says Roche, a cohesive elite dedicated to a particular set of political or economic assumptions beyond the simple need to create a national government that would be capable of reconciling disparate state interests. The Constitution was "a vivid demonstration of effective democratic political action, and of the forging of a national elite which literally persuaded its countrymen to hoist themselves by their own bootstraps."

1
John P. Roche

THE FOUNDING FATHERS: A REFORM CAUCUS IN ACTION

Over the last century and a half, the work of the Constitutional Convention and the motives of the Founding Fathers have been analyzed under a number of different ideological auspices. To one generation of historians, the hand of God was moving in the assembly; under a later dispensation, the dialectic (at various levels of philosophical sophistication) replaced the Deity: "relationships of production" moved into the niche previously reserved for Love of Country. Thus in counterpart to the *zeitgeist,* the framers have undergone miraculous metamorphoses: at one time acclaimed as liberals and bold social engineers, today they appear in the guise of sound Burkean conservatives, men who in our time would subscribe to *Fortune,* look to Walter Lippmann for political theory, and chuckle patronizingly at the antics of Barry Goldwater. The implicit assumption is that if James Madison were among us, he would be President of the Ford Foundation, while Alexander Hamilton would chair the Committee for Economic Development.

The "Fathers" have thus been admitted to our best circles; the revolutionary ferocity which confiscated all Tory property in reach and populated New Brunswick with outlaws has been converted by the "Miltown School" of American historians into a benign dedication to "consensus" and "prescriptive rights." The Daughters of the American Revolution have, through the ministrations of Professors Boorstin, Hartz, and Rossiter, at last found ancestors worthy of their descendants. It is not my purpose here to argue that the "Fathers" were, in fact, radical revolutionaries; that proposition has been brilliantly demonstrated by Robert R. Palmer in his *Age of the Democratic Revolution.* My concern is with the future position that not only were they revolutionaries, but also they were democrats. Indeed, in my view, there is one fundamental truth about the Founding Fathers that *every* generation of zeitgeisters has done its best to obscure: they were first and foremost superb democratic politicians. I suspect that in a contemporary setting, James Madison would be Speaker of the House of Representatives and Hamilton would be the *eminence grise* dominating

From John P. Roche, "The Founding Fathers: A Reform Caucus in Action," *American Political Science Review* (December 1961). Reprinted by permission.

(*pace* Theodore Sorensen or Sherman Adams) the Executive Office of the President. They were, with their colleagues, *political men*—not metaphysicians, disembodied conservatives or Agents of History—and as recent research into the nature of American politics in the 1780s confirms, they were committed (perhaps willy-nilly) to working within the democratic framework, within a universe of public approval. Charles Beard *and* the filiopietists to the contrary notwithstanding, the Philadelphia Convention was not a College of Cardinals or a council of Platonic guardians working within a manipulative, predemocratic framework; it was a *nationalist* reform caucus which had to operate with great delicacy and skill in a political cosmos full of enemies to achieve the one definitive goal—popular approbation.

Perhaps the time has come, to borrow Walton Hamilton's fine phrase, to raise the framers from immortality to mortality, to give them credit for their magnificent demonstration of the art of democratic politics. The point must be reemphasized; they *made* history and did it within the limits of consensus. There was nothing inevitable about the future in 1787; the *zeitgeist,* that fine Hegelian technique of begging causal questions, could only be discerned in retrospect. What they did was to hammer out a pragmatic compromise which would both bolster the "national interest" and be acceptable to the people. What inspiration they got came from their collective experience as professional politicians in a democratic society. As John Dickinson put it to his fellow delegates on August 13, "Experience must be our guide. Reason may mislead us."

In this context, let us examine the problems they confronted and the solutions they evolved. The Convention has been described picturesquely as a counter-revolutionary junta and the Constitution as a coup d'état, but this has been accomplished by withdrawing the whole history of the movement for constitutional reform from its true context. No doubt the goals of the constitutional elite were "subversive" to the existing political order, but it is overlooked that their subversion could only have succeeded if the people of the United States endorsed it by regularized procedures. Indubitably they were "plotting" to establish a much stronger central government than existed under the Articles, but only in the sense in which one could argue equally well that John F. Kennedy was, from 1956 to 1960, "plotting" to become President. In short, on the fundamental *procedural* level, the Constitutionalists had to work according to the prevailing rules of the game. Whether they liked it or not is a topic for spiritualists—and is irrelevant: one may be quite certain that had Washington agreed to play the de Gaulle (as the Cincinnati once urged), Hamilton would willingly have held his horse, but such fertile speculation in no way alters the actual context in which events took place.

I

When the Constitutionalists went forth to subvert the Confederation, they utilized the mechanisms of political legitimacy. And the roadblocks which confronted them were formidable. At the same time, they were endowed with certain potent political assets. The history of the United States from 1786 to 1790 was largely one of a masterful employment of political expertise by the Constitutionalists as against bumbling, erratic behavior by the opponents of reform. Effectively, the Constitutionalists had to induce the states, by democratic techniques of coercion, to emasculate themselves. To be specific, if New York had refused to join the new Union, the project was doomed; yet before New York was safely in, the reluctant state legislature had *suasponte* to take the following steps: (1) agree to send delegates to the Philadelphia Convention; (2) provide maintenance for these delegates (these were distinct stages: New Hampshire was early in naming delegates, but did not provide for their maintenance until July); (3) set up the special ad hoc convention to decide on ratification; and (4) concede to the decision of the ad hoc convention that New York should participate. New York admittedly was a tricky state, with a strong interest in a status quo which permitted her to exploit New Jersey and Connecticut, but the same legal hurdles existed in every state. And at the risk of becoming boring, it must be reiterated that the *only* weapon in the Constitutionalist arsenal was an effective mobilization of public opinion.

The group which undertook this struggle was an interesting amalgam of a few dedicated nationalists with the self-interested spokesmen of various parochial bailiwicks. The Georgians, for example, wanted a strong central authority to provide military protection for their huge, underpopulated state against the Creek Confederacy; Jerseymen and Connecticuters wanted to escape from economic bondage to New York; the Virginians hoped to establish a system which would give that great state its rightful place in the councils of the republic. The dominant figures in the politics of these states therefore cooperated in the call for the Convention. In other states, the thrust towards national reform was taken up by opposition groups who added the "national interest" to their weapons system; in Pennsylvania, for instance, the group fighting to revise the Constitution of 1776 came out four-square behind the Constitutionalists, and in New York, Hamilton and the Schuyler *ambiance* took the same tack against George Clinton. There was, of course, a large element of personality in the affair: there is reason to suspect that Patrick Henry's opposition to the Convention and the Constitution was founded on his conviction that Jefferson was behind both, and a close study of local politics elsewhere would surely reveal that others supported the Constitution for the simple (and politically quite sufficient) reason that the "wrong" people were against it.

To say this is not to suggest that the Constitution rested on a foundation of impure or base motives. It is rather to argue that in politics there are no immaculate conceptions, and that in the drive for a stronger general government, motives of all sorts played a part. Few men in the history of mankind have espoused a view of the "common good" or "public interest" that militated against their private status; even Plato with all his reverence for disembodied reason managed to put philosophers on top of the pile. Thus it is not surprising that a number of diversified private interests joined to push the nationalist public interest; what would have been surprising was the absence of such a pragmatic united front. And the fact remains that, however motivated, these men did demonstrate a willingness to compromise their parochial interests in behalf of an ideal which took shape before their eyes and under their ministrations.

As Stanley Elkins and Eric McKitrick have suggested in a perceptive essay [76 *Political Science Quarterly* 181 (1961)], what distinguished the leaders of the Constitutionalist caucus from their enemies was a "Continental" approach to political, economic and military issues. To the extent that they shared an institutional base of operations, it was the Continental Congress (thirty-nine of the delegates to the Federal Convention had served in Congress), and this was hardly a locale which inspired respect for the state governments. Robert de Jouvenal observed French politics half a century ago and noted that a revolutionary Deputy had more in common with a nonrevolutionary Deputy than he had with a revolutionary non-Deputy; similarly one can surmise that membership in the Congress under the Articles of Confederation worked to establish a continental frame of reference, that a Congressman from Pennsylvania and one from South Carolina would share a universe of discourse which provided them with a conceptual common denominator vis-à-vis their respective state legislatures. This was particularly true with respect to external affairs: the average state legislator was probably about as concerned with foreign policy then as he is today, but Congressmen were constantly forced to take the broad view of American prestige, were compelled to listen to the reports of Secretary John Jay and to the dispatches and pleas from their frustrated envoys in Britain, France and Spain. From considerations such as these, a "Continental" ideology developed which seems to have demanded a revision of our domestic institutions primarily on the ground that only by invigorating our general government could we assume our rightful place in the international arena. Indeed, an argument with great force—particularly since Washington was its incarnation—urged that our very survival in the Hobbesian jungle of world politics depended upon a reordering and strengthening of our national sovereignty.

The great achievement of the Constitutionalists was their ultimate success in convincing the elected representatives of a majority of the white male population that change was imperative. A small group of political leaders with a Continental vision and essentially a consciousness of the

United States' *international* impotence, provided the matrix of the movement. To their standard other leaders rallied with their own parallel ambitions. Their great assets were (1) the presence in their caucus of the one authentic American "father figure," George Washington, whose prestige was enormous; (2) the energy and talent of their leadership (in which one must include the towering intellectuals of the time, John Adams and Thomas Jefferson, despite their absence abroad), and their communications "network," which was far superior to anything on the opposition side; (3) the preemptive skill which made "their" issue The Issue and kept the locally oriented opposition permanently on the defensive; and (4) the subjective consideration that these men were spokesmen of a new and compelling credo: *American* nationalism, that ill-defined but nonetheless potent sense of collective purpose that emerged from the American Revolution.

Despite great institutional handicaps, the Constitutionalists managed in the mid-1780s to mount an offensive which gained momentum as years went by. Their greatest problem was lethargy, and paradoxically, the number of barriers in their path may have proved an advantage in the long run. Beginning with the initial battle to get the Constitutional Convention called and delegates appointed, they could never relax, never let up the pressure. In practical terms, this meant that the local "organizations" created by the Constitutionalists were perpetually in movement building up their cadres for the next fight. (The word *organization* has to be used with great caution: a political organization in the United States—as in contemporary England—generally consisted of a magnate and his following, or a coalition of magnates. This did not necessarily mean that it was "undemocratic" or "aristocratic," in the Aristotelian sense of the word: while a few magnates such as the Livingstons could draft their followings, most exercised their leadership without coercion on the basis of popular endorsement. The absence of organized opposition did not imply the impossibility of competition any more than low public participation in elections necessarily indicated an undemocratic suffrage.)

The Constitutionalists got the jump on the "opposition" (a collective noun: oppositions would be more correct) at the outset with the demand for a Convention. Their opponents were caught in an old political trap: they were not being asked to approve any specific program of reform, but only to endorse a meeting to discuss and recommend needed reforms. If they took a hard line at the first stage, they were put in the position of glorifying the status quo and of denying the need for *any* changes. Moreover, the Constitutionalists could go to the people with a persuasive argument for "fair play"—"How can you condemn reform before you know precisely what is involved?" Since the state legislatures obviously would have the final say on any proposals that might emerge from the Convention, the Constitutionalists were merely reasonable men asking for a chance. Besides, since they did not make any concrete proposals at that stage, they were in a position to capitalize on every sort of generalized discontent with the Confederation.

Perhaps because of their poor intelligence system, perhaps because of overconfidence generated by the failure of all previous efforts to alter the Articles, the opposition awoke too late to the dangers that confronted them in 1787. Not only did the Constitutionalists manage to get every state but Rhode Island (where politics was enlivened by a party system reminiscent of the "Blues" and the "Greens" in the Byzantine Empire) to appoint delegates to Philadelphia, but when the results were in, it appeared that they dominated the delegations. Given the apathy of the opposition, this was a natural phenomenon: in an ideologically nonpolarized political atmosphere those who get appointed to a special committee are likely to be the men who supported the movement for its creation. Even George Clinton, who seems to have been the first opposition leader to awake to the possibility of trouble, could not prevent the New York legislature from appointing Alexander Hamilton—though he did have the foresight to send two of his henchmen to dominate the delegation. Incidentally, much has been made of the fact that the delegates to Philadelphia were not elected by the people; some have adduced this fact as evidence of the "undemocratic" character of the gathering. But put in the context of the time, this argument is wholly specious: the central government under the Articles was considered a creature of the component states and in all the states but Rhode Island, Connecticut, and New Hampshire, members of the national Congress were chosen by the state legislatures. This was not a consequence of elitism or fear of the mob; it was a logical extension of states' rights doctrine to guarantee that the national institution did not end-run the state legislatures and make direct contact with the people.

II

With delegations safely named, the focus shifted to Philadelphia. While waiting for a quorum to assemble, James Madison got busy and drafted the so-called Randolph or Virginia Plan with the aid of the Virginia delegation. This was a political master-stroke. Its consequence was that once business got underway, the framework of discussion was established on Madison's terms. There was no interminable argument over agenda; instead the delegates took the Virginia Resolutions—"just for purposes of discussion"—as their point of departure. And along with Madison's proposals, many of which were buried in the course of the summer, went his major premise: a new start on a Constitution rather than piecemeal amendment. This was not necessarily revolutionary—but Madison's proposal that this "lump sum" amendment go into effect after approval by nine states (the Articles required unanimous state approval for any amendment) was thoroughly subversive.

Standard treatments of the Convention divide the delegates into "nationalists" and "states' righters" with various improvised shadings ("moderate nationalists," etc.), but these are *a posteriori* categories which obfuscate more than they clarify. What is striking to one who analyzes the Convention as a case study in democratic politics is the lack of clear-cut ideological divisions in the Convention. Indeed, I submit that the evidence— Madison's *Notes,* the correspondence of the delegates, and debates on ratification—indicates that this was a remarkably homogeneous body on the ideological level. Yates and Lansing, Clinton's two chaperones for Hamilton, left in disgust on July 10. (Is there anything more tedious than sitting through endless disputes on matters one deems fundamentally misconceived? It takes an iron will to spend a hot summer as an ideological *agent provocateur.*) Luther Martin, Maryland's bibulous narcissist, left on September 4 in a huff when he discovered that others did not share his self-esteem; others went home for personal reasons. But the hard core of delegates accepted a grinding regimen throughout the attrition of a Philadelphia summer precisely because they shared the Constitutionalist goal.

Basic differences of opinion emerged, of course, but these were not ideological; they were *structural.* If the so-called "states' rights" group had not accepted the fundamental purposes of the Convention, they could simply have pulled out and by doing so have aborted the whole enterprise. Instead of bolting, they returned day after day to argue and to compromise. An interesting symbol of this basic homogeneity was the initial agreement on secrecy: these professional politicians did not want to become prisoners of publicity; they wanted to retain that freedom of maneuver which is only possible when men are not forced to take public stands in the preliminary stages of negotiation. There was no legal means of binding the tongues of the delegates: at any stage in the game a delegate with basic principled objections to the emerging project could have taken the stump (as Luther Martin did after his exit) and denounced the convention to the skies. Yet Madison did not even inform Thomas Jefferson in Paris of the course of the deliberations and available correspondence indicates that the delegates generally observed the injunction. Secrecy is certainly uncharacteristic of any assembly marked by strong ideological polarization. This was noted at the time: the *New York Daily Advertiser,* August 14, 1787, commented that the "profound secrecy hitherto observed by the Convention [we consider] a happy omen, as it demonstrates that the spirit of party on any great and essential point cannot have arisen to any height."

Commentators on the Constitution who have read *The Federalist* in lieu of reading the actual debates have credited the Fathers with the invention of a sublime concept called "Federalism." Unfortunately *The Federalist* is probative evidence for only one proposition: that Hamilton and Madison were inspired propagandists with a genius for retrospective symmetry. Federalism, as the theory is generally defined, was an improvisation which was later promoted into a political theory. Experts on "federalism" should take to heart the advice of David Hume, who warned in his *Of the Rise and Progress of the Arts and Sciences* that "there is no subject in which we must proceed with more caution than in [history], lest we assign causes which never existed and reduce what is merely contingent to stable and universal principles." In any event, the final balance in the Constitution between the states and the nation must have come as a great disappointment to Madison, while Hamilton's unitary views are too well known to need elucidation.

It is indeed astonishing how those who have glibly designated James Madison the "father" of Federalism have overlooked the solid body of fact which indicates that he shared Hamilton's quest for a unitary central government. To be specific, they have avoided examining the clear import of the Madison-Virginia Plan, and have disregarded Madison's dogged inch-by-inch retreat from the bastions of centralization. The Virginia Plan envisioned a unitary national government effectively freed from and dominant over the states. The lower house of the national legislature was to be elected directly by the people of the states with membership proportional to population. The upper house was to be selected by the lower and the two chambers would elect the executive and choose the judges. The national government would be thus cut completely loose from the states.

The structure of the general government was freed from state control in a truly radical fashion, but the scope of the authority of the national sovereign as Madison initially formulated it was breathtaking—it was a formulation worthy of the Sage of Malmesbury himself. The national legislature was to be empowered to disallow the acts of state legislatures, and the central government was vested, in addition to the powers of the nation under the Articles of Confederation, with plenary authority wherever "the separate States are incompetent or in which the harmony of the United States may be interrupted by the exercise of individual legislation." Finally, just to lock the door against state intrusion, the national Congress was to be given the power to use military force on recalcitrant states. This was Madison's "model" of an ideal national government, though it later received little publicity in *The Federalist.*

The interesting thing was the reaction of the Convention to this militant program for a strong autonomous central government. Some delegates were startled, some obviously leery of so comprehensive a project of reform, but nobody set off any fireworks and nobody walked out. Moreover, in the two weeks that followed, the Virginia Plan received substantial endorsement *en principe;* the initial temper of the gathering can be deduced from the approval "without debate or dissent," on May 31, of the Sixth Resolution which granted Congress the authority to disallow state legislation "contravening *in its opinion* the Articles of Union." Indeed, an amendment was included to bar states from contravening national treaties.

The Virginia Plan may therefore be considered, in ideological terms, as the delegates' Utopia, but as the discussions continued and became more specific, many of those present began to have second thoughts. After all, they were not residents of Utopia or guardians in Plato's Republic who could simply impose a philosophical ideal on subordinate strata of the population. They were practical politicians in a democratic society, and no matter what their private dreams might be, they had to take home an acceptable package and defend it—and their own political futures—against predictable attack. On June 14 the breaking point between dream and reality took place. Apparently realizing that under the Virginia Plan, Massachusetts, Virginia, and Pennsylvania could virtually dominate the national government—and probably appreciating that to sell this program to "the folks back home" would be impossible—the delegates from the small states dug in their heels and demanded time for a consideration of alternatives. One gets a graphic sense of the inner politics from John Dickinson's reproach to Madison: "You see the consequences of pushing things too far. Some of the members from the small States wish for two branches in the General Legislature and are friends to a good National Government; but we would sooner submit to a foreign power than . . . be deprived of an equality of suffrage in both branches of the Legislature, and thereby be thrown under the domination of the large States."

The bare outline of the *Journal* entry for Tuesday, June 14, is suggestive to anyone with extensive experience in deliberative bodies. "It was moved by Mr. Patterson [*sic,* Paterson's name was one of those consistently misspelled by Madison and everybody else] seconded by Mr. Randolph that the further consideration of the report from the Committee of the whole House [endorsing the Virginia Plan] be postponed till tomorrow and before the question for postponement was taken. It was moved by Mr. Randolph seconded by Mr. Patterson that the House adjourn." The House adjourned by obvious prearrangement of the two principals: since the preceding Saturday when Brearley and Paterson of New Jersey had announced their fundamental discontent with the representational features of the Virginia Plan, the informal pressure had certainly been building up to slow down the steamroller. Doubtless there were extended arguments at the Indian Queen between Madison and Paterson, the latter insisting that events were moving rapidly towards a probably disastrous conclusion, towards a political suicide pact. Now the process of accommodation was put into action smoothly—and wisely, given the character and strength of the doubters. Madison had the votes, but this was one of those situations where the enforcement of mechanical majoritarianism could easily have destroyed the objectives of the majority: the Constitutionalists were in quest of a qualitative as well as a quantitative consensus. This was hardly from deference to local Quaker custom; it was a political imperative if they were to attain ratification.

III

According to the standard script, at this point the "states' rights" group intervened in force behind the New Jersey Plan, which has been characteristically portrayed as a reversion to the status quo under the Articles of Confederation with but minor modifications. A careful examination of the evidence indicates that only in a marginal sense is this an accurate description. It is true that the New Jersey Plan put the states back into the institutional picture, but one could argue that to do so was a recognition of political reality rather than an affirmation of states' rights. A serious case can be made that the advocates of the New Jersey Plan, far from being ideological addicts of states' rights, intended to substitute for the Virginia Plan a system which would both retain strong national power and have a chance of adoption in the states. The leading spokesman for the project asserted quite clearly that his views were based more on counsels of expediency than on principle; said Paterson on June 16: "I came here not to speak my own sentiments, but the sentiments of those who sent me. Our object is not such a Governmt. as may be best in itself, but such a one as our Constituents have authorized us to prepare, and as they will approve." This is Madison's version; in Yates's transcription, there is a crucial sentence following the remarks above: "I believe that a little practical virtue is to be preferred to the finest theoretical principles, which cannot be carried into effect." In his preliminary speech on June 9, Paterson had stated "to the public mind we must accommodate ourselves," and in his notes for this and his later effort as well, the emphasis is the same. The *structure* of government under the Articles should be retained:

> 2. Because it accords with the Sentiments of the People
>   [Proof:] 1. Coms. [Commissions from state legislatures defining the jurisdiction of the delegates]
> 2. News-papers—Political Barometer. Jersey never would have sent Delegates under the first [Virginia] Plan—
>   Not here to sport Opinions of my own. Wt. [What] can be done. A little practicable Virtue preferrable to Theory.

This was a defense of political acumen, not of states' rights. In fact, Paterson's notes of his speech can easily be construed as an argument for attaining the substantive objectives of the Virginia Plan by a sound political route, i.e., pouring the new wine in the old bottles. With a shrewd eye, Paterson queried:

> Will the Operation, and Force of the [central] Govt. depend upon the mode of Representn.—No—it will depend upon the Quantum of Power lodged in the leg. ex. and judy. Departments—Give [the existing] Congress the same Powers that you intend to give the two Branches, [under

the Virginia Plan] and I apprehend they will act with as much Propriety and more Energy....

In other words, the advocates of the New Jersey Plan concentrated their fire on what they held to be the *political liabilities* of the Virginia Plan— which were matters of institutional structure—rather than on the proposed scope of national authority. Indeed, the Supremacy Clause of the Constitution first saw the light of day in Paterson's Sixth Resolution; the New Jersey Plan contemplated the use of military force to secure compliance with national law; and finally Paterson made clear his view that under either the Virginia or the New Jersey systems, the general government would " . . . act on individuals and not on states." From the states' rights viewpoint, this was heresy: the fundament of that doctrine was the proposition that any central government had as its constituents the states, not the people, and could only reach the people through the agency of the state government.

Paterson then reopened the agenda of the Convention, but he did so within a distinctly nationalist framework. Paterson's position was one of favoring a strong central government in principle, but opposing one which in fact *put the big states in the saddle.* (The Virginia Plan, for all its abstract merits, did very well by Virginia.) As evidence for this speculation, there is a curious and intriguing proposal among Paterson's preliminary drafts of the New Jersey Plan:

> Whereas it is necessary in Order to form the People of the U.S. of America in to a Nation, that the States should be consolidated, by which means all the Citizens thereof will become equally intitled to and will equally participate in the same Privileges and Rights . . . it is therefore resolved, that all the Lands contained within the Limits of each state individually, and of the U.S. generally be considered as constituting one Body or Mass, and be divided into thirteen or more integral parts.
>
> Resolved, That such Divisions or integral Parts shall be styled Districts.

This makes it sound as though Paterson was prepared to accept a strong unified central government along the lines of the Virginia Plan if the existing states were eliminated. He may have gotten the idea from his New Jersey colleague Judge David Brearley, who on June 9 had commented that the only remedy to the dilemma over representation was "that a map of the U.S. be spread out, that all the existing boundaries be erased, and that a new partition of the whole be made into 13 equal parts." According to Yates, Brearley added at this point, "then a government on the present [Virginia Plan] system will be just."

This proposition was never pushed—it was patently unrealistic—but one can appreciate its purpose: it would have separated the men from the boys in the large-state delegations. How attached would the Virginians have been to their reform principles if Virginia were to disappear as a component geographical unit (the largest) for representational purposes? Up to this point, the Virginians had been in the happy position of supporting high ideals with that inner confidence born of knowledge that the "public interest" they endorsed would nourish their private interest. Worse, they had shown little willingness to compromise. Now the delegates from the small states announced that they were unprepared to be offered up as sacrificial victims to a "national interest" which reflected Virginia's parochial ambition. Caustic Charles Pinckney was not far off when he remarked sardonically that "the whole [conflict] comes to this": "Give N. Jersey an equal vote, and she will dismiss her scruples, and concur in the Natl. system." What he rather unfairly did not add was that the Jersey delegates were not free agents who could adhere to their private convictions; they had to take back, sponsor and risk their reputations on the reforms approved by the Convention—and in New Jersey, not in Virginia.

Paterson spoke on Saturday, and one can surmise that over the weekend there was a good deal of consultation, argument, and caucusing among the delegates. One member at least prepared a full length address: on Monday Alexander Hamilton, previously mute, rose and delivered a six-hour oration. It was a remarkably apolitical speech; the gist of his position was that *both* the Virginia and New Jersey Plans were inadequately centralist, and he detailed a reform program which was reminiscent of the Protectorate under the Cromwellian *Instrument of Government* of 1653. It has been suggested that Hamilton did this in the best political tradition to emphasize the moderate character of the Virginia Plan, to give the cautious delegates something *really* to worry about; but this interpretation seems somehow too clever. Particularly since the sentiments Hamilton expressed happened to be completely consistent with those he privately—and sometimes publicly—expressed throughout his life. He wanted, to take a striking phrase from a letter to George Washington, a "strong well mounted government"; in essence, the Hamilton Plan contemplated an elected life monarch, virtually free of public control, on the Hobbesian ground that only in this fashion could strength and stability be achieved. The other alternatives, he argued, would put policy-making at the mercy of the passions of the mob; only if the sovereign was beyond the reach of selfish influence would it be possible to have government in the interests of the whole community.

From all accounts, this was a masterful and compelling speech, but (aside from furnishing John Lansing and Luther Martin with ammunition for later use against the Constitution) it made little impact. Hamilton was simply transmitting on a different wavelength from the rest of the delegates; the latter adjourned after his great effort, admired his rhetoric, and then returned to business. It was rather as if they had taken a day off to attend the opera. Hamilton, never a particularly patient man or much of a negotiator, stayed for another ten days and then left, in considerable disgust, for New York. Although he came back to Philadelphia sporadically and attended the last two weeks of the Convention, Hamilton played no part in the laborious task of hammering out the Constitution. His day came later when he led the New York Constitutionalists into the savage imbroglio over ratification—an arena in which his unmatched talent for dirty political infighting may well have won the day. For instance, in the New York Ratifying Convention, Lansing threw back into Hamilton's teeth the sentiments the latter had expressed in his June 18 oration in the Convention. However, having since retreated to the fine defensive positions immortalized in *The Federalist,* the Colonel flatly denied that he had ever been an enemy of the states, or had believed that conflict between states and nation was inexorable! As Madison's authoritative *Notes* did not appear until 1840, and there had been no press coverage, there was no way to verify his assertions, so in the words of the reporter, "a warm personal altercation between [Lansing and Hamilton] engrossed the remainder of the day [June 28, 1788]."

IV

On Tuesday morning, June 19, the vacation was over. James Madison led off with a long, carefully reasoned speech analyzing the New Jersey Plan which, while intellectually vigorous in its criticisms, was quite conciliatory in mood. "The great difficulty," he observed, "lies in the affair of Representation; and if this could be adjusted, all others would be surmountable." (As events were to demonstrate, this diagnosis was correct.) When he finished, a vote was taken on whether to continue with the Virginia Plan as the nucleus for a new constitution: seven states voted "Yes"; New York, New Jersey, and Delaware voted "No"; and Maryland, whose position often depended on which delegates happened to be on the floor, divided. Paterson, it seems, lost decisively; yet in a fundamental sense he and his allies had achieved their purpose: from that day onward, it could never be forgotten that the state governments loomed ominously in the background and that no verbal incantations could exorcise their power. Moreover, nobody bolted the Convention: Paterson and his colleagues took their defeat in stride and set to work to modify the Virginia Plan, particularly with respect to its provisions on representation in the national legislature. Indeed, they won an immediate rhetorical bonus; when Oliver Ellsworth of Connecticut rose to move that the word "national" be expunged from the Third Virginia Resolution ("Resolved that a *national* Government ought to be established consisting of a *supreme* Legislative, Executive and Judiciary"), Randolph agreed and the motion passed unanimously. The process of compromise had begun.

For the next two weeks, the delegates circled around the problem of legislative representation. The Connecticut delegation appears to have evolved a possible compromise quite early in the debates, but the Virginians and particularly Madison (unaware that he would later be acclaimed as the prophet of "federalism") fought obdurately against providing for equal representation of states in the second chamber. There was a good deal of acrimony and at one point Benjamin Franklin—of all people—proposed the institution of a daily prayer; practical politicians in the gathering, however, were meditating more on the merits of a good committee than on the utility of Divine intervention. On July 2, the ice began to break when through a number of fortuitous events—and one that seems deliberate—the majority against equality of representation was converted into a dead tie. The Convention had reached the stage where it was "ripe" for a solution (presumably all the therapeutic speeches had been made), and the South Carolinians proposed a committee. Madison and James Wilson wanted none of it, but with only Pennsylvania dissenting, the body voted to establish a working party on the problem of representation.

The members of this committee, one from each state, were elected by the delegates—and a very interesting committee it was. Despite the fact that the Virginia Plan had held majority support up to that date, neither Madison nor Randolph was selected (Mason was the Virginian) and Baldwin of Georgia, whose shift in position had resulted in the tie, was chosen. From the composition, it was clear that this was not to be a "fighting" committee: the emphasis in membership was on what might be described as "second-level political entrepreneurs." On the basis of the discussions up to that time, only Luther Martin of Maryland could be described as a "bitter-ender." Admittedly, some divination enters into this sort of analysis, but one does get a sense of the mood of the delegates from these choices—including the interesting selection of Benjamin Franklin, despite his age and intellectual wobbliness, over the brilliant and incisive Wilson or the sharp, polemical Gouverneur Morris, to represent Pennsylvania. His passion for conciliation was more valuable at this juncture than Wilson's logical genius, or Morris's acerbic wit.

There is a common rumor that the framers divided their time between philosophical discussions of government and reading the classics in political theory. Perhaps this is as good a time as any to note that their concerns were highly practical, that they spent little time canvassing abstractions. A number of them had some acquaintance with the history of political theory (probably gained from reading John Adams's monumental compilation *A Defense of the Constitutions of Government,* the first volume of which appeared in 1786), and it was a poor rhetorician indeed who could not cite Locke, Montesquieu, or Harrington *in support* of a desired goal. Yet up to this point in the deliberations, no one had expounded a defense of states' rights or the "separation of powers" on anything resembling a theoretical basis. It should be reiterated that the Madison model had no room either for the states or for the "separation of powers": effectively *all* governmental power was vested in the national legislature. The merits of Montesquieu did not turn up until *The Federalist;* and although a perverse argument could be made that Madison's ideal was truly in the tradition of John Locke's *Second Treatise of Government,* the Locke whom the American rebels treated as an honorary president was a pluralistic defender of vested rights, not of parliamentary supremacy.

It would be tedious to continue a blow-by-blow analysis of the work of the delegates; the critical fight was over representation of the states and once the Connecticut Compromise was adopted on July 17, the Convention was over the hump. Madison, James Wilson, and Gouverneur Morris of New York (who was there representing Pennsylvania!) fought the compromise all the way in a last-ditch effort to get a unitary state with parliamentary supremacy. But their allies deserted them and they demonstrated after their defeat the essential opportunist character of their objections—using "opportunist" here in a nonpejorative sense, to indicate a willingness to swallow their objections and get on with the business. Moreover, once the compromise had carried (by five states to four, with one state divided), its advocates threw themselves vigorously into the job of strengthening the general government's substantive powers—as might have been predicted, indeed, from Paterson's early statements. It nourishes an increased respect for Madison's devotion to the art of politics, to realize that this dogged fighter could sit down six months later and prepare essays for *The Federalist* in contradiction to his basic convictions about the true course the Convention should have taken.

V

Two tricky issues will serve to illustrate the later process of accommodation. The first was the institutional position of the Executive. Madison argued for an executive chosen by the national legislature and on May 29 this had been adopted with a provision that after his seven-year term was concluded, the chief magistrate should not be eligible for reelection. In late July this was reopened and for a week the matter was argued from several different points of view. A good deal of desultory speech-making ensued, but the gist of the problem was the opposition from two sources to election by the legislature. One group felt that the states should have a hand in the process; another small but influential circle urged direct election by the people. There were a number of proposals: election by the people, election by state governors, by electors chosen by state legislatures, by the national legislature (James Wilson, perhaps ironically, proposed at one point that an Electoral College be chosen by lot from the national legislature!), and there was some resemblance to three-dimensional chess in the dispute because of the presence of two other variables, length of tenure and reeligibility. Finally, after opening, reopening, and re-reopening the debate, the thorny problem was consigned to a committee for absolution.

The Brearley Committee on Postponed Matters was a superb aggregation of talent and its compromise on the Executive was a masterpiece of political improvisation. (The Electoral College, its creation, however, had little in its favor as an *institution* — as the delegates well appreciated.) The point of departure for all discussion about the presidency in the Convention was that in immediate terms, the problem was nonexistent; in other words, everybody present knew that under any system devised, George Washington would be President. Thus they were dealing in the future tense and to a body of working politicians the merits of the Brearley proposal were obvious: everybody got a piece of cake. (Or to put it more academically, each viewpoint could leave the Convention and argue to its constituents that it had *really* won the day.) First, the state legislatures had the right to determine the mode of selection of the electors; second, the small states received a bonus in the Electoral College in the form of a guaranteed minimum of three votes while the big states got acceptance of the principle of proportional power; third, if the state legislatures agreed (as six did in the first presidential election), the people could be involved directly in the choice of electors; and finally, if no candidate received a majority in the College, the right of decision passed to the national legislature with each state exercising equal strength. (In the Brearley recommendation, the election went to the Senate, but a motion from the floor substituted the House; this was accepted on the ground that the Senate already had enough authority over the executive in its treaty and appointment powers.)

This compromise was almost too good to be true, and the framers snapped it up with little debate or controversy. No one seemed to think well of the College as an *institution;* indeed, what evidence there is suggests that there was an assumption that once Washington had finished his tenure as President, the electors would cease to produce majorities and the Chief Executive would usually be chosen in the House. George Mason observed casually that the selection would be made in the House nineteen times in twenty and no one seriously disputed this point. The vital aspect of the Electoral College was that it got the Convention over the hurdle and protected everybody's interests. The future was left to cope with the problem of what to do with this Rube Goldberg mechanism.

In short, the framers did not in their wisdom endow the United States with a college of Cardinals — the Electoral College was neither an exercise in applied Platonism nor an experiment in indirect government based on elitist distrust of the masses. It was merely a jerry-rigged improvisation which has subsequently been endowed with a high theoretical content. When an elector from Oklahoma in 1960 refused to cast his vote for Nixon (naming Byrd and Goldwater instead) on the ground that the Founding Fathers intended him to exercise his great independent wisdom, he was indulging in historical fantasy. If one were to indulge in counter-fantasy, he would be tempted to suggest that the Fathers would be startled to find the College still in operation — and perhaps even dismayed at their descendants' lack of judgment or inventiveness.

The second issue on which some substantial practical bargaining took place was slavery. The morality of slavery was, by design, not at issue; but in its other concrete aspects, slavery colored the arguments over taxation, commerce, and representation. The "Three-Fifths Compromise," that three-fifths of the slaves would be counted both for representation and for purposes of direct taxation (which was drawn from the past—it was a formula of Madison's utilized by Congress in 1783 to establish the basis of state contributions to the Confederation treasury) had allayed some Northern fears about Southern overrepresentation (no one then foresaw the trivial role that direct taxation would play in later federal financial policy), but doubts still remained. The Southerners, on the other hand, were afraid that Congressional control over commerce would lead to the exclusion of slaves or to their excessive taxation as imports. Moreover, the Southerners were disturbed over "navigation acts," i.e., tariffs, or special legislation providing, for example, that exports be carried only in American ships; as a section depending upon exports, they wanted protection from the potential voracity of their commercial brethren of the Eastern states. To achieve this end, Mason and others urged that the Constitution include a proviso that navigation and commercial laws should require a two-thirds vote in Congress.

These problems came to a head in late August and, as usual, were handed to a committee in the hope that, in Gouverneur Morris's words, "these things may form a bargain among the Northern and Southern States." The Committee reported its measures of reconciliation on August 25, and on August 29 the package was wrapped up and delivered. What occurred can best be described in George Mason's dour version (he anticipated Calhoun in his conviction that permitting navigation acts to pass by majority vote would put the South in economic bondage to the North—it was mainly on this ground that he refused to sign the Constitution):

> The Constitution as agreed to till a fortnight before the Convention rose was such a one as he would have set his hand and heart to. . . . [Until that time] The 3 New England States were constantly with us in all questions . . . so that it was these three States with the 5 Southern ones against Pennsylvania, Jersey and Delaware. With respect to the importation of slaves, [decision-making] was left to Congress. This disturbed the two Southern-most States who knew that Congress would immediately suppress the importation of slaves. Those two States therefore struck up a bargain with the three New England States. If they would join to admit slaves for some years, the two Southern-most States would join in changing the clause which required the 2/3 of the Legislature in any vote [on navigation acts]. It was done.

On the floor of the Convention there was a virtual love-feast on this happy occasion. Charles Pinckney of South Carolina attempted to overturn the committee's decision, when the compromise was reported to the Convention, by insisting that the South needed protection from the imperialism of the Northern states. But his Southern colleagues were not prepared to rock the boat and General C. C. Pinckney arose to spread oil on the suddenly ruffled waters; he admitted that:

> It was in the true interest of the S[outhern] States to have no regulation of commerce; but considering the loss brought on the commerce of the Eastern States by the Revolution, their liberal conduct towards the views of South Carolina [on the regulation of the slave trade] and the interests the weak Southn. States had in being united with the strong Eastern states, he thought it proper that no fetters should be imposed on the power of making commercial regulations; *and that his constituents, though prejudiced against the Eastern States, would be reconciled to this liberality.* He had himself prejudices agst the Eastern States before he came here, but would acknowledge that he had found them as liberal and candid as any men whatever. (Italics added.)

Pierce Butler took the same tack, essentially arguing that he was not too happy about the possible consequences, but that a deal was a deal. Many Southern leaders were later—in the wake of the "Tariff of Abominations"—to rue this day of reconciliation; Calhoun's *Disquisition on Government* was little more than an extension of the argument in the Convention against permitting a Congressional majority to enact navigation acts.

VI

Drawing on their vast collective political experience, utilizing every weapon in the politician's arsenal, looking constantly over their shoulders at their constituents, the delegates put together a Constitution. It was a makeshift affair; some sticky issues (for example, the qualification of voters) they ducked entirely; others they mastered with that ancient instrument of political sagacity, studied ambiguity (for example, citizenship); and some they just overlooked. In this last category, I suspect, fell the matter of the power of the federal courts to determine the constitutionality of acts of Congress. When the judicial article was formulated (Article III of the Constitution), deliberations were still in the stage where the legislature was endowed with broad power under the Randolph formulation, authority which by its own terms was scarcely amenable to judicial review. In essence, courts could hardly determine when "the separate States are incompetent or . . . the harmony of the United States may be interrupted"; the national legislature, as critics pointed out, was free to define its own jurisdiction. Later the definition of legislative authority was changed into the form we know, a series of stipulated powers, *but the delegates never seriously reexamined the jurisdiction of the judiciary under this new lim-*

ited formulation. All arguments on the intention of the framers in this matter are thus deductive and *a posteriori,* though some obviously make more sense than others.

The framers were busy and distinguished men, anxious to get back to their families, their positions, and their constituents, not members of the French Academy devoting a lifetime to a dictionary. They were trying to do an important job, and do it in such a fashion that their handiwork would be acceptable to very diverse constituencies. No one was rhapsodic about the final document, but it was a beginning, a move in the right direction, and one they had reason to believe the people would endorse. In addition, since they had modified the impossible amendment provisions of the Articles (the requirement of unanimity which could always be frustrated by "Rogues Island") to one demanding approval by only three-quarters of the states, they seemed confident that gaps in the fabric which experience would reveal could be rewoven without undue difficulty.

So with a neat phrase introduced by Benjamin Franklin (but devised by Gouverneur Morris) which made their decision sound unanimous, and an inspired benediction by the Old Doctor urging doubters to doubt their own infallibility, the Constitution was accepted and signed. Curiously, Edmund Randolph, who had played so vital a role throughout, refused to sign, as did his fellow Virginian George Mason and Elbridge Gerry of Massachusetts. Randolph's behavior was eccentric, to say the least—his excuses for refusing his signature have a factitious ring even at this late date; the best explanation seems to be that he was afraid that the Constitution would prove to be a liability in Virginia politics, where Patrick Henry was burning up the countryside with impassioned denunciations. Presumably, Randolph wanted to check the temper of the populace before he risked his reputation, and perhaps his job, in a fight with both Henry and Richard Henry Lee. Events lend some justification to this speculation: after much temporizing and use of the conditional subjunctive tense, Randolph endorsed ratification in Virginia and ended up getting the best of both worlds.

Madison, despite his reservations about the Constitution, was the campaign manager in ratification. His first task was to get the Congress in New York to light its own funeral pyre by approving the "amendments" to the Articles and sending them on to the state legislatures. Above all, momentum had to be maintained. The anti-Constitutionalists, now thoroughly alarmed and no novices in politics, realized that their best tactic was attrition rather than direct opposition. Thus they settled on a position expressing qualified approval but calling for a second Convention to remedy various defects (the one with the most demagogic appeal was the lack of a Bill of Rights). Madison knew that to accede to this demand would be equivalent to losing the battle, nor would he agree to conditional approval (despite wavering even by Hamilton). This was an all-or-nothing proposition: national salvation or national impotence with no intermediate positions possible. Unable to get Congressional approval, he settled for second best: a unanimous resolution of Congress transmitting the Constitution to the states for whatever action they saw fit to take. The opponents then moved from New York and the Congress, where they had attempted to attach amendments and conditions, to the states for the final battle.

At first the campaign for ratification went beautifully: within eight months after the delegates set their names to the document, eight states had ratified. Only in Massachusetts had the result been close (187-168). Theoretically, a ratification by one more state convention would set the new government in motion, but in fact until Virginia and New York acceded to the new Union, the latter was a fiction. New Hampshire was the next to ratify; Rhode Island was involved in its characteristic political convulsions (the legislature there sent the Constitution out to the towns for decision by popular vote and it got lost among a series of local issues); North Carolina's convention did not meet until July and then postponed a final decision. This is hardly the place for an extensive analysis of the conventions of New York and Virginia. Suffice it to say that the Constitutionalists clearly outmaneuvered their opponents, forced them into impossible political positions, and won both states narrowly. The Virginia Convention could serve as a classic study in effective floor management: Patrick Henry had to be contained, and a reading of the debates discloses a standard two-stage technique. Henry would give a four- or five-hour speech denouncing some section of the Constitution on every conceivable ground (the federal district, he averred at one point, would become a haven for convicts escaping from state authority!); when Henry subsided, "Mr. Lee of Westmoreland" would rise and literally poleax him with sardonic invective (when Henry complained about the militia power, "Lighthorse Harry" really punched below the belt: observing that while the former Governor had been sitting in Richmond during the Revolution, *he* had been out in the trenches with the troops and thus felt better qualified to discuss military affairs). Then the gentlemanly Constitutionalists (Madison, Pendleton, and Marshall) would pick up the matters at issue and examine them in the light of reason.

Indeed, modern Americans who tend to think of James Madison as a rather desiccated character should spend some time with this transcript. Probably Madison put on his most spectacular demonstration of nimble rhetoric in what might be called "The Battle of the Absent Authorities." Patrick Henry in the course of one of his harangues alleged that Jefferson was known to be opposed to Virginia's approving the Constitution. This was clever: Henry hated Jefferson, but was prepared to use any weapon that came to hand. Madison's riposte was superb: First, he said that with all due respect to the great reputation of Jefferson, he was not in the country and therefore could not formulate an adequate judgment; second, no one should utilize the reputation of an outsider—the Virginia Convention was there to think for itself; third, if there were to be recourse to outsiders, the opinions of George Washington should certainly be taken into consideration; and finally, he knew from privileged personal communications from Jefferson that in fact the latter *strongly favored* the Constitution. To devise an assault route into this rhetorical fortress was literally impossible.

VII

The fight was over; all that remained now was to establish the new frame of government in the spirit of its framers. And who were better qualified for this task than the framers themselves? Thus victory for the Constitution meant simultaneous victory for the Constitutionalists; the anti-Constitutionalists either capitulated or vanished into limbo—soon Patrick Henry would be offered a seat on the Supreme Court and Luther Martin would be known as the Federalist "bull-dog." And irony of ironies, Alexander Hamilton and James Madison would shortly accumulate a reputation as the formulators of what is often alleged to be our political theory, the concept of "federalism." Also, on the other side of the ledger, the arguments would soon appear over what the framers "really meant"; while these disputes have assumed the proportions of a big scholarly business in the last century, they began almost before the ink on the Constitution was dry. One of the best early ones featured Hamilton versus Madison on the scope of presidential power, and other framers characteristically assumed positions in this and other disputes on the basis of their political convictions.

Probably our greatest difficulty is that we know so much more about what the framers *should have meant* than they themselves did. We are intimately acquainted with the problems that their Constitution should have been designed to master; in short, we have read the mystery story backwards. If we are to get the right "feel" for their time and their circumstances, we must in Maitland's phrase, "think ourselves back into a twilight." Obviously, no one can pretend completely to escape from the solipsistic web of his own environment, but if the effort is made, it is possible to appreciate the past roughly on its own terms. The first step in this process is to abandon the academic premise that because we can ask a question, there must be an answer.

Thus we can ask what the framers meant when they gave Congress the power to regulate interstate and foreign commerce, and we emerge, reluctantly perhaps, with the reply that they may not have known what they meant, that there may not have been any semantic consensus. The Convention was not a seminar in analytic philosophy or linguistic analysis. Commerce was *commerce* —and if different interpretations of the word arose, later generations could worry about the problem of definition. The delegates were in a hurry to get a new government established; when definitional arguments arose, they characteristically took refuge in ambiguity. If different men voted for the same proposition for varying reasons, that was politics (and still is); if later generations were unsettled by this lack of precision, that would be their problem.

There was a good deal of definitional pluralism with respect to the problems the delegates did discuss, but when we move to the question of extrapolated intentions, we enter the realm of spiritualism. When men in our time, for instance, launch into elaborate talmudic exegesis to demonstrate that federal aid to parochial schools is (or is not) in accord with the intentions of the men who established the Republic and endorsed the Bill of Rights, they are engaging in historical Extra-Sensory Perception. (If one were to join this E.S.P. contingent for a minute, he might suggest that the hard-boiled politicians who wrote the Constitution and Bill of Rights would chuckle scornfully at such an invocation of authority: obviously a politician would chart his course on the intentions of the living, not of the dead, and count the number of Catholics in his constituency.)

The Constitution, then, was not an apotheosis of "constitutionalism," a triumph of architectonic genius; it was a patch-work sewn together under the pressure of both time and events by a group of extremely talented democratic politicians. They refused to attempt the establishment of a strong, centralized sovereignty on the principle of legislative supremacy for the excellent reason that the people would not accept it. They risked their political fortunes by opposing the established doctrines of state sovereignty because they were convinced that the existing system was leading to national impotence and probably foreign domination. For two years, they worked to get a convention established. For over three months, in what must have seemed to the faithful participants an endless process of give-and-take, they reasoned, cajoled, threatened, and bargained amongst themselves. The result was a Constitution which the people, in fact, by democratic processes, did accept, and a new and far better national government was established.

Beginning with the inspired propaganda of Hamilton, Madison, and Jay, the ideological build-up got under way. *The Federalist* had little impact on the ratification of the Constitution, except perhaps in New York, but this volume had enormous influence on the image of the Constitution in the minds of future generations, particularly on historians and political scientists who have an innate fondness for theoretical symmetry. Yet, while the shades of Locke and Montesquieu *may* have been hovering in the background, and the delegates *may* have been unconscious instruments of a transcendent *telos,* the careful observer of the day-to-day work of the Convention finds no overarching principles. The "separation of powers" to him seems to be a by-product of suspicion, and "federalism" he views as a *pis aller,* as the farthest point the delegates felt they could go in the destruction of state power without themselves inviting repudiation.

To conclude, the Constitution was neither a victory for abstract theory nor a great practical success. Well over half a million men had to die on the battlefields of the Civil War before certain constitutional principles could be defined—a baleful consideration which is somehow overlooked in our customary tributes to the farsighted genius of the framers and to the supposed American talent for "constitutionalism." The Constitution was, however, a vivid demonstration of effective democratic political action, and of the forging of a national elite which literally persuaded its countrymen to hoist themselves by their own boot straps. American pro-consuls would be wise not to translate the Constitution into Japanese, or Swahili, or treat if as a work of semi-Divine origin; but when students of comparative politics examine the process of nation-building in countries newly freed from colonial rule, they may find the American experience instructive as a classic example of the potentialities of a democratic elite.

□   John Roche's article on the framing of the Constitution was written as an attack upon a variety of views that suggested the Constitution was not so much a practical political document, as an expression of elitist views based upon political philosophy and economic interests. One such elitist view was that of Charles A. Beard, who published his famous *An Economic Interpretation of the Constitution* in 1913. He suggested that the Constitution was nothing more than the work of an economic elite that was seeking to preserve its property. This elite, according to Beard, consisted of landholders, creditors, merchants, public bondholders, and wealthy lawyers. Beard demonstrated that many of the delegates to the convention fell into one of these categories.

According to Beard's thesis, as the delegates met, the primary concern of most of them was to limit the power of popular majorities and thus protect their own property interests. To Beard, the antimajoritarian attributes that he felt existed in the Constitution were a reflection of the less numerous creditor class attempting to protect itself against incursions by the majority. Specific provisions as well were put into the Constitution with a view towards protecting property, such as the clause prohibiting states from impairing contracts, coining money, or emitting bills of credit. Control over money was placed in the hands of the national government, and in Article VI of the Constitution it was provided that the new government was to guarantee all debts that had been incurred by the national government under the Articles of Confederation.

Ironically, Beard, like Roche, was attempting to dispel the prevailing notions of his time that the Constitution had been formulated by philosopher kings whose wisdom could not be challenged. But while Roche postulates a loosely knit practical political elite, Beard suggests the existence of a cohesive and even conspiratorial economic elite. The limitation on majority rule was an essential component of this economic conspiracy.

The Constitution does contain many provisions that limit majority rule. Beard claimed that the Constitution from initial adoption to final ratification was never supported by the majority of the people. Holding a constitutional convention in the first place was never submitted to a popular vote, nor was the Constitution that was finally agreed upon ratified by a popular referendum. The selection of delegates to state ratifying conventions was not executed through universal suffrage, but on the basis of the suffrage qualifications that applied in the states and that were within the discretion of state legislatures. The limited suffrage in the states severely restricted popular participation in ratification of the Constitution.

Beard's thesis was startling at the time it was published in 1913. As it came under close examination, it was revealed that the evidence simply did not support Beard's hypothesis. Key leaders of the convention, including Madison, were not substantial property owners. Several important opponents to ratification of the Constitution were the very members of the economic elite that Beard said conspired to thrust the Constitution upon an unknowing public.

Before Beard presented his narrow thesis in 1913, he had published in 1912 *The Supreme Court and the Constitution*. The major theme of the book was that the Supreme Court was intended to have the authority to review acts of Congress under the terms of the original Constitution. At the same time, the book presents Beard's elitist view of the framing of the Constitution in a somewhat broader context than it was presented in *An Economic Interpretation of the Constitution* published a year later. But the earlier work clearly contains the economic theme, as in the passage where Beard states that the framers of the Constitution were "anxious above everything else to safeguard the rights of private property against any levelling tendencies on the part of the propertyless masses." The following selection contains Beard's overview of the framing and adoption of the Constitution and highlights his economic theme and his belief in the antimajoritarian attributes of the Constitution.

2

Charles A. Beard

FRAMING THE CONSTITUTION

As Blackstone[1] shows by happy illustration the reason and spirit of a law are to be understood only by an inquiry into the circumstances of its enactment. The underlying purposes of the Constitution [of the United States], therefore, are to be revealed only by a study of the conditions and events which led to its formation and adoption.

At the outset it must be remembered that there were two great parties at the time of the adoption of the Constitution—one laying emphasis on strength and efficiency in government and the other on its popular aspects. Quite naturally the men who led in stirring up the revolt against Great Britain and in keeping the fighting temper of the Revolutionists at the proper heat were the boldest and most radical thinkers—men like Samuel Adams, Thomas Paine, Patrick Henry, and Thomas Jefferson. They were not, generally speaking, men of large property interests or of much practical business experience. In a time of disorder, they could consistently lay more stress upon personal liberty than upon social control; and they pushed to the extreme limits those doctrines of individual rights which had been evolved in England during the struggles of the small landed proprietors and commercial classes against royal prerogative, and which corresponded to the economic conditions prevailing in America at the close of the eighteenth century. They associated strong government with monarchy, and came to believe that the best political system was one which governed least. A majority of the radicals viewed all government, especially if highly centralized, as a species of evil, tolerable only because necessary and always to be kept down to an irreducible minimum by a jealous vigilance.

Jefferson put the doctrine in concrete form when he declared that he preferred newspapers without government to government without newspapers. The Declaration of Independence, the first state Constitutions, and the Articles of Confederation bore the impress of this philosophy. In their anxiety to defend the individual against all federal interference and to preserve to the states a large sphere of local autonomy, these Revolutionists had set up a system too weak to accomplish the accepted objects of

---

Chapter X from *The Economic Basis of Politics and Related Writings by Charles A. Beard,* compiled and annotated by William Beard, Vintage Books, Inc., © 1957 by William Beard and Miriam B. Vagts. Reprinted with permission of William Beard and the Estate of Miriam B. Vagts.

[1]*Compiler's Note:* Blackstone, Sir William (1723-1780). Distinguished commentator on the laws of England, judge, and teacher.

government; namely, national defense, the protection of property, and the advancement of commerce. They were not unaware of the character of their handiwork, but they believed with Jefferson that "man was a rational animal endowed by nature with rights and with an innate sense of justice and that he could be restrained from wrong and protected in right by moderate powers confided to persons of his own choice." Occasional riots and disorders, they held, were preferable to too much government.

The new American political system based on these doctrines had scarcely gone into effect before it began to incur opposition from many sources. The close of the Revolutionary struggle removed the prime cause for radical agitation and brought a new group of thinkers into prominence. When independence had been gained, the practical work to be done was the maintenance of social order, the payment of the public debt, the provision of a sound financial system, and the establishment of conditions favorable to the development of the economic resources of the new country. The men who were principally concerned in this work of peaceful enterprise were not the philosophers, but men of business and property and the holders of public securities. For the most part they had had no quarrel with the system of class rule and the strong centralization of government which existed in England. It was on the question of policy, not of governmental structure, that they had broken with the British authorities. By no means all of them, in fact, had even resisted the policy of the mother country, for within the ranks of the conservatives were large numbers of Loyalists who had remained in America, and, as was to have been expected, cherished a bitter feeling against the Revolutionists, especially the radical section which had been boldest in denouncing the English system root and branch. In other words, after the heat and excitement of the War of Independence were over and the new government, state and national, was tested by the ordinary experiences of traders, financiers, and manufacturers, it was found inadequate, and these groups accordingly grew more and more determined to reconstruct the political system in such a fashion as to make it subserve their permanent interests.

Under the state constitutions and the Articles of Confederation established during the Revolution, every powerful economic class in the nation suffered either immediate losses or from impediments placed in the way of the development of their enterprises. The holders of the securities of the Confederate government did not receive the interest on their loans. Those who owned Western lands or looked with longing eyes upon the rich opportunities for speculation there chaffed at the weakness of the government and its delays in establishing order on the frontiers. Traders and commercial men found their plans for commerce on a national scale impeded by local interference with interstate commerce. The currency of the states and the nation was hopelessly muddled. Creditors everywhere were angry about the depreciated paper money which the agrarians had made and were attempting to force upon those from whom they had borrowed specie. In short, it was a war between business and populism. Under the Articles of Confederation populism had a free hand, for majorities in the state legislatures were omnipotent. Anyone who reads the economic history of the time will see why the solid conservative interests of the country were weary of talk about the "rights of the people" and bent upon establishing firm guarantees for the rights of property.

The Congress of the Confederation was not long in discovering the true character of the futile authority which the Articles had conferred upon it. The necessity for new sources of revenue became apparent even while the struggle for independence was yet undecided, and, in 1781, Congress carried a resolution to the effect that it should be authorized to lay a duty of five percent on certain goods. This moderate proposition was defeated because Rhode Island rejected it on the grounds that "she regarded it the most precious jewel of sovereignty that no state shall be called upon to open its purse but by the authority of the state and by her own officers." Two years later Congress prepared another amendment to the Articles providing for certain import duties, the receipts from which, collected by state officers, were to be applied to the payment of the public debt; but three years after the introduction of the measure, four states, including New York, still held out against its ratification, and the project was allowed to drop. At last, in 1786, Congress in a resolution declared that the requisitions for the last eight years had been so irregular in their operation, so uncertain in their collection, and so evidently unproductive, that a reliance on them in the future would be no less dishonorable to the understandings of those who entertained it than it would be dangerous to the welfare and peace of the Union. Congress, thereupon, solemnly added that it had become its duty "to declare most explicitly that the crisis had arrived when the people of the United States, by whose will and for whose benefit the federal government was instituted, must decide whether they will support their rank as a nation by maintaining the public faith at home and abroad, or whether for the want of a timely exertion in establishing a general revenue and thereby giving strength to the Confederacy, they will hazard not only the existence of the Union but those great and invaluable privileges for which they have so arduously and so honorably contended."

In fact, the Articles of Confederation had hardly gone into effect before the leading citizens also began to feel that the powers of Congress were wholly inadequate. In 1780, even before their adoption, Alexander Hamilton proposed a general convention to frame a new constitution, and from that time forward he labored with remarkable zeal and wisdom to extend and popularize the idea of a strong national government. Two years later, the Assembly of the State of New York recommended a convention to revise the Articles and increase the power of Congress. In 1783, Washington, in a circular letter to the governors, urged that it was indispensable to the happiness of the individual states that there should be lodged somewhere a supreme power to regulate and govern the general concerns of the confederation. Shortly afterward (1785), Governor Bowdoin, of Massachusetts, suggested to his state legislature the advisability of calling a national assembly to settle upon and define the powers of Congress; and the legislature resolved that the government under the Articles of Confederation was inadequate and should be reformed; but the resolution was never laid before Congress.

In January, 1786, Virginia invited all the other states to send delegates to a convention at Annapolis to consider the question of duties on imports and commerce in general. When this convention assembled in 1786, delegates from only five states were present, and they were disheartened at the limitations on their powers and the lack of interest the other states had shown in the project. With characteristic foresight, however, Alexander Hamilton seized the occasion to secure the adoption of a recommendation advising the states to choose representatives for another convention to meet in Philadelphia the following year "to consider the Articles of Confederation and to propose such changes therein as might render them adequate to the exigencies of the union." This recommendation was cautiously worded, for Hamilton did not want to raise any unnecessary alarm. He doubtless believed that a complete revolution in the old system was desirable, but he knew that, in the existing state of popular temper, it was not expedient to announce his complete program. Accordingly no general reconstruction of the political system was suggested; the Articles of Confederation were merely to be "revised"; and the amendments were to be approved by the state legislatures as provided by that instrument.

The proposal of the Annapolis convention was transmitted to the state legislatures and laid before Congress. Congress thereupon resolved in February, 1787, that a convention should be held for the sole and express purpose of revising the Articles of Confederation and reporting to itself and the legislatures of the several states such alterations and provisions as would when agreed to by Congress and confirmed by the states render the federal constitution adequate to the exigencies of government and the preservation of the union.

In pursuance of this call, delegates to the new convention were chosen by the legislatures of the states or by the governors in conformity to authority conferred by the legislative assemblies.[2] The delegates were given instructions of a general nature by their respective states, none of which, apparently, contemplated any very far-reaching changes. In fact, almost all of them expressly limited their representatives to a mere revision

---

[2]Rhode Island alone was unrepresented. In all, sixty-two delegates were appointed by the states; fifty-five of these attended sometime during the sessions; but only thirty-nine signed the finished document.

of the Articles of Confederation. For example, Connecticut authorized her delegates to represent and confer for the purpose mentioned in the resolution of Congress and to discuss such measures "agreeable to the general principles of Republican government" as they should think proper to render the Union adequate. Delaware, however, went so far as to provide that none of the proposed alterations should extend to the fifth part of the Articles of Confederation guaranteeing that each state should be entitled to one vote.

It was a truly remarkable assembly of men that gathered in Philadelphia on May 14, 1787, to undertake the work of reconstructing the American system of government. It is not merely patriotic pride that compels one to assert that never in the history of assemblies has there been a convention of men richer in political experience and in practical knowledge, or endowed with a profounder insight into the springs of human action and the intimate essence of government. It is indeed an astounding fact that at one time so many men skilled in statecraft could be found on the very frontiers of civilization among a population numbering about four million whites. It is no less a cause for admiration that their instrument of government should have survived the trials and crises of a century that saw the wreck of more than a score of paper constitutions.

All the members had had a practical training in politics. Washington, as commander-in-chief of the Revolutionary forces, had learned well the lessons and problems of war, and mastered successfully the no less difficult problems of administration. The two Morrises had distinguished themselves in grappling with financial questions as trying and perplexing as any which statesmen had ever been compelled to face. Seven of the delegates had gained political wisdom as governors of their native states; and no less than twenty-eight had served in Congress either during the Revolution or under the Articles of Confederation. These were men trained in the law, versed in finance, skilled in administration, and learned in the political philosophy of their own and all earlier times. Moreover, they were men destined to continue public service under the government which they had met to construct—Presidents, Vice-Presidents, heads of departments, Justices of the Supreme Court were in that imposing body. . . .

As Woodrow Wilson has concisely put it, the framers of the Constitution represented "a strong and intelligent class possessed of unity and informed by a conscious solidarity of interests."[3] . . .

The makers of the federal Constitution represented the solid, conservative, commercial and financial interests of the country—not the interests which denounced and proscribed judges in Rhode Island, New Jersey, and North Carolina, and stoned their houses in New York. The conserva-

---

[3]Woodrow Wilson, *Division and Reunion* (New York: Longmans, Green, & Co., 1893), p. 12.

tive interests, made desperate by the imbecilities of the Confederation and harried by state legislatures, roused themselves from their lethargy, drew together in a mighty effort to establish a government that would be strong enough to pay the national debt, regulate interstate and foreign commerce, provide for national defense, prevent fluctuations in the currency created by paper emissions, and control the propensities of legislative majorities to attack private rights.... The radicals, however, like Patrick Henry, Jefferson, and Samuel Adams, were conspicuous by their absence from the convention.[4] ...

[The makers of the Constitution were convened] to frame a government which would meet the practical issues that had arisen under the Articles of Confederation. The objections they entertained to direct popular government, and they were undoubtedly many, were based upon their experience with popular assemblies during the immediately preceding years. With many of the plain lessons of history before them, they naturally feared that the rights and privileges of the minority would be insecure if the principle of majority rule was definitely adopted and provisions made for its exercise. Furthermore, it will be remembered that up to that time the right of all men, as men, to share in the government had never been recognized in practice. Everywhere in Europe the government was in the hands of a ruling monarch or at best a ruling class; everywhere the mass of the people had been regarded principally as an arms-bearing and tax-paying multitude, uneducated, and with little hope or capacity for advancement. Two years were to elapse after the meeting of the grave assembly at Philadelphia before the transformation of the Estates General into the National Convention in France opened the floodgates of revolutionary ideas on human rights before whose rising tide old landmarks of government are still being submerged. It is small wonder, therefore, that, under the circumstances, many of the members of that august body held popular government in slight esteem and took the people into consideration only as far as it was imperative "to inspire them with the necessary confidence," as Mr. Gerry frankly put it.[5]

Indeed, every page of the laconic record of the proceedings of the convention preserved to posterity by Mr. Madison shows conclusively that the members of that assembly were not seeking to realize any fine notions about democracy and equality, but were striving with all the resources of political wisdom at their command to set up a system of government that would be stable and efficient, safeguarded on one hand against the possibili-

---

[4]*Compiler's Note:* The contents of this paragraph have been taken from positions on pp. 75–76 and 88 of the original text of *The Supreme Court and the Constitution* and placed here to emphasize the economic theme.

[5]Jonathan Elliot, *The Debates in the Several State Conventions on the Adoption of the Federal Constitution* (Washington, D.C.: The Editor, 1827–1830), vol. v, p. 160.

ties of despotism and on the other against the onslaught of majorities. In the mind of Mr. Gerry, the evils they had experienced flowed "from the excess of democracy," and he confessed that while he was still republican, he "had been taught by experience the danger of the levelling spirit."[6] Mr. Randolph in offering to the consideration of the convention his plan of government, observed "that the general object was to provide a cure for the evils under which the United States labored; that, in tracing these evils to their origin, every man had found it in the turbulence and follies of democracy; that some check therefore was to be sought for against this tendency of our governments; and that a good Senate seemed most likely to answer the purpose."[7] Mr. Hamilton, in advocating a life term for Senators, urged that "all communities divide themselves into the few and the many. The first are rich and well born and the other the mass of the people who seldom judge or determine right."

Gouverneur Morris wanted to check the "precipitancy, changeableness, and excess" of the representatives of the people by the ability and virtue of men "of great and established property—aristocracy; men who from pride will support consistency and permanency.... Such an aristocratic body will keep down the turbulence of democracy." While these extreme doctrines were somewhat counterbalanced by the democratic principles of Mr. Wilson who urged that "the government ought to possess, not only first, the force, but second the mind or sense of the people at large," Madison doubtless summed up in a brief sentence the general opinion of the convention when he said that to secure private rights against majority factions, and at the same time to preserve the spirit and form of popular government, was the great object to which their inquiries had been directed.[8]

They were anxious above everything else to safeguard the rights of private property against any leveling tendencies on the part of the propertyless masses. Gouverneur Morris, in speaking on the problem of apportioning representatives, correctly stated the sound historical fact when he declared: "Life and liberty were generally said to be of more value than property. An accurate view of the matter would, nevertheless, prove that property was the main object of society.... If property, then, was the main object of government, certainly it ought to be one measure of the influence due to those who were to be affected by the government."[9] Mr. King also agreed that "property was the primary object of society"[10]; and Mr. Madison

---

[6]*Ibid.,* vol. v, p. 136.

[7]*Ibid.,* vol. v, p. 138.

[8]*The Federalist,* No. 10.

[9]Elliot's *Debates,* op. cit., vol. v, p. 279.

[10]Ibid., p. 280.

warned the convention that in framing a system which they wished to last for ages they must not lose sight of the changes which the ages would produce in the forms and distribution of property. In advocating a long term in order to give independence and firmness to the Senate, he described these impending changes: "An increase of population will of necessity increase the proportion of those who will labor under all the hardships of life and secretly sigh for a more equal distribution of its blessings. These may in time outnumber those who are placed above the feelings of indigence. According to the equal laws of suffrage, the power will slide into the hands of the former. No agrarian attempts have yet been made in this country, but symptoms of a levelling spirit, as we have understood have sufficiently appeared, in a certain quarter, to give notice of the future danger."[11] And again, in support of the argument for a property qualification on voters, Madison urged: "In future times, a great majority of the people will not only be without landed, but any other sort of property. These will either combine, under the influence of their common situation,—in which case the rights of property and the public liberty will not be secure in their hands,—or, what is more probable, they will become the tools of opulence and ambition; in which case there will be equal danger on another side."[12] Various projects for setting up class rule by the establishment of property qualifications for voters and officers were advanced in the convention, but they were defeated. . . .

The absence of such property qualifications is certainly not due to any belief in Jefferson's free-and-equal doctrine. It is due rather to the fact that the members of the convention could not agree on the nature and amount of the qualifications. Naturally a landed qualification was suggested, but for obvious reasons it was rejected. Although it was satisfactory to the landed gentry of the South, it did not suit the financial, commercial, and manufacturing gentry of the North. If it was high, the latter would be excluded; if it was low it would let in the populistic farmers who had already made so much trouble in the state legislatures with paper-money schemes and other devices for "relieving agriculture." One of the chief reasons for calling the convention and framing the Constitution was to promote commerce and industry and to protect personal property against the "depredations" of Jefferson's noble freeholders. On the other hand a personal-property qualification, high enough to please merchant princes like Robert Morris and Nathaniel Gorham would shut out the Southern planters. Again, an alternative of land or personal property, high enough to afford safeguards to large interests, would doubtless bring about the rejec-

---

[11]Ibid., p. 243.
[12]Ibid., p. 387.

tion of the whole Constitution by the troublemaking farmers who had to pass upon the question of ratification.[13] . . .

Nevertheless, by the system of checks and balances placed in the government, the convention safeguarded the interests of property against attacks by majorities. The House of Representatives, Mr. Hamilton pointed out, "was so formed as to render it particularly the guardian of the poorer orders of citizens,"[14] while the Senate was to preserve the rights of property and the interests of the minority against the demands of the majority.[15] In the tenth number of *The Federalist,* Mr. Madison argued in a philosophic vein in support of the proposition that it was necessary to base the political system on the actual conditions of "natural inequality." Uniformity of interests throughout the state, he contended, was impossible on account of the diversity in the faculties of men, from which the rights of property originated; the protection of these faculties was the first object of government; from the protection of different and unequal faculties of acquiring property the possession of different degrees and kinds of property immediately resulted; from the influence of these on the sentiments and views of the respective proprietors ensued a division of society into different interests and parties; the unequal distribution of wealth inevitably led to a clash of interests in which the majority was liable to carry out its policies at the expense of the minority; hence, he added, in concluding this splendid piece of logic, "the majority, having such coexistent passion or interest, must be rendered by their number and local situation unable to concert and carry into effect schemes of oppression"; and in his opinion it was the great merit of the newly framed Constitution that it secured the rights of the minority against "the superior force of an interested and overbearing majority."

This very system of checks and balances, which is undeniably the essential element of the Constitution, is built upon the doctrine that the popular branch of the government cannot be allowed full sway, and least of all in the enactment of laws touching the rights of property. The exclusion of the direct popular vote in the election of the President; the creation, again by indirect election, of a Senate which the framers hoped would represent the wealth and conservative interests of the country[16]; and the establishment of an independent judiciary appointed by the President with the concurrence of the Senate—all these devices bear witness to the fact

---

[13]*Compiler's Note:* This single paragraph from "Whom Does Congress Represent?" *Harper's Magazine,* Jan., 1930, pp. 144–152, has been inserted here because of its value in amplifying the passages from *The Supreme Court and the Constitution.* Reprinting from this article by Beard has been done with the permission of *Harper's Magazine.*

[14]Elliot's *Debates,* op. cit., vol. v, p. 244.

[15]*Ibid.,* vol. v, p. 203.

[16]*Compiler's Note:* Popular election of Senators was achieved in 1913 through the 17th Amendment to the Constitution.

that the underlying purpose of the Constitution was not the establishment of popular government by means of parliamentary majorities.

Page after page of *The Federalist* is directed to that portion of the electorate which was disgusted with the "mutability of the public councils." Writing on the presidential veto Hamilton says: "The propensity of the legislative department to intrude upon the rights, and absorb the powers, of the other departments has already been suggested and repeated. . . . It may perhaps be said that the power of preventing bad laws included the power of preventing good ones; and may be used to the one purpose as well as the other. But this objection will have little weight with those who can properly estimate the mischiefs of that inconstancy and mutability in the laws which form the greatest blemish in the character and genius of our governments. They will consider every institution calculated to restrain the excess of law-making and to keep things in the same state in which they happen to be at any given period, as more likely to do good than harm; because it is favorable to greater stability in the system of legislation. The injury which may be possibly done by defeating a few good laws will be amply compensated by the advantage of preventing a number of bad ones."

When the framers of the Constitution had completed the remarkable instrument which was to establish a national government capable of discharging effectively certain great functions and checking the propensities of popular legislatures to attack the rights of private property, a formidable task remained before them—the task of securing the adoption of the new frame of government by states torn with popular dissensions. They knew very well that the state legislatures which had been so negligent in paying their quotas [of money] under the Articles [of Confederation] and which had been so jealous of their rights, would probably stick at ratifying such a national instrument of government. Accordingly they cast aside that clause in the Articles requiring amendments to be ratified by the legislature of all the states; and advised that the new Constitution should be ratified by conventions in the several states composed of delegates chosen by the voters.[17] They furthermore declared—and this is a fundamental matter—that when the conventions of nine states had ratified the Constitution the new government should go into effect so far as those states were concerned. The chief reason for resorting to ratifications by conventions is laid down by Hamilton in the twenty-second number of *The Federalist:* "It has not a little contributed to the infirmities of the existing federal system that it never had a ratification by the people. Resting on no better foundation than the consent of the several legislatures, it has been exposed to frequent and intricate questions concerning the validity of its powers; and

---

[17]*Compiler's Note:* The original text, p. 75, comments: "It was largely because the framers of the Constitution knew the temper and class bias of the state legislatures that they arranged that the new Constitution should be ratified by conventions."

has in some instances given birth to the enormous doctrine of a right of legislative repeal. Owing its ratification to the law of a state, it has been contended that the same authority might repeal the law by which it was ratified. However gross a heresy it may be to maintain that a party to a compact has a right to revoke that compact, the doctrine itself has respectable advocates. The possibility of a question of this nature proves the necessity of laying the foundations of our national government deeper than in the mere sanction of delegated authority. The fabric of American empire ought to rest on the solid basis of the consent of the people. The streams of national power ought to flow immediately from that pure original fountain of all legitimate authority."

Of course, the convention did not resort to the revolutionary policy of transmitting the Constitution directly to the conventions of the several states. It merely laid the finished instrument before the Confederate Congress with the suggestion that it should be submitted to "a convention of delegates chosen in each state by the people thereof, under the recommendation of its legislature, for their assent and ratification; and each convention assenting thereto and ratifying the same should give notice thereof to the United States in Congress assembled." The convention went on to suggest that when nine states had ratified the Constitution, the Confederate Congress should extinguish itself by making provision for the elections necessary to put the new government into effect....

After the new Constitution was published and transmitted to the states, there began a long and bitter fight over ratification. A veritable flood of pamphlet literature descended upon the country, and a collection of these pamphlets by Hamilton, Madison, and Jay, brought together under the title of *The Federalist* — though clearly a piece of campaign literature — has remained a permanent part of the contemporary sources on the Constitution and has been regarded by many lawyers as a commentary second in value only to the decisions of the Supreme Court. Within a year the champions of the new government found themselves victorious, for on June 21, 1788, the ninth state, New Hampshire, ratified the Constitution, and accordingly the new government might go into effect as between the agreeing states. Within a few weeks, the nationalist party in Virginia and New York succeeded in winning these two states, and in spite of the fact that North Carolina and Rhode Island had not yet ratified the Constitution, Congress determined to put the instrument into effect in accordance with the recommendations of the convention. Elections for the new government were held; the date March 4, 1789, was fixed for the formal establishment of the new system; Congress secured a quorum on April 6; and on April 30 Washington was inaugurated at the Federal Hall in Wall Street, New York.

☐   Charles A. Beard suggests that there is a dichotomy between the values of the Constitution and those of the Declaration of Independence, between Jefferson and his followers on the one hand, and Madison and Hamilton on the other. He suggests that Jefferson and the Revolutionists supported political equality and individual freedom and opposed a strong central government. The spirit of the Revolution, argues Beard, spawned the Articles of Confederation, which purposely created a weak and ineffective government. The Revolutionists, in general, were not men of property and thus did not believe that a strong central government was necessary to protect their interests. By contrast, the framers of the Constitution reflected the spirit of Alexander Hamilton, who ironically was not a man of substantial property himself, but who advocated an energetic and dominant national government. Hamilton, like many of the framers, was a strong proponent of governmental protection of property interests.

Limitation of Governmental Power and of Majority Rule

The most accurate and helpful way to characterize our political system is to call it a constitutional democracy. The term implies a system in which the government is regulated by laws that control and limit the exercise of political power. In a constitutional democracy people participate in government on a limited basis. A distinction should be made between an unlimited democratic government and a constitutional democracy. In the former, the people govern through the operation of a principle such as majority rule without legal restraint; in the latter, majority rule is curtailed and checked through various legal devices. A constitutional system is one in which the formal authority of government is restrained. The checks upon government in a constitutional society customarily include a division or fragmentation of authority that prevents government from controlling all sectors of human life.

Hamilton noted in *Federalist 1*, "It seems to have been reserved to the people of this country, to decide by their conduct and example, the important question, whether societies of men are really capable or not, of establishing good government from reflection and choice, or whether they are forever destined to depend, for their political constitutions, on accident and force." The framers of our Constitution attempted to structure the government in such a way that it would meet the needs and aspirations of the people and at the same time check the arbitrary exercise of political power. The doctrine of the separation of powers was designed to prevent any one group from gaining control of the national governmental apparatus. The selections reprinted here from *The Federalist,* which was written between October, 1787, and August, 1788, outline the theory and mechanism of the separation of powers.

3

Alexander Hamilton

FEDERALIST 1

I propose, in a series of papers to discuss the following interesting particulars . . . The utility of the UNION to your political prosperity . . . The insufficiency of the present confederation to preserve that Union . . . The necessity of a government, at least equally energetic with the one proposed, to the attainment of this object . . . The conformity of the proposed constitution to the true principles of republican government . . . Its analogy to your own state constitution . . . and lastly, The additional security, which its adoption will afford to the preservation of that species of government, to liberty, and to property.

4

James Madison

FEDERALIST 47

I proceed to examine the particular structure of this government, and the distribution of this mass of power among its constituent parts.

One of the principal objections inculcated by the more respectable adversaries to the constitution, is its supposed violation of the political maxim, that the legislative, executive, and judiciary departments, ought to be separate and distinct. In the structure of the federal government, no regard, it is said, seems to have been paid to this essential precaution in favor of liberty. The several departments of power are distributed and blended in such a manner, as at once to destroy all symmetry and beauty of form; and to expose some of the essential parts of the edifice to the danger of being crushed by the disproportionate weight of other parts.

No political truth is certainly of greater intrinsic value, or is stamped with the authority of more enlightened patrons of liberty, than that on which the objection is founded. The accumulation of all powers, legislative, executive, and judiciary, in the same hands, whether of one, a few, or many, and whether hereditary, self-appointed, or elective, may justly be pronounced the very definition of tyranny. Were the federal constitution, therefore, really chargeable with this accumulation of power, or with a mixture of powers, having a dangerous tendency to such an accumulation, no further arguments would be necessary to inspire a universal reprobation of the system. I persuade myself, however, that it will be made apparent to every one, that the charge cannot be supported, and that the maxim on which it relies has been totally misconceived and misapplied.

The oracle who is always consulted and cited on this subject, is the celebrated Montesquieu. If he be not the author of this invaluable precept in the science of politics, he has the merit of at least displaying and recommending it most effectually to the attention of mankind. . . .

From . . . facts, by which Montesquieu was guided, it may clearly be inferred, that in saying, "there can be no liberty, where the legislative and executive powers are united in the same person, or body of magistrates"; or "if the power of judging, be not separated from the legislative and executive powers," he did not mean that these departments ought to have no *partial agency* in, or no *control* over, the acts of each other. His meaning . . . can amount to no more than this, that where the *whole* power of one department is exercised by the same hands which possess the *whole* power of another department, the fundamental principles of a free constitution are subverted. . . .

If we look into the constitutions of the several states, we find, that notwithstanding the emphatical, and, in some instances, the unqualified terms in which this axiom has been laid down, there is not a single instance in which the several departments of power have been kept absolutely separate and distinct. . . .

The constitution of Massachusetts has observed a sufficient, though less pointed caution, in expressing this fundamental article of liberty. It declares, "that the legislative department shall never exercise the executive and judicial powers, or either of them: the executive shall never exercise the legislative and judicial powers, or either of them: the judicial shall never exercise the legislative and executive powers, or either of them." This declaration corresponds precisely with the doctrine of Montesquieu. . . . It goes no farther than to prohibit any one of the entire departments from exercising the powers of another department. In the very constitution to which it is prefixed, a partial mixture of powers has been admitted. . . .

FEDERALIST 48

. . . I shall undertake in the next place to show, that unless these departments be so far connected and blended, as to give to each a constitutional control over the others, the degree of separation which the maxim requires, as essential to a free government, can never in practice be duly maintained.

It is agreed on all sides, that the powers properly belonging to one of the departments ought not to be directly and completely administered by either of the other departments. It is equally evident, that neither of them ought to possess, directly or indirectly, an overruling influence over the others in the administration of their respective powers. It will not be denied, that power is of an encroaching nature, and that it ought to be effectually restrained from passing the limits assigned to it. After discriminating, therefore, in theory, the several classes of power, as they may in their nature be legislative, executive, or judiciary; the next, and most difficult task, is to provide some practical security for each, against the invasion of the others. What this security ought to be, is the great problem to be solved.

Will it be sufficient to mark, with precision, the boundaries of these departments, in the constitution of the government, and to trust to these parchment barriers against the encroaching spirit of power? This is the security which appears to have been principally relied on by the compilers of most American constitutions. But experience assures us, that the efficacy of the provision has been greatly overrated; and that some more adequate defense is indispensably necessary for the more feeble, against the more powerful members of the government. The legislative department is everywhere extending the sphere of its activity, and drawing all power into its impetuous vortex. . . .

In a government where numerous and extensive prerogatives are placed in the hands of an hereditary monarch, the executive department is very justly regarded as the source of danger, and watched with all the jealousy which a zeal for liberty ought to inspire. In a democracy, where a multitude of people exercise in person the legislative functions, and are continually exposed, by their incapacity for regular deliberation and concerted measures, to the ambitious intrigues of their executive magistrates, tyranny may well be apprehended on some favorable emergency, to start up in the same quarter. But in a representative republic, where the executive magistracy is carefully limited, both in the extent and the duration of its power; and where the legislative is exercised by an assembly, which is inspired by a supposed influence over the people, with an intrepid confidence in its own strength; which is sufficiently numerous to feel all the passions which actuate a multitude; yet not so numerous as to be incapable of pursuing the objects of its passions, by means which reason prescribes; it is against the enterprising ambition of this department, that the people ought to indulge all their jealousy and exhaust all their precautions.

The legislative department derives a superiority in our governments from other circumstances. Its constitutional powers being at once more extensive, and less susceptible of precise limits, it can, with the greater facility, mask, under complicated and indirect measures, the encroachment which it makes on the coordinate departments. It is not infrequently a question of real nicety in legislative bodies, whether the operation of a particular measure will, or will not extend beyond the legislative sphere. On the other side, the executive power being restrained within a narrower compass, and being more simple in its nature; and the judiciary being described by landmarks, still less uncertain, projects of usurpation by either of these departments would immediately betray and defeat themselves. Nor is this all: as the legislative department alone has access to the pockets of the people, and has in some constitutions full discretion, and in all a prevailing influence over the pecuniary rewards of those who fill the other departments; a dependence is thus created in the latter, which gives still greater facility to encroachments of the former. . . .

FEDERALIST 51

To what expedient then shall we finally resort, for maintaining in practice the necessary partition of power among the several departments, as laid down in the constitution? The only answer that can be given is, that as all these exterior provisions are found to be inadequate, the defect must be supplied, by so contriving the interior structure of the government, as that its several constituent parts may, by their mutual relations, be the means of keeping each other in their proper places. . . .

In order to lay a due foundation for that separate and distinct exercise of the different powers of government, which, to a certain extent, is admitted on all hands to be essential to the preservation of liberty, it is evident that each department should have a will of its own; and consequently should be so constituted, that the members of each should have as little agency as possible in the appointment of the members of the others. . . .

It is equally evident, that the members of each department should be as little dependent as possible on those of the others, for the emoluments annexed to their offices. Were the executive magistrate, or the judges, not independent of the legislature in this particular, their independence in every other, would be merely nominal.

But the great security against a gradual concentration of the several powers in the same department, consists in giving to those who administer each department, the necessary constitutional means, and personal motives, to resist encroachments of the others. The provision for defense must in this, as in all other cases, be made commensurate to the danger of attack. Ambition must be made to counteract ambition. The interest of the man must be connected with the constitutional rights of the place. It may be a reflection on human nature, that such devices should be necessary to control the abuses of government. But what is government itself, but the greatest of all reflections on human nature? If men were angels, no government would be necessary. If angels were to govern men, neither external nor internal controls on government would be necessary. In framing a government, which is to be administered by men over men, the great difficulty lies in this: You must first enable the government to control the governed; and in the next place, oblige it to control itself. A dependence on the people is, no doubt, the primary control on the government; but experience has taught mankind the necessity of auxiliary precautions.

This policy of supplying by opposite and rival interests, the defect of better motives, might be traced through the whole system of human affairs, private as well as public. We see it particularly displayed in all the subordinate distributions of power; where the constant aim is, to divide and arrange the several offices in such a manner, as that each may be a check on the other; that the private interest of every individual, may be a sentinel over the public rights. These inventions of prudence cannot be less requisite to the distribution of the supreme powers of the state.

But it is not possible to give to each department an equal power of self-defense. In republican government, the legislative authority necessarily predominates. The remedy for this inconvenience is, to divide the legislature into different branches; and to render them by different modes of election, and different principles of action, as little connected with each other, as the nature of their common functions, and their common dependence on the society will admit. It may even be necessary to guard against dangerous encroachments, by still further precautions. As the weight of the legislative authority requires that it should be thus divided, the weakness of the executive may require, on the other hand, that it should be fortified. An absolute negative on the legislature, appears, at first view, to be the natural defense with which the executive magistrate should be armed. But perhaps it would be neither altogether safe, nor alone sufficient. On ordinary occasions, it might not be exerted with the requisite firmness; and on extraordinary occasions, it might be perfidiously abused. May not this defect of an absolute negative be supplied by some qualified connection between this weaker department, and the weaker branch of the stronger department, by which the latter may be led to support the constitutional rights of the former, without being too much detached from the rights of its own department?

Constitutional Democracy:
The Rule of Law

☐   The Western political heritage has emphasized the importance of democracy and the rule of law. As early as Aristotle's *Politics,* the viability of democracy, provided there are sufficient checks upon unlimited popular rule, has been stressed.

The American constitutional tradition reflects the beliefs of many political philosophers. One of the most dominating figures is John Locke. It is not suggested that Locke was read by most of the colonists, but only that his ideas invariably found their way into many writings of eighteenth-century America, most importantly the Declaration of Independence. In a letter to Henry Lee in 1825, Thomas Jefferson wrote:

"When forced ... to resort to arms for redress, an appeal to the tribunal of the world was deemed proper for our justification. This was the object of the Declaration of Independence. Not to find out new principles, or new arguments, never before thought of, not merely to say things which had never been said before; but to place before mankind the common sense of the subject, in terms so plain and firm as to command their assent, and to justify ourselves in the independent stand we are compelled to take. Neither aiming at originality of principle or sentiment, nor yet copied from any particular and previous writing, it was intended to be an expression of the American mind, and to give to that expression the proper tone and spirit called for by the occasion. All its authority rests then on the harmonizing sentiments of the day, whether expressed in conversation, in letters, printed essays, or in the elementary books of public right [such] as Aristotle, Cicero, Locke, Sidney, etc. . . . "

In May of 1790, Jefferson wrote: "Locke's little book on government is perfect as far as it goes." Although Jefferson's admiration of Locke was perhaps greater than that of many other colonists, his views did reflect a mood of eighteenth-century America. Locke's *Second Treatise, Of Civil Government* attempted to trace the reasons why men enter into political societies in the first place. The eighteenth century, no less than the twentieth, was an era characterized by attempts to be "scientific" in political formulations. Locke's *Second Treatise,* first published in 1690, reflected the scientific emphasis that was to prevail so widely beginning in the eighteenth century. To Locke, natural law was objectively valid, and therefore once ascertained, governments based upon it would have a superior claim to legitimacy. Locke is notable for his discussions of natural law, from which he derived the "best" form of government. In reading Locke, one should observe how much importance he placed upon property rights and the right of the people to dissolve government once it no longer meets their legitimate expectations.

5
John Locke

SECOND TREATISE,
OF CIVIL GOVERNMENT

OF THE STATE OF NATURE

To understand political power aright, and derive it from its original, we must consider what estate all men are naturally in, and that is, a state of perfect freedom to order their actions, and dispose of their possessions and persons as they think fit, within the bounds of the laws of Nature, without asking leave or depending upon the will of any other man.

A state also of equality, wherein all the power and jurisdiction is reciprocal, no one having more than another, there being nothing more evident than that creatures of the same species and rank, promiscuously born to all the same advantages of Nature, and the use of the same faculties, should also be equal one amongst another, without subordination or subjection, unless the lord and master of them all should, by any manifest declaration of his will, set one above another, and confer on him, by an evident and clear appointment, an undoubted right to dominion and sovereignty. . . .

But though this be a state of liberty, yet it is not a state of license; though man in that state have an uncontrollable liberty to dispose of his person or possessions, yet he had not liberty to destroy himself, or so much as any creature in his possession, but where some nobler use than its bare preservation calls for it. The state of Nature has a law of Nature to govern it, which obliges every one, and reason, which is that law, teaches all mankind who will but consult it, that being all equal and independent, no one ought to harm another in his life, health, liberty or possessions. . . . And, being furnished with like faculties, sharing all in one community of Nature, there cannot be supposed any such subordination among us that may authorize us to destroy one another, as if we were made for one another's uses, as the inferior ranks of creatures are for ours. Every one as he is bound to preserve himself, and not to quit his station wilfully, so by the like reason, when his own preservation comes not in competition, ought he as much as he can to preserve the rest of mankind, and not unless it be to do justice on an offender, take away or impair the life, or what tends to the preservation of the life, the liberty, health, limb, or goods of another.

And that all men may be restrained from invading others' rights, and from doing hurt to one another, and the law of Nature be observed, which willeth the peace and preservation of all mankind, the execution of the law of Nature is in that state put into every man's hands, whereby every one has a right to punish the transgressors of that law to such a degree as may hinder its violation. For the law of Nature would, as all other laws that concern men in this world, be in vain if there were nobody that in the state of Nature had a power to execute that law, and thereby preserve the innocent and restrain offenders; and if any one in the state of Nature may punish another for any evil he has done, every one may do so. For in that state of perfect equality, where naturally there is no superiority or jurisdiction of one over another, what any may do in prosecution of that law, every one must needs have a right to do.

And thus, in the state of Nature, one man comes by a power over another, but yet no absolute or arbitrary power to use a criminal, when he has got him in his hands, according to the passionate heats or boundless extravagancy of his own will, but only to retribute to him so far as calm reason and conscience dictate, what is proportionate to his transgression, which is so much as may serve for reparation and restraint. . . .

Every offence that can be committed in the state of Nature may, in the state of Nature, be also punished equally, and as far forth, as it may, in a commonwealth. For—though it would be beside my present purpose to enter here into the particulars of the law of Nature, or its measures of punishment, yet it is certain there is such a law, and that too as intelligible and plain to a rational creature and a studier of that law as the positive laws of commonwealths, nay, possibly plainer; as much as reason is easier to be understood than the fancies and intricate contrivances of men, following contrary and hidden interests put into words. . . .

OF THE ENDS OF POLITICAL SOCIETY AND GOVERNMENT

If man in the state of Nature be so free as has been said, if he be absolute lord of his own person and possessions, equal to the greatest and subject to nobody, why will he part with his freedom, this empire, and subject himself to the dominion and control of any other power? To which it is obvious to answer, that though in the state of Nature he hath such a right, yet the enjoyment of it is very uncertain and constantly exposed to the invasion of others; for all being kings as much as he, every man his equal, and the greater part no strict observers of equity and justice, the enjoyment of the property he has in this state is very unsafe, very insecure. This makes him willing to quit this condition which, however free, is full of fears and continual dangers; and it is not without reason that he seeks out and is willing to join in society with others who are already united, or have a mind to unite for the mutual preservation of their lives, liberties, and estates, which I call by the general name—property.

The great and chief end, therefore, of men uniting into commonwealths, and putting themselves under government, is the preservation of their property; to which in the state of Nature there are many things wanting.

Firstly, there wants an established, settled, known law, received and allowed by common consent to be the standard of right and wrong, and the common measure to decide all controversies between them. For though the law of Nature be plain and intelligible to all rational creatures, yet men, being biased by their interest, as well as ignorant for want of study of it, are not apt to allow of it as a law binding to them in the application of it to their particular cases.

Secondly, in the state of Nature there wants a known and indifferent judge, with authority to determine all differences according to the established law. For every one in that state being both judge and executioner of the law of Nature, men being partial to themselves, passion and revenge is very apt to carry them too far, and with too much heat in their own cases, as well as negligence and unconcernedness, make them too remiss in other men's.

Thirdly, in the state of Nature there often wants power to back and support the sentence when right, and to give it due execution. They who by any injustice offended will seldom fail where they are able by force to make good their injustice. Such resistance many times makes the punishment dangerous, and frequently destructive to those who attempt it.

Thus mankind, notwithstanding all the privileges of the state of Nature, being but in an ill condition while they remain in it are quickly driven into society. Hence it comes to pass, that we seldom find any number of men live any time together in this state. The inconveniences that they are therein exposed to by the irregular and uncertain exercise of the power every man has of punishing the transgressions of others, make them take sanctuary under the established laws of government, and therein seek the preservation of their property. It is this makes them so willingly give up every one his single power of punishing to be exercised by such alone as shall be appointed to it amongst them, and by such rules as the community, or those authorised by them to that purpose, shall agree on. And in this we have the original right and rise of both the legislative and executive power as well as of the governments and societies themselves.

For in the state of Nature to omit the liberty he has of innocent delights, a man has two powers. The first is to do whatsoever he thinks fit for the preservation of himself and others within the permission of the law of Nature; by which law, common to them all, he and all the rest of mankind are one community, make up one society distinct from all other creatures, and were it not for the corruption and viciousness of degenerate men, there would be no need of any other, no necessity that men should separate from this great and natural community, and associate into lesser combinations. The other power a man has in the state of Nature is the power to punish the crimes committed against that law. Both these he gives up when he joins in a private, if I may so call it, or particular political society, and incorporates into any commonwealth separate from the rest of mankind.

The first power—viz., of doing whatsoever he thought fit for the preservation of himself and the rest of mankind, he gives up to be regulated by laws made by the society, so far forth as the preservation of himself and the rest of that society shall require; which laws of the society in many things confine the liberty he had by the law of Nature.

Secondly, the power of punishing he wholly gives up, and engages his natural force, which he might before employ in the execution of the law of Nature, by his own single authority, as he thought fit, to assist the executive power of the society as the law thereof shall require. For being now in a new state, wherein he is to enjoy many conveniences from the labor, assistance, and society of others in the same community, as well as protection from its whole strength, he is to part also with as much of his natural liberty, in providing for himself, as the good, prosperity, and safety of the society shall require, which is not only necessary but just, since the other members of the society do the like.

But though men when they enter into society give up the equality, liberty, and executive power they had in the state of Nature into the hands of the society, to be so far disposed of by the legislative as the good of the society shall require, yet it being only with an intention in every one the better to preserve himself, his liberty and property (for no rational creature can be supposed to change his condition with an intention to be worse), the power of the society or legislative constituted by them can never be supposed to extend farther than the common against those three defects above mentioned that made the state of Nature so unsafe and uneasy. And so, whoever has the legislative or supreme power of any commonwealth, is bound to govern by established standing laws, promulgated and known to the people, and not by extemporary decrees, by indifferent and upright judges, who are to decide controversies by those laws; and to employ the force of the community at home only in the execution of such laws, or abroad to prevent or redress foreign injuries and secure the community from inroads and invasion. And all this to be directed to no other end but the peace, safety, and public good of the people. . . .

OF THE EXTENT OF THE LEGISLATIVE POWER

The great end of men's entering into society being the enjoyment of their properties in peace and safety, and the great instrument and means of that being the laws established in that society, the first and fundamental positive law of all commonwealths is the establishing of the legislative power, as the first and fundamental natural law, which is to govern even the legislative itself, is the preservation of the society and (as far as will consist with the public good) of every person in it. This legislative is not only the supreme power of the commonwealth, but sacred and unalterable in the hands where the community have once placed it. Nor can any edict of anybody else, in what form soever conceived, or by what power soever backed, have the force and obligation of a law which has not its sanction from that legislative which the public has chosen and appointed; for without this the law could not have that which is absolutely necessary to its being a law, the consent of the society, over whom nobody can have a power to make laws but by their own consent and by authority received from them. . . .

These are the bounds which the trust that is put in them by the society and the law of God and Nature have set to the legislative power of every commonwealth, in all forms of government. First: They are to govern by promulgated established laws, not to be varied in particular cases, but to have one rule for rich and poor, for the favorite at Court and the countryman at plough. Secondly: These laws also ought to be designed for no other end ultimately but the good of the people. Thirdly: They must not raise taxes on the property of the people without the consent of the people given by themselves or their deputies. And this properly concerns only such governments where the legislative is always in being, or at least where the people have not reserved any part of the legislative to deputies, to be from time to time chosen by themselves. Fourthly: Legislative neither must nor can transfer the power of making laws to anybody else, or place it anywhere but where the people have. . . .

OF THE DISSOLUTION OF GOVERNMENT

The constitution of the legislative [authority] is the first and fundamental act of society, whereby provision is made for the continuation of their union under the direction of persons and bonds of laws, made by persons authorised thereunto, by the consent and appointment of the people, without which no one man, or number of men, amongst them can have authority of making laws that shall be binding to the rest. When any one, or more, shall take upon them to make laws whom the people have not appointed so to do, they make laws without authority, which the people are not therefore bound to obey; by which means they come again to be out of subjection, and may constitute to themselves a new legislative, as they think best, being in full liberty to resist the force of those who, without authority, would impose anything upon them. . . .

Whosoever uses force without right—as every one does in society who does it without law—puts himself into a state of war with those against whom he so uses it, and in that state all former ties are cancelled, all other rights cease, and every one has a right to defend himself, and to resist the aggressor. . . .

Here it is like the common question will be made: Who shall be judge whether the prince or legislative act contrary to their trust? This, perhaps, ill-affected and factious men may spread amongst the people, when the prince only makes use of his due prerogative. To this I reply, The people shall be judge; for who shall be judge whether his trustee or deputy acts well and according to the trust reposed in him, but he who deputes him and must, by having deputed him, have still a power to discard him when he fails in his trust? If this be reasonable in particular cases of private men, why should it be otherwise in that of the greatest moment, where the welfare of millions is concerned and also where the evil, if not prevented, is greater, and the redress very difficult, dear, and dangerous? . . .

To conclude. The power that every individual gave the society when he entered into it can never revert to the individuals again, as long as the society lasts, but will always remain in the community; because without this there can be no community—no commonwealth, which is contrary to the original agreement; so also when the society hath placed the legislative in any assembly of men, to continue in them and their successors, with direction and authority for providing such successors, the legislative can never revert to the people whilst that government lasts; because, having provided a legislative with power to continue for ever, they have given up their political power to the legislative, and cannot resume it. But if they have set limits to the duration of their legislative, and made this supreme power in any person or assembly only temporary; or else when, by the miscarriages of those in authority, it is forfeited; upon the foreferiture of their rulers, or at the determination of the time set, it reverts to the society, and the people have a right to act as supreme, and continue the legislative in themselves or place it in a new form, or new hands, as they think good.

☐ The influence of John Locke goes far beyond his impact on the thinking of the founding fathers of the United States, such as Thomas Jefferson. Some scholars (among them, Louis Hartz, *The Liberal Tradition in America*) have interpreted the American political tradition in terms of the pervasive attachment to the ideas and values set forth in the writings of Locke. There is little question that American political life has been uniquely characterized by widespread adherence to the fundamental principles about the relations among men, society, and government expressed in Locke's writings.

It is not just that we have representative government, with institutions similar in structure and function to those of the constitutional democracy described in Locke's *Second Treatise*, but that through the years we have probably maintained, more than any other society, a widespread agreement about the fundamental human values cherished by Locke. His emphasis upon the sanctity of private property has been paramount in the American political tradition from the very beginning. Moreover, Locke's views on the nature of man are shared by most Americans. All our governmental institutions, processes, and traditions rest upon principles such as the primacy of the individual, man's inborn ability to exercise reason in order to discern truth and higher principles of order and justice, and a political and social equality among men in which no man shall count for more than another in determining the actions of government and their application. We may not have always practiced these ideals, but we have been *theoretically* committed to them.

An Overview of the Framing and Purpose of the Constitution

The preceding selections have offered contrasting views on the framing, nature, and purpose of the Constitution. To John Roche, the Constitution was a practical political document reflecting compromises among state delegations with contrasting political and economic interests, and between advocates of strong national power and proponents of states' rights. Charles Beard saw the Constitution as a reflection of the interests of property owners and creditors who feared that the rule of the debtor majority would inflate currency, cancel debts, and deprive creditors of their rightful property. James Madison's selections from *The Federalist* suggest a mistrust of government, a wary view of both political leaders and the people, and an emphasis upon the need for governmental checks and balances to prevent the arbitrary exercise of political power. Madison also distrusted what he termed "faction," by which he meant political parties or special interest groups, which he considered intrinsically to be opposed to the national interest (see Federalist 10, Chapter 4). Finally, John Locke's political philosophy expressed in his *Second Treatise, Of Civil Government* (1690) supported the political beliefs of many eighteenth-century Americans in government as a social contract between rulers and ruled to protect the natural rights of citizens to life, liberty, and, very importantly, property.

CHAPTER 2

Federalism

The United States government utilizes a "federal" form to secure certain political and economic objectives. This chapter identifies both the traditional and modern goals of American federalism from the writings of important theorists who have examined general and specific problems in national–state relationships. The validity of federalism is also analyzed.

Constitutional Background: National v. State Power

No subject attracted greater attention or was more carefully analyzed at the time of the framing of the Constitution than federalism. *The Federalist* devoted a great deal of space to proving the advantages of a federal form of government relative to a confederacy, since the Constitution was going to take some of the power traditionally within the jurisdiction of state governments and give it to a newly constituted national government.

The victory of the nationalists at the Constitutional Convention of 1787, which resulted in sovereign states giving up a significant portion of their authority to a new national government, is remarkable by any standard of measurement. Today, when the creation of the Union is largely taken for granted, it is difficult to appreciate the environment of the Revolutionary period, a time when the states wanted at all costs to protect their newly won freedom from an oppressive British government. The constitution of 1787 was accepted as a matter of necessity as much as desire.

It was against the background of the Articles of Confederation that Hamilton wrote in *The Federalist* about the advantages of the new "federal" system that would be created by the Constitution. The Articles of Confederation had been submitted to the states in 1777 and was finally ratified by all of the states in 1781, Maryland being the only holdout after 1779. The "League of Friendship" that had been created among the states by the Articles had proved inadequate to meeting even the minimum needs of union. The government of the Articles of Confederation had many weaknesses, for it was essentially a league of sovereign states, joined together more in accordance with principles of international agreement than in accordance with the rules of nation states. Most of the provisions of the Articles of Confederation concerned the foreign relations of the new government, and matters of national defense and security. For this purpose a minimum number of powers were granted to the national government, which, however, had no executive or judicial authority and was therefore incapable of independent enforcement. National actions were dependent upon the states for enforcement, and under Article Two "each state retains its sovereignty, freedom and independence, and every power, jurisdiction and right, which is not by this confederation expressly delegated to the United States, in Congress assembled." The paucity of authority delegated to the central government under the Articles left the sovereignty of the states intact. And the national government was totally dependent upon the states as agents of enforcement of what little authority it could exercise. The government of the Articles of Confederation then, without an executive or judicial branch, and without such crucial authority as the power to tax and regulate commerce, required a drastic overhaul if it was to become a national government in fact as well as in name.

In the following selections from *The Federalist* Alexander Hamilton argues the advantages of the new federal Constitution, and at the same time attempts to alleviate the fears of his opponents that the new government would intrude upon and possibly eventually destroy the sovereignty of the states. The national government, he wrote, must be able to act directly upon the citizens of the states to regulate the common concerns of the nation. He found the system of the Articles of Confederation too weak, allowing state evasion of national power. Augmenting the authority of the national government would not destroy state sovereignty, because of the inherent strength of the individual states (which at the time Hamilton wrote were singly and collectively far more powerful than any proposed national government). Moreover, there would be no incentives for ambitious politicians to look to the states to realize their goals, for the scope of national power was sufficient to occupy temptations for political aggrandizement.

6

Alexander Hamilton

FEDERALIST 16

The . . . death of the confederacy . . . is what we now seem to be on the point of experiencing, if the federal system be not speedily renovated in a more substantial form. It is not probable, considering the genius of this country, that the complying states would often be inclined to support the authority of the union, by engaging in a war against the non-complying states. They would always be more ready to pursue the milder course of putting themselves upon an equal footing with the delinquent members, by an imitation of their example. And the guilt of all would thus become the security of all. Our past experience has exhibited the operation of this spirit in its full light. There would, in fact, be an insuperable difficulty in ascertaining when force would with propriety be employed. In the article of pecuniary contribution, which would be the most usual source of delinquency, it would often be impossible to decide whether it had proceeded from disinclination, or inability. The pretense of the latter would always be at hand. And the case must be very flagrant in which its fallacy could be detected with sufficient certainty to justify the harsh expedient of compulsion. It is easy to see that this problem alone, as often as it should occur, would open a wide field to the majority that happened to prevail in the national council, for the exercise of factious views, of partiality, and of oppression.

It seems to require no pains to prove that the states ought not to prefer a national constitution, which could only be kept in motion by the instrumentality of a large army, continually on foot to execute the ordinary requisitions or decrees of the government. And yet this is the plain alternative involved by those who wish to deny it the power of extending its operations to individuals. Such a scheme, if practicable at all, would instantly degenerate into a military despotism; but it will be found in every light impracticable. The resources of the union would not be equal to the maintenance of any army considerable enough to confine the larger states within the limits of their duty; nor would the means ever be furnished of forming such an army in the first instance. Whoever considers the populousness and strength of several of these states singly at the present juncture, and looks forward to what they will become, even at the distance of half a century, will at once dismiss as idle and visionary any scheme which aims at regulating their movements by laws, to operate upon them in their collective capacities, and to be executed by a coercion applicable to them in the same capacities. A project of this kind is little less romantic than the monster-taming spirit attributed to the fabulous heroes and demigods of antiquity. . . .

The result of these observations to an intelligent mind must clearly be this, that if it be possible at any rate to construct a federal government capable of regulating the common concerns, and preserving the general tranquillity, it must be founded, as to the objects committed to its case, upon the reverse of the principle contended for by the opponents of the proposed constitution [i.e., a confederacy]. It must carry its agency to the persons of the citizens. It must stand in need of no intermediate legislations; but must itself be empowered to employ the arm of the ordinary magistrate to execute its own resolutions. The majesty of the national authority must be manifested through the medium of the courts of justice. The government of the union, like that of each state, must be able to address itself immediately to the hopes and fears of individuals; and to attract to its support, those passions which have the strongest influence upon the human heart. It must, in short, possess all the means, and have a right to resort to all the methods, of executing the powers with which it is entrusted, that are possessed and exercised by the governments of the particular states.

To this reasoning it may perhaps be objected, that if any state should be disaffected to the authority of the union, it could at any time obstruct the execution of its laws, and bring the matter to the same issue of force, with the necessity of which the opposite scheme is reproached.

The plausibility of this objection will vanish the moment we advert to the essential difference between a mere NONCOMPLIANCE and a DIRECT and ACTIVE RESISTANCE. If the interposition of the state legislatures be necessary to give effect to a measure of the union [as in a confederacy], they have only NOT TO ACT, OR TO ACT EVASIVELY, and the measure is defeated. This neglect of duty may be disguised under affected but unsubstantial provisions so as not to appear, and of course not to excite any alarm in the people for the safety of the constitution. The state leaders may even make a merit of their surreptitious invasions of it, on the ground of some temporary convenience, exemption, or advantage.

But if the execution of the laws of the national government should not require the intervention of the state legislatures; if they were to pass into immediate operation upon the citizens themselves, the particular governments could not interrupt their progress without an open and violent exertion of an unconstitutional power. No omission, nor evasions, would answer the end. They would be obliged to act, and in such a manner, as would leave no doubt that they had encroached on the national rights. An experiment of this nature would always be hazardous in the face of a constitution in any degree competent to its own defense, and of a people enlightened enough to distinguish between a legal exercise and an illegal usurpation of authority. The success of it would require not merely a factious majority in the legislature, but the concurrence of the courts of justice, and of the body of the people....

FEDERALIST 17

An objection, of a nature different from that which has been stated and answered in my last address, may, perhaps, be urged against the principle of legislation for the individual citizens of America. It may be said, that it would tend to render the government of the union too powerful, and to enable it to absorb those residuary authorities, which it might be judged proper to leave with the states for local purposes. Allowing the utmost latitude to the love of power, which any reasonable man can require, I confess I am at a loss to discover what temptation the persons entrusted with the administration of the general government could ever feel to divest the states of the authorities of that description. The regulation of the mere domestic police of a state, appears to me to hold out slender allurements to ambition. Commerce, finance, negotiation, and war, seem to comprehend all the objects which have charms for minds governed by that passion; and all the powers necessary to those objects, ought, in the first instance, to be lodged in the national depository. The administration of private justice between the citizens of the same state; the supervision of agriculture, and of other concerns of a similar nature; all those things, in short, which are proper to be provided for by local legislation, can never be desirable cares of a general jurisdiction. It is therefore improbable, that there should exist a disposition in the federal councils, to usurp the powers with which they are connected; because the attempt to exercise them would be as troublesome as it would be nugatory; and the possession of them, for that reason, would contribute nothing to the dignity, to the importance, or to the splendor, of the national government.

But let it be admitted, for argument's sake, that mere wantonness, and lust of domination, would be sufficient to beget that disposition; still, it may be safely affirmed, that the sense of the constituent body of the national representatives, or in other words, of the people of the several states, would control the indulgence of so extravagant an appetite. It will always be far more easy for the state governments to encroach upon the national authorities, than for the national government to encroach upon the state authorities. The proof of this proposition turns upon the greater degree of influence which the state governments, if they administer their affairs with uprightness and prudence, will generally possess over the people; a circumstance which at the same time teaches us, that there is an inherent and intrinsic weakness in all federal constitutions; and that too much pain cannot be taken in their organization, to give them all the force which is compatible with the principles of liberty.

The superiority of influence in favor of the particular governments, would result partly from the diffusive construction of the national government; but chiefly from the nature of the objects to which the attention of the state administrations would be directed.

It is a known fact in human nature, that its affections are commonly weak in proportion to the distance of diffusiveness of the object. Upon the same principle that a man is more attached to his family than to his neighborhood, to his neighborhood than to the community at large, the people of each state would be apt to feel a stronger bias towards their local governments, than towards the government of the union, unless the force of that principle should be destroyed by a much better administration of the latter.

This strong propensity of the human heart, would find powerful auxiliaries in the objects of state regulation.

The variety of more minute interests, which will necessarily fall under the superintendence of the local administrations, and which will form so many rivulets of influence, running through every part of the society, cannot be particularized, without involving a detail too tedious and uninteresting to compensate for the instruction it might afford.

There is one transcendent advantage belonging to the province of the state governments, which alone suffices to place the matter in a clear and satisfactory light—I mean the ordinary administration of criminal and civil justice. This, of all others, is the most powerful, most universal and most attractive source of popular obedience and attachment. It is this, which, being the immediate and visible guardian of life and property; having its benefits and its terrors in constant activity before the public eye; regulating all those personal interests, and familiar concerns, to which the sensibility of individuals is more immediately awake; contributes, more than any other circumstance, to impress upon the minds of the people affection, esteem, and reverence towards the government. This great cement of society, which will diffuse itself almost wholly through the channels of the particular governments, independent of all other causes of influence, would insure them so decided an empire over their respective citizens, as to render them at all times a complete counterpoise, and not infrequently dangerous rivals to the power of the union.

☐ In *Federalist 39,* James Madison stated that the new Constitution was both federal and national. He attempted to answer arguments that the Constitution destroyed the confederacy of sovereign states and replaced it with a national government. In answering this argument Madison used the term "federal" as it was used by the objectors to the Constitution he was attempting to answer. They essentially used "federal" and "confederacy" interchangeably, each term referring to a system requiring agreement among the states before certain actions could be taken. Because agreement was required among the states for ratification, for example, Madison referred to the establishment of the Constitution as a *federal* and not a national act. Madison suggested that the character of the House of Representatives, which derives its powers from the people, was national rather than federal. Conversely, the Senate, representing the states equally, was federal, not national. With regard to the powers of the national government, Madison claimed that in operation they are national because they allow the national government to act directly upon the people, but in extent they are federal because they are limited, the states having agreed to delegate only a certain number of powers to the national government. A truly national government would not be limited in the scope of its powers.

7

James Madison

FEDERALIST 39

The last paper having concluded the observations which were meant to introduce a candid survey of the plan of government reported by the convention, we now proceed to the execution of that part of our undertaking.

The first question that offers itself is whether the general form and aspect of the government be strictly republican. It is evident that no other form would be reconcilable with the genius of the people of America; with the fundamental principles of the Revolution; or with that honorable determination which animates every votary of freedom to rest all our political experiments on the capacity of mankind for self-government. If the plan of the convention, therefore, be found to depart from the republican character, its advocates must abandon it as no longer defensible.

What, then, are the distinctive characters of the republican form? Were an answer to this question to be sought, not by recurring to principles but in the application of the term by political writers to the constitutions of different States, no satisfactory one would ever be found. Holland, in which no particle of the supreme authority is derived from the people, has passed almost universally under the denomination of a republic. The same title has been bestowed on Venice, where absolute power over the great body of the people is exercised in the most absolute manner by a small body of hereditary nobles. Poland, which is a mixture of aristocracy and of monarchy in their worst forms, has been dignified with the same appellation. The government of England, which has one republican branch only, combined with an hereditary aristocracy and monarchy, has with equal impropriety been frequently placed on the list of republics. These examples, which are nearly as dissimilar to each other as to a genuine republic, show the extreme inaccuracy with which the term has been used in political disquisitions.

If we resort for a criterion to the different principles on which different forms of government are established, we may define a republic to be, or at least may bestow that name on, a government which derives all its powers directly or indirectly from the great body of the people, and is administered by persons holding their offices during pleasure for a limited period, or during good behavior. It is *essential* to such a government that it be derived from the great body of the society, not from an inconsiderable proportion or a favored class of it; otherwise a handful of tyrannical nobles, exercising their oppressions by a delegation of their powers, might aspire to the rank of republicans and claim for their government the honorable title of republic. It is *sufficient* for such a government that the persons administering it be appointed, either directly or indirectly, by the people; and that they hold their appointments by either of the tenures just specified; otherwise every government in the United States, as well as every other popular government that has been or can be well organized or well executed, would be degraded from the republican character. According to the constitution of every State in the Union, some or other of the officers of government are appointed indirectly only by the people. According to most of them, the chief magistrate himself is so appointed. And according to one, this mode of appointment is extended to one of the co-ordinate branches of the legislature. According to all the constitutions, also, the tenure of the highest offices is extended to a definite period, and in many instances, both within the legislative and executive departments, to a period of years. According to the provisions of most of the constitutions, again, as well as according to the most respectable and received opinions on the subject, the members of the judiciary department are to retain their offices by the firm tenure of good behavior.

On comparing the Constitution planned by the convention with the standard here fixed, we perceived at once that it is, in the most rigid sense, comformable to it. The House of Representatives, like that of one branch at least of all the State legislatures, is elected immediately by the great body of the people. The Senate, like the present Congress and the Senate of Maryland, derives its appointment indirectly from the people. The President is indirectly derived from the choice of the people, according to the example in most of the States. Even the judges, with all other officers of the Union, will, as in the several States, be the choice, though a remote choice, of the people themselves. The duration of the appointments is equally conformable to the republican standard and to the model of State constitutions. The House of Representatives is periodically elective, as in all the States; and for the period of two years, as in the State of South Carolina. The Senate is elective for the period of six years, which is but one year more than the period of the Senate of Maryland, and but two more than that of the Senates of New York and Virginia. The President is to continue in office for the period of four years; as in New York and Delaware the chief magistrate is elected for three years, and in South Carolina for two years. In the other States the election is annual. In several of the States, however, no explicit provision is made for the impeachment of the chief magistrate. And in Delaware and Virginia he is not impeachable till out of office. The President of the United States is impeachable at any time during his continuance in office. The tenure by which the judges are to hold their places is, as it unquestionably ought to be, that of good behavior. The tenure of the ministerial offices generally will be a subject of legal regulation, conformable to the reason of the case and the example of the State constitutions.

Could any further proof be required of the republican complexion of this system, the most decisive one might be found in its absolute prohibition of titles of nobility, both under the federal and the State governments; and in its express guaranty of the republican form to each of the latter.

"But it was not sufficient," say the adversaries of the proposed Constitution, "for the convention to adhere to the republican form. They ought with equal care to have preserved the *federal* form, which regards the Union as a *Confederacy* of sovereign states; instead of which they have framed a *national* government, which regards the Union as a *consolidation* of the States." And it is asked by what authority this bold and radical innovation was undertaken. The handle which has been made of this objection requires that it should be examined with some precision.

Without inquiring into the accuracy of the distinction on which the objection is founded, it will be necessary to a just estimate of its force, first, to ascertain the real character of the government in question; secondly, to inquire how far the convention were authorized to propose such a government; and thirdly, how far the duty they owed to their country could supply any defect of regular authority.

First.—In order to ascertain the real character of the government, it may be considered in relation to the foundation on which it is to be established; to the sources from which its ordinary powers are to be drawn; to the operation of those powers; to the extent of them; and to the authority by which future changes in the government are to be introduced.

On examining the first relation, it appears, on one hand, that the Constitution is to be founded on the assent and ratification of the people of America, given by deputies elected for the special purpose; but, on the other, that this assent and ratification is to be given by the people, not as individuals composing one entire nation, but as composing the distinct and independent States to which they respectively belong. It is to be the assent and ratification of the several States, derived from the supreme authority in each State—the authority of the people themselves. The act, therefore, establishing the Constitution will not be a *national* but a *federal* act.

That it will be a federal and not a national act, as these terms are understood by the objectors—the act of the people, as forming so many independent States, not as forming one aggregate nation—is obvious from this single consideration: that it is to result neither from the decision of a *majority* of the people of the Union, nor from that of a *majority* of the States. It must result from the *unanimous* assent of the several States that are parties to it, differing not otherwise from their ordinary assent than in its being expressed, not by the legislative authority, but by that of the people themselves. Were the people regarded in this transaction as forming one nation, the will of the majority of the whole people of the United States would bind the minority, in the same manner as the majority in each State must bind the minority; and the will of the majority must be determined either by a comparison of the individual votes, or by considering the will of the majority of the States as evidence of the will of a majority of the people of the United States. Neither of these rules has been adopted. Each State, in ratifying the Constitution, is considered as a sovereign body independent of all others, and only to be bound by its own voluntary act. In this relation, then, the new Constitution will, if established, be a *federal* and not a *national* constitution.

The next relation is to the sources from which the ordinary powers of government are to be derived. The House of Representatives will derive its powers from the people of America; and the people will be represented in the same proportion and on the same principle as they are in the legislature of a particular State. So far the government is *national,* not *federal.* The Senate, on the other hand, will derive its powers from the States as political and coequal societies; and these will be represented on the principle of equality in the Senate, as they now are in the existing Congress. So far the government is *federal,* not *national.* The executive power will be derived from a very compound source. The immediate election of the President is to be made by the States in their political characters. The votes allotted to them are in a compound ratio, which considers them partly as distinct and coequal societies, partly as unequal members of the same society. The eventual election, again, is to be made by that branch of the legislature which consists of the national representatives; but in this particular act they are to be thrown into the form of individual delegations from so many distinct and co-equal bodies politic. From this aspect of the government it appears to be of a mixed character, presenting at least as many *federal* as *national* features.

The difference between a federal and national government, as it relates to the *operation of the government,* is by the adversaries of the plan of the convention supposed to consist in this, that in the former the powers operate on the political bodies composing the confederacy in their political capacities; in the latter, on the individual citizens composing the nation in their individual capacities. On trying the Constitution by this criterion, it falls under the *national* not the *federal* character; though perhaps not so completely as has been understood. In several cases, and particularly in the trial of controversies to which States may be parties, they must be viewed and proceeded against in their collective and political capacities only. But the operation of the government on the people in their individual capacities, in its ordinary and most essential proceedings, will, in the sense of its opponents, on the whole, designate it, in this relation, a *national* government.

But if the government be national with regard to the *operation* of its powers, it changes its aspect again when we contemplate it in relation to the extent of its powers. The idea of a national government involves in it not only an authority over the individual citizens, but an indefinite supremacy over all persons and things, so far as they are objects of lawful government. Among a people consolidated into one nation, this supremacy is completely vested in the national legislature. Among communities united for particular purposes, it is vested partly in the general and partly in the municipal legislatures. In the former case, all local authorities are subordinate to the supreme; and may be controlled, directed, or abolished by it at pleasure. In the latter, the local or municipal authorities form distinct and independent portions of the supremacy, no more subject, within their respective spheres, to the general authority than the general authority is subject to them, within its own sphere. In this relation, then, the proposed government cannot be deemed a *national* one; since its jurisdiction extends to certain enumerated objects only, and leaves to the several States a residuary and inviolable sovereignty over all other objects. It is true that in controversies relating to the boundary between the two jurisdictions, the tribunal which is ultimately to decide is to be established under the general government. But this does not change the principle of the case. The decision is to be impartially made, according to the rules of the Constitution; and all the usual and most effectual precautions are taken to secure this impartiality. Some such tribunal is clearly essential to prevent an appeal to the sword and a dissolution of the compact; and that it ought to be established under the general rather than under the local governments, or, to speak more properly, that it could be safely established under the first alone, is a position not likely to be combated.

If we try the Constitution by its last relation to the authority by which amendments are to be made, we find it neither wholly *national* nor wholly *federal*. Were it wholly national, the supreme and ultimate authority would reside in the *majority* of the people of the Union; and this authority would be competent at all times, like that of a majority of every national society to alter or abolish its established government. Were it wholly federal, on the other hand, the concurrence of each State in the Union would be essential to every alteration that would be binding on all. The mode provided by the plan of the convention is not founded on either of these principles. In requiring more than a majority, and particularly in computing the proportion by *States,* not by *citizens,* it departs from the national and advances towards the *federal* character; in rendering the concurrence of less than the whole number of States sufficient, it loses again the *federal* and partakes of the *national* character.

The proposed Constitution, therefore, even when tested by the rules laid down by its antagonists, is, in strictness, neither a national nor a federal Constitution, but a composition of both. In its foundation it is federal, not national; in the sources from which the ordinary powers of the government are drawn, it is partly federal and partly national; in the operation of these powers, it is national, not federal; in the extent of them, again, it is federal, not national; and, finally in the authoritative mode of introducing amendments, it is neither wholly federal nor wholly national.

PUBLIUS

☐ In *The Federalist,* Alexander Hamilton and James Madison were careful to point out the advantages of the federal form of government that would be established by the Constitution, both over the government that had existed under the Articles of Confederation and in general terms. Because many state political leaders were highly suspicious of the national government that would be created by the new Constitution, much of the efforts of Hamilton and Madison were directed toward allaying their fears. Above all, they both stated, the energy of the national government would never be sufficient to coerce the states into giving up any portion of their sovereignty. Moreover, Hamilton stated in *Federalist 17* that there would be no incentive for national politicians to take away the reserved powers of the states. The sphere of national power, although limited, was considered entirely adequate to absorb even the most ambitious politicians. And James Madison, *Federalist 39,* was careful to point out that the jurisdiction of the national government extended only to certain enumerated objects, implying that the residual sovereignty of the states was in fact greater than the sovereignty of the national government.

Alexis de Tocqueville, an aristocratic French observer of the American political and social scene in the early 1830s, acknowledged his debt to the writers of *The Federalist* in helping him to understand American government. Many of the sanguine views of Hamilton and Madison about the prospects for the new Constitution were echoed in Tocqueville's analysis of American institutions forty years later.

Tocqueville had set out for the United States in 1831, with his friend Gustave de Beaumont, ostensibly to examine the American prison system with a view toward prison reform in France. Tocqueville was a French judicial officer, who after the July Revolution of 1830 became disenchanted with the new government of Louis Philippe, and, in a broader context, with the continual turmoil that he saw in French political institutions. While the investigation of prisons served as a ready excuse for a leave of absence from governmental duties, Tocqueville and Beaumont's real interest was in studying American society and government. It was their feeling that democracy was probably the wave of the future and whatever lessons that could be learned from the American experiment would undoubtedly be a useful guide to the future of European society.

Tocqueville was in the United States for only nine months, from May 1831 until February 1832, but during this time he traveled over most of the country east of the Mississippi, staying long enough in various places to gain wide knowledge of local customs and institutions. Most of Tocqueville's observations about the United States were objectively optimistic about the future of democracy, yet his most hopeful expectations were not always realized. In particular, after leaving the United States, he became concerned with the possibility of what he called "tyranny of the majority" which he wrote would be an inevitable consequence of egalitarian tendencies in democratic societies such as the United States. The framers of the Constitution too were worried about unbridled majority rule in government, and felt that governmental tyranny by the majority would be curtailed by such institutional devices as the separation of powers, checks and balances, and federalism, the latter being a division of authority between the national government and the states. While the framers of the Constitution felt that the possibility of the tyranny of the majority was primarily a governmental problem, Tocqueville saw it as a societal dilemma, produced by the egalitarian ethic. Therefore, to Tocqueville, constitutional devices by themselves would not be sufficient to control the inevitable tendency toward majority despotism in an egalitarian society.

The following selection is taken from Tocqueville's discussion of the characteristics of federalism as he saw it in operation in 1831. In his discussion Tocqueville uses the terms "confederation" and "federalism" interchangeably. To him, the American federal system was one type of confederation. This is important to note because Hamilton, in his discussion of federalism in *The Federalist,* spoke of federalism in the new Constitution as replacing the "confederacy," by which he meant the government that existed under the Articles of Confederation. Most American writers on politics distinguish federalism and confederacy in the same way that Hamilton did, essentially by identifying federalism with the system of the Constitution, and a confederacy with the system of the Articles of Confederation. Under this more common definition of federalism, a federal system is one in which the national government has authority that is separate and distinct from that of the constituent states, an authority that operates directly upon the citizens of the states rather than upon the states as entities. Dual sovereignty is a characteristic of American federalism, whereas under the Articles of Confederation the national government had no authority distinct from the states, and it could not operate without their consent.

The breadth of Tocqueville's analytical method is revealed in his discussion of American federalism. He examines the broad social and political forces operating in society, refers to historical and comparative experience, and analyzes constitutional forms and institutional characteristics. His approach is both empirical and analytical. Tocqueville recognizes that while the theory of federalism may be clear, it is very difficult to apply it without some further clarification. This has certainly been true of the American federal system. As Tocqueville noted: "The sovereignty of the union is so involved in that of the states that it is impossible to distinguish its boundaries at the first glance. The whole structure of the government is artificial and conventional, and it would be ill adapted to a people which has not been long accustomed to conduct its own affairs, or to one in which the science of politics has not descended to the humblest classes of society. I have never been more struck by the good sense and the practical judgment of the Americans than in the manner in which they elude the numberless difficulties resulting from their federal constitution." Tocqueville implied that after all is said and done, federalism as well as other constitutional forms worked because of the good sense and pragmatism of the American people, which overcame constitutional ambiguity. This is why federalism worked in the United States, but, according to Tocqueville, failed in other countries that attempted to imitate the United States Constitution.

In reading the following selection, students should look for Tocqueville's views on (1) the outstanding characteristics of American federalism; (2) the major advantages of federalism; (3) significant disadvantages of the federal form of government. What evidence does Tocqueville use to buttress his arguments for the advantages and disadvantages of federalism? What changes have occurred since 1831 that might lead to a different perspective on federalism today?

8
Alexis de Tocqueville

DEMOCRACY IN AMERICA:
THE FEDERAL CONSTITUTION

CHARACTERISTICS OF THE FEDERAL CONSTITUTION
OF THE UNITED STATES OF AMERICA AS COMPARED
WITH ALL OTHER FEDERAL CONSTITUTIONS

The United States of America does not afford the first or the only instance of a confederation, several of which have existed in modern Europe, without referring to those of antiquity. Switzerland, the Germanic Empire, and the Republic of the Low Countries either have been or still are confederations. In studying the constitutions of these different countries one is surprised to see that the powers with which they invested the federal government are nearly the same as those awarded by the American Constitution to the government of the United States. They confer upon the central power the same rights of making peace and war, of raising money and troops, and of providing for the general exigencies and the common interests of the nation. Nevertheless, the federal government of these different states has always been as remarkable for its weakness and inefficiency as that of the American Union is for its vigor and capacity. Again, the first American Confederation perished through the excessive weakness of its government; and yet this weak government had as large rights and privileges as those of the Federal government of the present day, and in some respects even larger. But the present Constitution of the United States contains certain novel principles which exercise a most important influence, although they do not at once strike the observer.

This Constitution, which may at first sight be confused with the federal constitutions that have preceded it, rests in truth upon a wholly novel theory, which may be considered as a great discovery in modern political science. In all the confederations that preceded the American Constitution of 1789, the states allied for a common object agreed to obey the injunctions of a federal government; but they reserved to themselves the right of ordaining and enforcing the execution of the laws of the union. The American states which combined in 1789 agreed that the Federal government should not only dictate the laws, but execute its own enactments. In both cases the right is the same, but the exercise of the right is different; and this difference produced the most momentous consequences.

In all the confederations that preceded the American Union the federal government, in order to provide for its wants, had to apply to the separate governments; and if what it prescribed was disagreeable to any one of them, means were found to evade its claims. If it was powerful, it then had recourse to arms; if it was weak, it connived at the resistance which the law of the union, its sovereign, met with, and did nothing, under the plea of inability. Under these circumstances one of two results invariably followed: either the strongest of the allied states assumed the privileges of the federal authority and ruled all the others in its name;[1] or the federal government was abandoned by its natural supporters, anarchy arose between the confederates, and the union lost all power of action.[2]

In America the subjects of the Union are not states, but private citizens: the national government levies a tax, not upon the state of Massachusetts, but upon each inhabitant of Massachusetts. The old confederate governments presided over communities, but that of the Union presides over individuals. Its force is not borrowed, but self-derived; and it is served by its own civil and military officers, its own army, and its own courts of justice. It cannot be doubted that the national spirit, the passions of the multitude, and the provincial prejudices of each state still tend singularly to diminish the extent of the Federal authority thus constituted and to facilitate resistance to its mandates; but the comparative weakness of a restricted sovereignty is an evil inherent in the federal system. In America each state has fewer opportunities and temptations to resist; nor can such a design be put in execution (if indeed it be entertained) without an open violation of the laws of the Union, a direct interruption of the ordinary course of justice, and a bold declaration of revolt; in a word, without taking the decisive step that men always hesitate to adopt.

In all former confederations the privileges of the union furnished more elements of discord than of power, since they multiplied the claims of the nation without augmenting the means of enforcing them; and hence the real weakness of federal governments has almost always been in the exact ratio of their nominal power. Such is not the case in the American Union, in which, as in ordinary governments, the Federal power has the means of enforcing all it is empowered to demand. . . .

---

[1]This was the case in Greece when Philip undertook to execute the decrees of the Amphictyons; in the Low Countries, where the province of Holland always gave the law; and in our own time in the Germanic Confederation, in which Austria and Prussia make themselves the agents of the Diet and rule the whole confederation in its name.

[2]Such has always been the situation of the Swiss Confederation, which would have perished ages ago but for the mutual jealousies of its neighbors.

ADVANTAGES OF THE FEDERAL SYSTEM IN GENERAL, AND ITS SPECIAL UTILITY IN AMERICA

... In small states, the watchfulness of society penetrates everywhere, and a desire for improvement pervades the smallest details; the ambition of the people being necessarily checked by its weakness, all the efforts and resources of the citizens are turned to the internal well-being of the community and are not likely to be wasted upon an empty pursuit of glory. The powers of every individual being generally limited, his desires are proportionally small. Mediocrity of fortune makes the various conditions of life nearly equal, and the manners of the inhabitants are orderly and simple. Thus, all things considered, and allowance being made for the various degrees of morality and enlightenment, we shall generally find more persons in easy circumstances, more contentment and tranquillity, in small nations than in large ones.

When tyranny is established in the bosom of a small state, it is more galling than elsewhere, because, acting in a narrower circle, everything in that circle is affected by it. It supplies the place of those great designs which it cannot entertain, by a violent or exasperating interference in a multitude of minute details; and it leaves the political world, to which it properly belongs, to meddle with the arrangements of private life. Tastes as well as actions are to be regulated; and the families of the citizens, as well as the state, are to be governed. This invasion of rights occurs but seldom, however, freedom being in truth the natural state of small communities. The temptations that the government offers to ambition are too weak and the resources of private individuals are too slender for the sovereign power easily to fall into the grasp of a single man; and should such an event occur, the subjects of the state can easily unite and overthrow the tyrant and the tyranny at once by a common effort.

Small nations have therefore always been the cradle of political liberty; and the fact that many of them have lost their liberty by becoming larger shows that their freedom was more a consequence of their small size than of the character of the people.

The history of the world affords no instance of a great nation retaining the form of republican government for a long series of years;[3] and this has led to the conclusion that such a thing is impracticable. For my own part, I think it imprudent for men who are every day deceived in relation to the actual and the present, and often taken by surprise in the circumstances with which they are most familiar, to attempt to limit what is possible and to judge the future. But it may be said with confidence, that a great republic will always be exposed to more perils than a small one.

---

[3] I do not speak of a confederation of small republics, but of a great consolidated republic.

All the passions that are most fatal to republican institutions increase with an increasing territory, while the virtues that favor them do not augment in the same proportion. The ambition of private citizens increases with the power of the state; the strength of parties with the importance of the ends they have in view; but the love of country, which ought to check these destructive agencies, is not stronger in a large than in a small republic. It might, indeed, be easily proved that it is less powerful and less developed. Great wealth and extreme poverty, capital cities of large size, a lax morality, selfishness, and antagonism of interests are the dangers which almost invariably arise from the magnitude of states. Several of these evils scarcely injure a monarchy, and some of them even contribute to its strength and duration. In monarchical states the government has its peculiar strength; it may use, but it does not depend on, the community; and the more numerous the people, the stronger is the prince. But the only security that a republican government possesses against these evils lies in the support of the majority. This support is not, however, proportionably greater in a large republic than in a small one; and thus, while the means of attack perpetually increase, in both number and influence, the power of resistance remains the same; or it may rather be said to diminish, since the inclinations and interests of the people are more diversified by the increase of the population, and the difficulty of forming a compact majority is constantly augmented. It has been observed, moreover, that the intensity of human passions is heightened not only by the importance of the end which they propose to attain, but by the multitude of individuals who are animated by them at the same time. Everyone has had occasion to remark that his emotions in the midst of a sympathizing crowd are far greater than those which he would have felt in solitude. In great republics, political passions become irresistible, not only because they aim at gigantic objects, but because they are felt and shared by millions of men at the same time.

It may therefore be asserted as a general proposition that nothing is more opposed to the well-being and the freedom of men than vast empires. Nevertheless, it is important to acknowledge the peculiar advantages of great states. For the very reason that the desire for power is more intense in these communities than among ordinary men, the love of glory is also more developed in the hearts of certain citizens, who regard the applause of a great people as a reward worthy of their exertions and an elevating encouragement to man. If we would learn why great nations contribute more powerfully to the increase of knowledge and. the advance of civilization than small states, we shall discover an adequate cause in the more rapid and energetic circulation of ideas and in those great cities which are the intellectual centers where all the rays of human genius are reflected and combined. To this it may be added that most important discoveries demand a use of national power which the government of a small state is unable to make: in great nations the government has more enlarged ideas, and is more completely disengaged from the routine of precedent and the selfishness of local feeling; its designs are conceived with more talent and executed with more boldness.

In time of peace the well-being of small nations is undoubtedly more general and complete; but they are apt to suffer more acutely from the calamities of war than those great empires whose distant frontiers may long avert the presence of the danger from the mass of the people, who are therefore more frequently afflicted than ruined by the contest.

But in this matter, as in many others, the decisive argument is the necessity of the case. If none but small nations existed, I do not doubt that mankind would be more happy and more free; but the existence of great nations is unavoidable.

Political strength thus becomes a condition of national prosperity. It profits a state but little to be affluent and free if it is perpetually exposed to be pillaged or subjugated; its manufactures and commerce are of small advantage if another nation has the empire of the seas and gives the law in all the markets of the globe. Small nations are often miserable, not because they are small, but because they are weak; and great empires prosper less because they are great than because they are strong. Physical strength is therefore one of the first conditions of the happiness and even of the existence of nations. Hence it occurs that, unless very peculiar circumstances intervene, small nations are always united to large empires in the end, either by force or by their own consent. I do not know a more deplorable condition than that of a people unable to defend itself or to provide for its own wants.

The federal system was created with the intention of combining the different advantages which result from the magnitude and the littleness of nations; and a glance at the United States of America discovers the advantages which they have derived from its adoption.

In great centralized nations the legislator is obliged to give a character of uniformity to the laws, which does not always suit the diversity of customs and of districts; as he takes no cognizance of special cases, he can only proceed upon general principles; and the population are obliged to conform to the requirements of the laws, since legislation cannot adapt itself to the exigencies and the customs of the population, which is a great cause of trouble and misery. This disadvantage does not exist in confederations; Congress regulates the principal measures of the national government, and all the details of the administration are reserved to the provincial legislatures. One can hardly imagine how much this division of sovereignty contributes to the well-being of each of the states that compose the Union. In these small communities, which are never agitated by the desire of aggrandizement or the care of self-defense, all public authority and private energy are turned towards internal improvements. The central government of each state, which is in immediate relationship with the citizens, is daily apprised of the wants that arise in society; and new projects are proposed every year, which are discussed at town meetings or by the legislature, and which are transmitted by the press to stimulate the zeal and to excite the interest of the citizens. This spirit of improvement is constantly alive in the American republics, without compromising their tranquillity; the ambition of power yields to the less refined and less dangerous desire for well-being. It is generally believed in America that the existence and the permanence of the republican form of government in the New World depend upon the existence and the duration of the federal system; and it is not unusual to attribute a large share of the misfortunes that have befallen the new states of South America to the injudicious erection of great republics instead of a divided and confederate sovereignty.

It is incontestably true that the tastes and the habits of republican government in the United States were first created in the townships and the provincial assemblies. In a small state, like that of Connecticut, for instance, where cutting a canal or laying down a road is a great political question, where the state has no army to pay and no wars to carry on, and where much wealth or much honor cannot be given to the rulers, no form of government can be more natural or more appropriate than a republic. But it is this same republican spirit, it is these manners and customs of a free people, which have been created and nurtured in the different states, that must be afterwards applied to the country at large. The public spirit of the Union is, so to speak, nothing more than an aggregate or summary of the patriotic zeal of the separate provinces. Every citizen of the United States transfers, so to speak, his attachment to his little republic into the common store of American patriotism. In defending the Union he defends the increasing prosperity of his own state or county, the right of conducting its affairs, and the hope of causing measures of improvement to be adopted in it which may be favorable to his own interests; and these are motives that are wont to stir men more than the general interests of the country and the glory of the nation.

On the other hand, if the temper and the manners of the inhabitants especially fitted them to promote the welfare of a great republic, the federal system renders their task less difficult. The confederation of all the American states presents none of the ordinary inconveniences resulting from large associations of men. The Union is a great republic in extent, but the paucity of objects for which its government acts assimilates it to a small state. Its acts are important, but they are rare. As the sovereignty of the Union is limited and incomplete, its exercise is not dangerous to liberty; for it does not excite those insatiable desires for fame and power which have proved so fatal to great republics. As there is no common center to the country, great capital cities, colossal wealth, abject poverty, and sudden revolutions are alike unknown; and political passion, instead of spreading over the land like a fire on the prairies, spends its strength against the interests and the individual passions of every state.

Nevertheless, tangible objects and ideas circulate throughout the Union as freely as in a country inhabited by one people. Nothing checks the spirit of enterprise. The government invites the aid of all who have talents or knowledge to serve it. Inside of the frontiers of the Union profound peace prevails, as within the heart of some great empire; abroad it ranks with the most powerful nations of the earth: two thousand miles of coast are open to the commerce of the world; and as it holds the keys of a new world, its flag is respected in the most remote seas. The Union is happy and free as a small people, and glorious and strong as a great nation.

WHY THE FEDERAL SYSTEM IS NOT PRACTICABLE FOR ALL NATIONS, AND HOW THE ANGLO-AMERICANS WERE ENABLED TO ADOPT IT

... I have shown the advantages that the Americans derive from their federal system; it remains for me to point out the circumstances that enabled them to adopt it, as its benefits cannot be enjoyed by all nations. The accidental defects of the federal system which originate in the laws may be corrected by the skill of the legislator, but there are evils inherent in the system which cannot be remedied by any effort. The people must therefore find in themselves the strength necessary to bear the natural imperfections of their government.

The most prominent evil of all federal systems is the complicated nature of the means they employ. Two sovereignties are necessarily in presence of each other. The legislator may simplify and equalize as far as possible the action of these two sovereignties, by limiting each of them to a sphere of authority accurately defined; but he cannot combine them into one or prevent them from coming into collision at certain points. The federal system, therefore, rests upon a theory which is complicated at the best, and which demands the daily exercise of a considerable share of discretion on the part of those it governs. . . .

In examining the Constitution of the United States, which is the most perfect federal constitution that ever existed, one is startled at the variety of information and the amount of discernment that it presupposes in the people whom it is meant to govern. The government of the Union depends almost entirely upon legal fictions; the Union is an ideal nation, which exists, so to speak, only in the mind, and whose limits and extent can only be discerned by the understanding.

After the general theory is comprehended, many difficulties remain to be solved in its application; for the sovereignty of the Union is so involved in that of the states that it is impossible to distinguish its boundaries at the first glance. The whole structure of the government is artificial and conventional, and it would be ill adapted to a people which has not been long accustomed to conduct its own affairs, or to one in which the science of politics has not descended to the humblest classes of society. I have never been more struck by the good sense and the practical judgment of the Americans than in the manner in which they elude the numberless difficulties resulting from their Federal Constitution. I scarcely ever met with a plain American citizen who could not distinguish with surprising facility the obligations created by the laws of Congress from those created by the laws of his own state, and who, after having discriminated between the matters which come under the cognizance of the Union and those which the local legislature is competent to regulate, could not point out the exact limit of the separate jurisdictions of the Federal courts and the tribunals of the state.

The Constitution of the United States resembles those fine creations of human industry which ensure wealth and renown to their inventors, but which are profitless in other hands. . . .

The second and most fatal of all defects, and that which I believe to be inherent in the federal system, is the relative weakness of the government of the Union. The principle upon which all confederations rest is that of a divided sovereignty. Legislators may render this partition less perceptible, they may even conceal it for a time from the public eye, but they cannot prevent it from existing; and a divided sovereignty must always be weaker than an entire one. The remarks made on the Constitution of the United States have shown with what skill the Americans, while restraining the power of the Union within the narrow limits of a federal government, have given it the semblance, and to a certain extent the force, of a national government. By this means the legislators of the Union have diminished the natural danger of confederations, but have not entirely obviated it.

The American government, it is said, does not address itself to the states, but transmits its injunctions directly to the citizens and compels them individually to comply with its demands. But if the Federal law were to clash with the interests and the prejudices of a state, it might be feared that all the citizens of that state would conceive themselves to be interested in the cause of a single individual who refused to obey. If all the citizens of the state were aggrieved at the same time and in the same manner by the authority of the Union, the Federal government would vainly attempt to subdue them individually; they would instinctively unite in a common defense and would find an organization already prepared for them in the sovereignty that their state is allowed to enjoy. Fiction would give way to reality, and an organized portion of the nation might then contest the central authority.

The same observation holds good with regard to the Federal jurisdiction. If the courts of the Union violated an important law of a state in a private case, the real though not the apparent contest would be between the aggrieved state represented by a citizen and the Union represented by its courts of justice.

He would have but a partial knowledge of the world who should imagine that it is possible by the aid of legal fictions to prevent men from finding out and employing those means of gratifying their passions which have been left open to them. The American legislators, though they have rendered a collision between the two sovereignties less probable, have not destroyed the causes of such a misfortune. It may even be affirmed that, in case of such a collision, they have not been able to ensure the victory of the Federal element. The Union is possessed of money and troops, but the states have kept the affections and the prejudices of the people. The sovereignty of the Union is an abstract being, which is connected with but few external objects; the sovereignty of the states is perceptible by the senses, easily understood, and constantly active. The former is of recent creation, the latter is coeval with the people itself. The sovereignty of the Union is factitious, that of the states is natural and self-existent, without effort, like the authority of a parent. The sovereignty of the nation affects a few of the chief interests of society; it represents an immense but remote country, a vague and ill-defined sentiment. The authority of the states controls every individual citizen at every hour and in all circumstances; it protects his property, his freedom, and his life; it affects at every moment his well-being or his misery. When we recollect the traditions, the customs, the prejudices of local and familiar attachment with which it is connected, we cannot doubt the superiority of a power that rests on the instinct of patriotism, so natural to the human heart.

Since legislators cannot prevent such dangerous collisions as occur between the two sovereignties which coexist in the Federal system, their first object must be, not only to dissuade the confederate states from warfare, but to encourage such dispositions as lead to peace. Hence it is that the Federal compact cannot be lasting unless there exists in the communities which are leagued together a certain number of inducements to union which render their common dependence agreeable and the task of the government light. The Federal system cannot succeed without the presence of favorable circumstances added to the influence of good laws. All the nations that have ever formed a confederation have been held together by some common interests, which served as the intellectual ties of association. . . .

The circumstance which makes it easy to maintain a Federal government in America is not only that the states have similar interests, a common origin, and a common language, but they have also arrived at the same stage of civilization, which almost always renders a union feasible. I do not know of any European nation, however small, that does not present less uniformity in its different provinces than the American people, which occupy a territory as extensive as one half of Europe. The distance from Maine to Georgia is about one thousand miles; but the difference between the civilization of Maine and that of Georgia is slighter than the difference between the habits of Normandy and those of Brittany. Maine and Georgia, which are placed at the opposite extremities of a great empire, have therefore more real inducements to form a confederation than Normandy and Brittany, which are separated only by a brook.

The geographical position of the country increased the facilities that the American legislators derived from the usages and customs of the inhabitants; and it is to this circumstance that the adoption and the maintenance of the Federal system are mainly attributable.

The most important occurrence in the life of a nation is the breaking out of a war. . . . A long war almost always reduces nations to the wretched alternative of being abandoned to ruin by defeat or to despotism by success. War therefore renders the weakness of a government most apparent and most alarming; and I have shown that the inherent defect of federal governments is that of being weak.

The federal system not only has no centralized administration, and nothing that resembles one, but the central government itself is imperfectly organized, which is always a great cause of weakness when the nation is opposed to other countries which are themselves governed by a single authority. In the Federal Constitution of the United States, where the central government has more real force than in any other confederation, this evil is extremely evident. . . .

How does it happen, then, that the American Union, with all the relative perfection of its laws, is not dissolved by the occurrence of a great war? It is because it has no great wars to fear. Placed in the center of an immense continent, which offers a boundless field for human industry, the Union is almost as much insulated from the world as if all its frontiers were girt by the ocean. . . .

The great advantage of the United States does not, then, consist in a Federal Constitution which allows it to carry on great wars, but in a geographical position which renders such wars extremely improbable.

No one can be more inclined than I am to appreciate the advantages of the federal system, which I hold to be one of the combinations most favorable to the prosperity and freedom of man. I envy the lot of those nations which have been able to adopt it; but I cannot believe that any confederate people could maintain a long or an equal contest with a nation of similar strength in which the government is centralized. A people which, in the presence of the great military monarchies of Europe, should divide its sovereignty into fractional parts would, in my opinion, by that very act abdicate its power, and perhaps its existence and its name. But such is the admirable position of the New World that man has no other enemy than himself, and that, in order to be happy and to be free, he has only to determine that he will be so.

The Supremacy of National Law

☐   Tracing the historical development of nation-state relationships, one finds that there has been constant strife over the determination of the boundaries of national power in relation to the reserved powers of the states. The Civil War did not settle once and for all the difficult question of national versus state power. The Supreme Court has played an important role in the development of the federal system, and some of its most historic opinions have upheld national power at the expense of the states. In the early period of the Court, Chief Justice John Marshall in *McCulloch* v. *Maryland,* 4 Wheaton 316 (1819), stated two doctrines that have had a profound effect upon the federal system: (1) the doctrine of implied powers; (2) the doctrine of the supremacy of national law. The former enables Congress to expand its power into numerous areas affecting states directly. By utilizing the commerce clause, for example, Congress may now regulate what is essentially *intrastate* commerce, for the Court has held that this is implied in the original clause giving Congress the power to regulate commerce among the several states. The immediate issues in *McCulloch* v. *Maryland* were, first, whether or not Congress had the power to incorporate, or charter, a national bank; second, if Congress did have such a power, although nowhere stated in the Constitution, did the existence of such a bank prevent state action that would interfere in its operation?

9

McCULLOCH v. MARYLAND
4 Wheaton 316 (1819)

Mr. Chief Justice Marshall delivered the opinion of the Court, saying in part:

In the case now to be determined, the defendant, a sovereign state, denies the obligation of a law enacted by the legislature of the Union; and the plaintiff, on his part, contests the validity of an act which has been passed by the legislature of that state. The Constitution of our country, in its most interesting and vital parts, is to be considered; the conflicting powers of the government of the Union and of its members, as marked in that Constitution, are to be discussed; and an opinion given, which may essentially influence the great operations of the government. . . .

If any one proposition could command the universal assent of mankind, we might expect it would be this: that the government of the Union, though limited in its powers, is supreme within its sphere of action. This would seem to result necessarily from its nature. It is the government of all; its powers are delegated by all; it represents all, and acts for all. Though any one state may be willing to control its operations, no state is willing to allow others to control them. The nation, on those subjects on which it can act, must necessarily bind its component parts. But this question is not left to mere reason: the people have, in express terms, decided it, by saying, "this Constitution, and the laws of the United States, which shall be made in pursuance thereof," "shall be the supreme law of the land," and by requiring that the members of the state legislatures, and the officers of the executive and judicial departments of the states, shall take the oath of fidelity to it. . . .

A constitution, to contain an accurate detail of all the subdivisions of which its great powers will admit, and of all the means by which they may be carried into execution, would partake of the prolixity of a legal code, and could scarcely be embraced by the human mind. It would probably never be understood by the public. Its nature, therefore, requires that only its great outlines should be marked, its important objects designated, and the minor ingredients which compose those objects be deduced from the nature of the objects themselves. That this idea was entertained by the framers of the American Constitution, is not only to be inferred from the nature of the instrument, but from the language. . . .

Although, among the enumerated powers of government, we do not find the word "bank," or "incorporation," we find the great powers to lay and collect taxes; to borrow money; to regulate commerce; to declare and conduct a war; and to raise and support armies and navies. The sword and the purse, all the external relations, and no inconsiderable portion of the industry of the nation, are entrusted to its government. It can never be pretended that these vast powers draw after them others of inferior importance, merely because they are inferior. Such an idea can never be advanced. But it may, with great reason, be contended, that a government, entrusted with such ample powers, on the due execution of which the happiness and prosperity of the nation so vitally depends, must also be entrusted with ample means for their execution. The power being given, it is the interest of the nation to facilitate its execution. It can never be their interest, and cannot be presumed to have been their intention, to clog and embarrass its execution by withholding the most appropriate means. Throughout this vast republic, from the St. Croix to the Gulf of Mexico, from the Atlantic to the Pacific, revenue is to be collected and expended, armies are to be marched and supported. The exigencies of the nation may require, that the treasure raised in the North should be transported to the South, that raised in the East conveyed to the West, or that this order should be reversed. Is that construction of the Constitution to be preferred which would render these operations difficult, hazardous, and expensive? Can we adopt that construction (unless the words imperiously require it) which would impute to the framers of that instrument, when granting these powers for the public good, the intention of impeding their exercise by withholding a choice of means? If, indeed, such be the mandate of the Constitution, we have only to obey; but that instrument does not profess to enumerate the means by which the powers it confers may be executed; nor does it prohibit the creation of a corporation, if the existence of such a being be essential to the beneficial exercise of those powers. It is, then, the subject of fair inquiry, how far such means may be employed. . . .

We admit, as all must admit, that the powers of the government are limited, and that its limits are not to be transcended. But we think the sound construction of the Constitution must allow to the national legislature that discretion, with respect to the means by which the powers it confers are to be carried into execution, which will enable that body to perform the high duties assigned to it, in the manner most beneficial to the people. Let the end be legitimate, let it be within the scope of the Constitution, and all means which are appropriate, which are plainly adapted to that end, which are not prohibited, but consist with the letter and spirit of the Constitution, are constitutional. . . .

It being the opinion of the court that the act incorporating the bank is constitutional; and that the power of establishing a branch in the state of Maryland might be properly exercised by the bank itself, we proceed to inquire:

Whether the state of Maryland may, without violating the Constitution, tax that branch? . . .

That the power of taxation is one of vital importance; that it is retained by the states; that it is not abridged by the grant of a similar power to the government of the Union; that it is to be concurrently exercised by the two governments: are truths which have never been denied. But, such is the paramount character of the Constitution, that its capacity to withdraw any subject from the action of even this power, is admitted. The states are expressly forbidden to lay any duties on imports or exports, except what may be absolutely necessary for executing their inspection laws. If the obligation of this prohibition must be conceded—if it may restrain a state from the exercise of its taxing power on imports and exports; the same paramount character would seem to restrain, as it certainly may restrain, a state from such other exercise of this power, as is in its nature incompatible with, and repugnant to, the constitutional laws of the Union. A law, absolutely repugnant to another, as entirely repeals that other as if express terms of repeal were used.

On this ground the counsel for the bank place its claim to be exempted from the power of a state to tax its operations. There is no express provision for the case, but the claim has been sustained on a principle which so entirely pervades the Constitution, is so intermixed with the materials which compose it, so interwoven with its web, so blended with its texture, as to be incapable of being separated from it, without rending it into shreds.

This great principle is, that the Constitution and the laws made in pursuance thereof are supreme; that they control the Constitution and laws of the respective states, and cannot be controlled by them. From this, which may be almost termed an axiom, other propositions are deduced as corollaries, on the truth or error of which, and on their application to this case, the cause has been supposed to depend. These are, 1. That a power to create implies a power to preserve. 2. That a power to destroy, if wielded by a different hand, is hostile to, and incompatible with, these powers to create and preserve. 3. That where this repugnancy exists, that authority which is supreme must control, not yield to that over which it is supreme. . . .

If we apply the principle for which the state of Maryland contends, to the Constitution generally, we shall find it capable of changing totally the character of that instrument. We shall find it capable of arresting all the measures of the government, and of prostrating it at the foot of the states. The American people have declared their Constitution, and the laws made in pursuance thereof, to be supreme; but this principle would transfer the supremacy, in fact, to the states. . . .

The court has bestowed on this subject its most deliberate consideration. The result is a conviction that the states have no power, by taxation or otherwise, to retard, impede, burden, or in any manner control, the operations of the constitutional laws enacted by Congress to carry into execution the powers vested in the general government. That is, we think, the unavoidable consequence of that supremacy which the Constitution has declared. . . .

☐ Constitutional doctrine regarding the power of the national government to regulate commerce among the states to promote general prosperity has been clarified in a series of Supreme Court cases. At issue is the interpretation of the power to "regulate commerce with foreign nations, and among the several States," granted to Congress in Article 1. Some of these cases have emphasized the role of the national government as umpire, enforcing certain rules of the game within which the free enterprise system functions; others have emphasized the positive role of the government in regulating the economy.

A key case supporting the supremacy of the national government in commercial regulation was *Gibbons v. Ogden,* 9 Wheaton 1 (1824). The New York legislature, in 1798, granted Robert R. Livingston the exclusive privilege to navigate by steam the rivers and other waters of the state, provided he could build a boat that would travel at four miles an hour against the current of the Hudson River. A two-year time limitation was imposed, and the conditions were not met; however, New York renewed its grant for two years in 1803 and again in 1807. In 1807 Robert Fulton, who now held the exclusive license with Livingston, completed and put into operation a steamboat which met the legislative conditions. The New York legislature now provided that a five-year extension of their monopoly would be given to Livingston and Fulton for each new steamboat they placed into operation on New York waters. The monopoly could not exceed thirty years, but during that period anyone wishing to navigate New York waters by steam had first to obtain a license from Livingston and Fulton, who were given the power to confiscate unlicensed boats. New Jersey and Connecticut passed retaliatory laws, the former authorizing confiscation of any New York ship for each ship confiscated by Livingston and Fulton, the latter prohibiting boats licensed in New York from entering Connecticut waters. Ohio also passed retaliatory legislation. Open commercial warfare seemed a possibility among the states of the union.

In 1793 Congress passed an act providing for the licensing of vessels engaged in the coasting trade, and Gibbons obtained under this statute a license to operate boats between New York and New Jersey. Ogden was engaged in a similar operation under an exclusive license issued by Livingston and Fulton, and thus sought to enjoin Gibbons from further operation. The New York court upheld the exclusive grants given to Livingston and Fulton, and Gibbons appealed to the Supreme Court. Chief Justice Marshall made it quite clear that (1) states cannot interfere with a power granted to Congress by passing conflicting state legislation, and (2) the commerce power includes anything affecting "commerce among the states" and thus may include *intrastate* as well as interstate commerce. In this way the foundation was laid for broad national control over commercial activity.

☐   Over its history the Supreme Court has interpreted the commerce clause both to expand and contract the authority of the national government. After Chief Justice John Marshall's era ended in 1836, the Court gradually adopted a more restrictive view of the national commerce power, protecting state sovereignty over many areas of commercial regulation that Marshall clearly would have allowed Congress to regulate. The Supreme Court did not fully return to the broad commerce clause interpretation of the *Gibbons* case until 1937, when it reluctantly capitulated to Franklin D. Roosevelt's New Deal and the centralized government it represented. The restoration of the Marshall Court's definition of the commerce power removed constitutional restraints upon Congress.

Since 1937 the Supreme Court has essentially upheld congressional interpretations of its own authority under the commerce clause. While the commerce power is generally used to support economic regulation, Congress turned to the commerce clause for the legal authority to enact the Civil Rights Act of 1964. The public accommodations section of the bill, Title II, proscribed discrimination in public establishments, including inns, hotels, motels, restaurants, motion picture houses, and theaters. The law declared that the "operations of an establishment affects commerce . . . if . . . it serves or offers to serve interstate travelers or a substantial portion of the food which it serves or gasoline or other products which it sells, has moved in commerce . . . [or if] it customarily presents films, performances, athletic teams, exhibitions, or other sources of entertainment which move in commerce." In *Heart of Atlanta Motel, Inc.* v. *United States,* 379 US 241 (1964), the Supreme Court upheld the law under the commerce clause. The motel-plaintiff contended that it was in no way involved in interstate commerce, arguing that while some of its guests might be occasionally engaged in commerce, "persons and people are not part of trade or commerce. . . . people conduct commerce and engage in trade, but people are not part of commerce and trade." But the Court accepted the government's argument that racial discrimination in public accommodations impedes interstate travel by those discriminated against, causing disruption of interstate commerce which Congress has the authority to prevent.

The Supreme Court did briefly resurrect the commerce clause as a limit on congressional power over the states in *National League of Cities* v. *Usery,* 426 US 833 (1976). A sharply divided Court held that Congress could not regulate governmental activities that were an integral part of state sovereignty. The decision overturned provisions of the Fair Labor Standards Act that governed state employees. The Court's majority opinion argued that states had traditionally controlled their employees, a responsibility within state sovereignty because the states through their own democratic processes should have the autonomy to decide for themselves how they would manage their public sector.

It was not long, however, before the Court reversed the *National League of Cities* decision, holding in *Garcia* v. *San Antonio Metropolitan Transit Authority,* 83L Ed. 2d 10 16 (1985), that Congress could apply minimum-wage requirements to the states and their localities. Again the vote was closely divided, 5-4, and this time the majority opinion struck a distinct note of judicial self-restraint, concluding: "We doubt that courts ultimately can identify principled constitutional limitations on the scope of Congress' commerce clause powers over the states merely by relying on *a priori* definitions of state sovereignty." The Court found nothing in the Fair Labor Standards Act that violated state sovereignty, implying that it was up to Congress and not the courts to determine the extent of its power under the commerce clause. Sharp dissents were registered in the case, possibly indicating that in the future the issue once again may be joined and a more conservative Supreme Court majority uphold some commerce clause restraints against national regulation of state governments. The *Garcia* decision is directly in line with Court precedents since 1937 that have supported virtually unlimited congressional authority under the commerce clause.

A Perspective on Federalism: Present and Future

☐ In the following selection, the role of the states in the political system is discussed from the perspective that the nature of intergovernmental relations reflects underlying political conditions and realities. As James Madison pointed out in *Federalist 39,* the original constitutional scheme of federalism represented a delicate balance between national and state ("federal") interests. But, under the original constitutional design, the national government was not to intervene directly in the affairs of state governments; and the problems of subsidiary local governments within states were not considered to be separate from the problems of the states themselves, and therefore, they were a proper matter for resolution by the individual state governments.

Morton Grodzins points out that strict separation of national and state functions has never really existed, and that even before the Constitution of 1787 a national statute passed by the Continental Congress gave grants-in-aid of land to the states for public schools. Tocqueville also comments on the difficulties of formally separating, in theory, the responsibilities of national, state, and local governments. The history of the federal system has seen the ebb and flow of national dominance over the states; centralization and decentralization have been the cyclical themes of federalism and intergovernmental relations. The thrust of the New Deal was toward centralization through the use of federal grant-in-aid programs, a philosophy that dominated the government until the emergence of the "New Federalism" of the Nixon administration, which supported decentralization of power from the national to the state governments. The move toward decentralization was broadly supported by the Republican party. Revenue-sharing was inaugurated by President Nixon to transfer national funds to the states, without stipulation of how the money was to be spent. The revenue-sharing procedure was in direct contrast to the grant-in-aid programs, which allowed for state receipt of federal money upon the condition of state adherence to national standards. President Reagan's new Federalism proposed the merging of grant-in-aid programs into block grants to the states leading eventually to a reduced federal role in financing state and local governments. The continuing conflict between the themes and realities of centralization and decentralization are examined in the following selection.

10
Morton Grodzins

THE FEDERAL SYSTEM

Federalism is a device for dividing decisions and functions of government. As the constitutional fathers well understood, the federal structure is a means, not an end. The pages that follow are therefore not concerned with an exposition of American federalism as a formal, legal set of relationships. The focus, rather, is on the purpose of federalism, that is to say, on the distribution of power between central and peripheral units of government.

I. THE SHARING OF FUNCTIONS

The American form of government is often, but erroneously, symbolized by a three-layer cake. A far more accurate image is the rainbow or marble cake, characterized by an inseparable mingling of differently colored ingredients, the colors appearing in vertical and diagonal strands and unexpected whirls. As colors are mixed in the marble cake, so functions are mixed in the American federal system. Consider the health officer, styled "sanitarian," of a rural county in a border state. He embodies the whole idea of the marble cake of government.

The sanitarian is appointed by the state under merit standards established by the federal government. His base salary comes jointly from state and federal funds, the county provides him with an office and office amenities and pays a portion of his expenses, and the largest city in the county also contributes to his salary and office by virtue of his appointment

From Morton Grodzins, ed., *Goals for Americans,* pp. 265–82. © 1960 by The American Assembly, Columbia University, New York, New York. Reprinted by permission.

as a city plumbing inspector. It is impossible from moment to moment to tell under which governmental hat the sanitarian operates. His work of inspecting the purity of food is carried out under federal standards; but he is enforcing state laws when inspecting commodities that have not been in interstate commerce; and somewhat perversely he also acts under state authority when inspecting milk coming into the county from producing areas across the state border. He is a federal officer when impounding impure drugs shipped from a neighboring state; a federal-state officer when distributing typhoid immunization serum; a state officer when enforcing standards of industrial hygiene; a state-local officer when inspecting the city's water supply; and (to complete the circle) a local officer when insisting that the city butchers adopt more hygienic methods of handling their garbage. But he cannot and does not think of himself as acting in these separate capacities. All business in the county that concerns public health and sanitation he considers his business. Paid largely from federal funds, he does not find it strange to attend meetings of the city council to give expert advice on matters ranging from rotten apples to rabies control. He is even deputized as a member of both the city and county police forces.

The sanitarian is an extreme case, but he accurately represents an important aspect of the whole range of governmental activities in the United States. Functions are not neatly parceled out among the many governments. They are shared functions. It is difficult to find any governmental activity which does not involve all three of the so-called "levels" of the federal system. In the most local of local functions—law enforcement or education, for example—the federal and state governments play important roles. In what, a priori, may be considered the purest central government activities—the conduct of foreign affairs, for example—the state and local governments have considerable responsibilities, directly and indirectly.

The federal grant programs are only the most obvious example of shared functions. They also most clearly exhibit how sharing serves to disperse governmental powers. The grants utilize the greater wealth-gathering abilities of the central government and establish nationwide standards, yet they are "in aid" of functions carried out under state law, with considerable state and local discretion. The national supervision of such programs is largely a process of mutual accommodation. Leading state and local officials, acting through their professional organizations, are in considerable part responsible for the very standards that national officers try to persude all state and local officers to accept.

Even in the absence of joint financing, federal-state-local collaboration is the characteristic mode of action. Federal expertise is available to aid in the building of a local jail (which may later be used to house federal prisoners), to improve a local water purification system, to step up building inspections, to provide standards for state and local personnel in protecting housewives against dishonest butchers' scales, to prevent gas explosions, or to produce a land use plan. States and localities, on the other hand, take important formal responsibilities in the development of national programs for atomic energy, civil defense, the regulation of commerce, and the protection of purity in foods and drugs; local political weight is always a factor in the operation of even a post office or a military establishment. From abattoirs and accounting through zoning and zoo administration, any governmental activity is almost certain to involve the influence, if not the formal administration, of all three planes of the federal system.

II. ATTEMPTS TO UNWIND THE FEDERAL SYSTEM

[From 1947 to 1960] there [were] four major attempts to reform or reorganize the federal system: the first (1947–49) and second (1953–55) Hoover Commissions on Executive Organization; the Kestnbaum Commission on Intergovernmental Relations (1953–55); and the Joint Federal-State Action Committee (1957–59). All four of these groups . . . aimed to minimize federal activities. None of them . . . recognized the sharing of functions as the characteristic way American governments do things. Even when making recommendations for joint action, these official commissions [took] the view (as expressed in the Kestnbaum report) that "the main tradition of American federalism [is] the tradition of separateness." All four . . . in varying degrees, worked to separate functions and tax sources.

The history of the Joint Federal-State Action Committee is especially instructive. The committee was established at the suggestion of President Eisenhower, who charged it, first of all, "to designate functions which the States are ready and willing to assume and finance that are now performed or financed wholly or in part by the Federal Government." He also gave the committee the task of recommending "Federal and State revenue adjustments required to enable the States to assume such functions."[1]

The committee subsequently established seemed most favorably situated to accomplish the task of functional separation. It was composed of distinguished and able men, including among its personnel three leading members of the President's Cabinet, the director of the Bureau of the Budget, and ten state governors. It had the full support of the President at every point, and it worked hard and conscientiously. Excellent staff studies

---

[1]The President's third suggestion was that the committee "identify functions and responsibilities likely to require state or federal attention in the future and . . . recommend the level of state effort, or federal effort, or both, that will be needed to assure effective action." The committee initially devoted little attention to this problem. Upon discovering the difficulty of making separatist recommendations, i.e., for turning over federal functions and taxes to the states, it developed a series of proposals looking to greater effectiveness in intergovernmental collaboration. The committee was succeeded by a legislatively based, 26-member Advisory Commission on Intergovernmental Relations, established September 29, 1959.

were supplied by the Bureau of the Budget, the White House, the Treasury Department, and, from the state side, the Council of State Governments. It had available to it a large mass of research data, including the sixteen recently completed volumes of the Kestnbaum Commission. There existed no disagreements on party lines within the committee and, of course, no constitutional impediments to its mission. The President, his Cabinet members, and all the governors (with one possible exception) on the committee completely agreed on the desirability of decentralization-via-separation-of-functions-and-taxes. They were unanimous in wanting to justify the committee's name and to produce action, not just another report.

The committee worked for more than two years. It found exactly two programs to recommend for transfer from federal to state hands. One was the federal grant program for vocational education (including practical-nurse training and aid to fishery trades); the other was federal grants for municipal waste treatment plants. The programs together cost the federal government less than $80 million in 1957, slightly more than two per cent of the total federal grants for that year. To allow the states to pay for these programs, the committee recommended that they be allowed a credit against the federal tax on local telephone calls. Calculations showed that this offset device, plus an equalizing factor, would give every state at least 40 percent more from the tax than it received from the federal government in vocational education and sewage disposal grants. Some states were "equalized" to receive twice as much.

The recommendations were modest enough, and the generous financing feature seemed calculated to gain state support. The President recommended to Congress that all points of the program be legislated. None of them was, none has been since, and none is likely to be.

III. A POINT OF HISTORY

The American federal system has never been a system of separated governmental activities. There has never been a time when it was possible to put neat labels on discrete "federal," "state," and "local" functions. Even before the Constitution, a statute of 1785, reinforced by the Northwest Ordinance of 1787, gave grants-in-land to the states for public schools. Thus the national government was a prime force in making possible what is now taken to be the most local function of all, primary and secondary education. More important, the nation, before it was fully organized, established by this action a first principle of American federalism: the national government would use its superior resources to initiate and support national programs, principally administered by the states and localities.

The essential unity of state and federal financial systems was again recognized in the earliest constitutional days with the assumption by the federal government of the Revolutionary War debts of the states. Other points of federal-state collaboration during the Federalist period concerned the militia, law enforcement, court practices, the administration of elections, public health measures, pilot laws, and many other matters.

The nineteenth century is widely believed to have been the preeminent period of duality in the American system. Lord Bryce at the end of the century described (in *The American Commonwealth*) the federal and state governments as "distinct and separate in their action." The system, he said, was "like a great factory wherein two sets of machinery are at work, their revolving wheels apparently intermixed, their bands crossing one another, yet each set doing its own work without touching or hampering the other." Great works may contain gross errors. Bryce was wrong. The nineteenth century, like the early days of the republic, was a period principally characterized by intergovernmental collaboration.

Decisions of the Supreme Court are often cited as evidence of nineteenth-century duality. In the early part of the century the Court, heavily weighted with Federalists, was intent upon enlarging the sphere of national authority; in the later years (and to the 1930s) its actions were in the direction of paring down national powers and indeed all governmental authority. Decisions referred to "areas of exclusive competence" exercised by the federal government and the states; to their powers being "separated and distinct"; and to neither being able "to intrude within the jurisdiction of the other."

Judicial rhetoric is not always consistent with judicial action, and the Court did not always adhere to separatist doctrine. Indeed, its rhetoric sometimes indicated a positive view of cooperation. In any case, the Court was rarely, if ever, directly confronted with the issue of cooperation versus separation as such. Rather it was concerned with defining permissible areas of action for the central government and the states; or with saying with respect to a point at issue whether any government could take action. The Marshall Court contributed to intergovernmental cooperation by the very act of permitting federal operations where they had not existed before. Furthermore, even Marshall was willing to allow interstate commerce to be affected by the states in their use of the police power. Later courts also upheld state laws that had an impact on interstate commerce, just as they approved the expansion of the national commerce power, as in statutes providing for the control of telegraphic communication or prohibiting the interstate transportation of lotteries, impure foods and drugs, and prostitutes. Similar room for cooperation was found outside the commerce field, notably in the Court's refusal to interfere with federal grants-in-land or cash to the states. Although research to clinch the point has not been completed, it is probably true that the Supreme Court from 1800 to 1936 allowed far more federal-state collaboration than it blocked.

Political behavior and administrative action of the nineteenth century provide positive evidence that, throughout the entire era of so-called dual federalism, the many governments in the American federal system continued the close administrative and fiscal collaboration of the earlier period. Governmental activities were not extensive. But relative to what governments did, intergovernmental cooperation during the last century was comparable with that existing today.

Occasional presidential vetoes (from Madison to Buchanan) of cash and land grants are evidence of constitutional and ideological apprehensions about the extensive expansion of federal activities which produced widespread intergovernmental collaboration. In perspective, however, the vetoes are a more important evidence of the continuous search, not least by state officials, for ways and means to involve the central government in a wide variety of joint programs. The search was successful.

Grants-in-land and grants-in-services from the national government were of first importance in virtually all the principal functions undertaken by the states and their local subsidiaries. Land grants were made to the states for, among other purposes, elementary schools, colleges, and special educational institutions; roads, canals, rivers, harbors, and railroads; reclamation of desert and swamp lands; and veterans' welfare. In fact whatever was at the focus of state attention became the recipient of national grants. (Then, as today, national grants established state emphasis as well as followed it.) If Connecticut wished to establish a program for the care and education of the deaf and dumb, federal money in the form of a land grant was found to aid that program. If higher education relating to agriculture became a pressing need, Congress could dip into the public domain and make appropriate grants to states. If the need for swamp drainage and flood control appeared, the federal government could supply both grants-in-land and, from the Army's Corps of Engineers, the services of the only trained engineers then available.

Aid also went in the other direction. The federal government, theoretically in exclusive control of the Indian population, relied continuously (and not always wisely) on the experience and resources of state and local governments. State militias were an all-important ingredient in the nation's armed forces. State governments became unofficial but real partners in federal programs for homesteading, reclamation, tree culture, law enforcement, inland waterways, the nation's internal communications system (including highway and railroad routes), and veterans' aid of various sorts. Administrative contacts were voluminous, and the whole process of interaction was lubricated, then as today, by constituent-conscious members of Congress.

The essential continuity of the collaborative system is best demonstrated by the history of the grants. The land grant tended to become a cash grant based on the calculated disposable value of the land, and the cash grant tended to become an annual grant based upon the national government's superior tax powers. In 1887, only three years before the frontier was officially closed, thus signalizing the end of the disposable public domain, Congress enacted the first continuing cash grants.

A long, extensive, and continuous experience is therefore the foundation of the present system of shared functions characteristic of the American federal system, what we have called the marble cake of government. It is a misjudgment of our history and our present situation to believe that a neat separation of governmental functions could take place without drastic alterations in our society and system of government.

IV. DYNAMICS OF SHARING: THE POLITICS OF THE FEDERAL SYSTEM

Many causes contribute to dispersed power in the federal system. One is the simple historical fact that the states existed before the nation. A second is in the form of creed, the traditional opinion of Americans that expresses distrust of centralized power and places great value in the strength and vitality of local units of government. Another is pride in locality and state, nurtured by the nation's size and by variations of regional and state history. Still a fourth cause of decentralization is the sheer wealth of the nation. It allows all groups, including state and local governments, to partake of the central government's largesse, supplies room for experimentation and even waste, and makes unnecessary the tight organization of political power that must follow when the support of one program necessarily means the deprivation of another.

In one important respect, the Constitution no longer operates to impede centralized government. The Supreme Court since 1937 has given Congress a relatively free hand. The federal government can build substantive programs in many areas on the taxation and commerce powers. Limitations of such central programs based on the argument, "it's unconstitutional," are no longer possible as long as Congress (in the Court's view) acts reasonably in the interest of the whole nation. The Court is unlikely to reverse this permissive view in the foreseeable future.

Nevertheless, some constitutional restraints on centralization continue to operate. The strong constitutional position of the states—for example, the assignment of two Senators to each state, the role given the states in administering even national elections, and the relatively few limitations on their lawmaking powers—establishes the geographical units as natural centers of administrative and political strength. Many clauses of the Constitution are not subject to the same latitude of interpretation as the commerce and tax clauses. The simple, clearly stated, unambiguous phrases—for example, the President "shall hold his office during the term of four years"—are subject to change only through the formal amendment process. Similar provisions exist with respect to the terms of Senators and Congressmen and the amendment process. All of them have the effect of retarding or restraining centralizing action of the federal government. The fixed terms of the President and members of Congress, for example, greatly impede the development of nationwide, disciplined political parties that almost certainly would have to precede continuous large-scale expansion of federal functions.

The constitutional restraints on the expansion of national authority are less important and less direct today than they were in 1879 or in 1936. But to say that they are less important is not to say that they are unimportant.

The nation's politics reflect these decentralizing causes and add some of their own. The political parties of the United States are unique. They seldom perform the function that parties traditionally perform in other countries, the function of gathering together diverse strands of power and welding them into one. Except during the period of nominating and electing a President and for the essential but nonsubstantive business of organizing the houses of Congress, the American parties rarely coalesce power at all. Characteristically they do the reverse, serving as a canopy under which special and local interests are represented with little regard for anything that can be called a party program. National leaders are elected on a party ticket, but in Congress they must seek cross-party support if their leadership is to be effective. It is a rare President during rare periods who can produce legislation without facing the defection of substantial numbers of his own party. (Wilson could do this in the first session of the Sixty-Third Congress; but Franklin D. Roosevelt could not, even during the famous hundred days of 1933.) Presidents whose parties form the majority of the Congressional houses must still count heavily on support from the other party.

The parties provide the pivot on which the entire governmental system swings. Party operations, first of all, produce in legislation the basic division of functions between the federal government, on the one hand, and state and local governments, on the other. The Supreme Court's permissiveness with respect to the expansion of national powers has not in fact produced any considerable extension of exclusive federal functions. The body of federal law in all fields has remained, in the words of Henry M. Hart, Jr., and Herbert Wechsler, "interstitial in its nature," limited in objective and resting upon the principal body of legal relationships defined by state law. It is difficult to find any area of federal legislation that is not significantly affected by state law.

In areas of new or enlarged federal activity, legislation characteristically provides important roles for state and local governments. This is as true of Democratic as of Republican administrations and true even of functions for which arguments of efficiency would produce exclusive federal responsibility. Thus the unemployment compensation program of the New Deal and the airport program of President Truman's administration both provided important responsibilities for state governments. In both cases attempts to eliminate state participation were defeated by a cross-party coalition of pro-state votes and influence. A large fraction of the Senate is usually made up of ex-governors, and the membership of both houses is composed of men who know that their reelection depends less upon national leaders or national party organization than upon support from their home constituencies. State and local officials are key members of these constituencies, often central figures in selecting candidates and in turning out the vote. Under such circumstances, national legislation taking state and local views heavily into account is inevitable.

Second, the undisciplined parties affect the character of the federal system as a result of Senatorial and Congressional interference in federal administrative programs on behalf of local interests. Many aspects of the legislative involvement in administrative affairs are formalized. The Legislative Reorganization Act of 1946, to take only one example, provided that each of the standing committees "shall exercise continuous watchfulness" over administration of laws within its jurisdiction. But the formal system of controls, extensive as it is, does not compare in importance with the informal and extralegal network of relationships in producing continuous legislative involvement in administrative affairs.

Senators and Congressmen spend a major fraction of their time representing problems of their constituents before administrative agencies. An even larger fraction of Congressional staff time is devoted to the same task. The total magnitude of such "case work" operations is great. In one five-month period of 1943 the Office of Price Administration received a weekly average of 842 letters from members of Congress. If phone calls and personal contacts are added, each member of Congress on the average presented the OPA with a problem involving one of his constituents twice a day in each five-day work week. Data for less vulnerable agencies during less intensive periods are also impressive. In 1958, to take only one example, the Department of Agriculture estimated (and underestimated) that it received an average of 159 Congressional letters per working day. Special Congressional liaison staffs have been created to service this mass of business, though all higher officials meet it in one form or another. The Air Force in 1958 had, under the command of a major general, 137 people (55 officers and 82 civilians) working in its liaison office.

The widespread, consistent, and in many ways unpredictable character of legislative interference in administrative affairs has many consequences for the tone and character of American administrative behavior. From the perspective of this paper, the important consequence is the comprehensive, day-to-day, even hour-by-hour, impact of local views on national programs. No point of substance or procedure is immune from Congressional scrutiny. A substantial portion of the entire weight of this impact is on behalf of the state and local governments. It is a weight that can alter procedures for screening immigration applications, divert the course of a national highway, change the tone of an international negotiation, and amend a social security law to accommodate local practices or fulfill local desires.

The party system compels administrators to take a political role. This is a third way in which the parties function to decentralize the American system. The administrator must play politics for the same reason that the politician is able to play in administration: the parties are without program and without discipline.

In response to the unprotected position in which the party situation places him, the administrator is forced to seek support where he can find it. One ever-present task is to nurse the Congress of the United States, that crucial constituency which ultimately controls his agency's budget and program. From the administrator's view, a sympathetic consideration of Congressional requests (if not downright submission to them) is the surest way to build the political support without which the administrative job could not continue. Even the completely task-oriented administrator must be sensitive to the need for Congressional support and to the relationship between case work requests, on one side, and budgetary and legislative support, on the other. "You do a good job handling the personal problems and requests of a Congressman," a White House officer said, "and you have an easier time convincing him to back your program." Thus there is an important link between the nursing of Congressional requests, requests that largely concern local matters, and the most comprehensive national programs. The administrator must accommodate to the former as a price of gaining support for the latter.

One result of administrative politics is that the administrative agency may become the captive of the nationwide interest group it serves or presumably regulates. In such cases no government may come out with effective authority: the winners are the interest groups themselves. But in a very large number of cases, states and localities also win influence. The politics of administration is a process of making peace with legislators who for the most part consider themselves the guardians of local interests. The political role of administrators therefore contributes to the power of states and localities in national programs.

Finally, the way the party system operates gives American politics their overall distinctive tone. The lack of party discipline produces an openness in the system that allows individuals, groups, and institutions (including state and local governments) to attempt to influence national policy at every step of the legislative-administrative process. This is the "multiple-crack" attribute of the American government. "Crack" has two meanings. It means not only many fissures or access points; it also means, less statically, opportunities for wallops or smacks at government.

If the parties were more disciplined, the result would not be a cessation of the process by which individuals and groups impinge themselves upon the central government. But the present state of the parties clearly allows for a far greater operation of the multiple crack than would be possible under the conditions of centralized party control. American interest groups exploit literally uncountable access points in the legislative-administrative process. If legislative lobbying, from committee stages to the conference committee, does not produce results, a Cabinet secretary is called. His immediate associates are petitioned. Bureau chiefs and their aides are hit. Field officers are put under pressure. Campaigns are instituted by which friends of the agency apply a secondary influence on behalf of the interested party. A conference with the President may be urged.

To these multiple points for bringing influence must be added the multiple voices of the influencers. Consider, for example, those in a small town who wish to have a federal action taken. The easy merging of public and private interest at the local level means that the influence attempt is made in the name of the whole community, thus removing it from political partisanship. The Rotary Club as well as the City Council, the Chamber of Commerce and the mayor, eminent citizens and political bosses—all are readily enlisted. If a conference in a Senator's office will expedite matters, someone on the local scene can be found to make such a conference possible and effective. If technical information is needed, technicians will supply it. State or national professional organizations of local officials, individual Congressmen and Senators, and not infrequently whole state delegations will make the local cause their own. Federal field officers, who service localities, often assume local views. So may elected and appointed state officers. Friendships are exploited, and political mortgages called due. Under these circumstances, national policies are molded by local action.

In summary, then, the party system functions to devolve power. The American parties, unlike any other, are highly responsive when directives move from the bottom to the top, highly unresponsive from top to bottom. Congressmen and Senators can rarely ignore concerted demands from their home constituencies; but no party leader can expect the same kind of response from those below, whether he be a President asking for Congressional support or a Congressman seeking aid from local or state leaders.

Any tightening of the party apparatus would have the effect of strengthening the central government. The four characteristics of the system, discussed above, would become less important. If control from the top were strictly applied, these hallmarks of American decentralization might entirely disappear. To be specific, if disciplined and program-oriented parties were achieved: (1) It would make far less likely legislation that takes heavily into account the desires and prejudices of the highly decentralized power groups and institutions of the country, including the state and local governments. (2) It would to a large extent prevent legislators, individually and collectively, from intruding themselves on behalf of non-national interests in national administrative programs. (3) It would put an end to the administrator's search for his own political support, a search that often results in fostering state, local, and other non-national powers. (4) It would dampen the process by which individuals and groups, including state and local political leaders, take advantage of multiple cracks to steer national legislation and administration in ways congenial to them and the institutions they represent.

Alterations of this sort could only accompany basic changes in the organization and style of politics which, in turn, presuppose fundamental changes at the parties' social base. The sharing of functions is, in fact, the sharing of power. To end this sharing process would mean the destruction of whatever measure of decentralization exists in the United States today.

V. GOALS FOR THE SYSTEM OF SHARING

The Goal of Understanding. Our structure of government is complex, and the politics operating that structure are mildly chaotic. Circumstances are ever-changing. Old institutions mask intricate procedures. The nation's history can be read with alternative glosses, and what is nearest at hand may be furthest from comprehension. Simply to understand the federal system is therefore a difficult task. Yet without understanding there is little possibility of producing desired changes in the system. Social structures and processes are relatively impervious to purposeful change. They also exhibit intricate interrelationships so that change induced at point "A" often produces unanticipated results at point "Z." Changes introduced into an imperfectly understood system are as likely to produce reverse conse-quences as the desired ones.

This is counsel of neither futility nor conservatism for those who seek to make our government a better servant of the people. It is only to say that the first goal for those setting goals with respect to the federal system is that of understanding it.

Two Kinds of Decentralization. The recent major efforts to reform the federal system have in large part been aimed at separating functions and tax sources, at dividing them between the federal government and the states. All of these attempts have failed. We can now add that their success would be undesirable.

It is easy to specify the conditions under which an ordered separation of functions could take place. What is principally needed is a majority political party, under firm leadership, in control of both Presidency and Congress, and, ideally but not necessarily, also in control of a number of states. The political discontinuities, or the absence of party links, (1) between the governors and their state legislatures, (2) between the President and the governors, and (3) between the President and Con-gress clearly account for both the picayune recommendations of the Federal-State Action Committee and for the failure of even those recom-mendations in Congress. If the President had been in control of Con-gress (that is, consistently able to direct a majority of House and Senate votes), this alone would have made possible some genuine separation and devolution of functions. The failure to decentralize by order is a measure of the decentralization of power in the political parties.

Stated positively, party centralization must precede governmental decentralization by order. But this is a slender reed on which to hang decentralization. It implies the power to centralize. A majority party powerful enough to bring about ordered decentralization is far more likely to choose in favor of ordered centralization. And a society that produced centralized national parties would, by that very fact, be a society prepared to accept centralized government.

Decentralization by order must be contrasted with the different kind of decentralization that exists today in the United States. It may be called the decentralization of mild chaos. It exists because of the existence of dispersed power centers. This form of decentralization is less visible and less neat. It rests on no discretion of central authorities. It produces at times specific acts that many citizens may consider undesirable or evil. But power sometimes wielded even for evil ends may be desirable power. To those who find value in the dispersion of power, decentralization by mild chaos is infinitely more desirable than decentralization by order. The preservation of mild chaos is an important goal for the American federal system.

Oiling the Squeak Points. In a governmental system of genuinely shared responsibilities, disagreements inevitably occur. Opinions clash over proximate ends, particular ways of doing things become the subject of public debate, innovations are contested. These are not basic defects in the system. Rather, they are the system's energy-reflecting life blood. There can be no permanent "solutions" short of changing the system itself by elevating one partner to absolute supremacy. What can be done is to attempt to produce conditions in which conflict will not fester but be turned to constructive solutions of particular problems.

A long list of specific points of difficulty in the federal system can be easily identified. No adequate congressional or administrative mechanism exists to review the patchwork of grants in terms of national needs. There is no procedure by which to judge, for example, whether the national government is justified in spending so much more for highways than for education. The working force in some states is inadequate for the effective performance of some nationwide programs, while honest and not-so-honest graft frustrates efficiency in others. Some federal aid programs distort state budgets, and some are so closely supervised as to impede state action in meeting local needs. Grants are given for programs too narrowly defined, and overall programs at the state level consequently suffer. Administrative, accounting and auditing difficulties are the consequence of the multiplicity of grant programs. City officials complain that the states are intrusive fifth wheels in housing, urban redevelopment, and airport building programs.

Some differences are so basic that only a demonstration of strength on one side or another can solve them. School desegregation illustrates such an issue. It also illustrates the correct solution (although not the most desirable method of reaching it): in policy conflicts of fundamental importance, touching the nature of democracy itself, the view of the whole nation must prevail. Such basic ends, however, are rarely at issue, and sides are rarely taken with such passion that loggerheads are reached. Modes of settlement can usually be found to lubricate the squeak points of the system.

A pressing and permanent state problem, general in its impact, is the difficulty of raising sufficient revenue without putting local industries at a competitive disadvantage or without an expansion of sales taxes that press hardest on the least wealthy. A possible way of meeting this problem is to establish a state-levied income tax that could be used as an offset for federal taxes. The maximum level of the tax which could be offset would be fixed by federal law. When levied by a state, the state collection would be deducted from federal taxes. But if a state did not levy the tax, the federal government would. An additional fraction of the total tax imposed by the states would be collected directly by the federal government and used as an equalization fund, that is, distributed among the less wealthy states. Such a tax would almost certainly be imposed by all states since not to levy it would give neither political advantage to its public leaders nor financial advantage to its citizens. The net effect would be an increase in the total personal and corporate income tax.

The offset has great promise for strengthening state governments. It would help produce a more economic distribution of industry. It would have obvious financial advantages for the vast majority of states. Since a large fraction of all state income is used to aid political subdivisions, the local governments would also profit, though not equally as long as cities are underrepresented in state legislatures. On the other hand, such a scheme will appear disadvantageous to some low-tax states which profit from the in-migration of industry (though it would by no means end all state-by-state tax differentials). It will probably excite the opposition of those concerned over governmental centralization, and they will not be assuaged by methods that suggest themselves for making both state and central governments bear the psychological impact of the tax. Although the offset would probably produce an across-the-board tax increase, wealthier persons, who are affected more by an income tax than by other levies, can be expected to join forces with those whose fear is centralization. (This is a common alliance and, in the nature of things, the philosophical issue rather than financial advantage is kept foremost.)

Those opposing such a tax would gain additional ammunition from the certain knowledge that federal participation in the scheme would lead to some federal standards governing the use of the funds. Yet the political strength of the states would keep these from becoming onerous. Indeed, inauguration of the tax offset as a means of providing funds to the states might be an occasion for dropping some of the specifications for existing federal grants. One federal standard, however, might be possible because of the greater representation of urban areas in the constituency of Congress and the President than in the constituency of state legislatures: Congress might make a state's participation in the offset scheme dependent upon a periodic reapportionment of state legislatures.

The income tax offset is only one of many ideas that can be generated to meet serious problems of closely meshed governments. The fate of all such schemes ultimately rests, as it should, with the politics of a free people. But much can be done if the primary technical effort of those concerned with improving the federal system were directed not at separating its interrelated parts but at making them work together more effectively. Temporary commissions are relatively inefficient in this effort, though they may be useful for making general assessments and for generating new ideas. The professional organizations of government workers do part of the job of continuously scrutinizing programs and ways and means of improving them. A permanent staff, established in the President's office and working closely with state and local officials, could also perform a useful and perhaps important role.

The Strength of the Parts. Whatever governmental "strength" or "vitality" may be, it does not consist of independent decision-making in legislation and administration. Federal-state interpenetration here is extensive. Indeed, a judgment of the relative domestic strength of the two planes must take heavily into account the influence of one on the other's decisions. In such an analysis the strength of the states (and localities) does not weigh lightly. The nature of the nation's politics makes federal functions more vulnerable to state influence than state offices are to federal influence. Many states, as the Kestnbaum Commission noted, live with "self-imposed constitutional limitations" that make it difficult for them to "perform all of the services that their citizens require." If this has the result of adding to federal responsibilities, the states' importance in shaping and administering federal programs eliminates much of the sting.

The geography of state boundaries, as well as many aspects of state internal organization, are the products of history and cannot be justified on any grounds of rational efficiency. Who, today, would create major governmental subdivisions the size of Maryland, Delaware, New Jersey, or Rhode Island? Who would write into Oklahoma's fundamental law an absolute state debt limit of $500,000? Who would design (to cite only the most extreme cases) Georgia's and Florida's gross underrepresentation of urban areas in both houses of the legislature?

A complete catalogue of state political and administrative horrors would fill a sizeable volume. Yet exhortations to erase them have roughly the same effect as similar exhortations to erase sin. Some of the worst inanities—for example, the boundaries of the states, themselves—are fixed in the national constitution and defy alteration for all foreseeable time. Others, such as urban underrepresentation in state legislatures, serve the overrepresented groups, including some urban ones, and the effective political organization of the deprived groups must precede reform.

Despite deficiencies of politics and organizations that are unchangeable or slowly changing, it is an error to look at the states as static anachronisms. Some of them—New York, Minnesota, and California, to take three examples spanning the country—have administrative organizations that compare favorably in many ways with the national establishment. Many more in recent years have moved rapidly towards integrated administrative departments, statewide budgeting, and central leadership. The others have models-in-existence to follow, and active professional organizations (led by the Council of State Governments) promoting their development. Slow as this change may be, the states move in the direction of greater internal effectiveness.

The pace toward more effective performance at the state level is likely to increase. Urban leaders, who generally feel themselves disadvantaged in state affairs, and suburban and rural spokesmen, who are most concerned about national centralization, have a common interest in this task. The urban dwellers want greater equality in state affairs, including a more equitable share of state financial aid; nonurban dwellers are concerned that city dissatisfactions should not be met by exclusive federal, or federal-local, programs. Antagonistic, rather than amiable, cooperation may be the consequence. But it is a cooperation that can be turned to politically effective measures for a desirable upgrading of state institutions.

If one looks closely, there is scant evidence for the fear of the federal octopus, the fear that expansion of central programs and influence threatens to reduce the states and localities to compliant administrative arms of the central government. In fact, state and local governments are touching a larger proportion of the people in more ways than ever before; and they are spending a higher fraction of the total national product than ever before. Federal programs have increased, rather than diminished, the importance of the governors; stimulated professionalism in state agencies; increased citizen interest and participation in government; and, generally, enlarged and made more effective the scope of state action.[2] It may no longer be true in any significant sense that the states and localities are "closer" than the federal government to the people. It is true that the smaller governments remain active and powerful members of the federal system.

---

[2]See the valuable report, *The Impact of Federal Grants-in-Aid on the Structure and Functions of State and Local Governments,* submitted to the Commission on Intergovernmental Relations by the Governmental Affairs Institute (Washington, 1955).

Central Leadership: The Need for Balance. The chaos of party processes makes difficult the task of presidential leadership. It deprives the President of ready-made Congressional majorities. It may produce, as in the chairmen of legislative committees, power-holders relatively hidden from public scrutiny and relatively protected from presidential direction. It allows the growth of administrative agencies which sometimes escape control by central officials. These are prices paid for a wide dispersion of political power. The cost is tolerable because the total results of dispersed power are themselves desirable and because, where clear national supremacy is essential, in foreign policy and military affairs, it is easiest to secure.

Moreover, in the balance of strength between the central and peripheral governments, the central government has on its side the whole secular drift towards the concentration of power. It has on its side technical developments that make central decisions easy and sometimes mandatory. It has on its side potent purse powers, the result of superior tax-gathering resources. It has potentially on its side the national leadership capacities of the presidential office. The last factor is the controlling one, and national strength in the federal system has shifted with the leadership desires and capacities of the Chief Executive. As these have varied, so there has been an almost rhythmic pattern: periods of central strength put to use alternating with periods of central strength dormant.

Following a high point of federal influence during the early and middle years of the New Deal, the postwar years have been, in the weighing of central-peripheral strength, a period of light federal activity. Excepting the Supreme Court's action in favor of school desegregation, national influence by design or default has not been strong in domestic affairs. The danger now is that the central government is doing too little rather than too much. National deficiencies in education and health require the renewed attention of the national government. Steepening population and urbanization trend lines have produced metropolitan area problems that can be effectively attacked only with the aid of federal resources. New definitions of old programs in housing and urban redevelopment, and new programs to deal with air pollution, water supply, and mass transportation are necessary. The federal government's essential role in the federal system is that of organizing, and helping to finance, such nationwide programs.

The American federal system exhibits many evidences of the dispersion of power not only because of formal federalism but more importantly because our politics reflect and reinforce the nation's diversities-within-unity. Those who value the virtues of decentralization, which writ large are virtues of freedom, need not scruple at recognizing the defects of those virtues. The defects are principally the danger that parochial and private interests may not coincide with, or give way to, the nation's interest. The necessary cure for these defects is effective national leadership.

The centrifugal force of domestic politics needs to be balanced by the centripetal force of strong presidential leadership. Simultaneous strength at center and periphery exhibits the American system at its best, if also at its noisiest. The interests of both find effective spokesmen. States and localities (and private interest groups) do not lose their influence opportunities, but national policy becomes more than the simple consequence of successful, momentary concentrations of non-national pressures: it is guided by national leaders.

CHAPTER 3

Civil Liberties and Civil Rights

Civil liberties and civil rights cover a very broad area. Among the most fundamental civil liberties are those governing the extent to which individuals can speak, write, and read what they choose. The democratic process requires the free exchange of ideas. Constitutional government requires the protection of minority rights and, above all, the right to dissent.

The Nationalization of the Bill of Rights

It is clear from the debate over the inclusion of the Bill of Rights in the Constitution of 1787 that its provisions were certainly never intended to be prohibitions upon state action. The Bill of Rights was added to the Constitution to satisfy state governments that the same rights which they generally accorded to their own citizens under state constitutions would apply with respect to the national government, and act as a check upon abridgments by the national government of civil liberties and civil rights. Proponents of a separate bill of rights wanted specific provisions to limit the powers of the national government which, *in its own sphere,* could act directly upon citizens of the state.

Article Ten, which is not so much a part of the Bill of Rights as an expression of the balance of authority that exists between the national government and the states in the Constitution, provides that "the powers not delegated to the United States by the Constitution, nor prohibited by it to the states are reserved to the states respectively, or to the people." Under the federal system each member of the community is both (1) a citizen of the United States and (2) a citizen of the particular state in which he resides. The rights and obligations of each citizenship class are determined by the legal divisions of authority set up in the Constitution. Apart from specific limits upon state power to abridge civil liberties and civil rights, as for example the prohibitions of section ten against state passage of any bills of attainder or ex post facto laws, there is nothing in the main body of the Constitution or the Bill of Rights that controls state action. Originally it was up to the states to determine the protections they would give to their own citizens against state actions. The applicability of the Bill of Rights to national action only was affirmed in *Barron v. Baltimore,* 7 Peters 243 (1833).

The adoption of the Fourteenth Amendment in 1868 potentially limited the discretion that the states had possessed to determine the civil liberties and rights of citizens within their sphere of authority. The Fourteenth Amendment provided that:

> 1. All persons born or naturalized in the United States, and subject to the jurisdiction thereof, are citizens of the United States and of the state wherein they reside. No state shall make or enforce any law which shall abridge the privileges or immunities of citizens of the United States; nor shall any state deprive any person of life, liberty, or property, without due process of law; nor deny to any person within its jurisdiction the equal protection of the laws. . . .
>
> 5. The Congress shall have power to enforce, by appropriate legislation, the provisions of this article.

Although the Fourteenth Amendment appeared to be a tough restriction upon state action, its provisions were equivocal and required clarification by the Supreme Court before they could take effect. The history of the Fourteenth Amendment suggested that it was designed to protect the legal and political rights of blacks against state encroachment, and was not to have a broader application. In the *Slaughterhouse Cases,* 16 Wallace 36 (1873), the Supreme Court held that the privileges and immunities clause of the Fourteenth Amendment did nothing to alter the authority of the states to determine the rights and obligations of citizens subject to state action. Under this doctrine the Bill of Rights could not be made applicable to the states.

It was not until *Gitlow v. New York,* 268 U.S. 652 (1925), that the Court finally announced that the substantive areas of freedom of speech and of press of the First Amendment are part of the "liberty" protected by the Fourteenth Amendment due process clause; however, in Gitlow's case the Court found that the procedures that had been used in New York to restrict his freedom of speech did not violate due process. In *Near v. Minnesota,* 283 U.S. 697 (1931), the Court for the first time overturned a state statute as a violation of the Fourteenth Amendment due process clause because it permitted prior censorship of the press. *Gitlow* and *Near* were limited because they incorporated only the freedom of speech and press provisions of the First Amendment under the due process clause of the Fourteenth Amendment. The cases marked the beginning of a slow and tedious process of "incorporation" of most of the provisions of the Bill of Rights as part of the due process clause of the Fourteenth Amendment. The process of incorporation did not begin in earnest until the Warren Court, and then not until the 1960s. By the late 1970s all of the Bill of Rights were incorporated as protections against state action with the exceptions of the rights to grand jury indictment, trial by jury in *civil* cases, the right to bear arms, protection against excessive bail and fines, and against involuntary quartering of troops in private homes.[1]

The following case presents an example of incorporation of the right to counsel under the due process clause of the Fourteenth Amendment. In cases prior to *Gideon* v. *Wainwright,* decided in 1963, the Court had upheld an ad hoc right to counsel in individual cases. That is, it had held that the facts of a particular case warranted granting the right to counsel as part of due process under the Fourteenth Amendment for that particular case only. By such ad hoc determinations, the Court was able to exercise self-restraint in relation to federal-state relations, by not requiring a general right to counsel in all state criminal cases. *Powell* v. *Alabama,* 287 U.S. 45 (1932), was an example of such an ad hoc inclusion of the right to counsel in a specific case, where, in a one-day trial, seven blacks had been convicted of raping two white girls, and sentenced to death. The Court held that under the circumstances of the case the denial of counsel by the Alabama courts to the defendants violated the due process clause of the Fourteenth Amendment. In *Powell,* however, the Court did not incorporate the right to counsel in all criminal cases under this due process clause. It only provided that "in a capital case, where the defendant is unable to employ counsel, and is incapable adequately of making his own defense because of ignorance, feeblemindedness, illiteracy, or the like, it is the duty of the court, whether requested or not, to assign counsel for him as a necessary requisite of due process of law. . . . " The *Powell* case was widely interpreted as nationalizing (incorporating) the right to counsel in all *capital* cases. The Court reaffirmed its refusal to incorporate the right to counsel in all criminal cases in *Betts* v. *Brady,* 316 U.S. 455 (1942). There the Court held that the Sixth Amendment applies only to trials in federal courts and that the right to counsel is not a fundamental right, essential to a fair trial, and therefore is not required in all cases under the due process clause of the Fourteenth Amendment. The Court emphasized that whether

---

[1]For an excellent discussion of the incorporation of most of the Bill of Rights under the due process clause of the Fourteenth Amendment, see Henry J. Abraham, *Freedom and the Court* (3rd edition, New York: Oxford University Press, 1977), Chapter 3.

or not the right to counsel would be required depended upon the circumstances of the case in which it was requested.

In *Gideon* v. *Wainwright* the Court finally nationalized the right to counsel in all criminal cases under the due process clause of the Fourteenth Amendment. The case represented, in 1963, an important step in the progression toward nationalization of most of the Bill of Rights. While Justice Roberts, writing for the majority of the Court in the *Betts* case in 1942, found that the right to counsel was not fundamental to a fair trial, Justice Black, who had dissented in the *Betts* case, writing for the majority in *Gideon* v. *Wainwright* in 1962, held that the right to counsel was fundamental and essential to a fair trial and therefore was protected by the due process clause of the Fourteenth Amendment. In *Gideon*, Justice Black noted:

> We accept that the *Brady* assumption, based as it was on our prior cases, that a provision of the Bill of Rights which is "fundamental and essential to a fair trial" is made obligatory upon the states by the Fourteenth Amendment. We think the Court in *Betts* was wrong, however, in concluding that the Sixth Amendment's guarantee of counsel is not one of the fundamental rights.

The history of Supreme Court interpretation of the Fourteenth Amendment due process clause reveals the Court acting both politically and ideologically. In the period from 1868 to 1925 the Court was careful to exercise judicial self-restraint in interpreting the Fourteenth Amendment, in part because of the conservative views of most of the justices that the Court should not impose national standards of civil liberties and civil rights upon the states. The Court did not believe in self-restraint in all areas, as is demonstrated by its use of the due process clause of the Fourteenth Amendment to impose its own views on the proper relationship between the states and business. The Court read the Fourteenth Amendment due process clause in such a way as to protect the property interests of business against state regulation. Many such laws were found to be taking the liberty or property of business without due process. Beginning with *Gitlow* v. *New York* in 1925, the Court for the first time added substance to the due process clause of the Fourteenth Amendment in the area of civil liberties by including First Amendment freedoms of speech and press as part of the "liberty" of the due process clause.

While the Supreme Court is sensitive to the political environment in which it functions, the ways in which it has interpreted the due process clause of the Fourteenth Amendment suggest that ideological convictions are more important than pressure from political majorities. During the era of economic substantive due process under the Fourteenth Amendment, which ended in 1937, the Court was really taking an elitist position that did not agree with the political majorities in many states that were behind the regulatory laws that the Court struck down. Nor can it be said that when the Court began to add substance in civil liberties and civil rights to the due process clause and extend procedural protection that it was supported by political majorities. In fact, the Warren Court's extension of the Fourteenth Amendment due process clause, particularly in the area of criminal rights, caused a political outcry among the states and their citizens who felt that law enforcement efforts would be unduly impeded. When the Court, in *Griswold* v. *Connecticut* in 1965, went beyond the explicit provisions of the Bill of Rights to find a right of privacy to strike down Connecticut's birth control statute that prevented the use of contraceptives in the state, even Justice Black, a strong supporter of incorporating the Bill of Rights under the due process clause, took objection. He found in the *Griswold* decision a return to substantive due process in a form that was unacceptable, because it was adding substance to the clause that was not explicitly provided for in the intent of the Fourteenth Amendment, which he had held in *Adamson* v. *California* in 1946 to be total inclusion of the Bill of Rights. The *Griswold* decision was not unpopular politically, but when the Court in *Roe* v. *Wade* in 1973 used the right of privacy to strike down a Texas abortion statute, and in effect declare all state laws that absolutely prohibited abortion to be unconstitutional, a nationwide anti-abortion movement was organized to overturn the decision by mobilizing political support behind a constitutional amendment. The Supreme Court has certainly not, in the area of interpretation of the Fourteenth Amendment, acted solely out of political motives.[2]

The following case presents an example of the way in which the Supreme Court gradually incorporated the Bill of Rights under the Fourteenth Amendment. Behind the decision to nationalize the right to counsel in *Gideon* v. *Wainwright* a fascinating series of events had occurred.[3] By the time the *Gideon* case was called up the Court was purposely looking for an appropriate case from which it could incorporate the right to counsel under the due process clause of the Fourteenth Amendment. The Court felt that Gideon's case presented the kind of circumstances that would be publicly accepted as requiring the right to counsel to ensure fairness. In granting certiorari to Gideon's *in forma pauperis* petition ("in the manner of the pauper," a permission to sue without incurring liability for costs) the Court had in effect already made up its mind about the decision. By the appointment of Attorney Abe

[2]The forces affecting Supreme Court decision making are discussed in the selection by William J. Brennan, Jr., John P. Roche, and Earl Warren, in Chapter 9.
[3]The story of the case is brilliantly told by Anthony Lewis, in *Gideon's Trumpet* (New York: Random House, 1964).

Fortas, later to become a member of the Court (although eventually forced to resign because of conflict of interest charges), one of the most distinguished lawyers in the country, the Court guaranteed an eloquent and persuasive brief for the petitioner, Earl Gideon. The Court felt that the right to counsel was a right whose time had come by 1963.

11

GIDEON v. WAINWRIGHT
372 U.S. 335 (1963)

... Mr. Justice Black delivered the opinion of the Court, saying in part:
Petitioner was charged in a Florida state court with having broken and
entered a poolroom with intent to commit a misdemeanor. This offense is a
felony under Florida law. Appearing in court without funds and without a
lawyer, petitioner asked the court to appoint counsel for him, whereupon
the following colloquy took place:

> The COURT: Mr. Gideon, I am sorry, but I cannot appoint Counsel to
> represent you in this case. Under the laws of the State of Florida, the only
> time the Court can appoint Counsel to represent a Defendant is when that
> person is charged with a capital offense. I am sorry, but I will have to deny
> your request to appoint Counsel to defend you in this case.
>
> The DEFENDANT: The United States Supreme Court says I am entitled to
> be represented by Counsel.

Put to trial before a jury, Gideon conducted his defense about as well as
could be expected from a layman. He made an opening statement to the
jury, cross-examined the State's witnesses, presented witnesses in his own
defense, declined to testify himself, and made a short argument "emphasizing
his innocence to the charge contained in the Information filed in this case."
The jury returned a verdict of guilty, and petitioner was sentenced to serve
five years in the state prison. Later, petitioner filed in the Florida Supreme
Court this habeas corpus petition attacking his conviction and sentence on
the ground that the trial court's refusal to appoint counsel for him denied
him rights "guaranteed by the Constitution and the Bill of Rights by the
United States Government."[1] Treating the petition for habeas corpus as
properly before it, the State Supreme Court, "upon consideration thereof"
but without an opinion, denied all relief. Since 1942, when *Betts* v. *Brady,*
316 U.S. 455 ... was decided by a divided Court, the problem of a defendant's
federal constitutional right to counsel in a state court has been a continuing
source of controversy and litigation in both state and federal courts. To
give this problem another review here, we granted certiorari. 370 U.S.
908. ... Since Gideon was proceeding *in forma pauperis,* we appointed
counsel to represent him and requested both sides to discuss in their briefs

---

In this selection some footnotes are omitted; all are renumbered.

[1] Later in the petition for habeas corpus, signed and apparently prepared by the
petitioner himself, he stated, "I, Clarence Earl Gideon, claim that I was denied the rights of
the 4th, 5th and 14th amendments of the Bill of Rights."

and oral arguments the following: "Should this Court's holding in *Betts* v. *Brady* . . . be reconsidered?"

I.

The facts upon which Betts claimed that he had been unconstitutionally denied the right to have counsel appointed to assist him are strikingly like the facts upon which Gideon here bases his federal constitutional claim. Betts was indicted for robbery in a Maryland state court. On arraignment, he told the trial judge of his lack of funds to hire a lawyer and asked the court to appoint one for him. Betts was advised that it was not the practice in that county to appoint counsel for indigent defendants except in murder and rape cases. He then pleaded not guilty, had witnesses summoned, cross-examined the State's witnesses, examined his own, and chose not to testify himself. He was found guilty by the judge, sitting without a jury, and sentenced to eight years in prison. Like Gideon, Betts sought release by habeas corpus, alleging that he had been denied the right to assistance of counsel in violation of the Fourteenth Amendment. Betts was denied any relief, and on review this Court affirmed. It was held that a refusal to appoint counsel for an indigent defendant charged with a felony did not necessarily violate the Due Process Clause of the Fourteenth Amendment, which for reasons given the Court deemed to be the only applicable federal constitutional provision. The Court said:

> Asserted denial [of due process] is to be tested by an appraisal of the totality of facts in a given case. That which may, in one setting, constitute a denial of fundamental fairness, shocking to the universal sense of justice, may, in other circumstances, and in the light of other considerations, fall short of such denial. 316 U.S., at 462. . . .

Treating due process as "a concept less rigid and more fluid than those envisaged in other specific and particular provisions of the Bill of Rights," the Court held that refusal to appoint counsel under the particular facts and circumstances in the Betts case was not so "offensive to the common and fundamental ideas of fairness" as to amount to a denial of due process. Since the facts and circumstances of the two cases are so nearly indistinguishable, we think the *Betts* v. *Brady* holding if left standing would require us to reject Gideon's claim that the Constitution guarantees him the assistance of counsel. Upon full reconsideration we conclude that *Betts* v. *Brady* should be overruled.

II.

The Sixth Amendment provides, "In all criminal prosecutions, the accused shall enjoy the right . . . to have the Assistance of Counsel for his defence."

We have construed this to mean that in federal courts counsel must be provided for defendants unable to employ counsel unless the right is competently and intelligently waived. Betts argued that this right is extended to indigent defendants in state courts by the Fourteenth Amendment. In response the Court stated that, while the Sixth Amendment laid down "no rule for the conduct of the states, the question recurs whether the constraint laid by the amendment upon the national courts expresses a rule so fundamental and essential to a fair trial, and so, to due process of law, that it is made obligatory upon the states by the Fourteenth Amendment." 316 U.S., at 465. . . . In order to decide whether the Sixth Amendment's guarantee of counsel is of this fundamental nature, the Court in Betts set out and considered "[r]elevant data on the subject . . . afforded by constitutional and statutory provisions subsisting in the colonies and the states prior to the inclusion of the Bill of Rights in the national Constitution, and in the constitutional, legislative, and judicial history of the states to the present date." 316 U.S., at 465. . . . On the basis of this historical data the Court concluded that "appointment of counsel is not a fundamental right, essential to a fair trial." 316 U.S. at 471. . . . It was for this reason the Betts Court refused to accept the contention that the Sixth Amendment's guarantee of counsel for indigent federal defendants was extended to or, in the words of that Court, "made obligatory upon the states by the Fourteenth Amendment." Plainly, had the Court concluded that appointment of counsel for an indigent criminal defendant was "a fundamental right, essential to a fair trial," it would have held that the Fourteenth Amendment requires appointment of counsel in a state court, just as the Sixth Amendment requires in a federal court.

We think the Court in Betts had ample precedent for acknowledging that those guarantees of the Bill of Rights which are fundamental safeguards of liberty immune from federal abridgment are equally protected against state invasion by the Due Process Clause of the Fourteenth Amendment. This same principle was recognized, explained, and applied in *Powell* v. *Alabama,* 287 U.S. 45 (1932), a case upholding the right of counsel, where the Court held that despite sweeping language to the contrary in *Hurtado* v. *California,* 110 U.S. 516 (1884), the Fourteenth Amendment "embraced" those "fundamental principles of liberty and justice which lie at the base of all our civil and political institutions,' " even though they had been "specifically dealt with in another part of the Federal Constitution." 287 U.S., at 67. . . . In many cases other than Powell and Betts, this Court has looked to the fundamental nature of original Bill of Rights guarantees to decide whether the Fourteenth Amendment makes them obligatory on the States. Explicitly recognized to be of this "fundamental nature" and therefore made immune from state invasion by the Fourteenth, or some part of it, are the First Amendment's freedoms of speech, press, religion, assembly, association, and petition for redress of grievances. For the same reason, though not always in precisely the same terminology, the

Court has made obligatory on the States the Fifth Amendment's command that private property shall not be taken for public use without just compensation, the Fourth Amendment's prohibition of unreasonable searches and seizures, and the Eighth's ban on cruel and unusual punishment. On the other hand, this Court in *Palko* v. *Connecticut,* 302 U.S. 319 . . . (1937), refused to hold that the Fourteenth Amendment made the double jeopardy provision of the Fifth Amendment obligatory on the States. In so refusing, however, the Court, speaking through Mr. Justice Cardozo, was careful to emphasize that "immunities that are valid as against the federal government by force of the specific pledges of particular amendments have been found to be implicit in the concept of ordered liberty, and thus, through the Fourteenth Amendment, become valid as against the states" and that guarantees "in their origin . . . effective against the federal government alone" had by prior cases "been taken over from the earlier articles of the Federal Bill of Rights and brought within the Fourteenth Amendment by a process of absorption." 302 U.S., at 324-325, 326. . . .

We accept *Betts* v. *Brady's* assumption, based as it was on our prior cases, that a provision of the Bill of Rights which is "fundamental and essential to a fair trial" is made obligatory upon the States by the Four-teenth Amendment. We think the Court in Betts was wrong, however, in concluding that the Sixth Amendment's guarantee of counsel is not one of these fundamental rights. Ten years before *Betts* v. *Brady,* this Court, after full consideration of all the historical data examined in Betts, had unequivo-cally declared that "the right to the aid of counsel is of this fundamental character." *Powell* v. *Alabama,* 287 U.S. 45 . . . (1932). While the Court at the close of its Powell opinion did by its language, as this Court frequently does, limit its holding to the particular facts and circumstances of that case, its conclusions about the fundamental nature of the right to counsel are unmistakable. Several years later, in 1936, the Court reemphasized what it had said about the fundamental nature of the right to counsel in this language:

> We concluded that certain fundamental rights, safeguarded by the first eight amendments against federal action, were also safeguarded against state action by the due process of law clause of the Fourteenth Amendment, and among them the fundamental right of the accused to the aid of counsel in a criminal prosecution. *Grosjean* v. *American Press Co.,* 297 U.S. 233 . . . (1936).

And again in 1938 this Court said:

> [The assistance of counsel] is one of the safeguards of the Sixth Amend-ment deemed necessary to insure fundamental human rights of life and liberty. . . . The Sixth Amendment stands as a constant admonition that if the constitutional safeguards it provides be lost, justice will not 'still be done.' *Johnson* v. *Zerbst,* 304 U.S. 458 . . . (1938). To the same effect, see

Avery v. *Alabama,* 308 U.S. 444 . . . (1940), and *Smith* v. *O'Grady,* 312 U.S. 329 . . . (1941).

In light of these and many other prior decisions of this Court, it is not surprising that the Betts Court, when faced with the contention that "one charged with crime, who is unable to obtain counsel, must be furnished counsel by the state," conceded that "[e]xpressions in the opinions of this court lend color to the argument . . . " 316 U.S., at 462–463. . . . The fact is that in deciding as it did—that "appointment of counsel is not a fundamental right, essential to a fair trial"—the Court in *Betts* v. *Brady* made an abrupt break with its own well-considered precedents. In returning to these old precedents, sounder we believe than the new, we but restore constitutional principles established to achieve a fair system of justice. Not only these precedents but also reason and reflection require us to recognize that in our adversary system of criminal justice, any person haled into court, who is too poor to hire a lawyer, cannot be assured a fair trial unless counsel is provided for him. This seems to us to be an obvious truth. Governments, both state and federal, quite properly spend vast sums of money to establish machinery to try defendants accused of crime. Lawyers to prosecute are everywhere deemed essential to protect the public's interest in an orderly society. Similarly, there are few defendants charged with crime, few indeed, who fail to hire the best lawyers they can get to prepare and present their defenses. That government hires lawyers to prosecute and defendants who have the money hire lawyers to defend are the strongest indications of the widespread belief that lawyers in criminal courts are necessities, not luxuries. The right of one charged with crime to counsel may not be deemed fundamental and essential to fair trials in some countries, but it is in ours. From the very beginning, our state and national constitutions and laws have laid great emphasis on procedural and substantive safeguards designed to assure fair trials before impartial tribunals in which every defendant stands equal before the law. This noble ideal cannot be realized if the poor man charged with crime has to face his accusers without a lawyer to assist him. A defendant's need for a lawyer is nowhere better stated than in the moving words of Mr. Justice Sutherland in *Powell* v. *Alabama:*

The right to be heard would be, in many cases, of little avail if it did not comprehend the right to be heard by counsel. Even the intelligent and educated layman has small and sometimes no skill in the science of law. If charged with crime, he is incapable, generally, of determining for himself whether the indictment is good or bad. He is unfamiliar with the rules of evidence. Left without the aid of counsel he may be put on trial without a proper charge, and convicted upon incompetent evidence, or evidence irrelevant to the issue or otherwise inadmissible. He lacks both the skill and knowledge adequately to prepare his defense, even though he have a perfect one. He requires the guiding hand of counsel at every step in the proceedings against him. Without it, though he be not guilty, he faces the danger of conviction because he does not know how to establish his innocence. 287 U.S., at 68–69. . . .

The Court in *Betts* v. *Brady* departed from the sound wisdom upon which the Court's holding in *Powell* v. *Alabama* rested. Florida, supported by two other States, has asked that *Betts* v. *Brady* be left intact. Twenty-two States, as friends of the Court, argue that Betts was "an anachronism when handed down" and that it should now be overruled. We agree.

The judgment is reversed and the cause is remanded to the Supreme Court of Florida for further action not inconsistent with this opinion.

Reversed.

Chief Justice Warren, and Justices Brennan, Stewart, White, and Goldberg join in the opinion of the Court.

Mr. Justice Douglas joins the opinion, giving a brief historical resume of the relation between the Bill of Rights and the Fourteenth Amendment. Mr. Justice Clark concurs in the result. Mr. Justice Harlan concurs in the result.

Freedom of Speech and Press

☐   There are many reasons why we should support freedom of speech and press. One of these is the impossibility of proving the existence of an Absolute Truth. No person nor group can be infallible. The "best" decisions are those that are made on the basis of the most widespread information available pertaining to the subject at hand. Freedom of information is an integral part of the democratic process. In this selection from John Stuart Mill's famous essay *On Liberty,* published in 1859, the justifications for permitting liberty of speech and press are discussed.

12
John Stuart Mill

LIBERTY OF THOUGHT AND DISCUSSION

The time, it is to be hoped, is gone by when any defence would be necessary of the "liberty of the press" as one of the securities against corrupt or tyrannical government. No argument, we may suppose, can now be needed, against permitting a legislature or an executive, not identified in interest with the people, to prescribe opinions to them, and determine what doctrines or what arguments they shall be allowed to hear. This aspect of the question, besides, has been so often and so triumphantly enforced by preceding writers, that it needs not be specially insisted on in this place. Though the law of England, on the subject of the press, is as servile to this day as it was in the time of the Tudors, there is little danger of its being actually put in force against political discussion, except during some temporary panic, when fear of insurrection drives ministers and judges from their propriety; and, speaking generally, it is not, in constitutional countries, to be apprehended, that the government, whether completely responsible to the people or not, will often attempt to control the expression of opinion, except when in doing so it makes itself the organ of the general intolerance of the public. Let us suppose, therefore, that the government is entirely at one with the people, and never thinks of exerting any power of coercion unless in agreement with what it conceives to be their voice. But I deny the right of the people to exercise such coercion, either by themselves or by their government. The power itself is illegitimate. The best government has no more title to it than the worst. It is as noxious, or more noxious, when exerted in accordance with public opinion, than when in opposition to it. If all mankind minus one, were of one opinion, and only one person were of the contrary opinion, mankind would be no more justified in silencing that one person, than he, if he had the power, would be justified in silencing mankind. Were an opinion a personal possession of no value except to the owner; if to be obstructed in the enjoyment of it were simply a private injury, it would make some difference whether the injury was inflicted only on a few persons or on many. But the peculiar evil of silencing the expression of an opinion is, that it is robbing the human race; posterity as well as the existing generation; those who dissent from the opinion, still more than those who hold it. If the opinion is right, they are deprived of the opportunity of exchanging error for truth: if wrong, they lose, what is almost as great a benefit, the clearer perception and livelier impression of truth, produced by its collision with error.

It is necessary to consider separately these two hypotheses, each of which has a distinct branch of the argument corresponding to it. We can never be sure that the opinion we are endeavoring to stifle is a false opinion; and if we were sure, stifling it would be an evil still.

First: the opinion which it is attempted to suppress by authority may possibly be true. Those who desire to suppress it, of course deny its truth; but they are not infallible. They have no authority to decide the question for all mankind, and exclude every other person from the means of judging. To refuse a hearing to an opinion, because they are sure that it is false, is to assume that *their* certainty is the same thing as *absolute* certainty. All silencing of discussion is an assumption of infallibility. Its condemnation may be allowed to rest on this common argument, not the worse for being common.

Unfortunately for the good sense of mankind, the fact of their fallibility is far from carrying the weight in their practical judgment, which is always allowed to it in theory; for while every one well knows himself to be fallible, few think it necessary to take any precautions against their own fallibility, or admit the supposition that any opinion, of which they feel very certain, may be one of the examples of the error to which they acknowledge themselves to be liable. Absolute princes, or others who are accustomed to unlimited deference, usually feel this complete confidence in their own opinions on nearly all subjects. People more happily situated, who sometimes hear their opinions disputed, and are not wholly unused to be set right when they are wrong, place the same unbounded reliance only on such of their opinions as are shared by all who surround them, or to whom they habitually defer: for in proportion to a man's want of confidence in his own solitary judgment, does he usually repose, with implicit trust, on the infallibility of "the world" in general. And the world, to each individual, means the part of it with which he comes in contact; his party, his sect, his church, his class of society: the man may be called, by comparison, almost liberal and largeminded to whom it means anything so comprehensive as his own country or his own age. Nor is his faith in this collective authority at all shaken by his being aware that other ages, countries, sects, churches, classes, and parties have thought, and even now think, the exact reverse. He devolves upon his own world the responsibility of being in the right against the dissentient worlds of other people; and it never troubles him that mere accident has decided which of these numerous worlds is the object of his reliance, and that the same causes which make him a Churchman in London, would have made him a Buddhist or a Confucian in Peking. Yet it is as evident in itself, as any amount of argument can make it, that ages are no more infallible than individuals; every age having held many opinions which subsequent ages have deemed not only false but absurd; and it is as certain that many opinions, now general, will be rejected by future ages, as it is that many, once general, are rejected by the present.

The objection likely to be made to this argument, would probably take some such form as the following. There is no greater assumption of infallibility in forbidding the propagation of error, than in any other thing which is done by public authority on its own judgment and responsibility. Judgment is given to men that they may use it. Because it may be used erroneously, are men to be told that they ought not to use it at all? To prohibit what they think pernicious, is not claiming exemption from error, but fulfilling the duty incumbent on them, although fallible, of acting on their conscientious conviction. If we were never to act on our opinions, because those opinions may be wrong, we should leave all our interests uncared for, and all our duties unperformed. An objection which applies to all conduct, can be no valid objection to any conduct in particular. It is the duty of governments, and of individuals, to form the truest opinions they can; to form them carefully, and never impose them upon others unless they are quite sure of being right. But when they are sure (such reasoners may say), it is not conscientiousness but cowardice to shrink from acting on their opinions, and allow doctrines which they honestly think dangerous to the welfare of mankind, either in this life or in another, to be scattered abroad without restraint, because other people, in less enlightened times, have persecuted opinions now believed to be true. Let us take care, it may be said, not to make the same mistake: but governments and nations have made mistakes in other things, which are not denied to be fit subjects for the exercise of authority: they have laid on bad taxes, made unjust wars. Ought we therefore to lay on no taxes, and, under whatever provocation, make no wars? Men, and governments, must act to the best of their ability. There is no such thing as absolute certainty, but there is assurance sufficient for the purposes of human life. We may, and must, assume our opinion to be true for the guidance of our own conduct: and it is assuming no more when we forbid bad men to pervert society by the propagation of opinions which we regard as false and pernicious.

I answer, that it is assuming very much more. There is the greatest difference between presuming an opinion to be true, because, with every opportunity for contesting it, it had not been refuted, and assuming its truth for the purpose of not permitting its refutation. Complete liberty of contradicting and disproving our opinion, is the very condition which justifies us in assuming its truth for purposes of action; and on no other terms can a being with human faculties have any rational assurance of being right.

When we consider either the history of opinion, or the ordinary conduct of human life, to what is it to be ascribed that the one and the other are no worse than they are? Not certainly to the inherent force of the human understanding; for, on any matter not self-evident, there are ninety-nine persons totally incapable of judging of it, for one who is capable; and the capacity of the hundredth person is only comparative; for the majority of the eminent men of every past generation held many opinions now known to be erroneous, and did or approved numerous things which no one will now justify. Why is it, then, that there is on the whole a preponderance among mankind of rational opinions and rational conduct? If there really is this preponderance—which there must be, unless human affairs are, and have always been, in an almost desperate state—it is owing to a quality of the human mind, the source of everything respectable in man either as an intellectual or as a moral being, namely, that his errors are corrigible. He is capable of rectifying his mistakes, by discussion and experience. Not by experience alone. There must be discussion, to show how experience is to be interpreted. Wrong opinions and practices gradually yield to fact and argument: but facts and arguments, to produce any effect on the mind, must be brought before it. Very few facts are able to tell their own story, without comments to bring out their meaning. The whole strength and value, then, of human judgment, depending on the one property, that it can be set right when it is wrong, reliance can be placed on it only when the means of setting it right are kept constantly at hand. In the case of any person whose judgment is really deserving of confidence, how has it become so? Because he has kept his mind open to criticism of his opinions and conduct. Because it has been his practice to listen to all that could be said against him; to profit by as much of it as was just, and expound to himself, and upon occasion to others, the fallacy of what was fallacious. Because he has felt, that the only way in which a human being can make some approach to knowing the whole of a subject, is by hearing what can be said about it by persons of every variety of opinion, and studying all modes in which it can be looked at by every character of mind. No wise man ever acquired his wisdom in any mode but this; nor is it in the nature of human intellect to become wise in any other manner. The steady habit of correcting and completing his own opinion by collating it with those of others, so far from causing doubt and hesitation in carrying it into practice, is the only stable foundation for a just reliance on it: for, being cognizant of all that can, at least obviously, be said against him, and having taken up his position against all gainsayers—knowing that he has sought for objections and difficulties, instead of avoiding them, and has shut out no light which can be thrown upon the subject from any quarter—he has a right to think his judgment better than that of any person, or any multitude, who have not gone through a similar process.

It is not too much to require that what the wisest of mankind, those who are best entitled to trust their own judgment, find necessary to warrant their relying on it, should be submitted to by that miscellaneous collection of a few wise and many foolish individuals, called the public. The most intolerant of churches, the Roman Catholic Church, even at the canonization of a saint, admits, and listens patiently to, a "devil's advocate." The holiest of men, it appears, cannot be admitted to posthumous honors, until all that the devil could say against him is known and weighed. If even the Newtonian philosophy were not permitted to be questioned, mankind could not feel as complete assurance of its truth as they now do. The beliefs which we have most warrant for, have no safeguard to rest on, but a standing invitation to the whole world to prove them unfounded. . . .

We have now recognized the necessity to the mental well-being of mankind (on which all their other well-being depends) of freedom of opinion, and freedom of the expression of opinion, on four distinct grounds; which we will now briefly recapitulate.

First, if any opinion is compelled to silence, that opinion may, for aught we can certainly know, be true. To deny this is to assume our own infallibility.

Secondly, though the silenced opinion be an error, it may, and very commonly does, contain a portion of truth; and since the general or prevailing opinion on any subject is rarely or never the whole truth, it is only by the collision of adverse opinions that the remainder of the truth has any chance of being supplied.

Thirdly, even if the received opinion be not only true, but the whole truth; unless it is suffered to be, and actually is, vigorously and earnestly contested, it will, by most of those who receive it, be held in the manner of a prejudice, with little comprehension of feeling of its rational grounds. And not only this, but fourthly, the meaning of the doctrine itself will be in danger of being lost, or enfeebled, and deprived of its vital effect on the character and conduct: the dogma becoming a mere formal profession, inefficacious for good, but cumbering the ground, and preventing the growth of any real and heartfelt conviction from reason or personal experience.

Before quitting the subject of freedom of opinion, it is fit to take some notice of those who say, that the free expression of all opinions should be permitted, on condition that the manner be temperate, and do not pass the bounds of fair discussion. Much might be said on the impossibility of fixing where these supposed bounds are to be placed; for if the test be offence to those whose opinion is attacked, I think experience testifies that this offence is given whenever the attack is telling and powerful, and that every opponent who pushes them hard, and whom they find it difficult to answer, appears to them, if he shows any strong feeling on the subject, an intemperate opponent. But this, though an important consideration in a practical point of view, merges in a more fundamental objection. Undoubtedly the manner of asserting an opinion, even though it be a true one, may be very objectionable, and may justly incur severe censure. But the principal offences of the kind are such as it is mostly impossible, unless by accidental self-betrayal, to bring home to conviction. The gravest of them is, to argue sophistically, to suppress facts or arguments, to misstate the elements of the case, or misrepresent the opposite opinion. But all this, even to the most aggravated degree, is so continually done in perfect good faith, by persons who are not considered, and in many other respects may not deserve to be considered, ignorant or incompetent, that it is rarely possible on adequate grounds conscientiously to stamp the misrepresentation as morally culpable; and still less could law presume to interfere with this kind of controversial misconduct. With regard to what is commonly meant by intemperate discussion, namely, invective, sarcasm, personality, and the like, the denunciation of these weapons would deserve more sympathy if it were ever proposed to interdict them equally to both sides; but it is only desired to restrain the employment of them against the prevailing opinion: against the unprevailing they may not only be used without general disapproval, but will be likely to obtain for him who uses them the praise of honest zeal and righteous indignation. Yet whatever mischief arises from their use, is greatest when they are employed against the comparatively defenceless; and whatever unfair advantage can be derived by any opinion from this mode of asserting it, accrues almost exclusively to received opinions. The worst offence of this kind which can be committed by a polemic, is to stigmatize those who hold the contrary opinion as bad and immoral men. To calumny of this sort, those who hold any unpopular opinion are peculiarly exposed, because they are in general few and uninfluential, and nobody but themselves feels much interest in seeing justice done them; but this weapon is, from the nature of the case, denied to those who attack a prevailing opinion: they can neither use it with safety to themselves, nor, if they could, would it do anything but recoil on their own cause. In general, opinions contrary to those commonly received can only obtain a hearing by studied moderation of language, and the most cautious avoidance of unnecessary offence, from which they hardly ever deviate even in a slight degree without losing ground: while unmeasured vituperation employed on the side of the prevailing opinion, really does deter people from professing contrary opinions, and from listening to those who profess them. For the interest, therefore, of truth and justice, it is far more important to restrain this employment of vituperative language than the other; and, for example, if it were necessary to choose, there would be much more need to discourage offensive attacks on infidelity, than on religion. It is, however, obvious that law and authority have no business with restraining either, while opinion ought, in every instance, to determine its verdict by the circumstances of the individual case; condemning every one, on whichever side of the argument he places himself, in whose mode of advocacy either want of candor, or malignity, bigotry, or intolerance of feeling manifest themselves; but not inferring these vices from the side which a person takes, though it be the contrary side of the question to our own: and giving merited honor to every one, whatever opinion he may hold, who has calmness to see and honesty to state what his opponents and their opinions really are, exaggerating nothing to their discredit, keeping nothing back which tells, or can be supposed to tell, in their favor. This is the real morality of public discussion;

and if often violated, I am happy to think that there are many controversialists who to a great extent observe it, and a still greater number who conscientiously strive towards it.

☐ Mill does not justify absolute liberty of speech and press but implies that there are boundaries—although difficult to determine—to public debate. Democratic governments have always been faced with this dilemma: At what point can freedom of speech and press be curtailed? The Supreme Court has had difficulty in making decisions in areas involving censorship and loyalty and security. Freedom of speech and press cannot be used to destroy the very government that protects civil liberties.

Justice Holmes, in *Schenck v. United States,* 249 U.S. 47 (1919), stated his famous "clear and present danger" test, which subsequently was applied at both the national and state levels, for deciding whether or not Congress could abridge freedom of speech under the First Amendment:

"The most stringent protection of free speech would not protect a man in falsely shouting fire in a theatre and causing a panic. It does not protect a man from an injunction against uttering words that may have all the effects of force. . . . The question in every case is whether the words used are used in such circumstances and are of such a nature as to create a clear and present danger that they will bring about the substantive evils that Congress has a right to prevent. It is a question of proximity and degree. When a nation is at war many things that might be said in time of peace are such a hindrance to its efforts that their utterance will not be endured so long as men fight and that no Court could regard them as protected by any constitutional right."

In 1940 Congress passed the Smith Act, Section 2 of which made it unlawful for any person:

"(1) to knowingly or willfully advocate, abet, advise, or teach the duty, necessity, desirability, or propriety of overthrowing or destroying any government in the United States by force or violence . . . ; (2) with intent to cause the overthrow or destruction of any government in the United States, to print, publish, edit, issue, circulate, sell, distribute, or publicly display any written or printed matter advocating, advising, or teaching the duty, necessity, desirability, or propriety of overthrowing or destroying any government in the United States by force or violence; (3) to organize or help to organize any society, group, or assembly of persons who teach, advocate, or encourage the overthrow or destruction of any government in the United States by force or violence; or to be or become a member of, or affiliate with, any such society . . . , knowing the purposes thereof."

The constitutionality of this act was tested in *Dennis* v. *United States,* 341 U.S. 494 (1951), which contained five opinions. Vinson spoke for the Court, with Frankfurter and Jackson concurring; Black and Douglas dissented.

13

DENNIS v. UNITED STATES
341 U.S. 494 (1951)

Mr. Chief Justice Vinson announced the judgment of the Court, saying in part:

Petitioners were indicted in July, 1948, for violation of the conspiracy provisions of the Smith Act. . . . A verdict of guilty as to all the petitioners was returned by the jury on October 14, 1949. The Court of Appeals affirmed the convictions. . . . We granted certiorari. . . .

. . . Our limited grant of the writ of certiorari has removed from our consideration any question as to the sufficiency of the evidence to support the jury's determination that petitioners are guilty of the offense charged. Whether on this record petitioners did in fact advocate the overthrow of the government by force and violence is not before us, and we must base any discussion of this point upon the conclusions stated in the opinion of the Court of Appeals, which treated the issue in great detail. That court held that the record in this case amply supports the necessary finding of the jury that petitioners, the leaders of the Communist Party in this country, were unwilling to work within our framework of democracy, but intended to initiate a violent revolution whenever the propitious occasion appeared. . . .

I

It will be helpful in clarifying the issues to treat next the contention that the trial judge improperly interpreted the statute by charging that the statute required an unlawful intent before the jury could convict. More specifically, he charged that the jury could not find the petitioners guilty under the indictment unless they found that petitioners had the intent to "overthrow . . . the Government of the United States by force and violence as speedily as circumstances would permit."

. . . The structure and purpose of the statute demand the inclusion of intent as an element of the crime. Congress was concerned with those who advocate and organize for the overthrow of the government. Certainly those who recruit and combine for the purpose of advocating overthrow intend to bring about that overthrow. We hold that the statute requires as an essential element of the crime proof of the intent of those who are charged with its violation to overthrow the government by force and violence. . . .

II

The obvious purpose of the statute is to protect existing government, not from change by peaceable, lawful and constitutional means, but from change by violence, revolution, and terrorism. That it is within the *power* of the Congress to protect the government of the United States from armed rebellion is a proposition which requires little discussion. Whatever theoretical merit there may be to the argument that there is a "right" to rebellion against dictatorial governments is without force where the existing structure of the government provides for peaceful and orderly change. We reject any principle of governmental helplessness in the face of preparation for revolution, which principle, carried to its logical conclusion, must lead to anarchy. No one could conceive that it is not within the power of Congress to prohibit acts intended to overthrow the government by force and violence. The question with which we are concerned here is not whether Congress has such *power,* but whether the *means* that it has employed conflict with the First and Fifth Amendments to the Constitution.

One of the bases for the contention that the means which Congress has employed are invalid takes the form of an attack on the face of the statute on the grounds that by its terms it prohibits academic discussion of the merits of Marxism-Leninism, that it stifles ideas and is contrary to all concepts of a free speech and a free press. Although we do not agree that the language itself has that significance, we must bear in mind that it is the duty of the federal courts to interpret federal legislation in a manner not inconsistent with the demands of the Constitution. . . . This is a federal statute which we must interpret as well as judge. . . .

The very language of the Smith Act negates the interpretation which petitioners would have us impose on that Act. It is directed at advocacy, not discussion. Thus, the trial judge properly charged the jury that they could not convict if they found that petitioners did "no more than pursue peaceful studies and discussions or teaching and advocacy in the realm of ideas." He further charged that it was not unlawful "to conduct in an American college or university a course explaining the philosophical theories set forth in the books which have been placed in evidence." Such a charge is in strict accord with the statutory language, and illustrates the meaning to be placed on those words. Congress did not intend to eradicate the free discussion of political theories, to destroy the traditional rights of Americans to discuss and evaluate ideas without fear of governmental sanction. Rather Congress was concerned with the very kind of activity in which the evidence showed these petitioners engaged.

III

But although the statute is not directed at the hypothetical cases which petitioners have conjured, its application in this case has resulted in convictions for the teaching and advocacy of the overthrow of the government by force and violence, which, even though coupled with the intent to accomplish that overthrow, contains an element of speech. For this reason, we must pay special heed to the demands of the First Amendment marking out the boundaries of speech.

We pointed out in *Douds, supra,* that the basis of the First Amendment is the hypothesis that speech can rebut speech, propaganda will answer propaganda, free debate of ideas will result in the wisest governmental policies. It is for this reason that this Court has recognized the inherent value of free discourse. An analysis of the leading cases in this Court which have involved direct limitations on speech, however, will demonstrate that both the majority of the Court and the dissenters in particular cases have recognized that this is not an unlimited, unqualified right, but that the societal value of speech must, on occasion, be subordinated to other values and considerations. . . .

The rule we deduce from these cases [*Schenck* and others] is that where an offense is specified by a statute in nonspeech or nonpress terms, a conviction relying upon speech or press as evidence of violation may be sustained only when the speech or publication created a "clear and present danger" of attempting or accomplishing the prohibited crime, e.g. interference with enlistment. The dissents . . . in emphasizing the value of speech, were addressed to the argument of the sufficiency of the evidence. . . .

In this case we are squarely presented with the application of the "clear and present danger" test, and must decide what that phrase imports. We first note that many of the cases in which this Court has reversed convictions by use of this or similar tests have been based on the fact that the interest which the state was attempting to protect was itself too insubstantial to warrant restriction of speech. . . . Overthrow of the government by force and violence is certainly a substantial enough interest for the government to limit speech. Indeed, this is the ultimate value of any society, for if a society cannot protect its structure from armed internal attack, it must follow that no subordinate value can be protected. If, then, this interest may be protected, the literal problem which is presented is what has been meant by the use of the phrase "clear and present danger" of the utterances bringing about the evil within the power of Congress to punish.

Obviously, the words cannot mean that before the government may act, it must wait until the *putsch* is about to be executed, the plans have been laid and the signal is awaited. If government is aware that a group aiming at its overthrow is attempting to indoctrinate its members and to commit them to a course whereby they will strike when the leaders feel the circumstances permit, action by the government is required. The argument that there is no need for government to concern itself, for government is strong, it possesses ample powers to put down a rebellion, it may defeat the revolution with ease needs no answer. For that is not the question. Certainly an attempt to overthrow the government by force, even though doomed from the outset because of inadequate numbers or power of the revolutionists, is a sufficient evil for Congress to prevent. The damage which such attempts create both physically and politically to a nation makes it impossible to measure the validity in terms of the probability of success, or the immediacy of a successful attempt. In the instant case the trial judge charged the jury that they could not convict unless they found that petitioners intended to overthrow the government "as speedily as circumstances would permit." This does not mean, and could not properly mean, that they would not strike until there was certainty of success. What was meant was that the revolutionists would strike when they thought the time was ripe. We must therefore reject the contention that success or probability of success is the criterion.

The situation with which Justices Holmes and Brandeis were concerned in *Gitlow* was a comparatively isolated event [involving a conviction for criminal anarchy in New York of one Gitlow for circulating Communist literature], bearing little relation in their minds to any substantial threat to the safety of the community. . . . They were not confronted with any situation comparable to the instant one—the development of an apparatus designed and dedicated to the overthrow of the government, in the context of world crisis after crisis.

Chief Justice Learned Hand, writing for the majority below, interpreted the phrase as follows: "In each case [courts] must ask whether the gravity of the 'evil,' discounted by its improbability, justifies such invasion of free speech as is necessary to avoid the danger." 183 F.2d at 212. We adopt this statement of the rule. . . .

Likewise, we are in accord with the court below, which affirmed the trial court's finding that the requisite danger existed. The mere fact that from the period 1945 to 1948 petitioners' activities did not result in an attempt to overthrow the government by force and violence is of course no answer to the fact that there was a group that was ready to make the attempt. The formation by petitioners of such a highly organized conspiracy, with rigidly disciplined members subject to call when the leaders, these petitioners, felt that the time had come for action, coupled with the inflammable nature of world conditions, similar uprisings in other countries, and the touch-and-go nature of our relations with countries with whom petitioners were in the very least ideologically attuned, convince us that their convictions were justified on this score. And this analysis disposes of the contention that a conspiracy to advocate, as distinguished from the advocacy itself, cannot be constitutionally restrained, because it comprises only the preparation. It is the existence of the conspiracy which creates the danger. . . . If the ingredients of the reaction are present, we cannot bind the government to wait until the catalyst is added. . . .

We hold that § § 2(a) (1), 2(a) (2) and (3) of the Smith Act, do not inherently, or as construed or applied in the instant case, violate the First Amendment and other provisions of the Bill of Rights, or the First and Fifth Amendments because of indefiniteness. Petitioners intended to overthrow the government of the United States as speedily as the circumstances would permit. Their conspiracy to organize the Communist Party and to teach and advocate the overthrow of the government of the United States by force and violence created a "clear and present danger" of an attempt to overthrow the government by force and violence. They were properly and constitutionally convicted for violation of the Smith Act. The judgments of conviction are affirmed. . . .

Mr. Justice Black, dissenting, said in part:

. . . At the outset I want to emphasize what the crime involved in this case is, and what it is not. These petitioners were not charged with an attempt to overthrow the government. They were not charged with overt acts of any kind designed to overthrow the government. They were not even charged with saying anything or writing anything designed to over-throw the government. The charge was that they agreed to assemble and to talk and publish certain ideas at a later date: The indictment is that they conspired to organize the Communist Party and to use speech or newspapers and other publications in the future to teach and advocate the forcible overthrow of the government. No matter how it is worded, this is a virulent form of prior censorship of speech and press, which I believe the First Amendment forbids. . . .

But let us assume, contrary to all constitutional ideas of fair criminal procedure, that petitioners although not indicted for the crime of actual advocacy, may be punished for it. Even on this radical assumption, the other opinions in this case show that the only way to affirm these convictions is to repudiate directly or indirectly the established "clear and present danger" rule. This the Court does in a way which greatly restricts the protections afforded by the First Amendment. The opinions for affirmance indicate that the chief reason for jettisoning the rule is the expressed fear that advocacy of Communist doctrine endangers the safety of the Republic. Undoubtedly, a governmental policy of unfettered communication of ideas does entail dangers. To the Founders of this nation, however, the benefits derived from free expression were worth the risk. They embodied this philosophy in the First Amendment's command that "Congress shall make no law ... abridging the freedom of speech, or of the press. ... " I have always believed that the First Amendment is the keystone of our government, that the freedoms it guarantees provide the best insurance against destruction of all freedom. At least as to speech in the realm of public matters, I believe that the "clear and present danger" test does not "mark the furthermost constitutional boundaries of protected expression" but does "no more than recognize a minimum compulsion of the Bill of Rights." ...

So long as this Court exercises the power of judicial review of legislation, I cannot agree that the First Amendment permits us to sustain laws suppressing freedom of speech and press on the basis of Congress's or our own notions of mere "reasonableness." Such a doctrine waters down the First Amendment so that it amounts to little more than an admonition to Congress. The Amendment as so construed is not likely to protect any but those "safe" or orthodox views which rarely need its protection. I must also express my objection to the holding because, as Mr. Justice Douglas's dissent shows, it sanctions the determination of a crucial issue of fact by the judge rather than by the jury. Nor can I let this opportunity pass without expressing my objection to the severely limited grant of certiorari in this case which precluded consideration here of at least two other reasons for reversing these convictions: (1) the record shows a discriminatory selection of the jury panel which prevented trial before a representative cross-section of the community; (2) the record shows that one member of the trial jury was violently hostile to petitioners before and during the trial.

Public opinion being what it now is, few will protest the conviction of these Communist petitioners. There is hope, however, that in calmer times, when present pressure, passions and fears subside, this or some later Court will restore the First Amendment liberties to the high preferred place where they belong in a free society.

Mr. Justice Douglas, dissenting, said in part:

... [N]ever until today has anyone seriously thought that the ancient law of conspiracy could constitutionally be used to turn speech into seditious conduct. Yet that is precisely what is suggested. I repeat that we deal here with speech alone, not with speech *plus* acts of sabotage or unlawful conduct. Not a single seditious act is charged in the indictment. ...

Free speech has occupied an exalted position because of the high service it has given our society. Its protection is essential to the very existence of a democracy. The airing of ideas releases pressures which otherwise might become destructive. When ideas compete in the market for acceptance, full and free discussion exposes the false and they gain few adherents. Full and free discussion even of ideas we hate encourages the testing of our own prejudices and preconceptions. Full and free discussion keeps a society from becoming stagnant and unprepared for the stresses and strains that work to tear all civilizations apart.

Full and free discussion has indeed been the first article of our faith. We have founded our political system on it. It has been the safeguard of every religious, political, philosophical, economic, and racial group amongst us. We have counted on it to keep us from embracing what is cheap and false; we have trusted the common sense of our people to choose the doctrine true to our genius and to reject the rest. This has been the one single outstanding tenet that has made our institutions the symbol of freedom and equality. We have deemed it more costly to liberty to suppress a despised minority than to let them vent their spleen. We have above all else feared the political censor. We have wanted a land where our people can be exposed to all the diverse creeds and cultures of the world.

There comes a time when even speech loses its constitutional immunity. Speech innocuous one year may at another time fan such destructive flames that it must be halted in the interest of the safety of the Republic. That is the meaning of the clear and present danger test. When conditions are so critical that there will be no time to avoid the evil that the speech threatens, it is time to call a halt. Otherwise, free speech which is the strength of the nation will be the cause of its destruction.

Yet free speech is the rule, not the exception. The restraint to be constitutional must be based on more than fear, on more than passionate opposition against the speech, on more than a revolted dislike for its contents. There must be some immediate injury to society that is likely if speech is allowed. . . .

. . . This record . . . contains no evidence whatsoever showing that the acts charged, viz., the teaching of the Soviet theory of revolution with the hope that it will be realized, have created any clear and present danger to the nation. The Court, however, rules to the contrary. . . .

The political impotence of the Communists in this country does not, of course, dispose of the problem. Their numbers; their positions in industry and government; the extent to which they have in fact infiltrated the police, the armed services, transportation, stevedoring, power plants, munition works, and other critical places—these facts all bear on the likelihood that their advocacy of the Soviet theory of revolution will endanger the Republic. But the record is silent on these facts. If we are to proceed on the basis of judicial notice, it is impossible for me to say that the Communists in this country are so potent or so strategically deployed that they must be suppressed for their speech. I could not so hold unless I were willing to conclude that the activities in recent years of committees of Congress, of the Attorney General, of labor unions, of state legislatures, and of Loyalty Boards were so futile as to leave the country on the edge of grave peril. To believe that petitioners and their following are placed in such critical positions as to endanger the nation is to believe the incredible. It is safe to say that the followers of the creed of Soviet Communism are known to the

FBI; that in case of war with Russia they will be picked up overnight as were all prospective saboteurs at the commencement of World War II; that the invisible army of petitioners is the best known, the most beset, and the least thriving of any fifth column in history. Only those held by fear and panic could think otherwise. . . .

. . . The political censor has no place in our public debates. Unless and until extreme and necessitous circumstances are shown, our aim should be to keep speech unfettered and to allow the processes of law to be invoked only when the provocateurs among us move from speech to action.

Vishinsky wrote in 1938 in the Law of the Soviet state, "In our state, naturally, there is and can be no place for freedom of speech, press, and so on for the foes of socialism."

Our concern should be that we accept no such standard for the United States. Our faith should be that our people will never give support to those advocates of revolution, so long as we remain loyal to the purposes for which our nation was founded.

☐   The Supreme Court applied the clear and present danger test in the *Dennis* case to uphold the constitutionality of the Smith Act of 1940. Significantly, the Court's limited writ of certiorari prevented it from reviewing whether or not the facts of the case warranted a conclusion that a clear and present danger actually existed because of the actions of the Communist party officials involved. The Court accepted the findings of the trial court that such a danger did exist, and concluded that the law under which the defendants were convicted was a reasonable exercise of congressional power to prevent the overthrow of the government by force and violence. Federal prosecutors concluded that the *Dennis* decision gave them carte blanche to seek indictments and convictions of Communist party officials on the ground that their membership in the party per se supported the conclusion that they were forcibly attempting to overthrow the government. Supporting the prosecutors' view was the statement by the *Dennis* majority that "It is the existence of the conspiracy which creates the danger . . . if the ingredients of the reaction are present, we cannot bind the government to wait until the catalyst is added."

The Court modified its *Dennis* doctrine, however, in *Yates* v. *United States,* 354 U.S. 298 (1957), in which federal prosecutors had obtained convictions against lower level Communist party officials for conspiring to overthrow the government by force and violence in violation of the Smith Act. The trial court's charge to the jury failed to mention that in order to convict the defendants jurors would have to find that their advocacy of forceful governmental overthrow was intended and likely to bring action to that end. The Supreme Court's opinion stated: "We are . . . faced with the question whether the Smith Act prohibits advocacy and teaching of forcible overthrow as an abstract principle, divorced from any effort to instigate action to that end, so long as such advocacy or teaching is engaged in with evil intent. We hold that it does not."

In the following case the Court reaffirmed its interpretation of the clear and present danger doctrine to require more than mere advocacy of violent political change to sustain governmental suppression of freedoms of expression. The state of Ohio had used its outdated Criminal Syndicalism Statute, enacted in 1919, to prosecute and convict a Ku Klux Klan leader in the 1960s for advocating violent and forcible governmental change. The Court held the statute to be unconstitutional because of its punishment of mere advocacy without requiring the demonstration of a clear and present danger that lawless action would result.

14

BRANDENBURG v. OHIO
395 U.S. 444 (1969)

PER CURIAM:

The appellant, a leader of a Ku Klux Klan group, was convicted under the Ohio Criminal Syndicalism statute for "advocat[ing] . . . the duty, necessity, or propriety of crime, sabotage, violence, or unlawful methods of terrorism as a means of accomplishing industrial or political reform" and for "voluntarily assembl[ing] with any society, group, or assemblage of persons formed to teach or advocate the doctrines of criminal syndicalism." Ohio Rev. Code Ann. § 2923.13. He was fined $1,000 and sentenced to one to 10 years' imprisonment. The appellant challenged the constitutionality of the criminal syndicalism statute under the First and Fourth Amendments to the United States Constitution, but the intermediate appellate court of Ohio affirmed his conviction without opinion. The Supreme Court of Ohio dismissed his appeal . . . "for the reason that no substantial constitutional question exists herein." . . .

The record shows that a man, identified at trial as the appellant, telephoned an announcer-reporter on the staff of a Cincinnati television station and invited him to come to a Ku Klux Klan "rally" to be held at a farm in Hamilton County. With the cooperation of the organizers, the reporter and a cameraman attended the meeting and filmed the events.

Portions of the films were later broadcast on the local station and on a national network.

The prosecution's case rested on the films and on testimony identifying the appellant as the person who communicated with the reporter and who spoke at the rally. The State also introduced into evidence several articles appearing in the film, including a pistol, a rifle, a shotgun, ammunition, a Bible, and a red hood worn by the speaker in the films.

One film showed 12 hooded figures, some of whom carried firearms. They were gathered around a large wooden cross, which they burned. No one was present other than the participants and the newsmen who made the film. Most of the words uttered during the scene were incomprehensible when the film was projected, but scattered phrases could be understood that were derogatory of Negroes and, in one instance, of Jews. Another scene on the same film showed the appellant, in Klan regalia, making a speech. The speech, in full, was as follows:

> This is an organizers' meeting. We have had quite a few members here today which are—we have hundreds, hundreds of members throughout the State of Ohio. I can quote from a newspaper clipping from the Columbus, Ohio Dispatch, five weeks ago Sunday morning. The Klan has more members in the State of Ohio than does any other organization. We're not a revengent organization, but if our President, our Congress, our Supreme Court, continues to suppress the white, Caucasian race, it's possible that there might have to be some revengeance taken.
>
> We are marching on Congress July the Fourth, four hundred thousand strong. From there we are dividing into two groups, one group to march on St. Augustine, Florida, the other group to march into Mississippi. Thank you.

The second film showed six hooded figures one of whom, later identified as the appellant, repeated a speech very similar to that recorded on the first film. The reference to the possibility of "revengeance" was omitted, and one sentence was added: "Personally, I believe the nigger should be returned to Africa, the Jew returned to Israel." Though some of the figures in the films carried weapons, the speaker did not.

The Ohio Criminal Syndicalism Statute was enacted in 1919. From 1917 to 1920, identical or quite similar laws were adopted by 20 States and two territories. E. Dowell, A History of Criminal Syndicalism Legislation in the United States 21 (1939). In 1927, this Court sustained the constitutionality of California's Criminal Syndicalism Act, . . . the text of which is quite similar to that of the laws of Ohio. *Whitney* v. *California* [1927] . . . The Court upheld the statute on the ground that, without more, "advocating" violent means to effect political and economic change involves such danger to the security of the State that the State may outlaw it. . . . But *Whitney* has been thoroughly discredited by later decisions. See *Dennis* v. *United*

States. . . . These later decisions have fashioned the principle that the constitutional guarantees of free speech and free press do not permit a State to forbid or proscribe advocacy of the use of force or of law violation except where such advocacy is directed to inciting or producing imminent lawless action and is likely to incite or produce such action. As we said in *Noto* v. *United States* [1961] . . . "the mere abstract teaching . . . of the moral propriety or even moral necessity for a resort to force and violence, is not the same as preparing a group for violent action and steeling it to such action." . . . *Lowry.* A statute which fails to draw this distinction impermissibly intrudes upon the freedoms guaranteed by the First and Fourteenth Amendments. It sweeps within its condemnation speech which our Constitution has immunized from governmental control. . . .

Measured by this test, Ohio's Criminal Syndicalism Act cannot be sustained. The Act punishes persons who "advocate or teach the duty, necessity, or propriety" of violence "as a means of accomplishing industrial or political reform"; or who publish or circulate or display any book or paper containing such advocacy; or who "justify" the commission of violent acts "with intent to exemplify, spread or advocate the propriety of the doctrines of criminal syndicalism"; or who "voluntarily assemble" with a group formed "to teach or advocate the doctrines of criminal syndicalism." Neither the indictment nor the trial judge's instructions to the jury in any way refined the statute's bald definition of the crime in terms of mere advocacy not distinguished from incitement to imminent lawless action.

Accordingly, we are here confronted with a statute which, by its own words and as applied, purports to punish mere advocacy and to forbid, on pain of criminal punishment, assembly with others merely to advocate the described type of action. Such a statute falls within the condemnation of the First and Fourteenth Amendments. The contrary teaching of *Whitney* v. *California* . . . cannot be supported, and that decision is therefore overruled.

Reversed.

Mr. Justice Black, concurring:

I agree with the views expressed by Mr. Justice Douglas in his concurring opinion in this case that the "clear and present danger" doctrine should have no place in the interpretation of the First Amendment. I join the Court's opinion, which, as I understand it, simply cites *Dennis* v. *United States,* . . . but does not indicate any agreement on the Court's part with the "clear and present danger" doctrine on which *Dennis* purported to rely.

Mr. Justice Douglas, concurring:

While I join the opinion of the Court, I desire to enter a *caveat.*

[T]he World War I cases . . . of [*Schenck, Frohwerk, Debs,* and *Abrams*] put the gloss of "clear and present danger" on the First Amendment. Whether the war power—the greatest leveler of them all—is adequate to sustain that doctrine is debatable. The dissents in *Abrams, Schaefer,* and *Pierce* show how easily "clear and present danger" is manipulated to crush what Brandeis [in *Pierce*] called "[t]he fundamental right of free men to strive for better conditions through new legislation and new institutions" by argument and discourse . . . even in time of war. Though I doubt if the "clear and present danger" test is congenial to the First Amendment in time of a declared war, I am certain it is not reconcilable with the First Amendment in days of peace.

The Court quite properly overrules *Whitney* v. *California,* . . . which involved advocacy of ideas which the majority of the Court deemed unsound and dangerous.

Mr. Justice Holmes, though never formally abandoning the "clear and present danger" test, moved closer to the First Amendment ideal when he said in dissent in *Gitlow* v. *New York,* . . . "Every idea is an incitement. . . ." We have never been faithful to the philosophy of that dissent.

The Court in *Herndon* v. *Lowry* [1937] . . . overturned a conviction for exercising First Amendment rights to incite insurrection because of lack of evidence of incitement. . . . In *Bridges* v. *California* [1941] . . . we approved the "clear and present danger" test in an elaborate dictum that tightened it and confined it to a narrow category. But in *Dennis* v. *United States* [1951] . . . we opened wide the door, distorting the "clear and present danger" test beyond recognition.

. . . I see no place in the regime of the First Amendment for any "clear and present danger" test, whether strict and tight as some would make it, or free-wheeling as the Court in *Dennis* rephrased it.

When one reads the opinions closely and sees when and how the "clear and present danger" test has been applied, great misgivings are aroused. First, the threats were often loud but always puny and made serious only by judges so wedded to the *status quo* that critical analysis made them nervous. Second, the test was so twisted and perverted in *Dennis* as to make the trial of those teachers of Marxism an all-out political trial which was part and parcel of the cold war that has eroded substantial parts of the First Amendment.

Action is often a method of expression and within the protection of the First Amendment.

Suppose one tears up his own copy of the Constitution in eloquent protest to a decision of this Court. May he be indicted?

Suppose one rips his own Bible to shreds to celebrate his departure from one "faith" and his embrace of atheism. May he be indicted?

Last Term the Court held in *United States* v. *O'Brien* [1968] . . . that a registrant under Selective Service who burned his draft card in protest of the war in Vietnam could be prosecuted. The First Amendment was tendered as a defense and rejected. . . .

But O'Brien was not prosecuted for not having his draft card available when asked for by a federal agent. He was indicted, tried, and convicted for burning the card. And this Court's affirmance of that conviction was not, with all respect, consistent with the First Amendment. . . .

The line between what is permissible and not subject to control and what may be made impermissible and subject to regulation is the line between ideas and overt acts.

The example usually given by those who would punish speech is the case of one who falsely shouts fire in a crowded theatre.

This is, however, a classic case where speech is brigaded with action. . . . They are indeed inseparable and a prosecution can be launched for the overt acts actually caused. Apart from rare instances of that kind, speech is, I think, immune from prosecution. Certainly there is no constitutional line between advocacy of abstract ideas as in *Yates* and advocacy of political action as in *Scales.* The quality of advocacy turns on the depth of the conviction; and government has no power to invade that sanctuary of belief and conscience.

Equal Protection of the Laws: School Desegregation

☐   By now most students are thoroughly familiar with the evolution of the "separate but equal" doctrine first enunciated by the Supreme Court in *Plessy* v. *Ferguson,* 163 U.S. 537 (1896). Students should note that what is involved in cases in this area is legal interpretation of the provision in the Fourteenth Amendment that no state may deny "to any person within its jurisdiction the equal protection of the laws." The *Plessy* case stated that separate but equal accommodations, required by state law to be established on railroads in Louisiana, did not violate the equal protection of the laws clause of the Fourteenth Amendment. The Court went on to say that the object of the Fourteenth Amendment:

> . . . was undoubtedly to enforce the absolute equality of the two races before the law, but in the nature of things it could not have been intended to abolish distinction based upon color, or to enforce social, as distinguished from political, equality, or a commingling of the two races upon terms unsatisfactory to either. Laws permitting, and even requiring, their separation in places where they are liable to be brought into contact do not necessarily imply the inferiority of either race to the other, and have been generally, if not universally, recognized as within the competency of the state legislatures in the exercise of their police power. The most common instance of this is connected with the establishment of separate schools for white and colored children, which has been held to be a valid exercise of the legislative power even by courts of States where the political rights of the colored race have been longest and most earnestly enforced.

Both the police power and education are within the reserved powers of the states; they are reserved, however, only insofar as they do not conflict with provisions of the Constitution. The Supreme Court, in *Brown v. Board of Education,* 347 U.S. 483 (1954), finally crystallized its interpretation of the equal protection of the laws clause in a way that resulted in a significant decrease in state power in an area traditionally reserved to states, viz., education. In addition, a general principle was established which extended far beyond the field of education.

15

BROWN v. BOARD OF EDUCATION OF TOPEKA
347 U.S. 483 (1954)

Mr. Chief Justice Warren delivered the opinion of the Court, saying in part:

These cases come to us from the states of Kansas, South Carolina, Virginia, and Delaware. They are premised on different facts and different local conditions, but a common legal question justifies their consideration together in this consolidated opinion.

In each of the cases, minors of the Negro race, through their legal representatives, seek the aid of the courts in obtaining admission to the public schools of their community on a nonsegregated basis. In each instance, they had been denied admission to schools attended by white children under laws requiring or permitting segregation according to race. This segregation was alleged to deprive the plaintiffs of the equal protection of the laws under the Fourteenth Amendment. In each of the cases other than the Delaware case, a three-judge federal district court denied relief to the plaintiffs on the so-called "separate but equal" doctrine announced by this Court in *Plessy v. Ferguson.* . . .

The plaintiffs contend that segregated public schools are not "equal" and cannot be made "equal," and that hence they are deprived of the equal protection of the laws. Because of the obvious importance of the question presented, the Court took jurisdiction. . . .

In the first cases in this Court construing the Fourteenth Amendment, decided shortly after its adoption, the Court interpreted it as proscribing all state-imposed discriminations against the Negro race. The doctrine of "separate but equal" did not make its appearance in this Court until 1896 in the case of *Plessy v. Ferguson, supra,* involving not education but transportation. American courts have since labored with the doctrine for over half a century. In this Court, there have been six cases involving the "separate but equal" doctrine in the field of public education. . . . In more recent cases, all on the graduate school level, inequality was found in that specific benefits enjoyed by white students were denied to Negro students of the same educational qualifications. . . . In none of these cases was it necessary to reexamine the doctrine to grant relief to the Negro plaintiff. And in *Sweatt* v. *Painter* [339 U.S. 629 (1950)], the Court expressly reserved decision on the question whether *Plessy* v. *Ferguson* should be held inapplicable to public education.

In the instant cases, that question is directly presented. Here, unlike *Sweatt* v. *Painter,* there are findings below that the Negro and white schools involved have been equalized, or are being equalized, with respect to buildings, curricula, qualifications and salaries of teachers, and other "tangible" factors. Our decision, therefore, cannot turn on merely a comparison of these tangible factors in the Negro and white schools involved in each of the cases. We must look instead to the effect of segregation itself on public education.

In approaching this problem, we cannot turn the clock back to 1868 when the Amendment was adopted, or even to 1896 when *Plessy* v. *Ferguson* was written. We must consider public education in the light of its full development and its present place in American life throughout the Nation. Only in this way can it be determined if segregation in public schools deprives these plaintiffs of the equal protection of the laws.

Today, education is perhaps the most important function of state and local governments. Compulsory school attendance laws and the great expenditures for education both demonstrate our recognition of the importance of education to our democratic society. It is required in the performance of our most basic public responsibilities, even service in the armed forces. It is the very foundation of good citizenship. Today it is a principal instrument in awakening the child to cultural values, in preparing him for later professional training, and in helping him to adjust normally to his environment. In these days, it is doubtful that any child may reasonably be expected to succeed in life if he is denied the opportunity of an education. Such an opportunity, where the state has undertaken to provide it, is a right which must be made available to all on equal terms.

We come then to the question presented: Does segregation of children in public schools solely on the basis of race, even though the physical facilities and other "tangible" factors may be equal, deprive the children of the minority group of equal educational opportunities? We believe that it does.

In *Sweatt* v. *Painter, supra,* in finding that a segregated law school for Negroes could not provide them equal educational opportunities, this Court relied in large part on "those qualities which are incapable of objective measurement but which make for greatness in a law school." In

McLaurin v. *Oklahoma State Regents, supra* [339 U.S. 637 (1950)], the Court, in requiring that a Negro admitted to a white graduate school be treated like all other students, again resorted to intangible considerations: "his ability to study, to engage in discussions and exchange views with other students, and, in general, to learn his profession." Such considerations apply with added force to children in grade and high schools. To separate them from others of similar age and qualifications solely because of their race generates a feeling of inferiority as to their status in the community that may affect their hearts and minds in a way unlikely ever to be undone. The effect of this separation of their educational opportunities was well stated by a finding in the Kansas case by a court which nevertheless felt compelled to rule against the Negro plaintiffs:

> Segregation of white and colored children in public schools has a detrimental effect upon the colored children. The impact is greater when it has the sanction of the law; for the policy of separating the races is usually interpreted as denoting the inferiority of the Negro group. A sense of inferiority affects the motivation of a child to learn. Segregation with the sanction of law, therefore, has a tendency to retard the educational and mental development of Negro children and to deprive them of some of the benefits they would receive in a racially integrated school system.

Whatever may have been the extent of psychological knowledge at the time of *Plessy* v. *Ferguson,* this finding is amply supported by modern authority. Any language in *Plessy* v. *Ferguson* contrary to this finding is rejected.

We conclude that in the field of public education the doctrine of "separate but equal" has no place. Separate educational facilities are inherently unequal. Therefore, we hold that the plaintiffs and others similarly situated for whom the actions have been brought are by reason of the segregation complained of, deprived of the equal protection of the laws guaranteed by the Fourteenth Amendment. This disposition makes unnecessary any discussion whether such segregation also violates the Due Process Clause of the Fourteenth Amendment.

Because these are class actions, because of the wide applicability of this decision, and because of the great variety of local conditions, the formulation of decrees in these cases presents problems of considerable complexity. On re-argument, the consideration of appropriate relief was necessarily subordinate to the primary question—the constitutionality of segregation in public education. We have now announced that such segregation is a denial of the equal protection of the laws. In order that we may have the full assistance of the parties in formulating decrees, the cases will be restored to the docket, and the parties are requested to present further argument on Questions 4 and 5 previously propounded by the Court for the re-argument this Term [which deal with the implementation of desegregation]. The Attorney General of the United States is again invited to participate. The Attorneys General of the states requiring or permitting segregation in public education will also be permitted to appear as *amici curiae* upon request to do so by September 15, 1954, and submission of briefs by October 1, 1954. It is so ordered.

☐ On the same day the decision was announced in the *Brown* case (1954), the Court held that segregation in the District of Columbia was unconstitutional on the basis of the due process clause of the Fifth Amendment. (See *Bolling* v. *Sharpe*, 347 U.S. 497 [1954].) This situation reversed the normal one in that a protection explicitly afforded citizens of states was not expressly applicable against the national government, and could be made so only through interpreting it into the concept of due process of law.

After hearing the views of all interested parties in the *Brown* case the Court, on May 31, 1955, announced its decision concerning the implementation of desegregation in public schools.

16

BROWN v. BOARD OF EDUCATION OF TOPEKA
349 U.S. 294 (1955)

Mr. Chief Justice Warren delivered the opinion of the Court, saying in part:

These cases were decided on May 17, 1954. The opinions of that date, declaring the fundamental principle that racial discrimination in public education is unconstitutional, are incorporated herein by reference. All provisions of federal, state, or local law requiring or permitting such discrimination must yield to this principle. There remains for consideration the manner in which relief is to be accorded.

Because these cases arose under different local conditions and their disposition will involve a variety of local problems, we requested further argument on the question of relief. . . . The parties, the United States, and the states of Florida, North Carolina, Arkansas, Oklahoma, Maryland, and Texas filed briefs and participated in the oral argument.

These presentations were informative and helpful to the Court in its consideration of the complexities arising from the transition to a system of public education freed of racial discrimination. The presentations also demonstrated that substantial steps to eliminate racial discrimination in public schools have already been taken, not only in some of the communities in which these cases arose, but in some of the states appearing as *amici curiae,* and in other states as well. Substantial progress has been made in the District of Columbia and in the communities in Kansas and Delaware involved in this litigation. The defendants in the cases coming to us from South Carolina and Virginia are awaiting the decision of this Court concerning relief.

Full implementation of these constitutional principles may require solution of varied local school problems. School authorities have the primary responsibility for elucidating, assessing, and solving these problems; courts will have to consider whether the action of school authorities constitutes good faith implementation of the governing constitutional principles. Because of their proximity to local conditions and the possible need for further hearings, the courts which originally heard these cases can best perform this judicial appraisal. Accordingly, we believe it appropriate to remand the cases to those courts.

In fashioning and effectuating the decrees, the courts will be guided by equitable principles. Traditionally, equity has been characterized by a practical flexibility in shaping its remedies and by a facility for adjusting and reconciling public and private needs. These cases call for the exercise of these traditional attributes of equity power. At stake is the personal interest of the plaintiffs in admission to public schools as soon as practicable on a nondiscriminatory basis. To effectuate this interest may call for elimination of a variety of obstacles in making the transition to school systems operated in accordance with the constitutional principles set forth in our May 17, 1954, decision. Courts of equity may properly take into account the public interest in the elimination of such obstacles in a systematic and effective manner. But it should go without saying that the vitality of these constitutional principles cannot be allowed to yield simply because of disagreement with them.

While giving weight to these public and private considerations, the courts will require that the defendants make a prompt and reasonable start toward full compliance with our May 17, 1954, ruling. Once such a start has been made, the courts may find that additional time is necessary to carry out the ruling in an effective manner. The burden rests upon the defendants to establish such time as is necessary in the public interest and is consistent with good faith compliance at the earliest practicable date. To that end, the courts may consider problems related to administration, arising from the physical condition of the school plant, the school transportation system, personnel, revision of school districts and attendance areas into compact units to achieve a system of determining admission to the public schools on a nonracial basis, and revision of local laws and regulations which may be necessary in solving the foregoing problems. They will also consider the adequacy of any plans the defendants may propose to meet these problems and to effectuate a transition to a racially nondiscriminatory school system. During this period of transition, the courts will retain jurisdiction of these cases.

The judgments below, except that in the Delaware case, are accordingly reversed and the cases are remanded to the District Courts to take such proceedings and enter such orders and decrees consistent with this opinion as are necessary and proper to admit to public schools on a racially nondiscriminatory basis with all deliberate speed the parties to these cases. The judgment in the Delaware case—ordering the immediate admission of the plaintiffs to schools previously attended only by white children—is affirmed on the basis of the principles stated in our May 17, 1954, opinion, but the case is remanded to the Supreme Court of Delaware for such further proceedings as that Court may deem necessary in the light of this opinion.

It is so ordered.

☐   After the second decision of the Supreme Court in *Brown* v. *Board of Education* in 1955, it soon became clear that many Southern states would proceed with deliberate speed not to implement the desegregation of public schools but to obstruct the intent of the Supreme Court. The Southern Manifesto, signed by 101 Congressmen from 11 Southern states in 1956, clearly indicated the line that would be taken by many Southern Congressmen to justify defiance of the Supreme Court. The gist of the Manifesto was simply that the Supreme Court did not have the constitutional authority to interfere in an area such as education, which falls within the reserved powers of the states.

After the two *Brown* decisions in 1954 and 1955, the implementation for desegregation in the South was very slow. Ten years later, less than 10 percent of the black pupils in the lower educational levels in the Southern states that had had legally segregated education before were enrolled in integrated schools. It was not until 1970 that substantial progress was made in the South. Between 1968 and 1970 the percentage of black students in all-black schools in eleven Southern states decreased from 68.0 percent to 18.4 percent. One device used to circumvent the Supreme Court's decisions was to establish de facto dual school systems, similar to those that exist in most Northern cities, whereby students are assigned to schools on the basis of the neighborhoods in which they live. Such systems are not de jure segregation because they are not based upon a law requiring segregation per se, but simply upon school board regulations assigning pupils on the basis of where they live. De facto school systems can be as segregated as were the de jure systems previously existing in the South, but the question is to what extent can courts interfere to break up de facto segregation patterns since they are not based upon legal stipulations?

In *Swann v. Charlotte-Mecklenburg County Board of Education,* 402 U.S. 1 (1971), the Supreme Court held that in Southern states with a history of legally segregated education the District Courts have broad power to assure "unitary" school systems by requiring: (1) reassignment of teachers, so that each school faculty will reflect a racial balance similar to that which exists in the community as a whole; (2) reassignment of pupils to reflect a racial ratio similar to that which exists within the total community; (3) the use of noncontiguous school zones and the grouping of schools for the purpose of attendance to bring about racial balance; and (4) the use of busing of elementary and secondary school students within the school system to achieve racial balance.

This case and companion cases were referred to at the time as school "busing" cases, and caused tremendous controversy within the South because communities felt they were not being treated on an equal basis with their Northern counterparts, where de facto segregation is for the most part not subject to judicial intervention. The Nixon Administration, which favored neighborhood schools, was firmly opposed to the transportation of students beyond normal geographic school zones to achieve racial balance. Democratic Senator Ribicoff of Connecticut attempted to attach an amendment to an administration-sponsored bill providing $1.5 billion to aid school districts in the South in the desegregation of facilities that would have required nationwide integration of pupils from intercity schools with children from the suburbs. The amendment was defeated on April 21, 1971, by a vote of 51 to 35, with most Republicans voting against it and 13 of 34 Northern Democrats opposed. Busing remains a highly controversial political issue.

Swann v. Charlotte-Mecklenburg County Board (1971) held that the courts could order busing of school children within the limits of the city school district if necessary to achieve desegregated educational facilities. In the case of Charlotte-Mecklenburg the limits of the city school district included the surrounding county. However, only eighteen of the country's 100 largest city school districts contain both the inner city and the surrounding county. In cities such as San Francisco, Denver, Pasadena, and Boston, court-ordered busing plans pertained only to the central city school district. In 1974 the Supreme Court reviewed a busing plan for Detroit ordered by a federal District Court and sustained by the Court of Appeals that would have required the busing of students among fifty-four separate school districts in the Detroit metropolitan area to achieve racially balanced schools. The decision of the lower federal court in the Detroit case set a new precedent that required busing among legally separate school districts. Proponents of the Detroit busing plan argued that the central city of Detroit was 70 percent black, and that the only way integration could be achieved would be to link the school district of Detroit with the surrounding white suburban school districts. In *Milliken* v. *Bradley*, 418 U.S. 717 (1974), the Supreme Court held that the court-ordered Detroit busing plan could not be sustained under the Equal Protection Clause of the Fourteenth Amendment, which was the constitutional provision relied upon in the lower court's decision to require busing. The Supreme Court found that there was no evidence of disparate treatment of white and black students among the fifty-three outlying school districts that surround Detroit. The only evidence of discrimination was within the city limits of Detroit itself. Therefore, since the outlying districts did not violate the Equal Protection Clause they could not be ordered to integrate their systems with that of Detroit. Since discrimination was limited to Detroit, the court order to remedy the situation must be limited to Detroit also. The effect of the decision is to leave standing court orders for busing within school districts, but to prevent the forced merger of inner city schools with legally separate suburban school districts.

The Judicial Sources of Three Major Political Controversies over Civil Liberties and Rights

☐   Chief Justice John Marshall in the early nineteenth century laid the groundwork for Supreme Court involvement in politics when he declared that "it is emphatically the province and duty of the Judicial Department to say what the law is." Ironically, in the same case he invented the doctrine of "political questions," proclaiming that the courts should not become involved in those matters more appropriately decided by legislative bodies. Marshall muted that note of judicial self-restraint, however, by his implicit recognition that the courts and not legislatures ultimately would decide what matters fell within their jurisdiction.

Chief Justice Marshall's proclamation of judicial power in *Marbury* v. *Madison* also incorporated the doctrine of judicial review. The authority to declare what the law is included the power to review acts of Congress and judge their constitutionality. The *Marbury* case, however, did not involve a major confrontation with Congress. The Court merely held that Congress could not grant it the mandamus power in original jurisdiction, which had been done in the Judiciary Act of 1789. Essentially the Court was interpreting the scope of its own powers, not those of Congress.

Inevitably, however, the power of judicial review pushed the Supreme Court and lower federal courts as well into political controversies as they ruled not only on congressional laws but far more importantly on the actions of state legislatures and courts. As of early 1983 the Supreme Court had held only 127 provisions of federal laws to be unconstitutional in whole or in part out of a total of approximately 88,000 public and private bills that had been passed. By contrast, the Court had overturned on constitutional grounds 1,000 state laws and provisions of state constitutions, 900 of these rulings coming after 1870.[1] By far the greatest political controversies have been over Supreme Court rulings affecting the states, as the nation for most of its history struggled over the question of how far national power should intrude upon state sovereignty.

Controversies surrounding Supreme Court decisions on civil liberties and civil rights have almost entirely involved Supreme Court rulings on the permissible scope of state power. In the early nineteenth century Chief Justice John Marshall's decisions in the historic cases of *McCulloch v. Maryland* (1819) and *Gibbons v. Ogden* (1823) raised the ire of states' rights advocates who widely proclaimed that the Court's actions would bring about the dissolution of the Union. The Supreme Court had unequivocally upheld national supremacy and wide congressional powers over the states.

Almost a century and a half after the *McCulloch* decision, the Supreme Court was again embroiled in a political controversy, not concerning the extent of congressional power over the states, an issue that had finally been settled in favor of the national government during the New Deal, but over how far national civil liberties and rights standards should be applied to the states. Under the Chief Justiceship of former California governor Earl Warren, an activist and interventionist Supreme Court in the 1960s completed the process of applying most of the provisions of the Bill of Rights to the states under the due process clause of the Fourteenth Amendment. Before the Warren era the Court had been very reluctant to extend parts of the Bill of Rights to the states, weighing heavily against such action considerations of federalism that supported state sovereignty. It nationalized only what in the view of a majority of the justices were fundamental freedoms and rights without which the democratic process and individual liberty could not survive.

[1]Henry J. Abraham, *The Judiciary: The Supreme Court in the Governmental Process,* 6th edition (Boston: Allyn and Bacon, 1983), p. 164.

Religious Freedom and the Issue of School Prayer

As early as 1940 the Supreme Court nationalized the *free exercise* clause of the First Amendment, but it was not until 1947 that a majority of justices agreed that the *establishment* clause of the First Amendment was also a fundamental liberty protected by the due process clause of the Fourteenth Amendment.[1]

The First Amendment provision embodying the establishment and free exercise clauses states: "Congress shall make no law respecting an establishment of religion, or prohibiting the free exercise thereof." While little controversy surrounded the Supreme Court's nationalization of these provisions, its 1962 decision in *Engel* v. *Vitale,* given in the following selection, holding that religious freedom required a ban on prayers in public schools, caused a political backlash that continued into the 1980s, one that seemed to grow in intensity as the years passed. As the Moral Majority and the Christian Right became politically active in the 1980s, one of their major goals was the restoration of prayers in public schools. They supported state efforts to pass legislation that would get around the school prayer decision by requiring moments of silence rather than prayers to open school days. However, the Supreme Court held in 1985 that an Alabama moment of silence statute authorizing public school teachers to hold a one-minute period of silence for "meditation or voluntary prayer" each school day violated the establishment clause of the First Amendment.[2] Of particular concern to the Court were statements by the sponsors of the legislation that they intended the law to restore prayer to public schools. Even conservative justices, such as Sandra Day O'Connor, who supported completely voluntary moments of silence in public schools during which prayers might be given, agreed that the Alabama statute had no secular effect and was an impermissible official encouragement of prayers. The following case originated the school prayer controversy.

---

[1]The two cases nationalizing the First Amendment free exercise and establishment clauses were respectively *Cantwell* v. *Connecticut,* 310 U.S. 296 (1940) and *Everson* v. *Board of Education,* 330 U.S. 1 (1947).
[2]*Wallace* v. *Jaffree,* 86 L Ed. 2d 29 (1985).

17

ENGEL v. VITALE
370 U.S. 421 (1962)

Mr. Justice Black delivered the opinion of the Court, saying in part:
The respondent Board of Education of Union Free School District No. 9, New Hyde Park, New York, acting in its official capacity under state law, directed the School District's principal to cause the following prayer to be said aloud by each class in the presence of a teacher at the beginning of each school day:

> Almighty God, we acknowledge our dependence upon Thee, and we beg Thy blessings upon us, our parents, our teachers and our country.

This daily procedure was adopted on the recommendation of the State Board of Regents, a governmental agency created by the state Constitution to which the New York Legislature has granted broad supervisory, executive, and legislative powers over the state's public school system. These state officials composed the prayer which they recommended and published as a part of their "Statement on Moral and Spiritual Training in the Schools," saying: "We believe that this Statement will be subscribed to by all men and women of good will, and we call upon all of them to aid in giving life to our program."

Shortly after the practice of reciting the Regents' prayer was adopted by the School District, the parents of ten pupils brought this action in a New York State Court insisting that use of this official prayer in the public schools was contrary to the beliefs, religions, or religious practices of both themselves and their children. Among other things, these parents challenged the constitutionality of both the state law authorizing the School District to direct the use of prayer in public schools and the School District's regulation ordering the recitation of this particular prayer on the ground that these actions of official governmental agencies violate that part of the First Amendment of the federal Constitution which commands that "Congress shall make no law respecting an establishment of religion"—a command which was "made applicable to the state of New York by the Fourteenth Amendment of the said Constitution." The New York Court of Appeals, over the dissents of Judges Dye and Fuld, sustained an order of the lower state courts which had upheld the power of New York to use the Regents' prayer as a part of the daily procedures of its public schools so long as the schools did not compel any pupil to join in the prayer over his or her parents' objection. We granted certiorari to review this important decision involving rights protected by the First and Fourteenth Amendments.

We think that by using its public school system to encourage recitation of the Regents' prayer, the state of New York has adopted a practice wholly inconsistent with the Establishment Clause. There can, of course, be no doubt that New York's program of daily classroom invocation of God's blessings as prescribed in the Regents' prayer is a religious activity. It is a solemn avowal of divine faith and supplication for the blessings of the Almighty. The nature of such a prayer has always been religious, none of the respondents has denied this and the trial court expressly so found. . . .

The petitioners contend among other things that the state laws requiring or permitting use of the Regents' prayer must be struck down as a violation of the Establishment Clause because that prayer was composed by governmental officials as a part of a governmental program to further religious beliefs. For this reason, petitioners argue, the state's use of the Regents' prayer in its public school system breaches the constitutional wall of separation between church and state. We agree with that contention since we think that the constitutional prohibition against laws respecting an establishment of religion must at least mean that in this country it is no part of the business of government to compose official prayers for any group of the American people to recite as a part of a religious program carried on by government.

It is a matter of history that this very practice of establishing governmentally composed prayers for religious services was one of the reasons which caused many of our early colonists to leave England and seek religious freedom in America. The Book of Common Prayer, which was created under governmental direction and which was approved by Acts of Parliament in 1548 and 1549, set out in minute detail the accepted form and content of prayer and other religious ceremonies to be used in the established, tax-supported Church of England. The controversies over the Book and what should be its content repeatedly threatened to disrupt the peace of that country as the accepted forms of prayer in the established church changed with the views of the particular ruler that happened to be in control at the time. Powerful groups representing some of the varying religious views of the people struggled among themselves to impress their particular views upon the government and obtain amendments of the Book more suitable to their respective notions of how religious services should be conducted in order that the official religious establishment would advance their particular religious beliefs. Other groups, lacking the necessary political power to influence the government on the matter, decided to leave England and its established church and seek freedom in America from England's governmentally ordained and supported religion.

It is an unfortunate fact of history that when some of the very groups which had most strenuously opposed the established Church of England found themselves sufficiently in control of colonial governments in this country to write their own prayers into law, they passed laws making their own religion the official religion of their respective colonies. Indeed, as late as the time of the Revolutionary War, there were established churches in at least eight of the thirteen former colonies and established religions in at least four of the other five. But the successful Revolution against English political domination was shortly followed by intense opposition to the practice of establishing religion by law. . . .

By the time of the adoption of the Constitution, our history shows that there was a widespread awareness among many Americans of the dangers of a union of church and state. . . . The First Amendment was added to the Constitution to stand as a guarantee that neither the power nor the prestige of the federal government would be used to control, support or influence the kinds of prayer the American people can say—that the people's religions must not be subjected to the pressures of government for change each time a new political administration is elected to office. Under that amendment's prohibition against governmental establishment of religion, as reinforced by the provisions of the Fourteenth Amendment, government in this country, be it state or federal, is without power to prescribe by law any particular form of prayer which is to be used as an official prayer in carrying on any program of governmentally sponsored religious activity.

There can be no doubt that New York's state prayer program officially establishes the religious beliefs embodied in the Regents' prayer. The respondents' argument to the contrary, which is largely based upon the contention that the Regents' prayer is "nondenominational" and the fact that the program, as modified and approved by state courts, does not require all pupils to recite the prayer but permits those who wish to do so to remain silent or be excused from the room, ignores the essential nature of the program's constitutional defects. Neither the fact that the prayer may be denominationally neutral, nor the fact that its observance on the part of the students is voluntary can serve to free it from the limitations of the Establishment Clause, as it might from the Free Exercise Clause, of the First Amendment, both of which are operative against the states by virtue of the Fourteenth Amendment. Although these two clauses may in certain instances overlap, they forbid two quite different kinds of governmental encroachment upon religious freedom. The Establishment Clause, unlike the Free Exercise Clause, does not depend upon any showing of direct governmental compulsion and is violated by the enactment of laws which establish an official religion whether those laws operate directly to coerce nonobserving individuals or not. This is not to say, of course, that laws officially prescribing a particular form of religious worship do not involve coercion of such individuals. When the power, prestige and financial support of government is placed behind a particular religious belief, the indirect coercive pressure upon religious minorities to conform to the prevailing officially approved religion is plain. But the purposes underlying the Establishment Clause go much further than that. Its first and most immediate purpose rested on the belief that a union of government and religion tends to destroy government and to degrade religion. The history of governmentally established religion, both in England and in this country, showed that whenever government had allied itself with one particular form of religion, the inevitable result has been that it had incurred the hatred, disrespect and even contempt of those who held contrary beliefs. That same history showed that many people had lost their respect for any religion that had relied upon the support of government to spread its faith. The Establishment Clause thus stands as an expression of principle on the part of the Founders of our Constitution that religion is too personal, too sacred, too holy, to permit its "unhallowed perversion" by a civil magistrate. Another purpose of the Establishment Clause rested upon an awareness of the historical fact that governmentally established religions and religious persecutions go hand in hand. The founders knew that only a few years after the Book of Common Prayer became the only accepted form of religious services in the established Church of England, an Act of Uniformity was passed to compel all Englishmen to attend those services and to make it a criminal offense to conduct or attend religious gatherings of any other kind—a law which was consistently flouted by dissenting religious groups in England and which contributed to widespread persecutions of people like John Bunyan who persisted in holding "unlawful [religious] meetings . . . to the great disturbance and distraction of the good subjects of this kingdom. . . . " And they knew that similar persecutions had received the sanction of law in several of the colonies in this country soon after the establishment of official religions in those colonies. It was in large part to get completely away from this sort of systematic religious persecution that the Founders brought into being our Nation, our Constitution, and our Bill of Rights with its prohibition against any governmental establishment of religion. The New York laws officially prescribing the Regents' prayer are inconsistent with both the purposes of the Establishment Clause and with the Establishment Clause itself.

It has been argued that to apply the Constitution in such a way as to prohibit state laws respecting an establishment of religious services in public schools is to indicate a hostility toward religion or toward prayer. Nothing, of course, could be more wrong. The history of man is inseparable from the history of religion. And perhaps it is not too much to say that since the beginning of that history many people have devoutly believed that "More things are wrought by prayer than this world dreams of." It was doubtless largely due to men who believed this that there grew up a sentiment that caused men to leave the cross-currents of officially established state religions and religious persecution in Europe and come to this country filled with the hope that they could find a place in which they could pray when they pleased to the God of their faith in the language they chose. And there were men of this same faith in the power of prayer who led the fight for adoption of our Constitution and also for our Bill of Rights with the very guarantees of religious freedom that forbid the sort of governmental activity which New York has attempted here. These men knew that the First Amendment, which tried to put an end to governmental control of religion and of prayer, was not written to destroy either. They knew rather that it was written to quiet well-justified fears which nearly all of them felt arising out of an awareness that governments of the past had shackled men's tongues to make them speak only the religious thoughts that government wanted them to speak and to pray only to the God that government wanted them to pray to. It is neither sacrilegious nor antireligious to say that each separate government in this country should stay out of the business of writing or sanctioning official prayers and leave that purely religious function to the people themselves and to those the people choose to look to for religious guidance.

It is true that New York's establishment of its Regents' prayer as an officially approved religious doctrine of that state does not amount to a total establishment of one particular religious sect to the exclusion of all others—that, indeed, the governmental endorsement of that prayer seems relatively insignificant when compared to the governmental encroachments upon religion which were commonplace 200 years ago. To those who may subscribe to the view that because the Regents' official prayer is so brief and general there can be no danger to religious freedom in its governmental establishment, however, it may be appropriate to say in the words of James Madison, the author of the First Amendment:

> [I]t is proper to take alarm at the first experiment on our liberties. . . . Who does not see that the same authority which can establish Christianity, in exclusion of all other Religions, may establish with the same ease any particular sect of Christians, in exclusion of all other Sects? That the same authority which can force a citizen to contribute three pence only of his property for the support of any one establishment, may force him to conform to any other establishment in all cases whatsoever?

The judgment of the Court of Appeals of New York is reversed and the cause remanded for further proceedings not inconsistent with this opinion.

Reversed and remanded.

Mr. Justice Frankfurter took no part in the decision of this case.

Mr. Justice White took no part in the consideration or decision of this case.

Mr. Justice Douglas concurred in a separate opinion.

Mr. Justice Stewart, dissenting.

A local school board in New York has provided that those pupils who wish to do so may join in a brief prayer at the beginning of each school day, acknowledging their dependence upon God and asking His blessing upon them and upon their parents, their teachers, and their country. The court today decides that in permitting this brief nondenominational prayer the school board has violated the Constitution of the United States. I think this decision is wrong.

The Court does not hold, nor could it, that New York has interfered with the free exercise of anybody's religion. For the state courts have made clear that those who object to reciting the prayer must be entirely free of any compulsion to do so, including any "embarrassments and pressure." Cf. *West Virginia State Board of Education* v. *Barnette,* 319 U.S. 624. But the Court says that in permitting school children to say this simple prayer, the New York authorities have established "an official religion."

With all respect, I think the Court has misapplied a great constitutional principle. I cannot see how an "official religion" is established by letting those who want to say a prayer say it. On the contrary, I think that to deny the wish of these school children to join in reciting this prayer is to deny them the opportunity of sharing in the spiritual heritage of our nation.

The Court's historical review of the quarrels over the Book of Common Prayer in England throws no light for me on the issue before us in this case. England had then and has now an established church. Equally unenlightening, I think, is the history of the early establishment and later rejection of an official church in our own states. For we deal here not with the establishment of a state church, which would, of course, be constitutionally impermissible, but with whether school children who want to begin their day by joining in prayer must be prohibited from doing so. Moreover, I think that the Court's task, in this as in all areas of constitutional adjudication, is not responsibly aided by the uncritical invocation of metaphors like the "wall of separation," a phrase nowhere to be found in the Constitution. What is relevant to the issue here is not the history of an established church in sixteenth-century England or in eighteenth-century America, but the history of the religious traditions of our people, reflected in countless practices of the institutions and officials of our government.

At the opening of each day's session of this Court we stand, while one of our officials invokes the protection of God. Since the days of John Marshall our Crier has said, "God save the United States and this Honorable Court." Both the Senate and the House of Representatives open their daily sessions with prayer. Each of our Presidents, from George Washington to John F. Kennedy, has upon assuming his office asked the protection and help of God.

The Court today says that the state and federal governments are without constitutional power to prescribe any particular form of words to be recited by any group of the American people on any subject touching religion. The third stanza of "The Star-Spangled Banner," made our national anthem by Act of Congress in 1931, contains these verses:

Blest with victory and peace, may the heav'n rescued land
Praise the Pow'r that hath made and preserved us a nation!
Then conquer we must, when our cause it is just,
And this be our motto, "In God is our Trust."

In 1954 Congress added a phrase to the Pledge of Allegiance to the Flag so that it now contains the words "one Nation *under God* indivisible, with liberty and justice for all." In 1952 Congress enacted legislation calling upon the President each year to proclaim a National Day of Prayer. Since 1865 the words "IN GOD WE TRUST" have been impressed on our coins.

Countless similar examples could be listed, but there is no need to belabor the obvious. It was all summed up by this Court just ten years ago in a single sentence: "We are a religious people whose institutions presuppose a Supreme Being." *Zoarch* v. *Clauson,* 343 U.S. 306, 313.

I do not believe that this Court, or the Congress, or the President has by the actions and practices I have mentioned established an "official religion" in violation of the Constitution. And I do not believe the state of New York has done so in this case. What each has done has been to recognize and to follow the deeply entrenched and highly cherished spiritual traditions of our nation—traditions which come down to us from those who almost two hundred years ago avowed their "firm reliance on the Protection of Divine Providence" when they proclaimed the freedom and independence of this brave new world.

I dissent.

Abortion Rights

☐   Ironically, while the "liberal" Warren Court stirred political controversy with its school prayer and many other decisions extending civil liberties and rights to the states, it was the "conservative" Supreme Court under the Chief Justiceship of Warren Burger, who was appointed by Republican President Richard M. Nixon in 1969, that raised an even greater political storm by holding in the following case that the Fourteenth Amendment incorporates a right to privacy that grants women the absolute right to abortion during the first trimester of pregnancy. When the decision was handed down in 1973, all states strictly regulated abortions, which could be performed if at all only to protect the life of the mother. The moral codes of many religions, particularly the Catholic Church, forbid abortions under any circumstances.

Supporters of the abortion decision argued that while the issue was indeed a moral one for most people, women had a constitutionally protected right to decide whether or not they would have an abortion. Opponents not only emphatically opposed abortion on moral grounds, but also attacked the Court for acting as a supra-legislature by imposing its own values upon democratically elected state legislative bodies that were regulating abortion in response to the demands of popular majorities.

The Supreme Court's abortion decision did seem to resurrect "substantive due process," a doctrine under which the Court had in the past judged the fairness of state legislation in terms not of explicitly stated constitutional standards but on the basis of its own values. The Bill of Rights does not contain a general right of privacy, although it may be fairly implied, as Justice Douglas wrote for a majority of the Court in *Griswold v. Connecticut,* 381 U.S. 479 (1965), from First Amendment freedoms of association, Fourth Amendment protections against unreasonable searches and seizures, and the Fifth Amendment shield against self-incrimination.

Whether emanating indirectly from the Bill of Rights or considered to be part of the liberty protected by the Fourteenth Amendment, the right of privacy that the Supreme Court applied in its abortion decision is highly subjective and gives the justices great leeway to impose their own concepts of privacy rights upon legislative bodies. But judicial decisions, especially those of the Supreme Court, always express the values of those making them. The justices did go beyond a strict construction of the Bill of Rights in upholding a woman's right to abortion. However, they interpreted the Fourteenth Amendment due process clause just as subjectively in each case in the step-by-step process of nationalization of most of the provisions of the Bill of Rights.

The Anglo-American system of law and jurisprudence has always supported the concept of a higher law that ultimately the courts must interpret and apply. In Great Britain, however, Parliament became supreme after the Glorious Revolution of 1688, preventing judicial review of parliamentary laws. Our Supreme Court, on the other hand, continues to be the final judge of what the law is, and inevitably its decisions will, as has been the case in the following opinion, involve the Court in major political controversies.

18

ROE v. WADE
410 U.S. 113 (1973)

Mr. Justice Blackmun delivered the opinion of the Court:

V

The principal thrust of appellant's attack on the Texas statutes is that they improperly invade a right, said to be possessed by the pregnant woman, to choose to terminate her pregnancy. Appellant would discover this right in the concept of personal "liberty" embodied in the Fourteenth Amendment's Due Process Clause; or in personal, marital, familial, and sexual privacy said to be protected by the Bill of Rights or its penumbras, see *Griswold* v. *Connecticut* [1965] ... *Eisenstadt* v. *Baird* [1972] ... (White, J., concurring in result); or among those rights reserved to the people by the Ninth Amendment, *Griswold* v. *Connecticut*, ... (Goldberg, J., concurring). Before addressing this claim, we feel it desirable briefly to survey, in several aspects, the history of abortion, for such insight as that history may afford us, and then to examine the state purposes and interests behind the criminal abortion laws.

VI

It perhaps is not generally appreciated that the restrictive criminal abortion laws in effect in a majority of States today are of relatively recent vintage. Those laws, generally proscribing abortion or its attempt at any time during pregnancy except when necessary to preserve the pregnant woman's life, are not of ancient or even of common-law origin. Instead, they derive from statutory changes effected, for the most part, in the latter half of the 19th century. . . .

VII

Three reasons have been advanced to explain historically the enactment of criminal abortion laws in the 19th century and to justify their continued existence.

It has been argued occasionally that these laws were the product of a Victorian social concern to discourage illicit sexual conduct. Texas, however, does not advance this justification in the present case, and it appears that no court or commentator has taken the argument seriously. The appellants and amici contend, moreover, that this is not a proper state purpose at all and suggest that, if it were, the Texas statutes are overbroad in protecting it since the law fails to distinguish between married and unwed mothers.

A second reason is concerned with abortion as a medical procedure. When most criminal abortion laws were first enacted, the procedure was a hazardous one for the woman. This was particularly true prior to the development of antisepsis. Antiseptic techniques, of course, were based on discoveries by Lister, Pasteur, and others first announced in 1867, but were not generally accepted and employed until about the turn of the century. Abortion mortality was high. Even after 1900, and perhaps until as late as the development of antibiotics in the 1940's, standard modern techniques such as dilation and curettage were not nearly so safe as they are today. Thus, it has been argued that a State's real concern in enacting a criminal abortion law was to protect the pregnant woman, that is, to restrain her from submitting to a procedure that placed her life in serious jeopardy.

Modern medical techniques have altered this situation. Appellants and various amici refer to medical data indicating that abortion in early pregnancy, this is, prior to the end of the first trimester, although not without its risk, is now relatively safe. Mortality rates for women undergoing early abortions, where the procedure is legal, appear to be as low as or lower than the rates for normal childbirth. Consequently, any interest of the State in protecting the woman from an inherently hazardous procedure, except when it would be equally dangerous for her to forgo it, has largely disappeared. Of course, important state interests in the area of health and medical standards do remain.

The State has a legitimate interest in seeing to it that abortion, like any other medical procedure, is performed under circumstances that insure maximum safety for the patient. This interest obviously extends at least to the performing physician and his staff, to the facilities involved, to the availability of aftercare, and to adequate provision for any complication or emergency that might arise. The prevalence of high mortality rates at illegal "abortion mills" strengthens, rather than weakens, the State's interest in regulating the conditions under which abortions are performed. Moreover, the risk to the woman increases as her pregnancy continues. Thus, the State retains a definite interest in protecting the woman's own health and safety when an abortion is proposed at a late stage of pregnancy.

The third reason is the State's interest—some phrase it in terms of duty—in protecting prenatal life. Some of the argument for this justification rests on the theory that a new human life is present from the moment of conception. The State's interest and general obligation to protect life then extends, it is argued, to prenatal life. Only when the life of the pregnant mother herself is at stake, balanced against the life she carries within her, should the interest of the embryo or fetus not prevail. Logically, of course, a legitimate state interest in this area need not stand or fall on acceptance of the belief that life begins at conception or at some other point prior to live birth. In assessing the State's interest, recognition may be given to the less rigid claim that as long as at least *potential* life is involved, the State may assert interests beyond the protection of the pregnant woman alone.

Parties challenging state abortion laws have sharply disputed in some courts the contention that a purpose of these laws, when enacted, was to protect prenatal life. . . .

It is with these interests, and the weight to be attached to them, that this case is concerned.

VIII

The Constitution does not explicitly mention any right of privacy. In a line of decisions, however, going back perhaps as far as *Union Pacific R. Co. v. Botsford* [1891] . . . , the Court has recognized that a right of personal privacy, or a guarantee of certain areas or zones of privacy, does exist under the Constitution. In varying contexts, the Court or individual Justices have, indeed, found at least the roots of that right in the First Amendment, *Stanley* v. *Georgia* [1969] . . . ; in the Fourth and Fifth Amendments, *Terry* v. *Ohio* [1968] . . . , *Katz* v. *United States* [1967] . . . ; in the penumbras of the Bill of Rights, *Griswold* v. *Connecticut* [1965] . . . ; in the Ninth Amendment, id., at 486, . . . (Goldberg, J., concurring); or in the concept of liberty guaranteed by the first section of the Fourteenth Amendment, see *Meyer* v. *Nebraska* [1923]. . . . These decisions make it clear that only personal rights that can be deemed "fundamental" or "implicit in the concept of ordered liberty," *Palko* v. *Connecticut* [1937] . . . , are included in this guarantee of personal privacy. They also make it clear that the right has some extension to activities relating to marriage, *Loving* v. *Virginia* [1967] . . . ; procreation, *Skinner* v. *Oklahoma* [1942] . . . ; contraception, *Eisenstadt* v. *Baird* [1972]. . . .

This right of privacy, whether it be founded in the Fourteenth Amendment's concept of personal liberty and restrictions upon state action, as we feel it is, or, as the District Court determined, in the Ninth Amendment's reservation of rights to the people, is broad enough to encompass a woman's decision whether or not to terminate her pregnancy. The detriment that the State would impose upon the pregnant woman by denying this choice altogether is apparent. Specific and direct harm medically diagnosable even in early pregnancy may be involved. Maternity, or additional offspring, may force upon the woman a distressful life and future. Psychological harm may be imminent. Mental and physical health may be taxed by child care. There is also the distress, for all concerned, associated with the unwanted child, and there is the problem of bringing a child into a family already unable, psychologically and otherwise, to care for it. In other cases, as in this one, the additional difficulties and continuing stigma of unwed mother-hood may be involved. All these are factors the woman and her responsible physician necessarily will consider in consultation.

On the basis of elements such as these, appellant and some amici argue that the woman's right is absolute and that she is entitled to terminate her pregnancy at whatever time, in whatever way, and for whatever reason she alone chooses. With this we do not agree. Appellant's arguments that Texas either has no valid interest at all in regulating the abortion decision, or no interest strong enough to support any limitation upon the woman's sole determination, is unpersuasive. The Court's decisions recognizing a right of privacy also acknowledge that some state regulation in areas protected by that right is appropriate. As noted above, a State may properly assert important interests in safeguarding health, in maintaining medical standards, and in protecting potential life. At some point in pregnancy, these respec-tive interests become sufficiently compelling to sustain regulation of the factors that govern the abortion decision. The privacy right involved, therefore, cannot be said to be absolute. In fact, it is not clear to us that the claim asserted by some amici that one has an unlimited right to do with one's body as one pleases bears a close relationship to the right of privacy previously articulated in the Court's decisions. The Court has refused to recognize an unlimited right of this kind in the past. *Jacobson* v. *Massachusetts* [1905] . . . (vaccination); *Buck* v. *Bell* [1927] . . . (sterilization).

We, therefore, conclude that the right of personal privacy includes the abortion decision, but that this right is not unqualified and must be consid-ered against important state interests in regulation.

Where certain "fundamental rights" are involved, the Court has held that regulation limiting these rights may be justified only by a "compelling state interest," . . . and that legislative enactments must be narrowly drawn to express only the legitimate state interests at stake. . . .

IX

The District Court held that the appellee failed to meet his burden of demonstrating that the Texas statute's infringement upon Roe's rights was necessary to support a compelling state interest. . . . Appellee argues that the State's determination to recognize and protect prenatal life from and after conception constitutes a compelling state interest. As noted above, we do not agree fully with either formulation.

A. The appellee and certain amici argue that the fetus is a "person" within the language and meaning of the Fourteenth Amendment. In sup-port of this, they outline at length and in detail the well-known facts of fetal development. If this suggestion of personhood is established, the appellant's case, of course, collapses, for the fetus' right to life is then guaranteed specifically by the Amendment. The appellant conceded as much on reargument. On the other hand, the appellee conceded on reargument that no case could be cited that holds that a fetus is a person within the meaning of the Fourteenth Amendment.

The Constitution does not define "person" in so many words. Section 1 of the Fourteenth Amendment contains three references to "person." The first, in defining "citizens," speaks of "persons born or naturalized in the United States." The word also appears both in the Due Process Clause and in the Equal Protection Clause. "Person" is used in other places in the Constitution. . . . But in nearly all these instances, the use of the word is such that it has application only postnatally. None indicates, with any assurance, that it has any possible prenatal application.

All this, together with our observation, supra, that throughout the major portion of the 19th century prevailing legal abortion practices were far freer than they are today, persuades us that the word "person," as used in the Fourteenth Amendment, does not include the unborn. . . .

B. The pregnant woman cannot be isolated in her privacy. She carries an embryo and, later, a fetus, if one accepts the medical definitions of the developing young in the human uterus. . . . The situation therefore is inherently different from marital intimacy, or bedroom possession of obscene material, or marriage, or procreation, or education, with which *Eisenstadt, Griswold, Stanley, Loving, Skinner, Pierce,* and *Meyer* were respectively concerned. As we have intimated above, it is reasonable and appropriate for a State to decide that at some point in time another interest, that of health of the mother or that of potential human life, becomes significantly involved. The woman's privacy is no longer sole and any right of privacy she possesses must be measured accordingly.

Texas urges that, apart from the Fourteenth Amendment, life begins at conception and is present throughout pregnancy, and that, therefore, the State has a compelling interest in protecting that life from and after conception. We need not resolve the difficult question of when life begins. When those trained in the respective disciplines of medicine, philosophy, and theology are unable to arrive at any consensus, the judiciary, at this point in the development of man's knowledge, is not in a position to speculate as to the answer.

It should be sufficient to note briefly the wide divergence of thinking on this most sensitive and difficult question. . . .

X

In view of all this, we do not agree that, by adopting one theory of life, Texas may override the rights of the pregnant woman that are at stake. We repeat, however, that the State does have an important and legitimate interest in preserving and protecting the health of the pregnant woman, whether she be a resident of the State or a nonresident who seeks medical consultation and treatment there, and that it has still *another* important and legitimate interest in protecting the potentiality of human life. These interests are separate and distinct. Each grows in substantiality as the woman approaches term and, at a point during pregnancy, each becomes "compelling."

With respect to the State's important and legitimate interest in the health of the mother, the "compelling" point, in the light of present medical knowledge, is at approximately the end of the first trimester. This is so because of the now-established medical fact, referred to above . . . that until the end of the first trimester mortality in abortion may be less than mortality in normal childbirth. It follows that, from and after this point, a State may regulate the abortion procedure to the extent that the regulation reasonably relates to the preservation and protection of maternal health. Examples of permissible state regulation in this area are requirements as to the qualifications of the person who is to perform the abortion; as to the licensure of that person; as to the facility in which the procedure is to be performed, that is, whether it must be a hospital or may be a clinic or some other place of less-than-hospital status; as to the licensing of the facility; and the like.

This means, on the other hand, that, for the period of pregnancy prior to this "compelling" point, the attending physician, in consultation with his patient, is free to determine, without regulation by the State, that, in his medical judgment, the patient's pregnancy should be terminated. If that decision is reached, the judgment may be effectuated by an abortion free of interference by the State.

With respect to the State's important and legitimate interest in potential life, the "compelling" point is at viability. This is so because the fetus then presumably has the capability of meaningful life outside the mother's womb. State regulation protective of fetal life after viability thus has both logical and biological justifications. If the State is interested in protecting fetal life after viability, it may go so far as to proscribe abortion during that period, except when it is necessary to preserve the life or health of the mother.

Measured against these standards, Art. 1196 of the Texas Penal Code, in restricting legal abortions to those "procured or attempted by medical advice for the purpose of saving the life of the mother," sweeps too broadly. The statute makes no distinction between abortions performed early in pregnancy and those performed later, and it limits to a single reason, "saving" the mother's life, the legal justification for the procedure. The statute, therefore, cannot survive the constitutional attack made upon it here. . . .

XI

To summarize and to repeat:

1. A state criminal abortion statute of the current Texas type, that excepts from criminality only a *lifesaving* procedure on behalf of the mother, without regard to pregnancy stage and without recognition of the other interests involved, is violative of the Due Process Clause of the Fourteenth Amendment.

(a) For the stage prior to approximately the end of the first trimester, the abortion decision and its effectuation must be left to the medical judgment of the pregnant woman's attending physician.

(b) For the stage subsequent to approximately the end of the first trimester, the State, in promoting its interest in the health of the mother, may, if it chooses, regulate the abortion procedure in ways that are reasonably related to maternal health.

(c) For the stage subsequent to viability, the State in promoting its interest in the potentiality of human life may, if it chooses, regulate, and even proscribe, abortion except where it is necessary, in appropriate medical judgment, for the preservation of the life or health of the mother.

2. The State may define the term "physician," as it has been employed in the preceding numbered paragraphs of this Part XI of this opinion, to mean only a physician currently licensed by the State, and may proscribe any abortion by a person who is not a physician as so defined.

In *Doe v. Bolton* [1973] ... procedural requirements contained in one of the modern abortion statutes are considered. That opinion and this one, of course, are to be read together. ...

Mr. Chief Justice Burger concurred.

Mr. Justice Douglas concurred.

Mr. Justice Stewart, concurring:

In 1963, this Court, in *Ferguson* v. *Skrupa*, ... purported to sound the death knell for the doctrine of substantive due process, a doctrine under which many state laws had in the past been held to violate the Fourteenth Amendment. As Mr. Justice Black's opinion for the Court in *Skrupa* put it: "We have returned to the original constitutional proposition that courts do not substitute their social and economic beliefs for the judgment of legislative bodies, who are elected to pass laws." ...

Barely two years later, in *Griswold* v. *Connecticut*, ... the Court held a Connecticut birth control law unconstitutional. In view of what had been so recently said in *Skrupa*, the Court's opinion in *Griswold* understandably did its best to avoid reliance on the Due Process Clause of the Fourteenth Amendment as the ground for decision. Yet, the Connecticut law did not violate any provision of the Bill of Rights, nor any other specific provision of the Constitution. So it was clear to me then, and it is equally clear to me now, that the *Griswold* decision can be rationally understood only as a holding that the Connecticut statute substantively invaded the "liberty" that is protected by the Due Process Clause of the Fourteenth Amendment. As so understood, *Griswold* stands as one in a long line of pre-Skrupa cases decided under the doctrine of substantive due process, and I now accept it as such.

"In a Constitution for a free people, there can be no doubt that the meaning of 'liberty' must be broad indeed." . . . The Constitution nowhere mentions a specific right of personal choice in matters of marriage and family life, but the "liberty" protected by the Due Process Clause of the Fourteenth Amendment covers more than those freedoms explicitly named in the Bill of Rights. . . .

Several decisions of this Court make clear that freedom of personal choice in matters of marriage and family life is one of the liberties protected by the Due Process Clause of the Fourteenth Amendment. *Loving* v. *Virginia, . . . Griswold* v. *Connecticut. . . .* In *Eisenstadt* v. *Baird, . . .* we recognized "the right of the *individual,* married or single, to be free from unwarranted governmental intrusion into matters so fundamentally affecting a person as the decision whether to bear or beget a child." That right necessarily includes the right of a woman to decide whether or not to terminate her pregnancy. "Certainly the interests of a woman in giving of her physical and emotional self during pregnancy and the interests that will be affected throughout her life by the birth and raising of a child are of a far greater degree of significance and personal intimacy than the right to send a child to private school protected in *Pierce* v. *Society of Sisters* [1925] . . . , or the right to teach a foreign language protected in *Meyer* v. *Nebraska. . . .* "

Mr. Justice Rehnquist, dissenting:
. . . I have difficulty in concluding, as the Court does, that the right of "privacy" is involved in this case. Texas, by the statute here challenged, bars the performance of a medical abortion by a licensed physician on a plaintiff such as Roe. A transaction resulting in an operation such as this is not "private" in the ordinary usage of that word. . . .

If the Court means by the term "privacy" no more than that the claim of a person to be free from unwanted state regulation of consensual transactions may be a form of "liberty" protected by the Fourteenth Amendment, there is no doubt that similar claims have been upheld in our earlier decisions on the basis of that liberty. I agree with the statement of Mr. Justice Stewart in his concurring opinion that the "liberty," against deprivation of which without due process the Fourteenth Amendment protects, embraces more than the rights found in the Bill of Rights. But that liberty is not guaranteed absolutely against deprivation, only against deprivation without due process of law. The test traditionally applied in the area of social and economic legislation is whether or not a law such as that challenged has a rational relation to a valid state objective. . . . But the Court's sweeping invalidation of any restrictions on abortion during the first trimester is impossible to justify under that standard, and the conscious weighing of competing factors that the Court's opinion apparently substitutes for the established test is far more appropriate to a legislative judgment than to a judicial one.

The Court eschews the history of the Fourteenth Amendment in its reliance on the "compelling state interest" test. . . . But the Court adds a new wrinkle to this test by transposing it from the legal considerations associated with the Equal Protection Clause of the Fourteenth Amendment to this case arising under the Due Process Clause of the Fourteenth Amendment. Unless I misapprehend the consequences of this transplanting of the "compelling state interest test," the Court's opinion will accomplish the seemingly impossible feat of leaving this area of the law more confused than it found it.

While the Court's opinion quotes from the dissent of Mr. Justice Holmes in *Lochner* v. *New York,* the result it reaches is more closely attuned to the majority opinion of Mr. Justice Peckham in that case. As in *Lochner* and similar cases applying substantive due process standards to economic and social welfare legislation, the adoption of the compelling state interest standard will inevitably require this Court to examine the legislative policies and pass on the wisdom of these policies in the very process of deciding whether a particular state interest put forward may or may not be "compelling." The decision here to break pregnancy into three distinct terms and to outline the permissible restrictions the State may impose in each one, for example, partakes more of judicial legislation than it does of a determination of the intent of the drafters of the Fourteenth Amendment.

The fact that a majority of the States reflecting, after all the majority sentiment in those States, have had restrictions on abortions for at least a century is a strong indication, it seems to me, that the asserted right to an abortion is not "so rooted in the traditions and conscience of our people as to be ranked as fundamental," *Snyder* v. *Massachusetts* [1934]. . . . Even today, when society's views on abortion are changing, the very existence of the debate is evidence that the "right" to an abortion is not so universally accepted as the appellant would have us believe.

To reach its result, the Court necessarily has had to find within the scope of the Fourteenth Amendment a right that was apparently completely unknown to the drafters of the Amendment. As early as 1821, the first state law dealing directly with abortion was enacted by the Connecticut Legislature. . . . By the time of the adoption of the Fourteenth Amendment in 1868, there were at least 36 laws enacted by state or territorial legislatures limiting abortion. While many States have amended or updated their laws, 21 of the laws on the books in 1868 remain in effect today....

...The only conclusion possible from this history is that the drafters did not intend to have the Fourteenth Amendment withdraw from the States the power to legislate with respect to this matter....

Mr. Justice White, joined by Mr. Justice Rehnquist, dissented.

AFFIRMATIVE ACTION

☐   The Supreme Court has unequivocally ruled that racial discrimination by law is unconstitutional. When the law treats *racial* groups differently, it is almost invariably the case that the Court will declare the law to be a violation of the equal protection clause of the Fourteenth Amendment or, where federal action is involved, the standards of equal protection required under the due process clause of the Fifth Amendment.[1]

Before the era of the Warren court, which began in 1953 and led immediately to the *Brown* decision, the Supreme Court applied a "rational-relation" or "conceivable-basis" test to determine if legislative classifications that treated separate groups of people differently constituted a violation of equal protection standards. Generally, under these tests the Court upheld the legislative classifications if it found there was a rational relationship between the classifications and legislative goals. Such classifications were also upheld if the Court found a conceivable basis upon which to support the reasoning of the legislature in creating classifications. These equal protection standards are referred to as the "old equal protection."

The Warren court inaugurated the "new equal protection" standards to apply to legislative classifications based on race or other "suspect" group classifications. For example, gender-classifications have come to be regarded by the Burger court as at least semi-suspect.[2] The new equal protection standards required the demonstration of a "compelling" governmental interest to uphold the legislative classifications under review. The new equal protection standards also required the demonstration of a compelling governmental interest to sustain legislative classifications that burdened fundamental rights. For example, in *Shapiro* v.

[1]An important exception to the rigid application of equal protection standards to racial classification was the holding of the Supreme Court in *Korematsu* v. *United States,* 323 U.S. 214 (1944), which upheld a racial classification that treated Japanese-Americans differently than other citizens. The Court found that the federal government could exclude Japanese-Americans from military zones on the West Coast on the ground of national security, a holding that in effect supported the establishment of relocation centers for Japanese-American citizens during World War II.

[2]See, for example, *Frontiero* v. *Richardson,* 411 U.S. 677 (1973).

Thompson, 394 U.S. 618 (1969), the Warren court reviewed challenges to state and District of Columbia laws denying welfare assistance to persons who had not resided within their jurisdictions for at least one year immediately prior to applying for assistance. The Court found that the laws burdened the fundamental right to travel, and therefore could be sustained only upon the demonstration of a compelling governmental interest. The Court found no such compelling interest present and held the laws to be unconstitutional. The application of the new equal protection standard is called *strict judicial scrutiny.* When the Court employs this strict judicial scrutiny, the invariable effect is to declare unconstitutional the classification in the law under review.

In the *Bakke* case, presented below, the opinions of justices Powell and Brennan discuss the circumstances under which strict judicial scrutiny is required by the equal protection clause of the Fourteenth Amendment. This case arose out of a complex set of circumstances. Title VI of the Civil Rights Act of 1964 provided that no person was to be "subjected to discrimination under any program or activity receiving federal financial assistance." The Department of Health, Education and Welfare found this section to require affirmative action programs by private institutions receiving federal aid, to achieve a racial balance among employees and, in institutions of higher learning, within their student bodies as well. Under pressure from civil rights groups, women, and other minorities, many affirmative action plans were adopted throughout the country that contained racial classifications providing for the favored treatment of racial minorities in school admissions and private employment.

The *Bakke* case was initiated by Allan Bakke, a 36-year-old white engineer who decided that he wanted to become a doctor. In 1973 and 1974 he applied, unsuccessfully, for admission to the University of California Medical School at Davis. The school informed Bakke that there were too many qualified applicants and that it could admit only one out of 26 in 1973, and one out of 37 in 1974. However, 16 of the 100 openings in the Davis medical school were set aside for minority applicants. Bakke's objective qualifications, such as his Medical College Admission Test scores and his undergraduate grades, were better than those of some of the minority applicants that were accepted during the years when he was rejected. The minority applicants competed among themselves for the 16 places reserved for them, making it possible to admit minority students with different qualifications than were required of nonminority applicants. Bakke claimed that the admissions procedures violated the equal protection clause and Title VI of the Civil Rights Act of 1964.

The trial court in the *Bakke* case held that the admissions program established racial quotas in violation of the equal protection clause and

Title VI. However, the court refused to order the admission of Bakke to the medical school because of his failure to prove that he would have been admitted in the absence of the special program for minorities. The California Supreme Court sustained the trial court's finding that the program violated the equal protection clause and the Civil Rights Act but overruled the trial court's denial of an order that Bakke be admitted. The United States Supreme Court granted certiorari to the California Supreme Court to review the case.

The California Supreme Court, by a five-four vote, ruled that Bakke should be admitted to the Davis Medical School. The majority on the issue of admittance agreed that the racial quota system at the school was not an acceptable means to decide who should be admitted. The majority justices favoring admission and a ban on quotas were Powell, Burger, Stevens, Rehnquist, and Stewart. Brennan, White, Marshall, and Blackmun dissented on these issues, arguing that "Davis's special admissions program cannot be said to violate the Constitution simply because it has set aside a predetermined number of places for qualified minority applicants. . . . "

Justice Louis F. Powell, who was in the majority favoring admission and a ban on quotas, joined with the four justices who dissented from the Court's decision and opinion on those issues to form another majority that held that an applicant's race can be considered in deciding who should be admitted to a university program.

19

REGENTS OF THE UNIVERSITY OF CALIFORNIA v. BAKKE
438 U.S. 265 (1978)

Mr. Justice Powell announced the judgment of the Court and wrote an opinion:

For the reasons stated in the following opinion, I believe that so much of the judgment of the California court as holds petitioner's special admissions program unlawful and directs that respondent be admitted to the Medical School must be affirmed. For the reasons expressed in a separate opinion, my Brothers The Chief Justice, Mr. Justice Stewart, Mr. Justice Rehnquist, and Mr. Justice Stevens concur in this judgment.

I also conclude for the reasons stated in the following opinion that the portion of the court's judgment enjoining petitioner from according any consideration to race in its admissions process must be reversed. For reasons expressed in separate opinions, my Brothers Mr. Justice Brennan, Mr. Justice White, Mr. Justice Marshall, and Mr. Justice Blackmun concur in this judgment.

Affirmed in part and reversed in part.

II

B

The language of § 601 [of the Civil Rights Act of 1964], like that of the Equal Protection Clause, is majestic in its sweep:

> No person in the United States shall, on the ground of race, color, or national origin, be excluded from participation in, be denied the benefits of, or be subjected to discrimination under any program or activity receiving Federal financial assistance.

The concept of "discrimination," like the phrase "equal protection of the laws," is susceptible of varying interpretations, for as Mr. Justice Holmes declared, "[a] word is not a crystal, transparent and unchanged, it is the skin of a living thought and may vary greatly in color and content according to the circumstances and the time in which it is used." . . . We must, therefore, seek whatever aid is available in determining the precise meaning of the statute before us. . . . Examination of the voluminous legislative history of Title VI reveals a congressional intent to halt federal funding of entities that violate a prohibition of racial discrimination similar to that of the Constitution. Although isolated statements of various legislators, taken out of context, can be marshaled in support of the proposition that § 601 enacted a purely color-blind scheme, without regard to the reach of the Equal Protection Clause, these comments must be read against the background of both the problem that Congress was addressing and the broader view of the statute that emerges from a full examination of the legislative debates.

The problem confronting Congress was discrimination against Negro citizens at the hands of recipients of federal moneys. Indeed, the color blindness pronouncements [of Congress] generally occur in the midst of extended remarks dealing with the evils of segregation in federally funded programs. Over and over again, proponents of the bill detailed the plight of Negroes seeking equal treatment in such programs. There simply was no reason for Congress to consider the validity of hypothetical preferences that might be accorded minority citizens; the legislators were dealing with the real and pressing problem of how to guarantee those citizens equal treatment.

In addressing that problem, supporters of Title VI repeatedly declared that the bill enacted constitutional principles. . . .

In the Senate, Senator Humphrey declared that the purpose of Title VI was "to insure that Federal funds are spent in accordance with the Constitution and the moral sense of the Nation." . . .

Further evidence of the incorporation of a constitutional standard into Title VI appears in the repeated refusals of the legislation's supporters precisely to define the term "discrimination." Opponents sharply criticized this failure, but proponents of the bill merely replied that the meaning of "discrimination" would be made clear by reference to the Constitution or other existing law. . . .

In view of the clear legislative intent, Title VI must be held to proscribe only those racial classifications that would violate the Equal Protection Clause or the Fifth Amendment.

III

A

Petitioner does not deny that decisions based on race or ethnic origin by faculties and administrations of state universities are reviewable under the Fourteenth Amendment. . . . For his part, respondent does not argue that all racial or ethnic classifications are *per se* invalid. . . . The parties do disagree as to the level of judicial scrutiny to be applied to the special admissions program. Petitioner argues that the court below erred in applying strict scrutiny, as this inexact term has been applied in our cases. . . .

En route to this crucial battle over the scope of judicial review, the parties fight a sharp preliminary action over the proper characterization of the special admissions program. Petitioner prefers to view it as establishing a "goal" of minority representation in the Medical School. Respondent, echoing the courts below, labels it a racial quota.

This semantic distinction is beside the point: The special admissions program is undeniably a classification based on race and ethnic background. To the extent that there existed a pool of at least minimally qualified minority applicants to fill the 16 special admissions seats, white applicants could compete only for 84 seats in the entering class, rather than the 100 open to minority applicants. Whether this limitation is described as a quota or a goal, it is a line drawn on the basis of race and ethnic status.

The guarantees of the Fourteenth Amendment extend to all persons. Its language is explicit: "No State shall . . . deny to any person within its jurisdiction the equal protection of the laws." It is settled beyond question that the "rights created by the first section of the Fourteenth Amendment are, by its terms, guaranteed to the individual. The rights established are personal rights". . . . The guarantee of equal protection cannot mean one thing when applied to one individual and something else when applied to a person of another color. If both are not accorded the same protection, then it is not equal.

Nevertheless, petitioner argues that the court below erred in applying strict scrutiny to the special admissions program because white males, such as respondent, are not a "discrete and insular minority" requiring extraordinary protection from the majoritarian political process. . . . This rationale, however, has never been invoked in our decisions as a prerequisite to subjecting racial or ethnic distinctions to strict scrutiny. Nor has this Court held that discreteness and insularity constitute necessary preconditions to a holding that a particular classification is invidious. . . . These characteristics may be relevant in deciding whether or not to add new types of classifications to the list of "suspect" categories or whether a particular classification survives close examination. . . . Racial and ethnic classifications, however, are subject to stringent examination without regard to these additional characteristics. We declared as much in the first cases explicitly to recognize racial distinctions as suspect:

> Distinctions between citizens solely because of their ancestry are by their very nature odious to a free people whose institutions are founded upon the doctrine of equality. *Hirabayashi* [v. *United States* (1943)].
>
> [A]ll legal restrictions which curtail the civil rights of a single racial group are immediately suspect. That is not to say that all such restrictions are unconstitutional. It is to say that courts must subject them to the most rigid scrutiny. *Korematsu* [v. *United States* (1944)].

The Court has never questioned the validity of those pronouncements. Racial and ethnic distinctions of any sort are inherently suspect and thus call for the most exacting judicial examination. . . .

Although many of the Framers of the Fourteenth Amendment conceived of its primary function as bridging the vast distance between members of the Negro race and the white "majority" . . . the amendment itself was framed in universal terms, without reference to color, ethnic origin, or condition of prior servitude. As this Court recently remarked in interpreting the 1866 Civil Rights Act to extend to claims of racial discrimination against white persons, "the 39th Congress was intent upon establishing in the federal law a broader principle than would have been necessary simply to meet the particular and immediate plight of the newly freed Negro slaves." . . .

Over the past 30 years, this Court has embarked upon the crucial mission of interpreting the Equal Protection Clause with the view of assuring to all persons "the protection of equal laws . . ." in a Nation confronting a legacy of slavery and racial discrimination. . . . Because the landmark decisions in this area arose in response to the continued exclusion of Negroes from the mainstream of American society, they could be characterized as involving discrimination by the "majority" white race against the Negro minority. But they need not be read as depending upon that characterization for their results. It suffices to say that "[o]ver the years, this Court has consistently repudiated '[d]istinctions between citizens solely because of their ancestry' as being 'odious to a free people whose institutions are founded upon the doctrine of equality.'"...

Petitioner urges us to adopt for the first time a more restrictive view of the Equal Protection Clause and hold that discrimination against members of the white "majority" cannot be suspect if its purpose can be characterized as "benign." The clock of our liberties, however, cannot be turned back to 1868.... It is far too late to argue that the guarantee of equal protection to *all* persons permits the recognition of special wards entitled to a degree of protection greater than that accorded others. "The Fourteenth Amendment is not directed solely against discrimination due to a 'two-class theory'—that is, based upon differences between 'white' and Negro."...

Once the artificial line of a "two-class theory" of the Fourteenth Amendment is put aside, the difficulties entailed in varying the level of judicial review according to a perceived "preferred" status of a particular racial or ethnic minority are intractable. The concepts of "majority" and "minority" necessarily reflect temporary arrangements and political judgments. As observed above, the white "majority" itself is composed of various minority groups, most of which can lay claim to a history of prior discrimination at the hands of the State and private individuals. Not all of these groups can receive preferential treatment and corresponding judicial tolerance of distinctions drawn in terms of race and nationality, for then the only "majority" left would be a new minority of white Anglo-Saxon Protestants. There is no principled basis for deciding which groups would merit "heightened judicial solicitude" and which would not. Courts would be asked to evaluate the extent of the prejudice and consequent harm suffered by various minority groups. Those whose societal injury is thought to exceed some arbitrary level of tolerability then would be entitled to preferential classifications at the expense of individuals belonging to other groups. Those classifications would be free from exacting judicial scrutiny. As these preferences began to have their desired effect, and the consequences of past discrimination were undone, new judicial rankings would be necessary. The kind of variable sociological and political analysis necessary to produce such rankings simply does not lie within the judicial competence—even if they otherwise were politically feasible and socially desirable.

Moreover, there are serious problems of justice connected with the idea of preference itself. First, it may not always be clear that a so-called preference is in fact benign.... Second, preferential programs may only reinforce common stereotypes holding that certain groups are unable to achieve success without special protection based on a factor having no relationship to individual worth. . . . Third, there is a measure of inequity in forcing innocent persons in respondent's position to bear the burdens of redressing grievances not of their making.

By hitching the meaning of the Equal Protection Clause to these transitory considerations, we would be holding, as a constitutional principle, that judicial scrutiny of classifications touching on racial and ethnic background may vary with the ebb and flow of political forces. Disparate constitutional tolerance of such classifications well may serve to exacerbate racial and ethnic antagonisms rather than alleviate them. . . . Also, the mutability of a constitutional principle, based upon shifting political and social judgments, undermines the chances for consistent application of the Constitution from one generation to the next, a critical feature of its coherent interpretation. . . . In expounding the Constitution, the Court's role is to discern "principles sufficiently absolute to give them roots throughout the community and continuity over significant periods of time, and to lift them above the level of the pragmatic political judgments of a particular time and place." . . .

IV

We have held that in "order to justify the use of a suspect classification, a State must show that its purpose or interest is both constitutionally permissible and substantial, and that its use of the classification is 'necessary . . . to the accomplishment' of its purpose or the safeguarding of its interest." . . . The special admissions program purports to serve the purposes of: (i) "reducing the historic deficit of traditionally disfavored minorities in medical schools and in the medical profession"; (ii) countering the effects of societal discrimination; (iii) increasing the number of physicians who will practice in communities currently underserved; and (iv) obtaining the educational benefits that flow from an ethnically diverse student body. It is necessary to decide which, if any, of these purposes is substantial enough to support the use of a suspect classification.

A

If petitioner's purpose is to assure within its student body some specified percentage of a particular group merely because of its race or ethnic origin, such a preferential purpose must be rejected not as insubstantial but as facially invalid. Preferring members of any one group for no reason other than race or ethnic origin is discrimination for its own sake. This the Constitution forbids. . . .

B

... [T]he purpose of helping certain groups whom the faculty of the Davis Medical School perceived as victims of "societal discrimination" does not justify a classification that imposes disadvantages upon persons like respondent, who bear no responsibility for whatever harm the beneficiaries of the special admissions program are thought to have suffered. To hold otherwise would be to convert a remedy heretofore reserved for violations of legal rights into a privilege that all institutions throughout the Nation could grant at their pleasure to whatever groups are perceived as victims of societal discrimination. That is a step we have never approved. . . .

C

Petitioner identifies, as another purpose of its program, improving the delivery of health-care services to communities currently underserved. It may be assumed that in some situations a State's interest in facilitating the health care of its citizens is sufficiently compelling to support the use of a suspect classification. But there is virtually no evidence in the record indicating that petitioner's special admissions program is either needed or geared to promote that goal. . . .

D

The fourth goal asserted by petitioner is the attainment of a diverse student body. This clearly is a constitutionally permissible goal for an institution of higher education. Academic freedom, though not a specifically enumerated constitutional right, long has been viewed as a special concern of the First Amendment. . . .

... As the interest of diversity is compelling in the context of a university's admissions program, the question remains whether the program's racial classification is necessary to promote this interest. . . .

V

A

It may be assumed that the reservation of a specified number of seats in each class for individuals from the preferred ethnic groups would contribute to the attainment of considerable ethnic diversity in the student body. But petitioner's argument that this is the only effective means of serving the interest of diversity is seriously flawed. . . . Petitioner's special admissions program, focused *solely* on ethnic diversity, would hinder rather than further attainment of genuine diversity. . . .

The experience of other university admissions programs, which take race into account in achieving the educational diversity valued by the First Amendment, demonstrates that the assignment of a fixed number

CORNELL COLLEGE DROP/ADD FORM

Name __O'Brien__ (Last) __Christine__ (First) Date _____

COURSES DROPPED	COURSES ADDED	INSTRUCTORS' SIGNATURES
Dept. Name, Term Prefix, Course No. & Suffix	Dept. Name, Term Prefix, Course No. & Suffix	Only required after course has begun
FRE 7-102		dropped
		added
		dropped
		added
		dropped
		added
		dropped
		added
		dropped
		added
		dropped
		added

This form, properly filled out and signed, must be returned to the Registrar's Office in order for the change(s) to become official. Consult the current catalogue for the regulations, procedures, and deadlines concerning adding and dropping courses.

Signature of Faculty Adviser _____

of places to a minority group is not a necessary means toward that end. . . .

B

In summary, it is evident that the Davis special admissions program involves the use of an explicit racial classification never before countenanced by this Court. It tells applicants who are not Negro, Asian, or Chicano that they are totally excluded from a specific percentage of the seats in an entering class. No matter how strong their qualifications, quantitative and extracurricular, including their own potential for contribution to educational diversity, they are never afforded the chance to compete with applicants from the preferred groups for the special admissions seats. At the same time, the preferred applicants have the opportunity to compete for every seat in the class.

The fatal flaw in petitioner's preferential program is its disregard of individual rights as guaranteed by the Fourteenth Amendment. . . . Such rights are not absolute. But when a State's distribution of benefits or imposition of burdens hinges on ancestry or the color of a person's skin or ancestry, that individual is entitled to a demonstration that the challenged classification is necessary to promote a substantial state interest. Petitioner has failed to carry this burden. For this reason, that portion of the California court's judgment holding petitioner's special admissions program invalid under the Fourteenth Amendment must be affirmed.

C

In enjoining petitioner from ever considering the race of any applicant, however, the courts below failed to recognize that the State has a substantial interest that legitimately may be served by a properly devised admissions program involving the competitive consideration of race and ethnic origin. For this reason, so much of the California court's judgment as enjoins petitioner from any consideration of the race of any applicant must be reversed.

Opinion of Mr. Justice Brennan, Mr. Justice White, Mr. Justice Marshall, and Mr. Justice Blackmun, concurring in the judgment in part and dissenting in part:

The Court today, in reversing in part the judgment of the Supreme Court of California, affirms the constitutional power of Federal and State Governments to act affirmatively to achieve equal opportunity for all. The difficulty of the issue presented—whether government may use race-conscious programs to redress the continuing effects of past discrimination—and the mature consideration which each of our Brethren has brought to it have resulted in many opinions, no single one speaking for the Court. But this should not and must not mask the central meaning of today's opinions: Government may take race into account when it acts not to demean or insult any racial group, but to remedy disadvantages cast on minorities by past racial prejudice, at least when appropriate findings have been made by judicial, legislative, or administrative bodies with competence to act in this area.

The Chief Justice and our Brothers Stewart, Rehnquist, and Stevens, have concluded that Title VI of the Civil Rights Act of 1964, . . . as amended, . . . prohibits programs such as that at the Davis Medical School. On this statutory theory alone, they would hold that respondent Allan Bakke's rights have been violated and that he must, therefore, be admitted to the Medical School. Our Brother Powell, reaching the Constitution, concludes that, although race may be taken into account in university admissions, the particular special admissions program used by petitioner, which resulted in the exclusion of respondent Bakke, was not shown to be necessary to achieve petitioner's stated goals. Accordingly, these Members of the Court form a majority of five affirming the judgment of the Supreme Court of California insofar as it holds that respondent Bakke "is entitled to an order that he be admitted to the University." . . .

We agree with Mr. Justice Powell that, as applied to the case before us, Title VI goes no further in prohibiting the use of race than the Equal Protection Clause of the Fourteenth Amendment itself. We also agree that the effect of the California Supreme Court's affirmance of the judgment of the Superior Court of California would be to prohibit the University from establishing in the future affirmative action programs that take race into account. . . . Since we conclude that the affirmative admissions program at the Davis Medical School is constitutional, we would reverse the judgment below in all respects. Mr. Justice Powell agrees that some uses of race in university admissions are permissible and, therefore, he joins with us to make five votes reversing the judgment below insofar as it prohibits the University from establishing race-conscious programs in the future. . . .

II

. . . In our view, Title VI prohibits only those uses of racial criteria that would violate the Fourteenth Amendment if employed by a State or its agencies; it does not bar the preferential treatment of racial minorities as a means of remedying past societal discrimination to the extent that such action is consistent with the Fourteenth Amendment. The legislative history of Title VI, administrative regulations interpreting the statute, subsequent congressional and executive action, and the prior decisions of this Court compel this conclusion. None of these sources lends support to the proposition that Congress intended to bar all race-conscious efforts to extend the benefits of federally financed programs to minorities who have been historically excluded from the full benefits of American life. . . .

III

A

The assertion of human equality is closely associated with the proposition that differences in color or creed, birth or status, are neither significant nor relevant to the way in which persons should be treated. Nonetheless, the position that such factors must be "constitutionally an irrelevance" . . . summed up by the shorthand phrase "[o]ur Constitution is color-blind." *Plessy* v. *Ferguson* [1896] . . . has never been adopted by this Court as the proper meaning of the Equal Protection Clause. Indeed, we have expressly rejected this proposition on a number of occasions.

Our cases have always implied that an "overriding statutory purpose" . . . could be found that would justify racial classifications. . . .

We conclude, therefore, that racial classifications are not *per se* invalid under the Fourteenth Amendment. Accordingly, we turn to the problem of articulating what our role should be in reviewing state action that expressly classifies by race.

B

Respondent argues that racial classifications are always suspect and, consequently, that this Court should weigh the importance of the objectives served by Davis' special admissions program to see if they are compelling. . . .

Unquestionably we have held that a government practice or statute which restricts "fundamental rights" or which contains "suspect classifications" is to be subjected to "strict scrutiny" and can be justified only if it furthers a compelling government purpose and, even then, only if no less restrictive alternative is available. . . . But no fundamental right is involved here. . . . Nor do whites as a class have any of the "traditional indicia of suspectness: the class is not saddled with such disabilities, or subjected to such a history of purposeful unequal treatment, or relegated to such a position of political powerlessness as to command extraordinary protection from the majoritarian political process." . . .

On the other hand, the fact that this case does not fit neatly into our prior analytic framework for race cases does not mean that it should be analyzed by applying the very loose rational-basis standard of review that is the very least that is always applied in equal protection cases. " '[T]he mere recitation of a benign, compensatory purpose is not an automatic shield which protects against any inquiry into the actual purposes underlying a statutory scheme.' " . . . Instead, a number of considerations—developed in gender-discrimination cases but which carry even more force when applied to racial classifications—lead us to conclude that racial classifications designed to further remedial purposes " 'must serve important governmental objectives and must be substantially related to achievement of those objectives.'"...

First, race, like "gender-based classifications too often [has] been inexcusably utilized to stereotype and stigmatize politically powerless segments of society."... State programs designed ostensibly to ameliorate the effects of past racial discrimination obviously create the same hazard of stigma, since they may promote racial separatism and reinforce the views of those who believe that members of racial minorities are inherently incapable of succeeding on their own....

Second, race, like gender and illegitimacy... is an immutable characteristic which its possessors are powerless to escape or set aside. While a classification is not *per se* invalid because it divides classes on the basis of an immutable characteristic... it is nevertheless true that such divisions are contrary to our deep belief that "legal burdens should bear some relationship to individual responsibility or wrongdoing"... and that advancement sanctioned, sponsored, or approved by the State should ideally be based on individual merit or achievement, or at the least on factors within the control of an individual....

In sum, because of the significant risk that racial classification established for ostensibly benign purposes can be misused, causing effects not unlike those created by invidious classifications, it is inappropriate to inquire only whether there is any conceivable basis that might sustain such a classification. Instead, to justify such a classification an important and articulated purpose for its use must be shown. In addition, any statute must be stricken that stigmatizes any group or that singles out those least well represented in the political process to bear the brunt of a benign program. Thus, our review under the Fourteenth Amendment should be strict—not "'strict' in theory and fatal in fact," because it is stigma that causes fatality—but strict and searching nonetheless.

IV

Davis' articulated purpose of remedying the effects of past societal discrimination is, under our cases, sufficiently important to justify the use of race-conscious admissions programs where there is a sound basis for concluding that minority underrepresentation is substantial and chronic, and that the handicap of past discrimination is impeding access of minorities to the Medical School....

A

...If it was reasonable to conclude—as we hold that it was—that the failure of minorities to qualify for admission at Davis under regular procedures was due principally to the effects of past discrimination, then there is a reasonable likelihood that, but for pervasive racial discrimination, respondent would have failed to qualify for admission even in the absence of Davis' special admissions program.

Thus, our cases under Title VII of the Civil Rights Act have held that, in order to achieve minority participation in previously segregated areas of public life, Congress may require or authorize preferential treatment for those likely disadvantaged by societal racial discrimination. Such legislation has been sustained even without a requirement of findings of intentional racial discrimination by those required or authorized to accord preferential treatment, or a case-by-case determination that those to be benefited suffered from racial discrimination. These decisions compel the conclusion that States also may adopt race-conscious programs designed to overcome substantial, chronic minority underrepresentation where there is reason to believe that the evil addressed is a product of past racial discrimination. . . .

[Section B reviews the facts supporting the existence of discrimination and the underrepresentation of minorities in the Davis and other medical schools.]

C

The second prong of our test—whether the Davis program stigmatizes any discrete group or individual and whether race is reasonably used in light of the program's objectives—is clearly satisfied by the Davis program.

It is not even claimed that Davis' program in any way operates to stigmatize or single out any discrete and insular, or even any identifiable, nonminority group. Nor will harm comparable to that imposed upon racial minorities by exclusion or separation on grounds of race be the likely result of the program. It does not, for example, establish an exclusive preserve for minority students apart from and exclusive of whites. Rather, its purpose is to overcome the effects of segregation by bringing the races together. True, whites are excluded from participation in the special admissions program, but this fact only operates to reduce the number of whites to be admitted in the regular admissions program in order to permit admission of a reasonable percentage—less than their proportion of the California population—of otherwise under-represented qualified minority applicants.

Nor was Bakke in any sense stamped as inferior by the Medical School's rejection of him. Indeed, it is conceded by all that he satisfied those criteria regarded by the school as generally relevant to academic performance better than most of the minority members who were admitted. Moreover, there is absolutely no basis for concluding that Bakke's rejection as a result of Davis' use of racial preference will affect him throughout his life in the same way as the segregation of the Negro school children in *Brown I* would have affected them. Unlike discrimination against racial minorities, the use of racial preferences for remedial purposes does not inflict a pervasive injury upon individual whites in the sense that wherever they go or whatever they do there is a significant likelihood that they will be treated as second-class citizens because of their color. This distinction does not mean that the exclusion of a white resulting from the preferential use of race is not sufficiently serious to require justification; but it does mean that the injury inflicted by such a policy is not distinguishable from disadvantages caused by a wide range of government actions, none of which has ever been thought impermissible for that reason alone.

In addition, there is simply no evidence that the Davis program discriminates intentionally or unintentionally against any minority group which it purports to benefit. The program does not establish a quota in the invidious sense of a ceiling on the number of minority applicants to be admitted. Nor can the program reasonably be regarded as stigmatizing the program's beneficiaries or their race as inferior. The Davis program does not simply advance less qualified applicants; rather, it compensates applicants, who it is uncontested are fully qualified to study medicine, for educational disadvantages which it was reasonable to conclude were a product of state-fostered discrimination. Once admitted, these students must satisfy the same degree requirements as regularly admitted students; they are taught by the same faculty in the same classes; and their performance is evaluated by the same standards by which regularly admitted students are judged. Under these circumstances, their performance and degrees must be regarded equally with the regularly admitted students with whom they compete for standing. Since minority graduates cannot justifiably be regarded as less well qualified than nonminority graduates by virtue of the special admissions program, there is no reasonable basis to conclude that minority graduates at schools using such programs would be stigmatized as inferior by the existence of such programs.

D

We disagree with the lower courts' conclusion that the Davis program's use of race was unreasonable in light of its objectives. First, as petitioner argues, there are no practical means by which it could achieve its ends in the foreseeable future without the use of race-conscious measures. With respect to any factor (such as poverty or family educational background) that may be used as a substitute for race as an indicator of past discrimination, whites greatly outnumber racial minorities simply because whites make up a far larger percentage of the total population and therefore far outnumber minorities in absolute terms at every socioeconomic level. . . .

Second, the Davis admissions program does not simply equate minority status with disadvantage. Rather, Davis considers on an individual basis each applicant's personal history to determine whether he or she has likely been disadvantaged by racial discrimination. The record makes clear that only minority applicants likely to have been isolated from the mainstream of American life are considered in the special program;

other minority applicants are eligible only through the regular admissions program. . . .

V

Accordingly, we would reverse the judgment of the Supreme Court of California holding the Medical School's special admissions program unconstitutional and directing respondent's admission, as well as that portion of the judgment enjoining the Medical School from according any consideration to race in the admissions process.

Mr. Justice Marshall wrote a separate opinion.
Mr. Justice Blackmun wrote a separate opinion.
Mr. Justice Stevens, with whom the Chief Justice, Mr. Justice Stewart, and Mr. Justice Rehnquist join, concurring in the judgment in part and dissenting in part:

Both petitioner and respondent have asked us to determine the legality of the University's admissions program by reference to the Constitution. Our settled practice, however, is to avoid the decision of a constitutional issue if a case can be fairly decided on a statutory ground. "If there is one doctrine more deeply rooted than any other in the process of constitutional adjudication, it is that we ought not to pass on questions of constitutionality . . . unless such adjudication is unavoidable." . . . The more important the issue, the more force there is to this doctrine. In this case, we are presented with a constitutional question of undoubted and unusual importance. Since, however, a dispositive statutory claim was raised at the very inception of this case, and squarely decided in the portion of the trial court judgment affirmed by the California Supreme Court, it is our plain duty to confront it. Only if petitioner should prevail on the statutory issue would it be necessary to decide whether the University's admissions program violated the Equal Protection Clause of the Fourteenth Amendment.

Section 601 of the Civil Rights Act of 1964 . . . provides:

No person in the United States shall, on the ground of race, color, or national origin, be excluded from participation in, be denied the benefits of, or be subjected to discrimination under any program or activity receiving Federal financial assistance.

The University, through its special admissions policy, excluded Bakke from participation in its program of medical education because of his race. The University also acknowledges that it was, and still is, receiving federal financial assistance. The plain language of the statute therefore requires affirmance of the judgment below. A different result cannot be justified unless that language misstates the actual intent of the Congress that enacted the statute or the statute is not enforceable in a private action. Neither conclusion is warranted. . . .

. . . [I]t seems clear that the proponents of Title VI assumed that the Constitution itself required a colorblind standard on the part of government, but that does not mean that the legislation only codifies an existing constitutional prohibition. The statutory prohibition against discrimination in federally funded projects contained in § 601 is more than a simple paraphrasing of what the Fifth or Fourteenth Amendment would require. . . .

In short, nothing in the legislative history justifies the conclusion that the broad language of § 601 should not be given its natural meaning. We are dealing with a distinct statutory prohibition, enacted at a particular time with particular concerns in mind; neither its language nor any prior interpretation suggests that its place in the Civil Rights Act, won after long debate, is simply that of a constitutional appendage. In unmistakable terms the Act prohibits the exclusion of individuals from federally funded programs because of their race. As succinctly phrased during the Senate debate, under Title VI it is not "permissible to say 'yes' to one person; but to say 'no' to another person, only because of the color of his skin." . . .

The University's special admissions program violated Title VI of the Civil Rights Act of 1964 by excluding Bakke from the Medical School because of his race. It is therefore our duty to affirm the judgment ordering Bakke admitted to the University.

Accordingly, I concur in the Court's judgment insofar as it affirms the judgment of the Supreme Court of California. To the extent that it purports to do anything else, I respectfully dissent.

☐   How do the standards of judicial scrutiny differ in the Powell and Brennan opinions? Justice Powell wrote, "Racial and ethnic distinctions of any sort are inherently suspect and thus call for the most exacting judicial examination." Applying strict judicial scrutiny, Powell found no compelling justification for the use of racial quotas by the Davis Medical School. Powell reasoned that "The purpose of helping certain groups whom the faculty of the Davis Medical School perceived as victims of 'societal discrimination' does not justify a classification that imposes disadvantages upon persons like respondent [Bakke], who bear no responsibility for whatever harm the beneficiaries of the special admissions program are thought to have suffered." While Powell held that racial quotas are banned, he ruled that race may be taken into account in admissions programs because "the state has a substantial [i.e., compelling] interest that legitimately may be served by a properly devised admissions program involving the competitive consideration of race and ethnic origin."

The dissenting opinion of Justice Brennan supported the use of racial quotas in the Davis admissions program. Underlying Brennan's dissenting opinion was the finding that the classification under review was not "suspect," nor did it affect fundamental rights; therefore, strict judicial scrutiny, under which a compelling state interest has to be demonstrated to uphold the classification, was not required. Justice Brennan and his fellow dissenters used an intermediate standard of judicial scrutiny, which required more than the mere demonstration of a rational relationship between the classification and the goals sought but less than the demonstration of a compelling state interest to uphold the classification. The intermediate standard announced by Justice Brennan was that the classification "must serve important governmental objectives and be substantially related to achievement of those objectives." To uphold a racial classification, stated Brennan, "an important and articulated purpose for its use must be shown. In addition, any statute must be stricken that stigmatizes any group or that singles out those least well represented in the political process to bear the brunt of a benign program." Brennan concluded that the court's review should be "strict," but not at the level of strict judicial scrutiny, which, because it requires the demonstration of compelling state interests, is always fatal to the program under review.

☐ Affirmative action continued to be a major political issue after the Bakke decision. While the use of quotas was banned, race and gender considerations could still be taken into account in school admissions and employment programs. The push for affirmative action that began with President Lyndon B. Johnson, who issued an executive order requiring it for all government contractors and institutions receiving federal aid, continued unabated for over a decade, even during the Republican administrations of Nixon and Ford. However, President Ronald Reagan viewed affirmative action with suspicion, more as an undesirable governmental interference in private affairs than as a necessary policy to remedy the effects of past discrimination. Under Reagan affirmative action was muted, and the Justice Department even intervened in some cases on the side of plaintiffs challenging affirmative action programs. Opposition to affirmative action was not simply a conservative position as many liberals also came to feel that the enforcement of affirmative action, which benefited groups, denied individuals the right to be judged on their merits. However, the Supreme Court rejected blanket attacks on affirmative action, holding in several key cases in 1986 that race-conscious practices and even quotas could be used in employment and promotion to remedy the effects of past discrimination.[1]

---

[1]*Firefighters* v. *Cleveland* and *Sheet Metal Workers* v. *Equal Employment Opportunity Commission,* decided July 2, 1986.

PART TWO

Political Parties, Electoral Behavior, and Interest Groups

CHAPTER 4

Political Parties
and the Electorate

The political process involves the sources, distribution, and use of power in the state. All the institutions and processes of government relate to this area. The role of political parties and the electoral system in determining and controlling political power is examined in this chapter.

Constitutional Background

Political parties and interest groups have developed outside of the original constitutional framework to channel political power in the community, and for this reason they deserve special consideration from students of American government. The Constitution was designed to structure power relationships in such a way that the arbitrary exercise of political power by any one group or individual would be prevented. One important concept held by the framers of the Constitution was that faction, i.e., parties and interest groups, is inherently dangerous to political freedom and stable government. This is evident from *Federalist 10*.

20

James Madison

FEDERALIST 10

Among the numerous advantages promised by a well constructed Union, none deserves to be more accurately developed than its tendency to break and control the violence of faction. The friend of popular governments never finds himself so much alarmed for their character and fate as when he contemplates their propensity to this dangerous vice. He will not fail, therefore, to set a due value on any plan which, without violating the principles to which he is attached, provides a proper cure for it. The instability, injustice, and confusion, introduced into the public councils, have, in truth been the mortal diseases under which popular governments have everywhere perished; as they continue to be the favorite and fruitful topics from which the adversaries to liberty derive their most specious declamations. The valuable improvements made by the American constitutions on the popular models, both ancient and modern, cannot certainly be too much admired; but it would be an unwarrantable partiality, to contend that they have as effectually obviated the danger on this side, as was wished and expected. Complaints are everywhere heard from our most considerate and virtuous citizens, equally the friends of public and private faith, and of public and personal liberty, that our governments are too unstable; that the public good is disregarded in the conflicts of rival parties; and that measures are too often decided, not according to the rules of justice, and the rights of the minor party, but by the superior force of an interested and overbearing majority. However anxiously we may wish that these complaints had no foundation, the evidence of known facts will not permit us to deny that they are in some degree true. It will be found, indeed, on a candid review of our situation, that some of the distresses under which we labor, have been erroneously charged on the operation of our governments; but it will be found, at the same time, that other causes will not alone account for many of our heaviest misfortunes; and, particularly, for the prevailing and increasing distrust of public engagements, and alarm for private rights, which are echoed from one end of the continent to the other. These must be chiefly, if not wholly, effects of the unsteadiness and injustice, with which a factious spirit has tainted our public administrations.

By a faction, I understand a number of citizens, whether amounting to a majority or minority of the whole, who are united and actuated by some common impulse of passion, or of interest, adverse to the rights of other citizens, or to the permanent and aggregate interest of the community.

There are two methods of curing the mischiefs of faction: The one, by removing its causes; the other, by controlling its effects.

There are again two methods of removing the causes of faction: the one, by destroying the liberty which is essential to its existence; the other, by giving to every citizen the same opinions, the same passions, and the same interests.

It could never be more truly said, than of the first remedy, that it was worse than the disease. Liberty is to faction what air is to fire, an aliment, without which it instantly expires. But it could not be a less folly to abolish liberty, which is essential to political life because it nourishes faction, than it would be to wish the annihilation of air, which is essential to animal life, because it imparts to fire its destructive agency.

The second expedient is as impracticable, as the first would be unwise. As long as the reason of man continues fallible, and he is at liberty to exercise it, different opinions will be formed. As long as the connection subsists between his reason and his self-love, his opinions and his passions will have a reciprocal influence on each other; and the former will be objects to which the latter will attach themselves. The diversity in the faculties of men, from which the rights of property originate, is not less an insuperable obstacle to a uniformity of interests. The protection of those faculties is the first object of government. From the protection of different and unequal faculties of acquiring property, the possession of different degrees and kinds of property immediately results; and from the influence of these on the sentiments and views of the respective proprietors, ensues a division of the society into different interests and parties.

The latent causes of faction are thus sown in the nature of man; and we see them everywhere brought into different degrees of activity, according to the different circumstances of civil society. A zeal for different opinions concerning religion, concerning government, and many other points, as well of speculation as of practice; an attachment to different leaders, ambitiously contending for preeminence and power; or to persons of other descriptions, whose fortunes have been interesting to the human passions, have, in turn, divided mankind into parties, inflamed them with mutual animosity, and rendered them much more disposed to vex and oppress each other, than to cooperate for their common good. So strong is this propensity of mankind, to fall into mutual animosities, that where no substantial occasion presents itself, the most frivolous and fanciful distinctions have been sufficient to kindle their unfriendly passions, and excite their most violent conflicts. But the most common and durable source of factions has been the various and unequal distribution of property. Those who hold, and those who are without property, have even formed distinct interests in society. Those who are creditors, and those who are debtors, fall under a like discrimination. A landed interest, a manufacturing interest, a mercantile interest, a moneyed interest, with many lesser interests, grow up of necessity in civilized

nations, and divide them into different classes, actuated by different sentiments and views. The regulation of these various and interfering interests
forms the principle task of modern legislation, and involves the spirit of
party and faction in the necessary and ordinary operations of government.

No man is allowed to be a judge in his own cause; because his interest
will certainly bias his judgment, and, not improbably, corrupt his integrity.
With equal, nay, with greater reason, a body of men are unfit to be both
judges and parties at the same time; yet what are many of the most
important acts of legislation, but so many judicial determinations, not
indeed concerning the rights of single persons, but concerning the rights of
large bodies of citizens? And what are the different classes of legislators,
but advocates and parties to the cause which they determine? Is a law
proposed concerning private debts? It is a question to which the creditors
are parties on one side, and the debtors on the other. Justice ought to hold
the balance between them. Yet the parties are, and must be, themselves the
judges; and the most numerous party, or, in other words, the most powerful
faction, must be expected to prevail. Shall domestic manufactures be
encouraged, and in what degree, by restrictions on foreign manufactures?
are questions which would be differently decided by the landed and the
manufacturing classes; and probably by neither with a sole regard to justice
and the public good. . . .

It is in vain to say, that enlightened statesmen will be able to adjust
these clashing interests, and render them all subservient to the public good.
Enlightened statesmen will not always be at the helm; nor, in many cases,
can such an adjustment be made at all, without taking into view indirect
and remote considerations, which will rarely prevail over the immediate
interest which one party may find in disregarding the rights of another, or
the good of the whole.

The inference to which we are brought is, that the *causes* of faction
cannot be removed; and that relief is only to be sought in the means of
controlling its *effects*.

If a faction consists of less than a majority, relief is supplied by the
republican principle, which enables the majority to defeat its sinister views,
by regular vote. It may clog the administration, it may convulse the society;
but it will be unable to execute and mask its violence under the forms of
the constitution. When a majority is included in a faction, the form of
popular government, on the other hand, enables it to sacrifice to its ruling
passion or interest, both the public good and the rights of other citizens. To
secure the public good, and private rights, against the danger of such a
faction, and at the same time to preserve the spirit and the form of popular
government, is then the great object to which our inquiries are directed.
Let me add, that it is the great desideratum, by which alone this form of
government can be rescued from the opprobrium under which it has so
long labored, and be recommended to the esteem and adoption of mankind.

By what means is this object attainable? Evidently by one of two only. Either the existence of the same passion or interest in a majority, at the same time must be prevented; or the majority, having such coexistent passion or interest, must be rendered, by their number and local situation, unable to concert and carry into effect schemes of oppression. If the impulse and the opportunity be suffered to coincide, we well know, that neither moral nor religious motives can be relied on as an adequate control. They are not found to be such on the injustice and violence of individuals, and lose their efficacy in proportion to the number combined together; that is, in proportion as their efficacy becomes needful.

From this view of the subject, it may be concluded, that a pure democracy, by which I mean a society consisting of a small number of citizens, who assemble and administer the government in person, can admit of no cure from the mischiefs of faction. A common passion or interest will, in almost every case, be felt by a majority of the whole; a communication and concert, results from the form of government itself; and there is nothing to check the inducements to sacrifice the weaker party, or an obnoxious individual. Hence it is, that such democracies have ever been spectacles of turbulence and contention; have ever been found incompatible with personal security, or the rights of property; and have, in general, been as short in their lives, as they have been violent in their deaths. Theoretic politicians, who have patronized this species of government, have erroneously supposed that by reducing mankind to a perfect equality in their political rights, they would, at the same time, be perfectly equalized and assimilated in their possessions, their opinions, and their passions.

A republic, by which I mean a government in which the scheme of representation takes place, opens a different prospect, and promises the cure for which we are seeking. Let us examine the points in which it varies from pure democracy, and we shall comprehend both the nature of the cure and the efficacy which it must derive from the union.

The two great points of difference, between a democracy and a republic, are, first, the delegation of the government, in the latter, to a small number of citizens elected by the rest; secondly, the greater number of citizens, and greater sphere of country, over which the latter may be extended.

The effect of the first difference is on the one hand, to refine and enlarge the public views, by passing them through the medium of a chosen body of citizens, whose wisdom may best discern the true interest in their country, and whose patriotism and love of justice, will be least likely to sacrifice it to temporary or partial considerations. Under such a regulation, it may well happen, that the public voice, pronounced by the representatives of the people, will be more consonant to the public good, than if pronounced by the people themselves, convened for the purpose. On the other hand, the effect may be inverted. Men of factious tempers, of local prejudices, or of sinister designs, may by intrigue, by corruption, or by other means, first obtain the suffrages, and then betray the interest of the people. The question resulting is, whether small or extensive republics are most favorable to the election of proper guardians of the public weal; and it is clearly decided in favor of the latter by two obvious considerations.

In the first place, it is to be remarked, that however small the republic may be, the representatives must be raised to a certain number, in order to guard against the cabals of a few; and that however large it may be, they must be limited to a certain number, in order to guard against the confusion of a multitude. Hence, the number of representatives in the two cases not being in proportion to that of the constituents, and being proportionally greatest in the small republic, it follows that if the proportion of fit characters be not less in the large than in the small republic, the former will present a greater option, and consequently a greater probability of a fit choice.

In the next place, as each representative will be chosen by a greater number of citizens in the large than in the small republic, it will be more difficult for unworthy candidates to practice with success the vicious arts, by which elections are too often carried; and the suffrages of the people being more free, will be more likely to center in men who possess the most attractive merit, and the most diffusive and established characters. . . .

The other point of difference is, the greater number of citizens, and extent of territory, which may be brought within the compass of republican, than of democratic government; and it is this circumstance principally which renders factious combinations less to be dreaded in the former, than in the latter. The smaller the society, the fewer probably will be the distinct parties and interests composing it; the fewer the distinct parties and interests, the more frequently will a majority be found of the same party; and the smaller the number of individuals composing a majority, and the smaller the compass within which they are placed, the more easily they will concert and execute their plans of oppression. Extend the sphere, and you take in a greater variety of parties and interests; you make it less probable that a majority of the whole will have a common motive to invade the rights of other citizens; or if such a common motive exists, it will be more difficult for all who feel it to discover their own strength, and to act in unison with each other. . . .

Hence, it clearly appears, that the same advantage, which a republic has over a democracy, in controlling the effects of faction, is enjoyed by a large over a small republic—is enjoyed by the union over the states composing it. Does this advantage consist in the substitution of representatives, whose enlightened views and virtuous sentiments render them superior to local prejudices, and to schemes of injustice? It will not be denied, that the representation of the union will be most likely to possess these requisite endowments. Does it consist in the greater security afforded by a greater variety of parties, against the event of any one party being able to outnumber and oppress the rest? In an equal degree does the increased variety of parties, comprised within the union, increase this security? Does it, in fine, consist in the greater obstacles opposed to the concert and accomplishment of the secret wishes of an unjust and interested majority? Here, again, the extent of the union gives it the most palpable advantage.

The influence of factious leaders may kindle a flame within their particular states, but will be unable to spread a general conflagration through the other states; a religious sect may degenerate into a political faction in a part of the confederacy; but the variety of sects dispersed over the entire face of it, must secure the national councils against any danger from that source; a rage for paper money, for an abolition of debts, for an equal division of property, or for any other improper or wicked project, will be less apt to pervade the whole body of the union, than a particular member of it; in the same proportion as such a malady is more likely to taint a particular county or district, than an entire state.

In the extent and proper structure of the union, therefore, we behold a republican remedy for the diseases most incident to republican government. And according to the degree of pleasure and pride we feel in being republicans, ought to be our zeal in cherishing the spirit, and supporting the character of Federalists.

☐   The following selection is taken from E. E. Schattschneider's classic treatise, *Party Government*. In this material he examines both the implications of *Federalist 10* and counter-arguments to the propositions stated by Madison, with regard to political parties and interest groups.

PARTY GOVERNMENT

The Convention at Philadelphia produced a constitution with a dual attitude: it was proparty in one sense and antiparty in another. The authors of the Constitution refused to suppress the parties by destroying the fundamental liberties in which parties originate. They or their immediate successors accepted amendments that guaranteed civil rights and thus established a system of party tolerance, i.e., the right to agitate and to organize. This is the proparty aspect of the system. On the other hand, the authors of the Constitution set up an elaborate division and balance of powers within an intricate governmental structure designed to make parties ineffective. It was hoped that the parties would lose and exhaust themselves in futile attempts to fight their way through the labyrinthine framework of the government, much as an attacking army is expected to spend itself against the defensive works of a fortress. This is the antiparty part of the constitutional scheme. To quote Madison, the "great object" of the Constitution was "to preserve the public good and private rights against the danger of such a faction [party] and at the same time to preserve the spirit and form of popular government."

In Madison's mind the difference between an autocracy and a free republic seems to have been largely a matter of the precise point at which parties are stopped by the government. In an autocracy parties are controlled (suppressed) at the source; in a republic parties are tolerated but are invited to strangle themselves in the machinery of government. The result in either case is much the same, sooner or later the government checks the parties but *never do the parties control the government.* Madison was perfectly definite and unmistakable in his disapproval of party government as distinguished from party tolerance. In the opinion of Madison, parties were intrinsically bad, and the sole issue for discussion was the means by which bad parties might be prevented from becoming dangerous. What never seems to have occurred to the authors of the Constitution, however, is that parties might be *used* as beneficent instruments of popular government. It is at this point that the distinction between the modern and the antique attitude is made.

The offspring of this combination of ideas was a constitutional system having conflicting tendencies. The Constitution made the rise of parties inevitable yet was incompatible with party government. This scheme, in spite of its subtlety, involved a miscalculation. Political parties refused to be content

---

with the role assigned to them. The vigor and enterprise of the parties have therefore made American political history the story of the unhappy marriage of the parties and the Constitution, a remarkable variation of the case of the irresistible force and the immovable object, which in this instance have been compelled to live together in a permanent partnership . . .

THE RAW MATERIALS OF POLITICS

People who write about interests sometimes seem to assume that all interests are special and exclusive, setting up as a result of this assumption a dichotomy in which the interests on the one side are perpetually opposed to the public welfare on the other side. But there are common interests as well as special interests, and common interests resemble special interests in that they are apt to influence political behavior. The raw materials of politics are not all antisocial. Alongside of Madison's statement that differences in wealth are the most durable causes of faction there should be placed a corollary that the common possessions of the people are the most durable cause of unity. To assume that people have merely conflicting interests and nothing else is to invent a political nightmare that has only a superficial relation to reality. The body of agreement underlying the conflicts of a modern society ought to be sufficient to sustain the social order provided only that the common interests supporting this unity are mobilized. Moreover, not all differences of interest are durable causes of conflict. Nothing is apt to be more perishable than a political issue. In the democratic process, the nation moves from controversy to agreement to forgetfulness; politics is not a futile exercise like football, forever played back and forth over the same ground. The government creates and destroys interests at every turn.

There are, in addition, powerful factors inhibiting the unlimited pursuit of special aims by any organized minority. To assume that minorities will stop at nothing to get what they want is to postulate a degree of unanimity and concentration within these groups that does not often exist in real life. If every individual were capable of having only one interest to the exclusion of all others, it might be possible to form dangerous unions of monomaniacs who would go to great extremes to attain their objectives. In fact, however, people have many interests leading to a dispersion of drives certain to destroy some of the unanimity and concentration of any group. How many interests can an individual have? Enough to make it extremely unlikely that any two individuals will have the same combination of interests. Anyone who has ever tried to promote an association of people having some special interest in common will realize, first, that there are marked differences of enthusiasm within the group and, second, that interests compete with interests for the attention and enthusiasm of every individual. Every organized special interest consists of a group of busy, distracted individuals held together by the efforts of a handful of specialists and enthusiasts who sacrifice other matters in order to concentrate on one. The notion of resolute and unanimous minorities on the point of violence is largely the invention of paid lobbyists and press agents.

The result of the fact that every individual is torn by the diversity of his own interests, the fact that he is a member of many groups, is *the law of the imperfect political mobilization of interests.* That is, it has never been possible to mobilize any interest 100 percent. . . .

It is only another way of saying the same thing to state that conflicts of interests are not cumulative. If it were true that the dividing line in every conflict (or in all major conflicts) split the community identically in each case so that individuals who are opposed on one issue would be opposed to each other on all other issues also, while individuals who joined hands on one occasion would find themselves on the same side on all issues, always opposed to the same combination of antagonists, the cleavage created by the cumulative effect of these divisions would be fatal. But actually conflicts are not cumulative in this way. In real life the divisions are not so clearly marked, and the alignment of people according to interests requires an enormous shuffling back and forth from one side to the other, tending to dissipate the tensions created.

In view of the fact, therefore, (1) that there are many interests, including a great body of common interests, (2) that the government pursues a multiplicity of policies and creates and destroys interests in the process, (3) that each individual is capable of having many interests, (4) that interests cannot be mobilized perfectly, and (5) that conflicts among interests are not cumulative, it seems reasonable to suppose that the government is not the captive of blind forces from which there is no escape. There is nothing wrong about the raw materials of politics.

Functions and Types of Elections

☐ Most people transmit their political desires to government through elections. Elections are a critical part of the democratic process, and the existence of *free* elections is a major difference between democracies and totalitarian or authoritarian forms of government. Because elections reflect popular attitudes toward governmental parties, policies, and personalities, it is useful to attempt to classify different types of elections on the basis of changes and trends that take place within the electorate. Every election is not the same. For example, the election of 1932 with the resulting Democratic landslide was profoundly different from the election of 1960, in which Kennedy won by less than 1 percent of the popular vote.

Members of the Survey Research Center at the University of Michigan, as well as V. O. Key, Jr., have developed a typology of elections that is useful in analyzing the electoral system. The most prevalent type of election can be classified as a "maintaining election," "one in which the pattern of partisan attachments prevailing in the preceding period persists and is the primary influence on the forces governing the vote."[1] Most elections fall into the maintaining category, a fact significant for the political system because such elections result in political continuity and reflect a lack of serious upheavals within the electorate and government. Maintaining elections result in the continuation of the majority political party.

At certain times in American history, what V. O. Key, Jr., has called "critical elections" take place. He discusses this type of election, which results in permanent realignment of the electorate and reflects basic changes in political attitudes.

Apart from maintaining and critical elections, a third type, in which only temporary shifts take place within the electorate, occurs, which can be called "deviating elections." For example, the Eisenhower victories of 1952 and 1956 were deviating elections for several reasons, including the personality of Eisenhower and the fact that voters could register their choice for President without changing their basic partisan loyalties at Congressional and state levels. Deviating elections, with reference to the office of President, are probable when popular figures are running for the office.

In "reinstating elections," a final category that can be added to a typology of elections, there is a return to normal voting patterns. Reinstating elections take place after deviating elections as a result of the demise of the temporary forces that caused the transitory shift in partisan choice. The election of 1960, in which most of the Democratic majority in the electorate returned to the fold and voted for John F. Kennedy,[2] has been classified as a reinstating election.

---

[1]Angus Campbell, Philip E. Converse, Warren E. Miller, and Donald E. Stokes, *The American Voter* (New York: John Wiley & Sons, 1960), Chap. 19.

[2]See Philip E. Converse, Angus Campbell, Warren E. Miller, and Donald E. Stokes, "Stability and Change in 1960: A Reinstating Election," *The American Political Science Review*, vol. 55 (June 1961), pp. 269–80.

22
V. O. Key, Jr.

A THEORY OF CRITICAL ELECTIONS

Perhaps the basic differentiating characteristic of democratic order consists in the expression of effective choice by the mass of the people in
elections. The electorage occupies, at least in the mystique of such orders,
the position of the principal organ of governance; it acts through elections.
An election itself is a formal act of collective decision that occurs in a
stream of connected antecedent and subsequent behavior. Among democratic orders elections, so broadly defined, differ enormously in their
nature, their meaning, and their consequences. Even within a single nation
the reality of election differs greatly from time to time. A systematic
comparative approach, with a focus on variations in the nature of elections
would doubtless be fruitful in advancing the understanding of the democratic governing process. In behavior antecedent to voting, elections differ
in the proportions of the electorate psychologically involved, in the intensity of attitudes associated with campaign cleavages, in the nature of
expectations about the consequences of the voting, in the impact of objective events relevant to individual political choice, in individual sense of
effective connection with community decision, and in other ways. These
and other antecedent variations affect the act of voting itself as well as
subsequent behavior. An understanding of elections and, in turn, of the
democratic process as a whole must rest partially on broad differentiations
of the complexes of behavior that we call elections.

While this is not the occasion to develop a comprehensive typology of
elections, the foregoing remarks provide an orientation for an attempt
to formulate a concept of one type of election—based on American
experience—which might be built into a more general theory of elections.
Even the most fleeting inspection of American elections suggests the
existence of a category of elections in which voters are, at least from
impressionistic evidence, unusually deeply concerned, in which the extent
of electoral involvement is relatively quite high, and in which the decisive
results of the voting reveal a sharp alteration of the preexisting cleavage
within the electorate. Moreover, and perhaps this is the truly differentiating
characteristic of this sort of election, the realignment made manifest in the
voting in such elections seems to persist for several succeeding elections.
All these characteristics cumulate to the conception of an election type in

From V. O. Key, Jr., "A Theory of Critical Elections," *The Journal of Politics,* 17:1
(February 1955). Reprinted by permission.

which the depth and intensity of electoral involvement are high, in which more or less profound readjustments occur in the relations of power within the community, and in which new and durable electoral groupings are formed. These comments suppose, of course, the existence of other types of complexes of behavior centering about formal elections, the systematic isolation and identification of which, fortunately, are not essential for the present discussion.

I

The presidential election of 1928 in the New England states provides a specific case of the type of critical election that has been described in general terms. In that year Alfred E. Smith, the Democratic presidential candidate, made gains in all the New England states. The rise in Democratic strength was especially notable in Massachusetts and Rhode Island. When one probes below the surface of the gross election figures it becomes apparent that a sharp and durable realignment also occurred within the electorate, a fact reflective of the activation by the Democratic candidate of low-income, Catholic, urban voters of recent immigrant stock. In New England, at least, the Roosevelt revolution of 1932 was in large measure an Al Smith revolution of 1928, a characterization less applicable to the remainder of the country.

The intensity and extent of electoral concern before the voting of 1928 can only be surmised, but the durability of the realignment formed at the election can be determined by simple analyses of election statistics. An illustration of the new division thrust through the electorate by the campaign of 1928 is provided by the graphs in Figure A, which show the Democratic percentages of the presidential vote from 1916 through 1952 for the city of Somerville and the town of Ashfield in Massachusetts. Somerville, adjacent to Boston, had a population in 1930 of 104,000 of which 28 percent was foreign born and 41 percent was of foreign-born or mixed parentage. Roman Catholics constituted a large proportion of its relatively low-income population. Ashfield, a farming community in western Massachusetts with a 1930 population of 860, was predominantly native born (8.6 percent foreign born), chiefly rural-farm (66 percent), and principally Protestant.

The impressiveness of the differential impact of the election of 1928 on Somerville and Ashfield may be read from the graphs in Figure A. From 1920 the Democratic percentage in Somerville ascended steeply while the Democrats in Ashfield, few in 1920, became even less numerous in 1928. Inspection of graphs also suggests that the great reshuffling of voters that occurred in 1928 was perhaps the final and decisive stage in a process that had been under way for some time. That antecedent process involved a relatively heavy support in 1924 for La Follette in those towns in which

Smith was subsequently to find special favor. Hence, in Figure A, as in all the other charts, the 1924 figure is the percentage of the total accounted for by the votes of both the Democratic and Progressive candidates rather than the Democratic percentage of the two-party vote. This usage conveys a minimum impression of the size of the 1924-1928 Democratic gain but probably depicts the nature of the 1920-1928 trend.

For present purposes, the voting behavior of the two communities shown in Figure A after 1928 is of central relevance. The differences established between them in 1928 persisted even through 1952, although the two series fluctuated slightly in response to the particular influences of individual campaigns. The nature of the process of maintenance of the cleavage is, of course, not manifest from these data. Conceivably the impress of the events of 1928 on individual attitudes and loyalties formed partisan attachments of lasting nature. Yet it is doubtful that the new crystallization of 1928 projected itself through a quarter of a century solely from the momentum given it by such factors. More probably subsequent events operated to reenforce and to maintain the 1928 cleavage. Whatever the mechanism of its maintenance, the durability of the realignment is impressive.

Somerville and Ashfield may be regarded more or less as samples of major population groups within the electorate of Massachusetts. Since no sample survey data are available for 1928, about the only analysis feasible is inspection of election returns for geographic units contrasting in their population composition. Lest it be supposed, however, that the good citizens of Somerville and Ashfield were aberrants simply unlike the remainder of the people of the Commonwealth, examination of a large number of towns and cities is in order. In the interest of both compression and comprehensibility, a mass of data is telescoped into Figure B. The graphs in that figure compare over the period 1916-1952 the voting behavior of the 29 Massachusetts towns and cities having the sharpest Democratic increases, 1920-1928, with that of the 30 towns and cities having the most marked Democratic loss, 1920-1928. In other words, the figure averages out a great many Ashfields and Somervilles. The data of Figure B confirm the expectation that the pattern exhibited by the pair of voting units in Figure A represented only a single case of a much more general phenomenon. Yet by virtue of the coverage of the data in the figure, one gains a stronger impression of the difference in the character of the election of 1928 and the other elections recorded there. The cleavage confirmed by the 1928 returns persisted. At subsequent elections the voters shifted to and fro within the outlines of the broad division fixed in 1928.

Examination of the characteristics of the two groups of cities and towns of Figure B—those with the most marked Democratic gains, 1920-1928, and those with the widest movement in the opposite direction—reveals the expected sorts of differences. Urban, industrial, foreign-born, Catholic

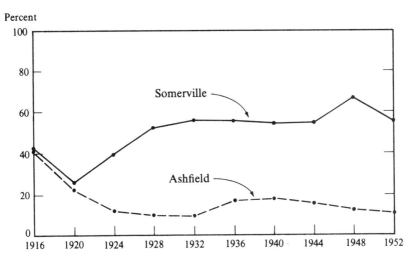

Figure A   Democratic Percentages of Major-Party Presidential Vote, Somerville and Ashfield, Massachusetts, 1916-1952

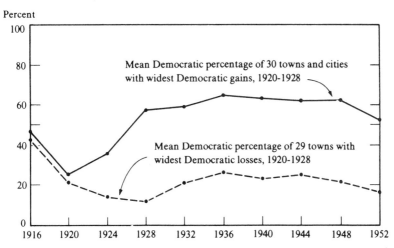

Figure B   Persistence of Electoral Cleavage of 1928 in Massachusetts: Mean Democratic Percentage of Presidential Vote in Towns with Sharpest Democratic Gains, 1920-1928, and in Towns of Widest Democratic Losses, 1920-1928

areas made up the bulk of the first group of towns, although an occasional rural Catholic community increased its Democratic vote markedly. The towns with a contrary movement tended to be rural, Protestant, native born. The new Democratic vote correlated quite closely with a 1930 vote on state enforcement of the national prohibition law.

Melancholy experience with the eccentricities of data, be they quantitative or otherwise, suggests the prudence of a check on the interpretation of 1928. Would the same method applied to any other election yield a similar result, i.e., the appearance of a more or less durable realignment? Perhaps there can be no doubt that the impact of the events of any election on many individuals forms lasting party loyalties; yet not often is the number so affected so great as to create sharp realignment. On the other hand, some elections are characterized by a large-scale transfer of party affection that is quite short-term, a different sort of phenomenon from that which occurs in elections marked by broad and durable shifts in party strength. The difference is illustrated by the data on the election of 1932 in New Hampshire in Figure C. The voting records of the twenty-five towns with the widest Democratic gains from 1928 to 1932 are there traced from 1916 to 1952. Observe that Democratic strength in these towns shot up in 1932 but fairly quickly resumed about the same position in relation to other towns that it had occupied in 1928. It is also evident from the graph that this group of towns had on the whole been especially strongly repelled by the Democratic appeal of 1928. Probably the depression drove an appreciable number of hardened Republicans of these towns to vote for a change in 1932, but they gradually found their way back to the party of their fathers. In any case, the figure reflects a type of behavior differing markedly from that of 1928. To the extent that 1932 resembled 1928 in the recrystallization of party lines, the proportions of new Democrats did not differ significantly among the groups of towns examined. In fact, what probably happened to a considerable extent in New England was that the 1928 election broke the electorate into two new groups that would have been formed in 1932 had there been no realignment in 1928.

The Massachusetts material has served both to explain the method of analysis and to present the case of a single state. Examinations of the election of 1928 in other New England states indicate that in each a pattern prevailed similar to that of Massachusetts. The total effect of the realignment differed, of course, from state to state. In Massachusetts and Rhode Island the number of people affected by the upheaval of 1928 was sufficient to form a new majority coalition. In Maine, New Hampshire, and Vermont the same sort of reshuffling of electors occurred, but the proportions affected were not sufficient to overturn the Republican combination, although the basis was laid in Maine and New Hampshire for later limited Democratic success. To underpin these remarks the materials on Connecticut, Maine, New Hampshire, and Rhode Island are presented in Figure D. The data on Vermont, excluded for lack of space, form a pattern similar to that emerging from the analysis of the other states.

In the interpretation of all these 1928 analyses certain limitations of the technique need to be kept in mind. The data and the technique most

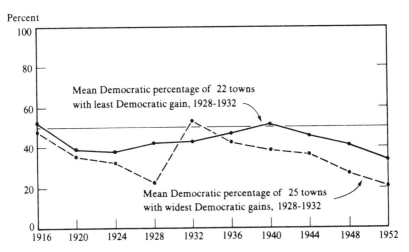

Figure C Impact of Election of 1932 in New Hampshire: Mean Democratic Percentage of Presidential Vote of Towns with Sharpest Democratic Gain, 1928-1932, Compared with Mean Vote of Towns at Opposite Extreme of 1928-1932 Change

clearly reveal a shift when voters of different areas move in opposite directions. From 1928 to 1936 apparently a good deal of Democratic growth occurred in virtually all geographic units, a shift not shown up sharply by the technique. Hence, the discussion may fail adequately to indicate the place of 1928 as the crucial stage in a process of electoral change that began before and concluded after that year.

II

One of the difficulties with an ideal type is that no single actual case fits exactly its specifications. Moreover, in any system of categorization the greater the number of differentiating criteria for classes, the more nearly one tends to create a separate class for each instance. If taxonomic systems are to be of analytical utility, they must almost inevitably group together instances that are unlike at least in peripheral characteristics irrelevant to the purpose of the system. All of which serves to warn that an election is about to be classified as critical even though in some respects the behavior involved differed from that of the 1928 polling.

Central to our concept of critical elections is a realignment within the electorate both sharp and durable. With respect to these basic criteria the election of 1896 falls within the same category as that of 1928, although it differed in other respects. The persistence of the new division of 1896 was perhaps not so notable as that of 1928; yet the Democratic defeat was so demoralizing and so thorough that the party could make little headway in regrouping its forces until 1916. Perhaps the significant feature of the 1896 contest was that, at least in New England, it did not form a new division in which partisan lines became more nearly congruent with lines separating classes, religions, or other such social groups. Instead, the Republicans succeeded in drawing new support, in about the same degree, from all sorts of economic and social classes. The result was an electoral coalition formidable in mass but which required both good fortune and skill in political management for its maintenance, given its latent internal contradictions.

If the 1896 election is described in our terms as a complex of behavior preceeding and following the formal voting, an account of the action must include the panic of 1893. Bank failures, railroad receiverships, unemployment, strikes, Democratic championship of deflation and of the gold standard, and related matters created the setting for a Democratic setback in 1894. Only one of the eight New England Democratic Representatives survived the elections of 1894. The two 1892 Democratic governors fell by the wayside and in all the states the Democratic share of the gubernatorial vote fell sharply in 1894. The luckless William Jennings Bryan and the free-silver heresy perhaps did not contribute as much as is generally supposed to the 1892-1896 decline in New England Democratic strength; New England Democrats moved in large numbers over to the Republican ranks in 1894.

The character of the 1892-1896 electoral shift is suggested by the data of Figure E, which presents an analysis of Connecticut and New Hampshire made by the technique used earlier in examining the election of 1928. The graphs make plain that in these states (and the other New England states show the same pattern) the rout of 1896 produced a basic realignment that persisted at least until 1916. The graphs in Figure E also make equally plain that the 1892-1896 realignment differed radically from that of 1928 in certain respects. In 1896 the net movement in all sorts of geographic units was toward the Republicans; towns differed not in the direction of their movement but only in the extent. Moreover, the persistence of the realignment of 1896 was about the same in those towns with the least Democratic loss from 1892 to 1896 as it was in those with the most marked decline in Democratic strength. Hence, the graphs differ from those on 1928 which took the form of opening scissors. Instead, the 1896 realignment appears as a parallel movement of both groups to a lower plateau of Democratic strength.

If the election of 1896 had had a notable differential impact on geographically segregated social groups, the graphs in Figure E of towns at the extremes of the greatest and least 1892-1896 change would have taken the form of opening scissors as they did in 1928. While the election of 1896 is often pictured as a last-ditch fight between the haves and the have-nots, that understanding of the contest was, at least in New England, evidently restricted to planes of leadership and oratory. It did not extend to the

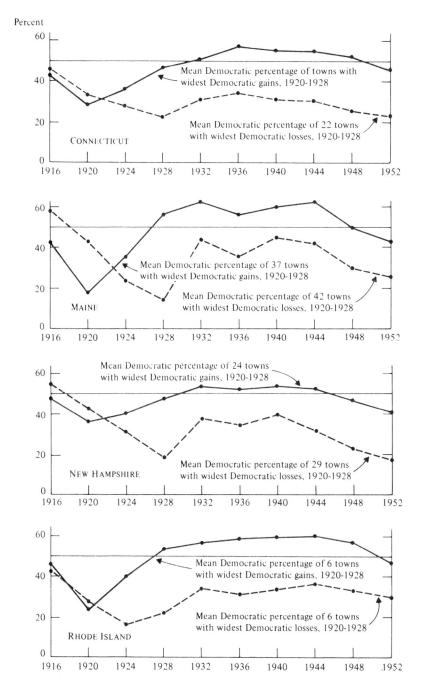

Figure D Realignment of 1928 in Connecticut, Maine, New Hampshire, and Rhode Island

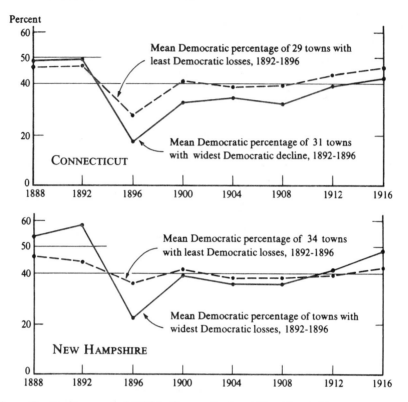

Figure E   Realignment of 1896 in Connecticut and New Hampshire

voting actions of the electorate. These observations merit some buttressing, although the inference emerges clearly enough from Figure E.

Unfortunately the census authorities have ignored the opportunity to advance demographic inquiry by publishing data of consequence about New England towns. Not much information is available on the characteristics of the populations of these small geographic areas. Nevertheless, size of total population alone is a fair separator of towns according to politically significant characteristics. Classification of towns according to that criterion groups them roughly according to industrialization and probably generally also according to religion and national origin. Hence, with size of population of towns and cities as a basis, Table 1 contrasts the elections of 1896 and 1928 for different types of towns. Observe from the table that the mean shift between 1892 and 1896 was about the same for varying size groups of towns. Contrast this lack of association between size and political movement with the radically different 1920–1928 pattern which also appears in the table.

Table 1 makes clear that in 1896 the industrial cities, in their aggregate vote at least, moved toward the Republicans in about the same degree as did the rural farming communities. Some of the misinterpretations of the election of 1896 flow from a focus on that election in isolation rather than in comparison with the preceding election. In 1896, even in New England cities, the Democrats tended to be strongest in the poor, working-class, immigrant sections. Yet the same relation had existed, in a sharper form, in 1892. In 1896 the Republicans gained in the working-class wards, just as they did in the silk-stocking wards, over their 1892 vote. They were able to place the blame for unemployment upon the Democrats and to propagate successfully the doctrine that the Republican Party was the party of prosperity and the "full dinner pail." On the whole, the effect apparently was to reduce the degree of coincidence of class affiliation and partisan inclination. Nor was the election of 1896, in New England at least, a matter of heightened tension between city and country. Both city and country voters shifted in the same direction. Neither urban employers nor industrial workers could generate much enthusiasm for inflation and free trade; rather they joined in common cause. Instead of a sharpening of class cleavages within New England the voting apparently reflected more a sectional antagonism and anxiety, shared by all classes, expressed in opposition to the dangers supposed to be threatening from the West.

Other contrasts between the patterns of electoral behavior of 1896 and 1928 could be cited but in terms of sharpness and durability of realignment both elections were of roughly the same type, at least in New England. In these respects they seem to differ from most other elections over a period of a half century, although it may well be that each round at the ballot boxes involves realignment within the electorate similar in kind but radically different in extent.

III

The discussion points toward the analytical utility of a system for the differentiation of elections. A concept of critical elections has been developed to cover a type of election in which there occurs a sharp and durable electoral realignment between parties, although the techniques employed do not yield any information of consequence about the mechanisms for the maintenance of a new alignment, once it is formed. Obviously any sort of system for the gross characterization of elections presents difficulties in application. The actual election rarely presents in pure form a case fitting completely any particular concept. Especially in a large and diverse electorate a single polling may encompass radically varying types of behavior among different categories of voters; yet a dominant characteristic often makes itself apparent. Despite such difficulties, the attempt to move toward a better understanding of elections in the terms here employed could provide a means for better integrating the study of electoral behavior with the analysis of political systems. In truth, a considerable proportion of the study of electoral behavior has only a tenuous relation to politics.

Table 1   Contrasts between Elections of 1896 and 1928 in Massachusetts: Shifts in Democratic Strength, 1892–1896 and 1920–1928, in Relation to Population Size of Towns

Population size group	Mean Democratic percentage 1892	1896	Mean change 1892–96	Mean Democratic percentage 1920	1928	Mean change 1920–28
1–999	34.0	14.7	– 19.3	16.5	18.6	+ 2.1
2000–2999	38.8	18.3	– 20.5	21.0	33.1	+12.1
10,000–14,999	46.7	26.9	– 19.8	25.8	43.7	+17.9
50,000+	47.7	30.1	– 17.6	29.5	55.7	+26.2

The sorts of questions here raised, when applied sufficiently broadly on a comparative basis and carried far enough, could lead to a consideration of basic problems of the nature of democratic orders. A question occurs, for example, about the character of the consequences for the political system of the temporal frequency of critical elections. What are the consequences for public administration, for the legislative process, for the operation of the economy of frequent serious upheavals within the electorate? What are the correlates of that pattern of behavior? And, for those disposed to raise such questions, what underlying changes might alter the situation? Or, when viewed from the contrary position, what consequences flow from an electorate which is disposed, in effect, to remain largely quiescent over considerable periods? Does a state of moving equilibrium reflect a pervasive satisfaction with the course of public policy? An indifference about matters political? In any case, what are the consequences for the public order? Further, what are the consequences when an electorate builds up habits and attachments, or faces situations, that make it impossible for it to render a decisive and clear-cut popular verdict that promises not to be upset by caprice at the next round of polling? What are the consequences of a situation that creates recurring, evenly balanced conflict over long periods? On the other hand, what characteristics of an electorate or what conditions permit sharp and decisive changes in the power structure from time to time? Such directions of speculation are suggested by a single criterion for the differentiation of elections. Further development of an electoral typology would probably point to useful speculation in a variety of directions.

Voting Behavior:
Rational or Irrational?

☐   Parties are supposed to bridge the gap between the people and their government. Theoretically they are the primary vehicles for translating the wishes of the electorate into public policy, sharing this role with interest groups and other governmental instrumentalities in varying degrees. If parties are to perform this aspect of their job properly, the party system must be conducive to securing meaningful debate and action. Party organization and procedure profoundly affect the ability of parties to act in a democratically responsible manner. It should also be pointed out, however, that the electorate has a responsibility in the political process—the responsibility to act rationally, debate the issues of importance, and record a vote for one party or the other at election time. These, at least, are electoral norms traditionally discussed. But does the electorate act in this manner? Is it desirable to have 100 percent electoral participation considering the characteristics of voting behavior? What are the determinants of electoral behavior? These questions are discussed in the following selection.

23

Bernard R. Berelson, Paul F. Lazarsfeld, and William N. Mcphee

DEMOCRATIC PRACTICE AND DEMOCRATIC THEORY

REQUIREMENTS FOR THE INDIVIDUAL

Perhaps the main impact of realistic research on contemporary politics has been to temper some of the requirements set by our traditional normative theory for the typical citizen. "Out of all this literature of political observation and analysis, which is relatively new," says Max Beloff, "there has come to exist a picture in our minds of the political scene which differs very considerably from that familiar to us from the classical texts of democratic politics."

Experienced observers have long known, of course, that the individual voter was not all that the theory of democracy requires of him. As [British Lord James] Bryce put it [in his 1888 treatise, *The American Commonwealth*]:

> How little solidity and substance there is in the political or social beliefs of nineteen persons out of every twenty. These beliefs, when examined, mostly resolve themselves into two or three prejudices and aversions, two or three prepossessions for a particular party or section of a party, two or three phrases or catch-words suggesting or embodying arguments which the man who repeats them has not analyzed.

While our data [from the Elmira study] do not support such an extreme statement, they do reveal that certain requirements commonly assumed for the successful operation of democracy are not met by the behavior of the "average" citizen. The requirements, and our conclusions concerning them, are quickly reviewed.

Interest, Discussion, Motivation. The democratic citizen is expected to be interested and to participate in political affairs. His interest and participation can take such various forms as reading and listening to campaign materials, working for the candidate or the party, arguing politics, donating money, and voting. In Elmira the majority of the people vote, but in general they do not give evidence of sustained interest. Many vote without real involvement in the election, and even the party workers are not typically motivated by ideological concerns or plain civic duty.

If there is one characteristic for a democratic system (besides the ballot itself) that is theoretically required, it is the capacity for and the practice of discussion. "It is as true of the large as of the small society," says [A. D.] Lindsay, "that its health depends on the mutual understanding which discussion makes possible; and that discussion is the only possible instrument of its democratic government." How much participation in political discussion there is in the community, what it is, and among whom—these questions have been given answers . . . earlier. . . . In this instance there was little true discussion between the candidates, little in the newspaper commentary, little between the voters and the official party representatives, some within the electorate. On the grass roots level there was more talk than debate, and, at least inferentially, the talk had important effects upon voting, in reinforcing or activating the partisans if not in converting the opposition.

An assumption underlying the theory of democracy is that the citizenry has a strong motivation for participation in political life. But it is a curious quality of voting behavior that for large numbers of people motivation is weak if not almost absent. It is assumed that this motivation would gain its strength from the citizen's perception of the difference that alternative decisions made to him. Now when a person buys something or makes other decisions of daily life, there are direct and immediate consequences for him. But for the bulk of the American people the voting decision is not followed by any direct, immediate, visible personal consequences. Most voters, organized or unorganized, are not in a position to foresee the distant and indirect consequences for themselves, let alone the society. The ballot is cast, and for most people that is the end of it. If their side is defeated, "it doesn't really matter."

Knowledge. The democratic citizen is expected to be well informed about political affairs. He is supposed to know what the issues are, what their history is, what the relevant facts are, what alternatives are proposed, what the party stands for, what the likely consequences are. By such standards the voter falls short. Even when he has the motivation, he finds it difficult to make decisions on the basis of full information when the subject is relatively simple and proximate; how can he do so when it is complex and remote? The citizen is not highly informed on details of the campaign, nor does he avoid a certain misperception of the political situation when it is to his psychological advantage to do so. The electorate's perception of what goes on in the campaign is colored by emotional feeling toward one or the other issue, candidate, party, or social group.

Principle. The democratic citizen is supposed to cast his vote on the basis of principle—not fortuitously or frivolously or impulsively or habitually, but with reference to standards not only of his own interest but of the common good as well. Here, again, if this requirement is pushed at all strongly, it becomes an impossible demand on the democratic electorate.

Many voters vote not for principle in the usual sense but "for" a group to which they are attached—their group. The Catholic vote or the hereditary vote is explainable less as principle than as a traditional social allegiance. The ordinary voter, bewildered by the complexity of modern political problems, unable to determine clearly what the consequences are of alternative lines of action, remote from the arena, and incapable of bringing information to bear on principle, votes the way trusted people around him are voting. . . .

On the issues of the campaign there is a considerable amount of "don't know"—sometimes reflecting genuine indecision, more often meaning "don't care." Among those with opinions the partisans *agree* on most issues, criteria, expectations, and rules of the game. The supporters of the different sides disagree on only a few issues. Nor, for that matter, do the candidates themselves always join the issue sharply and clearly. The partisans do not agree overwhelmingly with their own party's position, or, rather, only the small minority of highly partisan do; the rest take a rather moderate position on the political consideration involved in an election.

Rationality. The democratic citizen is expected to exercise rational judgment in coming to his voting decision. He is expected to have arrived at his principles by reason and to have considered rationally the implications and alleged consequences of the alternative proposals of the contending parties. Political theorists and commentators have always exclaimed over the seeming contrast here between requirement and fulfillment. . . . The upshot of this is that the usual analogy between the voting "decision" and the more or less carefully calculated decisions of consumers or businessmen or courts, incidentally, may be quite incorrect. For many voters political preferences may better be considered analogous to cultural tastes—in music, literature, recreational activities, dress, ethics, speech, social behavior. Consider the parallels between political preferences and general cultural tastes. Both have their origin in ethnic, sectional, class, and family traditions. Both exhibit stability and resistance to change for individuals but flexibility and adjustment over generations for the society as a whole. Both seem to be matters of sentiment and disposition rather than "reasoned preferences." While both are responsive to changed conditions and unusual stimuli, they are relatively invulnerable to direct argumentation and vulnerable to indirect social influences. Both are characterized more by faith than by conviction and by wishful expectation rather than careful prediction or consequences. The preference for one party rather than another must be highly similar to the preference for one kind of literature or music rather than another, and the choice of the same political party every four years may be parallel to the choice of the same old standards of conduct in new social situations. In short, it appears that a sense of fitness is a more striking feature of political preference than reason and calculation.

REQUIREMENTS FOR THE SYSTEM

If the democratic system depended solely on the qualifications of the individual voter, then it seems remarkable that democracies have survived through the centuries. After examining the detailed data on how individuals misperceive political reality or respond to irrelevant social influences, one wonders how a democracy ever solves its political problems. But when one considers the data in a broader perspective—how huge segments of the society adapt to political conditions affecting them or how the political system adjusts itself to changing conditions over long periods of time—he cannot fail to be impressed with the total result. Where the rational citizen seems to abdicate, nevertheless angels seem to tread. . . .

That is the paradox. *Individual voters* today seem unable to satisfy the requirements for a democratic system of government outlined by political theorists. But the *system of democracy* does meet certain requirements for a going political organization. The individual members may not meet all the standards, but the whole nevertheless survives and grows. This suggests that where the classic theory is defective is in its concentration on the *individual citizen.* What are undervalued are certain collective properties that reside in the electorate as a whole and in the political and social system in which it functions.

The political philosophy we have inherited, then, has given more consideration to the virtues of the typical citizen of the democracy than to the working of the *system* as a whole. Moreover, when it dealt with the system, it mainly considered the single constitutive institutions of the system, not those general features necessary if the institutions are to work as required. For example, the rule of law, representative government, periodic elections, the party system, and the several freedoms of discussion, press, association, and assembly have all been examined by political philosophers seeking to clarify and to justify the idea of political democracy. But liberal democracy is more than a political system in which individual voters and political institutions operate. For political democracy to survive, other features are required: the intensity of conflict must be limited, the rate of change must be restrained, stability in the social and economic structure must be maintained, a pluralistic social organization must exist, and a basic consensus must bind together the contending parties.

Such features of the system of political democracy belong neither to the constitutive institutions nor to the individual voter. It might be said that they form the atmosphere or the environment in which both operate. In any case, such features have not been carefully considered by political philosophers, and it is on these broader properties of the democratic political system that more reflection and study by political theory is called for. In the most tentative fashion let us explore the values of the political system, as they involve the electorate, in the light of the foregoing considerations.

Underlying the paradox is an assumption that the population is homogeneous socially and should be homogeneous politically: that everybody is about the same in relevant social characteristics; that, if something is a political virtue (like interest in the election), then everyone should have it; that there is such a thing as "the" typical citizen on whom uniform requirements can be imposed. The tendency of classic democratic literature to work with an image of "the" voter was never justified. For, as we will attempt to illustrate here, some of the most important requirements that democratic values impose on a system require a voting population that is not homogeneous but heterogeneous in its political qualities.

The need for heterogeneity arises from the contradictory functions we expect our voting system to serve. We expect the political system to adjust itself and our affairs to changing conditions; yet we demand too that it display a high degree of stability. We expect the contending interests and parties to pursue their ends vigorously and the voters to care; yet, after the election is over, we expect reconciliation. We expect the voting outcome to serve what is best for the community; yet we do not want disinterested voting unattached to the purposes and interests of different segments of that community. We want voters to express their own free and self-determined choices; yet, for the good of the community, we would like voters to avail themselves of the best information and guidance available from the groups and leaders around them. We expect a high degree of rationality to prevail in the decision; but were all irrationality and mythology absent, and all ends pursued by the most coldly rational selection of political means, it is doubtful if the system would hold together.

In short, our electoral system calls for apparently incompatible properties —which, although they cannot all reside in each individual voter, can (and do) reside in a heterogeneous electorate. What seems to be required of the electorate as a whole is a *distribution* of qualities along important dimensions. We need some people who are active in a certain respect, others in the middle, and still others passive. The contradictory things we want from the total require that the parts be different. This can be illustrated by taking up a number of important dimensions by which an electorate might be characterized.

Involvement and Indifference. How could a mass democracy work if all the people were deeply involved in politics? Lack of interest by some people is not without its benefits, too. True, the highly interested voters vote more, and know more about the campaign, and read and listen more, and participate more; however, they are also less open to persuasion and less likely to change. Extreme interest goes with extreme partisanship and might culminate in rigid fanaticism that could destroy democratic processes if generalized throughout the community. Low affect toward the election—not caring much—underlies the resolution of many political problems; votes can be resolved into a two-party split instead of fragmented into many parties (the splinter parties of the left, for example, splinter because their advocates are *too* interested in politics). Low interest provides maneuvering room for political shifts necessary for a complex society in a period of rapid change. Compromise might be based upon sophisticated awareness of costs and returns—perhaps impossible to demand of a mass society—but it is more often induced by indifference. Some people are and should be highly interested in politics, but not everyone is or needs to be. Only the doctrinaire would deprecate the moderate indifference that facilitates compromise.

Hence, an important balance between action motivated by strong sentiments and action with little passion behind it is obtained by heterogeneity within the electorate. Balance of this sort is, in practice, met by a distribution of voters rather than by a homogeneous collection of "ideal" citizens.

Stability and Flexibility. A similar dimension along which an electorate might be characterized is stability-flexibility. The need for change and adaptation is clear, and the need for stability ought equally to be (especially from observation of current democratic practice in, say, certain Latin American countries). . . . [I]t may be that the very people who are most sensitive to changing social conditions are those most susceptible to political change. For, in either case, the people exposed to membership in overlapping strata, those whose former life-patterns are being broken up, those who are moving about socially or physically, those who are forming new families and new friendships—it is they who are open to adjustments of attitudes and tastes. They may be the least partisan and the least interested voters, but they perform a valuable function for the entire system. Here again is an instance in which an individual "inadequacy" provides a positive service for society: The campaign can be a reaffirming force for the settled majority and a creative force for the unsettled minority. There is stability on both sides and flexibility in the middle.

Progress and Conservation. Closely related to the question of stability is the question of past versus future orientation of the system. In America a progressive outlook is highly valued, but, at the same time, so is a conservative one. Here a balance between the two is easily found in the party system and in the distribution of voters themselves from extreme conservatives to extreme liberals. But a balance between the two is also achieved by a distribution of political dispositions through time. There are periods of great political agitation (i.e., campaigns) alternating with periods of political dormancy. Paradoxically, the former—the campaign period—is likely to be an instrument of conservatism, often even of historical regression. . . .

Again, then, a balance (between preservation of the past and receptivity to the future) seems to be required of a democratic electorate. The heterogeneous electorate in itself provides a balance between liberalism and conservatism; and so does the sequence of political events from periods of drifting change to abrupt rallies back to the loyalties of earlier years.

Consensus and Cleavage. . . . [T]here are required *social* consensus and cleavage—in effect pluralism—in politics. Such pluralism makes for enough consensus to hold the system together and enough cleavage to make it move. Too much consensus would be deadening and restrictive of liberty; too much cleavage would be destructive of the society as a whole. . . . Thus again a requirement we might place on an electoral system—balance between total political war between segments of the society and total political indifference to group interests of that society—translates into varied requirements for different individuals. With respect to group or bloc voting, as with other aspects of political behavior, it is perhaps not unfortunate that "some do and some do not."

Individualism and Collectivism. Lord Bryce pointed out the difficulties in a theory of democracy that assumes that each citizen must himself be capable of voting intelligently:

> Orthodox democratic theory assumes that every citizen has, or ought to have, thought out for himself certain opinions, i.e., ought to have a definite view, defensible by argument, of what the country needs, of what principles ought to be applied in governing it, of the man to whose hands the government ought to be entrusted. There are persons who talk, though certainly very few who act, as if they believed this theory, which may be compared to the theory of some ultra-Protestants that every good Christian has or ought to have . . . worked out for himself from the Bible a system of theology.

In the first place, however, the information available to the individual voter is not limited to that directly possessed by him. True, the individual casts his own personal ballot. But, as we have tried to indicate . . . that is perhaps the most individualized action he takes in an election. His vote is formed in the midst of his fellows in a sort of group decision—if, indeed, it may be called a decision at all—and the total information and knowledge possessed in the group's present and past generations can be made available for the group's choice. Here is where opinion-leading relationships, for example, play an active role.

Second, and probably more important, the individual voter may not have a great deal of detailed information, but he usually has picked up the crucial *general* information as part of his social learning itself. He may not know the parties' position on the tariff, or who is for reciprocal trade treaties, or what are the differences on Asiatic policy, or how the parties split on civil rights, or how many security risks were exposed by whom. But he cannot live in an American community without knowing broadly where the parties stand. He has learned that the Republicans are more conservative and the Democrats more liberal—and he can locate his own sentiments and cast his vote accordingly. After all, he must vote for one or the other party, and, if he knows the big thing about the parties, he does not need to know all the little things. The basic role a party plays as an institution in American life is more important to his voting than a particular stand on a particular issue.

It would be unthinkable to try to maintain our present economic style of life without a complex system of delegating to others what we are not competent to do ourselves, without accepting and giving training to each other about what each is expected to do, without accepting our dependence on others in many spheres and taking responsibility for their dependence on us in some spheres. And, like it or not, to maintain our present political style of life, we may have to accept much the same interdependence with others in collective behavior. We have learned slowly in economic life that it is useful not to have everyone a butcher or a baker, any more than it is useful to have no one skilled in such activities. The same kind of division of labor—as repugnant as it may be in some respects to our individualistic tradition—is serving us well today in mass politics. There is an implicit division of political labor within the electorate.

The Role of Parties in the Political Process

☐   In the classical liberal democratic model of democracy political parties play a key role in bridging the gap between people and government. The purpose of parties is to develop meaningful programs and present choices to the electorate, and after the electorate has made its choice the parties are to implement programs in accordance with the wishes of the voters. The classical model of democracy can best be described as "government by discussion." Discussion proceeds in a sequential manner through three stages: (1) discussion within the parties on the formulation of issues that will be presented to the electorate; (2) discussion within the electorate of the party platforms that have been presented; (3) discussion within the legislature and the executive after the election to refine party programs in light of voter preferences. This model ideally presumes two-party government, a disciplined political party system, and a rational electorate. In the American political system, the electorate does not always vote rationally in accordance with issue preferences. Moreover, a major development reaching fruition in the last decade is the decline in the role of political parties that may spell, to use Walter Dean Burnham's description, the "end of American party politics."[1] If people cease to identify with political parties and no longer relate to government through parties then the usefulness of the electoral process as a vehicle of democratic participation is diminished.

Events since political scientists began to write about the end of American party politics in the late 1960s have continued to lend support to their theses. A virtual plethora of books and articles heralding the decline of parties has reinforced the theme. Common conclusions from the studies of political parties are: (1) the electorate is becoming more independent and less identified with one of the two major parties than in the past; (2) voters increasingly view electoral politics more in terms of individual candidates' styles, personalities, and issues, rather than in terms of those of the parties; (3) the electorate's image of parties has declined as its skepticism about the ability of parties to govern responsibly and effectively has risen.

Because parties play such an important role in democratic theory, providing an essential link between people and government, as well as

[1]W. D. Burnham, "The End of American Party Politics," *Society* 7:2 (December 1969).

ensuring governmental accountability, effectiveness, and responsiveness to change, it is disturbing to find such pervasive evidence of party decline. Yet, as a prominent political scientist observes in the following selection, the "party" is not over as political parties continue to function effectively on many levels.

24
Samuel J. Eldersveld

PARTY DECLINE:
FACT OR FICTION?

Political parties are complex institutions and processes, and as such they are difficult to understand and evaluate. There are several different yardsticks by which parties could be evaluated: whether they are democratic structures in which rank-and-file supporters can participate effectively; whether they produce competent leaders who deserve public support; whether they propose (and adopt) policies which meet the needs of our society; whether they are coherent and responsible organizations; and whether they communicate in such a way with the public that citizens feel confident about parties and their performance in our political system. These concerns about parties as "linkage structures" have been a major focus of this study of parties. Controversies abound today over these questions, and the complex issues they pose. An attempt shall be made here to present some concluding observations about the state of our parties today. . . .

There have always been serious criticism of, and attacks on, the American party system. At the level of government the role of parties has been seen as anarchic, fragmented, leaderless, and undisciplined. In leadership selection it has often been criticized as too decentralized in control, or undemocratic, or both. In the way parties conduct campaigns they have regularly been characterized as nonrational, uncoordinated, improvisational, unsystematic. As organizations they are viewed, aside from the big city machines (which are denounced as too efficient oligarchies), as loose aggregations of factional subgroups, ideologically at odds and minimally active. All these criticisms have been heard for years, and yet the United States party system has been far from dysfunctional. To many citizens this party system has remained through all these trying years, years of serious threats, as a meaningful set of social and political groups to which they can relate and be loyal. They have remained important linkage and mobilizational structures, performing critical functions. In the last analysis, the great policy decisions are those that parties, and the leaders produced by parties, have had a major role in—whether it was the Emancipation Proclamation, the anti-trust legislation, the New Deal legislation, the civil rights acts, energy legislation, or any other piece of significant legislation. The *parties* —not the Chamber of Commerce, not the UAW, not the American Legion, not the American Medical Association—usually are the *prime movers* in the adoption of such landmark laws *and* are usually held responsible for such actions.

Nevertheless, despite the recognition of their contributions of the past, parties and party systems change. The United States party system has been changing also, so much, as a matter of fact, that serious question is now raised as to the suitability, centrality, indeed the viability of the system. Students of parties see two major developments in recent years: demobilization (decline in involvement) and dealignment (decline in party identification). And they argue from this that the parties have been losing their "relevance," their critical capacity in responding to social needs and problems. Thus their support by the American public and their ability to maintain the loyalty of citizens in this party system is in decline. Today, many scholars do not see parties as great actors on the American scene. Rather, they see the decomposition, dismantling, and atrophying of parties. It may be, however, that what is occurring is a metamorphosis in the forms of party organization, not a decline. Our parties may be as active and relevant, but in new ways. This question of the changes in parties is the subject of this final evaluation.

THE MEANING OF PARTY "DECLINE"

Parties in all systems undergo "change"—in organizational nature, in types of leadership, in policy direction, in electoral strength, in social group support, and in competitive relationships to other parties. But in the United States the basic concern is over the decline in the *role* and *significance* of parties in the system. Two major foci of concern relate to our conceptions of "parties in the electorate" and "parties as organizational systems." Thus, one kind of change which observers of the American parties are primarily preoccupied with is the alleged decline in *the public's support relationship* to the party system. This can be variously specified as: (1) a decline in the strength and extent of partisan loyalty and commitment; (2) a decline in interest in elections and voting; and (3) a decline in a feeling that parties are important for policy decisions, and for governing generally.

Linked to these meanings of the decline of parties are the views of scholars that parties have declined as *organizational systems.* Again, there are several ways of operationalizing this concern, and the emphasis can be on the decline in (1) the existence and amount of organization; (2) the power of leaders and agencies in the organization; (3) the capacity and competence (particularly in the professional skills) of the party organizational leadership; (4) the activity of the organization; and (5) the importance of the organization in performing its key functions (such as nominations, campaigns, policy deliberation, decision making)—in comparison to the role of interest groups, mass media, candidate-centered committees or specialists in propaganda.

In essence, the decline conceived of often is in the institutional nature of parties—that the parties as organizational apparatuses have atrophied. The writings of many scholars . . . can be cited to document these observations— among them, [political scientists Walter] Burnham, [James] Wilson, and [Jeane] Kirkpatrick. Thus, Wilson in 1973 argued that parties, as organizations, "have become if anything weaker rather than stronger—parties are more important as labels than as organizations." And to Jeane Kirkpatrick, 1976 provided "fresh evidence of the parties' decreasing capacity to represent voters, mount campaigns, elicit resources, and recruit leaders who were devoted to the institution," and one of her central theses is that the decisions to reform the parties have been responsible for "hastening party deinstitutionalization."

Here is the convergence of two streams of concern or alarm—the alleged decline in the public's support for and interest in parties, and the decline of the party organizations as active and effective entities. Both of these streams emphasize the declining "relevance" of parties for the system, for the society, for the solution to our problems as important instrumentalities for political action, and, in the final analysis, for the lives of Americans as they are affected by government.

It is important to distinguish here between *what is alleged, what is perceived,* and *what is reality.* Scholars may assert that there is no organization, *but* that may be an inference not supported by reality. Or scholars may assert that the public is disillusioned with parties because parties have no important policy role, *but* to support such an argument two types of evidence are important: Is that in fact the public's perception? Is it factually correct that parties have no policy role? In analyzing party decline, then, both *perceptions* and *performance* must be examined. It may very well be argued that what is perceived is more important than what is reality, since attitudes of disillusionment by the public (and by scholars) reflect perceptions. But if there is a divergence between perception and reality, we have only begun to understand the problem and we then need a careful analysis of why. The analytical context for the discussion is suggested by Table 1.

Many scholars assume that the situation of Box D in the table obtains,

Table 1   Evaluations of parties: Four basic types

Perceptions of party performance and relevance	Party organizational preference	
	High	Low
Positive	A Healthy condition if it ever existed	B Very possibly what may have been true in the past
Negative	C Basic conflict	D Party role in system negative or neutral

and if it does, parties may well be responsible for negative attitudes. But this must yet be demonstrated. If, on the other hand, the conditions of Box C exist, then there is a conflict between perceptions and actual performance. This too needs to be demonstrated and the factors responsible for the disjunction identified. Box A suggests the conditions which many assume to have existed in the past when we had higher turnout, less independence, and so forth. But actually we may have had Box B conditions all along—to secure evidence on this historically is very difficult. In any event, when the "decline" in our parties is discussed it is necessary (1) to document the change in the level of party organizational performance; (2) to document the change in the content of public perceptions of parties; (3) to document the extent to which the decline in one is related to the decline in the other; and (4) if the two do not co-vary, to explore explanations for the decline in public affect for parties which may not be linked to party organizational effort. This is a major research task, and the evidence now available and relevant to that task will be presented here. But by no means is all the information needed to enlighten definitively and correctly all aspects of this phenomenon of party decline yet at hand. It is a puzzle which can only partially be pieced together at this point.

A FIRST MAJOR QUESTION:
HAS PARTY ORGANIZATION ACTIVISM DECLINED
AT THE LOCAL LEVEL?

The familiar refrain in commentaries on American parties these days is that the rise of the direct primary and of new campaign technology has meant the loss of control by the party organization, as presumably it existed in the past, over nominations, campaign strategies, candidates, issues, resources, elected leadership, *and* that this has meant "the decline of local party activism" . . . But what is the evidence of the decline in local party activism? None of the scholars making these general assertions have demonstrated that this is the case. In fact, there is evidence to suggest that the opposite may be true. Wolfe's careful analysis of the Center for Political Studies' data from 1952

Table 2   Percentage of United States public reporting contacts by local party
activists

Party	1952	1956	1972	1976
Democrat	6	11	19	17
Republican	7	11	13	13
	13	22	32	30
	13	22	32	30

Source: Michael Wolfe, "Personal Contact Campaigning in Presidential Elections" (A paper presented at the Annual Meeting of the Midwest Political Science Association, Chicago, April 1979), p. 11a.

on indicates that the proportion of the American public who have been contacted by party campaign workers in recent years is much greater than previously (see Table 2). Whereas in 1952 only 12 percent of the public report contacts, by 1976 it was close to 30 percent; in 1980 it was 24 percent.

What is interesting to note is the extension of such local party contact efforts in all parts of the country, to blacks, as well as whites, and to lower educational groups, as well as to the college educated (see Table 3). True, those with low socioeconomic status are not as frequently the targets of campaign activists as are those of higher status, but there is some evidence of expansionism in contacts, particularly for blacks and those with a middle (high school) educational status.

In this connection it is instructive to look at the results of the 1980 national surveys which also asked all those in the sample if they had been contacted in the campaign. Although there was a slight decline in the overall percentage (to 24.4 percent), the characteristics of those who were contacted are revealing (see Table 4). The Republican effort was slightly greater in 1980, particularly among conservatives (41 percent), young persons (44 percent) as well as the oldest citizens (41 percent) and, of course, among Republican identifiers. The Democrats seemed to spend more canvassing effort among liberals (46 percent), those with a lower educational status (50 percent) and, of course, among Democratic identifiers (55 percent). What is significant also, however, is that both parties appealed to all groups, including each other's partisans. One-fifth to one-fourth of strong partisans were called on by the opposite party. The same phenomenon holds true for other categories of voters. In the light of the election results perhaps the overall net advantage to the Republicans lies in their greater effort with Independents. They seemed to have contacted about 10 percent more of them than the Democrats did. And since 85 percent of those contacted said they voted (an exaggerated report, but nonetheless the proportion was still high), this extra Republican effort may have been relevant to Republican success.

Table 3   Extension of party activism efforts geographically, racially, and by educational level (as a percentage)

Category	Contacted by party canvassers each year				Increase 1952-76
	1952	1956	1972	1976	
Regions					
South	9	15	18	21	+12
Border	9	16	25	20	+11
Mountain and Far West	20	18	40	36	+16
Northeast	15	17.5	19	30	+15
Mid-Atlantic	12	15	26	28	+16
Midwest	12	20	40.5	32.5	+20.5
Race					
Whites	12	16	28	27	+15
Blacks	6	12	18	18	+12
Educational Level					
Completed college	15	22	33	35	+20
High school	13	22	29	27	+14
Less than high school	10	13	19	16	+ 6

Source: Michael Wolfe, "Personal Contact Campaigning in Presidential Elections" (A paper presented at the Annual Meeting of the Midwest Political Science Association, Chicago, April 1979), pp. 8a, 6a, 16a. Based on University of Michigan SRC/CPS data.

A great many questions can be asked of these data, including who the canvasser was (whether a party organization person or not), what the content of the contact was, and whether these recalls of contact are at all reliable. Obviously, many more adult citizens are being contacted now by party and campaign personnel than ever before. Although there is a continuous socioeconomic bias in these efforts, such contacts are reaching out to a larger proportion of blacks and less well-educated people than ever before, and this seems to be going on throughout the country. There has always been much organizational slack in the performance of the key tasks by the local party organization, except in certain big city machines, but there is really no convincing evidence that recently the local party is less active or less efficient than formerly. In fact, the data on Detroit and Los Angeles, comparing local party activity of 1980 with 1956, suggests no decline, as does the Wolfe analysis above.

A Subsidiary Question:
Are the Local Party Activists Less Likely
to Be Competent Workers than Previously?

Although it may be true that local parties are as active as previously, it is contended that the party activist today is different in two respects—he, or she, is more ideological and less pragmatic, and also less professional (and more amateur). This type of argument uses data particularly about the

Table 4   Characteristics of persons contacted by the parties and candidates, 1980 (as a percentage)

Respondents	Total for group	Contacted by Republicans	Democrats	Both parties	Other
Contacted in campaign	24.4	36.4	33.5	21.6	8.4
Ideology					
Liberal	31	23	46	23	
Moderate	25	39	31	22	
Conservative	26	41	22	28	
Party identification					
Strong Democrat	30	20	55	18	
Weak Democrat	21	36	34	18	
Independent Democrat	21	35	27	27	
Independent	23	42	20	29	
Independent Republican	21	42	36	23	
Weak Republican	27	44	24	24	
Strong Republican	30	53	24	18	
Age					
Young (18–29)	17	44	30	11	
Older	25	33	33	28	
Old	30	33	39	24	
Oldest (65 and over)	29	41	32	17	
Educational Level					
Grade school	17	21	50	14	
High School	22	37	37	16	
College	29	39	26	28	

Source: University of Michigan CPS/NES, 1980.

delegates to the national conventions, relying heavily on the 1972 delegate studies, a year which certainly on the Democratic side was perhaps somewhat abnormal. The Democratic National Convention in 1972 certainly did see what Jeane Kirkpatrick has called "new breed" of activists—more youth, more black, more women, and presumably more amateur and ideological. But, as Kirkpatrick herself has stated, the 1976 Democratic convention had more delegates with "prior party experience, more who had held party and public office, fewer who were indifferent to winning. . . ." Yet she is still concerned about the presence of activists in both parties who are not loyal to the party, who are candidate-oriented, who have limited professional competence, and who are unrepresentative in social and economic status in relationship to the parties' rank and file. [Washington Post columnist] David Broder is similarly concerned, citing figures that governors and congressmen are represented much less at recent Democratic conventions. But in 1980 this trend presumably was altered with the adoption of the new rule that 10 percent of the delegate seats in a state are set aside for elected party leaders.

The American parties have always been wide open structures. They have always had ideologues (a minority) and pragmatists, amateurs and professionals, those intermittently involved and those making a career out of party organizational work. To argue that our parties have changed radically, have declined, because there are today many more nonprofessional, nonpragmatic ideologues than formerly is not substantiated by any trend data available.

Another Subsidiary Question:
Is Party Organization at the Local Level
Less Important Today?

The point has been made by several writers that the local party organization is less critical today for our parties and for political campaigns, that state and national parties operate independently, that candidates depend less on the local organization, and that the mass media have replaced the local doorbell ringer as the major source of information about politics and the major stimulus to voting. As has been seen in the previous analysis of the research on the media, there can be no question but that since 1952 television particularly is relied on heavily by voters. But this has not meant a decline in the proportion of Americans exposed to the efforts of the local party organization. As for the extent to which candidates rely on the party organization in their districts, the evidence reviewed earlier by no means suggests that the new specialists in campaign technology have over time replaced the local organizations—for registration drives, for money, for mobilization of campaign personnel, for "getting out the vote." Scholars of Congress are inclined to emphasize the congressman's relationship to his constituency, and this includes his district party organization, through which he often rose to the top, whose views about politics he shares, and which could run an opposition candidate against him if that organization feels ignored. Again, the evidence on this point is not by any means overwhelming, and the importance of the local organization apparently varies greatly from state to state and from community to community. But to dismiss the local organization as superseded by the mass media or scorned by the candidate-centered campaign or ignored by the incumbent congressman (or state legislator), *particularly as something which has happened recently,* is not supported by the available data.

A SECOND MAJOR QUESTION:
HAS PARTY ORGANIZATION AT THE STATE AND
NATIONAL LEVELS BECOME WEAKER?

Have state and national party organizations declined in power and influence in the role they play in campaigns, leadership recruitment, and policy decisions? Contradictory arguments are advanced. One argument is that there is a nationalization trend and that state parties are losing out. But it is also maintained that the parties have lost control over nominations and campaigns to public relations agencies, professional consultants, and candidate organizations.

The evidence that state and national party organizations have lost power is not conclusive. Thus, the Democratic National Committee has expanded its control over the selection of delegates to the national convention both through the Compliance Review Commission, to which state organizations must submit descriptions of the process they use in selecting delegates, and in 1980, by informing the states that delegates selected in open primaries, not confined to declared Democrats, will not be acceptable at the national convention. The assertion of these two powers alone had meant a modest centralization tendency in American parties. True, those who would have "europeanized" our parties at the Kansas City mini-convention of 1974 by giving the national committee much more authority (over party policy, for example) were defeated. But the national committees have never been centers of party power, and thus recent developments represent, if anything, a slight increment in national committee power, rather than a decline.

As to the question of the decline in the role of the state and national organizations over nominations and campaigns, there is probably no question that some attrition has occurred. In 1980, and for the Democrats in 1976, the national convention did not make the final decision on the presidential nomination. The primaries selected over 70 percent of the delegates, and Reagan and Carter won the majority of the delegates needed for nomination long before the conventions met. This does depreciate the role of state organizations at the national convention—then and now. But, the national convention may still be important in nominations in the future. In the meantime it remains a major plenary body of party decision making—on the platform and on the rules and permanent organization of the party—as well as being a major forum for consensus building and party unity.

As for the role of the national parties in the campaigns for president and vice-president, the national organization was often only peripherally involved and rarely central in the planning and executing of campaign strategy. This role depended on the pleasure of the presidential candidate. Certainly Carter, Nixon, Johnson, Kennedy, to name only a few, did not place the national committee in the center of the campaign operation. It is true that the Federal Election Campaign acts since 1971, by providing public funds for presidential campaigns, most of which are given to the candidate, not to the committee, may appear to have weakened the role of the national committee. Yet, the Republican national organization under Chairman William Brock is credited with a major role in the 1980 presidential victory. Brock worked to renovate state and local organizations, organized training sessions on campaign techniques, the use of the media, and the use of surveys of public opinion, and actually ran a "campaign management college." Above all, large sums of money were collected and funneled through the national organization to United States senatorial, congressional, and state legislature candidates.

A major study of state party organizations recently has concluded that since 1960 the budgets of state organizations have more than tripled and their staffs have increased greatly. The authors conclude, "If state parties were in the undeveloped state ascribed to them by political scientists in the 1950s and early 1960s, they have since developed into relatively strong and durable organizations."

In short, to argue that party organization at the state and national levels has been decisively weakened in recent years is difficult to substantiate, and such claims assume strong parties in the past. In reality this country has always had a decentralized and stratarchical party organizational system, and some would argue that that is the strength of our parties. It has forced parties to be responsible to local interests, to adapt to local differences, to force upper-level party structures to be truly consultative of lower-level structures and to maintain, thus, a minimum of rapport in a very heterogeneous system. If anything, the national committee has more power today, and the party caucus in Congress is asserting its authority more than it has for many years. The decline in our parties, therefore, is difficult to demonstrate, empirically or in terms of a historical perspective.

THIRD BASIC QUESTION:
HAS THERE BEEN A DECLINE IN THE PUBLIC'S
AFFECT FOR, AND CONFIDENCE IN, THE PARTIES?

This may turn out to be the critical question in the party decline controversy. For, in the last analysis, it is *the* test of the viability of any particular party and of any particular party system. If there is a continuous decline in the public's positive evaluation of parties, rooted in disaffection over party capability and performance, then withdrawal of public support will occur which is meaningful and difficult to reverse, a concern about which empirical evidence is available.

There are several components of this concern which are separable. First, to what extent is there a change in the extent to which the public *thinks* in "party content" terms at all? If "party" is less salient to people, something they spontaneously talk and think about less frequently, that in itself is a significant development. The little data available on this matter indicates that, indeed, such seems to be the case today (see Table 5). Surveys show a decline in the 1970s in the public's inclination to evaluate candidates in "party" terms, a finding that holds true for party identifiers also. Second, when people do think of parties, they are less positive in their general evaluations of them than previously—a steady decline since the 1960 election, when 71 percent were positive, to 49 percent by 1976. Third, this does not necessarily mean an increase in negative evaluations but seems to be associated with more neutrality in the way people view parties. When people are asked, "Which party can do the best job in dealing with the most important problem(s), as you perceive those problems?" more citizens are inclined to say, "the parties are about the same," or "no party" or "neither party." And this is perhaps the most significant development of all—that close to 50 percent of the public today has great difficulty in identifying one or the other of the parties as best capable of solving our problems. In 1960 the proportion was 38 percent. These are the people who seem more inclined to stay home on election day.

The decline in the relevance of parties for the solution of problems may well be the nub of the matter. The general decline in affect for parties may be the result of a change in the image of the role of parties—from positive to neutral—in the policy process. It is not so troublesome that large proportions of the public over the years do not perceive clear-cut differences between the parties. That has been going on for years—the United States studies in the 1950s revealed that less than 20 percent of strong identifiers saw important differences between the parties on issues. Rather, what is new and significant is the declining relevance in public cognitions of parties combined with an increased neutralism and indifference to parties. This in turn may be linked (although scholars differ on this) to a decline in the correlation of partisanism to the vote—a drop after 1952 from .50 to .14 in 1976. To understand why that has occurred would lead to a closer understanding of the meaning of the decline of parties.

The "puzzle" as it has emerged thus far is: Compared to most other countries, the United States is unsurpassed in level of political activity and in amount of party identification, but far down in rank in voting turnout (54 percent in the presidential election of 1980, compared to 75 percent or more in most European countries and also Japan). Further, political activity is not declining in the United States, nor is party effort declining on the basis of the reports from the respondents in surveys since 1952. The parties are contacting a larger proportion of the citizens. At the same time our politics seem more competitive than before (closer elections in many parts of the country, including the South). There is more issue awareness and

Table 5   Measures of the public's interest and confidence in parties (as a percentage)

Interest	1952	1956	1960	1964	1968	1972	1976	1980
Use of "party" in evaluating candidates (all citizens)	46	41	41	34	40	24		
Use of "party" in evaluating candidates (identifiers)	52	46	47	37	44	27		
Positive evaluation of own or both parties	74	72	74	64	59	49	49	50
Feel parties "help a good deal in making the government pay attention" to the public				41	36	26	17	28
Do not mention one or the other of the parties as doing the best job on a problem the respondent considers most important (that is, the percentage who are neutral or indifferent)				38	34	48	51	54	50

Sources: Norman H. Nie, Sidney Verba and John R. Petrocik, *The Changing American Voter* (Cambridge: Harvard University Press, 1976), pp. 56, 58, 171; Jack Dennis, "Trends in Public Support for the American Party System," in Jeff Fischel, ed., *Parties and Elections in Anti-Party Age* (Bloomington: Indiana University Press, 1978), p. 10; Martin Wattenberg, "The Decline of Political Partisanship in America: Negativity or Neutrality?" *American Political Science Review* (December 1981); all data based on University of Michigan CPS/SRC/NES.

ideological involvement with politics recently which, at least in the interpretations of some scholars analyzing these data, indicates citizens are linking their issue positions to the vote more than they did before. In all of this, however, the image of parties has been declining, is less positive; parties are seen as less relevant to problem solving. Thus, the "puzzle" (see Table 6).

This poses the "why" question in a particular theoretical context. It suggests that the way *the image* of political parties is communicated recently, as having relevance for today's issues and problems, is changing, and this in turn may be partly responsible for nonvoting. Further, it suggests that all this is going on *because of, or despite,* the activities of political party organizational personnel and activists. It also suggests that the type of politics which interests people these days and with which parties and their activists must be engaged is different—special issue and special interest politics. Above all, it suggests that there should be a careful examination of *what is being communicated to the public about parties* and *by whom.* What is being communicated by party workers, by party organization leaders, by candidates for office, by incumbents in office, by television, by newspapers and other mass media, by opinion leaders, by interest group leaders? If the image of parties is declining despite a relatively consistent level of organizational contact work and political activity, then it is not the inactivity which is at fault, but *the message.*

Table 6   Relationship of party decline to party involvement

A. A decline in positive evaluations of parties, particularly as problem solvers **Plus** B. Decreasing voting turnout	At the same time there is	1. Much party activity 2. Still relatively high party identification 3. No decline in *personal* political activity 4. More issue politics

Much more research needs to be done on the question of why, before there can be any definitive answers. A configuration of forces seems to be at work which can be summarized in the following terms.

Party canvassing and contact efforts may today emphasize the party less frequently and less effectively than in the past. . . .

A second point to keep in mind is that the way party leaders and candidates think about parties and talk about parties in their appeals to the public may be a major factor in the public's image of parties. If the leadership plays down parties, if candidates de-emphasize their party affiliation or seek to maintain aloofness from the party organization, then indeed the public's rejection of parties will be encouraged. . . .

The third approach to explaining the decline in the public's positive images about parties is to lay the blame on the mass media, including not only television but also radio, newspapers, and other printed media. There has been some research on the role of the media in campaigns. The extent of the research directly related to the question of the impact of media content on the voter's images of political parties is much less, however. Some recent studies are more pertinent and do indeed suggest that the mass media role may be significant.

Much of the public is highly exposed to television and newspapers during campaigns as the only real source of political information, ideas, and images. Television has, since the 1960s, gradually become the major source, replacing newspapers, for certain types of voters, particularly those in the lower economic brackets. Both television and newspapers are extensively utilized and thus must be primary sources of political awareness. Certain scholars, such as [political scientist] Michael Robinson, have argued that persons relying on television have a lower sense of political efficacy than those relying on newspapers, radio, or magazines for their political information.

Implicit in [other] research is the clear implication that public feelings toward institutions are influenced by what the media communicate. Parties as key institutions are often treated poorly by the media. The criticism of our politics by the media appears clearly linked to cynicism, and this in turn may well exact its toll on the public's view of parties. Because of negative stories about parties and the cumulative impact of negative reporting a frame of reference emerges in terms of which the citizen judges what the party organizations and party leaders do, and this affects the nature of his identification with and belief in the party system.

CONCLUSION

If there is a weakness in our [party] system today, it is not that we have too much organizational control and leadership, but too little. There are obviously other reforms which should be sought—in Congress, party leadership, presidential nominations, state party organization, campaign techniques, and finance. But in all of this our major principles and objectives should be kept firmly in mind. Primarily we seek to make our parties more basic and useful instruments for the popular control of government, for the solution of social problems, and for the achievement of system integration. They have been functionally central for the achievement of these purposes in the past. Despite their defects they continue today to be major instruments for democratic government in this nation. With necessary reforms we can make them even more central to the governmental process and to the lives of American citizens. Eighty years ago Lord James Bryce, after studying our party system, said "In America the great moving forces are the parties. The government counts for less than in Europe, the parties count for more. . . . " If our citizens and their leaders wish it, American parties will still be the "great moving forces" of our system.

Political Campaigning

□   V. O. Key, Jr., suggested that the voice of the people is not capable of being manipulated by skillful politicians, nor is it apathetic.[1] Rather, his sanguine view was that individuals are indeed aware of government decisions affecting their lives and are capable of rendering rational judgments on the actions of political leaders. At the same time Key pointed out that voter rationality depends upon the rationality of political campaigns, although he argued that in many instances voters are clever enough to see through political propaganda. Joe McGinniss described in his book *The Selling of the President 1968* how public relations experts and political propagandists view the electorate and also demonstrated how these views affected the management of President Nixon's campaign in 1968. Readers should ask themselves how a rational democratic electorate can be maintained if the political leadership holds voters in such low esteem.

[1]V. O. Key, Jr., *The Responsible Electorate* (Cambridge, Mass.: The Belknap Press of Harvard University Press, 1966).

25
Joe McGinniss

THE SELLING OF THE PRESIDENT 1968

Politics, in a sense, has always been a con game.

The American voter, insisting upon his belief in a higher order, clings to his religion, which promises another, better life; and defends passionately the illusion that the men he chooses to lead him are of finer nature than he.

It has been traditional that the successful politician honor this illusion. To succeed today, he must embellish it. Particularly if he wants to be President.

"Potential presidents are measured against an ideal that's a combination of leading man, God, father, hero, pope, king, with maybe just a touch of the avenging Furies thrown in," an adviser to Richard Nixon wrote in a memorandum late in 1967. Then, perhaps aware that Nixon qualified only as father, he discussed improvements that would have to be made—not upon Nixon himself, but upon the image of him which was received by the voter.

That there is a difference between the individual and his image is human nature. Or American nature, at least. That the difference is exaggerated and exploited electronically is the reason for this book.

Advertising, in many ways, is a con game, too. Human beings do not need new automobiles every third year; a color television set brings little enrichment of the human experience; a higher or lower hemline no expansion of consciousness, no increase in the capacity to love.

It is not surprising, then, that politicians and advertising men should have discovered one another. And, once they recognized that the citizen did not so much vote for a candidate as make a psychological purchase of him, not surprising that they began to work together.

The voter, as reluctant to face political reality as any other kind, was hardly an unwilling victim. "The deeper problems connected with advertising," Daniel Boorstin has written in *The Image,* "come less from the unscrupulousness of our 'deceivers' than from our pleasure in being deceived, less from the desire to seduce than from the desire to be seduced. . . .

"In the last half-century we have misled ourselves . . . about men . . . and how much greatness can be found among them. . . . We have become so

From Joe McGinniss, *The Selling of the President 1968,* Chapter 2. Copyright © 1969, by Joemac, Inc. Reprinted by permission of Simon & Schuster, Inc.

accustomed to our illusions that we mistake them for reality. We demand them. And we demand that there be always more of them, bigger and better and more vivid."

The presidency seems the ultimate extension of our error.

Advertising agencies have tried openly to sell presidents since 1952. When Dwight Eisenhower ran for reelection in 1956, the agency of Batton, Barton, Durstine and Osborn, which had been on a retainer throughout his first four years, accepted his campaign as a regular account. Leonard Hall, national Republican chairman, said: "You sell your candidates and your programs the way a business sells its products."

The only change over the past twelve years has been that, as technical sophistication has increased, so has circumspection. The ad men were removed from the parlor but were given a suite upstairs.

What Boorstin says of advertising: "It has meant a reshaping of our very concept of truth," is particularly true of advertising on TV.

With the coming of television, and the knowledge of how it could be used to seduce voters, the old political values disappeared. Something new, murky, undefined started to rise from the mists. "In all countries," Marshall McLuhan writes, "the party system has folded like the organization chart. Policies and issues are useless for election purposes, since they are too specialized and hot. The shaping of a candidate's integral image has taken the place of discussing conflicting points of view."

Americans have never quite digested television. The mystique which should fade grows stronger. We make celebrities not only of the men who cause events but of the men who read reports of them aloud.

The televised image can become as real to the housewife as her husband, and much more attractive. Hugh Downs is a better breakfast companion, Merv Griffin cozier to snuggle with on the couch.

Television, in fact, has given status to the "celebrity" which few real men attain. And the "celebrity" here is the one described by Boorstin: "Neither good nor bad, great nor petty . . . the human pseudoevent . . . fabricated on purpose to satisfy our exaggerated expectations of human greatness."

This is, perhaps, where the twentieth century and its pursuit of illusion have been leading us. "In the last half-century," Boorstin writes, "the old heroic human mold has been broken. A new mold has been made, so that marketable human models—modern 'heroes'—could be mass-produced, to satisfy the market, and without any hitches. The qualities which now commonly make a man or woman into a 'nationally advertised' brand are in fact a new category of human emptiness."

The television celebrity is a vessel. An inoffensive container in which someone else's knowledge, insight, compassion, or wit can be presented. And we respond like the child on Christmas morning who ignores the gift to play with the wrapping paper.

Television seems particularly useful to the politician who can be charming but lacks ideas. Print is for ideas. Newspapermen write not about people but policies; the paragraphs can be slid around like blocks. Everyone is colored gray. Columnists—and commentators in the more polysyllabic magazines—concentrate on ideology. They do not care what a man sounds like; only how he thinks. For the candidate who does not, such exposure can be embarrassing. He needs another way to reach the people.

On television it matters less that he does not have ideas. His personality is what the viewers want to share. He need be neither statesman nor crusader, he must only show up on time. Success and failure are easily measured: How often is he invited back? Often enough and he reaches his goal—to advance from "politician" to "celebrity," a status jump bestowed by grateful viewers who feel that finally they have been given the basis for making a choice.

The TV candidate, then, is measured not against his predecessors—not against a standard of performance established by two centuries of democracy—but against Mike Douglas. How well does he handle himself? Does he mumble, does he twitch, does he make me laugh? Do I feel warm inside?

Style becomes substance. The medium is the massage and the masseur gets the votes.

In office, too, the ability to project electronically is essential. We were willing to forgive John Kennedy his Bay of Pigs; we followed without question the perilous course on which he led us when missiles were found in Cuba; we even tolerated his calling of reserves for the sake of a bluff about Berlin.

We forgave, followed, and accepted because we liked the way he looked. And he had a pretty wife. Camelot was fun, even for the peasants, as long as it was televised to their huts.

Then came Lyndon Johnson, heavy and gross, and he was forgiven nothing. He might have survived the sniping of the displaced intellectuals had he only been able to charm. But no one taught him how. Johnson was syrupy. He stuck to the lens. There was no place for him in our culture.

"The success of any TV performer depends on his achieving a low-pressure style of presentation," McLuhan has written. The harder a man tries, the better he must hide it. Television demands gentle wit, irony, understatement: the qualities of Eugene McCarthy. The TV politician cannot make a speech; he must engage in intimate conversation. He must never press. He should suggest, not state; request, not demand. Nonchalance is the key word. Carefully studied nonchalance.

Warmth and sincerity are desirable but must be handled with care. Unfiltered, they can be fatal. Television did great harm to Hubert Humphrey.

His excesses—talking too long and too fervently, which were merely annoy-ing in an auditorium—became lethal in a television studio. The performer must talk to one person at a time. He is brought into the living room. He is a guest. It is improper for him to shout. Humphrey vomited on the rug.

It would be extremely unwise for the TV politician to admit such knowledge of his medium. The necessary nonchalance should carry beyond his appearance while *on* the show; it should rule his attitude *toward* it. He should express distaste for television; suspicion that there is something "phony" about it. This guarantees him good press, because newspaper reporters, bitter over their loss of prestige to the television men, are certain to stress anti-television remarks. Thus, the sophisticated candidate, while analyzing his own on-the-air technique as carefully as a golf pro studies his swing, will state frequently that there is no place for "public relations gimmicks" or "those show business guys" in his campaign. Most of the television men working for him will be unbothered by such remarks. They are willing to accept anonymity, even scorn, as long as the pay is good.

Into this milieu came Richard Nixon: grumpy, cold, and aloof. He would claim privately that he lost elections because the American voter was an adolescent whom he tried to treat as an adult. Perhaps. But if he treated the voter as an adult, it was as an adult he did not want for a neighbor.

This might have been excused had he been a man of genuine vision. An explorer of the spirit. Martin Luther King, for instance, got by without being one of the boys. But Richard Nixon did not strike people that way. He had, in Richard Rovere's words, "an advertising man's approach to his work," acting as if he believed "policies [were] products to be sold the public—this one today, that one tomorrow, depending on the discounts and the state of the market."

So his enemies had him on two counts: his personality, and the convictions—or lack of such—which lay behind. They worked him over heavily on both.

Norman Mailer remembered him as "a church usher, of the variety who would twist a boy's ear after removing him from church."

McLuhan watched him debate Kennedy and thought he resembled "the railway lawyer who signs leases that are not in the best interests of the folks in the little town."

But Nixon survived, despite his flaws, because he was tough and smart, and—some said—dirty when he had to be. Also, because there was nothing else he knew. A man to whom politics is all there is in life will almost always beat one to whom it is only an occupation.

He nearly became President in 1960, and that year it would not have been by default. He failed because he was too few of the things a President had to be—and because he had no press to lie for him and did not know how to use television to lie about himself.

It was just Nixon and John Kennedy and they sat down together in a television studio and a little red light began to glow and Richard Nixon was finished. Television would be blamed but for all the wrong reasons.

They would say it was makeup and lighting, but Nixon's problem went deeper than that. His problem was himself. Not what he said but the man he was. The camera portrayed him clearly. America took its Richard Nixon straight and did not like the taste.

The content of the programs made little difference. Except for startling lapses, content seldom does. What mattered was the image the viewers received, though few observers at the time caught the point.

McLuhan read Theodore White's *The Making of the President* book and was appalled at the section on the debates. "White offers statistics on the number of sets in American homes and the number of hours of daily use of these sets, but not one clue as to the nature of the TV image or its effects on candidates or viewers. White considers the 'content' of the debates and the deportment of the debaters, but it never occurs to him to ask why TV would inevitably be a disaster for a sharp intense image like Nixon's and a boon for the blurry, shaggy texture of Kennedy." In McLuhan's opinion: "Without TV, Nixon had it made."

What the camera showed was Richard Nixon's hunger. He lost, and bitter, confused, he blamed it on his beard.

He made another, lesser thrust in 1962, and that failed, too. He showed the world a little piece of his heart the morning after and then he moved East to brood. They did not want him, the hell with them. He was going to Wall Street and get rich.

He was afraid of television. He knew his soul was hard to find. Beyond that, he considered it a gimmick; its use in politics offended him. It had not been part of the game when he had learned to play, he could see no reason to bring it in now. He half suspected it was an eastern liberal trick: one more way to make him look silly. It offended his sense of dignity, one of the truest senses he had.

So his decision to use it to become President in 1968 was not easy. So much of him argued against it. But in his Wall Street years, Richard Nixon had traveled to the darkest places inside himself and come back numbed. He was, as in the Graham Greene title, a burnt-out case. All feeling was behind him; the machine inside had proved his hardiest part. He would run for President again and if he would have to learn television to run well, then he would learn it.

America still saw him as the 1960 Nixon. If he were to come at the people again, as candidate, it would have to be as something new; not this scarred, discarded figure from their past.

He spoke to men who thought him mellowed. They detected growth, a new stability, a sense of direction that had been lacking. He would return with fresh perspective, a more unselfish urgency.

His problem was how to let the nation know. He could not do it through the press. He knew what to expect from them, which was the same as he had always gotten. He would have to circumvent them. Distract them with coffee and doughnuts and smiles from his staff and tell his story another way.

Television was the only answer, despite its sins against him in the past. But not just any kind of television. An uncommitted camera could do irreparable harm. His television would have to be controlled. He would need experts. They would have to find the proper settings for him, or if they could not be found, manufacture them. These would have to be men of keen judgment and flawless taste. He was, after all, Richard Nixon, and there were certain things he could not do. Wearing love beads was one. He would need men of dignity. Who believed in him and shared his vision. But more importantly, men who knew television as a weapon: from broadest concept to most technical detail. This would be Richard Nixon, the leader, returning from exile. Perhaps not beloved, but respected. Firm but not harsh; just but compassionate. With flashes of warmth spaced evenly throughout.

Nixon gathered about himself a group of young men attuned to the political uses of television. They arrived at his side by different routes. One, William Gavin, was a thirty-one-year-old English teacher in a suburban high school outside Philadelphia in 1967, when he wrote Richard Nixon a letter urging him to run for President and base his campaign on TV. Gavin wrote on stationery borrowed from the University of Pennsylvania because he thought Nixon would pay more attention if the letter seemed to be from a college professor.

> Dear Mr. Nixon:
> May I offer two suggestions concerning your plans for 1968?
> 1. Run. You can win. Nothing can happen to you, politically speaking, that is worse than what has happened to you. Ortega y Gasset in his *The Revolt of the Masses* says: "These ideas are the only genuine ideas: the ideas of the shipwrecked. All the rest is rhetoric, posturing, farce. He who does not really feel himself lost, is lost without remission . . . " You, in effect, are "lost"; that is why you are the only political figure with a vision to see things the way they are and not as Leftist or Rightist kooks would have them be. Run. You will win.
> 2. A tip for television: instead of those wooden performances beloved by politicians, instead of a glamorboy technique, instead of safety, be bold. Why not have live press conferences as your campaign on television? People will see you daring all, asking and answering questions from reporters, and not simply answering phony "questions" made up by your staff. This would be dynamic; it would be daring. Instead of the medium using you, you would be using the medium. Go on "live" and risk all. It is the only way to convince people of the truth: that you are beyond rhetoric, that you can face reality, unlike your opponents, who will rely on

public relations. Television hurt you because you were not yourself; it didn't hurt the "real" Nixon. The real Nixon can revolutionize the use of television by dynamically going "live" and answering everything, the loaded and the unloaded question. Invite your opponents to this kind of a debate.

Good luck, and I know you can win if you see yourself for what you are; a man who had been beaten, humiliated, hated, but who can still see the truth.

A Nixon staff member had lunch with Gavin a couple of times after the letter was received and hired him.

William Gavin was brought to the White House as a speech writer in January of 1969.

Harry Treleaven, hired as creative director of advertising in the fall of 1967, immediately went to work on the more serious of Nixon's personality problems. One was his lack of humor.

"Can be corrected to a degree," Treleaven wrote, "but let's not be too obvious about it. Romney's cornball attempts have hurt him. If we're going to be witty, let a pro write the words."

Treleaven also worried about Nixon's lack of warmth, but decided that "he can be helped greatly in this respect by how he is handled. . . . Give him words to say that will show his *emotional* involvement in the issues. . . . Buchanan wrote about RFK talking about the starving children in Recife. *That's* what we have to inject. . . .

"He should be presented in some kind of 'situation' rather than cold in a studio. The situation should look unstaged even if it's not."

Some of the most effective ideas belonged to Raymond K. Price, a former editorial writer for the *New York Herald Tribune,* who became Nixon's best and most prominent speech writer in the campaign. Price later composed much of the inaugural address.

In 1967, he began with the assumption that, "The natural human use of reason is to support prejudice, not to arrive at opinions." Which led to the conclusion that rational arguments would "only be effective if we can get the people to make the *emotional* leap, or what theologians call [the] 'leap of faith.' "

Price suggested attacking the "personal factors" rather than the "historical factors" which were the basis of the low opinion so many people had of Richard Nixon.

"These tend to be more a gut reaction," Price wrote, "unarticulated, non-analytical, a product of the particular chemistry between the voter and the *image* of the candidate. *We have to be very clear on this point: that the response is to the image, not to the man.* . . . It's not what's *there* that counts, it's what's projected—and carrying it one step further, it's not what *he* projects but rather what the voter receives. It's not the man we have to change, but rather the *received impression.* And this impression often depends more on the medium and its use than it does on the candidate himself."

So there would not have to be a "new Nixon." Simply a new approach to television.

"What, then, does this mean in terms of our uses of time and of media?" Price wrote.

"For one thing, it means investing whatever time RN needs in order to work out firmly in his own mind that vision of the nation's future that he wants to be identified with. This is crucial. . . . "

So, at the age of fifty-four, after twenty years in public life, Richard Nixon was still felt *by his own staff* to be in need of time to "work out firmly in his own mind that vision of the nation's future that he wants to be identified with."

"Secondly," Price wrote, "it suggests that we take the time and the money to experiment, in a controlled manner, with film and television techniques, with particular emphasis on pinpointing those *controlled* uses of the television medium that can *best* convey the *image* we want to get across. . . . "

"The TV medium itself introduces an element of distortion, in terms of its effect on the candidate and of the often subliminal ways in which the image is received. And it inevitably is going to convey a partial image—thus ours is the task of finding how to control its use so the part that gets across is the part we want to have gotten across. . . . "

"Voters are basically lazy, basically uninterested in making an *effort* to understand what we're talking about . . . ," Price wrote. "Reason requires a high degree of discipline, of concentration; impression is easier. Reason pushes the viewer back, it assaults him, it demands that he agree or disagree; impression can envelop him, invite him in, without making an intellectual demand. . . . When we argue with him we demand that he make the effort of replying. We seek to engage his intellect, and for most people this is the most difficult work of all. The emotions are more easily roused, closer to the surface, more malleable. . . . "

So, for the New Hampshire primary, Price recommended "saturation with a film, in which the candidate can be shown better than he can be shown in person because it can be edited, so only the best moments are shown; then a quick parading of the candidate in the flesh so that the guy they've gotten intimately acquainted with on the screen takes on a living presence—not saying anything, just being seen. . . .

"[Nixon] has to come across as a person larger than life, the stuff of legend. People are stirred by the legend, including the living legend, not by the man himself. It's the aura that surrounds the charismatic figure more than it is the figure itself, that draws the followers. Our task is to build that aura. . . .

"So let's not be afraid of television gimmicks . . . get the voters to like the guy and the battle's two-thirds won."

So this was how they went into it. Trying, with one hand, to build the illusion that Richard Nixon, in addition to his attributes of mind and heart, considered, in the words of Patrick J. Buchanan, a speech writer, "communicating with the people . . . one of the great joys of seeking the Presidency"; while with the other they shielded him, controlled him, and controlled the atmosphere around him. It was as if they were building not a President but an Astrodome, where the wind would never blow, the temperature never rise or fall, and the ball never bounce erratically on the artificial grass.

They could do this, and succeed, because of the special nature of the man. There was, apparently, something in Richard Nixon's character which sought this shelter. Something which craved regulation, which flourished best in the darkness, behind clichés, behind phalanxes of antiseptic advisers. Some part of him that could breathe freely only inside a hotel suite that cost a hundred dollars a day.

And it worked. As he moved serenely through his primary campaign, there was new cadence to Richard Nixon's speech and motion; new confidence in his heart. And, a new image of him on the television screen.

TV both reflected and contributed to his strength. Because he was winning he looked like a winner on the screen. Because he was suddenly projecting well on the medium he had feared, he went about his other tasks with assurance. The one fed upon the other, building to an astonishing peak in August as the Republican convention began and he emerged from his regal isolation, traveling to Miami not so much to be nominated as coronated. On live, but controlled, TV.

☐   The entrance of the professional public relations person into politics, the extensive use of television to "sell" the candidate, all of which began in 1952, has changed the landscape of presidential politics. The advertising of presidential candidates has changed little over the years, because their public relations advisers basically take the same approach to the campaign and the electorate. The images of candidates are to be shaped to optimize their appeal to the voters. The loss of elections is now blamed as much on media advisers as on the candidates and their public policy stances. Joe McGinniss, in the preceding selection, puts this idea in its most cynical form in his comment on President Nixon's campaign in 1960: "He nearly became President in 1960, and that year it would not have been by default. He failed because he was too few of the things that a President had to be—and because he had no press to lie for him and did not know how to use television to lie about himself." Nixon's defeat in 1960 is often said to have been caused by deficiencies in his popular image, including his *physical* appearance in the first television debate with John F. Kennedy. Thus, his television advisers in 1968 were very careful to structure the television environment in such a way as to project a favorable Nixon image.

The McGinniss description of the 1968 election could, with very few changes, have been applied to the 1976 and 1980 presidential elections. The candidates were different, but the public relations advisers took the same approach to selling them to the public. On the whole, the emphasis was on *images,* not issues. One seeks in vain through the verbiage of the 1976 and 1980 presidential campaigns to find many concrete statements on public policy. And, as is always the case, what public issues were highlighted were largely selected on the basis of their supposed appeal to the electorate.

Long before the 1976 presidential campaigns got under way Jimmy Carter had become a media event, if not a media creation. Hundreds of newspaper and magazine articles had portrayed him as an exciting new face on the political scene, which had helped him (admittedly with a highly effective political organization) to gain widespread support in the presidential primaries throughout the nation. People felt that they "knew" Jimmy Carter. The popular image of Carter raised expectations to a point where people were bound to be disappointed. The 1980 election reflected widespread cynicism about the role of government, perhaps in part the result of belief in the continuous media hype of the candidates as persons who would solve the nation's problems.

Political Consultants

Electoral politics has become a big business. Running for office is extraordinarily expensive, particularly at the national level. Successful House candidates spend an average of approximately $250,000 to be elected, while Senate races cost in the millions of dollars. Political consultants contribute to the high cost of campaigns, not only by the large fees they charge, but also because they have convinced candidates that widespread use of the media, particularly television, which is very expensive, is indispensable to a successful campaign. National, state, and even local candidates for office have come to consider political consultants indispensable. The consultants themselves have become an important political force, shaping the electoral process and even influencing public policy formation because of their access to office holders. The following selection analyzes the impact of consultants upon the political process.

26

Ron Suskind

THE POWER OF POLITICAL CONSULTANTS

I've got this senator in his office," says Robert Goodman, "and I'm shooting for three hours." The 55-year-old media consultant leans over the dinner table in a Maryland restaurant, sharing the events of his day. As he talks, his taut, wiry body begins to vibrate, hands waving, voice rising with the measured beat of a theatrical entertainer. "I fire questions at him. I berate him. I say, 'Don't give me that stuff. Answer the question. Tell me what you feel.' The whole time, he's on camera. I've never brought the camera in this close. Finally he forgets it's there. He's sweating, getting mad, tie loosened, vulnerable."

There is no script to the television commercial Goodman is describing, just the lights and cameras and the consultant peppering the candidate with questions. The goal of the advertisements is to change the voters' perception of an already well-known public figure, and Goodman wants his subject—in this case, Senator Roger W. Jepsen, Republican of Iowa—with his defenses down. "That works," he says. "The voters have heard about this person, or seen him from a distance, but now they're close. Here's who he really is. Voters are saying, 'Hey, I didn't know him before.' "

Goodman is among the masters of political imagery, one of a handful of high-priced, much-sought-after experts who have spent the last decade remaking the political landscape.

Media consultants design and produce all their clients' advertising—print and radio as well as television—and often decide where and when it will appear. They set themes for their candidates, raise funds and mobilize networks of longtime friends and allies to work in the campaigns.

Together with television, the consultants have produced a new kind of candidate—attractive, well-connected and docile—attractive enough to come across on television, well-connected enough to bring in the kind of money needed to buy television time and docile enough to tailor words, and even ideas, to a consultant's instructions.

Such stars as Goodman, who specializes in Republicans, and Robert D. Squier, a Democratic counterpart, spend most of their time on gubernatorial and senatorial races and usually avoid the Presidential primaries. "It's a crapshoot," says Squier, who was courted last year by several Democratic Presidential hopefuls. A primary contest leaves him no time for other races, and, as Squier puts it, "You can end up at the convention with

From *The New York Times,* August 12, 1984. Copyright © 1984 by The New York Times Company. Reprinted by permission.

nothing." What's more, a collection of six or seven statewide races can earn a consultant substantially more than a single primary race. Squier commonly receives $60,000 up front for each statewide race, plus a 15 percent commission on the millions of dollars spent to air his commercials.

Consultants rely on data from sophisticated polltakers and money from professional fund-raisers. The old-style politics of the precinct clubhouse are fading into distant memory. Even the traditional campaign events that are still used—such as the candidate shaking hands at a factory gate—are used as backgrounds for media coverage, not principally as a way to win votes at the factory. Austin Ranney, resident scholar at the American Enterprise Institute, says that consultants "are just short of being dictators of the modern campaign."

Critics fear that the public is being misled and manipulated by the half-truths the consultants build into many of the subtle new political ads. "Most people," says Larry J. Sabato, professor of government at the University of Virginia, "still think what you see is what you get."

For all their impact and the controversy they cause, the practices and practitioners of political advertising are little understood. "Squier and Goodman may be two of the most powerful men in America," says Susan Bennett King, who has directed the Washington office of the National Committee for an Effective Congress and was chairman of the Consumer Product Safety Commission, "and somehow no one knows who they are."

For Bob Squier, as for other top media consultants, success depends to an important degree on a vast network of the politically involved, including elected officials, journalists, wealthy contributors and veteran campaign staffers. The preparation for a race starts in the fall before the campaign year, with a kind of mating dance as candidates and consultants pair off. Most matches have been made by spring, and the first ads begin to appear on television in early summer. But the heavy flood of ads that signals the real start of the campaign is an August event.

Consider the candidacy of William Winter. Last fall, Winter, then Governor of Mississippi, made several exploratory trips to visit Squier and Democratic leaders in Washington to discuss the possibility of challenging Senator Thad Cochran, a first-term Republican. Winter and Squier paid a visit to Audrey Sheppard, director of campaign services for the Democratic Senatorial Campaign Committee, and other committee members. They discussed what assistance the committee—which offers candidates various campaign services, as well as funds—might offer Winter. No final commitments were made.

A few days later, Squier was having dinner with his wife, Prudence, at a restaurant not far from Capitol Hill. Across the room he spotted Audrey Sheppard, who was just finishing dinner with one of his major competitors, Jill Buckley. On their way out, the two women stopped. "Audrey," Squier said, "we need it in writing." He motions as though signing a document. "Winter is not going to ask you for it. He's just not that kind of guy."

By December, Winter had decided to leave politics and announced publicly that he would become chancellor of the University of Mississippi when his term as Governor expired in mid-January. But, as Winter now recalls, he was actually "very distraught" about the decision to leave the political arena. Over the next few days, he had a dozen telephone conversations with Squier, who had helped get him elected Governor. The main problem, Squier says, was a shortage of financial backing for Winter within Mississippi, and the consultant spent part of the weekend of December 17–18 plugging into his network.

One of the many calls Squier made in Winter's behalf was to a longtime friend, Senator Lloyd M. Bentsen of Texas, chairman of the Democratic Senatorial Campaign Committee. And one of Bentsen's calls that weekend was to Winter. None of the parties will discuss just how big a role Squier played in the placement of that call or exactly what the Senator and the Governor talked about. But on Monday, the Governor announced that he would not join Ole Miss after all. On February 6, he announced for the Senate.

In March, the Winter campaign received $17,500 from the Democratic Senatorial Campaign Committee and may receive as much as $144,000 more. The money will help fund a media blitz starting, most likely, in late August. Up to this point, the Winter campaign, which is starting to catch up with Senator Thad Cochran in money raised, has run no television ads. But Guy Land, Winter's campaign manager, says that "Squier has really helped fund raising by talking up the campaign around the country."

On a cold day in December, Bob Squier, a blond, broad-shouldered 49-year-old, sits in front of a fireplace at his Victorian house in the foothills of the Blue Ridge Mountains of Virginia and dreams about the coming campaigns for seats in the Senate. "It may be possible for the Democrats to seize control of the Senate this year," he says. "William Winter is important in that calculation."

Today there are 55 Republicans in the Senate and only 45 Democrats, but two powerful Republican incumbents are retiring this year, and in a handful of the 33 races the Democrats are given a good chance of picking up seats. Squier is involved in three of those contests. (He is also handling three incumbent Senators.) Albert Gore Jr., son of the former Senator from Tennessee, is running for the seat to be vacated by Majority Leader Howard H. Baker Jr. Paul Simon, a liberal Congressman, is challenging Illinois's three-term Senator, Charles Percy. And then there is William Winter.

Squier has a variety of reasons for being high on Winter. Tall, rugged, earnest, the 61-year-old politician has a large following in Mississippi.

What's more, Winter's opponent, Thad Cochran, was substantially helped in 1978 when a third-party candidate split the Democratic vote, and no serious third-party challenge is expected this year.

Though Squier wants to win every campaign, he likes to take chances, too. "One can't make a career out of doing home movies for sure winners," he says. "You've got to try races where you will make the difference of victory, instead of just increasing the point spread." That's why, Squier claims, he often chooses to represent challengers, and three out of seven candidates he has this year are challenging for the Senate. Another reason for working with challengers: "Very few fancy themselves as campaign experts. They listen."

Beyond the immediate race in Mississippi, Winter has other attractions for the consultant. Squier doesn't put it in these terms, but the Governor is seen inside the party as a possible candidate for President, or at least Vice President.

Races for national office are familiar to Bob Squier. In fact, his first political contract was for a Presidential race. In 1968, he embarked on his consulting career by handling television for Hubert H. Humphrey in his race for the Presidency. He had begun in the film medium in 1955 when, as a senior at the University of Minnesota, he put together the first of the 200 film documentaries he has since made. It was a version of Edward Steichen's photographic exhibition "The Family of Man." In the years that followed, he worked as a producer at National Educational Television and as director of television production at the United States Information Agency. Since going to work for Hubert Humphrey, Squier has taken on 89 campaigns, most of them statewide contests.

That kind of experience can hone political and television skills to a fine edge, and consultants as a group, like Squier, are not bashful about their achievements. But the way they use the skills they have developed sometimes provokes criticism.

When Squier joined Senator Gary Hart's re-election campaign in 1980, it was already the first week in September. According to a Denver Post poll, Hart was trailing his opponent, Mary Estill Buchanan, by 15 points. In return for a $50,000 fee, Squier rapidly created a series of new ads for Hart. The candidate was shown in a blue-collar locale—a coal mine, for example—where the workers did most of the talking and Hart looked tough and down-home in fatigues and jeans. It was a new image for the urbane, intellectual Senator, and there were charges in the press that the ads were purposely "macho," designed to exploit the fact that Hart was running against a woman. Hart won the election by less than 2 percent of the vote.

Political analysts believe the ads helped Hart, but they drew the fire of women's groups. "It is the conscious manipulation of people's biases," says Judy Goldsmith, president of the National Organization for Women. The ads, she says, subliminally conveyed a "very destructive stereotype"—that women "lack confidence, which they don't, or are timid, which they're not." Squier insists that he had no such intention.

Alan K. Simpson, the 6-foot, 7-inch junior Senator from Wyoming, slouches easily at his desk in the Hart Senate Office Building. He is recalling an evening early in 1978 when, for the first time, he spoke seriously with Bob Goodman about running for the Senate. They are an unlikely pair, the relaxed, folksy Wyoming rancher and the supercharged salesman, but they formed a successful partnership in the 1978 election, and Goodman is handling Simpson's campaign this year.

"He came over to my house for dinner and drinks," Simpson says of their first meeting, "but I didn't drink anything. I wanted a clear head. Of course, Goodman doesn't just arrive. He bursts onto the scene. He's saying, 'Who are you? Do you usually sit that way? Do you wear cowboy boots?'

"Well, I just said, 'Hold it a minute, Mister. I don't want you to tell me how to do anything. You're not going to package me, make me something I'm not.'

"He says, 'Right, right. Don't worry.' Next thing, he's up. It's like watching the Sorcerer's Apprentice—dancing, singing, bringing the waters down."

Simpson is not the first candidate to worry that he would be taken over by Goodman or one of the other superstar consultants. In the case of another Wyoming Republican, Malcolm Wallop, the tensions between the candidate and the consultant led to a bitter severing of ties.

In 1976, Wallop, then a 43-year-old State Senator from Big Horn, hired Bob Goodman to run his campaign for the United States Senate. From Goodman's point of view, Wallop had certain disadvantages as a candidate in Wyoming. He was born in New York (although he was raised in Wyoming), educated at Yale and descended from British nobility. Goodman's television commercial sought to compensate for all that.

It showed Malcolm Wallop riding at the head of a troop of 75 galloping cowboys. "Ride with us, Wyoming," the narrator intoned at the end of the spot as the music swelled. By most accounts, the ad—which is shown in university communications classes as the epitome of political salesmanship— was a crucial factor in Wallop's eventual victory.

Six years later, when Wallop ran for re-election, he chose another consultant. "Bob," says the Senator angrily, "has a tendency to dramatize— like he discovered me or something." Their relationship was strained further recently when Goodman was quoted as saying, "I invented Mal Wallop."

The University of Virginia's Larry Sabato speaks of the fine line consultants must walk. On one hand, they must be well-known enough to attract the strongest, richest clients; on the other hand, he says, "Consultants can become an albatross around the candidate's neck by being too willing to take credit." The result of the consultant's self-promotion: "The candidate's own leadership qualities are questioned."

In fact, the use of ever more artful ads to alter dramatically a candidate's image is seen by many political analysts as a clear and present danger to representative government. According to Sabato: "The voters really have no idea about the sophistication of the message, or, for that matter, how powerful these media men are. People just react to what they see."

How can a voter discover the real candidate, given the subtle skill with which the media consultants labor to paper over the cracks? The consultants answer by saying that, in any race, the crossfire of advertising claims and the live television appearances of candidates give the public a better chance than ever before to know whom they're voting for.

According to Bob Squier, an election is something like a trial, with attorneys presenting their clients in the best light and the media trying to make sense of it all. "It is the responsibility of the free press," he says, "to understand what goes on behind the camera. They have to keep up with the fast-rushing technology and keep the public informed about what they are seeing."

However, by presenting candidates through carefully controlled "media events," consultants like Squier and Goodman are constantly trying to limit the ways the press can cover a candidate and, in that way, manipulate coverage. They design their campaigns to limit the chances a candidate has to make a gaffe when he encounters the press and the public. For example, when a candidate is making a short public statement, he is advised by his consultant to follow the script and conclude with a brief summation of the speech. Often, the candidate is given some carefully planned anecdote or quip that is felt by the campaign staff to be "quotable." The idea is that the television and radio stations and newspapers should have nothing else of interest to seize upon besides that which is intended by the campaign.

"The magic words this year," according to Squier, "are, 'Are we live?'"

Unedited coverage of an event as it happens raises the ratings of news programs, so many television stations tend to cooperate with a candidate who arranges to fly into an airport just as the evening news gets under way. "The plane happens to land at 6:32," Squier says, "and the candidate can bypass the news editing process and go directly to the public."

News coverage of campaigns "deals predominantly with tactics, with 'horse race' questions of who is winning," says Thomas Patterson, a Syracuse University political scientist, "often because they are offered very little else by a campaign beyond the carefully orchestrated media event."

The press is aware of how it is being treated, and news reports will sometimes point out the artificiality of a staged event. But most consultants are willing to risk such criticism, as long as the event gets on television.

Despite the efforts of consultants, press coverage can destroy a media campaign if a candidate's commercials conflict with the image of the candidate as it is reflected in the press. Experts cite John Glenn's primary campaign as a case in point. His advertising spots stressed his image as an astronaut and a dynamic American hero, but during campaign appearances he spent his time discoursing dryly on policy issues instead of waving the flag. According to some analysts, the disparity between the two images damaged his campaign.

It is ironic that candidates like Glenn, who fail to conform to the image conveyed by their advertisements, are often viewed by the public as artificial because their advertising appears at odds with news coverage. Conversely, the candidate whose public appearances, as conveyed by the press, are in tune with his advertising is viewed as being authentic.

The feelings of many experts about television campaign spots and news coverage are summed up by James L. Sundquist, a senior fellow at the Brookings Institution: "The voters are picking up more information now than they would get otherwise. On the bad side, however, is the quality of the information they are getting. The voters are not informed in depth about a candidate. There is so much emphasis on the personality factor. Looks figure so importantly." The problem, he says, is that "a television image does not mean a capacity to govern."

Media consultants offer a variety of approaches and specialties. The team of Douglas Bailey and John Deardourff, who handle moderate Republican candidates, is largely issue-oriented. Tony Schwartz is a New York media consultant whose ads often rely upon subliminal techniques. David Garth, a pioneer of the trade, offers Democratic and some Republican candidates a total package of services, from polling to fund raising, and in return wants nearly total control. David Sawyer, who handles Democrats, is known as an expert at campaign technology and a master of cinéma vérité. Roger Ailes, who works on Republican campaigns, has made his reputation as a supreme strategist.

Since the early days of political advertisements on television, two formats have been consistently noted. "Feel-good" spots, as they are sometimes called, concentrate on the candidate's personal qualities. "Issue" spots emphasize the candidate's support of particular positions and groups of voters. Bob Goodman has made it his business to break out of those molds.

When he graduated from Haverford College in 1949, Goodman's aspiration was to be a star of Tin Pan Alley. "Ever since I was young, I wanted to be a songwriter," he reflected late one night in his office, a converted grist mill in tiny Brooklandville, Md., 20 minutes from Baltimore. When he came to New York, after a stint as a public information officer with the Air Force, Goodman had high hopes and a collection of songs for a Broadway show. After some hard months, he landed a job at the now-defunct Joseph Katz Company, a major advertising firm.

Goodman's wit, energy and songwriting ability were perfect for Madison Avenue. He rose fast at the agency and started his own firm in 1959.

"Handling just private clients—well, there was something missing," Goodman says now. "Maybe it was drama." In 1966, Spiro Agnew wanted to be Governor of Maryland, and Goodman, wanting a change, signed on.

Since then he has handled more than 100 clients, including George Bush and 10 Republican senators currently in office. This year, he is involved in 11 races, including those of several "safe" incumbent Republican senators and one Democratic representative. He will also be trying to save the careers of three first-term Republicans "targeted" for defeat by the Democrats—as well as the Republican Party's control of the Senate—by handling Senator Roger Jepsen of Iowa, Senator Thad Cochran of Mississippi, and Senator Rudy Boschwitz of Minnesota.

One of the closest and most interesting races this year is expected to be that pitting Boschwitz against Joan Growe, Minnesota's Secretary of State, who is the favorite to win the Democratic primary there on Sept. 11. With Goodman's help, Boschwitz won election in 1978 by a substantial margin, but Minnesota traditionally sends Democrats to the Senate.

The first task of the media consultant is to determine the political strengths and weaknesses of the candidate. To discover how the public felt about Boschwitz, Goodman used a technique known as "concept testing." A group of representative voters was gathered to fill out questionnaires and discuss among themselves Boschwitz's qualities as a Senator and as a person. They were asked, for example, to rate him on the extent to which he is "someone who cares for and helps the people of Minnesota" and "a leader, or policymaker."

Boschwitz scored highest on the help-the-people category, and Goodman designed the early spots in the campaign to play to this strength. The voters, he felt, needed to be reminded of why they liked the candidate. The following commercial was one of the four he created.

A farmer walks past a herd of cattle, his boots crunching on the snow. Steam rises from the cows' nostrils. Not until a third of the ad has run does the narration begin, a voice-over of the farmer himself. "I've been farming since I could walk," he says. "Can't imagine doing something else."

The farmer enters his house, takes off his boots—there's a hole in one sock—and joins his big family for dinner. They say grace. The spot is more than halfway through when Boschwitz's name is first mentioned: "It used to be that taxes could keep you from passing your farm on. But Senator Rudy Boschwitz stood up for us. Brought down inheritance taxes."

Fifty-two seconds into the spot, the farmer turns to face the camera. "Senator Boschwitz," he says, "you sure came through for us. Just want to say thanks." Finally, a small picture of Boschwitz appears in the corner of the screen.

Goodman says he held back the political message of the Boschwitz spots "until you're completely involved." Understatement, he says, is critical: "If there is one thing that smacks of persuasion or manipulation, it is ruined. If anyone is saying, 'I stand for this and that, and I want your vote,' then greed is portrayed." Goodman wants to sneak up on the viewer. "If you love the little person on the screen," he says, "and you will, some of it will transfer to the candidate. You won't even know it's happening."

Once the spots were completed, Goodman made use of a new testing service that has been offered by the National Republican Senatorial Committee to all Republican incumbents and challengers. Before they appear, the ads are screened in front of groups. According to William J. Feltus, of Market Opinion Research, the firm that created and conducted the tests, members of the groups are selected on the basis of "attitudinal, as opposed to demographic," characteristics to represent "the soft middle of the electorate, not strongly committed, not especially knowledgeable about the candidate and, for the most part, nonpartisan."

The 80 or so members of each group, who are paid between $10 and $20, are split into smaller groups of 15 to 40 people and put together in a room. They are given a questionnaire before they see the spots, and another after they finish. They are also asked to evaluate each spot as to the influence it will have on other people—on the assumption that they will thereby reveal their own feelings.

The results of the questionnaires are fed into a computer for analysis. "You have to immediately send the television stations instructions about which spots to run, where to run them, and how strong a concentration is needed," Feltus says. The group results must be used before they go stale. "Political races are so volatile, and the voters so sensitive, you can't afford to wait."

For eight weeks, starting in February, Goodman ran four spots designed to make voters feel that Boschwitz cares about Minnesotans and their problems. A poll sponsored by the Minneapolis Star and Tribune compared Boschwitz's standing at the beginning of that period and at the end. The number of respondents who gave him an "approval" rating rose from 65 percent to 75 percent; his "strong approval" rating jumped from 15 percent to 35 percent.

Even as the spots were running throughout Minnesota, Bob Goodman was responding to a major negative comment that emerged from the Market Opinion Research tests. Some viewers wanted more information about what Boschwitz had actually done for the farmer and for the senior citizen, foundry owner and drug counselor shown in the other spots.

Four 60-second follow-up spots were produced. They begin with a 10-second clip from the first series, like a "scenes-from-the-last-episode" segment of a television miniseries, and then present what they describe as "the story behind the story." This is followed by a flurry of photographs of

Boschwitz during his five years on Capitol Hill. The photos appear to document the narration—in the case of the farmer ad, Boschwitz's effort to lower the inheritance tax—though, in fact, they are stock photos.

The dissecting of viewer behavior and the careful testing of ads before they air are all elements of the imperfect—but constantly advancing—science of polltaking. The 30-second spot is the end result of all the analysis and expertise; the first step is knowing the voter. For that, consultants rely on polltakers—well-paid, independent professionals who are a vital part of the network of campaign specialists.

With the rise of the media consultant, polltaking has become more and more important in planning and conducting races. According to Bob Squier, "It used to be you'd take a poll, set up a media plan, and six months later find out how it worked. Nowadays, you can send out your media, check out how it worked by the very next day and fine-tune the message accordingly."

Polltaking starts early in a campaign, often a year or more before the election, and consists of extensive phone interviewing of voters. The data are updated and cross-referenced regularly until election day. By pinpointing the issues that the voters care most about and the qualities they like about a candidate, polls enable a consultant to decide which issues or images to stress, and which to sidestep.

"Now you can put it all into a computer model," said the consultant David Sawyer, "and then begin to do your analysis. You can punch in attitudinal distinctions, or your different target groups. Now you have instant access to your data."

The data can also disclose an opponent's weaknesses—and the media consultant can exploit these weaknesses through so-called "negative advertising." Bob Goodman is renowned for his humorous negative advertisements, such as the classic one he used for Malcolm Wallop against Senator Gail McGee, Democrat of Wyoming, in 1976. Polls showed that voters were opposed to government regulation and felt that Washington was out of touch with Wyoming. Goodman decided to make an ad attacking a single regulation, and let the viewers make the connection between government controls and Senator McGee.

For the ad, Goodman picked a regulation, then being considered by the Occupational Safety and Health Administration, that would have required employers to provide sanitary facilities for agricultural workers on the job. (McGee had no involvement with the regulation, and it was never adopted.) The spot—known among consultants as the "potty spot"—began by quoting a brief excerpt from the Federal Register about the proposed regulation. Following the quote, the ad showed a cowboy riding the range with a portable toilet strapped to his saddle. Voters laughed, and Senator McGee went down to defeat.

Negative advertising can help a campaign in two ways: it can remind voters of something they don't like about the opposing candidate, and it can put the opposition on the defensive. The spot challenges the opposing candidate to respond, often with emotion and in his own words, and that is politically dangerous. All the care that has gone into crafting an image for a candidate can be destroyed if the candidate responds to a negative advertisement by lashing out angrily at his opponent. With issues playing a smaller part in today's campaigns, more attention is paid to any mistake a politician makes in the course of a race.

If elected officials are more and more dependent upon media consultants, the dependence does not end on Election Day. With television lights permanently fixed on Washington, the media consultant's skill in presenting ideas and images to the public has become indispensable to the politician, whether he is running for office or between elections.

"In the early days," says Bob Squier, "it was always a search for new magic, a new consultant with every election. No more. I talk to Jim Sasser more now than during his election," he added, referring to Senator James R. Sasser, Democrat of Tennessee.

Some critics contend that the line between candidacy and government service, always blurred, has now virtually disappeared; that senators and representatives are perpetually engaged in "media events," and that drawing the cameras has become an end in itself. The never-ending campaign, they say, distracts elected officials from the undramatic business of building coalitions that can enact legislation, and the fear of making a mistake results in cautious and unimaginative legislators.

"It really doesn't make any difference," says Representative Tony Coelho, Democrat of California, and chairman of the Democratic Congressional Campaign Committee, "what kind of law you create. Today, it's only the perception you create that's important. And the perception is created on TV."

"Men who came to Congress 30 years ago," Speaker of the House Thomas P. O'Neill Jr. said recently, "usually served in their local state legislature, or in the city council, or were mayors, or a part of the party organization, and they had discipline when they came.

"Today, about 60 percent of the members of Congress never served before in any legislative body. You don't have to have the party organization out there that you once had.

"Today, new members depend on their ability to get their message across through the television."

Ultimately, it is a question of shifting loyalties. Political parties traditionally provided a candidate with workers and funds to help him get elected, and in return expected him to restrict both his personal ambitions and his legislative independence in order to build coalitions and maintain party discipline. Today, the political consultant is often the most important fund-raiser a candidate has, and television commercials are more valued than campaign volunteers.

"Elected officials are accountable to voters and loyal to their consultants," says Larry Sabato. "They no longer have any reason to be loyal to the parties."

The consultant does not require a candidate he has helped elect to restrain his ambitions—in fact, he welcomes the chance to take his client higher. But his reputation as a winner is what brings in the business, so he wants the candidate to give him credit for his victory, or at least to remain silent when the consultant takes responsibility for a win. The consultant does not care about party discipline, but he does care about his political network. He wants, and usually gets, access to the new senators and governors, and to their staffs. These staff members replenish the consultant's network of powerful contacts and provide fresh troops for the next campaign.

"Entree to the right people is important," Sabato says. "Many consultants are hired by lobby groups as well, because the lobbies know consultants have access to elected officials. It's all in the family."

CHAPTER 5

Interest Groups

Interest groups are vital cogs in the wheels of the democratic process. Although *Federalist 10* suggests that one major purpose of the separation of powers system is to break and control the "evil effects" of faction, modern political theorists take a much more sanguine view of the role that political interest groups as well as parties play in government. No longer are interest groups defined as being opposed to the "public interest." They are vital channels through which particular publics participate in the governmental process. This chapter examines the nature of interest groups and shows how they function.

The Nature and Functions of Interest Groups

Group theory is an important component of democratic political theory. The essence of group theory is that in the democratic process interest groups interact naturally and properly to produce public policy. In American political thought, the origins of this theory can be found in the theory of concurrent majority in John C. Calhoun's *Disquisition on Government.*

It is very useful to discuss the operation of interest groups within the framework of what can best be described as a concurrent majority system. In contemporary usage the phrase "concurrent majority" means a system in which major government policy decisions must be approved by the dominant interest groups directly affected. The word *concurrent* suggests that each group involved must give its consent before policy can be enacted. Thus a concurrent majority is a majority of each group considered separately. If we take as an example an area such as agricultural policy, in which three or four major private interest groups can be identified, we can say that the concurrent majority is reached when each group affected gives its approval before agricultural policy is passed.

The extent to which such a system of concurrent majority is actually functioning is a matter that has not been fully clarified by empirical research. Nevertheless, it does seem tenable to conclude that in many major areas of public policy, it is necessary at least to achieve a concurrent majority of the *major* or *dominant* interests affected.

The *theory* of concurrent majority originated with John C. Calhoun. Calhoun, born in 1781, had a distinguished career in public service at both the national and state levels. The idea of concurrent majority evolved from the concept of state nullification of federal law. Under this states' rights doctrine, states would be able to veto any national action. The purpose of this procedure was theoretically to protect states in a minority from encroachment by a national majority that could act through Congress, the President, and even the Supreme Court. Those who favored this procedure had little faith in the separation of powers doctrine as an effective device to prevent the arbitrary exercise of national power. At the end of his career Calhoun decided to incorporate his earlier views on state nullification into a more substantial theoretical treatise in political science; thus he wrote his famous *Disquisition on Government* (New York: D. Appleton & Co., 1853) in the decade between 1840 and 1850. He attempted to develop a general theory of constitutional (limited) government, the primary mechanism of which would be the ability of the major interest groups (states in Calhoun's time) to veto legislation adverse to their interests. Students should overlook some of the theoretical inconsistencies in Calhoun and concentrate upon the basic justification he advances for substituting his system of concurrent majority for the separation of powers device. Under the latter, group interests are not necessarily taken into account, for national laws can be passed on the basis of a numerical majority. And even though this majority may reflect the interests of some groups, it will not necessarily reflect the interests of all groups affected. Calhoun argued that a system in which the major interest groups can dominate the policy process is really more in accord with constitutional democracy than the system established in our Constitution and supported in *Federalist 10*.

The group theory of John C. Calhoun has been updated and carried over into modern political science by several writers, one of the most important being David B. Truman. David Truman's selection, taken from *The Governmental Process* (1951), contains (1) a definition of the term "interest group" and (2) a brief outline of the frame of reference within which the operations of interest groups should be considered. A fairly articulate interest group theory of the governmental process is sketched by Truman. It will become evident to the student of American government that interest groups, like political parties, form an integral part of our political system. Further, interest group theory suggests an entirely new way of looking at government.

27

David B. Truman

THE GOVERNMENTAL PROCESS

INTEREST GROUPS

Interest group refers to any group that, on the basis of one or more shared attitudes, makes certain claims upon other groups in the society for the establishment, maintenance, or enhancement of forms of behavior that are implied by the shared attitudes. . . . [F]rom interaction in groups arise certain common habits of response, which may be called norms, or shared attitudes. These afford the participants frames of reference for interpreting and evaluating events and behaviors. In this respect all groups are interest groups because they are shared-attitude groups. In some groups at various points in time, however, a second kind of common response emerges, in addition to the frame of reference. These are shared attitudes toward what is needed or wanted in a given situation, as demands or claims upon other groups in the society. The term "interest group" will be reserved here for those groups that exhibit both aspects of the shared attitudes. . . .

Definition of the interest group in this fashion . . . permits the identification of various potential as well as existing interest groups. That is, it invites examination of an interest whether or not it is found at the moment as one of the characteristics of a particular organized group. Although no group that makes claims upon other groups in society will be found without an interest or interests, it is possible to examine interests that are not at a particular point in time the basis of interactions among individuals, but that may become such. . . .

GROUPS AND GOVERNMENT:
DIFFICULTIES IN A GROUP INTERPRETATION OF POLITICS

Since we are engaged in an effort to develop a conception of the political process in the United States that will account adequately for the role of groups, particularly interest groups, it will be appropriate to take account of some of the factors that have been regarded as obstacles to such a conception and that have caused such groups to be neglected in many explanations of the dynamics of government. Perhaps the most important practical reason for this neglect is that the significance of groups has only fairly recently been forced to the attention of political scientists by the

From *The Governmental Process,* by David Truman. Copyright 1951 by Alfred A. Knopf, Inc. Reprinted by permission of the publisher.

tremendous growth in the number of formally organized groups in the United States within the last few decades. It is difficult and unnecessary to attempt to date the beginning of such attention, but Herring in 1929, in his groundbreaking book, *Group Representation Before Congress,* testified to the novelty of the observations he reported when he stated: "There has developed in this government an extra-legal machinery of as integral and of as influential a nature as the system of party government that has long been an essential part of the government. . . . " Some implications of this development are not wholly compatible with some of the proverbial notions about representative government held by specialists as well as laymen. . . . This apparent incompatibility has obstructed the inclusion of group behaviors in an objective description of the governmental process.

More specifically, it is usually argued that any attempt at the interpretation of politics in terms of group patterns inevitably "leaves something out" or "destroys something essential" about the processes of "our" government. On closer examination, we find this argument suggesting that two "things" are certain to be ignored: the individual, and a sort of totally inclusive unity designated by such terms as "society" and "the state."

The argument that the individual is ignored in any interpretation of politics as based upon groups seems to assume a differentiation or conflict between "the individual" and some such collectivity as the group. . . .

Such assumptions need not present any difficulties in the development of a group interpretation of politics, because they are essentially unwarranted. They simply do not square with . . . evidence concerning group affiliations and individual behavior. . . . We do not, in fact, find individuals otherwise than in groups; complete isolation in space and time is so rare as to be an almost hypothetical situation. It is equally demonstrable that the characteristics of any interest group, including the activities by which we identify it, are governed by the attitudes and the circumstances that gave rise to the interactions of which it consists. There are variable factors, and, although the role played by a particular individual may be quite different in a lynch mob from that of the same individual in a meeting of the church deacons, the attitudes and behaviors involved in both are as much a part of his personality as is his treatment of his family. "The individual" and "the group" are at most merely convenient ways of classifying behavior, two ways of approaching the same phenomena, not different things.

The persistence among nonspecialists of the notion of an inherent conflict between "the individual" and "the group" or "society" is understandable in view of the doctrines of individualism that have underlain various political and economic conflicts over the past three centuries. The notion persists also because it harmonizes with a view of the isolated and independent individual as the "cause" of complicated human events. The personification of events, quite apart from any ethical considerations, is a kind of shorthand convenient in everyday speech and, like supernatural explanations of natural phenomena, has a comforting simplicity. Explanations that take into account multiple causes, including group affiliations, are difficult. The "explanation" of a national complex like the Soviet Union wholly in terms of a Stalin or the "description" of the intricacies of the American government entirely in terms of a Roosevelt is quick and easy. . . .

The second major difficulty allegedly inherent in any attempt at a group interpretation of the political process is that such an explanation inevitably must ignore some greater unity designated as society or the state. . . .

Many of those who place particular emphasis upon this difficulty assume explicitly or implicitly that there is an interest of the nation as a whole, universally and invariably held and standing apart from and superior to those of the various groups included within it. This assumption is close to the popular dogmas of democratic government based on the familiar notion that if only people are free and have access to "the facts," they will all want the same thing in any political situation. It is no derogation of democratic preferences to state that such an assertion flies in the face of all that we know of the behavior of men in a complex society. Were it in fact true, not only the interest group but even the political party should properly be viewed as an abnormality. The differing experiences and perceptions of men not only encourage individuality but also . . . inevitably result in differing attitudes and conflicting group affiliations. "There are," says Bentley in his discussion of this error of the social whole, "always some parts of the nation to be found arrayed against other parts." [From *The Process of Government* (1908).] Even in war, when a totally inclusive interest should be apparent if it is ever going to be, we always find pacifists, conscientious objectors, spies, and subversives, who reflect interests opposed to those of "the nation as a whole."

There is a political significance in assertions of a totally inclusive interest within a nation. Particularly in times of crisis, such as an international war, such claims are a tremendously useful promotional device by means of which a particularly extensive group or league of groups tries to reduce or eliminate opposing interests. Such is the pain attendant upon not "belonging" to one's "own" group that if a normal person can be convinced that he is the lone dissenter to an otherwise universally accepted agreement, he usually will conform. This pressure accounts at least in part for the number of prewar pacifists who, when the United States entered World War II, accepted the draft or volunteered. Assertion of an inclusive "national" or "public interest" is an effective device in many less critical situations as well. In themselves, these claims are part of the data of politics. However, they do not describe any actual or possible political situation within a complex modern nation. In developing a group interpretation of politics, therefore, we do not need to account for a totally inclusive interest, because one does not exist.

Denying the existence of an interest of the nation as a whole does not completely dispose of the difficulty raised by those who insist that a group interpretation must omit "the state." We cannot deny the obvious fact that we are examining a going political system that is supported or at least accepted by a large proportion of the society. We cannot account for such a system by adding up in some fashion the National Association of Manufacturers, the Congress of Industrial Organizations, the American Farm Bureau Federation, The American Legion, and other groups that come to mind when "lobbies" and "pressure groups" are mentioned. Even if the political parties are added to the list, the result could properly be designated as "a view which seems hardly compatible with the relative stability of the political system. . . . " Were such the exclusive ingredients of the political process in the United States, the entire system would have torn itself apart long since.

If these various organized interest groups more or less consistently reconcile their differences, adjust, and accept compromises, we must acknowledge that we are dealing with a system that is not accounted for by the "sum" of the organized interest groups in the society. We must go further to explain the operation of such ideals or traditions as constitutionalism, civil liberties, representative responsibility, and the like. These are not, however, a sort of disembodied metaphysical influence, like Mr. Justice Holmes's "brooding omnipresence." We know of the existence of such factors only from the behavior and the habitual interactions of men. If they exist in this fashion, they are interests. We can account for their operation and for the system by recognizing such interests as representing what . . . we called potential interest groups in the "becoming" stage of activity. "It is certainly true," as Bentley has made clear, "that we must accept a . . . group of this kind as an interest group itself." It makes no difference that we cannot find the home office and the executive secretary of such a group. Organization in this formal sense, as we have seen, represents merely a stage or degree of interaction that may or may not be significant at any particular point in time. Its absence does not mean that these interests do not exist, that the familiar "pressure groups" do not operate as if such potential groups were organized and active, or that these interests may not move from the potential to the organized stage of activity.

It thus appears that the two major difficulties supposedly obstacles to a group interpretation of the political process are not insuperable. We can employ the fact of individuality and we can account for the existence of the state without doing violence to the evidence available from the observed behaviors of men and groups. . . .

INTEREST GROUPS AND THE NATURE OF THE STATE

Men, wherever they are observed, are creatures participating in those established patterns of interaction that we call groups. Excepting perhaps the most casual and transitory, these continuing interactions, like all such interpersonal relationships, involve power. This power is exhibited in two closely interdependent ways. In the first place, the group exerts power over its members; an individual's group affiliations largely determine his attitudes, values, and the frames of reference in terms of which he interprets his experiences. For a measure of conformity to the norms of the group is the price of acceptance within it. . . . In the second place, the group, if it is or becomes an interest group, which any group in society may be, exerts power over other groups in the society when it successfully imposes claims upon them.

Many interest groups, probably an increasing proportion in the United States, are politicized. That is, either from the outset or from time to time in the course of their development they make their claims through or upon the institutions of government. Both the forms and functions of govern-ment in turn are a reflection of the activities and claims of such groups. . . .

The institutions of government are centers of interest-based power; their connections with interest groups may be latent or overt and their activities range in political character from the routinized and widely accepted to the unstable and highly controversial. In order to make claims, political interest groups will seek access to the key points of decision within these institutions. Such points are scattered throughout the structure, including not only the formally established branches of government but also the political parties in their various forms and the relationships between govern-mental units and other interest groups.

The extent to which a group achieves effective access to the institu-tions of government is the resultant of a complex of interdependent factors. For the sake of simplicity these may be classified in three somewhat overlapping categories: (1) factors relating to a group's strategic position in the society; (2) factors associated with the internal characteristics of the group; and (3) factors peculiar to the governmental institutions themselves. In the first category are: the group's status or prestige in the society, affecting the ease with which it commands deference from those outside its bounds; the standing it and its activities have when measured against the widely held but largely unorganized interests or "rules of the game"; the extent to which government officials are formally or informally "members" of the group; and the usefulness of the group as a source of technical and political knowledge. The second category includes: the degree and appro-priateness of the group's organization; the degree of cohesion it can achieve in a given situation, especially in the light of competing group demands upon its membership; the skills of the leadership; and the group's resources in numbers and money. In the third category are: the operating structure of the government institutions, since such established features involve relatively fixed advantages and handicaps; and the effects of the group life of particular units or branches of the government. . . .

A characteristic feature of the governmental system in the United States is that it contains a multiplicity of points of access. The federal system establishes decentralized and more or less independent centers of power, vantage points from which to secure privileged access to the national government. Both a sign and a cause of the strength of the constituent units in the federal scheme is the peculiar character of our party system, which has strengthened parochial relationships, especially those of national legislators. National parties, and to a lesser degree those in the states, tend to be poorly cohesive leagues of locally based organizations rather than unified and inclusive structures. Staggered terms for executive officials and various types of legislators accentuate differences in the effective electorates that participate in choosing these officers. Each of these different, often opposite, localized patterns (constituencies) is a channel of independent access to the larger party aggregation and to the formal government. Thus, especially at the national level, the party is an electing-device and only in limited measure an integrated means of policy determination. Within the Congress, furthermore, controls are diffused among committee chairmen and other leaders in both chambers. The variety of these points of access is further supported by relationships stemming from the constitutional doctrine of separation of powers, from related checks and balances, and at the state and local level from the common practice of choosing an array of executive officials by popular election. At the federal level the formal simplicity of the executive branch has been complicated by a Supreme Court decision that has placed a number of administrative agencies beyond the removal power of the President. The position of these units, however, differs only in degree from that of many that are constitutionally within the Executive Branch. In consequence of alternative lines of access available through the legislature and the Executive and of divided channels for the control of administrative policy, many nominally executive agencies are at various times virtually independent of the Chief Executive.

. . . Within limits, therefore, organized interest groups, gravitating toward responsive points of decision, may play one segment of the structure against another as circumstances and strategic considerations permit. The total pattern of government over a period of time thus presents a protean complex of crisscrossing relationships that change in strength and direction with alternations in the power and standing of interests, organized and unorganized.

☐   From Truman's definition *any* group, organized or unorganized, that has a shared attitude toward goals and methods for achieving them should be classified as an interest group. Truman is essentially saying that, since people generally function as members of groups, it is more useful and accurate for the political observer to view the governmental process as the interaction of political interest groups. If one accepts the sociologist's assumption that people act and interact only as members of groups, then it is imperative that the governmental process be viewed as one of interest group interaction.

Within the framework of Truman's definition it is possible to identify both *public* and *private* interest groups. In the political process, governmental groups sometimes act as interest groups in the same sense as private organizations. In many public policies, governmental groups may have more at stake than private organizations. Thus administrative agencies, for example, may lobby as vigorously as their private counterparts to advance their own interests.

Theodore Lowi refers to group theory as "interest group liberalism." The following selection is taken from his well-known book *The End of Liberalism* (1969), in which he severely criticizes group theory and its pervasive influence upon governmental decision makers. In reading the following selection, remember that the author does not use the term "liberal" in its ordinary sense. The political "liberal" in Lowi's terminology is much like the "economic Liberal" of the early 19th century. Just as economic liberalism preached that the public good emerged automatically from the free clash of private interests, the political liberal (in Lowi's terms) supports group theory which holds that the public interest in government is automatically achieved through the interaction of pressure groups.

28
Theodore J. Lowi

THE END OF LIBERALISM: THE INDICTMENT

The corruption of modern democratic government began with the emergence of interest-group liberalism as the public philosophy. Its corrupting influence takes at least four important forms, four counts, therefore, of an indictment for which most of the foregoing chapters are mere documentation. Also to be indicted, on at least three counts, is the philosophic component of the ideology, pluralism.

SUMMATION 1:
FOUR COUNTS AGAINST THE IDEOLOGY

1. Interest-group liberalism as public philosophy corrupts democratic government because it deranges and confuses expectations about democratic institutions. Liberalism promotes popular decision-making but derogates from the decisions so made by misapplying the notion to the implementation as well as the formulation of policy. It derogates from the processes by treating all values in the process as equivalent interests. It derogates from democratic rights by allowing their exercise in foreign policy, and by assuming they are being exercised when access is provided. Liberal practices reveal a basic disrespect for democracy. Liberal leaders do not wield the authority of democratic government with the resoluteness of men certain of the legitimacy of their positions, the integrity of their institutions, or the justness of the programs they serve.

2. Interest-group liberalism renders government impotent. Liberal governments cannot plan. Liberals are copious in plans but irresolute in planning. Nineteenth-century liberalism was standard without plans. This was an anachronism in the modern state. But twentieth-century liberalism turned out to be plans without standards. As an anachronism it, too, ought to pass. But doctrines are not organisms. They die only in combat over the minds of men, and no doctrine yet exists capable of doing the job. All the popular alternatives are so very irrelevant, helping to explain the longevity of interest-group liberalism. Barry Goldwater most recently proved the irrelevance of one. The *embourgeoisement* of American unions suggests the irrelevance of others.

Reprinted from *The End of Liberalism* by Theodore J. Lowi, with the permission of W. W. Norton & Company, Inc. Copyright © 1969 by W. W. Norton & Company, Inc.

The Departments of Agriculture, Commerce, and Labor provide illustrations, but hardly exhaust illustrations, of such impotence. Here clearly one sees how liberalism has become a doctrine whose means are its ends, whose combatants are its clientele, whose standards are not even those of the mob but worse, are those the bargainers can fashion to fit the bargain. Delegation of power has become alienation of public domain—the gift of sovereignty to private satrapies. The political barriers to withdrawal of delegation are high enough. But liberalism reinforces these through the rhetoric of justification and often even permanent legal reinforcement: Public corporations—justified, oddly, as efficient planning instruments— permanently alienate rights of central coordination to the directors and to those who own the corporation bonds. Or, as Walter Adams finds, the "most pervasive method . . . for alienating public domain is the certificate of convenience and necessity, or some variation thereof in the form of an exclusive franchise, license or permit. . . . [G]overnment has become increasingly careless and subservient in issuing them. The net result is a general legalization of private monopoly. . . . " While the best examples still are probably the 10 self-governing systems of agriculture policy, these are obviously only a small proportion of all the barriers the interest-group liberal ideology has erected to democratic use of government.

3. Interest-group liberalism demoralizes government, because liberal governments cannot achieve justice. The question of justice has engaged the best minds for almost as long as there have been notions of state and politics, certainly ever since Plato defined the ideal as one in which republic and justice were synonymous. And since that time philosophers have been unable to agree on what justice is. But outside the ideal, in the realms of actual government and citizenship, the problem is much simpler. We do not have to define justice at all in order to weight and assess justice in government, because in the case of liberal policies we are prevented by what the law would call a "jurisdictional fact." In the famous jurisdictional case of *Marbury* v. *Madison* Chief Justice Marshall held that even if all the Justices hated President Jefferson for refusing to accept Marbury and the other "midnight judges" appointed by Adams, there was nothing they could do. They had no authority to judge President Jefferson's action one way or another because the Supreme Court did not possess such jurisdiction over the President. In much the same way, there is something about liberalism that prevents us from raising the question of justice at all, no matter what definition of justice is used.

Liberal governments cannot achieve justice because their policies lack the *sine qua non* of justice—that quality without which a consideration of justice cannot even be initiated. Considerations of the justice in or achieved by an action cannot be made unless a deliberate and conscious attempt was made by the actor to derive his action from a general rule or moral principle governing such a class of acts. One can speak personally of good rules and bad rules, but a homily or a sentiment, like liberal legislation, is not a rule at all. The best rule is one which is relevant to the decision or action in question and is general in the sense that those involved with it have no direct control over its operation. A general rule is, hence, *a priori.* Any governing regime that makes a virtue of avoiding such rules puts itself totally outside the context of justice.

Take the homely example of the bull and the china shop. Suppose it was an op art shop and that we consider op worthy only of the junk pile. That being the case, the bull did us a great service, the more so because it was something we always dreamed of doing but were prevented by law from entering and breaking. But however much we may be pleased, we cannot judge the act. We can only like or dislike the consequences. The consequences are haphazard; the bull cannot have intended them. The act was a thoughtless, animal act which bears absolutely no relation to any aesthetic principle. We don't judge the bull. We only celebrate our good fortune. Without the general rule, the bull can reenact his scenes of creative destruction daily and still not be capable of achieving, in this case, aesthetic justice. The whole idea of justice is absurd.

The general rule ought to be a legislative rule because the United States espouses the ideal of representative democracy. However, that is merely an extrinsic feature of the rule. All that counts is the character of the rule itself. Without the rule we can only like or dislike the consequences of the governmental action. In the question of whether justice is achieved, a government without good rules, and without acts carefully derived therefrom, is merely a big bull in an immense china shop.

4. Finally, interest-group liberalism corrupts democratic government in the degree to which it weakens the capacity of governments to live by democratic formalisms. Liberalism weakens democratic institutions by opposing formal procedure with informal bargaining. Liberalism derogates from democracy by derogating from all formality in favor of informality. Formalism is constraining; playing it "by the book" is a role often unpopular in American war films and sports films precisely because it can dramatize personal rigidity and the plight of the individual in collective situations. Because of the impersonality of formal procedures, there is inevitably a separation in the real world between the forms and the realities, and this kind of separation gives rise to cynicism, for informality means that some will escape their collective fate better than others. There has as a consequence always been a certain amount of cynicism toward public objects in the United States, and this may be to the good, since a little cynicism is the father of healthy sophistication. However, when the informal is elevated to a positive virtue, and hard-won access becomes a share of official authority, cynicism becomes distrust. It ends in reluctance to submit one's fate to the governmental process under any condition, as is the case in the United States in the mid-1960s.

Public officials more and more frequently find their fates paradoxical and their treatment at the hands of the public fickle and unjust when in fact they are only reaping the results of their own behavior, including their direct and informal treatment of the public and the institutions through which they serve the public. The more government operates by the spreading of access, the more public order seems to suffer. The more public men pursue their constituencies, the more they seem to find their constituencies alienated. Liberalism has promoted concentration of democratic authority but deconcentration of democratic power. Liberalism has opposed privilege in policy formulation only to foster it, quite systematically, in the implementation of policy. Liberalism has consistently failed to recognize, in short, that in a democracy forms are important. In a medieval monarchy all formalisms were at court. Democracy proves, for better or worse, that the masses like that sort of thing too.

Another homely parable may help. In the good old days, everyone in the big city knew that traffic tickets could be fixed. Not everyone could get his ticket fixed, but nonetheless a man who honestly paid his ticket suffered in some degree a dual loss: his money, and his self-esteem for having so little access. Cynicism was widespread, violations were many, but perhaps it did not matter, for there were so few automobiles. Suppose, however, that as the automobile population increased a certain city faced a traffic crisis and the system of ticket fixing came into ill repute. Suppose a mayor, victorious on the Traffic Ticket, decided that, rather than eliminate fixing by universalizing enforcement, he would instead reform the system by universalizing the privileges of ticket fixing. One can imagine how the system would work. One can imagine that some sense of equality would prevail, because everyone could be made almost equally free to bargain with the ticket administrators. But one would find it difficult to imagine how this would make the total city government more legitimate. Meanwhile, the purpose of the ticket would soon have been destroyed.

Traffic regulation, fortunately, was not so reformed. But many other government activities were. The operative principles of interest-group liberalism possess the mentality of a world of universalized ticket fixing: Destroy privilege by universalizing it. Reduce conflict by yielding to it. Redistribute power by the maxim of each according to his claim. Reserve an official place for every major structure of power. Achieve order by worshipping the processes (as distinguished from the forms and the procedures) by which order is presumed to be established.

If these operative principles will achieve equilibrium—and such is far from proven—that is all they will achieve. Democracy will have disappeared, because all of these maxims are founded upon profound lack of confidence in democracy. Democracy fails when it lacks confidence in its own authority.

Democratic forms were supposed to precede and accompany the formulation of policies so that policies could be implemented authoritatively and firmly. Democracy is indeed a form of absolutism, but ours was fairly well contrived to be an absolutist government under the strong control of consent-building prior to taking authoritative action in law. Interest-group liberalism fights the absolutism of democracy but succeeds only in taking away its authoritativeness. Whether it is called "creative federalism" by President Johnson, "cooperation" by the farmers, "local autonomy" by the Republicans, or "participatory democracy" by the New Left, the interest-group liberal effort does not create democratic power but rather negates it.

☐   The following discussion by V. O. Key, Jr., concentrates on private pressure groups and the extent to which they are links between public opinion and government. One interesting conclusion is that the elites of interest groups are not able to influence their members' attitudes to anywhere near the degree commonly thought possible. Pressure group participation in government more often than not reflects highly limited participation by the active elements of the groups. Public policy is often hammered out by very small numbers of individuals both in the government and in the private sphere. Political leaders can never stray too far beyond the boundaries of consent, but these are often very broad.

29
V. O. Key, Jr.

PRESSURE GROUPS

Pressure groups occupy a prominent place in analyses of American politics. In a regime characterized by official deference to public opinion and by adherence to the doctrine of freedom of association, private organizations may be regarded as links that connect the citizen and government. They are differentiated in both composition and function from political parties. Ordinarily they concern themselves with only a narrow range of policies, those related to the peculiar interests of the group membership. Their aim is primarily to influence the content of public policy rather than the results of elections. Those groups with a mass membership, though, may oppose or support particular candidates; in that case they are treated as groups with power to affect election results and, thereby, with capacity to pressure party leaders, legislators, and others in official position to act in accord with their wishes. . . .

PUZZLES OF PRESSURE POLITICS

. . . [There is] a series of puzzles as we seek to describe the role of pressure groups as links between opinion and government. Clearly the model of the lobbyist who speaks for a united following, determined in its aims and prepared to reward its friends and punish its enemies at the polls, does not often fit reality. Nor is it probable that the unassisted effort of pressure organizations to mold public opinion in support of their position has a large effect upon mass opinion. Yet legislators listen respectfully to the representations of the spokesmen of private groups, which in turn spend millions of dollars every year in propagandizing the public. Leaders of private groups articulate the concerns of substantial numbers of persons, even though they may not have succeeded in indoctrinating completely the members of their own groups. All this activity must have some functional significance in the political system. The problem is to identify its functions in a manner that seems to make sense. In this endeavor a distinction of utility is that made . . . between mass-membership organizations and nonmass organizations, which far outnumber the former.

Representation of Mass-Membership Groups. Only the spokesmen for mass-membership organizations can give the appearance of representing voters in sufficient numbers to impress (or intimidate) government. The influence of nonmass groups, which often have only a few hundred or a few thousand members, must rest upon something other than the threat of electoral retribution. As has been seen, the reality of the behavior of members of mass organizations is that in the short run they are not manipulable in large numbers by their leaders. Their party identification anchors many of them to a partisan position, and over the longer run they seem to be moved from party to party in presidential elections by the influences that affect all types and classes of people.

The spokesmen of mass-membership groups also labor under the handicap that they may be made to appear to be unrepresentative of the opinions of their members. When the president of an organization announces to a Congressional committee that he speaks for several million people, the odds are that a substantial proportion of his members can be shown to have no opinion or even to express views contrary to those voiced by their spokesmen. This divergency is often explained as a wicked betrayal of the membership or as a deliberate departure from the mass mandate. Yet it is not unlikely that another type of explanation more often fits the facts. Opinions, as we have seen in many contexts, do not fall into blacks and whites. It may be the nature of mass groups that attachment to the positions voiced by the peak spokesmen varies with attachment to and involvement in the group. At the leadership level the group position is voiced in its purest and most uncompromising form. A substantial layer of group activists subscribes to the official line, but among those with less involvement the faith wins less general acceptance. At the periphery of the group, though, the departure from the official line may be more a matter of indifference than of dissent. Leadership policy is often pictured as the consequence of interaction between leadership and group membership, which may be only partially true. Leaders may be more accurately regarded as dedicated souls who bid for group support of their position. Almost invariably they receive something less than universal acquiescence. This may be especially true in mass organizations in which political endeavor is to a degree a side issue—as, for example, in trade unions and farm organizations. As one traces attitudes and opinions across the strata of group membership, the clarity of position and the extremeness of position become more marked at the level of high involvement and activism.

If it is more or less the nature of mass organizations to encompass a spectrum of opinion rather than a single hue, much of the discussion of the representativeness of group leadership may be beside the point. However that may be, circumstances surrounding the leadership elements of mass organizations place them, in their work of influencing government, in a position not entirely dissimilar to that of leaders of nonmass groups. They must rely in large measure on means not unlike those that must be employed by groups with only the smallest membership. The world of pressure politics becomes more a politics among the activists than a politics that involves many people. Yet politics among the activists occurs in a context of concern about public opinion, a concern that colors the mode of action if not invariably its substance.

Arenas of Decision and Norms of Action. The maneuvers of pressure-group politics thus come ordinarily to occur among those highly involved and immediately concerned about public policy; the connection of these maneuvers with public opinion and even with the opinions of mass-membership organizations tends to be tenuous. Many questions of policy are fought out within vaguely bounded arenas in which the activists concerned are clustered. A major factor in the determination of the balance of forces within each arena is party control of the relevant governmental apparatus. Included among the participants in each issue-cluster of activists are the spokesmen for the pressure groups concerned, the members of the House and Senate committees with jurisdiction, and the officials of the administrative departments and agencies concerned. In the alliances of pressure politics those between administrative agencies and private groups are often extremely significant in the determination of courses of action. The cluster of concerned activists may include highly interested persons, firms, and organizations scattered over the country, though the boundaries delimiting those concerned vary from question to question, from arena to arena. In short, pressure politics among the activists takes something of the form that it would take if there were no elections or no concern about the nature of public opinion; that is, those immediately concerned make themselves heard in the process of decision.

In the give and take among the activists, norms and values with foundations in public opinion are conditioning factors. The broad values of the society determine to a degree who will be heard, who can play the game. Those who claim to speak for groups that advocate causes outside the range of consensus may be given short shrift. Some groups advocating perfectly respectable causes may be heard with less deference than others. Subtle standards define what David Truman calls "access" to the decision makers. To some extent this is a party matter: an AFL–CIO delegation does not expect to be heard with much sympathy by a committee dominated by right-wing Republicans. The reality of access, too, may provide an index to the tacit standards in definition of those interests regarded as having a legitimate concern about public policy. The spokesmen of groups both large and small are often heard with respect, not because they wield power, but because they are perceived as the representatives of interests entitled to be heard and to be accorded consideration as a matter of right.

Within the range of the permissible, the process of politics among the activists is governed to some extent by the expectation that all entitled to play the game shall get a fair deal (or at least a fair hearing before their noses are rubbed in the dirt). Doubtless these practices parallel a fairly widespread set of attitudes within the population generally. Probably those attitudes could be characterized as a disposition to let every group—big business and labor unions as well—have its say, but that such groups should not be permitted to dominate the government. In the implementation of these attitudes the legalism of American legislators plays a role. Frequently Congressional committeemen regard themselves as engaged in a judicial role of hearing the evidence and of arriving at decisions based on some sort of standards of equity.

Rituals of the Activists. The maneuvers of group spokesmen, be they spokesmen for mass or nonmass organizations, are often accompanied by rituals in obeisance to the doctrine that public opinion governs. The belief often seems to be that Congressmen will be impressed by a demonstration that public opinion demands the proposed line of action or inaction. Hence, groups organize publicity campaigns and turn up sheaves of editorials in support of their position. They stimulate people to write or to wire their Congressmen; if the labor of stimulation is too arduous, they begin to sign to telegrams names chosen at random from the telephone directory. They solicit the endorsement of other organizations for their position. They lobby the American Legion and the General Federation of Women's

Clubs for allies willing to permit their names to be used. On occasion they buy the support of individuals who happen to hold official positions in other organizations. They form fraudulent organizations with impressive letterheads to advance the cause. They attempt to anticipate and to soften the opposition of organizations that might be opposed to their position. Groups of similar ideological orientation tend to "run" together or to form constellations in confederation for mutual advantage.

All these maneuvers we have labeled "rituals"; that is, they are on the order of the dance of the rainmakers. They may be too brutal a characterization, for sometimes these campaigns have their effects—just as rain sometimes follows the rainmakers' dance. Yet the data make it fairly clear that most of these campaigns do not affect the opinion of many people and even clearer that they have small effect by way of punitive or approbative feedback in the vote. Their function in the political process is difficult to divine. The fact that organizations engage in these practices, though, is in itself a tribute to the importance of public opinion. To some extent, too, these opinion campaigns are not so much directed to mass opinion as to other activists who do not speak for many people either but have access to the arena of decision-making and perhaps have a viewpoint entitled to consideration. In another direction widespread publicity, by its creation of the illusion of mass support, may legitimize a position taken by a legislator. If a legislator votes for a measure that seems to arouse diverse support, his vote is not so likely to appear to be a concession to a special interest.

Barnums among the Businessmen. An additional explanation that apparently accounts for a good deal of group activity is simply that businessmen (who finance most of the campaigns of public education by pressure groups) are soft touches for publicity men. The advertising and public-relations men have demonstrated that they can sell goods; they proceed on the assumption that the business of obtaining changes in public policy is analogous to selling soap. They succeed in separating businessmen from large sums of money to propagate causes, often in a manner that sooner or later produces a boomerang effect.

Professional bureaucrats of the continuing and well-established organizations practice restraint in their public-relations campaigns. They need to gain the confidence of Congressmen and other officials with whom they also need to be able to speak the next time they meet. The fly-by-night organization or the business group that falls into the clutches of an unscrupulous public relations firm is more likely to indulge in the fantastic public relations and pressure campaign. Thus the National Tax Equality Association raised some $600,000 to finance a campaign against the tax exemptions of cooperatives, the most important of which are farm coops. Contributions came from concerns as scattered as the Central Power & Light Co., of Corpus Christi, Texas; Fairmont Foods Co., of Omaha, Nebraska; Central

Hudson Gas Electric Corporation, of Poughkeepsie, New York; and the Rheem Manufacturing Co., of San Francisco. The late Representative Reed, of New York, who was not one to attack business lightly, declared:

> Mr. Speaker, an unscrupulous racket, known as the National Tax Equality Association, has been in operation for some time, directing its vicious propaganda against the farm co-operatives. To get contributions from businessmen, this racketeering organization has propagandized business-men with false statements to the effect that if farm co-operatives were taxed and not exempted the revenue to the government would mount annually to over $800,000,000. [The treasury estimate was in the neighborhood of $20,000,000.] This is, of course, absolutely false and nothing more nor less than getting money under false pretenses. . . . This outfit of racketeers known as the Tax Equality Association has led honest businessmen to believe that their contributions were deductible from gross income as ordinary and necessary business expense with reference to their Federal income-tax return.

The Tax Equality Association provided its subscribers with the following form letter to send to their Congressmen:

> Dear Mr. Congressman: You raised my income taxes. Now I hear you are going to do it again. But you still let billions in business and profits escape. How come you raise my taxes, but let co-ops, mutuals, and other profit-making corporations get off scot free, or nearly so? I want a straight answer—and I want these businesses fully taxed before you increase my or anyone else's income taxes again.

Letters so phrased are not well designed to produce favorable Congressional response. The ineptness of this sort of campaign creates no little curiosity about the political judgment of solvent businessmen who put their money or their corporation's money into the support of obviously stupidly managed endeavors.

Autonomous Actors or Links? This review of the activities of pressure groups may raise doubts about the validity of the conception of these groups as links between public opinion and government. The reality seems to be that the conception applies with greater accuracy to some groups than to others. Certainly group spokesmen may represent a shade of opinion to government even though not all their own members share the views they express. Yet to a considerable degree the work of the spokesmen of private groups, both large and small, proceeds without extensive involvement of either the membership or a wider public. Their operations as they seek to influence legislation and administration, though, occur in a milieu of concern about opinion, either actual or latent. That concern also disposes decision makers to attend to shades of opinion and preference relevant to decision though not necessarily of great electoral strength—a disposition of no mean importance in the promotion of the equitable treatment of people in a democratic order. The chances are that the effects of organized groups on public opinion occur mainly over the long run rather than in short-run maneuvers concerned with particular congressional votes. Moreover, group success may be governed more by the general balance of partisan strength than by the results of group endeavors to win friends in the mass public. An industry reputed to be led by swindlers may not expect the most cordial reception from legislative committees, especially at times when the balance of strength is not friendly to any kind of business. If the industry can modify its public image, a task that requires time, its position as it maneuvers on particulars (about which few of the public can ever know anything) may be less unhappy. That modification may be better attained by performance than by propaganda.

Case Studies in Pressure Group Politics

☐   Ironically, the campaign finance laws of the 1970s, which were designed to restrict the influence of money in politics by limiting contributions to political campaigns, spawned PACs, or political action committees. The laws explicitly allowed corporations, labor unions, and any other group to create political action committees that would voluntarily solicit funds from employees, shareholders, union and group members to build war chests that could be used directly and indirectly to help finance congressional campaigns. PACs focused primarily on congressional elections, because presidential campaigns are publicly financed when the candidates, as they always do, accept public funds. Even in presidential races, however, political action committees can make their presence felt by indirectly spending money in behalf of candidates of their choice.

While a political action committee can contribute directly only $10,000 to a candidate—$5,000 each for the primary and general elections—there is no limit on the amount of money that can be indirectly spent, for example, for media advertising to elect or defeat candidates. Moreover, some interests have geometrically expanded their political clout by creating and encouraging confederations of PACs who advance a single cause. Labor union PACs, for example, may be created by local union organizations as well as by the national AFL-CIO, Teamsters, and the United Auto Workers. The National Rifle Association, the National Association of Realtors, the American Medical Association, and Right-to-Life groups have encouraged networks of PACs that collectively can have an enormous impact on congressional campaigns. While political action committees are generally pictured as conservative ideologically, liberal groups, particularly labor interests, have created PACs of their own to advance their causes.

It has become fashionable in the rhetoric of American politics to picture PACs as an unhealthy if not evil influence, creating a Congress that is the "best that money can buy." The term "PAC" has developed a pejorative connotation. The contemporary rhetoric of PACs reflects a strand in American political thought that originated with James Madison's skeptical view of "faction" that he expressed in *Federalist 10*. The popular press has throughout history given interest groups an evil coloration, helping to perpetuate a suspicious popular view of their influence in the political process. James Madison set a theme that has recurred consistently in political commentary since his day.

The following selection describes how political action committees have become an integral part of interest group and electoral politics.

30
Walter Isaacson

RUNNING WITH THE PACs

Like electronic images gobbling dots across a video screen, the PAC-men darted among the elegant rooms of the National Republican Club on Capitol Hill. At a fund raiser for Congressman Eldon Rudd of Arizona, they dropped their checks into a basket by the door or pressed them into the candidate's palm, before heading for the shrimp rolls and meatballs. Downstairs, other PAC-men crowded into a reception for Delaware Congressman Tom Evans, which featured piano music and White House luminaries. A few stopped in at the party for Deborah Cochran of Massachusetts. Because she is a long-shot challenger, they mainly left business cards rather than checks. But still she came out ahead; the cost of the event was picked up by the National Rifle Association.

Although Congress has adjourned and most members have headed home for the final stretch of the 1982 campaign, candidates can still be found buzzing back to Capitol Hill. They know that Washington is where the money is these days, or at least where one dips into the honeypot of contributions from political action committees (PACs). In a circular chase that is dominating congressional politics as never before, the candidates are courting the PACs, and the PAC-men are courting the candidates. "Harry Truman said that some people like government so much that they want to buy it," says Democratic Congressman David Obey of Wisconsin. "The 1982 elections will see Truman proved right."

There is nothing inherently evil about PACs: they are merely campaign committees established by organizations of like-minded individuals to raise money for political purposes, a valid aspect of the democratic process. In the wake of Watergate, Congress amended the federal election laws in 1974 to limit the role of wealthy contributors and end secretive payoffs by corporations and unions. The new law formalized the role of PACs, which were supposed to provide a well-regulated channel for individuals to get together and support candidates. But as with many well-intended reforms, there were unintended consequences. Instead of solving the problem of campaign financing, PACs became the problem. They proliferated beyond any expectation, pouring far more money into campaigns than ever before. Today the power of PACs threatens to undermine America's system of representative democracy.

This year there are 3,149 PACs placing their antes into the political pot, up from 2,551 in 1980 and 113 in 1972. The estimated total of funds they will dispense for campaigns this year: a staggering $240 million. There is Back Pac, PeacePac and Cigar-Pac. Beer distributors have a committee named—what else?—SixPAC. Whataburger Inc. has one called Whata-Pac. The Concerned Rumanians for a Stronger America has a PAC, as does the Hawaiian Golfers for Good Government. And so do most major corporations and unions.

By law a PAC can give $5,000 to both a candidate's primary and general election campaigns, while an individual contributor can give only $1,000 to each. Presidential elections are financed by federal funds, so most of the money is channeled into congressional, state and local races. Since PACs tend to run in packs, a popular candidate, particularly a powerful incumbent, may raise more than half his war chest from these special-interest groups. One example: Democratic Congressman Thomas Luken of Ohio, who has sponsored numerous special-interest bills and raised some $100,000 from PACs.

During Campaign '82, PACs will directly donate at least $80 million to House and Senate candidates—a leap of more than 45 percent from 1980. Another $160 million may be spent by PACs on local races, independent political advertising, and administrative activities. Says Democrat James Shannon of Massachusetts: "PACs are visibly corrupting the system."

Critics charge that PACs have distorted the democratic process by making candidates beholden to narrow interests rather than to their constituents. "Dependency on PACs has grown so much that PACs, not constituents, are the focus of a Congressman's attention," says Common Cause President Fred Wertheimer, whose citizens' lobby is fighting to reform the system. Special interests, of course, should be able to fight for their own concerns, but the power of PACs has upset the delicate balance between private interests and the public good. Indeed, PAC victories— continued price supports for dairy farmers, the defeat of a proposed fee on commodity trades, a proposed exemption from antitrust laws for shipping companies—often come at taxpayer expense. "It is not surprising there are no balanced budgets," says Republican Jim Leach of Iowa, who is one of fewer than a dozen members of Congress who refuse to take PAC money.

In addition, the close correlation between special-interest donations and legislative votes sometimes makes it seem that Congress is up for sale. Says Republican Senator Robert Dole of Kansas: "When these PACs give money they expect something in return other than good government." Democratic Congressman Thomas Downey of New York is more blunt: "You can't buy a Congressman for $5,000. But you can buy his vote. It's done on a regular basis." This is one reason why Michigan Democrat William Brodhead decided to quit Congress this year. Says he: "I got sick of feeling indebted to PACs. There is no reason they give money except in the expectation of votes."

Another problem is that PACs have helped raise the cost of campaigning, just as the desire to buy more and more expensive television time increases a candidate's dependency on PACs. Says Democrat Andrew Jacobs of Indiana, a critic of PACs: "It's like getting addicted by a pusher. You become accustomed to lavish campaigns." In 1974 the average cost of campaigning for the House was $50,000; in 1980 the average was $150,000, and this year races costing $500,000 are not uncommon. Says House Republican Leader Robert Michel of Illinois, who has raised more than $220,000 from PACs: "This year I'll pay several hundred thousand dollars for a job that pays $60,000."

Before the sanctioning of PACs in the early 1970s, corporations and unions were generally prohibited from donating to campaigns. Money from large special interests, however, was often funneled secretly in stuffed envelopes; Lyndon Johnson built his power base by serving as a conduit for campaign donations from oil tycoons and construction companies, and one of the key Watergate revelations was the pernicious influence of large corporate payoffs made under the table. But the national parties, and the local political machines, remained the dominant force in the control of campaign funds. By diminishing the role of parties, PACs tend to make elected officials more narrow in their allegiances. This lessens the chance for broad coalitions that balance competing interests. Says Stuart Eizenstat, former domestic affairs adviser to Jimmy Carter: "PACs balkanize the political process."

Labor unions, which organized the first political action committees, will pump some $20 million into the 1982 campaign through 350 separate PACs. Business followed the union lead and soon overtook them: this year 1,497 corporate PACs will give $30 million to the candidates. Trade associations such as the National Association of Realtors and the American Medical Association (A.M.A.) account for 613 PACs, which will chip in another $22 million. An additional 45 PACs are run by cooperatives like the Associated Milk Producers, and will give $2 million this election. By far the greatest, and most worrisome, growth has been among the loose cannons of the PAC arsenal, ideological PACs not connected to any organization. Among them: the National Conservative Political Action Committee

(NCPAC) and North Carolina Senator Jesse Helms' Congressional Club. The 644 nonconnected PACs are expected to donate only $6 million directly to candidates. But they will use most of their money for negative propaganda unauthorized by any candidate and for building up direct-mail lists that will help fund future political wars.

PAC money is mainly helping incumbents, since most PACs are guided by the pragmatic desire for access to power. Many corporate PACs that supported successful conservative challengers in 1980 are concentrating this year on solidifying Republican gains. Only 15 percent of the PAC money has gone to challengers so far this election. In the past this bias toward incumbents meant that Democrats fared slightly better with PACs than Republicans, but now the increasing strength of corporate PACs (which give 65 percent of their money to Republicans) relative to labor PACs (which channel 90 percent of their funds to Democrats) could mean that G.O.P. candidates receive slightly more money.

The PACs are playing a dominant role in many races around the country. When Ohio Republican Paul Pfeifer launched his challenge against Senator Howard Metzenbaum last spring, he was given so little chance that the pragmatic PACs shunned him. Metzenbaum's $3 million campaign fund, on the other hand, included $350,000 in PAC money by the end of the summer, mainly from unions. But last month, while Metzenbaum was in Washington conducting a maverick crusade against special-interest bills, Pfeifer began showing strength in the polls. Suddenly PAC money started flowing to the challenger. Says a Pfeifer aide: "More than anything else, a poll will speak to the PAC community. They're like a business trying to invest." One-third of Pfeifer's campaign donations are now from PACs.

Congressmen Ike Skelton and Wendell Bailey of Missouri have been pitted against each other by redistricting. Such a clash of incumbents inevitably triggers heavy PAC spending, and some groups like the A.M.A. have hedged their bets by donating to both. With dairy and labor PACs lining up behind Democrat Skelton, and corporate ones behind Republican Bailey, each side has raised $100,000 from special interests.

Another heated PAC showdown is the California race between Democrat Phillip Burton and Republican Milton Marks. When Marks first flew to Washington to solicit PAC money, he ran into Burton at a restaurant. "I'm here to raise money to run against you," Marks proclaimed jovially. Of his 800 PAC solicitations, Marks hooked 100 donors, raising almost $100,000. Burton piously proclaims he will never take corporate PAC money. But he will take it from labor, progressive groups and conservationist clubs. More than half of his $450,000 reelection fund will come from such PACs.

A far different type of political influence develops when an ideological PAC targets a race. NCPAC, for example, is notorious for mounting negative campaigns against candidates it hopes to see defeated. In these races, NCPAC rarely makes direct contributions to a candidate, and thus can spend as much as it wishes. (In 1976 the Supreme Court ruled that parts of the federal election law violated the right of free speech. It said that candidates may personally use as much of their own money as they want, and that unaffiliated groups, like NCPAC, can spend unlimited amounts on their own advocacy campaigns as long as their activity is not authorized by any candidate's official organization.) Moreover, since NCPAC is not affiliated with a candidate, it is less accountable for the tone and content of its campaign. As NCPAC Chairman Terry Dolan has admitted, "A group like ours could lie through its teeth, and the candidate it helps stays clean." NCPAC played a loud but indefinite role in the defeat of four liberal Senators in 1980, but since then it has waned in power if not in dollars.

Liberal groups have responded to NCPAC and other right-wing organizations by forming PACs of their own. Among the new groups is Progressive PAC (ProPAC), which will spend $150,000 in the election, most of it having gone into now abandoned negative campaigns against conservatives. Another is Democrats for the '80s (nicknamed PamPAC for Founder Pamela Harriman), which is spending $500,000. One of the richest ideological PACs is that of the National Organization for Women, which hopes to donate more than $2 million this year to candidates who support its feminist positions and who oppose Reaganomics. Says newly elected NOW President Judy Goldsmith: "We will proceed with work on defeating the right wing."

The growing importance of PAC donations means that the scramble for such money has become an integral part of campaigning. "It used to be that lobbyists lobbied congressmen," says PAC Critic Mike Synar, a Democratic Congressman from Oklahoma. "Now, Congressmen lobby lobbyists— for money." When that inevitable creature of the PAC explosion, the National Association for Association PACs, threw a party, 80 Congressmen showed up. "I've never seen such a group grope," says Democrat Dan Glickman of Kansas. Republican James Coyne of Pennsylvania playfully installed five PacMan video games near the bar of one of his Washington fund raisers in honor of the real PAC-men who have donated $126,000 to his 1982 campaign. Other lawmakers shower the PACs with glossy brochures soliciting money.

Republican Senator Orrin Hatch of Utah has already collected an astounding $750,000 from 531 PACs. Over scrambled eggs at a breakfast last Tuesday in Salt Lake City, he graciously accepted $5,000 more from the Association of Trial Lawyers. Such support, his campaign manager says, "shows a level of commitment to Hatch nationwide by thousands of people." It also shows, critics say, that he is intensely pro-business and chairs the powerful Labor and Human Resources Committee.

Indeed, the pursuit of PAC money has given a national flavor to state campaigns. Two Democratic congressional hopefuls from California, Doug

Bosco and Barbara Boxer, ran into each other this year in the Washington waiting room of a PAC they were both courting. Says Bosco: "You get kind of bored with yourself going from PAC to PAC to PAC. You get the feeling you are being processed." San Diego's Republican mayor Pete Wilson, running for the Senate, made a pilgrimage to Washington a few weeks ago and met with Bernadette Budde of the Business Industry PAC (BIPAC). He also held a $500-per-PAC-man reception at a hotel near the White House. Total take: $75,000.

Houston and Dallas, where the oil money runs thick, have become hubs of PAC activity. "We had a congressional candidate here from North Carolina recently and gave him a few thousand dollars," says Jack Webb, executive director of the Houston PAC. "Then we took him around and introduced him to other oil folks and I'm pretty sure he left with more than $10,000 in pledges." HouPAC plans to give away $200,000 this year, ten times its donations for 1980.

Deciding how to divvy up their bounty can be a complex process for PACs. The 20 trustees of the Realtors PAC held the last of a dozen strategy sessions in Chicago's downtown Marriott Hotel two weeks ago, working late into the night and through the next day to cull the 150 worthy candidates who would receive the last of the $2.5 million allotted for 1982. Each trustee had a folder on supplicants that included voting records and "campaign intelligence reports" prepared with the aid of eight full-time field specialists. Washington staffers gave briefings on where incumbents stand on such issues as the balanced-budget amendment and the mortgage subsidy bill.

Candidates seeking the Realtors' money must submit answers to a six-page questionnaire. In some cases the "correct" answers are all too obvious. "Do you agree or disagree [that] trade associations have a right and a responsibility to hold members of Congress accountable for their votes?" Others are trickier. One asks candidates to rank what contributes most to high interest rates: record deficits, restrictive monetary policy, excessive tax cuts, etc. (A: The Realtors have fought strongly against high deficits.) "Sometimes candidates plead with me to give them the correct answers," says Political Resources Director Randall Moorhead.

Typical of the Realtors' deliberation was their discussion of the Texas Senate race between Democratic Incumbent Lloyd Bentsen and Challenger Jim Collins. Although Republican Collins was very sympathetic to the Realtors' philosophy and had been a supporter in the House, Bentsen is the incumbent and likely victor. He got the $4,250. Challengers are referred to as "risk capital ventures."

The choices for smaller PACs are simpler. At a meeting this month to hand out the last of its $225,000 congressional donations, the PAC of the Grumman Corp., maker of fighter jets, gave another $1,000 to Democrat

William Chappell of Florida, who is on the Defense Appropriations Subcommittee. Says Grumman PAC Chairman Dave Walsh: "We have selfish interests. We dole out money to those on committees dealing with defense and those whose viewpoint is in line with ours."

Small PACs often look to larger ones for guidance. The Chamber of Commerce, BIPAC and the AFL–CIO publish "opportunity lists" to lead like-minded PAC money where it will do the most good. The Chamber recently produced a video version of its list by broadcasting a four-hour, closed-circuit television show called *See How They Run* to 150 PAC managers in seven cities. It opens with patriotic music and a waving flag as Chamber President Richard Lesher extols "a brighter future for America through political action." Presidential Assistant Kenneth Duberstein joins Chamber analysts in handicapping 50 key races. One of the Chamber choices, Pennsylvania's Coyne, expresses the sentiment of the rest of the all-Republican lineup: "The key to my race is, Can we marshal the resources?"

An article in *INC.* magazine, which is aimed at independent businessmen, offers advice on "some ways to measure your return" from PAC donations. It explains how to compute the "equity share" and "cost-vote ratio" that can be "bought" for each candidate. "Special interests don't contribute to congressional candidates for the fun of it," the article advises. "They do so to get things done." It dismisses any moral qualms: "If politicians want to sell and the public wants to buy, there is not much you can do to stop the trade."

The question of whether PAC donations actually buy votes or only reward members who tend to vote properly is akin to that of the chicken and the egg. One thing is certain: the combination of chickens and eggs fertilizes the legislative process. The National Automobile Dealers Association, which will contribute more than $850,000 to congressional candidates this election, was able to kill a regulation requiring that buyers be informed of known defects in used cars for sale. The United Auto Workers (U.A.W.) is handing out more than $1 million this year while it lines up support for a "domestic content" bill that requires foreign firms to use a high percentage of American parts and labor in cars they sell in the U.S. Lockheed Corp., like its competitor Boeing, donated heavily to the House and Senate armed services committees as it fought to win a Government contract for its C-5B cargo plane. The National Rifle Association (N.R.A.) will give away $1.3 million this year, some of it to help Senate Judiciary Committee members who approved a law loosening gun-control regulations.

Although lobbyists and Congressmen deny that votes are for sale, the link to donations is often uncomfortably clear. The U.A.W. PAC in New Jersey has long backed Congressman Peter Rodino. But last month Rodino was informed that future support would be contingent on his agreeing to co-sponsor the domestic content bill. When his office said he would, the union publicly announced that its endorsement came "following Rodino's decision to sign on as a co-sponsor" of the bill. The appearance of coercion annoyed Rodino. Said an aid: "He thought it was the most heavyhanded thing he had seen during his career." Rodino withdrew as a co-sponsor, although he is still backing the bill.

An example of how donations and votes go hand in palm is the House passage of a bill that would allow the shipping industry to fix prices, which could raise freight costs by about 20 percent. The Merchant Marine and Fisheries Committee has long been a safe harbor for special interests. "Any bill coming out of the Merchant Marine ought to go straight to the grand jury," jokes one Congressman. Both labor and business groups formed an alliance to pass the price fixing bill, with the Seafarers' Union and Lykes Bros. Steamship Co. leading the lobbying by 13 interested PACs. Their total donations to Merchant Marine Committee members: $47,850. After passing the bill 33 to 0, the committee got the House rules suspended to allow only 40 minutes of debate. Since most Congressmen had little idea of what was in the bill, many voted in response to thumbs-up signs from committee members. The bill passed 350 to 33.

Among other PAC-man specials:

The Professionals Bill. The A.M.A. and American Dental Association have been lobbying for a law that would exempt professionals from Federal Trade Commission regulation and thus permit them to fix prices. The bill is still awaiting House action. Since 1979 the two groups have given $2.3 million to House members, 72 percent of it to 213 co-sponsors of the bill. Each sponsor got an average of $7,598, according to Consumer Advocate Ralph Nader's Congress Watch. Thomas Luken, the prime sponsor, got $14,750. Luken, one of Congress's most notorious PAC-men, also sponsored the bill revoking the used-car regulation.

The Beer Bill. Brewers want to be allowed to designate monopoly territories for their distributors, which could raise the cost of beer 20 percent. The legislation is pending in the House. SixPAC has handed out $35,000 to members of the Judiciary Subcommittee on Monopolies. Democrat Jack Brooks of Texas, the chief sponsor, got a $10,000 contribution, a $1,000 honorarium for a speech and a trip to Las Vegas from SixPAC this year.

The Bankruptcy Bill. The credit industry is pushing for a law that would fundamentally change the legal concept of a "fresh start" for those who go broke. The pending bill would require individual debtors, but not businesses, to pay back debts after declaring bankruptcy. Six credit PACs, led by the American Bankers Association and Household Finance Corp., have donated $704,297 to 255 Congressmen co-sponsoring the bill.

Commodity Traders' Fee. PACs representing three major groups of commodities brokers have been fighting a Reagan Administration proposal to set a 6¢ to 12¢ fee on each trade to finance the Commodity Futures Trading Commission. They have contributed to most members of the House and Senate agriculture committees, both of which voted to reject the fee. "It isn't buying votes," said Michael McLeod, a lobbyist with the Chicago Board of Trade. "It's just how the political system works."

Clean Air. The House Health and the Environment Subcommittee voted this year to weaken considerably the Clean Air Act. The twelve members who voted for the relaxation got a total of $197,325 from the PACs of the seven major industries affected. Republican Senator Steve Symms of Idaho, who got $97,500 during his 1980 campaign from affected industries, dutifully introduced one industry amendment after another. "It was clear he had no idea what was in those amendments," says one Senator. Members of his committee even privately mocked him, asking, "Which campaign check had that amendment attached to it?"

When a bill emerges from committee, and the debate becomes publicized, it becomes harder for special interests to be effective. Grassroots pressure by those in favor of the Clean Air Act, and perhaps also the growth of environmental PACs, make it likely that the act will pass without being significantly weakened.

Defenders of the PAC system say that contributions are an effect, not a cause; and that they are given to those who are already known to be supportive of a PAC's position. "The idea that there's a *quid pro quo* is balderdash," says Republican Congressman Bill Frenzel of Minnesota. Argues BIPAC's Budde: "Pacs are not buying anyone. They're rewarding." Because a single PAC is limited to $5,000 a race, the power it can command, while large, is not overwhelming. The most you can purchase, proponents claim, is access. Says Grumman PAC Chairman Walsh: "We don't expect contracts because we gave someone $5,000. But the likelihood of us getting in to see the Congressman is much higher."

The backers of PACs point out that, like rivers to the sea, special-interest money will find a way to flow into campaigns, and the PAC channel keeps the process regulated and open to public scrutiny. Small donors, who once felt they had no impact, can now pool their money with like-minded voters. "PACs have redistributed political influence," says Phil Gramm of Texas. "They've taken power away from the smoke-filled room." Agrees Jack Webb of HouPAC: "PACs get people involved who otherwise might not be. They're a damned good thing."

There is no argument about one major PAC fact: within ten years, PACs have become a significant method of financing congressional campaigns, accounting for more than one-fourth of all money raised by candidates, and more than one-third of all money raised by incumbents. The average candidate now gets three times as much money from PACs as from a political party. This year, the national campaign committees of the Republican Party have been revitalized by a surge of donations. Even so, unless the laws are changed, PACs are destined to remain much more important than national parties as a source of funds for candidates. Says Herbert Alexander, a professor at the University of Southern California who was written about campaign finance: "The decline of the parties is, in part, a consequence of election reform gone awry."

PACs have become so important and controversial that they are now an issue of their own on the campaign trail. Their proper role is being debated, for example, in the Senate race in Montana. Democratic Incumbent John Melcher is receiving contributions from a wide array of labor, corporate and association PACs. They have given him more than $350,000, over half his campaign fund. "How can you work for your constituents when you've got $10,000 chits out?" demands Republic Challenger Larry Williams, a self-made millionaire. Melcher is countering by making an issue of the fact that NCPAC has waged an irresponsible $250,000 independent effort to defeat him. One of Melcher's television ads depicts NCPAC operatives flying into the state with money-stuffed briefcases to "defeat Doc Melcher."

Democrat Joseph Kolter is also trying to turn PAC donations into an issue in his bid to unseat Republican Congressman Eugene Atkinson of Pennsylvania. Last year Atkinson made a dramatic switch in party allegiance. As a Democrat, he had piously refused on principle to accept PAC money, but since becoming a Republican he has raised $40,000 from business-oriented PACs. In his campaign speeches, Kolter reels off a list of Atkinson donors, referring to General Public Utilities Corp. as "the people who brought you Three Mile Island" and to a group of major industries as "the filthy five." Kolter has his own PAC sources; he is drawing the maximum donations from the United Steel Workers, the U.A.W. and other unions.

Any attempt to reform the PAC system is vulnerable to the law of unintended consequences. Individuals, groups, corporations and unions will continue to have the desire and resources to support favored candidates. They also have the right, and even the responsibility, to do so. Trying to restrict such efforts too severely could just divert them into other, less worthy approaches, like the one followed by NCPAC. Says Michael Malbin, a political analyst at the American Enterprise Institute: "Unless you repeal the First Amendment, people with private interests in legislation will be active."

Public financing of campaigns would solve many of the problems. The same arguments that were persuasive at the presidential level—the need to lower the role of fat-cat donors and special interests—are at least as compelling when it comes to Congress. (In the primaries, presidential candidates raise money, some of it from PACs, that is matched by federal funds. The general election is fully financed by federal money.) But such a process presents practical difficulties: some districts and states are much more expensive to campaign in than others, and incumbents (who make the laws) are unlikely to vote for a system that removes their own built-in advantage. "It's like sending goats to guard the cabbage patch," says Andrew Jacobs of Indiana, one of the Congressmen who refuse PAC money. Moreover, public financing could be expensive.

Raising the $1,000 limit that an individual can contribute to a campaign would help dilute the power of PACs. The individual limit had stayed the same since 1974, despite inflation. "Individual contributions are far less effective than those from a PAC," says Republican Congresswoman Millicent Fenwick of New Jersey. "The PAC's lobbyist will come and twist arms." In her race for a Senate seat, Fenwick has refused PAC money.

Individual donations from corporate leaders, of course, can exert the same type of influence as money from PACs. Indeed, the PAC-stemious Fenwick has raised $13,650 from the top executives of a Wall Street investment firm, far more than the limit imposed on the firm's PAC. But the greatest threat posed by individual contributions in the past was the secrecy surrounding them and their disproportionate amounts. A new $5,000 limit would seem reasonable in light of today's strict reporting requirements.

Another option would be to limit the total amount each candidate can accept from PACs. A bill setting a $70,000 limit on the amount a House candidate could raise from PACs passed the House in 1979, but died in the Senate. A new measure has been introduced in the House setting the PAC money ceiling at $75,000.

The ideal reform would incorporate elements of each of these proposals. Partial federal financing, either by direct grants or matching funds, could water down the importance of PACs. So could raising the private contribution limit. Increasing the amount people can donate to the national parties, currently $20,000 each year, could strengthen the role of the parties. Finally, setting a reasonable limit on the amount a candidate can get from PACs, certainly no more than $75,000 an election, would rein in the PAC-men.

The difficulty is not so much finding solutions, but persuading Congressmen, who benefit so handsomely, to change the present situation. "It is a lot easier to raise money from PACs than from other sources," observes PAC Critic Barney Frank, a Democratic Congressman from Massachusetts. "You sit there, somebody hands you a check for $3,000, and you say 'Thank you.'" In the end, it is pressure from the voters that may limit the power of the PACs. Some lawmakers, like Missouri Democrat Richard Gephardt, detect rumblings of reform. Says he: "There is a growing sense that the system is getting out of hand."

☐   Although the PAC phenomenon is a development of the 1970s and 1980s, lobbyists of one kind or another have represented special interests since the earliest days of the Republic, practicing their craft in state capitals and in Washington. The word "lobbyist" derives from the fact that individuals seeking to influence government gathered in the corridors or large anterooms—the "lobbies"—of legislatures to buttonhole and pressure the elected representatives of the people.

The poet Walt Whitman expressed the view of his countrymen when he wrote in the nineteenth century that lobbyists, whom he called "lobbiers," should be included among the "lousy combinings and born freedom sellers of the earth."[1] Long before Whitman wrote, James Madison's antifaction views in *Federalist 10* set the hostile tone toward interest groups that surfaced in future political rhetoric.

While lobbying is considered to be more respectable in the twentieth than it was in the nineteenth century, journalistic barbs and political attacks nevertheless continue against those who practice the fine art of putting pressure upon government. Even the title and many of the descriptions of modern-day lobbying in the following lively account have a pejorative ring. However one views lobbying, its practice is, as Madison himself observed, a fundamental freedom that constitutional governments must protect lest political liberty itself be stamped out altogether.

31
Evan Thomas

PEDDLING INFLUENCE

The hallway is known as Gucci Gulch, after the expensive Italian shoes they wear. At tax-writing time, the Washington lobbyists line up by the hundreds in the corridor outside the House Ways and Means Committee room, ever vigilant against the attempts of lawmakers to close their prized loopholes. Over near the House and Senate chambers, Congressmen must run a gauntlet of lobbyists who sometimes express their views on legislation by pointing their thumbs up or down. Not long ago, Senator John Danforth, chairman of the Senate Commerce Committee, could be seen on the

[1]William Safire, *Safire's Political Dictionary* (New York: Random House, 1978), p. 383.

Capitol steps trying to wrench his hand from the grip of a lobbyist for the textile industry seeking new protectionist legislation. Though Danforth himself wants help for the shoe, auto and agricultural industries in his native Missouri, the Senator, an ordained Episcopal minister, rolled his eyes heavenward and mumbled, "Save me from these people."

There have been lobbyists in Washington for as long as there have been lobbies. But never before have they been so numerous or quite so brazen. What used to be, back in the days of Bobby Baker, a somewhat shady and disreputable trade has burst into the open with a determined show of respectability. Tempted by the staggering fees lobbyists can command, lawmakers and their aides are quitting in droves to cash in on their connections. For many, public service has become a mere internship for a lucrative career as a hired gun for special interests.

With so many lobbyists pulling strings, they may sometimes seem to cancel one another out. But at the very least, they have the power to obstruct, and their overall effect can be corrosive. At times the halls of power are so glutted with special pleaders that government itself seems to be gagging. As Congress and the Administration begin working this month to apportion the deepest spending cuts in America's history and to sort out the most far-reaching reform of the tax laws since World War II, the interests of the common citizen seem to stand no chance against the onslaught of lobbyists. Indeed, the tax bill that emerged from the House already bears their distinctive Gucci prints, and the budget is still filled with programs they have been able to protect.

Of course, the common citizen often benefits from various "special interest" breaks (for example, a deduction for home mortgages or state and local taxes). One man's loophole is another man's socially useful allowance, and one's man's lobbyist is another man's righteous advocate. Nonetheless, the voices most likely to be heard are often the ones that can afford the best-connected access brokers.

As the legislative year cranks up, the whine of special pleaders resonates throughout the Capitol:

• In the Senate Finance Committee, heavy industries like steel and autos, led by Veteran Lobbyist Charls Walker, are working to restore tax breaks for investment in new equipment that were whittled down last fall by the House Ways and Means Committee.

• In the House and Senate Armed Services Committees, lobbyists for weapons manufacturers are fanning out to make sure that lawmakers do not trim their pet projects from the defense budget.

• In the Senate Commerce Committee, business lobbyists are pressing for legislation to limit liability for defective products. They face fierce opposition from consumer groups and personal-injury lawyers.

• Throughout the House and Senate, lobbyists for interests ranging from commercial-waterway users to child-nutrition advocates are laboring to spare their favorite federal subsidies from the exigencies of deficit reduction.

A superlobbyist like Robert Gray, a former minor official in the Eisenhower Administration who parlayed his promotional genius and friendship with the Reagans into a $20 million-a-year p.r. and lobbying outfit, is in the papers more than most congressional committee chairmen. He would have his clients believe that he is at least as powerful. "In the old days, lobbyists never got any publicity," says Veteran Lobbyist Maurice Rosenblatt, who has prowled the halls of Congress for several decades. "Congressmen didn't want to be seen with notorious bagmen." But now, he shrugs, "the so-called best lobbyists get the most publicity."

Influence peddling, says Jack Valenti, head of the Motion Picture Association and no mean practitioner of the craft, "is the biggest growth industry around." The number of registered domestic lobbyists has more than doubled since 1976, from 3,420 to 8,800. That figure is understated, however, since reporting requirements under a toothless 1946 law are notoriously lax. Most experts put the influence-peddling population at about 20,000, or more than 30 for every member of Congress. Registered lobbyists reported expenditures of $50 million last year, twice as much as a decade ago, but the true figure is estimated at upwards of $1.5 billion, including campaign contributions.

What does the money buy? "Everybody needs a Washington representative to protect their hindsides, even foreign governments," says Senator Paul Laxalt. "So the constituency for these people is the entire free-world economy." Joseph Canzeri, a former Reagan aide who calls himself a Washington "facilitator," notes, "It's a competitive business. There are a lot of wolves out there. But there are a lot of caribou in government too."

In the amoral revolving-door world of Washington, it has become just as respectable to lobby as to be lobbied. Ronald Reagan may have come to Washington to pare down the size of the Federal Government, but many of his former top aides have quit to profit off Big Government as influence peddlers. None has been more successful more swiftly than Reagan's former deputy chief of staff Michael Deaver, who may multiply his White House income sixfold in his first year out of government by offering the nebulous blend of access, influence and advice that has become so valued in Washington. Other Reaganauts now prowling Gucci Gulch include ex-Congressional Liaison Kenneth Duberstein and two former White House political directors, Lyn Nofziger and Ed Rollins. "I spent a lot of years doing things for love. Now I'm going to do things for money," Rollins told the Washington *Post* after he left the White House. By representing clients like the Teamsters Union, Rollins, who never earned more than $75,000 a year in government, boasts that he can earn ten times as much.

Former Administration officials are often paid millions of dollars by special interests to oppose policies they once ardently promoted. This is particularly true in the area of foreign trade, as documented by the Washington *Post* a week ago. For example, Reagan has ordered an investigation into the unfair trade practices of South Korea. That country will pay former Reagan Aide Deaver $1.2 million over three years to "protect, manage and expand trade and economic interests" of the nation's industry. Deaver refuses to say exactly what he will do to earn his fee, but he has hired Doral Cooper, a former deputy trade representative in the Reagan Administration, as a lobbyist for his firm. Japanese semiconductor and machine-tool firms are also charged by the Administration with engaging in unfair trade practices. They have hired Stanton Anderson, who had served as director of economic affairs for the Administration's 1980 transition team.

Foreign governments are particularly eager to retain savvy Washington insiders to guide them through the bureaucratic and congressional maze and polish their sometimes unsavory images in the U.S. The Marcos government in the Philippines has retained the well-connected lobbying firm of Black, Manafort & Stone for a reported fee of $900,000. Another Black, Manafort client is Angolan Rebel Jonas Savimbi. Not to be outdone, the Marxist regime of Angola hired Bob Gray's firm to front for it in Washington. Two years ago, Gray told TIME that he checks with his "good friend," CIA Director William Casey, before taking on clients who might be inimical to U.S. interests. It is unclear just what Casey could have said this time, since the CIA is currently funneling $15 million in covert aid to Savimbi to help his rebellion against the Angolan regime. Last week outraged Savimbi backers chained themselves to a railing in Gray's posh offices in Georgetown and had to be forcibly removed by local police.

Lobbyists call themselves lawyers, government-affairs specialists, public relations consultants, sometimes even lobbyists. They offer a wide array of increasingly sophisticated services, from drafting legislation to creating slick advertisements and direct-mail campaigns. But what enables the big-time influence peddlers to demand upwards of $400 an hour is their connections. "I'll tell you what we're selling," says Lobbyist Frank Mankiewicz. "The returned phone call."

Old-time fixers such as Tommy ("the Cork") Corcoran and Clark Clifford were not merely practiced lawyers but had some genuine legislative expertise to offer. Lately, however, Washington has seen the rise of a new breed of influence peddler, whose real value is measured by his friends in high places—particularly in the White House. Clifford prospered no matter who was in office; after the Reagans go home to California, it is hard to believe that Deaver or Gray will remain quite such hot commodities.

There is, and has long been, a strong whiff of scam about the influence-peddling business. Its practitioners like to imply that they have more clout than they truly do. In the post-Watergate era, power has been fractionated on Capitol Hill. Where a few powerful committee chairmen once held sway, Congress has become a loose federation of 535 little fiefdoms. This has made a lobbyist's job more difficult, but it hardly means that Congress has been liberated from the thrall of special interests. Well-intentioned congressional reform has been subverted over the years by the proliferation of lobbyists and the spiraling cost of election campaigns, two trends that go together like a hand and a pocket. The result has often been institutional paralysis. The very fact that Congress and the White House felt compelled to enact the Gramm-Rudman measure, requiring automatic spending cuts, is a monument to the inability of weak-willed legislators to say no to the lobbyists who buzz around them.

President Reagan has tried to sell his tax-reform bill as the supreme test of the public interest vs. the special interests. In pitching his campaign to the public, he has accused special interests of "swarming like ants through every nook and cranny of Congress," overlooking, perhaps, that many of the most prominent ants are his former aides. Few lobbyists, however, seem especially offended by his rhetoric, and certainly their livelihoods are not threatened. Indeed, many lobbyists candidly admit that true tax reform would actually mean more business for them, since they would have a fresh slate upon which to write new loopholes.

The way lobbyists have feasted on the President's tax-reform bill illustrates why the bill is known in the law firms and lobbying shops of K Street as the "Lobbyists' Full Employment Act." The 408-page proposal first drafted by the Treasury Department 16 months ago, known as Treasury I, was called a model of simplicity and fairness. It would have swept the tax code virtually clean of loopholes for the few in order to cut tax rates sharply for the many. But the 1,363-page tax bill sent by the House to the Senate last December is so riddled with exemptions and exceptions that the goal of fairness was seriously compromised, and simplicity abandoned altogether.

The lobbyists wasted no time biting into Treasury I. Insurance executives calculated that such loophole closings as taxing employer-paid life insurance and other fringe benefits would cost the industry about $100 billion over five years. Led by Richard Schweiker, who was President Reagan's Secretary of Health and Human Services before becoming head of the American Council of Life Insurance, the industry launched a $5 million lobbying campaign that can only be described as state of the art.

Even before Treasury had finished drafting its original plan, the insurers were showing 30-second spots on TV that depicted a bird nibbling away at a loaf of bread labeled "employee benefits." An actress in the role of frightened housewife exclaimed, "We shouldn't have to pay taxes for protecting our family!" Life insurance agents around the country were revved up by a twelve-minute film entitled *The Worst Little Horror Story in Taxes.* In the film, Senate Finance Chairman Robert Packwood, a strong advocate of preserving tax breaks for fringe benefits, was shown urging the public to write their Congressmen. The insurers also mounted a direct-mail campaign that inundated Congress last year with 7 million preprinted, postage-paid cards. The campaign was successful: by the time the bill passed the House of Representatives last December, the insurance lobby figured that it had managed to restore about $80 billion of the $100 billion in tax breaks cut out by Treasury I. The insurers hope to win back most of the rest when the bill is reported out by the Senate Finance Committee this spring.

Threats to close a single loophole can bring scores of lobbyists rallying round. The original Treasury proposal sought to eliminate Section 936 of the U.S. Tax Code, which gives tax breaks worth some $600 million to companies that invest in Puerto Rico. Treasury Department officials conceded that the tax break helped create jobs by luring business to the island, but figured that each new job was costing the U.S. Treasury about $22,000. To defend Section 936, a coalition of some 75 U.S. companies with factories on the island formed a million-dollar "Puerto Rico-U.S.A. Foundation" and hired more than a dozen lobbyists, including Deaver. Last fall Section 936 advocates flew some 50 Congressmen and staffers to Puerto Rico on fact-finding trips.

Deaver, meanwhile, coordinated a lobbying campaign aimed at National Security staffers and officials in the State, Commerce and Defense Departments. The strategy was to cast Section 936 as a way to revive the President's moribund Caribbean Basin Initiative and erect a bulwark against Communism in the region. Some two dozen companies with plants in Puerto Rico promised that if Section 936 was retained, they would reinvest their profits in new factories on other Caribbean islands. During a tense moment in the negotiations with the Administration, Deaver even managed to place a ground-to-air call to Air Force One as it flew to the Geneva Summit last November. He wanted to alert Secretary of State George Shultz to stand fast against the maneuverings of the tax reformers at Treasury. Not surprisingly, the Treasury gnomes were overwhelmed. Later that month the Administration committed itself to preserving Section 936.

The fabled three-martini lunch, threatened by the Treasury Department's proposal to end tax deductions for business entertainment, was preserved as at least a two-martini lunch after heavy lobbying by the hotel and restaurant industry. In the House-passed bill, 80% of the cost of a business lunch can still be deducted. The oil-and-gas lobby managed to restore over half the tax breaks for well drilling removed by the original Treasury bill. Lawyers, doctors and accountants won an exemption from more stringent new accounting rules. The lobbying by lawyers was a bit crude: Congressmen received letters that were supposedly written by partners of different law firms but were all signed by the same hand. No matter. Though congressional etiquette demands that each constituent's letter be answered personally, "We just let our word processors talk to their word processors," shrugged a congressional staffer.

The real deal making was done over so-called transition rules, which postpone or eliminate new taxes for certain individual businesses. The House-passed bill is studded with some 200 transition rules, which have been written to protect pet projects in a Congressman's district or large industries with particular clout on the Hill. Drafted behind closed doors, these rules are written in language designed to make it difficult to identify the real beneficiaries. One transition rule, for instance, waives the cutbacks on investment tax credits and depreciation for the fiberoptic networks of telecommunications companies that have committed a certain number of dollars for construction by a certain date. It turns out that just two companies profit from the exemption: AT&T and United Telecom.

Not every lobbyist made out in the wheeling and dealing, by any means. Some were a little too greedy. The banking lobby pushed an amendment that would actually *increase* its tax breaks for bad-debt reserves. The lobbyists figured that they were just making an opening bid; their real aim was to protect existing tax breaks. To their surprise, however, the amendment passed in the confusion of an early Ways and Means Committee drafting session. When jubilant banking lobbyists began shouting "We won! We won!" outside the hearing room, some Congressmen became angry. Giving more tax breaks to the already well-sheltered banking industry was no way to sell voters on tax reform. The amendment was repealed.

Despite the predations of lobbyists, a tax-reform bill may be signed into law this year. But it must first survive the Senate, and already the advocates are queuing up to be heard. "I wish there were a secret elevator into the committee room," laments Senator David Pryor of Arkansas, a member of the Finance Committee. "Whenever I go there to vote, I try to walk fast and be reading something."

Some Congressmen may try to avoid lobbyists, but many have come to depend on them. "God love 'em," quips Vermont Senator Patrick Leahy. "Without them we would have to decide how to vote on our own." Sarcasm aside, lobbyists do serve a useful purpose by showing busy legislators the virtues and pitfalls of complex legislation. "There's a need here," says Anne Wexler, a former Carter Administration aide turned lobbyist. "Government officials are not comfortable making these complicated decisions by themselves." Says Lobbyist Van Boyette, a former aide to Senator Russell Long of Louisiana: "We're a two-way street. Congress often legislates on issues without realizing that the marketplace has changed. We tell Congress what business is up to, and the other way around."

Lobbyists and Government officials alike are quick to point out that lobbying is cleaner than in earlier eras, when railroad barons bought Senators as if they were so much rolling stock. "It's an open process now," says Jack Albertine, president of the American Business Conference, a trade association of medium-size, high-growth companies. "All sides are represented, the contributions are reported, and the trade-offs are known to everybody. In the old days you never knew who got what until a waterway project suddenly appeared in someone's district."

In some ways the growth of interest groups is healthy. Capitol Hill at times seems like a huge First Amendment jamboree, where Americans of all persuasions clamor to be heard. Movie stars plead on behalf of disease prevention, Catholic clerics inveigh against abortion, farmers in overalls ask for extended credit, Wall Street financiers extol the virtues of lower capital-gains taxes. No single group dominates. When the steel, auto and rubber industries saw the Reagan Administration as an opening to weaken the Clean Air and Clean Water acts, the "Green Lobby," a coalition of environmental groups, was able to stop them.

But not every voter has a lobby in Washington. "Sometimes I think the only people not represented up here are the middle class," says Democratic Congressman Barney Frank of Massachusetts. "The average folks—that's what bothers me." Of course, that is not entirely true; many ordinary citizens are represented by such lobbies as the National Association of Retired Persons and Common Cause.

Lobbyists cannot afford to rely solely on well-reasoned arguments and sober facts and figures to make their case. In the scramble to win a hearing, they have developed all manner of stratagems designed to ingratiate themselves and collect IOUs.

Helping Congressmen get re-elected is an increasingly popular device. Veteran Washington Lobbyist Thomas Hale Boggs Jr. is on no fewer than 50 "steering committees" set up to raise money for congressional election campaigns. By night, Good Ole Boy Boggs can be found shmoozing at Capitol Hill fund raisers, where lobbyists drop off envelopes containing checks from Political Action Committees (PACs) at the door before digging into the hors d'oeuvres. By day, Boggs lobbies Congressmen, often the same ones for whom he has raised money the night before. Lately high-power political consulting firms such as Black, Manafort & Stone have taken not only to raising money for candidates but actually to running their campaigns: planning strategy, buying media, and polling. These firms get paid by the candidates for electioneering services, and then paid by private clients to lobby the Congressmen they have helped elect. In the trade this cozy arrangement is known as double dipping.

Special-interest giving to federal candidates has shot up eightfold since 1974, from $12.5 million to more than $100 million by the 1984 election. Nonetheless, PACs can give no more than $5,000 to a single campaign, and all contributions are publicly filed with the Federal Election Commission. "Elections are so expensive that the idea of a PAC's having inordinate influence is ridiculous," says Boggs.

Some Congressmen are not so sure. "Somewhere there may be a race of humans who will take $1,000 from perfect strangers and be unaffected by it," dryly notes Congressman Frank. Says Congressman Leon Panetta of

California: "There's a danger that we're putting ourselves on the auction block every election. It's now tough to hear the voices of the citizens in your district. Sometimes the only things you can hear are the loud voices in three-piece suits carrying a PAC check."

Even the most reputable influence peddlers use their political connections to build leverage. As director of the 1984 G.O.P. Convention, Lobbyist William Timmons, a quietly genial man who represents such blue-chippers as Boeing, Chrysler, ABC and Anheuser-Busch, controlled access to the podium. G.O.P. Senators lobbied *him* for prime-time appearances. A *Wall Street Journal* reporter described Senator Pete Domenici of New Mexico, who was running for re-election in the fall of 1984, thanking Timmons a bit too effusively for allotting time for him to address the convention. "You told me you'd give me a shot," gushed Domenici. "So I appreciate it, brother."

Family ties help open doors. Tommy Boggs' mother Lindy is a Congresswoman from Louisiana; his father, the late Hale Boggs, was House majority leader. Other congressional progeny who as lobbyists have traded on their names for various interests: Speaker Tip O'Neill's son Kip (sugar, beer, cruise ships); Senate Majority Leader Robert Dole's daughter Robin (Century 21 real estate); Senator Paul Laxalt's daughter Michelle (oil, Wall Street, Hollywood); and House Appropriations Committee Chairman Jamie Whitten's son Jamie Jr. (steel, barges, cork).

Then there is so-called soft core (as opposed to hard-core) lobbying. Since the real business of Washington is often conducted by night, a whole cottage industry has grown up around the party-giving business. Michael Deaver's wife Carolyn is one of half a dozen Washington hostesses who can be hired to set up power parties, which bring top Government officials together with private businessmen. "Facilitator" Canzeri puts on charitable events to burnish corporate images, like a celebrity tennis tournament that drew scores of Washington lobbyists and netted $450,000 for Nancy Reagan's antidrug campaign. Lobbyists, not surprisingly, work hard not just at re-electing Congressmen but also at befriending them. Congressman Tony Coelho of California describes the methods of William Cable, a former Carter Administration aide who lobbies for Timmons & Co. "Three out of four times," says Coelho, "he talks to you not about lobbying, but about sports, or tennis—I play a lot of tennis with him—or your family. He's a friend, a sincere friend." Congressman Thomas Luken of Ohio is so chummy with lobbyists that he has been known to wave at them from the dais at committee hearings.

Congressmen often find themselves being lobbied by their former colleagues. More than 200 ex-Congressmen have stayed on in the capital to represent interest groups, sometimes lobbying on the same legislation they helped draft while serving in office. Former Congressmen are free to go onto the floor of Congress and into the cloakrooms, though they are not supposed to lobby there. "Well, they don't call it lobbying," shrugs Senator Pryor. "They call it visiting. But you know exactly what they're there for." Congressional staffers also cash in by selling their expertise and connections. Indeed, members of the House Ways and Means Committee were concerned that the President's tax-reform bill would provoke an exodus of staffers into the lobbying ranks. Their fears were not unfounded: the committee's chief counsel, John Salmon, quit to work as a lobbyist for the law firm of Dewey, Ballantine; James Healey, former aide to Committee Chairman Dan Rostenkowski, quit to join Black, Manafort.

As Congressmen became more independent of committee chairmen and party chieftains, they have tended to listen more to the folks back home. Predictably, however, lobbyists have skillfully found ways to manipulate so-called grassroots support. Direct-mail outfits, armed with computer banks that are stocked with targeting groups, can create "instant constituencies" for special-interest bills. To repeal a 1982 provision requiring tax withholding on dividends and interest, the small banks and thrifts hired a mass-mailing firm to launch a letter-writing campaign that flooded congressional offices with some 22 million pieces of mail. The bankers' scare tactics were dubious—they managed to convince their depositors that the withholding provision was a tax hike, when in fact it was set up merely to make people pay taxes that they legally owed. But the onslaught worked. Over the objections of President Reagan and most of the congressional leadership, Congress voted overwhelmingly in 1983 to repeal withholding.

Onetime liberal activists who learned grass-roots organizing for such causes as opposition to the Viet Nam War now employ these same techniques on behalf of business clients. Robert Beckel, Walter Mondale's campaign manager in 1984, has set up an organization with the grandiose title of the Alliance to Save the Ocean. Its aim is to stop the burning of toxic wastes at sea. Beckel's fee is being paid by Rollins Environmental Services, a waste-disposal company that burns toxic waste on land.

Grass-roots organizations sometimes collide. Lobbyist Jack Albertine recently established the Coalition to Encourage Privatization. Its public policy purpose: to enable private enterprise to run services now performed by the Government. Its more immediate goal: to persuade Congress to sell Conrail to the Norfolk Southern railroad. In the meantime, Anne Wexler has been building the Coalition for a Competitive Conrail, a farm-dominated group pushing for Morgan Guaranty as the prospective purchaser.

Booze, broads and bribes—what 19th century Congressional Correspondent Edward Winslow Martin called "the levers of lust"—are no longer the tools of the trade. This is not to say, however, that lobbyists have stopped wining and dining Congressman and their staffs. Public records indicate that Ways and Means Chairman Rostenkowski spends about as much time playing golf as the guest of lobbyists at posh resorts as he does holding hearings in Washington.

Though it has become more difficult to slip a special-interest bill through Congress in the dead of night, it is not impossible. In 1981, when a group of commodity traders began lobbying for a tax loophole worth $300 million, then Senate Finance Chairman Dole poked fun at the commodity traders on the Senate floor. "They are great contributors. They haven't missed a fund raiser. If you do not pay any taxes, you can afford to go to all the fund raisers." But then commodity PACs and individual traders increased their contributions to Dole's own political action committee from $11,000 in 1981–82 to $70,500 in 1983–84. Dole, engaged in a campaign to become Senate majority leader, badly needed the money (his PAC contributed some $300,000 to 47 of the Senate's 53 Republicans). In a late-night tax-writing session in the summer of 1984, Dole quietly dropped his opposition to the tax break for the commodity traders, and it became law.

Such victories inspire other loophole-seeking businessmen to hire guides through the congressional maze, at any price. There is no shortage of hungry lobbyists ready to relieve them of their money. "You get hustlers in Washington who get hooked up with hustlers outside of Washington, and the money moves very quickly," says Peter Teeley, former press aide to Vice President George Bush and now a Washington p.r. man. "Some people are getting ripped off." Says Senator Pryor: "Businessmen are very, very naive. It's amazing what they pay these lobbyists. The businessmen panic. They really don't understand Washington."

As one of the most successful lobbyists in town, Bob Gray naturally has his detractors, and they accuse him of overselling businessmen on his ability to solve all their Washington problems with a few phone calls. "Gray is so overrated it's unbelievable," says one U.S. Senator. "He makes a big splash at parties, but his clients aren't getting a lot for their money." Gray insists that he never promises more than he can deliver. But his own clients sometimes grumble that, for a fat fee, they get little more than a handshake from a Cabinet member at a cocktail party.

When the big lobbying guns line up on opposite sides of an issue, they tend to cancel each other out. Threatened with a takeover by Mobil Oil in 1981, Marathon Oil hired Tommy Boggs' firm to push a congressional bill that would block the merger. The firm managed to get the bill through the House by using a little-known procedural rule at a late-night session. In the Senate, however, Mobil—represented by former Carter Aide Stuart Eizenstat—was able to stop the bill when Senator Howell Heflin of Alabama blocked consideration on the Senate floor. Heflin is a friend of Mobil Chairman Rawleigh Warner.

"We're getting to the point of lobbylock now," says Lobbyist Carl Nordberg. "There are so many lobbyists here pushing and pulling in so many different directions that, at times, nothing seems to go anywhere." The most pernicious effect of the influence-peddling game may simply be that it consumes so much of a Congressman's working day. Every time a Congressmen takes a PAC check, he is obliged at least to grant the contributor an audience. The IOUs mount up. "Time management is a serious problem," says Frank. "I find myself screening out people who just want to bill their clients for talking to a Congressman." The lobbyists are not unmindful of congressional impatience. Lobbyist Dan Dutko, for instance, has a "five-second rule"—all background documents must be simple enough to be absorbed by a Congressman at the rate of five seconds per page. It is no wonder that Congress rarely takes the time to debate such crucial national security questions as whether the U.S. really needs to build a 600-ship Navy, as the Reagan Administration contends; most Congressmen are too preoccupied listening to lobbyists for defense contractors telling them how many jobs building new ships will create back in the district.

In theory at least, there is a partial cure to the growing power of the influence-peddling pack: further limits on campaign expenditures and public financing of elections. But Congress is not likely to vote for these reforms any time soon, in large part because as incumbents they can almost always raise more money than challengers can. Certainly, most Congressmen have become wearily resigned to living with lobbyists. They are sources of money, political savvy, even friendship. In the jaded culture of Washington, influence peddlers are more envied than disdained. Indeed, to lawmakers on the Hill and policymakers throughout the Executive Branch, the feeling increasingly seems to be: well, if you can't beat 'em, join 'em.

The Media as the Fourth Estate

☐   The press, joined by the electronic media, is a unique kind of interest group. Often called the "fourth estate," and sometimes the "fourth branch of government,"[1] the press and the media act as part of government at the same time that they criticize it. Objectivity is a journalistic standard that reporters widely herald, but the process of news gathering and reporting inevitably has a highly subjective content. What is or is not covered reflects an editor's or reporter's view of what is or is not important, what the public should or should not know. Policies that do not receive publicity have little chance of passage through the intricate maze of government. The press and the media can be an important ally of government agencies, politicians, and interest groups as well in their quest for the enactment of particular public policies.

The following selection describes the world of the Washington reporter and the forces that shape the news.

[1]See, for example, Douglass Cater, The Fourth Branch of Government (Boston: Houghton Mifflin, 1959).

32

Stephen Hess

THE WASHINGTON REPORTERS

Washington is more and more the center of attention in the nation's news media, dominating even when nothing very special happens in the capital. There are consequences for public policy when the information that citizens receive is overwhelmingly about one level of government.

The television networks and the weekly newsmagazines must be national in character, of course, yet a conclusion of this study is that so too are newspapers, to a surprising degree.

News comes from where reporters are: the increase in Washington stories reflects growth in the Washington press corps. This growth in personnel, argues a reporter for Knight-Ridder, "is a miracle in that Washington coverage drains, rather than produces, revenue." While true, most newspapers get most of their Washington stories from the wire services and, increasingly, from the supplemental news services, where the costs to local papers are constant regardless of the amount used. In comparison with state and local stories, which are more apt to be staff-produced, Washington stories are a bargain. Thus the increase in Washington stories is a product both of newspapers' willingness to spend money on coverage that they think is important and prestigious and of a system that provides them with plentiful and inexpensive copy.

Given the limits to the size of newspapers' news holes, a rise in Washington stories presages a decline in news of municipal and state governments, most often the latter. . . .

The sheer volume of words that flows from Washington is remarkable; there has never been a place so extensively covered on a permanent basis. Yet Washington reporters currently feel themselves under attack. . . .

Of all the problems of Washington news gathering, the one that reporters find most serious has been given the name pack journalism. Only 8 percent of the press do not feel it is a problem. The responses isolate two separate conditions: one, reporters are packed together, that is, they cover the same events, such as presidential news conferences, rather than venturing out on their own; two, they arrive at pack decisions, often based on pooling information. Eugene McCarthy once compared the press to blackbirds on

From Stephen Hess, *The Washington Reporters.* Copyright © 1981 by The Brookings Institution. Reprinted by permission.

a telephone line. One flies off, the others fly off; one comes back, the others come back. All in a row. It is the second condition that reporters consider more troubling, for it implies that they do not form independent judgments or even that they are somehow cheating.

Yet how different could their judgments be when—as Timothy Crouse notes—the reporters live in the same city, use the same sources, belong to the same professional groups, and swear by the same omens? He concludes of those covering presidential campaigns: "They arrived at their answers just as independently as a class of honest seventh graders using the same geometry text—they did not have to cheat off each other to come up with the same answer."[1] Crouse is right in stressing common vantage point rather than socioeconomic similarities. When women or blacks are on the beats that most often produce pack journalism, they are not immune. From the same perspective, there is one view. It is a matter of optics.

Still, there is more than meets the eye. Editors wonder—perhaps properly—when their reporters too often see events in a very different light from other reporters. Presumably there are "right" answers. And if the majority answer turns out to be wrong, there is comfort for the reporters in knowing that they were not wrong alone. What occupation wishes to maximize risk? Even Hollywood stuntmen take precautions to survive. When the work has to be done very fast, when events are subject to different interpretations, when participants are unknown or not available, when the situation is complicated, it is useful to have colleagues to compare impressions with. But unlike doctors, for whom it is a matter of pride to make the same diagnosis, reporters sharing diagnoses feel almost conspiratorial. They prefer to think of themselves as lone rangers, and even having research assistants creates problems for their self-image. They take precautions, then feel uneasy. (The great politicians whom they admire are notorious risk takers.) Again, one wonders about this as part of the journalist personality.

Of course, the press corps could be concerned about pack journalism not because their individualism is in doubt but because it has produced mistaken perceptions so often. In recent presidential politics the press saw Edmund Muskie as the frontrunner in 1972, discounting George McGovern; Henry Jackson as the frontrunner in 1976, discounting Jimmy Carter. It is debatable whether their shared perceptions were any different from their individual perceptions, but limiting the number of perspectives does limit the opportunities to see things differently. Which suggests the criticism of the other form of pack journalism.

Is not something wrong when all the firemen rush to the same fire? In theory at least, Americans, including news workers, are offended by inefficiency; the United States pioneered time-and-motion studies. Adjusting

---

[1]*The Boys on the Bus* (Random House, 1973), p. 44.

resources, however, requires an adjuster controlling where reporters are located and what they are covering; and this, of course, is exactly what news workers wish to avoid. Instead, Washington news gathering is procedural pluralism, or "let a hundred flowers bloom."

The results are that the sum of Washington reporting does not add up to the universe of government activities; it is excessive in some areas, nonexistent in others. This cannot accurately be called a system if a system is defined as an arrangement that molds the parts into an organic whole. Rather, Washington news is produced by a large number of small, fiercely competitive units, each functioning independently and without regard for how its operation affects other news-gathering agencies or the totality of information that reaches the public.

When an event is public—such as a trial—and all reporters must rely on the same equally available resources, procedural pluralism is hard to justify. A rule of thumb should be, Can a reporter get information that will not be available to the wire services and reported as adequately by them? Washington reporters rarely criticize the quality of AP and UPI stories, as they once did. In practice, however, there are few Washington stories on which different reporters do not produce some different information. (Because the popular media often use the same lead stories, resources appear to be more redundant than they actually are.) Only a handful of the press corps waits at the White House or travels on the campaign buses. While some could be moved to other assignments without diminishing the news flow, this would not greatly expand Washington coverage. Only at the television networks is a substantial portion of resources devoted to overlapping stories. To operate otherwise would require pooling arrangements on all major beats, which, though it would free reporters to cover other stories, would produce uniform coverage of the top news. Would this be an improvement? Duplicating resources at least leaves open the possibility that correspondents, spurred on by the competition, will do a better job. But the most important effect of procedural pluralism is as a check on the influence of any one news gatherer.

[My] study [of Washington reporters] provides new answers to the question, Who is deciding what is news? The findings, if surprising, are less so when the study's vantage point is recalled. Many recent attempts to explain the news media have been directed at the top, recounting life and times in corporate headquarters and home offices. In this study the sightings were taken at the bottom, looking at the worker in the field, usually far from headquarters. Things, including organizations, look different from different angles.

The news business also may look different from a nonjournalist's perspective. For example, Washington reporters bridle at home-office requests for stories, although we find that these requests consume a very small percentage of their time. They worry, too, about bureaucratization in their operations. News organizations are bureaucracies, of course, and they may become more bureaucratic as they grow larger, but they are considerably less hierarchical than other types of enterprises of comparable size. To news workers, newswork seems to be much more controlled from the top than it appears to an outsider.

Moreover, many recent studies concentrate on national operations—television networks, weekly newsmagazines, newspapers of reputation beyond their immediate circulation areas—and ignore the many smaller operations whose reporters and collective impact play an important role in the dissemination of information. Centralized control is a by-product of the technology of television and is part of the basic design at the newsmagazines, where reports from the outposts are blended into a finished product. Prestige organizations often grant the least autonomy to their workers (and thus prestige reporters at prestige organizations may be the most conflicted; they are also the most likely to write books explaining the media).

A conclusion that the more national the character of the news operation, the greater the home-office control—while generally true—misses a key point: the nature of news gathering vests considerable autonomy in all news gatherers. And the nature of Washington news gathering (regardless of an organization's size) adds to their freedom. Reporters' autonomy is greater (1) the greater their distance from their home offices; (2) the more prestige they have; (3) the longer they have worked at their jobs; (4) the greater their specialized knowledge; (5) the more complex the news they cover; (6) the more sources they grant anonymity; and (7) the less revenue related their stories. Using these formulations, the Washington reporter with least autonomy is a young person on general assignment for a television network; the most autonomous is an older specialist reporter for a noninfluential newspaper.

This survey shows that Washington reporters initiate the vast majority of their stories and that the stories get good placement and hardly any editing. When Washington is also the home office, the reporters' autonomy is lessened, but in general, Washington reporters are freer of supervision than any other type of news gatherer save the foreign correspondent. Washington reporters are, almost by definition, the stars of their organizations. Few are under thirty years old. Their reporting is becoming more specialized and the news more complex. Sources are granted anonymity more than in other parts of the country. And unlike stories about automobiles, real estate, or food, news from Washington is rarely related to an operation's receipts and hence not as susceptible to management's influence.

True, constraints are imposed on reporters by the type of organization they work for (copy must fit time, space, style, and technical requirements); by the beat system (they can gather information only within prescribed areas); by the parameters of permissible news (defined for them by tradition,

libel law, and consumer acceptance); and by profitability or other management considerations that determine the amount of money they can have for
travel and expenses. Other limitations are self-imposed and can be ignored,
but not without cost: if they treat a news source roughly, they could
endanger their access to news; if they fail to take into account what
competitors are writing, they could endanger their standing within their
own organization. Moreover, news events are largely determined by natural
forces or governments, beyond the control of either editor or reporter. It is
not the journalist who calls the press conference, casts the vote, or pulls the
trigger. (Still, the *form* of human events increasingly adjusts to the needs of
the media, and these accommodations affect the *nature* of the events. Only
the most unperceptive news workers believe that they function merely as
flies on the wall and that their presence does not affect the behavior of
newsmakers.)

Yet to the degree that the media decide what is Washington news, the
decisions are most often made in the field, not in executive suites. The
reporters, collectively, cover what interests them, and do not cover what
does not interest them. In public administration it is said, "Let me write the
option paper, I'll let you make the decisions."[2] In newswork, organizations make the decisions (What will be the front page lead? Will the
evening news be expanded to an hour?), but day to day, the options on the
content of news are written by Washington reporters.

Headquarters allows control to drift out of its hands in part because the
events that interest or fail to interest Washington reporters are roughly the
same events that interest or do not interest editors. When there is a
conflict, editors probably could get their way. (A participant in a shake-up
by the *Chicago Sun-Times* of its Washington bureau says, "It reminds us all
who cracks the whip.") But most editors do not bother, for a variety of
reasons—not caring very much, not knowing very much, being too busy,
deferring to experts, wanting to maintain morale. Probably the most frequent reason is inertia. It is in the interests of reporters to leave as vague as
possible the exact balance of autonomy and control.

The autonomy of Washington reporters has consequences for what will
be covered. The gradual shifting from regional news, for example, is a
direct result of reporters' freedom of choice. Editors—at least so they
say—would like more stories about how government in Washington affects
their circulation areas, but they do not get them because the Washington
press corps prefers to write about other matters. What reporters do not
want to cover is not necessarily what consumers need not be informed
about—economics, for example. Conversely, there are subjects—notably
international affairs—that reporters cover extensively despite survey evidence that consumers are less interested than they are.

---

[2]The aphorism is attributed to Herbert Kaufman.

Reporters spend relatively little time in their circulation areas once they take up residence in Washington. Their travels, while extensive, are always on specific assignments, always rushed, often to places that do not help them stay in touch with readers. Consumers rarely write them. Those who do, reporters feel, are not representative. Home offices rarely share unpublished letters to the editor or the results of consumer surveys. As Washington journalism becomes more specialized, reporters are hired for subject-area expertise rather than knowledge of the city in which their reporting appears. Consumers are even easier than editors to forget. In their isolated world, reporters find their satisfactions and status from their peers in the press corps. How to break the isolation is a problem that reporters and their organizations recognize but seem unwilling to seriously address, partly because the answers can be expensive for management and uncomfortable for labor.

What has been happening, perhaps slowly and subtly enough to escape broad notice, is that over time the proprietors gave up control of content to the editors, and the editors, in turn, are losing control to the reporters. At least this is the way it appears from Washington to this observer. Three phenomena are at the root of this shift: the changing ownership of news organizations, their growth, and the professional status of editorial workers.

The steady movement is from politically motivated newspaper publishers—the William Randolph Hearsts and Robert R. McCormicks in the United States, Lord Beaverbrooks and Cecil Kings in Great Britain—to the corporate managers. The new breed is not concerned with ideology. Indeed, a highly politicized product can be bad for business. To a lesser degree—because they are designed to be interpretive—this is even the case at the newsmagazines in the post-Henry Luce era. The television networks, unlike their news divisions, are always run by nonjournalists, which creates frictions but does not negate the general rule. (Reporters do not worry that media corporations will use their properties for political purposes. Reporters also know that this is the sort of threat that they are very good at turning into very bad publicity, and public corporations have a fierce aversion to bad publicity.)

The news business is highly profitable, and the proprietors' implicit bargain with their reporters makes it even more profitable. Reporters have fewer management prerogatives than workers of comparable status in most other industries. At the same time, Washington reporters could cite almost no examples of management imposing editorial judgments on their copy. This is a trade-off that seems to satisfy both management and labor. Reporters, who are not business people and care little even for the business of their own business, want to appear in print or on the air; the new proprietors, who are or become business people, want to make a profit. Each side gets what it most wants. This is not to say that reporters are exploited or that proprietors take no pride in their product. On the contrary. Reporters are well paid by the standards and expectations they set for themselves when they chose journalism as a career, and proprietors, especially in monopoly situations, usually make greater investments than are necessary to retain consumers and advertisers. Whether this will change if the news business should become less profitable is a question that rightly worries editorial workers.

As news organizations grow bigger, the reporters gain greater control over content. Reporters think the opposite happens, but this is because they confuse red tape with control. As the organizations that they work for get larger and more far-flung, reporters will have to learn to live with more bureaucratic management. There will be elaborate travel vouchers to fill out; bureau chiefs, and perhaps even reporters, will have to prepare detailed budgets—and these should give news workers a sufficiency to complain about. But if they look closely they will find that there is less interference with the gathering and reporting of news. In Washington, bureaus of newspaper chains have more independence than bureaus of independent newspapers; regional reporters for multiple papers have more independence than regional reporters for a single newspaper. Control weakens as the distance increases from top to bottom. Reporters write about this when it occurs in government, but do not relate span-of-control doctrines to their own work.

The reporters' control over content also increases in direct proportion to their rise in professional status. The professionalism movement was designed to correct the abuses of yellow journalism in the late nineteenth century. From this laudable beginning the press has created for itself most of the trappings of a profession. Once an occupation is accepted as a profession, the only acceptable controls are self-controls and peer-controls; those not trained or otherwise qualified are not entitled to pass judgment. The increasing expectation of reporters that their stories will appear as written is founded on professional virtue, not on property rights.

The editorial independence of reporters may be more pronounced in Washington than in other locations. And even in Washington there are wide differences among organizations and types of organizations. The overall impression, however, is that Washington news gathering fragments the power of the media, while at the same time it shifts decisions on what is news and how it should be covered to the reporters.

PART THREE

National Governmental Institutions

CHAPTER 6

The Presidency

The American presidency is the only unique political institution that the United States has contributed to the world. It developed first in this country and later was imitated, usually unsuccessfully, in many nations. In no country and at no time has the institution of the presidency achieved the status and power that it possesses in the United States. This chapter will analyze the basis, nature, and implications of the power of this great American institution.

Constitutional Background: Single v. Plural Executive

The change that has taken place in the presidency since the office was established in 1789 is dramatic and significant. The framers of the Constitution were primarily concerned with the control of the arbitrary exercise of power by the legislature; thus they were willing to give the president broad power since he was not to be popularly elected and would be constantly under attack by the coordinate legislative branch. Although the framers were not afraid of establishing a vigorous presidency, there was a great deal of opposition to a potentially strong executive at the time the Constitution was drafted. In *Federalist 70* Alexander Hamilton attempts to persuade the people of the desirability of a strong presidential office, and, while persuading, he sets forth the essential constitutional basis of the office.

33
Alexander Hamilton

FEDERALIST 70

There is an idea, which is not without its advocates, that a vigorous executive is inconsistent with the genius of republican government. The enlightened well-wishers to this species of government must at least hope that the supposition is destitute of foundation; since they can never admit its truth, without, at the same time, admitting the condemnation of their own principles. Energy in the executive is a leading character in the definition of good government. It is essential to the protection of the community against foreign attacks; it is not less essential to the steady administration of the laws, to the protection of property against those irregular and high-handed combinations, which sometimes interrupt the ordinary course of justice, to the security of liberty against the enterprises and assaults of ambition, of faction, and of anarchy. Every man, the least conversant in Roman story, knows how often that republic was obliged to take refuge in the absolute power of a single man, under the formidable title of dictator, as well as against the intrigues of ambitious individuals, who aspired to the tyranny, and the seditions of whole classes of the community, whose conduct threatened the existence of all government, as against the invasions of external enemies, who menaced the conquest and destruction of Rome.

There can be no need, however, to multiply arguments or examples on this head. A feeble executive implies a feeble execution of the government. A feeble execution is but another phrase for a bad execution; and a government ill executed, whatever it may be in theory, must be, in practice, a bad government.

Taking it for granted, therefore, that all men of sense will agree in the necessity of an energetic executive, it will only remain to inquire, what are the ingredients which constitute this energy? How far can they be combined with those other ingredients, which constitute safety in the republican sense? And how far does this combination characterize the plan which has been reported by the convention?

The ingredients which constitute energy in the executive are: unity; duration; and adequate provision for its support; competent powers.

The ingredients which constitute safety in the republican sense are: a due dependence on the people; a due responsibility.

Those politicians and statesmen, who have been the most celebrated for the soundness of their principles, and for the justness of their views, have declared in favor of a single executive, and a numerous legislature. They have, with great propriety, considered energy as the most necessary qualification of the former, and have regarded this as most applicable to power in a single hand; while they have, with equal propriety, considered the latter as the best adapted to deliberation and wisdom, and best calculated to conciliate the confidence of the people, and to secure their privileges and interests.

That unity is conducive to energy will not be disputed. Decision, activity, secrecy, and dispatch, will generally characterize the proceedings of one man, in a much more eminent degree than the proceedings of any greater number; and in proportion as the number is increased, these qualities will be diminished.

This unity may be destroyed in two ways; either by vesting the power in two or more magistrates, of equal dignity and authority; or by vesting it ostensibly in one man, subject, in whole or in part, to the control and cooperation of others, in the capacity of counsellors to him. . . .

The experience of other nations will afford little instruction on this head. As far, however, as it teaches anything, it teaches us not to be enamoured of plurality in the executive. . . .

Wherever two or more persons are engaged in any common enterprise or pursuit, there is always danger of difference of opinion. If it be a public trust of office, in which they are clothed with equal dignity and authority, there is peculiar danger of personal emulation and even animosity. From either, and especially from all these causes, the most bitter dissentions are apt to spring. Whenever these happen, they lessen the respectability, weaken the authority, and distract the plans and operations of those whom they divide. If they should unfortunately assail the supreme executive magistracy of a country, consisting of a plurality of persons, they might impede or frustrate the most important measures of the government, in the most critical emergencies of state. And what is still worse, they might split the community into violent and irreconcilable factions, adhering differently to the different individuals who composed the magistracy. . . .

Upon the principles of a free government, inconveniences from the source just mentioned, must necessarily be submitted to in the formation of the legislature; but it is unnecessary, and therefore unwise, to introduce them into the constitution of the executive. It is here, too, that they may be most pernicious. In the legislature, promptitude of decision is oftener an evil than a benefit. The differences of opinion, and the jarrings of parties in that department of the government, though they may sometimes obstruct salutary plans, yet often promote deliberation and circumspection; and serve to check excesses in the majority. When a resolution, too, is once taken, the opposition must be at an end. That resolution is a law, and resistance to it punishable. But no favorable circumstances palliate, or atone for the disadvantages of dissention in the executive department. Here they are pure and unmixed. There is no point at which they cease to operate. They serve to embarrass and weaken the execution of the plan or measure to which they relate, from the first step to the final conclusion of it. They constantly counteract those qualities in the executive, which are the most necessary ingredients in its composition—vigor and expedition; and this without any counterbalancing good. In the conduct of war, in which the energy of the executive is the bulwark of the national security, everything would be to be apprehended from its plurality.

It must be confessed, that these observations apply with principal weight to the first case supposed, that is, to a plurality of magistrates of equal dignity and authority, a scheme, the advocates for which are not likely to form a numerous sect; but they apply, though not with equal, yet with considerable weight, to the project of a council, whose concurrence is made constitutionally necessary to the operations of the ostensible executive. An artful cabal in that council would be able to distract and to enervate the whole system of administration. If no such cabal should exist, the mere diversity of views and opinions would alone be sufficient to tincture the exercise of the executive authority with the spirit of habitual feebleness and dilatoriness.

But one of the weightiest objections to a plurality in the executive, and which lies as much against the last as the first plan, is, that it tends to conceal faults, and destroy responsibility. . . . It often becomes impossible, amidst mutual accusations, to determine on whom the blame or the punishment of a pernicious measure . . . ought really to fall. It is shifted from one to another with so much dexterity, and under such plausible appearances, that the public opinion is left in suspense about the real author. . . .

A little consideration will satisfy us, that the species of security sought for in the multiplication of the executive, is unattainable. Numbers must be so great as to render combination difficult; or they are rather a source of danger than of security. The united credit and influence of several individuals must be more formidable to liberty than the credit and influence of either of them separately. When power, therefore, is placed in the hands of so small a number of men, as to admit of their interests and views being easily combined in a common enterprise, by an artful leader, it becomes more liable to abuse, and more dangerous when abused, than if it be lodged in the hands of one man; who, from the very circumstances of his being alone, will be more narrowly watched and more readily suspected, and who cannot unite so great a mass of influence as when he is associated with others. . . .

I will only add, that prior to the appearance of the constitution, I rarely met with an intelligent man from any of the states, who did not admit as the result of experience, that the unity of the executive of this state was one of the best of the distinguishing features of our constitution.

The Nature of the Presidency:
Power and Persuasion

☐ What is the position of the presidential office today? There is little doubt that it has expanded far beyond the expectations of the framers of the Constitution. The presidency is the only governmental branch with the necessary unity and energy to meet many of the most crucial problems of twentieth-century government in the United States; people have turned to the president in times of crisis to supply the central direction necessary for survival. In the next selection Clinton Rossiter, one of the leading American scholars of the presidency, gives his view of the role of the office.

34
Clinton Rossiter

THE PRESIDENCY—
FOCUS OF LEADERSHIP

No American can contemplate the presidency ... without a feeling of solemnity and humility—solemnity in the face of a historically unique concentration of power and prestige, humility in the thought that he has had a part in the choice of a man to wield the power and enjoy the prestige.

Perhaps the most rewarding way to grasp the significance of this great office is to consider it as a focus of democratic leadership. Free men, too, have need of leaders. Indeed, it may well be argued that one of the decisive forces in the shaping of American democracy has been the extraordinary capacity of the presidency for strong, able, popular leadership. If this has been true of our past, it will certainly be true of our future, and we should therefore do our best to grasp the quality of this leadership. Let us do this by answering the essential question: For what men and groups does the president provide leadership?

First, the president is *leader of the Executive Branch*. To the extent that our federal civil servants have need of common guidance, he alone is in a position to provide it. We cannot savor the fullness of the president's duties unless we recall that he is held primarily accountable for the ethics,

From *The New York Times,* November 11, 1956. Copyright © 1956 by The New York Times Company. Reprinted by permission.

loyalty, efficiency, frugality, and responsiveness to the public's wishes of the two and one-third million Americans in the national administration.

Both the Constitution and Congress have recognized his power to guide the day-to-day activities of the Executive Branch, strained and restrained though his leadership may often be in practice. From the Constitution, explicitly or implicitly, he receives the twin powers of appointment and removal, as well as the primary duty, which no law or plan or circumstances can ever take away from him, to "take care that the laws be faithfully executed."

From Congress, through such legislative mandates as the Budget and Accounting Act of 1921 and the succession of Reorganization Acts, the president has received further acknowledgment of his administrative leadership. Although independent agencies such as the Interstate Commerce Commission and the National Labor Relations Board operate by design outside his immediate area of responsibility, most of the government's administrative tasks are still carried on within the fuzzy-edged pyramid that has the president at its lonely peak; the laws that are executed daily in his name and under his general supervision are numbered in the hundreds.

Many observers, to be sure, have argued strenuously that we should not ask too much of the president as administrative leader, lest we burden him with impossible detail, or give too much to him, lest we inject political considerations too forcefully into the steady business of the civil service. Still, he cannot ignore the blunt mandate of the Constitution, and we should not forget the wisdom that lies behind it. The president has no more important tasks than to set a high personal example of integrity and industry for all who serve the nation, and to transmit a clear lead downward through his chief lieutenants to all who help shape the policies by which we live.

Next, the president is *leader of the forces of peace and war.* Although authority in the field of foreign relations is shared constitutionally among three organs—president, Congress, and, for two special purposes, the Senate—his position is paramount, if not indeed dominant. Constitution, laws, customs, the practice of other nations and the logic of history have combined to place the president in a dominant position. Secrecy, dispatch, unity, continuity, and access to information—the ingredients of successful diplomacy—are properties of his office, and Congress, needless to add, possesses none of them. Leadership in foreign affairs flows today from the president—or it does not flow at all.

The Constitution designates him specifically as "Commander in Chief of the Army and Navy of the United States." In peace and war he is the supreme commander of the armed forces, the living guarantee of the American belief in "the supremacy of the civil over military authority."

In time of peace he raises, trains, supervises and deploys the forces that Congress is willing to maintain. With the aid of the Secretary of Defense, the Joint Chiefs of Staff and the National Security Council—all of whom are his personal choices—he looks constantly to the state of the nation's defenses. He is never for one day allowed to forget that he will be held accountable by the people, Congress and history for the nation's readiness to meet an enemy assault.

In time of war his power to command the forces swells out of all proportion to his other powers. All major decisions of strategy, and many of tactics as well, are his alone to make or to approve. Lincoln and Franklin Roosevelt, each in his own way and time, showed how far the power of military command can be driven by a president anxious to have his generals and admirals get on with the war.

But this, the power of command, is only a fraction of the vast responsibility the modern president draws from the Commander in Chief clause. We need only think back to three of Franklin D. Roosevelt's actions in World War II—the creation and staffing of a whole array of emergency boards and offices, the seizure and operation of more than sixty strike-bound or strike-threatened plants and industries, and the forced evacuation of 70,000 American citizens of Japanese descent from the West Coast—to understand how deeply the president's authority can cut into the lives and liberties of the American people in time of war. We may well tremble in contemplation of the kind of leadership he would be forced to exert in a total war with the absolute weapon.

The president's duties are not all purely executive in nature. He is also intimately associated, by Constitution and custom, with the legislative process, and we may therefore consider him as *leader of Congress.* Congress has its full share of strong men, but the complexity of the problems it is asked to solve by a people who still assume that all problems are solvable has made external leadership a requisite of effective operation.

The president alone is in a political, constitutional, and practical position to provide such leadership, and he is therefore expected, within the limits of propriety, to guide Congress in much of its lawmaking activity. Indeed, since Congress is no longer minded or organized to guide itself, the refusal or inability of the president to serve as a kind of prime minister results in weak and disorganized government. His tasks as leader of Congress are difficult and delicate, yet he must bend to them steadily or be judged a failure. The president who will not give his best thoughts to leading Congress, more so the president who is temperamentally or politically unfitted to "get along with Congress," is now rightly considered a national liability.

The lives of Jackson, Lincoln, Wilson, and the two Roosevelts should be enough to remind us that the president draws much of his real power from his position as *leader of his party.* By playing the grand politician with unashamed zest, the first of these men gave his epic administration a unique sense of cohesion, the second rallied doubting Republican leaders and their followings to the cause of the Union, and the other three achieved genuine triumphs as catalysts of Congressional action. That gifted amateur, Dwight D. Eisenhower, has also played the role for every drop of drama and power in it. He has demonstrated repeatedly what close observers of the presidency know well: that its incumbent must devote an hour or two of every working day to the profession of Chief Democrat or Chief Republican.

It troubles many good people, not entirely without reason, to watch the president dabbling in politics, distributing loaves and fishes, smiling on party hacks, and endorsing candidates he knows to be unfit for anything but immediate delivery to the county jail. Yet if he is to persuade Congress, if he is to achieve a loyal and cohesive administration, if he is to be elected in the first place (and reelected in the second), he must put his hand firmly to the plow of politics. The president is inevitably the nation's No. 1 political boss.

Yet he is, at the same time, if not in the same breath, *leader of public opinion.* While he acts as political chieftain of some, he serves as moral spokesman for all. It took the line of presidents some time to sense the nation's need for a clear voice, but since the day when Andrew Jackson thundered against the Nullifiers of South Carolina, no effective president has doubted his prerogative to speak the people's mind on the great issues of his time, to serve, in Wilson's words, as "the spokesman for the real sentiment and purpose of the country."

Sometimes, of course, it is no easy thing, even for the most sensitive and large-minded presidents, to know the real sentiment of the people or to be bold enough to state it in defiance of loudly voiced contrary opinion. Yet the president who senses the popular mood and spots new tides even before they start to run, who practices shrewd economy in his appearances as spokesman for the nation, who is conscious of his unique power to compel discussion on his own terms and who talks the language of Christian morality and the American tradition, can shout down any other voice or chorus of voices in the land. The president is the American people's one authentic trumpet, and he has no higher duty than to give a clear and certain sound.

The president is easily the most influential leader of opinion in this country principally because he is, among all his other jobs, our Chief of State. He is, that is to say, the ceremonial head of the government of the United States, the *leader of the rituals of American democracy.* The long catalogue of public duties that the Queen discharges in England and the Governor General in Canada is the President's responsibility in this country, and the catalogue is even longer because he is not a king, or even the agent of one, and is therefore expected to go through some rather undignified paces by a people who think of him as a combination of scoutmaster, Delphic oracle, hero of the silver screen, and father of the multitudes.

The role of Chief of State may often seem trivial, yet it cannot be neglected by a president who proposes to stay in favor and, more to the point, in touch with the people, the ultimate support of all his claims to leadership. And whether or not he enjoys this role, no president can fail to realize that his many powers are invigorated, indeed are given a new dimension of authority, because he is the symbol of our sovereignty, continuity and grandeur as a people.

When he asks a senator to lunch in order to enlist his support for a pet project, when he thumps his desk and reminds the antagonists in a labor dispute of the larger interests of the American people, when he orders a general to cease caviling or else be removed from his command, the senator and the disputants and the general are well aware—especially if the scene is laid in the White House—that they are dealing with no ordinary head of government. The framers of the Constitution took a momentous step when they fused the dignity of a king and the power of a prime minister in one elective office—when they made the president a national leader in the mystical as well as the practical sense.

Finally, the president has been endowed—whether we or our friends abroad like it or not—with a global role as *a leader of the free nations.* His leadership in this area is not that of a dominant executive. The power he exercises is in a way comparable to that which he holds as a leader of Congress. Senators and congressmen can, if they choose, ignore the president's leadership with relative impunity. So, too, can our friends abroad; the action of Britain and France in the Middle East is a case in point. But so long as the United States remains the richest and most powerful member of any coalition it may enter, then its president's words and deeds will have a direct bearing on the freedom and stability of a great many other countries.

Having engaged in this piecemeal analysis of the categories of presidential leadership, we must now fit the pieces back together into a seamless unity. For that, after all, is what the presidency is, and I hope this exercise in political taxonomy has not obscured the paramount fact that this focus of democratic leadership is a single office filled by a single man.

The president is not one kind of leader one part of the day, another kind in another part—leader of the bureaucracy in the morning, of the armed forces at lunch, of Congress in the afternoon, of the people in the evening. He exerts every kind of leadership every moment of the day, and every kind feeds upon and into all the others. He is a more exalted leader of ritual because he can guide opinion, a more forceful leader in diplomacy because he commands the armed forces personally, a more effective leader of Congress because he sits at the top of his party. The conflicting demands of these categories of leadership give him trouble at times, but in the end all unite to make him a leader without any equal in the history of democracy.

I think it important to note the qualification: "the history of democracy." For what I have been talking about here is not the Fuehrerprinzip of Hitler or the "cult of personality," but the leadership of free men. The presidency, like every other instrument of power we have created for our use, operates within a grand and durable pattern of private liberty and public morality, which means that the president can lead successfully only when he honors the pattern—by working towards ends to which a "persistent and undoubted" majority of people has given support, and by selecting means that are fair, dignified and familiar.

The president, that is to say, can lead us only in the direction we are accustomed to travel. He cannot lead the gentlemen of Congress to abdicate their functions; he cannot order our civil servants to be corrupt and slothful; he cannot even command our generals to bring off a coup d'état. And surely he cannot lead public opinion in a direction for which public opinion is not prepared—a truth to which our strongest presidents would make the most convincing witnesses. The leadership of free men must honor their freedom. The power of the presidency can move as a mighty host only with the grain of liberty and morality.

The president, then, must provide a steady focus of leadership—of administrators, ambassadors, generals, congressmen, party chieftains, people and men of good will everywhere. In a constitutional system compounded of diversity and antagonism, the presidency looms up as the countervailing force of unity and harmony. In a society ridden by centrifugal forces, it is the only point of reference we all have in common. The relentless progress of this continental republic has made the presidency our truly national political institution.

There are those, to be sure, who would reserve this role to Congress, but, as the least aggressive of our presidents, Calvin Coolidge, once testified, "It is because in their hours of timidity the Congress becomes subservient to the importunities of organized minorities that the president comes more and more to stand as the champion of the rights of the whole country." The more Congress becomes, in Burke's phrase, "a confused and scuffling bustle of local agency" the more the presidency must become a clear beacon of national purpose.

It has been such a beacon at most great moments in our history. In this great moment, too, we may be confident it will burn brightly.

☐   The constitutional and statutory *authority* of the president is indeed extraordinary. However, it is more important to point out that the actual power of the president depends upon his political abilities. The president must act within the framework of a complex and diversified political constituency. He can use the authority of his office to buttress his strength, but this alone is not sufficient. Somehow he must be able to persuade those with whom he deals to follow him; otherwise, he will be weak and ineffective.

35
Richard E. Neustadt

PRESIDENTIAL POWER

In the United States we like to "rate" a president. We measure him as "weak" or "strong" and call what we are measuring his "leadership." We do not wait until a man is dead; we rate him from the moment he takes office. We are quite right to do so. His office has become the focal point of politics and policy in our political system. Our commentators and our politicians make a speciality of taking the man's measurements. The rest of us join in when we feel "government" impinging on our private lives. In the third quarter of the twentieth century millions of us have that feeling often.

... Although we all make judgments about presidential leadership, we often base our judgments upon images of office that are far removed from the reality. We also use those images when we tell one another whom to choose as president. But it is risky to appraise a man in office or to choose a man for office on false premises about the nature of his job. When the job is the presidency of the United States the risk becomes excessive ...

We deal here with the president himself and with his influence on governmental action. In institutional terms the presidency now includes 2,000 men and women. The president is only one of them. But *his* performance scarcely can be measured without focusing on *him*. In terms of party, or of country, or the West, so-called, his leadership involves far more than governmental action. But the sharpening of spirit and of values and of purposes is not done in a vacuum. Although governmental action may not be the whole of leadership, all else is nurtured by it and gains meaning from it. Yet if we treat the presidency as the president, we cannot measure him as though he were the government. Not action as an outcome but his impact on the outcome is the measure of the man. His strength or weakness, then, turns on his personal capacity to influence the conduct of the men who make up government. His influence becomes the mark of leadership. To rate a president according to these rules, one looks into the

Reprinted with permission of Macmillan Publishing Company from *Presidential Power* by Richard E. Neustadt (New York: Macmillan, 1960).

man's own capabilities as seeker and as wielder of effective influence upon the other men involved in governing the country. . . .

"Presidential" . . . means nothing but the president. "Power" means *his* influence. It helps to have these meanings settled at the start.

There are two ways to study "presidential power." One way is to focus on the tactics, so to speak, of influencing certain men in given situations: how to get a bill through Congress, how to settle strikes, how to quiet Cabinet feuds, or how to stop a Suez. The other way is to step back from tactics on those "givens" and to deal with influence in more strategic terms: what is its nature and what are its sources? What can *this* man accomplish to improve the prospect that he will have influence when he wants it? Strategically, the question is not how he masters Congress in a peculiar instance, but what he does to boost his chance for mastery in any instance, looking toward tomorrow from today. The second of these two ways has been chosen for this [selection]. . . .

In form all presidents are leaders, nowadays. In fact this guarantees no more than that they will be clerks. Everybody now expects the man inside the White House to do something about everything. Laws and customs now reflect acceptance of him as the Great Initiator, an acceptance quite as widespread at the Capitol as at his end of Pennsylvania Avenue. But such acceptance does not signify that all the rest of government is at his feet. It merely signifies that other men have found it practically impossible to do *their* jobs without assurance of initiatives from him. Service for themselves, not power for the president, has brought them to accept his leadership in form. They find his actions useful in their business. The transformation of his routine obligations testifies to their dependence on an active White House. A president, these days, is an invaluable clerk. His services are in demand all over Washington. His influence, however, is a very different matter. Laws and customs tell us little about leadership in fact.

Why have our presidents been honored with this clerkship? The answer is that no one else's services suffice. Our Constitution, our traditions, and our politics provide no better source for the initiatives a president can take. Executive officials need decisions, and political protection, and a referee for fights. Where are these to come from but the White House? Congressmen need an agenda from outside, something with high status to respond to or react against. What provides it better than the program of the president? Party politicians need a record to defend in the next national campaign. How can it be made except by "their" Administration? Private persons with a public ax to grind may need a helping hand or they may need a grinding stone. In either case who gives more satisfaction than a president? And outside the United States, in every country where our policies and postures influence home politics, there will be people needing just the "right" thing said and done or just the "wrong" thing stopped in *Washington.* What symbolizes Washington more nearly than the White House?

A modern president is bound to face demands for aid and service from five more or less distinguishable sources: the Executive officialdom, from Congress, from his partisans, from citizens at large, and from abroad. The presidency's clerkship is expressive of these pressures. In effect they are constituency pressures and each president has five sets of constituents. The five are not distinguished by their membership; membership is obviously an overlapping matter. And taken one by one they do not match the man's electorate; one of them, indeed, is outside his electorate. They are distinguished, rather, by their different claims upon him. Initiatives are what they want, for five distinctive reasons. Since government and politics have offered no alternative, our laws and customs turn those wants into his obligations.

Why, then, is the president not guaranteed an influence commensurate with services performed? Constituent relations are relations of dependence. Everyone with any share in governing this country will belong to one (or two, or three) of his "constituencies." Since everyone depends on him why is he not assured of everyone's support? The answer is that no one else sits where he sits, or sees quite as he sees; no one else feels the full weight of his obligations. Those obligations are a tribute to his unique place in our political system. But just because it is unique they fall on him alone. *The same conditions that promote his leadership in form preclude a guarantee of leadership in fact.* No man or group at either end of Pennsylvania Avenue shares his peculiar status in our government and politics. That is why his services are in demand. By the same token, though, the obligations of all other men are different from his own. His Cabinet officers have departmental duties and constituents. His legislative leaders head *Congressional* parties, one in either House. His national party organization stands apart from his official family. His political allies in the states need not face Washington, or one another. The private groups that seek him out are not compelled to govern. And friends abroad are not compelled to run in our elections. Lacking his position and prerogatives, these men cannot regard his obligations as their own. They have their jobs to do; none is the same as his. As they perceive their duty they may find it right to follow him, in fact, or they may not. Whether they will feel obliged *on their responsibility* to do what he wants done remains an open question. . . .

There is reason to suppose that in the years immediately ahead the power problems of a president will remain what they have been in the decades just behind us. If so there will be equal need for presidential expertise of the peculiar sort . . . that has [been] stressed [i.e., political skill]. Indeed, the need is likely to be greater. The president himself and with him the whole government are likely to be more than ever at the mercy of his personal approach.

What may the sixties do to politics and policy and to the place of presidents in our political system? The sixties may destroy them as we know them; that goes without saying. But barring deep depression or unlimited war, a total transformation is the least of likelihoods. Without catastrophes of those dimensions nothing in our past experience suggests that we shall see either consensus of the sort available to F.D.R. in 1933 and 1942, or popular demand for institutional adjustments likely to assist a president. Lacking popular demand, the natural conservatism of established institutions will keep Congress and the party organizations quite resistant to reforms that could give him a clear advantage over them. Four-year terms for congressmen and senators might do it, if the new terms ran with his. What will occasion a demand for that? As for crisis consensus it is probably beyond the reach of the next president. We may have priced ourselves out of the market for "productive" crises on the pattern Roosevelt knew—productive in the sense of strengthening his chances for sustained support *within* the system. Judging from the fifties, neither limited war nor limited depression is productive in those terms. Anything unlimited will probably break the system.

In the absence of productive crises, and assuming that we manage to avoid destructive ones, nothing now forseeable suggests that our next president will have assured support from any quarter. There is no use expecting it from the bureaucracy unless it is displayed on Capitol Hill. Assured support will not be found in Congress unless contemplation of their own electorates keeps a majority of members constantly aligned with him. In the sixties it is to be doubted . . . that pressure from electors will move the same majority of men in either House toward consistent backing for the president. Instead the chances are that he will gain majorities, when and if he does so, by ad hoc coalition-building, issue after issue. In that respect the sixties will be reminiscent of the fifties; indeed, a closer parallel may well be in the late forties. As for "party discipline" in English terms— the favorite cure-all of political scientists since Woodrow Wilson was a youth—the first preliminary is a party link between the White House and the leadership on both sides of the Capitol. But even this preliminary has been lacking in eight of the fifteen years since the Second World War. If ballot-splitting should continue through the sixties it will soon be "un-American" for president and Congress to belong to the same party.

Even if the trend were now reversed, there is no short-run prospect that behind each party label we would find assembled a sufficiently like-minded bloc of voters, similarly aligned in states and districts all across the country, to negate the massive barriers our institutions and traditions have erected against "discipline" on anything like the British scale. This does not mean that a reversal of the ballot-splitting trend would be without significance. If the White House and the legislative leadership were linked by party ties again, a real advantage would accrue to both. Their opportunities for mutually productive bargaining would be enhanced. The policy results might surprise critics of our system. Bargaining "within the family" has a rather different quality than bargaining with members of the rival clan. But we would still be a long way from "party government." Bargaining, not "discipline," would still remain the key to Congressional action on a president's behalf. The crucial distinctions between presidential party and Congressional party are not likely to be lost in the term of the next president.

Presidential Politics

☐   Whether the Founding Fathers intended that the president would be a king or a clerk they clearly did not foresee the deep involvement of the presidency in *partisan* politics. All presidents after George Washington were party chiefs, a role that grew more important as national parties expanded their electoral bases and began to act in a more disciplined fashion to facilitate their control of government. American parties have never been disciplined in the European sense, but they have managed to achieve sufficient organizational unity at both national and more importantly state and local levels to affect and sometimes determine the course of government.

Presidential parties help to identify and translate the political demands of popular majorities into government action. At least theoretically, presidents should be able to use their role as party chief to bridge the constitutional gap between the presidency and Congress that the separation of powers created. However, as the author of the following selection observes, the chasm between presidential and party politics may be as great as that between the president and Congress. A president cannot rely upon the rather tenuous and often vaguely defined role of party chief to build the kinds of political coalitions that are necessary to govern effectively.

36

Austin Ranney

THE PRESIDENT AND HIS PARTY

Any discussion of the relations between the president and Congress should keep in mind that the men who wrote the Constitution of the United States believed that those relations should consist mainly of checks and balances, not of cooperation and certainly not of presidential leadership.

They proceeded from three basic convictions: that government is a necessary evil required by people's tendency to pursue their particular interests by methods and to lengths excessively damaging to the interests of others; that swift and concerted government action is likely to advance the interests of some groups at the expense of others; and that it is therefore better for government to do little or nothing than to do something over the strong objections of any of the nation's significant groups.

The authors of the Constitution sought to implement these convictions in two main ways. First, they fragmented and dispersed governmental jurisdiction between the nation and the states. Second, they fragmented and dispersed the power of the national government mainly between the president and Congress, with a bit left over for the Supreme Court.

The central concern of this [article] is the current condition of the various devices by which American presidents and other politicians have tried to join together, for purposes of getting the government to work, what the Constitution so successfully put asunder. Most of these devices fall under the general heading of "presidential leadership of Congress." The ideas underlying all of them are that America, like every other country, must sometimes take swift, coherent, and purposive action; that Congress is an assembly of independent ambassadors from semisovereign states and districts and therefore cannot by itself initiate such action; that the president, who has the enormous advantages of being one person and of being the only public official elected by all the people, is the only official who can take the lead; and that the basic problem of American government is finding and perfecting institutions that will enable the president to lead Congress with maximum effectiveness.

In the opinion of many analysts over the years, one of the most promising devices stems from the fact that every president since George Washington has been a member of the political party to which many members of Congress—ideally majorities in both chambers—also belong.

From Anthony King (ed.), *Both Ends of the Avenue* (Washington, DC: The American Enterprise Institute, 1983). Reprinted by permission.

Moreover, the president is not just an ordinary member of his party. He is its leader, and he can and should use his party leadership as a way—perhaps the most effective way—of inducing Congress to adopt his programs. . . . [H]ow important [is] the president's role as head of his party . . . in his efforts to lead the government[?]

HOW PARTISAN ARE AMERICAN PRESIDENTS?

Some Rankings. Let us imagine a presidential partisanship scale. At one extreme (let us set it, as it should be set in all good scales, at 100) is the most partisan president we can imagine: one who has been active in party affairs at all levels for many years; who both says and believes that all wisdom and most patriotism reside in his party; who believes that any candidate of his party for any office should be elected over any candidate of the opposition party, and who regularly and intensively campaigns for his party's ticket from top to bottom; who takes a strong and active interest in his national committee's activities, insists that it be well led, well staffed, and well financed; who makes past party service and party loyalty prime criteria in making all his major and minor appointments; who works closely with his party's leaders in Congress in developing his programs and considers the party one of his most important instruments of leadership; and who places high priority on leaving his party in the best possible condition to win elections after he has left the White House.

At the other extreme (let us score it 0) is the least partisan president we can imagine: one whose acceptance of a party's nomination is his first official association with it; who campaigns strictly for himself and his policies and never mentions his party or its other candidates; who has no interest in his party's national committee or other organizational affairs except when they threaten to cause him embarrassment; who treats with the leaders and members of Congress entirely on a nonpartisan basis and never makes any special appeals to his nominal fellow partisans or does special favors for them; who pays no attention whatever to partisan affiliation in making his appointments; and who has no concern whatever for the state of his party after he has left office.

In my highly subjective judgment, the only presidents in the twentieth century who would score close to 50 on such a scale would be Woodrow Wilson and Franklin D. Roosevelt, with Wilson ranking a notch above Roosevelt. (A few early signs suggest that Ronald Reagan may rank among the high-partisanship presidents, but at the present writing it is too early to say so with confidence.) Ranking the lowest would probably be Warren Harding, Calvin Coolidge, Herbert Hoover, and Jimmy Carter. And the average score for all fifteen twentieth-century presidents would be, say, 33.3.

Why Are American Presidents So Unpartisan? Such an average score would surely be far lower than any we would assign to the head of govern-ment in any other modern democratic country. Why is it so low for American presidents? No doubt there are too many reasons to be covered in detail here, but let me briefly outline a few of the most important.

Weak congressional parties. Most of the time, especially in the twentieth century, American political parties have been too weak and uncohesive to constitute an agency capable of providing a president with the votes he needs to get his programs adopted. He can and often does work closely with his party leaders in both chambers, as we have seen; but their powers over their rank and file are those of scheduling the business and trying to persuade the members to support the president. They certainly do not include any power to order the members to get behind the president or to expel them if they oppose him. Given the parties' weakness, what is remarkable about the fact that the president usually gets the support of about two-thirds of his congressional party is that he gets so much, not that he gets so little.

The need for support from the opposition party. Given that on almost any issue before Congress a president will lose from a quarter to more than half of his own party, there are very few issues on which he will not need at least some support from members of the opposition party, and not infrequently he will need quite substantial support from them. Such sup-port has, of course, been crucial for all Republican presidents since Herbert Hoover; for in the total of twenty years in which they held office from 1929 to 1977, in only four years (1929–1931 and 1953–1955) did any of them enjoy a Congress with Republican majorities in both houses. (Ronald Reagan, dealing with a Republican senate and a Democratic house, was better off than most Republican presidents.) Democratic presidents have been much better situated in this regard; even so, in order to get most of the important parts of their programs through Congress, most of them have needed at least some Republican votes to make up for defecting Democrats. Hence no president has felt that he could afford to be so completely partisan in word and deed that he would offend all the members of the opposition party so much that they would never support him on anything.

The increasing irrelevance of party to presidential politics. . . . [P]arty organizations and leaders at all levels have been largely stripped of their once-considerable power to select national convention delegates and deliver them to one candidate or another. Hence no presidential aspirant today bothers much with the party organizations in his drive for the nomination; indeed it may be most effective, as it certainly was for Jimmy Carter in 1974–1976, to run for the nomination as the candidate who is not in any way involved with or supported by the "party bosses."

The increasing antiparty tone of American political culture. I have argued elsewhere that from the nation's beginnings most ordinary Americans have had a poor opinion of political parties in general, as institutions—though most of them have most of the time "identified" with one party over the other. Since the mid-1960s, however, even these party identifications have weakened substantially; there are more independents now than there have been for a long time, and party has a worse name than ever. Most Americans evidently want to weaken parties still further, not strengthen them.

The antipolitician bias of network television. These traditionally strong antiparty strains in American political culture have been considerably reinforced in recent years by the manner in which the television networks have portrayed American politics. In America, as in all other modern democratic countries, most people get most of their information about politics from television; but, unlike many other democracies, America has no party-controlled broadcasts, except for a few thirty-second "commercials" shown in election years. Hence most broadcasting about politics emanates from the local stations' news programs, the three national commercial networks' news programs, and an occasional longer documentary on a particular issue or person. For a variety of reasons—including the nonparty backgrounds and attitudes of most correspondents and producers and the antiestablishment, adversary posture of the broadcasting profession—political parties do not fare well in these broadcasts. Being collectivities, they are much harder to portray in dramatic pictures than personalities. Being such ancient features of the political landscape (the Republicans go back to 1854 and the Democrats to 1792), they are not novel or exciting in the way that a new issue or a new personality is. Worst of all, they are composed entirely of politicians, and everyone—certainly every network correspondent—is sure that politicians are by nature tricky, deceitful, and often dishonest characters who do what they do entirely because they want to be reelected, not because they have any sincere concern for the public interest.

The President's Objectives. For all these reasons, any president is likely to pay a considerable price for appearing to be a strong party man. If he acts—or is portrayed—too much as Mr. Democrat or Mr. Republican, he is almost certain to lose some of the support from the opposition party that he needs in Congress. He will also present a very large target for the networks' tireless snipers. Worst of all, he will deeply offend a good many ordinary people who believe he should be "president of all the people," not an all-out leader of some gang of self-seeking politicians.

If the president were to set as one of his prime objectives strengthening his party organizationally, financially, and in public esteem so that it would go on to even greater success after he had left office, then these prices might be well worth paying. But most presidents give the highest priority to making a presidential record that will secure them a high position in history; and being a strong partisan and strong leader of a party has struck most presidents in this century as a poor way of winning good notices from contemporary or future historians.

There is no reason to suppose that Ronald Reagan and his successors will see things differently.

☐   The presidential nominating process continues to be the subject of intense political debate in the 1980s. Austin Ranney notes in the previous selection the weakening impact grass-roots presidential nominating politics has had upon parties in general and the president's power as party chief in particular. The author of the following selection presents a contrasting point of view, arguing that the current arrangement for choosing presidential candidates has neither weakened parties nor undermined the president's role as chief of his party. The reforms in presidential nominating politics were, in the author's view, a proper response to a changing political and social environment that required parties to adapt to new electoral forces.

37
Michael Nelson

THE CASE FOR THE CURRENT PRESIDENTIAL NOMINATING PROCESS

The current process by which Americans nominate their parties' candidates for president is the product of nearly two centuries of historical evolution and two decades of deliberate procedural reform. It can be judged successful because it satisfies reasonably well the three main criteria by which any presidential nominating process may be judged:

• Does the process strengthen or weaken the two major parties, which our political system relies on to provide some measure of coherence to a constitutionally fragmented government?

• Does the process foster or impede the selection of presidents who are suitably skilled for the office?

From George Grassmuck (ed.), *Before Nomination: Our Primary Problems* (Washington, DC: The American Enterprise Institute, 1985). Reprinted by permission.

• Is the process regarded as legitimate by the public? Is it seen to be fair and democratic?

POLITICAL PARTIES

Have the two major parties been weakened by the reforms of the presidential nominating process that were instituted by the McGovern-Fraser commission and its successors? Much scholarly talent and energy have been devoted to answering this question in the affirmative. Implicit in such analyses are the beliefs that the parties were basically strong before the post-1968 reforms and that they have been considerably weaker ever since. In truth, neither of these beliefs is fully accurate. The parties were in a state of decline during the 1950s and 1960s, a decline that has been arrested and in most cases reversed during the 1970s and 1980s, as the parties, aided by the reforms, have adapted to the changed social and political environment that underlay their decline. This is true of all three of the components of parties that political scientists, following V. O. Key, have identified as fundamental: the party-in-the-electorate, the party-in-government, and the party organization.

Party-in-the-Electorate. Americans are no longer as loyal to the parties as they were in the early 1950s, when modern survey research on voting behavior first took form. On this there is little room for dispute: as Figure A indicates, voters are far less likely now than in the past to think of themselves as either Democrats or Republicans, to vote a straight-party ticket (even for presidential and House candidates), or to express a favorable evaluation of one or both political parties.

Natural though the tendency may be to explain dramatic changes by equally dramatic causes, one cannot attribute the decline of the party-in-the-electorate to the reform era that began in 1968. The largest falloff in party identification, which had remained steadily high through the 1950s and early 1960s, came between 1964 and 1966. An additional large drop occurred between 1970 and 1972, but since then the decline in party identification seems to have leveled off or even been reversed. The share of voters who evaluate at least one party favorably, which fell steadily during the 1960s, has stayed very close to 50 percent ever since, rising to 52 percent in 1984. Similarly, split-ticket voting, a more explicitly behavioral indicator of weak voter loyalty to the parties, underwent its greatest increases before the reform era and has declined since 1980.

Whether Ronald Reagan's presidency has reversed the "dealignment" of voters that occurred mainly during the 1960s remains to be seen. But well before 1980 most of the indexes of party strength in the electorate at least had stopped falling.

Party-in-Government. Historically, Americans have used the political par-

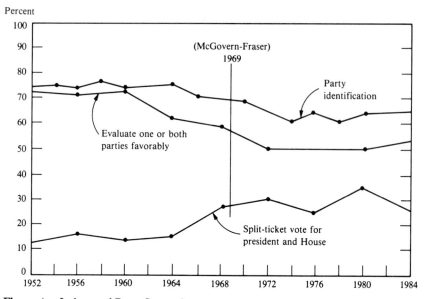

Figure A   Indexes of Party Strength
Sources: Stephen J. Wayne, *The Road to the White House*, 2d ed. (New York: St. Martin's Press, 1984), pp. 57, 59; David E. Price, *Bringing Back the Parties* (Washington, D.C.: Congressional Quarterly Press, 1984), p. 18; and Martin P. Wattenberg, "Realignment without Party Revitalization" (unpublished manuscript).

ties to join what the Constitution put asunder, namely, the executive and legislative branches. The electorate's habit of straight-ticket voting in twentieth-century elections before 1956 meant that the party that controlled the White House also controlled both houses of Congress in forty-six of fifty-four years.

The rise of split-ticket voting weakened such interbranch aspects of party-in-government: nowadays control by the same party of the presidency and Congress is the exception rather than the rule. As with the party-in-the-electorate, however, the evidence indicates that the party-weakening trend in government began well before the reform era: indeed, it was in 1954 that the new pattern of Republican presidents and divided or Democratic congresses emerged.

Even more significant than the trend in interbranch party strength, perhaps, is the intrabranch trend. During the supposedly halcyon days of parties in the 1950s and 1960s, party unity voting in Congress, as measured by the *Congressional Quarterly*, declined fairly steadily in both parties in both houses, bottoming out in the Ninety-first Congress. During the 1970s and 1980s, in direct contradiction to what the "reform-killed-the-parties" theory would predict, party unity voting has been on the increase. (So has the share of all congressional votes that unite one party against the other.) Nor has this intrabranch development been devoid of interbranch consequences:

in 1981 Senate Republicans demonstrated the highest degree of support for a president ever recorded by either party in either house of Congress since the *Congressional Quarterly* began making measurements in 1953.

Party Organization. It is as organizations that the parties were affected most directly by the post-1968 reforms; if party-weakening effects are to be found anywhere, it should be in the realm of party organization. Yet it is here, recent research increasingly is showing, that the opposite is most true: the parties in the 1970s and 1980s are institutionally stronger than they were in the 1950s and 1960s.

The regeneration of the parties as organizations has occurred at all levels of the federal system. In the localities and counties there is now far more party activity in the areas of fund raising, campaign headquarters, voter registration, and get-out-the-vote efforts than during the mid-1960s. About twice as many citizens as in the 1950s (some 24 to 32 percent) report that they have been approached personally by party workers in recent presidential campaigns. The share of state party organizations that have permanent headquarters rose from less than half in 1960 to 95 percent in 1982; the size and professionalism of salaried state party staffs have also grown considerably. Judging from his study of party budgets, political scientist Cornelius Cotter concludes that the percentage of state parties whose organization is "marginal" fell from 69 in 1961 to 31 in 1979; the proportion of highly organized state parties rose from 12 percent to 26 percent.

National party organizations, long the stepchild of the party system, have undergone the most striking transformation of all. Since the mid-1970s, when William Brock became chairman, the Republican National Committee has developed a capacity to recruit candidates to run for local office and provide them with funds and professional assistance in such activities as voter registration and television campaigning; to help state parties enhance their own organizational abilities; to do institutional advertising on a "Vote Republican" theme; and so on. As for the opposition, journalist David Broder reports, "Since 1980 the Democrats have been doing what the Republicans did under Brock: raising money and pumping it back to party-building projects at the state and local level."

The Fall and Rise of the Parties. Political parties in the 1980s have arrested or reversed the decline that they were suffering before the reform era that began in 1968 but only because they are different from what they used to be. The recent reforms have helped the parties to adapt relatively successfully to a changing social and political environment.

Organizationally and procedurally, the parties on the eve of the post-1968 reforms were relics of an earlier era. Virtually since the Andrew Jackson years, party strength had continued to rest on the same foundations.

Patronage, in the form of government jobs and contracts, had long been one reliable source of workers and funds for party organizations. Party-sponsored charity work—memorably, the Thanksgiving turkey and the winter bucket of coal—helped to cement the loyalties of many voters. Such tangible inducements aside, voters also found the party label the best device for ordering their choices in elections that involved numerous offices, candidates, and issues.

For some years before 1968, developments in government and society had been weakening these foundations. A merit-based civil service and competitive contracting replaced the patronage system of government hiring and purchasing. Income security programs reduced dependence on charity. After World War II education, income, and leisure time rose rapidly throughout the population—voters now had more ability and opportunity to sort out information for themselves about candidates and issues. During the 1950s television sets became fixtures in the American home, bringing such information to voters in more accessible (if not always more valuable) form.

From these developments, which eroded some of the main props of the traditional political parties, came others that created the basis for new-style parties. First, the issue basis of political participation intensified, both in the movements of the 1960s (civil rights, antiwar, environmental, feminist, and others), which originated mainly outside the party system, and in the parties themselves. In 1962 James Q. Wilson chronicled the rise during the 1950s of the "amateur Democrat," an upper-middle-class reformer whose main concern was for issues and who saw the party as a vehicle for advancing causes, in opposition to professional party people, who viewed elections mainly as a means of achieving the satisfactions and spoils of victory. In 1964 the amateur Democrat's conservative Republican cousin, whom Aaron Wildavsky dubbed the "purist," seized control of the Republican national convention.

Second, the candidate basis of politics intensified, both in presidential politics, where individual aspirants, following John F. Kennedy in 1960, sought to take their own popular paths to the nomination even if that meant detouring around the party professionals, and in congressional politics, where reelection-oriented incumbents, with increasing success, forged personal bonds with their constituents that freed them from much of their dependency on party. Finally, the media basis of politics intensified. As television, radio, and direct mail became available and highly effective routes for reaching voters, media professionals became more valuable politically, as did fundraising specialists who could help to pay for the expensive new forms of campaigning.

Political parties in all their aspects—in the electorate, in government, and as organizations—were weakened during the 1950s and 1960s by these social and political developments. To recover and thrive the parties had to adapt. To adapt they had to accommodate the rise of four main groups: new-style voters, who by virtue of greater education and leisure no longer needed to depend on parties to order their choices in elections; amateur political activists who regarded the parties mainly as vehicles for political change; entrepreneurial candidates who had ceased to regard party fealty as the necessary or even the most desirable strategy for electoral success; and modern political tacticians who practiced the now essential crafts of polling, advertising, press relations, and fund raising. In sum, the reinvigoration of the parties would have to come on terms that accepted the "new politics" in both that label's common uses: policy as the basis for political participation, and modern campaign professionalism as the incentive to channel such participation through the parties.

What made the transformation and reinvigoration of the parties possible was the organizational and procedural fluidity that was hastened by the post-1968 reforms. Once the lingering hold of party professionals of the *ancien régime* on the nominating process was broken, the new groups of voters, activists, candidates, and campaign professionals were able to establish a new equilibrium of power within the parties that reflected the changed social and political realities. Republicans realized this first and strengthened their party by committing it to conservative political ideology and professional campaign services, which in turn tied the party-in-the-electorate, the party-in-government, and the party organization together. Democrats, preoccupied with the reform process more than with the fruits of reform, were slower to adapt. But, responding to the Republican party's success, they now seem to be following a parallel path: new policies and a new professionalism to rebuild the party.

Perhaps the best evidence of the parties' successful adaptation to change is that the old amateurs have become the new professionals: committed to policy but also to party. Summarizing several studies of delegates to recent Republican and Democratic national conventions, William Crotty and John Jackson conclude that "the new professionals are likely to be college graduates working in a service profession . . . familiar with all the paraphernalia of modern campaigning . . . [and] likely to care deeply about at least some issues. . . . They also care, sometimes passionately, about their party . . . and they see the parties as the best vehicles for advancing both their concept of the public interest and their own political careers."

PRESIDENTS

Many political analysts have argued vigorously that the influence of the presidential nominating process on the selection of suitably skilled presidents, like its influence on the parties, was benign before the post-1968 reforms were instituted but has been malignant ever since. "In the old way," according to Broder, "whoever wanted to run for president of the United

States took a couple of months off from public service in the year of the presidential election and presented his credentials to the leaders of his party, who were elected officials, party officials, leaders of allied interest groups, and bosses in some cases. These people had known the candidate over a period of time and had carefully examined his work." As it happened, the qualities those political peers were looking for, argues political scientist Jeane Kirkpatrick, were the very qualities that make for good presidents: "the ability to deal with diverse groups, ability to work out compromises, and the ability to impress people who have watched a candidate over many years." In contrast, under the post-1968 rules, "the skills required to be successful in the nominating process are almost entirely irrelevant to, perhaps even negatively correlated with, the skills required to be successful at governing."

In a real sense, the old nominating process did work reasonably well to increase the chances of selecting skillful presidents. But then so does the new process. The difference underlying this similarity is the contrast between the political and social environment in which contemporary presidents must try to govern and the environment in which their predecessors as recently as the 1950s and 1960s had to operate.

The contrast is most obvious and significant in the nation's capital. As Samuel Kernell notes, the "old" Washington that was described so accurately by Richard Neustadt in his 1960 success manual for presidents, *Presidential Power,* was "a city filled with hierarchies. To these hierarchies were attached leaders or at least authoritative representatives"—committee chairmen and party leaders in Congress, press barons, umbrella-style interest groups that represented broad sectors such as labor, business, and agriculture, and so on. In this setting to lead was to bargain—the same political "whales," to use Harry MacPherson's term, who could thwart a president's desires could also satisfy them, and in the same way: by directing the activities of their associates and followers. Clearly a presidential nominating process that placed some emphasis on a candidate's ability to pass muster with Washington power brokers was functional for the governing system.

As the 1960s drew to a close, however, the same social and political changes—and some others as well—that were undermining the foundations of the old party system also were undermining the old ways of conducting the nation's business in Washington. The capital came under the intense and—to many elected politicians—alluring spotlight of television news; a more educated and active citizenry took its heightened policy concerns directly to government officials; interest group activity both flourished and fragmented; and careerism among members of Congress prompted a steady devolution of legislative power to individual representatives and senators and to proliferating committees and subcommittees. From the president's perspective this wave of decentralization meant that

Washington had become "a city of free agents" in which "the number of exchanges necessary to secure others' support ha[d] increased dramatically." What skills do contemporary presidents need if they are to lead in this changed environment, or, to phrase the question more pertinently, what skills should the presidential nominating process foster? Two presidential leadership requirements are familiar and longstanding; first, a strategic sense of the public's disposition to be led during the particular term of office—an ability to sense, shape, and fulfill the historical possibilities of the time; second, some talent for the management of authority, both of lieutenants in the administration who can help the president form policy proposals and of the large organizations in the bureaucracy that are charged with implementing existing programs. Other skills required by presidents are more recent in origin, at least in the form they must take and their importance. Presidents must be able to present themselves and their policies to the public through rhetoric and symbolic action, especially on television. Because reelection-oriented members of Congress "are hypersensitive to anticipated constituent reaction," it is not surprising that the best predictor of a president's success with Congress is his standing in the public opinion polls. Finally, presidents need tactical skills of bargaining, persuasion, and other forms of political gamesmanship to maximize their support among other officials whose help they need to secure their purposes. But in the new Washington these tactical skills must be employed not merely or even mainly on the sort of old-style power brokers who used to be able to help presidents sustain reliable coalitions but on the many elements of a fragmented power system in which tactics must be improvised for new coalitions on each issue.

In several nonobvious and even inadvertent ways, the current nominating process rewards, perhaps requires, most of these skills. The process is, for would-be presidents, self-starting and complex. To a greater extent than ever before, candidates must raise money, develop appealing issues, devise shrewd campaign strategies, impress national political reporters, attract competent staff, and build active organizations largely on their own. They then must dance through a minefield of staggered and varied state primaries and caucuses, deciding and reevaluating weekly or even daily where to spend their time, money, and other resources. What better test of a president's ability to manage lieutenants and lead in a tactically skillful way in the equally complex, fragmented, and uncertain environment of modern Washington or, for that matter, the modern world?

The fluidity of the current nominating process also has opened it to Washington "outsiders." This development, although much lamented by critics of the post-1968 reforms, has done nothing more than restore the traditional place of those who have served as state governors in the ranks of plausible candidates for the presidency, thus broadening the talent pool to include more than senators and vice-presidents. (From 1960 to 1972 every-major party nominee for president was a senator or a vice-president who previously had been a senator.) As chief executives of their states, governors may be presumed to have certain skills in the management of large public bureaucracies that senators do not.

Self-presentational skills also are vital for candidates in the current nominating process—not just "looking good on television" but being able to persuade skeptical journalists and others to accept one's interpretation of the complex reality of the campaign. If it does nothing else, the endless contest, which carries candidates from place to place for months and months in settings that range from living rooms to stadiums, probably sensitizes candidates to citizens in ways that uniquely facilitate the choice of a president who has a strong strategic sense of his time.

No earthly good is unalloyed, of course. The length and complexity of the current nominating process, to which so much good can be ascribed, are nonetheless sources of real distraction to incumbent presidents who face renomination challenges and to other contenders who hold public office. To be sure, the post-1968 rules cannot be blamed for all of this. Unpopular presidents have always had to battle, to some extent, for renomination; popular presidents still do not. (In 1984 Reagan not only was unopposed for his party's nomination—the first such president since 1956—but received millions of dollars in federal matching funds for his renomination "campaign.") Most challengers seem to be able to arrange time to campaign, either while holding office (Gary Hart, Alan Cranston, Ernest Hollings, and others in 1984) or by abandoning office for the sake of pursuing the presidency (Walter Mondale in 1984, Howard Baker in 1988). Still, by any standard, the same nominating process that tests a would-be president's leadership skills so well must be said to carry at least a moderate price tag.

PUBLIC

Ironically, democratic legitimacy, the paramount value sought by the post-1968 reformers, must be judged as the least achieved of the three main criteria for judging the presidential nominating process: strengthened political parties, skilled presidents, and a satisfied public. Everyone, including journalists, decries the responsibility that the hybrid nature of the process places on the media to interpret who is winning and even which candidates will be taken seriously. Few think it proper that voters in the late primary states have their choices circumscribed by the decisions of voters in Iowa, New Hampshire, and other states with early contests.

The characteristic of the current nominating process that is most corrosive of legitimacy is its sheer complexity. As Henry Mayo notes in his *Introduction to Democratic Theory:*

> If the purpose of the election is to be carried out—to enable the voter to share in political power—the voter's job must not be made more difficult and confusing for him. It ought, on the contrary, to be made as simple as the electoral machinery can be devised to make it.

Yet nothing could be less descriptive of the way we choose presidential candidates. "No school, no textbook, no course of instruction," writes Theodore H. White, "could tell young Americans how their system worked." Or, as Richard Stearns, chief delegate hunter for Senator George McGovern in 1972 and Senator Edward Kennedy in 1980, put it: "I am fully confident that there aren't more than 100 people in the country who fully understand the rules."

What would the public prefer? Nothing that will prove consoling to those who dislike the current process for its excesses of democracy and absence of "peer review." Overwhelmingly, citizens want to select the parties' nominees for president through national primaries: in the most recent Gallup survey on this issue, which was completed in June 1984, 67 percent were in favor, 21 percent were opposed, and 12 percent were undecided. And there are ample reasons to believe that citizens mean what they are saying. For one, the national primary idea has received consistently high support by margins ranging from two-to-one to six-to-one—in Gallup surveys that date back to 1952. More important, the direct primary is the method by which voters are accustomed to nominating almost all party candidates for almost all other offices in the federal system.

A vigorous case can be made for a national primary, and not solely because of the heightened legitimacy it would bring to the nomination process. Still, there are good reasons to stay with the current arrangement. First, the very constancy of rules rewriting is in itself subversive of legitimacy. Second, it also is distracting to the parties, diverting them from the more important task of deciding what they have to offer voters. Finally, to bring the argument of this essay full circle, to the extent that the current process helps the political parties to grow stronger and the presidency to work more effectively, voters ultimately will grow not just used to it but pleased with it, and the legitimacy problem will take care of itself.

The Presidential Establishment

☐   The expansion of the Executive Office of the President is a major development of the modern presidency. Created in 1939 by an executive order of President Roosevelt under the reorganization authority granted to him by Congress, the Executive Office has expanded over the years and now occupies a pivotal position in government. The Executive Office was devised originally to act as a staff arm of the presidency. It was to consist of his closest personal advisers, as well as a small number of agencies, such as the Bureau of the Budget (now the Office of Management and Budget) and was to function as an aid to him in carrying out his presidential responsibilities.

The Executive Office was not to be an independent bureaucracy but was to be accountable to the president and to act in accordance with his wishes. However, the tremendous expansion that has occurred in the Executive Office has raised the question of whether or not it has become an "invisible presidency," not accountable to anyone within or without government. The relationships between President Nixon and the Executive Office, particularly, raised this question. President Nixon's emphasis upon managerial techniques led him to expand very significantly the number of agencies within the Executive Office. Moreover, he delegated to his personal staff a wide range of responsibilities over which he failed to exercise continuous supervision. Ehrlichman and Haldeman, before they resigned because of their involvement in events surrounding the Watergate affairs, ruthlessly wielded power around Washington in the name of the president. It was the lack of presidential supervision over his own staff that may have accounted for the Watergate break-in in the first place, as well as other questionable activities, including the burglary of Daniel Ellsberg's psychiatrist's office and the solicitation of unreported funds during the 1972 presidential election year.

President Carter came into office with a promise to reduce the presidential bureaucracy, a promise that he made in conjunction with another to reorganize the regular bureaucracy of the federal government. Both of these promises had a ring of great familiarity, as they had been part of the campaigns of many prior presidents. Carter in particular wanted to reinstate the Cabinet as a major policy-making group that would act as a collegial body advising the president directly. He wanted to reverse the flow of power from the Cabinet to the presidential bureaucracy, reinstating Cabinet secretaries as the primary spokespersons for presidential policy in the areas under their jurisdiction. President Carter soon found, like presidents before him, however, that Cabinet government does not work to the advantage of the president. The only bureaucracy the president can trust is the presidential bureaucracy. Cabinet secretaries tend to develop their own power bases and soon become independent of, and even antagonistic to, the president. By the summer of 1979 Carter fully recognized the strains on his leadership being produced by a weak presidential bureaucracy and by antagonistic cabinet secretaries. He fired HEW Secretary Joseph A. Califano, Jr., and Treasury Secretary W. Michael Blumenthal, both of whom had flouted the White House staff by going their own ways. At the same time, Carter strengthened the presidential bureaucracy by centralizing responsibility in the White House in the hands of his principal adviser, Hamilton Jordan, whom he made chief of the White House staff. Carter's initial promises to decentralize power and reduce the size of the presidential bureaucracy failed. Centralization of power within the White House continued to be the theme of the Reagan administration. In the following selection Thomas E. Cronin examines the politics, structure, and responsibilities of the presidential establishment.

38
Thomas E. Cronin

THE SWELLING OF THE PRESIDENCY: CAN ANYONE REVERSE THE TIDE?

In 1939 President Franklin D. Roosevelt created the Executive Office of the President. In his executive order, Roosevelt stated that "in no event shall the Administrative Assistants to the President be interposed between the President and the head of any department or agency."

More than forty-five years later, the size and importance of the White House staff and the Executive Office of the President have been controversial precisely because they seem to be frequently interposed between president and heads of departments and agencies. In campaigning for the presidency in 1976, Jimmy Carter had pledged to reduce the size of the presidential establishment by 30 percent. Further he claimed he would reverse the flow of power away from the White House staffers and back to his cabinet heads. About halfway through his term, however, Carter fired about half his cabinet secretaries and strengthened the hand of his chief White House aides. And though he had tried to reduce somewhat the number of White House aides by one means or another, the size and importance of the presidential establishment was just as great as it had been in the Nixon and Ford years. Nor has Ronald Reagan, that well-known advocate of a slimmer federal government, reduced the size or importance of the White House staff. (See Table 1.) If anything, Reagan centralized political influence even further.

Ronald Reagan came to the White House pledging to cut back on government. He said he would abolish the Departments of Education and Energy. He stated that "government was not the solution, government is the problem." He shied away from saying he would cut the White House staff

Table 1   Expanding the White House Staff

Year	President	Full time employees	Employees temporarily detailed to the White House from outside agencies	Total
1937	Franklin D. Roosevelt	45	112 (June 30)	157
1947	Harry S Truman	190	27 (June 30)	217
1957	Dwight D. Eisenhower	364	59 (June 30)	423
1967	Lyndon B. Johnson	251	246 (June 30)	497
1972	Richard M. Nixon	550	34 (June 30)	584
1975	Gerald R. Ford	533	27 (June 30)	560
1980	Jimmy Carter	488	75 (June 30)	570
1984	Ronald Reagan	575*	17 (June 1983)	592

Source: U.S. Budget and White House interviews and letters.

*Two former explicitly White House staff units, the Office of Administration and the Office of Policy Development, are now formally in the Executive Office of the President and not in the White House. But this misleads. These staffs are indeed White House and presidential staffs and thus are included here. The vice-president employs another 22 White House staffers and the National Security Council another 75 to 100, but these are not included in this 575 person staff of President Reagan.

and its influence. As Governor of California he was decidedly a "delegator," but he delegated to top aides. He also formed a number of cabinet clusters—headed by his top Sacramento aides, William Clark and Edwin Meese.

Reagan followed the same administrative design soon after he came to Washington. In fact, he brought along Ed Meese and later William Clark to perform many of the same "inner circle" responsibilities they had performed back in California. Reagan recruited many able and experienced persons to serve in his cabinet. Plainly, however, he increasingly favored doing business with his small band of White House aides. The White House inner circle of James Baker, William Clark, Michael Deaver, and Edwin Meese became known as the people with clout in the Reagan Administration. They were the ones that would decide that Alexander Haig must go, that Richard Allen, a national security aide, must go, that Anne Gorsuch, the Environmental Protection Agency Administrator, must go, and so on. They increasingly loomed large as both an inner circle and virtually as an inner cabinet. To be sure, the Secretary of Defense, the Secretary of State, the Attorney General and the Secretary of Treasury were regularly consulted—but they seemed "on call" rather than "on top."

Why has the presidential bureaucracy become a problem? Many analysts feel it is too bloated and too top-heavy with aides, counselors, and advisers who invariably intrude themselves between the president and the department heads—thereby breaking FDR's old promise.

A few months after Carter was in office, the White House staff had grown to nearly 700 aides—although perhaps as many as 175 of these were "on loan" from other governmental departments to assist with energy program planning, appointments and the sizeable increase of mail pouring into the Carter White House. In addition to the White House staff there were several support agencies in the Executive Office, such as the National Security Office and the Office of Management and Budget.

Plainly, the cabinet has lost power and the Executive Office has grown in status, in size, and in powers. In light of experience, should Roosevelt's promise be revised? Can the performance of the Executive Office be made to conform to Roosevelt's promise? Can the presidential establishment really be cut back?

After they were elected, some of Carter's and Reagan's aides discounted the importance of staff cutbacks. Improved delivery of services, better public understanding, and fixing accountability are more important than reducing numbers and costs.

We have heard many plans and promises about government reorganization before. President Nixon was genuinely worried that the presidency had "grown like Topsy" so that it weakened rather than strengthened his ability to manage the federal government. Nixon proposed a sweeping consolidation of Cabinet Departments into four functionally oriented super-departments— Community Development, Natural Resources, Human Resources, and Economic Affairs—and at one point wanted to cut the White House workforce in half. But he did not prevent one of the largest expansions of the presidency in history, nor the aggrandizement of power in his White House that contributed to his isolation and downfall. Rather than assisting the president, Nixon's aides often became assistant presidents.

Nixon had little success in these efforts. The Office of the President increased 13 percent during the Eisenhower and Kennedy years, and another 13 percent under LBJ. But it rose approximately another 25 percent under Nixon. Many of President Nixon's cabinet members say they had difficulty in seeing the president. One joked that "Nixon should have told me I was being appointed to a secret mission when I was made Secretary of Commerce." It was said of another that he had to take the public tour of the White House to get in.

Unchecked growth of the White House establishment and its battalion of "faceless ministers" continued to grow even under Gerald Ford. Mr. Ford had always promised to curb bureaucratic growth. His favorite motto was "A government big enough to give you everything you want is a government big enough to take from you everything you have." But Ford was unsuccessful in reversing the trend. Midway through his brief presidential term, one account indicated there were about seventy-five more White House aides on his staff than when Richard Nixon departed.

The expansion of the presidency, it should be emphasized, was by no means only a phenomenon of the Nixon-Ford years. The number of employees directly under the president has been growing steadily since the New Deal days, when only a few dozen people served in the White

House entourage at a cost of less than a few hundred thousand dollars annually.

According to the traditional civics textbook picture, the executive branch is more or less neatly divided into Cabinet departments and their secretaries, agencies and their heads, and the president. A more contemporary view takes note of a few prominent presidential aides, and refers to them as the "White House staff." Neither view adequately recognizes the large and growing coterie surrounding the president, which comprises dozens of assistants, hundreds of presidential advisers, and thousands of members of an institutional amalgam called the Executive Office of the President. The men and women in these categories all fall directly under a president in organizational charts—not under the Cabinet departments—and may best be considered by the term the Presidential Establishment (see Figure A).

In the mid-1970s the Presidential Establishment embraced nearly a score of support staffs (the White House Office, National Security Council, Office of Management and Budget, etc.) and advisory office (Council of Economic Advisors, Office of Science and Technology Policy, Office of Telecommunications Policy, etc.). It spawned a vast proliferation of ranks and titles to go with its proliferation of functions (Counsel to the President, Assistant to the President, Special Consultant, Director, Staff Director, etc.). "The White House now has enough people with fancy titles to populate a Gilbert and Sullivan comic opera," Congressman Morris Udall once observed.

Official figures on the size of the Presidential Establishment, and standard body counts vary widely, depending on exactly who is included, but by one frequently used reckoning, between two to two and a half thousand people work directly for the President of the United States. Payroll and maintenance costs for this staff run to several hundred million dollars annually. Salary alone for the 488 White House aides in 1980 was estimated at over 22 million dollars.

Under President Nixon, there was a systematic bureaucratization of the Presidential Establishment, in which more new councils and offices were established and more specialization, division of labor, and layers of staffing added than at any time except during World War II. Among the major Nixon additions were the Council of Environmental Quality, the Council on International Economic Policy, the Office of Consumer Affairs, and the Domestic Council. Nixon aide John Ehrlichman wanted the Domestic Council as a base from which to control domestic policy and bypass the Office of Management and Budget as well as the domestic department heads. This may not have been the formal intent exactly, but it was plainly the result.

President Nixon in 1973 moved a number of trusted domestic-policy assistants from the White House rolls and dispersed them to key subCabinet posts across the span of government, virtually setting up White House outposts throughout the Cabinet departments. One of Nixon's most important staffing actions, after his landslide victory in 1972, was to set up formally a second office, with space and a staff in the White House, for Treasury Secretary George Shultz, as chairman of yet another new presidential body,

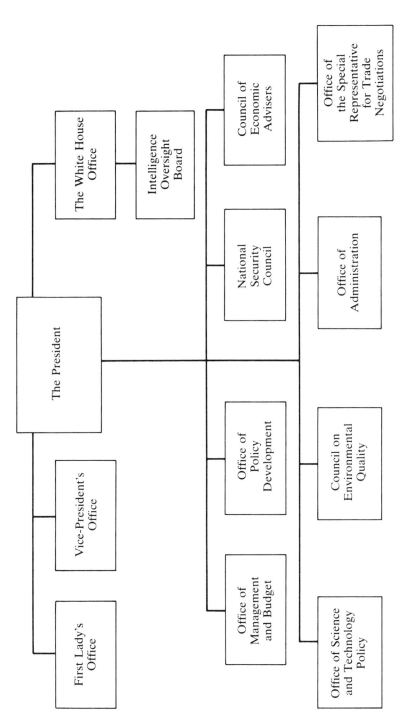

Figure A   The Presidential Establishment, 1984

the Council on Economic Policy. With Shultz as over-secretary of economic affairs, and John Ehrlichman as over-secretary for domestic affairs, Nixon attempted to accomplish the cabinet consolidation that Congress had denied him a year earlier. This super-cabinet was dismantled almost immediately with the Watergate-pressured resignations of Haldeman and Ehrlichman.

President Ford made few changes in the organizational structure of the Executive Office that he inherited from Nixon. He established the Nixon-proposed Council on Wage and Price Stability and a few other councils and boards, most notably an Economic Policy Board that served as a kind of National Security Council and staff for major economic issues. He also allowed the Congress to establish the Office of Science and Technology Policy. Ford continued the Nixon practice of double appointments, such as Kissinger as Secretary of State and head of the National Security Council, and William Simon as Secretary of Treasury and chief spokesman for the White House-based Economic Policy Board.

Carter pledged to cut the White House staff and its importance, and in his first year he earnestly tried to act upon this pledge. He reduced the White House staff by over one hundred persons, but he did so merely by transferring most of the administrative personnel to a newly created Office of Administration within the Executive Office of the President. In fact, many, if not most, of these aides did not even move from their regular offices. They were already located in the Old Executive Office Building, and there they remained. What was labeled a "reduction" was simply a rejuggling of the organizational boxes. Representative Clarence E. Miller of Ohio, who kept tabs on the Carter White House, declared in 1979 that "It appears we are fooling the American people," and he called the Carter reductions "really a shuffling of the deck." White House reporters who studied the growth of the payroll at the White House said appropriations for the White House Office have jumped from $8.3 million in 1971 to a proposed $18.2 million for 1980.

Early in 1980 I had an opportunity to meet with Carter's staff director at the White House, a Mr. Alonzo McDonald. McDonald was a former managing director of McKinsey & Company, the management-consultant firm. He was brought to the Carter White House to reduce the chaos that developed under the decidedly unmanagerial Hamilton Jordan, then the chief of staff. After being in the White House for less than a year, McDonald told me: "Frankly, I would increase the size of the White House staff. It requires more staff. We need larger groups for congressional relations, for dealing with important interest groups; they deserve to be listened to and I now feel that these kinds of staffs can't be cut, they actually should be larger." What did he think, then, of Jimmy Carter's 1976 pledge to cut the White House staff? He diplomatically avoided answering that one.

Carter probably talked more about reorganizing the executive branch than any recent president. Yet, after about two years in office he seemed to have given up. One of his early reorganization aides later summed up Carter's problem as a reorganizer this way:

For Carter, reorganization was an end in itself, unconnected with the higher purposes of government. He never really linked it together with other policy goals. He gave it up after the first couple of years. Perhaps it was because the rest of government resisted because policy ends and reorganization ends were never discussed or dealt with in any coherent way. Carter, to repeat, had kind of an engineer's notion that organization itself was a policy area. (Personal interview with the writer, February 1980.)

However the names and numbers have changed recently, or may be shifted about in the near future, the Presidential Establishment has not declined in terms of functions, power, or prerogatives; in fact, it has grown.

Does it matter? A number of political analysts have argued recently that it does, and I agree with them. To be sure, the debate about the size of the White House establishment is less important than the purposes to which it is put. But size and purposes are hard to separate. Perhaps the most disturbing aspect of the expansion of the Presidential Establishment is that it has become a powerful inner sanctum of government, isolated from traditional, constitutional checks and balances. It has become common practice for anonymous, unelected, and unratified aides to negotiate sensitive international commitments that are free from congressional oversight. Other aides in the Presidential Establishment wield fiscal authority over billions of dollars in funds that Congress appropriates yet a president refuses to spend, or that Congress assigns to one purpose and the administration routinely redirects to another—all with no semblance of public scrutiny. Such exercises of power pose an important, perhaps vital, question of governmental philosophy: Should a political system that has made a virtue of periodic electoral accountability accord an ever-increasing policy-making role to White House counselors who are neither confirmed by the U.S. Senate nor, because of the doctrine of "executive privilege," subject to questioning by Congress?

Another disquieting aspect of the growth of the Presidential Establishment is that the increase of its powers has been largely at the expense of the traditional sources of executive power and policy-making—the Cabinet members and their departments. When I asked a former Kennedy-Johnson Cabinet member a while ago what he would like to do if he ever returned to government, he said he would rather be a presidential assistant than a Cabinet member. And this is an increasingly familiar assessment of the relative influence of the two levels of the executive branch. In Carter's White House, it was pretty clear from the very beginning that Stuart Eisenstadt, the domestic issues advisor, Hamilton Jordan, the virtual Chief of Staff, and Zbigniew Brzezinski, the National Security Council aide, were among the most powerful members of the Carter administration. Their influence increased the longer Carter kept them.

The Presidential Establishment has become, in effect, a whole layer of government between the president and the Cabinet, and it often stands above the Cabinet in terms of influence with the president. In spite of the exalted position that Cabinet members hold in textbooks and protocol, a number of Cabinet members in recent administrations have complained that they could not even get the President's ear except through a presidential assistant. In his book *Who Owns America?*, former Secretary of the Interior Walter Hickel recounts his combat with a dozen different presidential functionaries and tells how he needed clearance from them before he could get to talk to the president, or how he frequently had to deal with the assistants themselves because the president was "too busy." During an earlier administration, President Eisenhower's chief assistant, Sherman Adams, was said to have told two Cabinet members who could not resolve a matter of mutual concern: "Either make up your mind or else tell me and I will do it. We must not bother the President with this. He is trying to keep the world from war." Several of President Kennedy's Cabinet members regularly battled with White House aides who blocked them from seeing the President. And McGeorge Bundy, as Kennedy's chief assistant for national security affairs, simply sidestepped the State Department in one major area of department communications. He had all important incoming State Department cables transmitted simultaneously to his office in the White House, part of an absorption of traditional State Department functions that visibly continues to this day.

Carter began his presidency by holding weekly Cabinet meetings—two and three hours in length—every Monday morning. He was the first President in recent years to try to get the Cabinet working, talking, and arguing about wide-ranging issues. His intent was not to turn his Cabinet into a parliamentary decision-making collegium, but to establish a team of advisors who could assist and advise him on matters above and beyond the narrow functions of their departments. It was also a recognition by Carter that so many of the problems for a president and for Cabinet members are interdepartmental in character.

Did Carter's Cabinet system work? One White House aide who attended some of these sessions told a *New York Times* reporter that most of the Cabinet members "just sit there, go through their little recitations of what's happening in their departments and nod agreeably when the President speaks." Said another: "These [weekly] meetings . . . are essentially a waste of everybody's time, including the President's."

By his third year, Carter had fired just about half of his Cabinet in the summer of 1978, and he had grown accustomed to relying more heavily than ever on his own proximate White House aides. To his credit, he tried to use the Cabinet more responsibly than his immediate predecessors. He even held more than 60 Cabinet meetings during his first two years. Most of the cabinet meetings had no agendas. The President raised issues that were on his mind, and then solicited the views of those around the table, both on the subjects he had raised and on other matters they thought appropriate. Some of the meetings were criticized as nothing less than adult versions of a grade-school "show-and-tell" session. As the months wore on, several of his Cabinet members, especially Joseph Califano, Michael Blumenthal, Brock Adams, and Andrew Young made their differences of views with the

President a public matter. Many of them, from the vantage point of the White House, seemed to be going into business for themselves. Carter and his aides worried about this, and with the tough 1980 elections in mind they decided to "clean house." Secretary of State Cyrus Vance quit somewhat later, in part because he had lost power and influence to his White House counterpart, Zbigniew Brzezinski.

When the Carter Administration is studied in the years to come, the verdict will probably be that the Cabinet failure of his first two years or so was caused more by the president and his aides than by the members of his Cabinet. If Carter had been more experienced in the ways of Washington, if he had been a stronger, more effective coalition builder, he might have molded these talented individuals into a positive force in his Administration. If he had been more popular in the country as a whole, higher in the polls, he would have had greater respect from his Cabinet officers—and they, in turn, would have probably tried fewer end-runs around him in pursuit of their own particular interests.

Perhaps the more things change, the more they stay the same—as the old saying goes.

In a speech in 1971, Senator Ernest Hollings of South Carolina plaintively noted the lowering of Cabinet status. "It used to be," he said, "that if I had a problem with food stamps, I went to see the Secretary of Agriculture, whose department had jurisdiction over that problem. Not anymore. Now, if I want to learn the policy, I must go to the White House to consult John Price [a special assistant]. If I want the latest on textiles, I won't get it from the Secretary of Commerce, who has the authority and responsibility. No, I am forced to go to the White House and see Mr. Peter Flanigan. I shouldn't feel too badly. Secretary Stans [Maurice Stans, then Secretary of Commerce] has to do the same thing."

If Cabinet members individually have been downgraded in influence, the Cabinet as a council of government has become somewhat of a relic, replaced by more specialized policy clusters that as often as not are presided over by White House staffers. The Cabinet's decline has taken place over several administrations. John Kennedy started out his term intending to use the Cabinet as a major policy-making body, but Postmaster General J. Edward Day noted, "After the first two or three meetings, one had the distinct impression that the President felt that decisions on major matters were not made—or even influenced—at Cabinet sessions, and that discussion there was a waste of time. . . . When members spoke up to suggest or to discuss major administration policy, the President would listen with thinly disguised impatience and then postpone or otherwise bypass the question."

President Eisenhower held weekly well-structured Cabinet meetings. Johnson, however, was disenchanted with the Cabinet as a body and characteristically held Cabinet sessions only when the press talked about how the Cabinet was withering away. Under Nixon, the Cabinet was almost never convened at all. Former Nixon counsel John Dean suggested, "I would like to see a more dominant Cabinet. The Nixon Cabinet was totally controllable by the White House staff. A strong Cabinet member should be able to tell a White House staffer, 'Buzz off' or 'Have the President call me himself and I'll tell him why I'm doing what I am.' " Nixon aide John Ehrlichman was very blunt in his description of Nixon's relationship with the Cabinet, "The Cabinet officers are tied closely to the executive, or to put it in extreme terms, when he says jump, they only ask, 'How high?' "

President Ford met with his Cabinet about once a month, using it as a discussion group, not a decision-making body. Ford's Cabinet members have reported that little was accomplished at these sessions and rarely if ever did any arguments take place.

As the Presidential Establishment has taken over policy-making and even some operational functions from the Cabinet departments, the departments have been undercut continuously and the cost has been heavy. These intrusions can cripple the capacity of Cabinet officials to present policy alternatives, and they diminish self-confidence, morale, and initiative within the departments. George Ball, a former undersecretary of state, noted the effects on the State Department: "Able men, with proper pride in their professional skills, will not long tolerate such votes of no-confidence, so it should be no surprise that they are leaving the career service, and making way for mediocrity with the result that, as time goes on it may be hopelessly difficult to restore the Department. . . . "

The irony of this accretion of numbers and functions to the Presidential Establishment is that the presidency has been increasingly afflicted with the very ills of the traditional departments that expansion was intended to remedy. The presidency has become a large, complex bureaucracy itself, rapidly acquiring many dubious characteristics of large bureaucracies in the process: layering, overspecialization, communication gaps, interoffice rivalries, inadequate coordination, and an impulse to become consumed with short-term, urgent operational concerns at the expense of thinking systematically about the consequences of varying sets of policies and priorities and about important long-range problems.

White House aides, in assuming more and more responsibility for the management of government programs, inevitably lose the detachment and objectivity that is so essential for evaluating new ideas. Can a lieutenant vigorously engaged in implementing the presidential will admit the possibility that what the President wants is wrong or not working? Yet a President is increasingly dependent on the judgment of these same staff members, since he seldom sees some of his Cabinet members.

WHY HAS THE PRESIDENCY GROWN BIGGER AND BIGGER?

There is no single villain or systematically organized conspiracy promoting this expansion. A variety of factors is at work. The most significant is the expansion of the role of the presidency itself—an expansion that for the most part has taken place during national emergencies. It should be noted, too, that the business of government has dramatically increased and that the rise of the White House staff is a result of the same forces that have seen a tripling of Congress's staff and a marked increase in law clerks and aides to Supreme Court members. The public and Congress in recent decades have both tended to look to the president for the decisions that were needed in those emergencies. The Great Depression and World War II in particular brought sizeable increases in presidential staffs. And once in place, many stayed on, even after the emergencies that brought them had faded. Smaller national crises have occasioned expansion in the White House entourage, too. After the Russians successfully orbited Sputnik in 1957, President Eisenhower added several science advisors. After the Bay of Pigs, President Kennedy enlarged his national security staff.

Considerable growth in the Presidential Establishment, especially in the post World War II years, stems directly from the belief that critical societal problems require wise men be assigned to the White House to alert the President to appropriate solutions and to serve as the agents for implementing these solutions. Congress has frequently acted on the basis of this belief, legislating the creation of the National Security Council, the Council of Economic Advisors, and the Council on Environmental Quality, among others. Congress has also increased the chores of the presidency by making it a statutory responsibility for the President to prepare more and more reports on critical social areas—annual economic and manpower reports, a biennial report on national growth, etc.

President Nixon responded to a number of troublesome problems that defy easy relegation to any one department—problems like international trade and drug abuse—by setting up special offices in the Executive Office with sweeping authority and sizeable staffs. Once established, these units rarely get dislodged. And an era of permanent crisis ensures a continuing accumulation of such bodies.

Another reason for the growth of the Presidential Establishment is that occupants of the White House frequently distrust members of the permanent government. Nixon aides, for example, viewed most civil servants not only as Democratic but as wholly unsympathetic to such Nixon objectives as decentralization, revenue-sharing, and the curtailment of several Great Society programs. Departmental bureaucracies are viewed from the White House as independent, unresponsive, unfamiliar, and inaccessible. They are suspected again and again of placing congressional, special-interest, or their own priorities ahead of those communicated to them from the White House. Even the President's own Cabinet members soon become viewed in the same light; one of the strengths of Cabinet members, namely their capacity to make a compelling case for their programs, has proved to be their chief liability with presidents.

Presidents may want this type of advocacy initially, but they soon grow weary and wary of it. Efforts by former Interior Secretary Hickel to advance certain environmental programs and by departing Housing and Urban Development Secretary George Romney to promote innovative housing construction methods not only were unwelcome but after a while were viewed with considerable displeasure and suspicion at the White House. Similarly Ronald Reagan asked Alexander Haig, his first Secretary of State, to resign when Haig became too much of an advocate of his own foreign policy views.

Hickel writes poignantly of coming to this recognition during his final meeting with President Nixon, in the course of which the President frequently referred to him as an "adversary." "Initially," writes Hickel, "I considered that a compliment because, to me, an adversary is a valuable asset. It was only after the President had used the term many times and with a disapproving inflection that I realized he considered an adversary an enemy. I could not understand why he would consider me an enemy."

Not only have recent Presidents been suspicious about the depth of the loyalty of those in their Cabinets, but also they invariably become concerned about the possibility that sensitive administration secrets may leak out through the departmental bureaucracies; this is another reason why Presidents have come to rely more on their own personal staff and advisory groups.

Still another reason that more and more portfolios have been given to the presidency is that new federal programs frequently concern more than one federal agency, and it seems reasonable that someone at a higher level is needed to fashion a consistent policy and to reconcile conflicts. Attempts by Cabinet members themselves to solve sensitive jurisdictional questions frequently result in bitter squabbling. At times, too, Cabinet members themselves have recommended that these multidepartmental issues be settled at the White House. Sometimes new presidential appointees insist that new offices for program coordination be assigned directly under the President. Ironically, such was the plea of George McGovern, for example, when President Kennedy offered him the post of director of the Food-for-Peace program in 1961. Later, in his own campaign for the White House, McGovern attacked the buildup of the Presidential Establishment; but back in 1961 he wanted visibility (and no doubt celebrity status), and he successfully argued against his being located outside the White House—in either the State Department or the Department of Agriculture. President Kennedy and his then campaign manager Robert Kennedy felt indebted to McGovern because of his efforts in assisting the Kennedy campaign in South Dakota. Accordingly, McGovern was granted not only a berth in the Executive Office of the President but also the much-coveted title of Special Assistant to the President.

The Presidential Establishment has also been enlarged by the representation of interest groups within its fold. Even a partial listing of staff specializations that have been grafted onto the White House in recent years reveals how interest-group brokerage has become added to the more traditional staff activities of counseling and administration. These specializations form a veritable index of American society: budget and management, national security, economics, congressional matters, science and technology, drug abuse prevention, telecommunications, consumers, national goals, intergovernmental relations, environment, domestic policy, international economics, military affairs, civil rights, disarmament, labor relations, District of Columbia, cultural affairs, education, foreign trade and tariffs, the aged, health and nutrition, physical fitness, volunteerism, intellectuals, Blacks, youth, women, Wall Street, governors, mayors, "ethnics," regulatory agencies and related industry, state party chairmen.

Both President Ford and President Carter, in their efforts to "keep the door of the White House open," maintained a fairly large staff called the Public Liaison Office. William Baroody, Jr., ran Ford's office. Margaret "Midge" Costanza and later Anne Wexler served as Carter's top aides for this operation. Elizabeth Dole and Faith Whittlesey served Reagan in this position. Ford's and Carter's staffs were constantly meeting with ethnic groups, special interest organizations, and with everyone from poet Allen Ginsberg, who wanted to talk about his philosophy on food, to groups opposed to the B-1 bomber and the 1980 Olympic boycott. Reagan's staff tried to win women's support for Reagan's policies and claimed to work with several women's groups. Critics contend that this kind of White House staff is unnecessary, too much of an on-going campaign unit, or merely a staff that engages in "stroking" people who want to say they have taken their cause to the White House. White House aides, of course, claim that ensuring access to the White House for nearly every interest is a requirement of an open presidency.

One of the more fascinating elements in the growth of the Presidential Establishment is the development, particularly under recent administrations, of a huge public-relations apparatus. Scores of presidential aides are now engaged in various forms of press-agentry or public relations, busily selling and reselling the president. This activity—sometimes cynically called the politics of symbolism—is devoted to the particular occupant of the White House, but inevitably, it affects the presidency itself, expanding public expectations about the presidency.

Last, but by no means least, Congress, which has grown increasingly critical of the burgeoning power of the presidency, must itself take some blame for the expansion of the White House. Divided within itself, and often ill-equipped or simply disinclined to make some of the nation's toughest political decisions in recent decades, Congress often has abdicated significant authority to the presidency. In late 1972 Congress almost passed a grant of authority to the president that would have given him the right to determine which programs to cut whenever the budget went beyond the $250 billion ceiling limit—a bill which, in effect, would have handed over to the President some of Congress's long-cherished "power of the purse." Fortunately, Congress could not agree on how to yield this precious power to the executive.

Congress is now making better use of its own General Accounting Office and Congressional Research Service for chores that too often were assigned to the President. Perhaps, also, it might establish in each of its houses special subcommittees on Executive Office operations. Most congressional committees are organized to deal with areas such as labor, agriculture, armed services, or education, paralleling the organization of the Cabinet. What we need now are committees designed explicitly to oversee the White House, to probe how much it costs to run the White House, to probe the size and quality of White House staff arrangements, and to periodically review what might better be removed from the White House and decentralized to the Cabinet secretaries. Can the task of overseeing presidential operations be dispersed among dozens of committees and subcommittees, each of which can look at only small segments of the Presidential Establishment? Since Truman, presidents have had staffs to oversee and lobby the Congress; Congress might want to reciprocate.

While the number of functionaries is the most tangible and dramatic measure of the White House's expansion, its increasing absorption of governmental functions is more disturbing. The White House must understand the dangers inherent in a Presidential Establishment that has become swollen in functions as well as in numbers. The next White House occupant may consider cutting staff or consolidating a number of agencies, but it is yet another thing to reduce the accumulated prerogatives and responsibilities of the presidency.

It is important for presidents not only to criticize the swelling government and its inefficiencies, but also to move to deflate this swelling in the areas where it most needs to be deflated—at home, in the White House, and in the Executive Office of the President. But very likely the attempts to reorganize and reduce the presidential bureaucracy will not succeed, and the forces that buttress the large presidential establishment will remain unchanged.

Presidential Character and Style

☐   The preceding selections in this chapter have focused upon the institutional aspects of the presidency, and the constitutional and political responsibilities of the office. Richard Neustadt does focus upon certain personal dimensions of the power equation, the ability to persuade, but he does not deal with presidential character outside of the power context. The following selection is taken from one of the most important and innovative of the recent books dealing with the presidency, in which the author, James David Barber, presents the thesis that it is the *total character* of the person who occupies the White House that is the determinant of presidential performance. As he states, "The presidency is much more than an institution." It is not only the focus of the emotional involvement of most people in politics, but also occupied by an emotional person. How that person is able to come to grips with his feelings and emotions often shapes his orientation toward issues and the way in which he makes decisions. From the very beginning the office was thought of in highly personal terms, for the framers of the Constitution, in part at least, built the office around the character of George Washington who virtually everyone at the time thought would be the first occupant of the office. And evolution of the office since 1787 has added to its personal quotient. James David Barber provides a framework for the analysis of presidential character and its effect upon performance in the White House.

39
James David Barber

THE PRESIDENTIAL CHARACTER: WITH A SPECIAL FOCUS ON THE REAGAN PRESIDENCY

When a citizen votes for a presidential candidate he makes, in effect, a prediction. He chooses from among the contenders the one he thinks (or feels, or guesses) would be the best President. He operates in a situation of immense uncertainty. If he has a long voting history, he can recall time and time again when he guessed wrong. He listens to the commentators, the politicians, and his friends, then adds it all up in some rough way to produce his prediction and his vote. Earlier in the game, his anticipations have been taken into account, either directly in the polls and primaries or indirectly in the minds of politicians who want to nominate someone he will like. But he must choose in the midst of a cloud of confusion, a rain of phony advertising, a storm of sermons, a hail of complex issues, a fog of charisma and boredom, and a thunder of accusation and defense. In the

---

Excerpted from James David Barber, *The Presidential Character,* 2nd and 3rd Editions (Prentice-Hall, Inc.). © 1972, 1977, 1985 by James David Barber. Reprinted by permission of the author.

face of this chaos, a great many citizens fall back on the past, vote their old allegiances, and let it go at that. Nevertheless, the citizen's vote says that on balance he expects Mr. X would outshine Mr. Y in the presidency.

This [book] is meant to help citizens and those who advise them cut through the confusion and get at some clear criteria for choosing presidents. To understand what actual presidents do and what potential presidents might do, the first need is to see the man whole—not as some abstract embodiment of civic virtue, some scorecard of issue stands, or some reflection of a faction, but as a human being like the rest of us, a person trying to cope with a difficult environment. To that task he brings his own character, his own view of the world, his own political style. None of that is new for him. If we can see the pattern he has set for his political life we can, I contend, estimate much better his pattern as he confronts the stresses and chances of the presidency.

The presidency is a peculiar office. The founding fathers left it extraordinarily loose in definition, partly because they trusted George Washington to invent a tradition as he went along. It is an institution made a piece at a time by successive men in the White House. Jefferson reached out to Congress to put together the beginnings of political parties; Jackson's dramatic force extended electoral partisanship to its mass base; Lincoln vastly expanded the administrative reach of the office, Wilson and the Roosevelts showed its rhetorical possibilities—in fact every President's mind and demeanor has left its mark on a heritage still in lively development.

But the presidency is much more than an institution. It is a focus of feelings. In general, popular feelings about politics are low-key, shallow, casual. For example, the vast majority of Americans knows virtually nothing of what Congress is doing and cares less. The presidency is different. The presidency is the focus for the most intense and persistent emotions in the American polity. The president is a symbolic leader, the one figure who draws together the people's hopes and fears for the political future. On top of all his routine duties, he has to carry that off—or fail.

Our emotional attachment to presidents shows up when one dies in office. People were not just disappointed or worried when President Kennedy was killed; people wept at the loss of a man most had never even met. Kennedy was young and charismatic—but history shows that whenever a president dies in office, heroic Lincoln or debased Harding, McKinley or Garfield, the same wave of deep emotion sweeps across the country. On the other hand, the death of an ex-president brings forth no such intense emotional reaction.

The president is the first political figure children are aware of (later they add Congress, the Court, and others, as "helpers" of the president). With some exceptions among children in deprived circumstances, the president is seen as a "benevolent leader," one who nurtures, sustains, and inspires the citizenry. Presidents regularly show up among "most admired" contemporaries and forebears, and the president is the "best known" (in the sense of sheer name recognition) person in the country. At inauguration time, even presidents elected by close margins are supported by much larger majorities than the election returns show, for people rally round as he actually assumes office. There is a similar reaction when the people see their president threatened by crisis: if he takes action, there is a favorable spurt in the Gallup poll whether he succeeds or fails.

Obviously the president gets more attention in schoolbooks, press, and television than any other politician. He is one of very few who can make news by doing good things. *His* emotional state is a matter of continual public commentary, as is the manner in which his personal and official families conduct themselves. The media bring across the president not as some neutral administrator or corporate executive to be assessed by his production, but as a special being with mysterious dimensions.

We have no king. The sentiments English children—and adults—direct to the Queen have no place to go in our system but to the president. Whatever his talents—Coolidge-type or Roosevelt-type—the president is the only available object for such national-religious-monarchical sentiments as Americans possess.

The president helps people make sense of politics. Congress is a tangle of committees, the bureaucracy is a maze of agencies. The president is one man trying to do a job—a picture much more understandable to the mass of people who find themselves in the same boat. Furthermore, he is the top man. He ought to know what is going on and set it right. So when the economy goes sour, or war drags on, or domestic violence erupts, the president is available to take the blame. Then when things go right, it seems the president must have had a hand in it. Indeed, the flow of political life is marked off by presidents: the "Eisenhower Era," the "Kennedy Years."

What all this means is that the president's *main* responsibilities reach far beyond administering the Executive Branch or commanding the armed forces. The White House is first and foremost a place of public leadership. That inevitably brings to bear on the president intense moral, sentimental, and quasi-religious pressures which can, if he lets them, distort his own thinking and feeling. If there is such a thing as extraordinary sanity, it is needed nowhere so much as in the White House.

Who the president is at a given time can make a profound difference in the whole thrust and direction of national politics. Since we have only one president at a time, we can never prove this by comparison, but even the most superficial speculation confirms the commonsense view that the man himself weighs heavily among other historical factors. A Wilson reelected in 1920, a Hoover in 1932, a John F. Kennedy in 1964 would, it seems very likely, have guided the body politic along rather different paths from those their actual successors chose. Or try to imagine a Theodore Roosevelt ensconced behind today's "bully pulpit" of a presidency, or Lyndon Johnson as president in the age of McKinley. Only someone mesmerized by the lures of historical inevitability can suppose that it would have made little or no difference to government policy had Alf Landon replaced FDR in 1936, had Dewey beaten Truman in 1948, or Adlai Stevenson reigned through the 1950s. Not only would these alternative presidents have advocated different policies—they would have approached the office from very different psychological angles. It stretches credibility to think that Eugene McCarthy would have run the institution the way Lyndon Johnson did.

The burden of this book is that the crucial differences can be anticipated by an understanding of a potential president's character, his world view, and his style. This kind of prediction is not easy; well-informed observers often have guessed wrong as they watched a man step toward the White House. One thinks of Woodrow Wilson, the scholar who would bring reason to politics; of Herbert Hoover, the Great Engineer who would organize chaos into progress; of Franklin D. Roosevelt, that champion of the balanced budget; of Harry Truman, whom the office would surely overwhelm; of Dwight D. Eisenhower, militant crusader; of John F. Kennedy, who would lead beyond moralisms to achievements; of Lyndon B. Johnson, the Southern conservative; and of Richard M. Nixon, conciliator. Spotting the errors is easy. Predicting with even approximate accuracy is going to require some sharp tools and close attention in their use. But the experiment is worth it because the question is critical and because it lends itself to correction by evidence.

My argument comes in layers.

First, a president's personality is an important shaper of his presidential behavior on nontrivial matters.

Second, presidential personality is patterned. His character, world view, and style fit together in a dynamic package understandable in psychological terms.

Third, a president's personality interacts with the power situation he faces and the national "climate of expectations" dominant at the time he serves. The tuning, the resonance—or lack of it—between these external factors and his personality sets in motion the dynamics of his presidency.

Fourth, the best way to predict a president's character, world view, and style is to see how they were put together in the first place. That happened in his early life, culminating in his first independent political success.

But the core of the argument . . . is that presidential character—the basic stance a man takes toward his presidential experience—comes in four varieties. The most important thing to know about a president or candidate is where he fits among these types, defined according to (a) how active he is and (b) whether or not he gives the impression he enjoys his political life.

Let me spell out these concepts briefly before getting down to cases.

PERSONALITY SHAPES PERFORMANCE

I am not about to argue that once you know a president's personality you know everything. But as the cases will demonstrate, the degree and quality of a president's emotional involvement in an issue are powerful influences on how he defines the issue itself, how much attention he pays to it, which facts and persons he sees as relevant to its resolution, and, finally, what principles and purposes he associates with the issue. Every story of presidential decision-making is really two stories: an outer one in which a rational man calculates and an inner one in which an emotional man feels. The two are forever connected. Any real president is one whole man and his deeds reflect his wholeness.

As for personality, it is a matter of tendencies. It is not that one president "has" some basic characteristic that another president does not "have." That old way of treating a trait as a possession, like a rock in a basket, ignores the universality of aggressiveness, compliancy, detachment, and other human drives. We all have all of them, but in different amounts and in different combinations.

THE PATTERN OF CHARACTER, WORLD VIEW, AND STYLE

The most visible part of the pattern is style. *Style is the president's habitual way of performing his three political roles: rhetoric, personal relations, and homework.* Not to be confused with "stylishness," charisma, or appearance, style is how the president goes about doing what the office requires him to do—to speak, directly or through media, to large audiences; to deal face to face with other politicians, individually and in small, relatively private groups; and to read, write, and calculate by himself in order to manage the endless flow of details that stream onto his desk. No president can escape doing at least some of each. But there are marked differences in stylistic emphasis from president to president. The *balance* among the three style elements varies; one president may put most of himself into rhetoric, another may stress close, informal dealing, while still another may devote his energies mainly to study and cogitation. Beyond the balance, we want to see each president's peculiar habits of style, his mode of coping with and adapting to these presidential demands. For example, I think both Calvin Coolidge and John F. Kennedy were primarily rhetoricians, but they went about it in contrasting ways.

A president's *world view consists of his primary, politically relevant beliefs, particularly his conceptions of social causality, human nature, and the central moral conflicts of the time.* This is how he sees the world and his lasting opinions about what he sees. Style is his way of acting; world view is his way of seeing. Like the rest of us, a president develops over a lifetime certain conceptions of reality—how things work in politics, what people are like, what the main purposes are. These assumptions or conceptions help him make sense of his world, give some semblance of order to the chaos of existence. Perhaps most important: a man's world view affects what he pays attention to, and a great deal of politics is about paying attention. The name of the game for many politicians is not so much "Do this, do that" as it is "Look here!"

"Character" comes from the Greek word for engraving; in one sense it is what life has marked into a man's being. As used here, *character is the way the president orients himself toward life* — not for the moment, but enduringly. Character is the person's stance as he confronts experience. And at the core of character, a man confronts himself. The president's fundamental self-esteem is his prime personal resource; to defend and advance that, he will sacrifice much else he values. Down there in the privacy of his heart, does he find himself superb, or ordinary, or debased, or in some intermediate range? No president has been utterly paralyzed by self-doubt and none has been utterly free of midnight self-mockery. In between, the real presidents move out on life from positions of relative strength or weakness. Equally important are the criteria by which they judge themselves. A president who rates himself by the standard of achievement, for instance, may be little affected by losses of affection.

Character, world view, and style are abstractions from the reality of the whole individual. In every case they form an integrated pattern: the man develops a combination which makes psychological sense for him, a dynamic arrangement of motives, beliefs, and habits in the service of his need for self-esteem.

THE POWER SITUATION AND "CLIMATE OF EXPECTATIONS"

Presidential character resonates with the political situation the president faces. It adapts him as he tries to adapt it. The support he has from the public and interest groups, the party balance in Congress, the thrust of Supreme Court opinion together set the basic power situation he must deal with. An activist president may run smack into a brick wall of resistance, then pull back and wait for a better moment. On the other hand, a president who sees himself as a quiet caretaker may not try to exploit even the most favorable power situation. So it is the relationship between President and the political configuration that makes the system tick.

Even before public opinion polls, the president's real or supposed popularity was a large factor in his performance. Besides the power mix in Washington, the president has to deal with a national climate of expectations, the predominant needs thrust up to him by the people. There are at least three recurrent themes around which these needs are focused.

People look to the president for *reassurance,* a feeling that things will be all right, that the president will take care of his people. The psychological request is for a surcease of anxiety. Obviously, modern life in America involves considerable doses of fear, tension, anxiety, worry; from time to time, the public mood calls for a rest, a time of peace, a breathing space, a "return to normalcy."

Another theme is the demand for a *sense of progress and action.* The president ought to do something to direct the nation's course—or at least be in there pitching for the people. The president is looked to as a take-charge man, a doer, a turner of the wheels, a producer of progress— even if that means some sacrifice of serenity.

A third type of climate of expectations is the public need for a sense of *legitimacy* from, and in, the presidency. The president should be a master politician who is above politics. He should have a right to his place and a rightful way of acting in it. The respectability—even religiosity—of the office has to be protected by a man who presents himself as defender of the faith. There is more to this than dignity, more than propriety. The president is expected to personify our betterness in an inspiring way, to express in what he does and is (not just in what he says) a moral idealism which, in much of the public mind, is the very opposite of "politics."

Over time the climate of expectations shifts and changes. Wars, depressions, and other national events contribute to that change, but there also is a rough cycle, from an emphasis on action (which begins to look too "political") to an emphasis on legitimacy (the moral uplift of which creates its own strains) to an emphasis on reassurance and rest (which comes to seem like drift) and back to action again. One need not be astrological about it. The point is that the climate of expectations at any given time is the political air the President has to breathe. Relating to this climate is a large part of his task.

PREDICTING PRESIDENTS

The best way to predict a President's character, world view, and style is to see how he constructed them in the first place. Especially in the early stages, life is experimental; consciously or not, a person tries out various ways of defining and maintaining and raising self-esteem. He looks to his environment for clues as to who he is and how well he is doing. These lessons of life slowly sink in: certain self-images and evaluations, certain ways of looking at the world, certain styles of action get confirmed by his experience and he gradually adopts them as his own. If we can see that process of development, we can understand the product. The features to note are those bearing on presidential performance.

Experimental development continues all the way to death; we will not blind ourselves to midlife changes, particularly in the full-scale prediction case, that of Richard Nixon. But it is often much easier to see the basic patterns in early life histories. Later on a whole host of distractions—especially the image-making all politicians learn to practice—clouds the picture.

In general, character has its *main* development in childhood, world view in adolescence, style in early adulthood. The stance toward life I call character grows out of the child's experiments in relating to parents, brothers and sisters, and peers at play and in school, as well as to his own body and the objects around it. Slowly the child defines an orientation toward experience; once established, that tends to last despite much subsequent contradiction. By adolescence, the child has been hearing and seeing how people make their worlds meaningful, and now he is moved to relate himself—his own meanings—to those around him. His focus of attention shifts toward the future; he senses that decisions about his fate are coming and he looks into the premises for those decisions. Thoughts about the way the world works and how one might work in it, about what people are like and how one might be like them or not, and about the values people share and how one might share in them too—these are typical concerns for the post-child, pre-adult mind of the adolescent.

These themes come together strongly in early adulthood, when the person moves from contemplation to responsible action and adopts a style. In most biographical accounts this period stands out in stark clarity—the time of emergence, the time the young man found himself. I call it his first independent political success. It was then he moved beyond the detailed guidance of his family; then his self-esteem was dramatically boosted; then he came forth as a person to be reckoned with by other people. The *way* he did that is profoundly important to him. Typically he grasps that style and hangs onto it. Much later, coming into the presidency, something in him remembers this earlier victory and reemphasizes the style that made it happen.

Character provides the main thrust and broad direction—but it does not *determine,* in any fixed sense, world view and style. The story of development does not end with the end of childhood. Thereafter, the culture one grows in and the ways that culture is translated by parents and peers shape the meanings one makes of his character. The going world view gets learned and that learning helps channel character forces. Thus it will not necessarily be true that compulsive characters have reactionary beliefs, or that compliant characters believe in compromise. Similarly for style: historical accidents play a large part in furnishing special opportunities for action—and in blocking off alternatives. For example, however much anger a young man may feel, that anger will not be expressed in rhetoric unless and until his life situation provides a platform and an audience. Style thus has a stature and independence of its own. Those who would reduce all explanation to character neglect these highly significant later channelings. For beyond the root is the branch, above the foundation the superstructure, and starts do not pre-scribe finishes.

FOUR TYPES OF PRESIDENTIAL CHARACTER

The five concepts—character, world view, style, power situation, and climate of expectations—run through the accounts of presidents in [later chapters of Barber's book], which cluster the presidents since Theodore Roosevelt into four types. This is the fundamental scheme of the study. It offers a way to move past the complexities to the main contrasts and comparisons.

The first baseline in defining presidential types is *activity-passivity.* How much energy does the man invest in his presidency? Lyndon Johnson went at his day like a human cyclone, coming to rest long after the sun went down. Calvin Coolidge often slept eleven hours a night and still needed a nap in the middle of the day. In between the presidents array themselves on the high or low side of the activity line.

The second baseline is *positive-negative affect* toward one's activity— that is, how he feels about what he does. Relatively speaking, does he seem to experience his political life as happy or sad, enjoyable or discouraging, positive or negative in its main effect. The feeling I am after here is not grim satisfaction in a job well done, not some philosophical conclusion. The idea is this: is he someone who, on the surfaces we can see, gives forth the feeling that he has *fun* in political life? Franklin Roosevelt's Secretary of War, Henry L. Stimson wrote that the Roosevelts "not only understood the *use* of power, they knew the *enjoyment* of power, too. . . . Whether a man is burdened by power or enjoys power; whether he is trapped by responsibility or made free by it; whether he is moved by other people and outer forces or moves them—that is the essence of leadership."

The positive-negative baseline, then, is a general symptom of the fit between the man and his experience, a kind of register of *felt* satisfaction.

Why might we expect these two simple dimensions to outline the main character types? Because they stand for two central features of anyone's orientation toward life. In nearly every study of personality, some form of the active-passive contrast is critical; the general tendency to act or be acted upon is evident in such concepts as dominance-submission, extraversion-introversion, aggression-timidity, attack-defense, fight-flight, engagement-withdrawal, approach-avoidance. In everyday life we sense quickly the general energy output of the people we deal with. Similarly we catch on fairly quickly to the affect dimension—whether the person seems to be optimistic or pessimistic, hopeful or skeptical, happy or sad. The two baselines are clear and they are also independent of one another: all of us know people who are very active but seem discouraged, others who are quite passive but seem happy, and so forth. The activity baseline refers to what one does, the affect baseline to how one feels about what he does.

Both are crude clues to character. They are leads into four basic character patterns long familiar in psychological research. In summary form, these are the main configurations:

Active-positive: There is a congruence, a consistency, between much activity and the enjoyment of it, indicating relatively high self-esteem and relative success in relating to the environment. The man shows an orientation toward productiveness as a value and an ability to use his styles flexibly, adaptively, suiting the dance to the music. He sees himself as developing over time toward relatively well defined personal goals—growing toward his image of himself as he might yet be. There is an emphasis on rational mastery, on using the brain to move the feet. This may get him into trouble; he may fail to take account of the irrational in politics. Not everyone he deals with sees things his way and he may find it hard to understand why.

Active-negative: The contradiction here is between relatively intense effort and relatively low emotional reward for that effort. The activity has a compulsive quality, as if the man were trying to make up for something or to escape from anxiety into hard work. He seems ambitious, striving upward, power-seeking. His stance toward the environment is aggressive and he has a persistent problem in managing his aggressive feelings. His self-image is vague and discontinuous. Life is a hard struggle to achieve and hold power, hampered by the condemnations of a perfectionistic conscience. Active-negative types pour energy into the political system, but it is an energy distorted from within.

Passive-positive: This is the receptive, compliant, other-directed character whose life is a search for affection as a reward for being agreeable and cooperative rather than personally assertive. The contradiction is between low self-esteem (on grounds of being unlovable, unattractive) and a superficial optimism. A hopeful attitude helps dispel doubt and elicits encouragement from others. Passive-positive types help soften the harsh edges of politics. But their dependence and the fragility of their hopes and enjoyments make disappointment in politics likely.

Passive-negative: The factors are consistent—but how are we to account for the man's *political* role-taking? Why is someone who does little in politics and enjoys it less there at all? The answer lies in the passive-negative's character-rooted orientation toward doing dutiful service; this compensates for low self-esteem based on a sense of uselessness. Passive-negative types are in politics because they think they ought to be. They may well adapted to certain nonpolitical roles, but they lack the experience and flexibility to perform effectively as political leaders. Their tendency is to withdraw, to escape from the conflict and uncertainty of politics by emphasizing vague principles (especially prohibitions) and procedural arrangements. They become guardians of the right and proper way, above the sordid politicking of lesser men.

Active-positive Presidents want most to achieve results. Active-negatives aim to get and keep power. Passive-positives are after love. Passive-negatives emphasize their civic virtue. The relation of activity to enjoyment in a President thus tends to outline a cluster of characteristics, to set apart the adapted from the compulsive, compliant, and withdrawn types.

The first four Presidents of the United States, conveniently, ran through this gamut of character types. (Remember, we are talking about tendencies, broad directions; no individual man exactly fits a category.) George Washington—clearly the most important President in the pantheon— established the fundamental legitimacy of an American government at a time when this was a matter in considerable question. Washington's dignity, judiciousness, his aloof air of reserve and dedication to duty fit the passive-negative or withdrawing type best. Washington did not seek innovation, he sought stability. He longed to retire to Mount Vernon, but fortunately was persuaded to stay on through a second term, in which, by rising above the political conflict between Hamilton and Jefferson and inspiring confidence in his own integrity, he gave the nation time to develop the organized means for peaceful change.

John Adams followed, a dour New England Puritan, much given to work and worry, an impatient and irascible man—an active-negative President, a compulsive type. Adams was far more partisan than Washington; the survival of the system through his presidency demonstrated that the nation could tolerate, for a time, domination by one of its nascent political parties. As President, an angry Adams brought the United States to the brink of war with France, and presided over the new nation's first experiment in political repression: the Alien and Sedition Acts, forbidding, among other things, unlawful combinations "with intent to oppose any measure or measures of the government of the United States," or "any false, scandalous, and malicious writing or writings against the United States, or the President of the United States, with intent to defame . . . or to bring them or either of them, into contempt or disrepute."

Then came Jefferson. He too had his troubles and failures—in the design of national defense, for example. As for his presidential character (only one element in success or failure), Jefferson was clearly active-positive. A child of the Enlightenment, he applied his reason to organizing connections with Congress aimed at strengthening the more popular forces. A man of catholic interests and delightful humor, Jefferson combined a clear and open vision of what the country could be with a profound political sense, expressed in his famous phrase, "Every difference of opinion is not a difference of principle."

The fourth president was James Madison, "Little Jemmy," the constitutional philosopher thrown into the White House at a time of great international turmoil. Madison comes closest to the passive-positive, or compliant, type; he suffered from irresolution, tried to compromise his way out, and gave in too readily to the "warhawks" urging combat with Britain. The nation drifted into war, and Madison wound up ineptly commanding his collection of amateur generals in the streets of Washington. General Jackson's victory at New Orleans saved the Madison administration's historical reputation; but he left the presidency with the United States close to bankruptcy and secession.

These four Presidents—like all Presidents—were persons trying to cope with the roles they had won by using the equipment they had built over a lifetime. The President is not some shapeless organism in a flood of novelties, but a man with a memory in a system with a history. Like all of us, he draws on his past to shape his future. The pathetic hope that the White House will turn a Caligula into a Marcus Aurelius is as naive as the fear that ultimate power inevitably corrupts. The problem is to understand— and to state understandably—what in the personal past foreshadows the presidential future. . . .

REAGAN'S RISE AND RULE: PREDICTION AND RESULTS

At [the outset] Reagan's Presidency looked this way to me:

The *climate of expectations* would be dominated by "the tide of reaction against too long and hard a time of troubles, too much worry, too much tension and anxiety" through the Carter years. Reagan came on as "a friend, a pal, a guy to reassure us that the story is going to come out all right. . . . He is supposed to make it well again. That is very likely to prove difficult, if not impossible."

Reagan's *power situation* would be fragile. His "best bet for popular support in darker months to come may well be the fury of the radical right, whose indignant disillusionment with Reagan will help him gain acceptance with moderates." He would need help winning the public, having "won in an election with the lowest turnout in 32 years." He had a modest Senate majority and conservative Democratic allies in the House. Inflation would be tough to beat and he had "no terrible social disaster going for him, such as the collapse that brought in Franklin Roosevelt, to put steam behind a burst of effective legislation in his first 100 or 200 days." After an initial romance, the media would play up "the inevitable 'performance gap' stories, featuring bobbles and corruptions on the road to Utopia."

The Reagan Presidential *style* would be dominated by rhetoric, with "little interest in homework on the issues" and little taste for "the charms of personal negotiation. . . . particularly if they involve an element of disagreement or confrontation." Further, "his rhetoric is essentially ahistorical and apolitical. He is bound to contribute to the ever-widening gap in American politics between speech and meaning."

Reagan's *worldview*, despite various attributions of "ideology," would be simpler than supposed: "He is a Republican millionaire and hangs around with those folks. . . . As long as Reagan's business friends are happy with moderation, he will be, too. He is unlikely to go off the deep end with Milton Friedman. . . . His domestic economic policies may indeed turn out to be too watered down to be effective." In foreign policy, "a reasonable guess would be: distract attention by waving the fist at the Soviet Union, while quieter and more profitable arrangements are worked out 'realistically' in the Third World, unhampered by 'Utopian' human rights consideration. As president, Reagan is as likely to [be] 'business oriented' as ever, at home and abroad."

The Reagan *character* would be "passive-positive." That meant he would be "definitely no Nixon"—not a rigidified compulsive. Rather the danger was in "his type's tendency to drift, particularly with forces in the close-up environment. The danger is confusion, delay and then impulsiveness."

That day I thought, "The best hope is that, like Gerry Ford and Jimmy Carter, Ronald Reagan will leave the Constitution about as he found it and the nation, at peace. The worst fear is that Reagan, seeking affection, will have disaster thrust upon him."

As of [1986], a Reagan disaster has not befallen the nation as a whole, though certain sizeable categories of persons would disagree on the basis of personal experience. Indeed the subsequent business recovery made life easier for the better-off Americans, as the cycle of business rolled on. What we have witnessed is a dazzling kaleidoscope of political fireworks; seeing past the dazzle to the dynamics takes a calmer, theory-guided vision than day-to-day observation typically affords.

The basic outlines are clearer now than they were then. The climate of expectations when Reagan began his rule stressed the recurrent need for reassurance, for conciliation after a time of too much combat and moralizing. As he had when he ran for Governor of California against Pat Brown in 1966, Reagan managed to get his opponent to greet the Reagan candidacy with shocked indignation and alarm. Carter like Brown read the Reagan verbal record and recoiled in horror, supposing he might mean it. Reagan let the fear define itself and then came on in person—in his warm and amiable person—to dispel it. As Kevin Phillips noted, "The public took comfort and relaxed." Reagan thereafter appeared again and again to reassure the public that he was not as bad as they feared, not as frightening as he had been painted, not as wildly gaga as various columnists had made him out to be. Reagan the reassurer worked, in dramatic terms, through the Presidential honeymoon period. The public, if the polls are to be believed, suspended disbelief regarding his economic theories and opted to "give him a chance" to do his Presidential thing. As the honeymoon faded and the conflictful election of 1984 loomed ahead, Reagan the reassurer, old "Ease On Down The Road" Ron, came in for more and more concentrated criticism, especially from the press. As predicted, some of the fun started to leak out of his Presidency.

Similarly the fundamental balance of the Reagan style persisted as predicted: the antipathy for homework, the overwhelming emphasis on rhetoric. Reagan the President not only revived the one page "mini-memo" as his favorite homework-avoider, he also eventually brought its inventor, William Clark, into the White House as his National Security Advisor—thereby underlining doubly his disdain for mastering information, since Clark, whatever else he may have been guilty of, was innocent of national security expertise. As for negotiation, Reagan held many a meeting with Congressmen and the like—and typically charmed the socks off them. But he left the dealing to his staffers. He liked to play host. Others could arrange the terms of legislation. What he spent by far the most time and energy on was speaking and getting ready to speak—honing his performance. It was there, within that rhetorical emphasis, that the essential impact of the Reagan persona was to be found. Nearly three years into his Presidency, *Time* drew a summary portrait of the Reagan Presidential style:

> Reagan is remarkably disengaged from the substance of his job. His aides no longer dismiss as glib the theory that Reagan has a movie-star approach to governing. "In Reagan's mind," says a White House adviser, "somebody does the lighting, somebody else does the set, and Reagan takes care of his role, which is the public role."
>
> White House aides, adapting to his mellow managerial style, seldom prod the President, nor he them. Instead, Reagan waits for an amiable consensus to develop among advisers, who work within the boundaries of Reagan's ideology. Except for his unbudging devotion to a military buildup and opposition to tax increases, he often accepts uncritically his advisers' recommendations. . . .
>
> Even at the most pedestrian level, Reagan can be eerily detached, oblivious. He does not know where most of his closest advisers sit, even though some are only a few paces away from the Oval Office. . . .
>
> Reagan's curiosity, even after three years at the epicenter of events, seems stunted. . . . He occasionally dozes off during meetings, sometimes with outsiders. . . . Even when he makes a substantial policy recommendation, he rarely follows through on it. . . . Reagan's extreme reliance on his staff leaves him badly exposed when they muff their jobs. . . .
>
> When his staff is divided, Reagan can be caught in a crossfire. . . . "When the staff chooses up sides," says a White House adviser, "that's when the weakness of the system of delegating power is apparent. That's when it doesn't work." It does not work because Reagan lacks the temperament, and often the knowledge, to choose between the competing arguments."

Reagan the passive-positive political character kept his shape as he moved into the White House. His day began long after sunup and ended well before sundown. His favorite moment of the week, he said, was "climbing into that helicopter to go to Camp David," where he could get into his pajamas and watch "golden oldie" movies with his wife; he went out to his ranch in California for frequent long vacations. The passivity showed up dramatically on August 19, 1981, when two American F-14 fighter planes were attacked by Russian-built Libyan jets, which they promptly shot down. The President's advisors quickly established mutual communication— but they waited five hours and twenty minutes before they told the President. The call reached him at 4:24 a.m. He got the message—and went back to sleep.

Through the first half of 1981, the President's aides grew more and more doubtful that his economic plan could work, but that did not concern Ronald Reagan, because they did not tell him. "The evidence is in," the *New York Times* reported in mid-1982, "that Mr. Reagan does often serve simply as a ratifier of his advisors' decisions." "For a successful man," *Time* reported, "Reagan is very passive, with little fire or curiosity.... Indeed, Reagan makes little effort even to learn exactly what it is that his advisors are up to." One aide tried to explain the boss's languor: "He likes to lie dormant and then spring to life." Compared to the schedules of a Jimmy Carter or a Lyndon Johnson, or even a Jerry Ford, President Reagan's schedule was Tahitian.

Like Cupid, Ronald Reagan kept firing away from "his never-depleted quiver of smiles," as Francis X. Clines noted. If Carter had not done so much smiling, Reagan would be noted for it. He remained an egregious grinner, even when troubles loomed, even when he had, at his age, every reason to be tired and irritable, even when there was no need to be encouraging. In February 1983, Robert Kaiser tracked down and questioned nearly two dozen people who had met with the President that month: "Their accounts suggest a man who prefers fun to work, who loves to entertain and feel loved, who likes being President, but who rarely gets enthused about governing." The President began his third year by reporting, "How time flies when you're having fun." Reagan the booster, the eternal optimist, contrasted markedly with his negative counterparts in the Presidency.

And the main product of that combination, an emphasis on compliance, showed up and maintained itself in his White House life. He was not a hater, but he hated controversy up close. He "expected concord, and the appearance of concord, to prevail among his staff," as biographer Lou Cannon puts it. Reagan's regular equanimity collapses in the presence of real, I'm-not-kidding argument in his presence. When the unity of his top campaign aides fell apart and one of them had to be fired, Reagan agonized and suffered until Mrs. Reagan finally got him to end his suffering with a clean cut decision. Similarly in the administration, constant friction and confrontation between his self-styled "vicar of peace," Secretary of State Alexander Haig, and nearly every other top advisor so disrupted life within his "corral of cordiality" that Reagan was at last driven to perform an unkind act in person: he fired him. "Reagan likes quiet, easygoing, collegial people who can submerge themselves in a harmonic whole," Cannon notes. His wife concurs: "He doesn't function well if there are tensions," she reports. "He likes everyone to like one another and get along." Biographer Laurence Barrett wrote what that meant: "About one crucial fact there could be no doubt: Reagan trusted his aides not wisely but too well. He often leaned on them more often than their strength indicated."

Thus if there were those who stepped into the Reagan years expecting him to be the rigid ideologue his opponents had described him to be, or a withdrawn, philosopher-king President like his hero Calvin Coolidge, or a go-get-'em results achiever like the Roosevelts, they were wrong. They had significantly misdirected their attention to the wrong clues because they had begun with the wrong questions. Reagan was a passive-positive linked through his extraordinary rhetorical style to a public ready, for the moment, for just such a hopeful and reassuring personality. That combination would turn out to be the simplest and the most significant thing to point out as the world rolled over towards 1984.

We may see other Reagans in the years ahead. We are bound to see other rhetoricians attuned to the modern media. We may well see future conjunctions of the man and the mood of the nation which will mightily reinforce one another. As the transition from Carter to Reagan once again demonstrated, understanding the "institution" of the Presidency tells you far less than you want to know, and provides only the shape of the stage and the arrangement of the furniture on and around which the action will take place. Theory which fails to reach the person of the President will fall short of useful prediction and into the gap will step whatever speculations politicians can generate, as they struggle to bring power to bear on urgent problems. Therefore we ought to focus on those facets of the Reagan case that also shed light on his type and the types of conditions in which he operates.

Beyond the basic outlines, three questions are intriguing.

1. Within a few months of assuming the powers of the Presidency, Reagan the passive-positive got through Congress a startlingly novel package of economic legislation, overcoming what looked at the time like high odds against it. How that happened illuminates important aspects of the power situation.

2. Reagan came on as a "conservative," but, as predicted, he soon had the "conservatives" furious at him and at least some of the "liberals" appreciating his "flexibility." What practical meaning do these "ideological" elements take on in this Reagan worldview?

3. The connections linking Reagan's words with historical reality, on the one hand, and his own actions, on the other, were, to put it mildly, loosely knit. Yet his communicative ability was celebrated as extraordinarily powerful. What forces in the Reagan character sustain his rhetorical effectiveness? He may not be the last President whose style is significantly theatrical. What does that portend for the processes of persuasion and deliberation in a democracy?

The President and the Media

☐   The media spotlight is on the presidency more than on other governmental institutions. Theodore Roosevelt was the first president to undertake a major effort to co-opt the press, giving Washington reporters space in the White House in order to facilitate his use of them as much as to accommodate the growing presidential press corps. Teddy Roosevelt knew that the press could be an important ally of government, that publicity for presidential policies and actions help to build public support and ease the job of his administration.

Teddy Roosevelt set a precedent for twentieth-century presidents in recognizing the power of the press and the importance of turning the political reporters' craft to the advantage of the White House by managing the news. Teddy Roosevelt's cousin, Franklin D. Roosevelt, held regular informal press conferences with reporters in the Oval Office, knowing that by keeping them informed of his programs and progress the nation would learn about and, he hoped, support the New Deal.

From the vantage point of the White House, the press, while potentially a useful conduit of managed news, is seen more as a critic than an ally. Presidents tend to view the press as the enemy with which they have to deal. Charged with the responsibility of coping with the press is the presidential press secretary, who conducts daily briefings apprising White House reporters of the president's actions and plans.

A White House insider, George E. Reedy, now Nieman Professor of Journalism at Marquette University, portrays the world of the White House reporter and the way in which presidents view and treat the press in the following selection.

40

George E. Reedy

THE PRESS AND THE PRESIDENT

To the leisurely observer of the Washington scene, there is a distinct charm in the startled air of discovery with which the press greets each step in the entirely predictable course of its relationship with the president and the White House staff.

Actually, the patterns are as well-established and as foreseeable as the movements of a Javanese temple dance. The timing will vary as will the alternating degrees of adoration and bitterness. But the sequence of events, at least in modern times, appears to be inexorable. It is only the determination of the press to treat each new day as unprecedented that makes the specific events seem to be news.

Seen from a little distance, cries of outrage from the press over the discovery that Mr. Reagan seeks to "manage the news" have the flavor of an Ed Sullivan rerun show on after-midnight television. They are reminiscent of similar protests in the administrations of Presidents Carter, Nixon, Johnson, Kennedy, Eisenhower, Truman, and Roosevelt. Presidents before that do not offer much material for discussion simply because they served prior to the FDR era, when press-White House relations were put on a daily-contact basis for the first time in history.

The charge of management is a familiar one because it has a strong element of truth. All presidents seek to manage the news and all are successful to a degree. What is not taken into account is that legitimate management of the news from the White House is inescapable and, human nature being what it is, it is hardly surprising that presidents try to bend this necessity for their own ends. Few men will decline an opportunity to recommend themselves highly.

The press would not be happy with a White House that ended all efforts at news management and either threw the mansion wide open for coverage or closed it to outsiders altogether and told journalists to get facts any way they could. Since the early days of the New Deal, reporters have been relying on daily press briefings, prearranged press conferences, and press pools when the president travels. There would be chaos should all this come to an end.

The point is that the White House is covered by journalists through highly developed and formal organizational structures. It is inherent in the nature of such structures that they must be managed by somebody, and the

---

Reprinted from the *Columbia Journalism Review,* May/June, 1983. © 1983. By permission.

president's office is no exception. Management technique is employed every time the president decides what stories will be released on Monday and what stories will be released on Saturday; every time he decides that some meetings will be open to press coverage and others will not; every time he decides that some visitors will be fed to the press as they walk out of the Oval Office and others will not. Anybody who believes that he will make decisions on the basis of what makes him look bad will believe a hundred impossible things before breakfast.

There are actually times when the press literally does not want news. This became very clear early in the administration of Lyndon Johnson when he inaugurated the custom of unexpected Saturday morning news conferences. This meant disruption of newspaper production schedules all over the United States. Printing pressmen had to be recalled from weekend holidays to work at exorbitant rates; front pages that had been planned in leisurely fashion in the morning had to be scrapped for new layouts; rewrite men who had looked forward to quiet afternoons with their families worked into the evening hours. It was a mess.

After two such conferences, I began getting calls from top bureau chiefs in Washington pleading with me to put an end to them. They made it clear they wanted stories timed so that they would fit conveniently into news slots. It took some doing on my part; Johnson would have enjoyed the discovery that he was putting newspaper publishers to so much expense and trouble. (I think he started these conferences simply because he became lonely on Saturday mornings when there was little to do.) I talked him into dropping the custom by producing figures which showed that the weekend audiences were not large enough to justify the effort.

While it was actually going on, the episode struck me as just another example of the Johnsonian inability to comprehend the press. It was not until later that I realized the deeper significance. The press had not only acquiesced in news management but had actually asked that it be instituted. The fact that nothing was involved except timing was irrelevant. The ability to control the timing of news is the most potent weapon that any would-be news manipulator can have. No absolute line can be drawn between the occasions when he should have it and those when he should not.

This may well account for the indifference of the public to the periodic campaigns against news management. Even to an unsophisticated audience it is apparent that journalists are not objecting to news management per se but only to the kind of news management that makes their professional lives more difficult. However it may look in Washington, at a distance the issue appears as a dispute over control of the news for the convenience of the president or for the convenience of the press. In such a situation, Americans tend to come down on the side of the president.

Of course, if the president is caught in an outright lie—a lie about something in which the public is really concerned—the public will mobilize against him swiftly. But many charges of news management are directed at statements that Americans do not regard as outright lies. Americans have become so accustomed to the kind of exaggeration and misleading facts that are used to sell products on nightly television that a little White House puffery seems quite natural.

There is, of course, another side to the coin. While presidents always try to manipulate the news—and all too often succeed—there is a very real doubt whether the manipulation performs any real service for them, even in the crassest image-building sense. The presidency is a strange institution. The occupant must accept never-ending responsibilities and must act on never-ending problems. It may well be that what a president does speaks so much more loudly than anything he can say that the normal techniques of public relations are completely futile.

In the first place, a president may be able to time his public appearances but he cannot time his acts. He *is* the United States and anything that affects the United States must have a presidential response. He must react to international crises, to domestic disasters, to unemployment, and to inflation; if he chooses to do nothing in any of these instances his inaction will be writ large in the public media.

In the second place, a president may be able to keep his thoughts to himself but he cannot act in any direction without causing waves that sweep through the Washington community. The federal bureaucracy is shot through with holdovers from previous administrations who do not like him; the Congress is loaded with political opponents with whom he must deal; the lobbying offices of the capital are staffed by skilled president-watchers who can interpret his every act and who have sympathetic journalistic listeners. Finally, there is the overwhelming fact that the president has a direct impact on the lives of every citizen and there is a limit to his capacity to mislead. He cannot convince men and women that there is peace when their sons are dying in a war. He cannot hold up images of prosperity (although he will try) when men and women are out of work. He cannot persuade constituents that there is peace and harmony when there is rioting in the streets. There may be instances when he can escape the blame but only when his political opposition is not on its toes.

Against this background, the efficacy of manipulation is dubious at best. It may have a favorable impact on public opinion in the short run. But I know of no persuasive evidence that it helps to build the long-term support a politician needs. Every instance I have studied bears a close parallel to what happened when Lyndon Johnson held his meaningless meeting with the late Soviet premier Alexei Kosygin at Glassboro, New Jersey, in 1967. He was able to maneuver the press into treating it as a major summit conference for a few days, and his poll ratings rose accordingly.

But it soon became clear that the meeting had produced nothing of substance and that there had been no reason to expect that it would. The poll ratings went right back down again.

On the other hand, efforts at manipulation invariably challenge the press to dig deeper than journalists ordinarily would. The stories they write about manipulation have little effect. But the stories they write as a result of the digging may have the kind of substance that does make an impact. The whole exercise can well be merely an invitation to trouble on the part of the president.

The bottom line can be simply stated. The president can, within limits, manipulate that part of the press which covers the White House. But he cannot manipulate the press as a whole, and it is probable that his efforts to do so will always backfire.

Presidential Power and Executive Privilege

□   On July 24, 1974, the Supreme Court in *United States* v. *Richard M. Nixon* rendered a historic decision interpreting the meaning of the separation of powers. President Nixon had attempted to claim executive privilege in refusing to obey a district court order to turn over tape recordings and other data involving White House conversations pertaining to the Watergate coverup. Special Watergate Prosecutor Leon Jaworski had successfully sought from District Court Judge John Sirica a subpoena directing the president to produce the tapes and documents, to be used as evidence in the trial of six former Nixon aides who were accused of conspiring to conceal the burglary in 1972 of the Democratic National Headquarters in the Watergate complex. The court held unanimously (Justice Rehnquist, one of Nixon's four appointees to the court, disqualified himself) that the president is subject to the judicial process, and cannot claim executive privilege in refusing to turn over the subpoenaed material on the general grounds that the material contained "confidential conversations between a President and his close advisors that it would be inconsistent with the public interest to produce." The court stated that although the separation of powers requires that each branch give deference to the others, only the courts have the power to say what the law is with respect to the claim of executive privilege. The proper scope of judicial power in a particular case and controversy cannot in any way be subject to presidential control.

41

UNITED STATES v. RICHARD M. NIXON
418 U.S. 683 (1974)

Mr. Chief Justice Burger delivered the opinion of the Court:

These cases present for review the denial of a motion, filed on behalf of the President of the United States, in the case of *United States* v. *Mitchell et al.* (D.C. Crim. No. 74–110), to quash a third party subpoena duces tecum [requires the party who is summoned to appear in court to bring some document or piece of evidence to be used or inspected by the court] issued by the United States District Court for the District of Columbia, pursuant to Fed. Rule Crim. Proc. 17 (C). The subpoena directed the President to produce certain tape recordings and documents relating to his conversations with aides and advisors. The Court rejected the President's claims of absolute executive privilege, of lack of jurisdiction, and of failure to satisfy the requirements of Rule 17 (C) [that the evidence sought must be specific, relevant to the case, and admissible in court]. The President appealed to the Court of Appeals. We granted the United States petition for certiorari before judgment, and also the President's responsive cross-petition for certiorari before judgment, because of the public importance of the issues presented and the need for their prompt resolution.

On March 1, 1974, a grand jury of the United States District Court for the District of Columbia returned an indictment charging seven named individuals with various offenses, including conspiracy to defraud the United States and to obstruct justice. Although he was not designated as such in the indictment, the grand jury named the President, among others, as an unindicted co-conspirator. On April 18, 1974, upon motion of the special prosecutor . . . a subpoena duces tecum was issued pursuant to Rule 17 (C) to the President by the United States District Court and made returnable on May 2, 1974. This subpoena required the production, in advance of the September 9 trial date, of certain tapes, memoranda, papers, transcripts, or other writings relating to certain precisely identified meetings between the President and others. The Special Prosecutor was able to fix the time, place, and persons present at these discussions because the White House daily logs and appointment records had been delivered to him.

On April 30, 1974, the President publicly released edited transcripts of forty-three conversations; portions of twenty conversations subject to subpoena in the present case were included. On May 1, 1974, the President's counsel filed a "special appearance" and a motion to quash the subpoena, under Rule 17 (C). This motion was accompanied by a formal claim of privilege. At a subsequent hearing, further motions to expunge the grand jury's action naming the President as an unindicted co-conspirator and for protective orders against the disclosure of that information were filed or raised orally by counsel for the President.

On May 20, 1974, the District Court denied the motion to quash and the motions to expunge and for protective orders. It further ordered "the President or any subordinate officer, official or employee with custody or control of the documents or objects subpoenaed," to deliver to the District Court, on or before May 31, 1974, the originals of all subpoenaed items, as well as an index and analysis of those items, together with tape copies of those portions of the subpoenaed recordings for which transcripts had been released to the public by the President on April 30. . . .

The District Court held that the judiciary, not the President, was the final arbiter of a claim of executive privilege. The court concluded that, under the circumstances of this case, the presumptive privilege was overcome by the Special Prosecutor's prima facie "demonstration of need sufficiently compelling to warrant judicial examination in chambers. . . . "

THE CLAIM OF PRIVILEGE

A

Having determined that the requirements of Rule 17 (e) were satisfied, we turn to the claim that the subpoena should be quashed because it demands "confidential conversations between a President and his close advisors that it would be inconsistent with the public interest to produce." . . . The first contention is a broad claim that the separation of powers doctrine precludes judicial review of a president's claim of privilege. The second contention is that if he does not prevail on the claim of absolute privilege, the Court should hold as a matter of constitutional law that the privilege prevails over the subpoena duces tecum.

In the performance of assigned constitutional duties each branch of the Government must initially interpret the Constitution, and the interpretation of its powers by any branch is due great respect from the others.

The President's counsel, as we have noted, reads the Constitution as providing an absolute privilege of confidentiality for all presidential communications. Many decisions of this Court, however, have unequivocally reaffirmed the holding of *Marbury* v. *Madison,* 1 Cranch 137 (1803), that "it is emphatically the province and duty of the Judicial department to say what the law is." . . .

No holding of the Court has defined the scope of judicial power specifically relating to the enforcement of a subpoena for confidential presidential communications for use in a criminal prosecution, but other exercises of powers by the executive branch and the legislative branch have been found invalid as in conflict with the Constitution. . . .

Our system of government "requires that Federal courts on occasion interpret the Constitution in a manner at variance with the construction given the document by another branch." . . .

Notwithstanding the deference each branch must accord the others, the "judicial power of the United States" vested in the Federal courts by Art. 111, Section 1, of the Constitution can no more be shared with the executive branch than the chief executive, for example, can share with the judiciary the veto power, or the Congress share with the judiciary the power to override a presidential veto. Any other conclusion would be contrary to the basic concept of separation of powers and the checks and balances that flow from a scheme of a tripartite Government. [See] the Federalist, No. 47, . . . We therefore reaffirm that it is "emphatically the province and the duty" of this court "to say what the law is" with respect to the claim of privilege presented in this case. *Marbury* v. *Madison,* supra,. . . .

B

In support of his claim of absolute privilege, the President's counsel urges two grounds one of which is common to all governments and one of which is peculiar to our system of separation of powers. The first ground is the valid need for protection of communications between high government officials and those who advise and assist them in the performance of their manifold duties; the importance of this confidentiality is too plain to require further discussion. Human experience teaches that those who expect public dissemination of their remarks may well temper candor with a concern for appearances and for their own interests to the detriment of the decision-making process. Whatever the nature of the privilege of confidentiality of presidential communications in the exercise of Art. 8 powers, the privilege can be said to derive from the supremacy of each branch within its own assigned area of constitutional duties. Certain powers and privileges flow from the nature of enumerated powers; the protection of the confidentiality of presidential communications has similar constitutional underpinnings.

The second ground asserted by the President's counsel in support of the claim of absolute privilege rests on the doctrine of separation of powers. Here it is argued that the independence of the executive branch within its own sphere, *Humphrey's Executor* v. *United States,* 295 U.S. 602, 629-630 (1935): *Kilbourn* v. *Thompson,* 103 U.S. 168, 190-191 (1880), insulates a President from a judicial subpoena in an ongoing criminal prosecution, and thereby protects confidential presidential communications.

However, neither the doctrine of separation of powers, nor the need for confidentiality of high level communications, without more, can sustain an absolute unqualified presidential privilege of immunity from judicial process under all circumstances. The President's need for complete candor and objectivity from advisors calls for great deference from the courts. However, when the privilege depends solely on the broad, undifferentiated claim of public interest in the confidentiality of such conversations, a confrontation with other values arises. Absent a claim of need to protect military, diplomatic, or sensitive national security secrets, we find it difficult to accept the argument that even the very important interest in confidentiality of presidential communications is significantly diminished by production of such material for in camera inspection [in the judge's chambers] with all the protection that a District Court will be obliged to provide.

The impediment that an absolute, unqualified privilege would place in the way of the primary constitutional duty of the judicial branch to do justice in criminal prosecutions would plainly conflict with the function of the courts under Art. III. In designing the structure of our government and dividing and allocating the sovereign power among three co-equal branches, the framers of the Constitution sought to provide a comprehensive system, but the separate powers were not intended to operate with absolute independence.

"While the Constitution diffuses power the better to secure liberty, it also contemplates that practice will integrate the dispersed powers into a workable Government. It enjoins upon its branches separateness but interdependence, autonomy but reciprocity. *Youngstown Sheet & Tube Co. v. Sawyer,* 343 U.S. 579, 635 (1952) (Jackson, J., concurring)."

To read the Art. II powers of the President as providing an absolute privilege as against a subpoena essential to enforcement of criminal statutes on no more than a generalized claim of the public interest in confidentiality of nonmilitary and nondiplomatic discussions would upset the constitutional balance of "a workable government" and gravely impair the role of the courts under Art. III.

C

Since we conclude that the legitimate needs of the judicial process may outweigh presidential privilege, it is necessary to resolve those competing interests in a manner that preserves the essential functions of each branch. The right and indeed the duty to resolve that question does not free the judiciary from according high respect to the representations made on behalf of the President. *United States* v. *Burr,* 25 Fed. Cas. 187, 190, 191-192 (No. 14,694) (1807).

The expectation of a president to the confidentiality of his conversations and correspondence, like the claim of confidentiality of judicial deliberations, for example, has all the values to which we accord deference for the privacy of all citizens and added to those values the necessity for protection of the public interest in candid, objective, and even blunt or harsh opinions in presidential decision-making. A president and those who assist him must be free to explore alternatives in the process of shaping policies and making decisions and to do so in a way many would be unwilling to express except privately. These are the considerations justifying a presumptive privilege for presidential communications. The privilege is fundamental to the operation of government and inextricably rooted in the separation of powers under the Constitution. In *Nixon* v. *Sirica,* 487 F. 2d 700 (1973), the Court of Appeals held that such presidential communications are "presumptively privileged," id., at 717, and this position is accepted by both parties in the present litigation.

We agree with Mr. Chief Justice Marshall's observation, therefore, that "in no case of this kind would a Court be required to proceed against the President as against an ordinary individual." *United States* v. *Burr,* 25 Fed. Cas. 187, 191 (No. 14,694) (CCD Va. 1807).

But this presumptive privilege must be considered in light of our historic commitment to the rule of law. This is nowhere more profoundly manifest than in our view that "the twofold aim [of criminal justice] is that guilt shall not escape or innocence suffer." *Berger* v. *United States,* 295 U.S. 18, 88 (1935). We have elected to employ an adversary system of criminal justice in which the parties contest all issues before a court of law. The need to develop all relevant facts in the adversary system is both fundamental and comprehensive. The ends of criminal justice would be defeated if judgments were to be founded on a partial or speculative presentation of the facts. The very integrity of the judicial system and public confidence in the system depend on full disclosure of all the facts, within the framework of the rules of evidence.

To ensure that justice is done, it is imperative to the function of courts that compulsory process be available for the production of evidence needed either by the prosecution or by the defense.

Only recently the Court restated the ancient proposition of law, albeit in the context of a grand jury inquiry rather than a trial,

" 'That the public . . . has a right to every man's evidence' except for those persons protected by a constitutional, common law, or statutory privilege, *United States* v. *Bryan,* 339 U.S., at 331 (1949); *Blackmer* v. *United States,* 284 U.S. 421, 438, *Branzburg* v. *United States,* 408 U.S. 665, 638 (1972)."

The privileges referred to by the Court are designed to protect weighty and legitimate competing interests. Thus, the Fifth Amendment to the Constitution provides that no man "shall be compelled in any criminal case to be a witness against himself."

And, generally, an attorney or a priest may not be required to disclose what has been revealed in professional confidence. These and other interests are recognized in law by privileges against forced disclosure, established in the Constitution, by statute, or at common law. Whatever their origins, these exceptions to the demand for every man's evidence are not lightly created nor expansively construed, for they are in derogation of the search for truth.

In this case the President challenges a subpoena served on him as a third party requiring the production of materials for use in a criminal prosecution on the claim that he has a privilege against disclosure of confidential communications. He does not place his claim of privilege on the ground they are military or diplomatic secrets. As to these areas of Art. II duties the courts have traditionally shown the utmost deference to presidential responsibilities. In *C. & S. Air Lines* v. *Waterman Steamship Corp.,* 333 U.S. 103, 111 (1948), dealing with presidential authority involving foreign policy considerations, the Court said:

"The President, both as commander-in-chief and as the nation's organ for foreign affairs, has available intelligence services whose reports are not and ought not to be published to the world. It would be intolerable that courts, without the relevant information, should review and perhaps nullify actions of the executive taken on information properly held secret." Id., at 111.

In *United States* v. *Reynolds,* 345 U.S. 1 (1952), dealing with a claimant's demand for evidence in a damage case against the government the Court said:

"It may be possible to satisfy the Court, from all the circumstances of the case, that there is a reasonable danger that compulsion of the evidence will expose military matters which, in the interest of national security, should not be divulged. When this is the case, the occasion for the privilege is appropriate, and the Court should not jeopardize the security which the privilege is meant to protect by insisting upon an examination of the evidence, even by the judge alone, in chambers."

No case of the Court, however, has extended this high degree of deference to a President's generalized interest in confidentiality. Nowhere in the Constitution as we have noted earlier, is there any explicit reference to a privilege of confidentiality, yet to the extent this interest relates to the effective discharge of a President's powers, it is constitutionally based.

The right to the production of all evidence at a criminal trial similarly has constitutional dimensions. The Sixth Amendment explicitly confers upon every defendant in a criminal trial the right "to be confronted with the witnesses against him" and "to have compulsory process for obtaining witnesses in his favor." Moreover, the Fifth Amendment also guarantees that no person shall be deprived of liberty without due process of law. It is the manifest duty of the courts to vindicate those guarantees and to accomplish that it is essential that all relevant and admissible evidence be produced.

In this case we must weigh the importance of the general privilege of confidentiality of presidential communications in performance of his responsibilities against the inroads of such a privilege on the fair administration of criminal justice. The interest in preserving confidentiality is weighty indeed and entitled to great respect. However we cannot conclude that advisors will be moved to temper the candor of their remarks by the infrequent occasions of disclosure because of the possibility that such conversations will be called for in the context of a criminal prosecution.

On the other hand, the allowance of the privilege to withhold evidence that is demonstrably relevant in a criminal trial would cut deeply into the guarantee of due process of law and gravely impair the basic function of the courts. A President's acknowledged need for confidentiality in the communications of his office is general in nature, whereas the constitutional need for production of relevant evidence in a criminal proceeding is specific and central to the fair adjudication of a particular criminal case in the administration of justice.

Without access to specific facts a criminal prosecution may be totally frustrated. The President's broad interest in confidentiality of communications will not be vitiated by disclosure of a limited number of conversations preliminarily shown to have some bearing on the pending criminal cases.

We conclude that when the ground for asserting privilege as to subpoenaed materials sought for use in a criminal trial is based only on the generalized interest in confidentiality, it cannot prevail over the fundamental demands of due process of law in the fair administration of criminal justice. The generalized assertion of privilege must yield to the demonstrated, specific need for evidence in a pending criminal trial.

D

We have earlier determined that the District Court did not err in authorizing the issuance of the subpoena. If a President concludes that compliance with a subpoena would be injurious to the public interest he may properly, as was done here, invoke a claim of privilege on the return of the subpoena. Upon receiving a claim of privilege from the chief executive, it became the further duty of the District Court to treat the subpoenaed material as presumptively privileged and to require the Special Prosecutor to demonstrate that the presidential material was "essential to the justice of the [pending criminal] case." *United States* v. *Burr,* supra, at 192. Here the District Court treated the material as presumptively privileged, proceeded to find that the Special Prosecutor had made a sufficient showing to rebut the presumption and ordered an in camera examination of the subpoenaed material.

On the basis of our examination of the record we are unable to conclude that the District Court erred in ordering the inspection. Accordingly we affirm the order of the District Court that subpoenaed materials be transmitted to that court. We now turn to the important question of the District Court's responsibilities in conducting the in camera examination of presidential materials or communications delivered under the compulsion of the subpoena duces tecum.

E

Enforcement of the subpoena duces tecum was stayed pending this Court's resolution of the issues raised by the petitions for certiorari. Those issues now having been disposed of, the matter of implementation will rest with the district court. "[T]he guard, furnished to [The President] to protect him from being harassed by vexations and unnecessary subpoenas, is to be looked for in the conduct of the [District] Court after the subpoenas have issued; not in any circumstances which is to precede their being issued." *United States* v. *Burr,* supra, at 34. Statements that meet the test of admissibility and relevance must be isolated; all other material must be excised. At this stage, the District Court is not limited to representations of the Special Prosecutor as to the evidence sought by the subpoena; the material will be available to the District Court. It is elementary that in camera inspection of evidence is always a procedure calling for scrupulous protection against any release or publication of material not found by the Court, at that stage, probably admissible in evidence and relevant to the issues of the trial for which it is sought. That being true of an ordinary situation, it is obvious that the District Court has a very heavy responsibility to see to it that presidential conversations which are either not relevant or not admissible, are accorded that high degree of respect due the President of the United States. Mr. Chief Justice Marshall sitting as a trial judge in the Burr case, supra, was extraordinarily careful to point out that:

" ... [I]n no case of this kind would a court be required to proceed against the President as against an ordinary individual." *United States* v. *Burr,* 25 Fed. Cases 187, 191 (No. 14,694).

Marshall's statement cannot be read to mean in any sense that a president is above the law, but relates to the singularly unique role under Art. II of a President's communications and activities related to the performance of duties under the Article. Moreover, a President's communications and activities encompass a vastly wider range of sensitive material than would be true of any "ordinary individual." It is therefore necessary in the public interest to afford presidential confidentiality the greatest protection consistent with the fair administration of justice. The need for confidentiality even as to idle conversations with associates in which casual reference might be made concerning political leaders within the country or foreign statesmen is too obvious to call for further treatment. We have no doubt that the District Judge will at all times accord to presidential records that high degree of deference suggested in *United States* v. *Burr,* supra, and will discharge his responsibility to see to it that until released to the Special Prosecutor no in camera material is revealed to anyone. This burden applies with even greater force to excised material; once the decision is made to excise, the material is restored to its privileged status and should be returned under seal to its lawful custodian.

Since the matter came before the Court during the pendency of a criminal prosecution, and on representations that time is of the essence, the mandate shall issue forthwith.

Affirmed.

Mr. Justice Rehnquist took no part in the consideration or decision of these cases.

Judging the Presidency

☐ The presidency, standing as it does at the focal point of our political system and drawing into its vortex the expectations of the American people about government performance, virtually guarantees that presidents will strive to excel in their performance in the White House. In particular, presidents who view the office as the center of political activity and the major source of policy initiative hope to be judged as among the great presidents of history. Before Watergate Richard Nixon, who viewed the presidency as an active-conservative force, hoped to take his place among the great presidents in American history. Presidential "greatness" was almost surely an aspiration of Jimmy Carter, as it is of Ronald Reagan.

Running for the position of great president may have an important effect upon performance in the White House. All candidates for greatness are well aware that historians will judge them on the basis of what they have accomplished, the decisions they have made, and the actions they have taken that exhibit leadership. Sometimes presidents feel that the appearance of leadership is as important as the real thing. Style may be substituted for substance. Above all, a president seeking greatness will always strive to aggrandize the presidency in word and deed. This means raising the level of popular expectation about what the president can do to meet and solve national problems, and at the same time demanding support for unilateral presidential actions that may circumvent the carefully constructed constitutional processes of separation of powers and checks and balances. Many "great" presidents have not paid enough attention to constitutional niceties nor respected the co-equal role in the governmental process of Congress and the Supreme Court. In the following selection Nelson Polsby argues that while presidential performance may be enhanced because of aspirations to achieve greatness, it is more common for such strivings to produce difficulties and reduce effective leadership.

42

Nelson W. Polsby

AGAINST PRESIDENTIAL GREATNESS

Until election day is past, candidates for president campaign among their fellow citizens with the simple end in view of being elected. Once they are inaugurated, however, presidents frequently yearn for an even higher office—a niche in the pantheon of "great" presidents. Membership in this exclusive society is, on the whole, not to be achieved through sheer popularity. Was there ever a more popular president than Dwight D. Eisenhower? Yet we all "know" he was not a "great" president, nor even a "near great" one.

How do we know this? Essentially I think the answer is: we know it because historians tell us so. In each generation, or possibly over a shorter span, a consensus arises among the authors of political and historical texts about how well various presidents met the alleged needs of their times. These opinions are in turn the distillate of writings of journalists and other leading opinion-makers who were contemporaries of the various presidents, filtered through the ideological predispositions of the current batch of history writers.

This means that running for great president is a chancy business, since the admissions committee is small and self-conscious, somewhat shifty-eyed, and possibly even harder to please than, let us say, the wonderful folks who guard the lily-white portals of the Chevy Chase Club. Some presidents are smart enough to take out a little insurance. Surely that was one extremely good reason for John Kennedy to invite Arthur Schlesinger, Jr., to join his White House staff and to encourage him to keep notes. Schlesinger's father, also a distinguished historian, was after all the author of two well-publicized surveys of historians—in 1949 and 1962—that ranked presidents for overall greatness.

Lyndon Johnson and, evidently, Richard Nixon, pursued somewhat different strategies. Apparently neither found a court historian wholly to his liking—though after an unsatisfactory experience with Eric Goldman, perhaps Johnson found Doris Kearns more tractable and useful for somewhat similar purposes. Both recent presidents caused their administrations to engage in what might be called over-documentation of their official activities. Johnson hauled tons of stuff down to his museum in Texas where a staff composed "his" memoirs at leisure. One assumes the Nixon tapes,

From Nelson W. Polsby, "Against Presidential Greatness." Reprinted from *Commentary,* January 1977, by permission; all rights reserved.

had they remained undiscovered, would have been employed to some such similar end.

In general, authorized ex-presidential memoirs are pretty awful to read, and nobody takes them seriously as history. At best they can be self-revelatory, and hence grist for the analyst's mill, but they are mostly stale, dull, self-serving documents. By common repute the best ex-presidential memoir ever written was that of Ulysses S. Grant. It was about his Civil War service, not his presidency, and so it is probably too much to expect that it would have saved Grant's presidency from the adverse judgment of "history."

We must conclude that writing memoirs may be a respectable way to fatten the exchequer of an ex-president, but that it is of negligible value in running for great president. Hiring, or charming, a court historian is a somewhat better investment, and especially if, by calculation or misfortune, the court historian's account appears after the death of the president in question. Reflective readers may find it slightly loony that presidents would want to control what people think of them after they have died, but the desire to leave an admiring posterity is surely not all that unusual among Americans. Moreover, among those Americans who land in the White House one can frequently discern an above-average desire to control the rest of the world, future generations, if possible, included.

What is it that historians like to see on the record when they make their ratings? It is impossible to speak with assurance for all future generations of historians. Fads and cross-currents make it difficult even to read the contemporary scene in a perfectly straightforward way. Nevertheless, over the near term, I think it is fair to say that the predominant sentiments of historians about presidents have been shaped by the experience of the New Deal, a longish episode in which presidential leadership was generally perceived to have saved the country not merely in the sense of restoring a modicum of prosperity to the economy, but more fundamentally rescuing the political system from profound malaise and instability.

The evidence that the New Deal actually did either of these things is, as a matter of fact, rather thin. But I shall not argue that attentiveness to evidence is a strong point of the gatekeepers of presidential greatness. They do, however, appear very much to admire presidents who adopt an activist, aggrandizing, constitutional posture toward presidential power. As the senior Schlesinger wrote: "Mediocre Presidents believed in negative government, in self-subordination to the legislative power." My view is that this reflects a New Deal-tutored preference for a particular sort of political structure rather than a statement of constitutional principles about which there can be no two opinions.

William Howard Taft, later a notably activist Chief Justice, put the classic case for the passive presidency when he wrote:

The true view of the executive function is, as I conceive it, that the President can exercise no power which cannot be fairly and reasonably traced to some specific grant of power or justly implied and included within such express grant as proper and necessary to its exercise. Such specific grant must be either in the federal Constitution or in an act of Congress passed in pursuance thereof. There is no undefined residuum of power which he can exercise because it seems to him to be in the public interest....

Poor Taft! That sort of argument got him low marks for presidential greatness, and especially since he evidently acted on his beliefs. Says James David Barber, author of the recent study of *The Presidential Character,* "...he was from the start a genial, agreeable, friendly, compliant person, much in need of affection...."

Whereas the senior Arthur Schlesinger's 1962 survey rated Taft an "average" sixteenth, between McKinley and Van Buren on the all-time hit parade, Theodore Roosevelt, Taft's friend and patron, comes in a "near great" seventh, just below Andrew Jackson on the list. Roosevelt's theory of the presidency undoubtedly helped him in the sweepstakes. He said:

I declined to adopt the view that what was imperatively necessary for the Nation could not be done by the President unless he could find some specific authorization to do it. My belief was that it was not only his right but his duty to do anything that the needs of the Nation demanded unless such action was forbidden by the Constitution or by the laws. Under this interpretation of executive power I did and caused to be done many things not previously done by the President and the heads of the departments. I did not usurp power, but I did greatly broaden the use of executive power. In other words, I acted for the public welfare, I acted for the common well-being of all our people, whenever and in whatever manner was necessary, unless prevented by direct constitutional or legislative prohibition....

The beginnings of this conflict in constitutional interpretation and practice have been traced back to the founding of the Republic. In those early years, Leonard White found:

The Federalists emphasized the necessity for power in government and for energy in the executive branch. The Republicans emphasized the liberties of the citizen and the primacy of representative assemblies. The latter accused their opponents of sympathy to monarchy and hostility to republican institutions.... Hamilton... insisted on the necessity for executive leadership of an otherwise drifting legislature; Jefferson thought the people's representatives would readily find their way if left alone to educate each other by free discussion and compromise.... By 1792 Jefferson thought the executive power had swallowed up the legislative branch; in 1798 Hamilton thought the legislative branch had so curtailed executive power that an able man could find no useful place in the government.

In the present era there is no real conflict at the theoretical level. The last sitting president even half-heartedly to argue against a self-aggrandizing presidency was Eisenhower. To be sure, a few voices—notably Eugene McCarthy's—could be heard proposing structural limitations on presidential powers in the dark days of Vietnam, but the resonance of his argument has faded quickly.

Even the remarkable shenanigans of the Nixon years seem only slightly to have diminished the enthusiasm of opinion leaders for strong presidents. Theodore Sorensen has gone so far as to advance the comforting view that we have nothing to fear from a strong president because Nixon was not in fact a strong president. In the light of such ingenuity one can only conclude that even today the mantle of presidential greatness is available only to those presidents who subscribe to a constitutional theory affording the widest scope for presidential action.

Does the historical record suggest any other helpful hints to the aspiring presidential great? Indeed it does. Crises are good for presidential reputations. Over the short run, as countless public-opinion surveys have shown, a small crisis in foreign affairs followed by a small show of presidential decisiveness is always good for a boost in the president's ratings. These ratings, moreover, are evidently indifferent to the efficacy of the presidential decision; triumph or fiasco, it makes little short-run difference.

Presidential greatness, however, is not decided over the short run. Yet the things that mass publics like today are frequently attractive to historians when painted on a larger canvas. Our three "greatest" presidents were reputedly Washington, Lincoln, and Franklin Roosevelt. The service of all three is intimately associated with three incidents in American history when the entire polity was engaged in total war.

Total war—that is, war engaging some major fraction of the gross national product in its prosecution—creates vastly different conditions of psychological mobilization than the nagging, running sores of limited wars, which, in time, invariably become extremely unpopular. Lyndon Johnson was one president who showed awareness of the irony implicit in the popularity risks of restricting, as well as pursuing, a limited war.

To those scrupulous souls who shrink from manufacturing a war of total mobilization in the service of their future reputations, is there anything left to be said? Surely lessons can be drawn equally from our least successful as well as our most successful presidents. Harding, Grant, and, one surmises, Nixon, lurk somewhere near the bottom of the heap. The smell of very large-scale scandal (not the small potatoes of the Truman era) attaches to the administration of each.

Assuming, for the sake of argument, that presidents want to run an administration untainted by scandal, can they do it? Considering the scale of operations of the United States government, the general absence of corruption in the conduct of its business is an admirable achievement. One doubts that if some illegal and greedy scheme were discovered somewhere in the vast labyrinth of the executive bureaucracies, the president would be held strictly to account. One doubts it unless one of three conditions obtains: the president, once appraised of the scandal, failed to act promptly to set things right, or, second, trusted friends and close associates of the president were involved, or, worse yet, the president himself were involved.

Only Richard Nixon, it will be observed, with his well-known penchant for presidential firsts, hits the jackpot on this list of no-no's. Neither Harding nor Grant escaped blame for the criminal acts of others close to them, but both are commonly held to have been themselves free of wrongdoing.

A final arena in which presidents achieve greatness is in the legislative record. Normally, what is required is a flurry of action, like FDR's hundred days, or Woodrow Wilson's first term. A kindly fate can sweep a new president into office along with a heavy congressional majority of his own party. With a little more luck there can be a feeling abroad in the land that something must be done. Whereupon, for a little while at least, the president and Congress together do something. Great strides in the enactment of public policy are commonly made in this fashion. And it is now settled custom that the president gets the long-run credit.

Thus many of the factors that go into presidential greatness appear to boil down to being in the right place at the right time. Much of the rest consists of having others put the right construction on ambiguous acts. Understandably, quite a lot of White House effort consequently goes into cultivating favorable notice for the incumbent. And here, at this point, a worm begins to emerge from the apple. The scenery, cosmetics, and sound effects that go into good public relations, unless strongly resisted, can begin to overwhelm more substantive concerns. The aspiration to presidential greatness, which under ideal circumstances can provide an incentive for good presidential behavior, under less than ideal circumstances leads to a great variety of difficulties. For fear of being found out and downgraded, there is the temptation to deny failure, to refuse to readjust course when a program or a proposal doesn't work out. There is the temptation to hoard credit rather than share it with the agencies that actually do the work and produce the results. There is the temptation to export responsibility away from the White House for the honest shortfalls of programs, thus transmitting to the government at large an expectation that loyalty upward will be rewarded with disloyalty down. There is the temptation to offer false hopes and to proclaim spurious accomplishments to the public at large.

As Henry Fairlie and others point out, a presidency that inflates expectations can rarely deliver. Worse yet, such a presidency gives up a precious opportunity to perform essential tasks of civic education, to help ordinary people see both the limitations and the possibilities of democratic government. George Reedy and others have observed that a presidency made of overblown rhetoric and excessive pretension can lose touch with the realities of politics, can waste its resources on trivialities, can fail, consequently, to grasp opportunities to govern well.

This, such as it is, is the case against the pursuit of presidential greatness. It is a case based upon a hope that there can be something approximating a restoration of democratic manners in the presidency. There are, however, good reasons to suppose that such a restoration will be hard to accomplish.

Part of the problem is structural. The complex demands of modern governmental decision-making require that presidents receive plenty of help. They need advice, information, criticism, feedback. They also need people to take care of the endless round of chores that fall to a president's lot: press secretaries, congressional liaison, managers of paper work and the traffic of visitors. Presidents also need to be able to trust the help they are getting, to be able to feel that what is being said and done in their behalf does genuinely place presidential interests first. From these requirements comes the need for an entourage of people whose careers in the limelight are solely the product of presidential favor. And from this entourage invariably comes what I suppose could be called the First Circle of presidential Moonies.

These are the people who "sleep a little better at night," as Jack Valenti so memorably said, because the charisma of their chief powers the machinery of government. During the day, we can be sure, they wear sunglasses to keep from being dazzled by "that special grace" (as members of John Kennedy's entourage frequently put it).

Anybody who doubts Kennedy's impact to this day on his successors should look again at the "great" debates of 1960 and 1976. For his encounter with Richard Nixon, Kennedy was stuffed like a Christmas goose with small discrete facts. In the course of the debates, out they came, two and three at a time. By all accounts, Kennedy "won" the 1960 encounter, albeit by nearly as small a margin as he won the election itself.

This evidently established a standard presidential-candidate debating style which the candidates of 1976 dutifully aped: neither risked the variety of facial expressions that did Nixon in, both spouted facts—not all of them true or relevant—rather than risk explaining their points of view.

It is probably foolish to expect some sort of civic enlightenment to come from debates. They are, rather, as near as our society gets to a trial by ordeal. The debater's central task is neither to inform nor to enlighten, but rather to survive, to avoid saying something that newspaper and television commentators will fix upon as an error or that will require an endless round of "clarifications" and become the "issue" of the following week or two. No wonder both Ford and Carter stood like tethered goats for the twenty-seven-minutes' silence that interrupted their first debate. To have been there at all no doubt temporarily exhausted their capacity to take risks.

The needs of White House staff to bask in reflected glory, plus risk-aversion in the face of the work habits of the mass media, are a potent combination tending to sustain a president's interest in president-worship. Moreover, the mystique of the presidency can be useful politically, vesting the visit in the rose garden, the invitation to breakfast, even a beseeching telephone call to Capitol Hill, with an added value that can spell the difference between political victory and defeat. And of course a president may simply grow fond of being coddled.

Added to these are the powerful factors in the world and in the American political system that have brought the president to the forefront: the increased importance of foreign affairs in the life of the nation, an area in which the president has no serious constitutional rival; the creation and proliferation of federal bureaucracies, all of them subject to presidential influence and supervision; the growth of the mass media with their focus upon the personalities at the center of our national politics, and the decline of political parties as a countervailing force. No wonder the entire political system seems president-preoccupied.

Against this formidable array of forces a plea for modesty of presidential aims, for prudence and moderation in the choice of instruments, for a scaling-down of promises and claims of achievement, seems unlikely to attract widespread agreement, least of all from presidents and their entourages bent on making their mark on History.

CHAPTER 7

The Bureaucracy

American bureaucracy today is an important fourth branch of the government. Too frequently the administrative branch is lumped under the heading of the "Executive" and is considered to be subordinate to the president. But the following selections will reveal that the bureaucracy is often autonomous, acting outside of the control of Congress, the president, and even the judiciary. This fact raises an important problem for our constitutional democracy: How can the bureaucracy be kept responsible if it does not fit into the constitutional framework that was designed to guarantee limited and responsible government?

Constitutional Background

While the Constitution carefully outlined the responsibilities and powers of the president, Congress, and to a lesser extent the Supreme Court, it did not mention the bureaucracy. The position of the bureaucracy in the separation of powers scheme developed by custom and statutory law, rather than by explicit constitutional provisions. The following selection makes it clear that, although the constitution did not provide for an administrative branch, it did have bearing upon the development of the bureaucracy. Perhaps the most important result of constitutional bureaucracy is that the administrative agencies have become pawns in the constant power struggle between the president and Congress.

43

Peter Woll

CONSTITUTIONAL DEMOCRACY AND BUREAUCRATIC POWER

The administrative branch today stands at the very center of our governmental process; it is the keystone of the structure. And administrative agencies exercise legislative and judicial as well as executive functions—a fact that is often overlooked . . .

How should we view American bureaucracy? Ultimately, the power of government comes to rest in the administrative branch. Agencies are given the responsibility of making concrete decisions carrying out vague policy initiated in Congress or by the president. The agencies can offer expert advice, closely attuned to the most interested pressure groups, and they often not only determine the policies that the legislature and executive recommend in the first place, but also decisively affect the policy-making process. Usually it is felt that the bureaucracy is politically "neutral," completely under the domination of the president, Congress, or the courts. We will see that this is not entirely the case, and that the president and Congress have only sporadic control over the administrative process.

The bureaucracy is a semi-autonomous branch of the government, often dominating Congress, exercising strong influence on the president, and only infrequently subject to review by the courts. If our constitutional democracy is to be fully analyzed, we must focus attention upon the administrative branch. What is the nature of public administration? How are administration and politics intertwined? How are administrative constituencies determined? What is the relationship between agencies and their constituencies? What role should the president assume in relation to the administrative branch? How far should Congress go in controlling agencies which in fact tend to dominate the legislative process? Should judicial review be expanded? What are the conditions of judicial review? How do administrative agencies perform judicial functions, and how do these activities affect the ability of courts to oversee their actions? These questions confront us with what is called the problem of administrative responsibility: that is, how can we control the activities of the administrative branch? In order to approach an understanding of this difficult problem, it is necessary to appreciate the nature of the administrative process and how it interacts with other branches of the government and with the

From Peter Woll, editor, *Public Administration and Policy,* pp. 1-14. Copyright © 1966 by Peter Woll. Reprinted by permission.

general public. It is also important to understand the nature of our constitutional system, and the political context within which agencies function.

We operate within the framework of a constitutional democracy. This means, first, that the government is to be limited by the separation of powers and Bill of Rights. Another component of the system, federalism, is designed in theory to provide states with a certain amount of authority when it is not implied at the national level. Our separation of powers, the system of checks and balances, and the federal system help to explain some of the differences between administrative organization here and in other countries. But the Constitution does not explicitly provide for the administrative branch, which has become a new fourth branch of government. This raises the question of how to control the bureaucracy when there are no clear constitutional limits upon it. The second aspect of our system, democracy, is of course implied in the Constitution itself, but has expanded greatly since it was adopted. We are confronted, very broadly speaking, first with the problem of constitutional limitation, and secondly with the problem of democratic participation in the activities of the bureaucracy. The bureaucracy must be accommodated within the framework of our system of constitutional democracy. This is the crux of the problem of administrative responsibility.

Even though the Constitution does not explicitly provide for the bureaucracy, it has had a profound impact upon the structure, functions, and general place that the bureaucracy occupies in government. The administrative process was incorporated into the constitutional system under the heading of "The Executive Branch." But the concept of "administration" at the time of the adoption of the Constitution was a very simple one, involving the "mere execution" of "executive details," to use the phrases of Hamilton in *The Federalist*. The idea, at that time, was simply that the president as Chief Executive would be able to control the Executive Branch in carrying out the mandates of Congress. In *Federalist 72,* after defining administration in this very narrow way, Hamilton stated:

> ... The persons, therefore, to whose immediate management the different administrative matters are committed ought to be considered as Assistants or Deputies of the Chief Magistrate, and on this account, they ought to derive their offices from his appointment, at least from his nomination, and ought to be subject to his superintendence.

It was clear that Hamilton felt the president would be responsible for administrative action as long as he was in office. This fact later turned up in what can be called the "presidential supremacy" school of thought, which held and still holds that the president is *constitutionally* responsible for the administrative branch, and that Congress should delegate to him all necessary authority for this purpose. Nevertheless, whatever the framers of the Constitution might have planned if they could have foreseen the nature of bureaucratic development, the fact is that the system they constructed in many ways supported bureaucratic organization and functions independent of the president. The role they assigned to Congress in relation to administration assured this result, as did the general position of Congress in the governmental system as a check or balance to the power of the president. Congress has a great deal of authority over the administrative process.

If we compare the powers of Congress and the president over the bureaucracy it becomes clear that they both have important constitutional responsibility. Congress retains primary control over the organization of the bureaucracy. It alone creates and destroys agencies, and determines whether they are to be located within the executive branch or outside it. This has enabled Congress to create a large number of *independent* agencies beyond presidential control. Congress has the authority to control appropriations and may thus exercise a great deal of power over the administrative arm, although increasingly the Bureau of the Budget and the president have the initial, and more often than not the final say over the budget. Congress also has the authority to define the jurisdiction of agencies. Finally, the Constitution gives to the legislature the power to interfere in high level presidential appointments, which must be "by and with the advice and consent of the Senate."

Congress may extend the sharing of the appointive power when it sets up new agencies. It may delegate to the president pervasive authority to control the bureaucracy. But one of the most important elements of the separation of powers is the electoral system, which gives to Congress a constituency which is different from and even conflicting with that of the president. This means that Congress often decides to set up agencies beyond presidential purview. Only rarely will it grant the president any kind of final authority to structure the bureaucracy. During World War II, on the basis of the War Powers Act, the president had the authority to reorganize the administrative branch. Today he has the same authority, provided that Congress does not veto presidential proposals within a certain time limit. In refusing to give the president permanent reorganization authority, Congress is jealously guarding one of its important prerogatives.

Turning to the constitutional authority of the president over the bureaucracy, it is somewhat puzzling to see that it gives him a relatively small role. He appoints certain officials by and with the advice and consent of the Senate. He has directive power over agencies that are placed within his jurisdiction by Congress. His control over patronage, once so important, has diminished sharply under the merit system. The president is Commander-in-Chief of all military forces, which puts him in a controlling position over the Defense Department and agencies involved in military matters. In the area of international relations, the president is by constitutional authority the "Chief Diplomat," to use [presidential scholar Clinton] Rossiter's phrase.

This means that he appoints Ambassadors (by and with the advice and consent of the Senate), and generally directs national activities in the international arena—a crucially important executive function. But regardless of the apparent intentions of some of the framers of the Constitution as expressed by Hamilton in *The Federalist,* and in spite of the predominance of the presidency in military and foreign affairs, the fact remains that we seek in vain for explicit constitutional authorization for the president to be "Chief Administrator."

This is not to say that the president does not have an important responsibility to act as chief of the bureaucracy, merely that there is no constitutional mandate for this. As our system evolved, the president was given more and more responsibility until he became, in practice, Chief Administrator. At the same time the constitutional system has often impeded progress in this direction. The president's Committee on Administrative Management in 1937, and later the Hoover Commissions of 1949 and 1955, called upon Congress to initiate a series of reforms increasing presidential authority over the administrative branch. It was felt that this was necessary to make democracy work. The president is the only official elected nationally, and if the administration is to be held democratically accountable, he alone can stand as its representative. But meaningful control from the White House requires that the president have a comprehensive program which encompasses the activities of the bureaucracy. He must be informed as to what they are doing, and be able to control them. He must understand the complex responsibilities of the bureaucracy. Moreover, he must be able to call on sufficient political support to balance the support which the agencies draw from private clientele groups and congressional committees. This has frequently proven a difficult and often impossible task for the president. He may have the *authority* to control the bureaucracy in many areas, but not enough power.

On the basis of the Constitution, Congress feels it quite proper that when it delegates legislative authority to administrative agencies it can relatively often place these groups outside the control of the president. For example, in the case of the Interstate Commerce Commission . . . Congress has delegated final authority to that agency to control railroad mergers and other aspects of transportation activity, without giving the president the right to veto. The president may feel that a particular merger is undesirable because it is in violation of the antitrust laws, but the Interstate Commerce Commission is likely to feel differently. In such a situation, the president can do nothing because he does not have the *legal authority* to take any action. If he could muster enough political support to exercise influence over the ICC, he would be able to control it, but the absence of legal authority is an important factor in such cases and diminishes presidential power. Moreover, the ICC draws strong support from the railroad industry, which has been able to counterbalance the political support possessed by the president and other groups that have wished to control it. Analogous situations exist with respect to other regulatory agencies.

Besides the problem of congressional and presidential control over the bureaucracy, there is the question of judicial review of administrative decisions. The rule of law is a central element in our Constitution. The rule of law means that decisions judicial in nature should be handled by common law courts, because of their expertise in rendering due process of law. When administrative agencies engage in adjudication their decisions should be subject to judicial review—at least, they should if one supports the idea of the supremacy of law. Judicial decisions are supposed to be rendered on an independent and impartial basis, through the use of tested procedures, in order to arrive at the accurate determination of the truth. Administrative adjudication should not be subject to presidential or congressional control, which would mean political determination of decisions that should be rendered in an objective manner. The idea of the rule of law, derived from the common law and adopted within the framework of our constitutional system, in theory limits legislative and executive control over the bureaucracy.

The nature of our constitutional system poses very serious difficulties to the development of a system of administrative responsibility. The Constitution postulates that the functions of government must be separated into different branches with differing constituencies and separate authority. The idea is that the departments should oppose each other, thereby preventing the arbitrary exercise of political power. Any combination of functions was considered to lead inevitably to arbitrary government. This is a debatable point, but the result of the Constitution is quite clear. The administrative process, on the other hand, often combines various functions of government in the same hands. Attempts are made, of course, to separate those who exercise the judicial functions from those in the prosecuting arms of the agencies. But the fact remains that there is a far greater combination of functions in the administrative process than can be accommodated by strict adherence to the Constitution.

It has often been proposed, as a means of alleviating what may be considered the bad effects of combined powers in administrative agencies, to draw a line of control from the original branches of the government to those parts of the bureaucracy exercising similar functions. Congress would control the legislative activities of the agencies, the president the executive aspects, and the courts the judicial functions. This would maintain the symmetry of the constitutional system. But this solution is not feasible, because other parts of the Constitution, giving different authority to these three branches, make symmetrical control of this kind almost impossible. The three branches of the government are not willing to give up whatever powers they may have over administrative agencies. For example, Congress is not willing to give the President complete control over all executive functions, nor to give the courts the authority to review all the decisions of the agencies. At present, judicial review takes place only if Congress authorizes it, except in those rare instances where constitutional issues are involved.

Another aspect of the problem of control is reflected in the apparent paradox that the three branches do not always use to the fullest extent their authority to regulate the bureaucracy, even though they wish to retain their power to do so. The courts, for example, have exercised considerable self-restraint in their review of administrative decisions. They are not willing to use all their power over the bureaucracy. Similarly, both Congress and the President will often limit their dealings with the administrative branch for political and practical reasons.

In the final analysis, we are left with a bureaucratic system that has been fragmented by the Constitution, and in which administrative discretion is inevitable. The bureaucracy reflects the general fragmentation of our political system. It is often the battleground for the three branches of government, and for outside pressure groups which seek to control it for their own purposes.

The Political Roots and Consequences of Bureaucracy

☐   With the exception of those executive departments that all governments need, such as State, Treasury, and Defense, *private* sector political demands have led to the creation of American bureaucracy. In response to those demands Congress has over the years created more and more executive departments and agencies to solve economic, political, and social problems. It is important to realize that the bureaucracy is not, as many of its critics have suggested, a conspiracy by government officials to increase their power. The following selection traces the rise of the administrative state and particularly notes how political pluralism has affected the character of the bureaucracy by dividing it into clientele sectors.

44

James Q. Wilson

THE RISE OF THE
BUREAUCRATIC STATE

During its first 150 years, the American republic was not thought to have "bureaucracy," and thus it would have been meaningless to refer to the "problems" of a "bureaucratic state." There were, of course, appointed civilian officials: Though only about 3,000 at the end of the Federalist period, there were about 95,000 by the time Grover Cleveland assumed office in 1881, and nearly half a million by 1925. Some aspects of these numerous officials were regarded as problems—notably, the standards by which they were appointed and the political loyalties to which they were held—but these were thought to be matters of proper character and good management. The great political and constitutional struggles were not over the power of the administrative apparatus, but over the power of the President, of Congress, and of the states.

The Founding Fathers had little to say about the nature or function of the executive branch of the new government. The Constitution is virtually silent on the subject and the debates in the Constitutional Convention are almost devoid of reference to an administrative apparatus. This reflected no lack of concern about the matter, however. Indeed, it was in part because of the Founders' depressing experience with chaotic and inefficient management under the Continental Congress and the Articles of Confederation that they had assembled in Philadelphia. Management by committees composed of part-time amateurs had cost the colonies dearly in the War of Independence and few, if any, of the Founders wished to return to that system. The argument was only over how the heads of the necessary departments of government were to be selected, and whether these heads should be wholly subordinate to the President or whether instead they should form some sort of council that would advise the President and perhaps share in his authority. In the end, the Founders left it up to Congress to decide the matter.

There was no dispute in Congress that there should be executive departments, headed by single appointed officials, and, of course, the Constitution specified that these would be appointed by the President with the advice and consent of the Senate. The only issue was how such officials might be removed. After prolonged debate and by the narrowest of majorities, Congress agreed that the President should have the sole right of removal,

Reprinted with permission of the author from *The Public Interest,* No. 41 (Fall 1975). © 1975 by National Affairs, Inc.

thus confirming that the infant administrative system would be wholly subordinate—in law at least—to the President. Had not Vice-President John Adams, presiding over a Senate equally divided on the issue, cast the deciding vote in favor of presidential removal, the administrative departments might conceivably have become legal dependencies of the legislature, with incalculable consequences for the development of the embryonic government.

THE "BUREAUCRACY PROBLEM"

The original departments were small and had limited duties. The State Department, the first to be created, had but nine employees in addition to the Secretary. The War Department did not reach 80 civilian employees until 1801; it commanded only a few thousand soldiers. Only the Treasury Department had substantial powers—it collected taxes, managed the public debt, ran the national bank, conducted land surveys, and purchased military supplies. Because of this, Congress gave the closest scrutiny to its structure and its activities.

The number of administrative agencies and employees grew slowly but steadily during the 19th and early 20th centuries and then increased explosively on the occasion of World War I, the Depression, and World War II. It is difficult to say at what point in this process the administrative system became a distinct locus of power or an independent source of political initiatives and problems. What is clear is that the emphasis on the sheer *size* of the administrative establishment—conventional in many treatments of the subject—is misleading.

The government can spend vast sums of money—wisely or unwisely—without creating that set of conditions we ordinarily associate with the bureaucratic state. For example, there could be massive transfer payments made under government auspices from person to person or from state to state, all managed by a comparatively small staff of officials and a few large computers. In 1971, the federal government paid out $54 billion under various social insurance programs, yet the Social Security Administration employs only 73,000 persons, many of whom perform purely routine jobs.

And though it may be harder to believe, the government could in principle employ an army of civilian personnel without giving rise to those organizational patterns that we call bureaucratic. Suppose, for instance, that we as a nation should decide to have in the public schools at least one teacher for every two students. This would require a vast increase in the number of teachers and schoolrooms, but almost all of the persons added would be performing more or less identical tasks, and they could be organized into very small units (e.g., neighborhood schools). Though there would be significant overhead costs, most citizens would not be aware of any increase in the "bureaucratic" aspects of education—indeed, owing to the much greater time each teacher would have to devote to each pupil and his or her parents, the citizenry might well conclude that there actually had been a substantial reduction in the amount of "bureaucracy."

To the reader predisposed to believe that we have a "bureaucracy problem," these hypothetical cases may seem farfetched. Max Weber, after all, warned us that in capitalist and socialist societies alike, bureaucracy was likely to acquire an "overtowering" power position. Conservatives have always feared bureaucracy, save perhaps the police. Humane socialists have frequently been embarrassed by their inability to reconcile a desire for public control of the economy with the suspicion that a public bureaucracy may be as immune to democratic control as a private one. Liberals have equivocated, either dismissing any concern for bureaucracy as reactionary quibbling about social progress or embracing that concern when obviously nonreactionary persons (welfare recipients, for example) express a view toward the Department of Health and Human Services indistinguishable from the view businessmen take of the Internal Revenue Service.

POLITICAL AUTHORITY

There are at least three ways in which political power may be gathered undesirably into bureaucratic hands: by the growth of an administrative apparatus so large as to be immune from popular control, by placing power over a governmental bureaucracy of any size in private rather than public hands, or by vesting discretionary authority in the hands of a public agency so that the exercise of that power is not responsive to the public good. These are not the only problems that arise because of bureaucratic organization. From the point of view of their members, bureaucracies are sometimes uncaring, ponderous, or unfair; from the point of view of their political superiors, they are sometimes unimaginative or inefficient; from the point of view of their clients, they are sometimes slow or unjust. No single account can possibly treat of all that is problematic in bureaucracy; even the part I discuss here—the extent to which political authority has been transferred undesirably to an unaccountable administrative realm—is itself too large for a single essay. But it is, if not the most important problem, then surely the one that would most have troubled our Revolutionary leaders, especially those that went on to produce the Constitution. It was, after all, the question of power that chiefly concerned them, both in redefining our relationship with England and in finding a new basis for political authority in the Colonies.

To some, following in the tradition of [Max] Weber, bureaucracy is the inevitable consequence and perhaps necessary concomitant of modernity. A money economy, the division of labor, and the evolution of legal-rational norms to justify organizational authority require the efficient adaptation of means to ends and a high degree of predictability in the behavior of rulers.

To this, Georg Simmel added the view that organizations tend to acquire the characteristics of those institutions with which they are in conflict, so that as government becomes more bureaucratic, private organizations—political parties, trade unions, voluntary associations—will have an additional reason to become bureaucratic as well.

By viewing bureaucracy as an inevitable (or, as some would put it, "functional") aspect of society, we find ourselves attracted to theories that explain the growth of bureaucracy in terms of some inner dynamic to which all agencies respond and which makes all barely governable and scarcely tolerable. Bureaucracies grow, we are told, because of Parkinson's Law: Work and personnel expand to consume the available resources. Bureaucracies behave, we believe, in accord with various other maxims, such as the Peter Principle: In hierarchical organizations, personnel are promoted up to that point at which their incompetence becomes manifest—hence, all important positions are held by incompetents. More elegant, if not essentially different, theories have been propounded by scholars. The tendency of all bureaus to expand is explained by William A. Niskanen by the assumption, derived from the theory of the firm, that "bureaucrats maximize the total budget of their bureau during their tenure"—hence, "all bureaus are too large." What keeps them from being not merely too large but all-consuming is that fact that a bureau must deliver to some degree on its promised output, and if it consistently underdelivers, its budget will be cut by unhappy legislators. But since measuring the output of a bureau is often difficult—indeed, even *conceptualizing* the output of the State Department is mind-boggling—the bureau has a great deal of freedom within which to seek the largest possible budget.

Such theories, both the popular and the scholarly, assign little importance to the nature of the tasks an agency performs, the constitutional framework in which it is embedded, or the preferences and attitudes of citizens and legislators. Our approach will be quite different: Different agencies will be examined in historical perspective to discover the kinds of problems—if any, to which their operation give rise, and how those problems were affected—perhaps determined—by the tasks which they were assigned, the political system in which they operated, and the preferences they were required to consult. What follows will be far from a systematic treatment of such matters, and even farther from a rigorous testing of any theory of bureaucratization. Our knowledge of agency history and behavior is too sketchy to permit that.

BUREAUCRACY AND SIZE

During the first half of the 19th century, the growth in the size of the federal bureaucracy can be explained, not by the assumption of new tasks by the government or by the imperialistic designs of the managers of existing tasks, but by the addition to existing bureaus of personnel performing essentially routine, repetitive tasks for which the public demand was great and unavoidable. The principal problem facing a bureaucracy thus enlarged was how best to coordinate its activities toward given and noncontroversial ends.

The increase in the size of the executive branch of the federal government at this time was almost entirely the result of the increase in the size of the Post Office. From 1816 to 1861, federal civilian employment in the executive branch increased nearly eightfold (from 4,837 to 36,672), but 86 percent of this growth was the result of additions to the postal service. The Post Office Department was expanding as population and commerce expanded. By 1869 there were 27,000 post offices scattered around the nation; by 1901, nearly 77,000. In New York alone, by 1894 there were nearly 3,000 postal employees, the same number required to run the entire federal government at the beginning of that century.

The organizational shape of the Post Office was more or less fixed in the administration of Andrew Jackson. The Postmaster General, almost always appointed because of his partisan position, was aided by three (later four) assistant postmaster generals dealing with appointments, mail-carrying contracts, operations, and finance. There is no reason in theory why such an organization could not deliver the mails efficiently and honestly: The task is routine, its performance is measurable, and its value is monitored by millions of customers. Yet the Post Office, from the earliest years of the 19th century, was an organization marred by inefficiency and corruption. The reason is often thought to be found in the making of political appointments to the Post Office. "Political hacks," so the theory goes, would inevitably combine dishonesty and incompetence to the disservice of the nation; thus, by cleansing the department of such persons these difficulties could be avoided. Indeed, some have argued that it was the advent of the "spoils system" under Jackson that contributed to the later inefficiencies of the public bureaucracy.

The opposite is more nearly the case. The Jacksonians did not seek to make the administrative apparatus a mere tool of the Democratic party advantage, but to purify that apparatus not only of what they took to be Federalist subversion but also of personal decadence. The government was becoming not just large, but lax. Integrity and diligence were absent, not merely from government, but from social institutions generally. The Jacksonians were in many cases concerned about the decline in what the Founders had called "republican virtue," but what their successors were more likely to call simplicity and decency. As Matthew Crenson has recently observed in his book *The Federal Machine,* Jacksonian administrators wanted to "guarantee the good behavior of civil servants" as well as to cope with bigness, and to do this they sought both to place their own followers in office and—what is more important—to create a system of depersonalized, specialized bureaucratic rule. Far from being the enemies of bureaucracy, the Jacksonians were among its principal architects.

Impersonal administrative systems, like the spoils system, were "devices for strengthening the government's authority over its own civil servants"; these bureaucratic methods were, in turn, intended to "compensate for a decline in the disciplinary power of social institutions" such as the community, the professions, and business. If public servants, like men generally in a rapidly growing and diversifying society, could no longer be relied upon "to have a delicate regard for their reputations," accurate bookkeeping, close inspections, and regularized procedures would accomplish what character could not.

Amos Kendall, Postmaster General under President Jackson, set about to achieve this goal with a remarkable series of administrative innovations. To prevent corruption, Kendall embarked on two contradictory courses of action: He sought to bring every detail of the department's affairs under his personal scrutiny and he began to reduce and divide the authority on which that scrutiny depended. Virtually every important document and many unimportant ones had to be signed by Kendall himself. At the same time, he gave to the Treasury Department the power to audit his accounts and obtained from Congress a law requiring that the revenues of the department be paid into the Treasury rather than retained by the Post Office. The duties of his subordinates were carefully defined and arranged so that the authority of one assistant would tend to check that of another. What was installed was not simply a specialized management system, but a concept of the administrative separation of powers.

Few subsequent postmasters were of Kendall's ability. The result was predictable. Endless details flowed to Washington for decision, but no one in Washington other than the Postmaster General had the authority to decide. Meanwhile, the size of the postal establishment grew by leaps and bounds. Quickly the department began to operate on the basis of habit and local custom: Since everybody reported to Washington, in effect no one did. As Leonard D. White was later to remark, "the system could work only because it was a vast, repetitive, fixed, and generally routine operation." John Wanamaker, an able businessman who became Postmaster General under President Cleveland, proposed decentralizing the department under 26 regional supervisors. But Wanamaker's own assistants in Washington were unenthusiastic about such a diminution in their authority and, in any event, Congress steadfastly refused to endorse decentralization.

Civil service reform was not strongly resisted in the Post Office; from 1883 on, the number of its employees covered by the merit system expanded. Big-city postmasters were often delighted to be relieved of the burden of dealing with hundreds of place-seekers. Employees welcomed the job protection that civil service provided. In time, the merit system came to govern Post Office personnel almost completely, yet the problems of the department became, if anything, worse. By the mid-20th century, slow and inadequate service, an inability technologically to cope with the mounting flood of mail, and the inequities of its pricing system became all too evident. The problem with the Post Office, however, was not omnipotence but impotence. It was a government monopoly. Being a monopoly, it had little incentive to find the most efficient means to manage its services; being a government monopoly, it was not free to adopt such means even when found—communities, Congressmen, and special-interest groups saw to that.

THE MILITARY ESTABLISHMENT

Not all large bureaucracies grow in response to demands for service. The Department of Defense, since 1941 the largest employer of federal civilian officials, has become, as the governmental keystone of the "military-industrial complex," the very archetype of an administrative entity that is thought to be so vast and so well-entrenched that it can virtually ignore the political branches of government, growing and even acting on the basis of its own inner imperatives. In fact, until recently the military services were a major economic and political force only during wartime. In the late 18th and early 19th centuries, America was a neutral nation with only a tiny standing army. During the Civil War, over two million men served on the Union side alone and the War Department expanded enormously, but demobilization after the war was virtually complete, except for a small Indian-fighting force. Its peacetime authorized strength was only 25,000 enlisted men and 2,161 officers, and its actual strength for the rest of the century was often less. Congress authorized the purchase and installation of over 2,000 coastal defense guns, but barely 6 percent of these were put in place.

When war with Spain broke out, the army was almost totally unprepared. Over 300,000 men eventually served in that brief conflict, and though almost all were again demobilized, the War Department under Elihu Root was reorganized and put on a more professional basis with a greater capacity for unified central control. Since the United States had become an imperial power with important possessions in the Caribbean and the Far East, the need for a larger military establishment was clear; even so, the average size of the army until World War I was only about 250,000.

The First World War again witnessed a vast mobilization—nearly five million men in all—and again an almost complete demobilization after the war. The Second World War involved over 16 million military personnel. The demobilization that followed was less complete than after previous engagements owing to the development of the Cold War, but it was substantial nonetheless—the Army fell in size from over eight million men to only half a million. Military spending declined from $91 billion in the first quarter of 1945 to only slightly more than $10 billion in the second quarter of 1947. For the next three years it remained relatively flat. It began to rise rapidly in 1950, partly to finance our involvement in the Korean conflict and partly to begin the construction of a military force that could counterbalance the Soviet Union, especially in Europe.

In sum, from the Revolutionary War to 1950, a period of over 170 years, the size and deployment of the military establishment in this country was governed entirely by decisions made by political leaders on political grounds. The military did not expand autonomously, a large standing army did not find wars to fight, and its officers did not play a significant role except in wartime and occasionally as presidential candidates. No bureaucracy proved easier to control, at least insofar as its size and purposes were concerned.

A "MILITARY-INDUSTRIAL COMPLEX"?

The argument for the existence of an autonomous, bureaucratically led military-industrial complex is supported primarily by events since 1950. Not only has the United States assumed during this period worldwide commitments that necessitate a larger military establishment, but the advent of new, high-technology weapons has created a vast industrial machine with an interest in sustaining a high level of military expenditures, especially on weapons research, development, and acquisition. This machine, so the argument goes, is allied with the Pentagon in ways that dominate the political officials nominally in charge of the armed forces. There is some truth in all this. We have become a world military force, though that decision was made by elected officials in 1949–1950 and not dictated by a (then nonexistent) military-industrial complex. High-cost, high-technology weapons have become important and a number of industrial concerns will prosper or perish depending on how contracts for those weapons are let. The development and purchase of weapons is sometimes made in a wasteful, even irrational, manner. And the allocation of funds among the several armed services is often dictated as much by inter-service rivalry as by strategic or political decisions.

But despite all this, the military has not been able to sustain itself at its preferred size, to keep its strength constant or growing, or to retain for its use a fixed or growing portion of the Gross National Product. Even during the last two decades, the period of greatest military prominence, the size of the Army has varied enormously—from over 200 maneuver battalions in 1955, to 174 in 1965, rising to 217 at the peak of the Vietnam action in 1969, and then declining rapidly to 138 in 1972. Even military hardware, presumably of greater interest to the industrial side of the military-industrial complex, has often declined in quantity, even though per unit price has risen. The Navy had over 1,000 ships in 1955; it has only 700 today [in 1975]. The Air Force had nearly 24,000 aircraft in 1955; it has fewer than

14,000 today. This is not to say the combat strength of the military is substantially less than it once was, and there is greater firepower now at the disposal of each military unit, and there are various missile systems now in place, for which no earlier counterparts existed. But the total budget, and thus the total force level, of the military has been decided primarily by the President and not in any serious sense forced upon him by subordinates. (For example, President Truman decided to allocate one third of the federal budget to defense, President Eisenhower chose to spend no more than 10 percent of the Gross National Product on it, and President Kennedy strongly supported Robert McNamara's radical and controversial budget revisions.) Even a matter of as great significance as the size of the total military budget for research and development has proved remarkably resistant to inflationary trends: In constant dollars, since 1964 that appropriation has been relatively steady (in 1972 dollars, about $30 billion a year).

The principal source of growth in the military budget in recent years has arisen from Congressionally determined pay provisions. The legislature has voted for more or less automatic pay increases for military personnel with the result that the military budget has gone up even when the number of personnel in the military establishment has gone down.

The bureaucratic problems associated with the military establishment arise mostly from its internal management and are functions of its complexity, the uncertainty surrounding its future deployment, conflicts among its constituent services over mission and role, and the need to purchase expensive equipment without the benefit of a market economy that can control costs. Complexity, uncertainty, rivalry, and monopsony are inherent (and frustrating) aspects of the military as a bureaucracy, but they are very different problems from those typically associated with the phrase "the military-industrial complex." The size and budget of the military are matters wholly within the power of civilian authorities to decide—indeed, the military budget contains the largest discretionary items in the entire federal budget.

If the Founding Fathers were to return to review their handiwork, they would no doubt be staggered by the size of both the Post Office and the Defense Department, and in the case of the latter, be worried about the implications of our commitments to various foreign powers. They surely would be amazed at the technological accomplishments but depressed by the cost and inefficiency of both departments; but they would not, I suspect, think that our Constitutional arrangements for managing these enterprises have proved defective or that there had occurred, as a result of the creation of these vast bureaus, an important shift in the locus of political authority.

They would observe that there have continued to operate strong localistic pressures in both systems—offices are operated, often uneconomically, in some small communities because small communities have influential Congressmen; military bases are maintained in many states because states have powerful Senators. But a national government with localistic biases is precisely the system they believed they had designed in 1787, and though they surely could not have then imagined the costs of it, they just as surely would have said (Hamilton possibly excepted) that these costs were the defects of the system's virtues.

BUREAUCRACY AND CLIENTELISM

After 1861, the growth in the federal administrative system could no longer be explained primarily by an expansion of the postal service and other traditional bureaus. Though these continued to expand, new departments were added that reflected a new (or at least greater) emphasis on the enlargement of the scope of government. Between 1861 and 1901, over 200,000 civilian employees were added to the federal service, only 52 percent of whom were postal workers. Some of these, of course, staffed a larger military and naval establishment stimulated by the Civil War and the Spanish-American War. By 1901 there were over 44,000 civilian defense employees, mostly workers in government-owned arsenals and shipyards. But even those could account for less than one fourth of the increase in employment during the preceding 40 years.

What was striking about the period after 1861 was that the government began to give formal, bureaucratic recognition to the emergence of distinctive interest in a diversifying economy. As Richard L. Schott has written, "whereas earlier federal departments had been formed around specialized governmental functions (foreign affairs, war, finance, and the like), the new departments of this period—Agriculture, Labor, and Commerce—were devoted to the interests and aspirations of particular economic groups."

The original purpose behind these clientele-oriented departments was neither to subsidize nor to regulate, but to promote, chiefly by gathering and publishing statistics and (especially in the case of agriculture) by research. The formation of the Department of Agriculture in 1862 was to become a model, for better or worse, for later political campaigns for government recognition. A private association representing an interest—in this case the United States Agricultural Society—was formed. It made every President from Fillmore to Lincoln an honorary member, it enrolled key Congressmen, and it began to lobby for a new department. The precedent was followed by labor groups, especially the Knights of Labor, to secure creation in 1888 of a Department of Labor. It was broadened in 1903 to be a Department of Commerce and Labor, the parts were separated and the two departments we now know were formed.

There was an early 19th-century precedent for the creation of these client-serving departments: the Pension Office, then in the Department of the Interior. Begun in 1833 and regularized in 1849, the Office became one of the largest bureaus of the government in the aftermath of the Civil War, as hundreds of thousands of Union Army veterans were made eligible for pensions if they had incurred a permanent disability or injury while on military duty; dependent widows were also eligible if their husbands had died in service or of service-connected injuries. The Grand Army of the Republic (GAR), the leading veterans' organization, was quick to exert pressure for more generous pension laws and for more liberal administration of such laws as already existed. In 1879 Congressmen, noting the number of ex-servicemen living (and voting) in their states, made veterans eligible for pensions retroactively to the date of their discharge from the service, thus enabling thousands who had been late in filing applications to be rewarded for their dilatoriness. In 1890 the law was changed again to make it unnecessary to have been injured in the service—all that was necessary was to have served and then to have acquired a permanent disability by any means other than through "their own vicious habits." And whenever cases not qualifying under existing law came to the attention of Congress, it promptly passed a special act making those persons eligible by name.

So far as is known, the Pension Office was remarkably free of corruption in the administration of this windfall—and why not, since anything an administrator might deny, a legislator was only too pleased to grant. By 1891 the Commissioner of Pensions observed that this was "the largest executive bureau in the world." There were over 6,000 officials supplemented by thousands of local physicians paid on a fee basis. In 1900 alone, the Office had to process 477,000 cases. Fraud was rampant as thousands of persons brought false or exaggerated claims; as Leonard D. White was later to write, "pensioners and their attorneys seemed to have been engaged in a gigantic conspiracy to defraud their own government." Though the Office struggled to be honest, Congress was indifferent—or more accurately, complaisant: The GAR was a powerful electoral force and it was ably and lucratively assisted by thousands of private pension attorneys. The pattern of bureaucratic clientelism was set in a way later to become a familiar feature of the governmental landscape—a subsidy was initially provided, because it was either popular or unnoticed, to a group that was powerfully benefited and had few or disorganized opponents; the beneficiaries were organized to supervise the administration and ensure the funding of the program; the law authorizing the program, first passed because it seemed the right thing to do, was left intact or even expanded because politically it became the only thing to do. A benefit once bestowed cannot easily be withdrawn.

PUBLIC POWER AND PRIVATE INTERESTS

It was at the state level, however, that client-oriented bureaucracies prolif-erated in the 19th century. Chief among these were the occupational licensing agencies. At the time of Independence, professions and occupa-tions either could be freely entered (in which case the consumer had to judge the quality of service for himself) or entry was informally controlled by the existing members of the profession or occupation by personal tutelage and the management of reputations. The later part of the 19th century, however, witnessed the increased use of law and bureaucracy to control entry into a line of work. The state courts generally allowed this on the grounds that it was a proper exercise of the "police power" of the state, but as Morton Keller has observed, "when state courts approved the licensing of barbers and blacksmiths, but not of horseshoers, it was evident that the principles governing certification were—to put it charitably—elusive ones." By 1952, there were more than 75 different occupations in the United States for which one needed a license to practice, and the awarding of these licenses was typically in the hands of persons already in the occupation, who could act under color of law. These licensing boards—for plumbers, dry cleaners, beauticians, attorneys, undertakers, and the like—frequently have been criticized as particularly flagrant examples of the excesses of a bureaucratic state. But the problems they create—of restricted entry, higher prices, and lengthy and complex initiation procedures—are not primarily the result of some bureaucratic pathology but of the posses-sion of public power by persons who use it for private purposes. Or more accurately, they are the result of using public power in ways that benefited those in the profession in the sincere but unsubstantiated conviction that doing so would benefit the public generally.

The New Deal was perhaps the high water mark of at least the theory of bureaucratic clientelism. Not only did various sectors of society, notably agriculture, begin receiving massive subsidies, but the government proposed, through the National Industrial Recovery Act (NRA), to cloak with public power a vast number of industrial groupings and trade associations so that they might control production and prices in ways that would end the depression. The NRA's Blue Eagle fell before the Supreme Court—the wholesale delegation of public power to private interests was declared unconstitutional. But the piecemeal delegation was not, as the continued growth of specialized promotional agencies attests. The Civil Aeronautics Board, for example, erroneously thought to be exclusively a regulatory agency, was formed in 1938 "to promote" as well as regulate civil aviation and it has done so by restricting entry and maintaining above-market rate fares.

Agriculture, of course, provides the leading case of clientelism. Theodore J. Lowi finds "at least 10 separate, autonomous, local self-governing systems" located in or closely associated with the Department of Agriculture that control to some significant degree the flow of billions of dollars in expenditures and loans. Local committees of farmers, private farm organizations, agency heads, and committee chairmen in Congress dominate policy-making in this area—not, perhaps, to the exclusion of the concerns of other publics, but certainly in ways not powerfully constrained by them.

"COOPERATIVE FEDERALISM"

The growing edge of client-oriented bureaucracy can be found, however, not in government relations with private groups, but in the relations among governmental units. In dollar volume, the chief clients of federal domestic expenditures are state and local government agencies. To some degree, federal involvement in local affairs by the cooperative funding or management of local enterprises has always existed. The Northwest Ordinance of 1784 made public land available to finance local schools and the Morrill Act of 1862 gave land to support state colleges, but what Morton Grodzins and Daniel Elazar have called "cooperative federalism," though it always existed, did not begin in earnest until the passage in 1913 of the 16th Amendment to the Constitution allowed the federal government to levy an income tax on citizens and thereby to acquire access to vast sources of revenue. Between 1914 and 1917, federal aid to states and localities increased a thousandfold. By 1948 it amounted to over one tenth of all state and local spending; by 1970, to over one sixth.

The degree to which such grants, and the federal agencies that administer them, constrain or even direct state and local bureaucracies is a matter of dispute. No general answer can be given—federal support of welfare programs has left considerable discretion in the hands of the states over the size of benefits and some discretion over eligibility rules, whereas federal support of highway construction carries with it specific requirements as to design, safety, and (since 1968) environmental and social impact.

A few generalizations are possible, however. The first is that the states and not the cities have been from the first, and remain today, the principal client group for grants-in-aid. It was not until the Housing Act of 1937 that money was given in any substantial amount directly to local governments and though many additional programs of this kind were later added, as late as 1970 less than 12 percent of all federal aid went directly to cities and towns. The second general observation is that the 1960s mark a major watershed in the way in which the purposes of federal aid are determined. Before that time, most grants were for purposes initially defined by the states—to build highways and airports, to fund unemployment insurance programs, and the like. Beginning in the 1960s, the federal government, at the initiative of the President and his advisors, increasingly came to define the purposes of these grants—not necessarily over the objection of the states, but often without any initiative from them. Federal money was to be spent on poverty, ecology, planning, and other "national" goals for which, until the laws were passed, there were few, if any, well-organized and influential constituencies. Whereas federal money was once spent in response to the claims of distinct and organized clients, public or private, in the contemporary period federal money has increasingly been spent in ways that have *created* such clients.

And once rewarded or created, they are rarely penalized or abolished. What David Stockman has called the "social pork barrel" grows more or less steadily. Between 1950 and 1970, the number of farms declined from about 5.6 million to fewer than three million, but government payments to farmers rose about $283 million to $3.2 billion. In the public sector, even controversial programs have grown. Urban renewal programs have been sharply criticized, but federal support for the program rose from $281 million in 1965 to about $1 billion in 1972. Public housing has been enmeshed in controversy, but federal support for it rose from $206 million in 1965 to $845 million in 1972. Federal financial support for local poverty programs under the Office of Economic Opportunity has actually declined in recent years, but this cut is almost unique and it required the steadfast and deliberate attention of a determined President who was bitterly assailed both in the Congress and in the courts.

SELF-PERPETUATING AGENCIES

If the Founding Fathers were to return to examine bureaucratic clientelism, they would, I suspect, be deeply discouraged. James Madison clearly foresaw that American society would be "broken into many parts, interests and classes of citizens" and that this "multiplicity of interests" would help ensure against "the tyranny of the majority," especially in a federal regime with separate branches of government. Positive action would require a "coalition of a majority"; in the process of forming this coalition, the rights of all would be protected, not merely by self-interested bargains, but because in a free society such a coalition "could seldom take place on any other principles than those of justice and the general good." To those who wrongly believed that Madison thought of men as acting only out of base motives, the phrase is instructive: Persuading men who disagree to compromise their differences can rarely be achieved solely by the parceling out of relative advantage; the belief is also required that what is being agreed to is right, proper, and defensible before public opinion.

Most of the major new social programs of the United States, whether for the good of the few or the many, were initially adopted by broad coalitions appealing to general standards of justice or to conceptions of the public weal. This is certainly the case with most of the New Deal legislation — notably such programs as Social Security — and with most Great Society legislation—notably Medicare and aid to education; it was also conspicuously the case with respect to post-Great Society legislation pertaining to consumer and environmental concerns. State occupational licensing laws were supported by majorities instead in, among other things, the contribution of these statutes to public safety and health.

But when a program supplies particular benefits to an existing or newly created interest, public or private, it creates a set of political relationships that make exceptionally difficult further alteration of that program by coalitions of the majority. What was created in the name of the common good is sustained in the name of the particular interest. Bureaucratic clientelism becomes self-perpetuating, in the absence of some crisis or scandal, because a single interest group to which the program matters greatly is highly motivated and well-situated to ward off the criticisms of other groups that have a broad but weak interest in the policy.

In short, a regime of separated powers makes it difficult to overcome objections and contrary interests sufficiently to permit the enactment of a new program or the creation of a new agency. Unless the legislation can be made to pass either with little notice or at a time of crisis or extraordinary majorities—and sometimes even then—the initiation of new programs requires public interest arguments. But the same regime works to protect agencies, once created, from unwelcome change because a major change is, in effect, new legislation that must overcome the same hurdles as the original law, but this time with one of the hurdles—the wishes of the agency and its client—raised much higher. As a result, the Madisonian system makes it relatively easy for the delegation of public power to private groups to go unchallenged and, therefore, for factional interests that have acquired a supportive public bureaucracy to rule without submitting their interests to the effective scrutiny and modification of other interests.

BUREAUCRACY AND DISCRETION

For many decades, the Supreme Court denied to the federal government any general "police power" over occupations and businesses, and thus most such regulation occurred at the state level and even there under the constraint that it must not violate the notion of "substantive due process"—that is, the view that there were sharp limits to the power of any government to take (and therefore to regulate) property. What clearly was within the regulatory province of the federal government was interstate commerce, and thus it is not surprising that the first major federal regulatory body should be the Interstate Commerce Commission (ICC), created in 1887.

What does cause, if not surprise, then at least dispute, is the view that the Commerce Act actually was intended to regulate railroads in the public interest. It has become fashionable of late to see this law as a device sought by the railroads to protect themselves from competition. The argument has been given its best-known formulation by Gabriel Kolko. Long-haul railroads, facing ruinous price wars and powerless to resist the demands of big shippers for rebates, tried to create voluntary cartels or "pools" that would keep rates high. These pools always collapsed, however, when one railroad or another would cut rates in order to get more business. To prevent this, the railroads turned to the federal government seeking a law to compel what persuasion could not induce. But the genesis of the act was in fact more complex: Shippers wanted protection from high prices charged by railroads that operated monopolistic services in certain communities; many other shippers served by competing lines wanted no legal barriers to prevent competition from driving prices down as far as possible; some railroads wanted regulation to ease competition, while others feared regulation. And the law as finally passed in fact made "pooling" (or cartels to keep prices up) illegal.

The true significance of the Commerce Act is not that it allowed public power to be used to make secure private wealth but that it created a federal commission with broadly delegated powers that would have to reconcile conflicting goals (the desire for higher or lower prices) in a political environment characterized by a struggle among organized interests and rapidly changing technology. In short, the Commerce Act brought forth a new dimension to the problem of bureaucracy: not those problems, as with the Post Office, that resulted from size and political constraints, but those that were caused by the need to make binding choices without any clear standards for choice.

The ICC was not, of course, the first federal agency with substantial discretionary powers over important matters. The Office of Indian Affairs, for a while in the War Department but after 1849 in the Interior Department, coped for the better part of a century with the Indian problem equipped with no clear policy, beset on all sides by passionate and opposing arguments, and infected with a level of fraud and corruption that seemed impossible to eliminate. There were many causes of the problem, but at root was the fact that the government was determined to control the Indians but could not decide toward what end that control should be exercised (extermination, relocation, and assimilation all had their advocates) and, to the extent the goal was assimilation, could find no method by which to achieve it. By the end of the century, a policy of relocation had been adopted *de facto* and the worse abuses of the Indian service had been eliminated—if not by administrative skill, then by the exhaustion of things in Indian possession worth stealing. By the turn of the century, the management of the Indian question had become more or less routine administration of Indian schools and the allocation of reservation land among Indian claimants.

REGULATION VERSUS PROMOTION

It was the ICC and agencies and commissions for which it was the precedent that became the principal example of federal discretionary authority. It is important, however, to be clear about just what this precedent was. Not everything we now call a regulatory agency was in fact intended to be one. The ICC, the Antitrust Division of the Justice Department, the Federal Trade Commission (FTC), the Food and Drug Administration (FDA), the National Labor Relations Board (NLRB)—all these *were* intended to be genuinely regulatory bodies created to handle under public auspices matters once left to private arrangements. The techniques they were to employ varied: approving rates (ICC), issuing cease-and-desist orders (FTC), bringing civil or criminal actions in the courts (the Antitrust Division), defining after a hearing an appropriate standard of conduct (NLRB), or testing a product for safety (FDA). In each case, however, Congress clearly intended that the agency either define its own standards (a safe drug, a conspiracy in restraint of trade, a fair labor practice) or choose among competing claims (a higher or lower rate for shipping grain).

Other agencies often grouped with these regulatory bodies—the Civil Aeronautics Board, the Federal Communications Commission, the Maritime Commission—were designed, however, not primarily to regulate, but to *promote* the development of various infant or threatened industries. However, unlike fostering agriculture or commerce, fostering civil aviation or radio broadcasting was thought to require limiting entry (to prevent "unsafe" aviation or broadcast interference); but at the time these laws were passed few believed that the restrictions on entry would be many or that the choices would be made on any but technical or otherwise noncontroversial criteria. We smile now at their naïveté, but we continue to share it—today we sometimes suppose that choosing an approved exhaust emission control system or a water pollution control system can be done on the basis of technical criteria and without affecting production and employment.

MAJORITARIAN POLITICS

The creation of regulatory bureaucracies has occurred, as is often remarked, in waves. The first was the period between 1887 and 1890 (the Commerce Act and the Antitrust Act), the second between 1906 and 1915 (the Pure Food and Drug Act, the Meat Inspection Act, the Federal Trade Commission Act, the Clayton Act), the third during the 1930s (the Food, Drug, and Cosmetic Act, the Public Utility Holding Company Act, the Securities Exchange Act, the Natural Gas Act, the National Labor Relations Act), and the fourth during the latter part of the 1960s (the Water Quality Act, the Truth in Lending Act, the National Traffic and Motor Vehicle Safety

Act, various amendments to the drug laws, the Motor Vehicle Pollution Control Act, and many others).

Each of these periods was characterized by progressive or liberal Presidents in office (Cleveland, T. R. Roosevelt, Wilson, F. D. Roosevelt, Johnson); one was a period of national crisis (the 1930s); three were periods when the President enjoyed extraordinary majorities of his own party in both houses of Congress (1914-1916, 1932-1940, and 1964-1968); and only the first period preceded the emergence of the national mass media of communication. These facts are important because of the special difficulty of passing any genuinely regulatory legislation: A single interest, the regulated party, sees itself seriously threatened by a law proposed by a policy entrepreneur who must appeal to an unorganized majority, the members of which may not expect to be substantially or directly benefited by the law. Without special political circumstances—a crisis, a scandal, extraordinary majorities, an especially vigorous President, the support of media—the normal barriers to legislative innovation (i.e., to the formation of a "coalition of the majority") may prove insuperable.

Stated another way, the initiation of regulatory programs tends to take the form of majoritarian rather than coalition politics. The Madisonian system is placed in temporary suspense: Exceptional majorities propelled by a public mood and led by a skillful policy entrepreneur take action that might not be possible under ordinary circumstances (closely divided parties, legislative-executive checks and balances, popular indifference). The consequence of majoritarian politics for the administration of regulatory bureaucracies is great. To initiate and sustain the necessary legislative mood, strong, moralistic, and sometimes ideological appeals are necessary—leading, in turn, to the granting of broad mandates of power to the new agency (a modest delegation of authority would obviously be inadequate if the problem to be resolved is of crisis proportions) or to the specifying of exacting standards to be enforced (e.g., *no* carcinogenic products may be sold; 95 percent of the pollutants must be eliminated), or to both.

Either in applying a vague but broad rule ("the public interest, convenience, and necessity") or in enforcing a clear and strict standard, the regulatory agency will tend to broaden the range and domain of its authority, to lag behind technological and economic change, to resist deregulation, to stimulate corruption, and to contribute to the bureaucratization of private institutions.

It will broaden its regulatory reach out of a variety of motives: to satisfy the demand of the regulated enterprise that it be protected from competition, to make effective the initial regulatory action by attending to the unanticipated side effects of that action, to discover or stretch the meaning of vague statutory language, or to respond to new constituencies induced by the existence of the agency to convert what were once private demands into public pressures. For example, the Civil Aeronautics Board, out of a desire both to promote aviation and to protect the regulated price structure of the industry, will resist the entry into the industry of new carriers. If a Public Utilities Commission sets rates too low for a certain class of customers, the utility will allow service to those customers to decline in quality, leading in turn to a demand that the Commission also regulate the quality of service. If the Federal Communications Commission cannot decide who should receive a broadcast license by applying the "public interest" standard, it will be powerfully tempted to invest that phrase with whatever preferences the majority of the Commission then entertains, leading in turn to the exercise of control over many more aspects of broadcasting than merely signal interference—all in the name of deciding what the standard for entry shall be. If the Antitrust Division can prosecute conspiracies in restraint of trade, it will attract to itself the complaints of various firms about business practices that are neither conspiratorial nor restraining but merely competitive, and a "vigorous" antitrust lawyer may conclude that these practices warrant prosecution.

BUREAUCRATIC INERTIA

Regulatory agencies are slow to respond to change for the same reason all organizations with an assured existence are slow: There is no incentive to respond. Furthermore, the requirements of due process and of political conciliation will make any response time-consuming. For example, owing to the complexity of the matter and the money at stake, any comprehensive review of the long-distance rates of the telephone company will take years, and possibly may take decades.

Deregulation, when warranted by changed economic circumstances or undesired regulatory results, will be resisted. Any organization, and *a fortiori* any public organization, develops a genuine belief in the rightness of its mission that is expressed as a commitment to regulation as a process. This happened to the ICC in the early decades of this century as it steadily sought both enlarged powers (setting minimum as well as maximum rates) and a broader jurisdiction (over trucks, barges, and pipelines as well as railroads). It even urged incorporation into the Transportation Act of 1920 language directing it to prepare a comprehensive transportation plan for the nation. Furthermore, any regulatory agency will confer benefits on some group or interest, whether intended or not; those beneficiaries will stoutly resist deregulation. (But in happy proof of the fact that there are no iron laws, even about bureaucracies, we note the recent proposals emanating from the Federal Power Commission that the price of natural gas be substantially deregulated.)

The operation of regulatory bureaus may tend to bureaucratize the private sector. The costs of conforming to many regulations can be met most easily—often, *only*—by large firms and institutions with specialized bureaucracies of their own. Smaller firms and groups often must choose between unacceptably high overhead costs, violating the law, or going out of business. A small bakery producing limited runs of a high-quality product literally may not be able to meet the safety and health standards for equipment or to keep track of and administer fairly its obligations to its two employees; but unless the bakery is willing to break the law, it must sell out to a big bakery that can afford to do these things, but may not be inclined to make and sell good bread. I am not aware of any data that measure private bureaucratization or industrial concentration as a function of the economies of scale produced by the need to cope with the regulatory environment, but I see no reason why such data could not be found.

Finally, regulatory agencies that control entry, fix prices, or substantially affect the profitability of an industry create a powerful stimulus for direct or indirect forms of corruption. The revelations about campaign finance in the 1972 presidential election show dramatically that there will be a response to that stimulus. Many corporations, disproportionately those in regulated industries (airlines, milk producers, oil companies), made illegal or hard to justify campaign contributions involving very large sums.

THE ERA OF CONTRACT

It is far from clear what the Founding Fathers would have thought of all this. They were not doctrinaire exponents of laissez-faire, nor were 18th-century governments timid about asserting their powers over the economy. Every imaginable device of fiscal policy was employed by the states after the Revolutionary War. Mother England had, during the mercantilist era, fixed prices and wages, licensed merchants, and granted monopolies and subsidies. (What were the royal grants of American land to immigrant settlers but the greatest of subsidies, sometimes—as in Pennsylvania—almost monopolistically given?) European nations regularly operated state enterprises, controlled trade, and protected industry. But as William D. Grampp has noted, at the Constitutional Convention the Founders considered authorizing only four kinds of economic controls, and they rejected two of them. They agreed to allow the Congress to regulate international and interstate commerce and to give monopoly protection in the form of copyrights and patents. Even Madison's proposal to allow the federal government to charter corporations was rejected. Not one of the 85 *Federalist* papers dealt with economic regulation; indeed, the only reference to commerce was the value to it of a unified nation and a strong navy.

G. Warren Nutter has speculated as to why our Founders were so restrained in equipping the new government with explicit regulatory powers. One reason may have been the impact of Adam Smith's *Wealth of Nations,* published the same year as the Declaration of Independence, and certainly soon familiar to many rebel leaders, notably Hamilton. Smith himself sought to explain the American prosperity before the Revolution by the fact that Britain, through "salutary neglect," had not imposed mercantilist rules on the colonial economy. "Plenty of good land, and liberty to manage their own affairs in their own way" were the "two great causes" of colonial prosperity. As Nutter observes, there was a spirit of individualistic venture among the colonies that found economic expression in the belief that voluntary contracts were the proper organization principle of enterprise.

One consequence of this view was that the courts in many states were heavily burdened with cases testing the provisions of contracts and settling debts under them. In one rural county in Massachusetts the judges heard over 800 civil cases during 1785. As James Willard Hurst has written, the years before 1875 were "above all else, the years of contract in our law."

The era of contract came to an end with the rise of economic organizations so large or with consequences so great that contracts were no longer adequate, in the public's view, to adjust corporate behavior to the legitimate expectations of other parties. The courts were slower to accede to this change than were many legislatures, but in time they acceded completely, and the era of administrative regulation was upon us. The Founders, were they to return, would understand the change in the scale and social significance of enterprise, would approve of many of the purposes of regulation, perhaps would approve of the behavior of some of the regulatory bureaus seeking to realize those purposes, but surely would be dismayed at the political cost resulting from having vested vast discretionary authority in the hands of officials whose very existence—to say nothing of whose function—was not anticipated by the Constitutional Convention and whose effective control is beyond the capacity of the governing institutions which that Convention had designed.

THE BUREAUCRATIC STATE AND THE REVOLUTION

The American Revolution was not only a struggle for independence but a fundamental rethinking of the nature of political authority. Indeed, until that reformulation was completed the Revolution was not finished. What made political authority problematic for the colonists was the extent to which they believed Mother England had subverted their liberties despite the protection of the British constitution, until then widely regarded in America as the most perfect set of governing arrangements yet devised. The evidence of usurpation is now familiar: unjust taxation, the weakening of the independence of the judiciary, the stationing of standing armies, and the extensive use of royal patronage to reward office-seekers at colonial expense. Except for the issue of taxation, which raised for the colonists major questions of representation, almost all of their complaints involved the abuse of *administrative* powers.

The first solution proposed by Americans to remedy this abuse was the vesting of most (or, in the case of Pennsylvania and a few other states, virtually all) powers in the legislature. But the events after 1776 in many colonies, notably Pennsylvania, convinced the most thoughtful citizens that legislative abuses were as likely as administrative ones: In the extreme case, citizens would suffer from the "tyranny of the majority." Their solution to this problem was, of course, the theory of the separation of powers by which, as brilliantly argued in *The Federalist* papers, each branch of government would check the likely usurpations of the other.

This formulation went essentially unchallenged in theory and unmodified by practice for over a century. Though a sizable administrative apparatus had come into being by the end of the 19th century, it constituted no serious threat to the existing distribution of political power because it either performed routine tasks (the Post Office) or dealt with temporary crises (the military). Some agencies wielding discretionary authority existed, but they either dealt with groups whose liberties were not of much concern (the Indian Office) or their exercise of discretion was minutely scrutinized by Congress (the Land Office, the Pension Office, the Customs Office). The major discretionary agencies of the 19th century flourished at the very period of greatest Congressional domination of the political process—the decades after the Civil War—and thus, though their supervision was typically inefficient and sometimes corrupt, these agencies were for most practical purposes direct dependencies of Congress. In short, their existence did not call into question the theory of the separation of powers.

But with the growth of client-serving and regulatory agencies, grave questions began to be raised—usually implicitly—about that theory. A client-serving bureau, because of its relations with some source of private power, could become partially independent of both the executive and legislative branches—or in the case of the latter, dependent upon certain committees and independent of others and of the views of the Congress as a whole. A regulatory agency (that is to say, a truly regulatory one and not a clientelist or promotional agency hiding behind a regulatory fig leaf) was, in the typical case, placed formally outside the existing branches of government. Indeed, they were called "independent" or "quasi-judicial" agencies (they might as well have been called "quasi-executive" or "quasi-legislative") and thus the special status that clientelist bureaus achieved *de facto,* the regulatory ones achieved *de jure.*

It is, of course, inadequate and misleading to criticize these agencies, as has often been done, merely because they raise questions about the problem of sovereignty. The crucial test of their value is their behavior, and that can be judged only by applying economic and welfare criteria to the policies they produce. But if such judgments should prove damning, as increasingly has been the case, then the problem of finding the authority with which to alter or abolish such organizations becomes acute. In this regard the theory of the separation of powers has proved unhelpful.

The separation of powers makes difficult, in ordinary times, the extension of public power over private conduct—as a nation, we came more slowly to the welfare state than almost any European nation, and we still engage in less central planning and operate fewer nationalized industries than other democratic regimes. But we have extended the regulatory sway of our national government as far as or farther than that of most other liberal regimes (our environmental and safety codes are now models for much of Europe), and the bureaus wielding these discretionary powers are, once created, harder to change or redirect than would be the case if authority were more centralized.

The shift of power toward the bureaucracy was not inevitable. It did not result simply from increased specialization, the growth of industry, or the imperialistic designs of the bureaus themselves. Before the second decade of this century, there was no federal bureaucracy wielding substantial discretionary powers. That we have one now is the result of political decisions made by elected representatives. Fifty years ago, the people often wanted more of government than it was willing to provide—it was, in that sense, a republican government in which representatives moderated popular demands. Today, not only does political action follow quickly upon the stimulus of public interest, but government itself creates that stimulus and sometimes acts in advance of it.

All democratic regimes tend to shift resources from the private to the public sector and to enlarge the size of the administrative component of government. The particularistic and localistic nature of American democracy has created a particularistic and client-serving administration. If our bureaucracy often serves special interests and is subject to no central direction, it is because our legislature often serves special interests and is subject to no central leadership. For Congress to complain of what it has created and it maintains is, to be charitable, misleading. Congress could change what it has devised, but there is little reason to suppose it will.

CHAPTER 8

Congress

The United States Congress, exercising supreme legislative power, was at the beginning of the nineteenth century the most powerful political institution in the national government. It was feared by the framers of the Constitution, who felt that unless it was closely guarded and limited it would easily dominate both the presidency and the Supreme Court. Its powers were carefully enumerated, and it was made a bicameral body. This latter provision not only secured representation of different interests but also limited the power of the legislature which, when hobbled by two houses often working against each other, could not act as swiftly and forcefully as a single body could. Although still important, the power and prestige of Congress have declined while the powers of the President and the Supreme Court, not to mention those of the vast governmental bureaucracy, have increased. Congressional power, its basis, and the factors influencing the current position of Congress vis-à-vis coordinate governmental departments are discussed in this chapter.

Constitutional Background:
Representation of Popular, Group, and National Interests

Article I, Section 1 of the Constitution states that "all legislative powers herein granted shall be vested in a Congress of the United States, which shall consist of a Senate and House of Representatives." Section 8 specifically enumerates Congressional powers, and provides that Congress shall have power "to make all laws which shall be necessary and proper for carrying into execution the foregoing powers, and all other powers vested by this Constitution in the government of the United States, or in any department or officer thereof."

Apart from delineating the powers of Congress, Article I provides that the House shall represent the people, and the Senate the states through appointment of members by the state legislatures. The representative function of Congress is written into the Constitution, and at the time of the framing of the Constitution much discussion centered on the nature of representation and what constituted adequate representation in a national legislative body. Further, relating in part to the question of representation, the framers of the Constitution had to determine what the appropriate tasks for each branch of the legislature were, and to what extent certain legislative activities should be within the exclusive or initial jurisdiction of the House or the Senate. All these questions depended to some extent upon the conceptualization the framers had of the House as representative of popular interests on a short-term basis and the Senate as a reflection of conservative interests on a long-term basis. These selections from *The Federalist* indicate the thinking of the framers about the House of Representatives and the Senate.

45
James Madison

FEDERALIST 53

...No man can be a competent legislator who does not add to an upright intention and a sound judgment a certain degree of knowledge of the subjects on which he is to legislate. A part of this knowledge may be acquired by means of information, which lie within the compass of men in private, as well as public stations. Another part can only be attained, or at least thoroughly attained, by actual experience in the station which requires the use of it. The period of service ought, therefore, in all such cases, to bear some proportion to the extent of practical knowledge requisite to the due performance of the service....

In a single state the requisite knowledge relates to the existing laws, which are uniform throughout the state, and with which all the citizens are more or less conversant.... The great theater of the United States presents a very different scene. The laws are so far from being uniform that they vary in every state; whilst the public affairs of the union are spread throughout a very extensive region, and are extremely diversified by the local affairs connected with them, and can with difficulty be correctly learnt in any other place than in the central councils, to which a knowledge of them will be brought by representatives of every part of the empire. Yet some knowledge of the affairs, and even of the laws of all the states, ought to be possessed by the members from each of the states....

A branch of knowledge which belongs to the acquirements of a federal representative, and which has not been mentioned, is that of foreign affairs. In regulating our own commerce he ought to be not only acquainted with the treaties between the United States and other nations, but also with the commercial policy and laws of other nations. He ought not to be altogether ignorant of the law of nations; for that, as far as it is a proper object of municipal legislation, is submitted to the federal government. And although the House of Representatives is not immediately to participate in foreign negotiations and arrangements, yet from the necessary connection between the several branches of public affairs, those particular subjects will frequently deserve attention in the ordinary course of legislation, and will sometimes demand particular legislative sanction and cooperation. Some portion of this knowledge may, no doubt, be acquired in a man's closet; but some of it also can only be acquired to best effect, by a practical attention to the subject, during the period of actual service in the legislature....

FEDERALIST 56

The ... charge against the House of Representatives is, that it will be too small to possess a due knowledge of the interests of its constituents.

As this objection evidently proceeds from a comparison of the proposed number of representatives, with the great extent of the United States, the number of their inhabitants, and the diversity of their interests, without taking into view, at the same time, the circumstances which will distinguish the Congress from other legislative bodies, the best answer that can be given to it, will be a brief explanation of these pecularities.

It is a sound and important principle that the representative ought to be acquainted with the interests and circumstances of his constituents. But this principle can extend no farther than to those circumstances and interests to which the authority and care of the representative relate. An ignorance of a variety of minute and particular objects, which do not lie within the compass of legislation, is consistent with every attribute necessary to a due performance of the legislative trust. In determining the extent of information required in the exercise of a particular authority, recourse then must be had to the objects within the purview of that authority.

What are to be the objects of federal legislation? Those which are of most importance, and which seem most to require knowledge, are commerce, taxation, and the militia.

A proper regulation of commerce requires much information, as has been elsewhere remarked; but as far as this information relates to the laws, and local situation of each individual state, a very few representatives would be sufficient vehicles of it to the federal councils.

Taxation will consist, in great measure, of duties which will be involved in the regulation of commerce. So far the preceding remark is applicable to this object. As far as it may consist of internal collections, a more diffusive knowledge of the circumstances of the state may be necessary. But will not this also be possessed in sufficient degree by a very few intelligent men, diffusively elected within the state? ...

With regard to the regulation of the militia there are scarcely any circumstances in reference to which local knowledge can be said to be necessary.... The art of war teaches general principles of organization, movement, and discipline, which apply universally.

The attentive reader will discern that the reasoning here used, to prove the sufficiency of a moderate number of representatives, does not, in any respect, contradict what was urged on another occasion, with regard to the extensive information which the representatives ought to possess, and the time that might be necessary for acquiring it....

FEDERALIST 57

... The House of Representatives is so constituted as to support in the members an habitual recollection of their dependence on the people. Before the sentiments impressed on their minds by the mode of their elevation, can be effaced by the exercise of power, they will be compelled to anticipate the moment when their power is to cease, when their exercise of it is to be reviewed, and when they must descend to the level from which they were raised; there for ever to remain unless a faithful discharge of their trust shall have established their title to a renewal of it.

I will add, as a ... circumstance in the situation of the House of Representatives, restraining them from oppressive measures, that they can make no law which will not have its full operation on themselves and their friends, as well as on the great mass of the society. This has always been deemed one of the strongest bonds by which human policy can connect the rulers and the people together. It creates between them that communion of interest, and sympathy of sentiments, of which few governments have furnished examples; but without which every government degenerates into tyranny. If it be asked, what is to restrain the House of Representatives from making legal discriminations in favor of themselves, and a particular class of the society? I answer, the genius of the whole system; the nature of just and constitutional laws; and, above all, the vigilant and manly spirit which actuates the people of America; a spirit which nourishes freedom, and in return is nourished by it.

If this spirit shall ever be so far debased as to tolerate a law not obligatory on the legislature, as well as on the people, the people will be prepared to tolerate anything but liberty.

Such will be the relation between the House of Representatives and their constituents. Duty, gratitude, interest, ambition itself, are the cords by which they will be bound to fidelity and sympathy with the great mass of the people. It is possible that these may all be insufficient to control the caprice and wickedness of men. But are they not all that government will admit, and that human prudence can devise? Are they not the genuine, and the characteristic means, by which republican government provides for the liberty and happiness of the people? ...

FEDERALIST 58

... In this review of the constitution of the House of Representatives ... one observation ... I must be permitted to add ... as claiming, in my judgment, a very serious attention. It is, that in all legislative assemblies, the greater the number composing them may be, the fewer will be the men who will in fact direct their proceedings. In the first place, the more numerous any assembly may be, of whatever characters composed, the greater is known to be the ascendancy of passion over reason. In the next place, the larger the number, the greater will be the proportion of members of limited information and of weak capacities. Now it is precisely on characters of this description that the eloquence and address of the few are known to act with all their force. In the ancient republics, where the whole body of the people assembled in person, a single orator, or an artful statesman, was generally seen to rule with as complete a sway as if a sceptre had been placed in his single hands. On the same principle, the more multitudinous a representative assembly may be rendered, the more it will partake of the infirmities incident to collective meetings of the people. Ignorance will be the dupe of cunning; and passion the slave of sophistry and declamation. The people can never err more than in supposing, that by multiplying their representatives beyond a certain list, they strengthen the barrier against the government of a few. Experience will for ever admonish them, that, on the contrary, after securing a sufficient number for the purposes of safety, of local information, and of diffusive sympathy with the whole society, they will counteract their own views by every addition to their representatives. The countenance of the government may become more democratic; but the soul that animates it will be more oligarchic. The machine will be enlarged, but the fewer, and often the more secret, will be the springs by which its motions are directed. ...

FEDERALIST 62

Having examined the constitution of the House of Representatives ... I enter next on the examination of the Senate.

The heads under which this member of the government may be considered are—I. The qualifications of senators; II. The appointment of them by the state legislatures; III. The equality of representation in the Senate; IV. The number of senators, and the term for which they are to be elected; V. The powers vested in the Senate.

I

The qualifications proposed for senators, as distinguished from those of representatives, consist in a more advanced age and a longer period of citizenship. A senator must be thirty years of age at least; as a representative must be twenty-five. And the former must have been a citizen nine years; as seven years are required for the latter. The propriety of these distinctions is explained by the nature of the senatorial trust; which, requiring greater extent of information and stability of character, requires at the same time, that the senator should have reached a period of life most likely to supply these advantages. . . .

II

It is equally unnecessary to dilate on the appointment of senators by the state legislators. Among the various modes which might have been devised for constituting this branch of the government, that which has been proposed by the convention is probably the most congenial with the public opinion. It is recommended by the double advantage of favoring a select appointment, and of giving to the state governments such an agency in the formation of the federal government, as must secure the authority of the former, and may form a convenient link between the two systems.

III

The equality of representation in the Senate is another point, which, being evidently the result of compromise between the opposite pretensions of the large and the small states, does not call for much discussion. If indeed it be right, that among a people thoroughly incorporated into one nation, every district ought to have a *proportional* share in the government: and that among independent and sovereign states bound together by a simple league, the parties, however unequal in size, ought to have an *equal* share in the common councils, it does not appear to be without some reason, that in a compound republic, partaking both of the national and federal character, the government ought to be founded on a mixture of the principles of proportional [as found in the House of Representatives] and equal representation [in the Senate]. . . .

. . . [T]he equal vote allowed to each state, is at once a constitutional recognition of the portion of sovereignty remaining in the individual states, and an instrument for preserving that residuary sovereignty. So far the equality ought to be no less acceptable to the large than to the small states; since they are not less solicitous to guard by every possible expedient against an improper consolidation of the states into one simple republic.

Another advantage accruing from this ingredient in the constitution of the senate is, the additional impediment it must prove against improper acts of legislation. No law or resolution can now be passed without the concurrence, first, of a majority of the people, and then, of a majority of the states. It must be acknowledged that this complicated check on legislation may, in some instances, be injurious as well as beneficial; and that the peculiar defense which it involves in favor of the smaller states, would be more rational, if any interests common to them, and distinct from those of the other states, would otherwise be exposed to peculiar danger. But as the larger states will always be able, by their power over the supplies, to defeat unreasonable exertions of this prerogative of the lesser states; and as the facility and excess of law-making seem to be the diseases to which our governments are most liable, it is not impossible, that this part of the constitution may be more convenient in practice than it appears to many in contemplation.

IV

The number of senators, and the duration of their appointment, come next to be considered. In order to form an accurate judgment on both these points, it will be proper to inquire into the purposes which are to be answered by the Senate; and, in order to ascertain these, it will be necessary to review the inconveniences which a republic must suffer from the want of such an institution.

First. It is a misfortune incident to republican government, though in a lesser degree than to other governments, that those who administer it may forget their obligations to their constituents, and prove unfaithful to their important trust. In this point of view, a senate, as a second branch of the legislative assembly, distinct from, and dividing the power with, a first, must be in all cases a salutary check on the government. It doubles the security to the people by requiring the concurrence of two distinct bodies in schemes of usurpation or perfidy, where the ambition or corruption of one would otherwise be sufficient.... [A]s the improbability of sinister combinations will be in proportion to the dissimilarity in the genius of the two bodies, it must be politic to distinguish them from each other by every circumstance which will consist with a due harmony in all proper measures, and with the genuine principles of republican government.

Second. The necessity of a senate is not less indicated by the propensity of all single and numerous assemblies, to yield to the impulse of sudden and violent passions, and to be seduced by factious leaders into intemperate and pernicious resolutions. Examples on this subject might be cited without number; and from proceedings within the United States, as well as from the history of other nations. But a position that will not be contradicted need not be proved. All that need be remarked is, that a body which is to correct this infirmity ought itself to be free from it, and consequently ought to be less numerous. It ought, moreover, to possess great firmness, and consequently ought to hold its authority by a tenure of considerable duration.

Third. Another defect to be supplied by a senate lies in a want of due acquaintance with the objects and principles of legislation. It is not possible that an assembly of men, called, for the most part, from pursuits of a private nature, continued in appointments for a short time, and led by no permanent motive to devote the intervals of public occupation to a study of the laws, the affairs, and the comprehensive interests of their country, should, if left wholly to themselves, escape a variety of important errors in the exercise of their legislative trust. . . .

Fourth. The mutability in the public councils, arising from a rapid succession of new members, however qualified they may be, points out, in the strongest manner, the necessity of some stable institution in the government. Every new election in the states is found to change one-half of the representatives. From this change of men must proceed a change of opinions; and from a change of opinions, a change of measures. But a continual change even of good measures is inconsistent with every rule of prudence, and every prospect of success. . . .

FEDERALIST 63

A *fifth* desideratum, illustrating the utility of a senate, is the want of a due sense of national character. Without a select and stable member of the government, the esteem of foreign powers will not only be forfeited by an unenlightened and variable policy . . . ; but the national councils will not possess that sensibility to the opinion of the world, which is perhaps not less necessary in order to merit, than it is to obtain, its respect and confidence. . . .

I add, as a *sixth* defect, the want in some important cases of a due responsibility in the government to the people, arising from that frequency of elections, which in other cases produces this responsibility. . . .

Responsibility, in order to be reasonable, must be limited to objects within the power of the responsible party, and in order to be effectual, must relate to operations of that power, of which a ready and proper judgment can be formed by the constituents. The objects of government may be divided into two general classes; the one depending on measures, which have singly an immediate and sensible operation; the other depending on a succession of well chosen and well connected measures, which have a gradual and perhaps unobserved operation. The importance of the latter description to the collective and permanent welfare of every country, needs no explanation. And yet it is evident that an assembly elected for so short a term as to be unable to provide more than one or two links in a chain of measures, on which the general welfare may essentially depend, ought not to be answerable for the final result, any more than a steward or tenant, engaged for one year, could be justly made to answer for plans or improvements, which could not be accomplished in less than half a dozen years. Nor is it possible for the people to estimate the *share* of influence, which their annual assemblies may respectively have on events resulting from the mixed transactions of several years. It is sufficiently difficult, at any rate, to preserve a personal responsibility in the members of a *numerous* body, for such acts of the body as have an immediate, detached, and palpable operation on its constituents.

The proper remedy for this defect must be an additional body in the legislative department, which, having sufficient permanency to provide for such objects as require a continued attention, and a train of measures, may be justly and effectually answerable for the attainment of those objects.

Thus far I have considered the circumstances, which point out the necessity of a well constructed senate, only as they relate to the representatives of the people. To a people as little blinded by prejudice, or corrupted by flattery, as those whom I address, I shall not scruple to add, that such an institution may be sometimes necessary, as a defense to the people against their own temporary errors and delusions. As the cool and deliberate sense of the community ought, in all governments, and actually will, in all free governments, ultimately prevail over the views of its rulers; so there are particular moments in public affairs, when the people, stimulated by some irregular passion, or some illicit advantage, or misled by the artful misrepresentations of interested men, may call for measures which they themselves will afterwards be the most ready to lament and condemn. In these critical moments, how salutary will be the interference of some temperate and respectable body of citizens, in order to check the misguided career, and to suspend the blow meditated by the people against themselves, until reason, justice and truth can regain their authority over the public mind? What bitter anguish would not the people of Athens have often avoided, if their government had contained so provident a safeguard against the tyranny of their own passions? Popular liberty might then have escaped the indelible reproach of decreeing to the same citizens the hemlock on one day, and statues on the next.

It may be suggested that a people spread over an extensive region cannot, like the crowded inhabitants of a small district, be subject to the infection of violent passions; or to the danger of combining in the pursuit of unjust measures. I am far from denying that this is a distinction of peculiar importance. I have, on the contrary, endeavored in a former paper to show that it is one of the principal recommendations of a confederated republic. At the same time this advantage ought not to be considered as superseding the use of auxiliary precautions. It may even be remarked that the same extended situation, which will exempt the people of America from some of the dangers incident to lesser republics, will expose them to the inconveniency of remaining for a longer time under the influence of those misrepresentations which the combined industry of interested men may succeed in distributing among them. . . .

Congress and the Washington Political Establishment

☐   The author of the following selection agrees with David Mayhew (see selection No. 50) that the principal goal of members of Congress is reelection. That incentive, the author suggests, has led Congress to create a vast federal bureaucracy to implement programs that ostensibly benefit constituents. Congress has delegated substantial authority to administrative departments and agencies to carry out programs, inevitably resulting in administrative decisions that frequently step on constituents' toes. Congress, which has gained credit for establishing the programs in the first place, steps in once again to receive credit for handling constituent complaints against the bureaucracy. The author's provocative thesis is that both the establishment and maintenance of a vast federal bureaucracy is explained by the congressional reelection incentive.

46
Morris P. Fiorina

THE RISE OF THE
WASHINGTON ESTABLISHMENT

DRAMATIS PERSONAE

In this chapter, the heart of [my] book, I will set out a theory of the Washington establishment(s). The theory is quite plausible from a common-sense standpoint, and it is consistent with the specialized literature of academic political science. Nevertheless, it is still a theory, not proven fact. Before plunging in let me bring out in the open the basic axiom on which the theory rests: the self-interest axiom.

I assume that most people most of the time act in their own self-interest. This is not to say that human beings seek only to amass tangible wealth but rather to say that human beings seek to achieve their own ends—tangible and intangible—rather than the ends of their fellow men. I do not condemn such behavior nor do I condone it (although I rather sympathize with Thoreau's comment that "if I knew for a certainty that a man was coming to my house with the conscious design of doing me good, I should run for my life."). I only claim that political and economic theories which presume self-interested behavior will prove to be more widely applicable than those which build on more altruistic assumptions.

What does the axiom imply when used in the specific context of this book, a context peopled by congressmen, bureaucrats, and voters? I assume that the primary goal of the typical congressman is reelection. Over and above the $45,000 salary plus "perks" and outside money, the office of congressman carries with it prestige, excitement, and power. It is a seat in the cockpit of government. But in order to retain the status, excitement, and power (not to mention more tangible things) of office, the congressman must win reelection every two years. Even those congressmen genuinely concerned with good public policy must achieve reelection in order to continue their work. Whether narrowly self-serving or more publicly oriented, the individual congressman finds reelection to be at least a necessary condition for the achievement of his goals.

Moreover, there is a kind of natural selection process at work in the electoral arena. On average, those congressmen who are not primarily interested in reelection will not achieve reelection as often as those who

From Morris P. Fiorina, *Congress: Keystone of the Washington Establishment.* Copyright © 1977 by Yale University Press. Reprinted by permission.

are interested. We, the people, help to weed out congressmen whose primary motivation is not reelection. We admire politicians who courageously adopt the aloof role of the disinterested statesman, but we vote for those politicians who follow our wishes and do us favors.

What about the bureaucrats? A specification of their goals is somewhat more controversial—those who speak of appointed officials as public servants obviously take a more benign view than those who speak of them as bureaucrats. The literature provides ample justification for asserting that most bureaucrats wish to protect and nurture their agencies. The typical bureaucrat can be expected to seek to expand his agency in terms of personnel, budget, and mission. One's status in Washington (again, not to mention more tangible things) is roughly proportional to the importance of the operation one oversees. And the sheer size of the operation is taken to be a measure of importance. As with congressmen, the specified goals apply even to those bureaucrats who genuinely believe in their agency's mission. If they believe in the efficacy of their programs, they naturally wish to expand them and add new ones. All of this requires more money and more people. The genuinely committed bureaucrat is just as likely to seek to expand his agency as the proverbial empire-builder.

And what of the third element in the equation, us? What do we, the voters who support the Washington system, strive for? Each of us wishes to receive a maximum of benefits from government for the minimum cost. This goal suggests maximum government efficiency, on the one hand, but it also suggests mutual exploitation on the other. Each of us favors an arrangement in which our fellow citizens pay for our benefits.

With these brief descriptions of the cast of characters in hand, let us proceed.

TAMMANY HALL GOES TO WASHINGTON

What should we expect from a legislative body composed of individuals whose first priority is their continued tenure in office? We should expect, first, that the normal activities of its members are those calculated to enhance their chances of reelection. And we should expect, second, that the members would devise and maintain institutional arrangements which facilitate their electoral activities. . . .

For most of the twentieth century, congressmen have engaged in a mix of three kinds of activities: lawmaking, pork barreling, and casework. Congress is first and foremost a lawmaking body, at least according to constitutional theory. In every postwar session Congress "considers" thousands of bills and resolutions, many hundreds of which are brought to a record vote (over 500 in each chamber in the 93rd Congress). Naturally the critical consideration in taking a position for the record is the maximization of approval in the home district. If the district is unaffected by and unconcerned with the matter at hand, the congressman may then take into account the general welfare of the country. (This sounds cynical, but remember that "profiles in courage" are sufficiently rare that their occurrence inspires books and articles.) Abetted by political scientists of the pluralist school, politicians have propounded an ideology which maintains that the good of the country on any given issue is simply what is best for a majority of congressional districts. This ideology provides a philosophical justification for what congressmen do while acting in their own self-interest.

A second activity favored by congressmen consists of efforts to bring home the bacon to their districts. Many popular articles have been written about the pork barrel, a term originally applied to rivers and harbors legislation but now generalized to cover all manner of federal largesse. Congressmen consider new dams, federal buildings, sewage treatment plants, urban renewal projects, etc. as sweet plums to be plucked. Federal projects are highly visible, their economic impact is easily detected by constituents, and sometimes they even produce something of value to the district. The average constituent may have some trouble translating his congressman's vote on some civil rights issue into a change in his personal welfare. But the workers hired and supplies purchased in connection with a big federal project provide benefits that are widely appreciated. The historical importance congressmen attach to the pork barrel is reflected in the rules of the House. That body accords certain classes of legislation "privileged" status: they may come directly to the floor without passing through the Rules Committee, a traditional graveyard for legislation. What kinds of legislation are privileged? Taxing and spending bills, for one: the government's power to raise and spend money must be kept relatively unfettered. But in addition, the omnibus rivers and harbors bills of the Public Works Committee and public lands bills from the Interior Committee share privileged status. The House will allow a civil rights or defense procurement or environmental bill to languish in the Rules Committee, but it takes special precautions to insure that nothing slows down the approval of dams and irrigation projects.

A third major activity takes up perhaps as much time as the other two combined. Traditionally, constituents appeal to their congressman for myriad favors and services. Sometimes only information is needed, but often constituents request that their congressman intervene in the internal workings of federal agencies to affect a decision in a favorable way, to reverse an adverse decision, or simply to speed up the glacial bureaucratic process. On the basis of extensive personal interviews with congressmen, Charles Clapp writes:

> Denied a favorable ruling by the bureaucracy on a matter of direct concern to him, puzzled or irked by delays in obtaining a decision, confused by the administrative maze through which he is directed to proceed, or ignorant of whom to write, a constituent may turn to his congressman for help. These letters offer great potential for political

benefit to the congressman since they affect the constituent personally. If the legislator can be of assistance, he may gain a firm ally; if he is indifferent, he may even lose votes.

Actually congressmen are in an almost unique position in our system, a position shared only with high-level members of the executive branch. Congressmen possess the power to expedite and influence bureaucratic decisions. This capability flows directly from congressional control over what bureaucrats value most: higher budgets and new program authorizations. In a very real sense each congressman is a monopoly supplier of bureaucratic unsticking services for his district.

Every year the federal budget passes through the appropriations committees of Congress. Generally these committees make perfunctory cuts. But on occasion they vent displeasure on an agency and leave it bleeding all over the Capitol. The most extreme case of which I am aware came when the House committee took away the entire budget of the Division of Labor Standards in 1947 (some of the budget was restored elsewhere in the appropriations process). Deep and serious cuts are made occasionally, and the threat of such cuts keeps most agencies attentive to congressional wishes. Professors Richard Fenno and Aaron Wildavsky have provided extensive documentary and interview evidence of the great respect (and even terror) federal bureaucrats show for the House Appropriations Committee. Moreover, the bureaucracy must keep coming back to Congress to have its old programs reauthorized and new ones added. Again, most such decisions are perfunctory, but exceptions are sufficiently frequent that bureaucrats do not forget the basis of their agencies' existence. For example, the Law Enforcement Assistance Administration (LEAA) and the Food Stamps Program had no easy time of it this last Congress (94th). The bureaucracy needs congressional approval in order to survive, let alone expand. Thus, when a congressman calls about some minor bureaucratic decision or regulation, the bureaucracy considers his accommodation a small price to pay for the goodwill its cooperation will produce, particularly if he has any connection to the substantive committee or the appropriations subcommittee to which it reports.

From the standpoint of capturing voters, the congressman's lawmaking activities differ in two important respects from his pork-barrel and casework activities. First, programmatic actions are inherently controversial. Unless his district is homogeneous, a congressman will find his district divided on many major issues. Thus when he casts a vote, introduces a piece of nontrivial legislation, or makes a speech with policy content he will displease some elements of his district. Some constituents may applaud the congressman's civil rights record, but others believe integration is going too fast. Some support foreign aid, while others believe it's money poured down a rathole. Some advocate economic equality, others stew over welfare cheaters. On such policy matters the congressman can expect to make friends as well as enemies. Presumably he will behave so as to maximize the excess of the former over the latter, but nevertheless a policy stand will generally make some enemies.

In contrast, the pork barrel and casework are relatively less controversial. New federal projects bring jobs, shiny new facilities, and general economic prosperity, or so people believe. Snipping ribbons at the dedication of a new post office or dam is a much more pleasant pursuit than disposing of a constitutional amendment on abortion. Republicans and Democrats, conservatives and liberals, all generally prefer a richer district to a poorer one. Of course, in recent years the river damming and stream-bed straightening activities of the Army Corps of Engineers have aroused some opposition among environmentalists. Congressmen happily reacted by absorbing the opposition and adding environmentalism to the pork barrel: water treatment plants are currently a hot congressional item.

Casework is even less controversial. Some poor, aggrieved constituent becomes enmeshed in the tentacles of an evil bureaucracy and calls upon Congressman St. George to do battle with the dragon. Again Clapp writes;

> A person who has a reasonable complaint or query is regarded as providing an opportunity rather than as adding an extra burden to an already busy office. The party affiliation of the individual even when known to be different from that of the congressman does not normally act as a deterrent to action. Some legislators have built their reputations and their majorities on a program of service to all constituents irrespective of party. Regularly, voters affiliated with the opposition in other contests lend strong support to the lawmaker whose intervention has helped them in their struggle with the bureaucracy.

Even following the revelation of sexual improprieties, Wayne Hays won his Ohio Democratic primary by a two-to-one margin. According to a *Los Angeles Times* feature story, Hays's constituency base was built on a foundation of personal service to constituents:

> They receive help in speeding up bureaucratic action on various kinds of federal assistance—black lung benefits to disabled miners and their families, Social Security payments, veterans' benefits and passports.
>
> Some constituents still tell with pleasure of how Hays stormed clear to the seventh floor of the State Department and into Secretary of State Dean Rusk's office to demand, successfully, the quick issuance of a passport to an Ohioan.

Practicing politicians will tell you that word of mouth is still the most effective mode of communication. News of favors to constituents gets around and no doubt is embellished in the process.

In sum, when considering the benefits of his programmatic activities, the congressman must tote up gains and losses to arrive at a net profit. Pork barreling and casework, however, are basically pure profit.

A second way in which programmatic activities differ from casework and the pork barrel is the difficulty of assigning responsibility to the former as compared with the latter. No congressman can seriously claim that he is responsible for the 1964 Civil Rights Act, the ABM, or the 1972 Revenue Sharing Act. Most constituents do have some vague notion that their congressman is only one of hundreds and their senator one of an even hundred. Even committee chairmen may have a difficult time claiming credit for a piece of major legislation, let alone a rank-and-file congressman. Ah, but casework, and the pork barrel. In dealing with the bureaucracy, the congressman is not merely one vote of 435. Rather, he is a nonpartisan power, someone whose phone calls snap an office to attention. He is not kept on hold. The constituent who receives aid believes that his congressman and his congressman alone got results. Similarly, congressmen find it easy to claim credit for federal projects awarded their districts. The congressman may have instigated the proposal for the project in the first place, issued regular progress reports, and ultimately announced the award through his office. Maybe he can't claim credit for the 1965 Voting Rights Act, but he can take credit for Littletown's spanking new sewage treatment plant.

Overall then, programmatic activities are dangerous (controversial), on the one hand, and programmatic accomplishments are difficult to claim credit for, on the other. While less exciting, casework and pork barreling are both safe and profitable. For a reelection-oriented congressman the choice is obvious.

The key to the rise of the Washington establishment (and the vanishing marginals) is the following observation: *the growth of an activist federal government has stimulated a change in the mix of congressional activities.* Specifically, a lesser proportion of congressional effort is now going into programmatic activities and a greater proportion into pork-barrel and casework activities. As a result, today's congressmen make relatively fewer enemies and relatively more friends among the people of their districts.

To elaborate, a basic fact of life in twentieth-century America is the growth of the federal role and its attendant bureaucracy. Bureaucracy is the characteristic mode of delivering public goods and services. Ceteris paribus, the more the government attempts to do for people, the more extensive a bureaucracy it creates. As the scope of government expands, more and more citizens find themselves in direct contact with the federal government. Consider the rise in such contacts upon passage of the Social Security Act, work relief projects and other New Deal programs. Consider the millions of additional citizens touched by the veterans' programs of the postwar period. Consider the untold numbers whom the Great Society and its aftermath brought face to face with the federal government. In 1930 the federal bureaucracy was small and rather distant from the everyday concerns of Americans. By 1975 it was neither small nor distant.

As the years have passed, more and more citizens and groups have found themselves dealing with the federal bureaucracy. They may be seeking positive actions—eligibility for various benefits and awards of government grants. Or they may be seeking relief from the costs imposed by bureaucratic regulations—on working conditions, racial and sexual quotas, market restrictions, and numerous other subjects. While not malevolent, bureaucracies make mistakes, both of commission and omission, and normal attempts at redress often meet with unresponsiveness and inflexibility and sometimes seeming incorrigibility. Whatever the problem, the citizen's congressman is a source of succor. The greater the scope of government activity, the greater the demand for his services.

Private monopolists can regulate the demand for their product by raising or lowering the price. Congressmen have no such (legal) option. When the demand for their services rises, they have no real choice except to meet that demand—to supply more bureaucratic unsticking services—so long as they would rather be elected than unelected. This vulnerability to escalating constituency demands is largely academic, though. I seriously doubt that congressmen resist their gradual transformation from national legislators to errand boy-ombudsmen. As we have noted, casework is all profit. Congressmen have buried proposals to relieve the casework burden by establishing a national ombudsman or Congressman Reuss's proposed Administrative Counsel of the Congress. One of the congressmen interviewed by Clapp stated:

> Before I came to Washington I used to think that it might be nice if the individual states had administrative arms here that would take care of necessary liaison between citizens and the national government. But a congressman running for reelection is interested in building fences by providing personal services. The system is set to reelect incumbents regardless of party, and incumbents wouldn't dream of giving any of this service function away to any subagency. As an elected member I feel the same way.

In fact, it is probable that at least some congressmen deliberately stimulate the demand for their bureaucratic fixit services. (See [Figure A].) Recall that the new Republican in district A travels about his district saying:

> I'm your man in Washington. What are your problems? How can I help you?

And in district B, did the demand for the congressman's services rise so much between 1962 and 1964 that a "regiment" of constituency staff became necessary? Or, having access to the regiment, did the new Democrat stimulate the demand to which he would apply his regiment?

In addition to greatly increased casework, let us not forget that the growth of the federal role has also greatly expanded the federal pork barrel.

NEED HELP WITH A FEDERAL PROBLEM?

Please feel free to communicate with me in person by phone or by mail. Daily from 9 a.m. until 5 p.m. my Congressional District office in Fullerton is open to serve you and your family. The staff will be able to help you with information or assistance on proposed Federal legislation and procedures of Federal agencies. If you are experiencing a problem with Social Security, educational assistance, Veterans Administration, Immigration, Internal Revenue Service, Postal Service, Environmental Protection Agency, Federal Energy Office or any other Federal agency, please contact me through this office. If you decide to write to me, please provide a telephone number as many times I can call you with information within a day or two.

CONGRESSMAN CHARLES E. WIGGINS
Brashears Center, Suite 103
1400 N. Harbor Boulevard
Fullerton, Ca 92635 (714) 870-7266

My Washington address is
Room 2445 Rayburn Building, Washington, D.C.
20515. Telephone (202) 225-4111.

U.S. House of Representatives
WASHINGTON, D.C. 20515
PUBLIC DOCUMENT
OFFICIAL BUSINESS

Charles E. Wiggins
M.C.

POSTAL CUSTOMER-LOCAL
39th District
CALIFORNIA

Figure A   How the Congressman-as-Ombudsman Drums up Business

The creative pork barreler need not limit himself to dams and post offices— rather old-fashioned interests. Today, creative congressmen can cadge LEAA money for the local police, urban renewal and housing money for local politicians, educational program grants for the local education bureaucracy. And there are sewage treatment plants, worker training and retraining programs, health services, and programs for the elderly. The pork barrel is full to overflowing. The conscientious congressman can stimulate applications for federal assistance (the sheer number of programs makes it difficult for local officials to stay current with the possibilities), put in a good word during consideration, and announce favorable decisions amid great fanfare.

In sum, everyday decisions by a large and growing federal bureaucracy bestow significant tangible benefits and impose significant tangible costs. Congressmen can affect these decisions. Ergo, the more decisions the bureaucracy has the opportunity to make, the more opportunities there are for the congressman to build up credits.

The nature of the Washington system is now quite clear. Congressmen (typically the majority Democrats) earn electoral credits by establishing various federal programs (the minority Republicans typically earn credits by fighting the good fight). The legislation is drafted in very general terms, so some agency, existing or newly established, must translate a vague policy mandate into a functioning program, a process that necessitates the promulgation of numerous rules and regulations and, incidentally, the trampling of numerous toes. At the next stage, aggrieved and/or hopeful constituents petition their congressman to intervene in the complex (or at least obscure) decision processes of the bureaucracy. The cycle closes when the congressman lends a sympathetic ear, piously denounces the evils of bureaucracy, intervenes in the latter's decisions, and rides a grateful electorate to ever more impressive electoral showings. Congressmen take credit coming and going. They are the alpha and the omega.

The popular frustration with the permanent government in Washington is partly justified, but to a considerable degree it is misplaced resentment. *Congress is the linchpin of the Washington establishment.* The bureaucracy serves as a convenient lightning rod for public frustration and a convenient whipping boy for congressmen. But so long as the bureaucracy accommodates congressmen, the latter will oblige with ever larger budgets and grants of authority. Congress does not just react to big government—it creates it. All of Washington prospers. More and more bureaucrats promulgate more and more regulations and dispense more and more money. Fewer and fewer congressmen suffer electoral defeat. Elements of the electorate benefit from government programs, and all of the electorate is eligible for ombudsman services. But the general, long-term welfare of the United States is no more than an incidental by-product of the system.

Committee Chairmen as Part of the Washington Establishment

☐   In 1885 Woodrow Wilson was able to state categorically in his famous work *Congressional Government:*

> The leaders of the House are the chairmen of the principal Standing Committees. Indeed, to be exactly accurate, the House has as many leaders as there are subjects of legislation; for there are as many Standing Committees as there are leading classes of legislation, and in the consideration of every topic of business the House is guided by a special leader in the person of the chairman of the Standing Committee, charged with the superintendence of measures of the particular class to which that topic belongs. It is this multiplicity of leaders, this many-headed leadership, which makes the organization of the House too complex to afford uninformed people and unskilled observers any easy clue to its methods of rule. For the chairmen of the Standing Committees do not constitute a cooperative body like a ministry. They do not consult and concur in the adoption of homogeneous and mutually helpful measures; there is no thought of acting in concert. Each Committee goes its own way at its own pace. It is impossible to discover any unity or method in the disconnected and therefore unsystematic, confused, and desultory action of the House, or any common

purpose in the measures which its Committees from time to time recommend.

With regard to the Senate he noted:

It has those same radical defects of organization which weaken the House. Its functions also, like those of the House, are segregated in the prerogatives of numerous Standing Committees. In this regard Congress is all of a piece. There is in the Senate no more opportunity than exists in the House for gaining such recognized party leadership as would be likely to enlarge a man by giving him a sense of power, and to steady and sober him by filling him with a grave sense of responsibility. So far as its organization controls it, the Senate . . . proceedings bear most of the characteristic features of committee rule.

The Legislative Reorganization Act of 1946 was designed to stream-line Congressional committee structure and provide committees and individual Congressmen with increased expert staff; however, although the number of standing committees was reduced, subcommittees have increased so that the net numerical reduction is not as great as was originally intended. Further, because Congress still conducts its business through committees: (1) the senior members of the party with the majority in Congress dominate the formulation of public policy through the seniority rule; (2) policy formulation is fragmented with each committee maintaining relative dominance over policy areas within its jurisdiction; (3) stemming from this fragmentation, party control is weakened, especially when the President attempts to assume legislative dominance.

Although Congress is often pictured as powerless in confrontation with the executive branch, the fact is that the chairmen of powerful congressional committees often dominate administrative agencies over which they have jurisdiction. They are an important part of the broad Washington establishment. This is particularly true of the chairmen of appropriations committees and subcommittees, for they are able to wield far more influence over the bureaucracy because of their control of the purse strings than the chairmen of other committees. The appropriations committees have a direct weapon—money—that they can wield against administrative adversaries. And, the chairmen of all committees have seniority that often exceeds that of the bureaucrats with whom they are dealing. The secretaries and assistant secretaries of executive departments are political appointments who rarely stay in government more than two years, whereas powerful congressmen have been around for one or more decades. This gives the congressmen expertise that the political levels of the bureaucracy often lack. Political appointees in the bureaucracy must rely upon their professional staff in order to match the expertise of senior congressmen. The power of the chairmen of the appropriations committees often leads them to interfere directly in administrative operations. They become in effect part of the bureaucracy, often dominating it and determining what programs it will implement. The constant interaction between committee chairmen and agencies results in "government without passing laws," to use the phrase of Michael W. Kirst. (See Michael W. Kirst, *Government Without Passing Laws,* Chapel Hill: University of North Carolina Press, 1969.) The following selection deals with this process of legislative influence and describes how one senior Southern congressman established himself as the "permanent secretary of agriculture."[1]

47
Nick Kotz

JAMIE WHITTEN, PERMANENT SECRETARY OF AGRICULTURE

With the sensitive instincts of a successful career bureaucrat, Dr. George Irving scanned the list of states scheduled for the National Nutrition Survey, which was to measure the extent of hunger in America. Halfway down the column his glance froze, and he quickly dialed Congressman Jamie Whitten, the man known in Washington as the "permanent secretary of agriculture."

"Mr. Chairman, they've got Mississippi on that malnutrition study list, and I thought you'd want to know about it," dutifully reported Irving, Administrator of the Agriculture Department's Agricultural Research Service.

For the better part of eighteen years as chairman of the House Appropriations Subcommittee on Agriculture, dapper Jamie L. Whitten has held an iron hand over the budget of the Department of Agriculture (USDA). The entire 107,000-man department is tuned in to the Mississippi legislator's every whim.

"George, we're not going to have another smear campaign against Mississippi, are we?" declared Whitten to his informant. "You boys should be thinking about a *national* survey—and do some studies in Watts and Hough and Harlem!"

Dr. Irving alerted the government's food aid network. "Mr. Whitten

---

From the book *Let Them Eat Promises* by Nick Kotz. © 1969 by Nick Kotz. Published by Prentice-Hall, Inc., Englewood Cliffs, NJ 07632. Reprinted by permission.

[1]The selection deals with Mississippi Congressman Jamie Whitten, who has moved into the most powerful position in the House of Representatives since the piece was written—the chairmanship of the Appropriations Committee. At the same time he has retained his position as Chairman of the Appropriations Subcommittee on Agriculture.

wants Mississippi taken off that list," he told Department of Agriculture food administrator Rodney Leonard.

Leonard, in turn, called Dr. George Silver, a Deputy Assistant Secretary of Health, Education, and Welfare, who was responsible for the joint USDA-HEW malnutrition survey.

"Jamie Whitten's found out Mississippi is on the list and is raising hell. I think we'd better drop it," Leonard said.

Silver, recalling HEW Secretary Wilbur Cohen's order to "avoid unnecessary political friction" in choosing the sample states for the hunger survey, called Dr. Arnold Schaefer, the project chief.

"Mississippi's out—politics!" Silver said curtly.

Back at the Department of Agriculture, food administrator Leonard snapped at Jamie Whitten's informant, "You couldn't have killed the project any better if you had planned it!"

Thus, in August, 1967, the Johnson Administration's first meaningful attempt to ascertain the facts about hunger in Mississippi was stopped cold by an executive department's fear of one congressman. This kind of bureaucratic-congressional maneuvering, exercised between the lines of the law, is little understood, seldom given public scrutiny, and far too infrequently challenged. In the quiet process of hidden power, a bureaucrat in the Agriculture Department reacts more quickly to a raised eyebrow from Jamie Whitten than to a direct order from the Secretary himself. Time after time, a few words from Jamie Whitten can harden into gospel at the Department of Agriculture. Indeed, a casual Whitten statement may be so magnified, as it is whispered from official to official, that the response is more subservient than even the Congressman had in mind.

The stocky, 59-year-old Congressman is not shy about his meteoric rise from a country store in Tallahatchie County to a key position in the nation's capital. And his record is impressive—trial lawyer and state legislator at 21, district attorney for five counties at 23, U.S. Congressman at 31 (in 1941), and chairman of an appropriations subcommittee at 36. His steely self-confidence, studied informality, and carefully conservative clothes suggest anything but the stereotype of country-lawyer-come-to-Washington. Only the beginning of a paunch detracts from a physical sense of strength and energy that radiates from Jamie Whitten.

For all his dynamic presence, Whitten has a way of confounding a listener—or potential critic—with silky Southern rhetoric. It is a test of mental agility to remember the original course of a conversation, as one high USDA official noted: "When you check on things with him, Whitten can go all around the barn with you. Often-times you don't fully understand what he meant. So you latch onto the most obvious point you can find and act on that."

With his implicit power, Whitten doesn't *have* to threaten or be specific. In fact, as George Irving pointed out about his conversation with the Congressman that led to dropping Mississippi from the national hunger survey, "He wasn't saying 'don't go to Mississippi,' he was just suggesting that we think about other places."

Bureaucratic officials who are familiar with Whitten's oblique way of expressing his ideas know also that the Mississippian can rattle off complicated economic statistics and arguments with precise logic and organized thought.

Whitten legally holds the power of the purse, and he exercises it shrewdly. His appropriations subcommittee doles out funds for every item in the Agriculture Department's $7 billion budget, and it does not take long for Washington bureaucrats to realize that the chairman's wrath can destroy precious projects and throw hundreds of people out of jobs.

"He's got the most phenomenal information and total recall," one Agriculture official says of Whitten. "Once you fully understand his do's and don't's and establish rapport with him, life is a whole lot easier!"

Jamie Whitten's considerable power is enhanced by his scholarship. He is a conscientious student of every line of the Agriculture budget, and his hawk's-eye is legendary among Department officials. They, in turn, anticipate his scrutiny by checking planned moves with him, thus extending to him a virtual veto on the most minute details. "A suggestion, that's all you have to have in this business," admitted Rodney Leonard.

The key to this phenomenal power—which goes beyond that of budget control—lies in Whitten's network of informants within the Department, and his skill directing their activities and operations. Executive branch officials learn to protect their own jobs, adjusting their loyalties to the legislative branch in a way the Founding Fathers may not have envisioned when they devised their splendid system of checks and balances. Bureaucratic allies of a particular congressman may be able to inject that congressman's political views (or their own) into laws or programs sponsored by the Administration without the consent, or even the knowledge, of the Department head. Secretaries of Agriculture come and go, but Jamie Whitten remains, a product of Mississippi's political oligarchy and the seniority system in Congress.

In theory, an appropriations subcommittee only considers requests for funds to finance programs already approved by Congress. Thus, Whitten shares some power with Bob Poage (D-Tex.), chairman of the House Agriculture Committee. In actuality, a skillful chairman such as Whitten can control policy, alter the original authorizing legislation, and wind up virtually controlling the administration of a department.

In addition to Chairman Whitten, the Agriculture Appropriations Subcommittee has seven members: Democrats William H. Natcher of Kentucky, W. R. Hull, Jr., of Missouri, George Shipley of Illinois, and Frank Evans of Colorado, and Republicans Odin Langen of Minnesota, Robert H. Michel of Illinois, and Jack Edwards of Alabama. Because a majority of these members share Whitten's outlook on agriculture and his arch-conservative view of social action, the chairman's will becomes the subcommittee's will. As chairman, he also has a hold over staff appointments.

Much of Whitten's power derives from the system within the House of Representatives. Once a subcommittee makes a decision, the full House Appropriations Committee almost always backs it up. This is particularly true with agriculture appropriations, because House Appropriations Chairman George Mahon (D-Tex.) shares Whitten's views on farm policy, welfare spending, and racial issues. For years, Whitten has been in absolute control of all bills before his subcommittee, from the first markup session to the final House vote. "The lines in my face would be deeper except for you" Mahon inscribed on his own portrait in the Mississippian's office.

The House at large rarely has challenged Agriculture budgets because most non-farmbloc members find the subject too complex or dull and rarely take the trouble to inform themselves about it. If some members, or the public, are roused to the point where a challenge develops, the House's committee chairmen generally pull together to defeat the move. Committee members follow to ensure that they will have the chairman's support for their own pet bills—and to keep sacrosanct the whole system of mutual support and protection.

If a challenge happens to get out of hand, the first commandment of a subcommittee chairman is "Never let yourself in for a battle on the House floor if there is any chance for defeat." Part of the power of chairman stems from his apparent invincibility—and the image must be preserved! Therefore, Whitten went along with the Nixon Administration's full budget request for food aid in 1969, knowing there was sufficient pressure for a much bigger appropriation. Whitten responded here only to the politics of the issue, not the substance, for he still complained to Senator George McGovern that hunger was not a problem, that "Nigras won't work" if you give them free food, and that McGovern was promoting revolution by continuing to seek free food stamps for the poorest Americans.

Where agriculture legislation is concerned, Whitten must share power in some measure with Senator Spessard Holland, a Florida Democrat who chairs the Senate Appropriations Subcommittee on Agriculture. Holland is a blunt man who insists that Section 32 funds—food dollars from customs receipts—should be held in reserve to be used at the proper time to boost prices for his state's citrus, vegetable, and beef industries. When Whitten and Holland act in unison—as they often do—the results are predictable. After the School Lunch Act was liberalized in 1964, they managed to refuse funding free school lunches for more than two years. The Johnson administration had sought only $2–3 million to help some of the estimated 5 million poor children who got no benefits from the lunch program, but all the funds were held back in committee until Senator Philip Hart (D-Mich.) threatened to take the fight to the floor.

Jamie Whitten's power is greater than Holland's, however, not only because appropriations usually originate in the House, but also because in the smaller body of the Senate there is less hesitation to overturn subcommittee decisions than in the tradition-bound House of Representatives. The

House system, therefore, assures more *inherent* power for its subcommittee chairmen, and Jamie Whitten has been vigorous and skillful in pursuing it.

GETTING ALONG WITH WHITTEN

Even the Secretary himself feels he must bend to the power of the "permanent secretary." When a delegation headed by Richard Boone of the Citizens' Crusade Against Poverty had asked Orville Freeman to provide free stamps and commodities to help the hungry in Mississippi, the Secretary told them: "I've got to get along with two people in Washington—the President and Jamie Whitten. How can you help me with Whitten?"

Just back from a study of hunger in Mississippi in April, 1967, Dr. Robert Coles and three other doctors also found out about Whitten's influence when they appealed to Orville Freeman. They walked into the Secretary's office feeling that they would be welcomed as helpful, authoritative reporters of the facts, and they left feeling that they had been tagged as troublemakers.

"We were told that we and all the hungry children we had examined and all the other hungry Americans would have to reckon with Mr. Jamie L. Whitten, as indeed must the Secretary of Agriculture, whose funds come to him through the kindness of the same Mr. Whitten. We were told of the problems that the Agriculture Department has with Congress, and we left feeling we ought to weigh those problems as somehow of the same order as the problems we had met in the South—and that we know from our work elsewhere existed all over the country," recalled Coles.

Whitten's power goes beyond the secretary to the presidency itself. In the last year of his administration, President Johnson steadily refused to adopt proposals for broadened food aid that were drafted within his administration. Johnson was then trying to get his income surtax bill through the Congress, and he needed the support of Whitten and the rest of the small group of Southern hierarchs. Johnson declined to risk possible loss of critical votes on the war- and inflation-related surtax.

When Senator Jacob Javits (R-N.Y.) asked Agriculture Secretary Freeman, "What are you afraid of in Mississippi?" (at a July, 1967, hearing on hunger in Mississippi), he wanted to know why Freeman would not modify the food program to reach more of the hungry in Mississippi and elsewhere. The only response he got was ex-marine Freeman's outthrust jaw and a growl that he was not afraid of anyone and would not be intimidated.

Nevertheless, faced with Jamie Whitten's power over his department, and fed information by a Whitten-conscious bureaucracy, Freeman had failed for two years to take measures to feed more of the hungry poor in America. Moreover, the Secretary had stubbornly refused to acknowledge the chasm between his department's efforts and the real needs of the hungry.

From Freeman on down, every Agriculture Department official knew that hunger spelled "hound dog" to Jamie Whitten.

"You've got to understand how Jamie feels about 'hound dog' projects," a career official explained. (In Southern country jargon, a "hound dog" is always hanging around, useless, waiting to be thrown scraps.) Years before, the chairman had killed a small pilot project to teach unemployed Southern Negroes how to drive tractors. "Now, that's a 'hound dog' project, and I don't want to see any more of them" he had said.

Whitten's opposition to any program resembling social welfare—or aid to Negroes—contributed to the failure of War on Poverty programs for rural America. When President Johnson signed an executive order, giving the Agriculture Department responsibility for coordinating the rural war on poverty, Secretary Freeman created a Rural Community Development Service (RCDS) to give the Department a focal point for helping the poor. It was designed to coordinate programs meeting all the needs of the rural poor—housing, education, water, food—not only within the Agriculture Department, but throughout the federal government.

Within a year, the Rural Community Development Service was dead. "Whitten thought the Service smacked of social experimentation and civil rights," a Department of Agriculture official said. In addition, Whitten's brother-in-law, one of many cronies who have filled Agriculture jobs over the years, had clashed with Robert G. Lewis, the idealistic Wisconsin progressive who headed the program. Whitten simply cut off the funds and pigeonholed the coordinating powers of RCDS by placing the responsibility with the docile, conservative Farmers Home Administration. Freeman never fought the issue. There were too many other matters, other appropriations, that were more important to him, so the embryonic effort to coordinate rural poverty programs through the Department of Agriculture ended as little more than a passing idea.

(By assigning the broad rural poverty responsibility to the Department of Agriculture, President Johnson, like President Nixon after him, indicated either a great naïveté about the Department or a lack of seriousness in his proposals. The four congressional committees with which Agriculture must deal undoubtedly are the least receptive of any in Congress to attempts to provide meaningful help to the hard-core rural poor.)

Jamie Whitten has wielded that kind of influence since the mid-1940s, when he killed an emerging Agriculture study that tried to anticipate the social and economic problems of Negro GI's returning from World War II to the feudal cotton South. At that time, the Mississippi Congressman was the youngest chairman of an appropriations subcommittee. By opposing all studies exploring the effects of a changing agriculture upon people, Whitten helped ensure that Agriculture's farm policy would never include serious consideration of the effects of its programs on sharecroppers or farm workers. Whitten and the other powerful Southern congressmen who share his views ensured that the Department would focus only on the cotton planter and his crop. As a result, farm policies that have consistently ignored their toll on millions of black poor have contributed to a rural-urban migration, to a civil rights revolution, and to the ruin of many Americans.

There is no doubt as to the motives of Whitten and the other congressmen who run the Agriculture Department. Testifying on the proposed food stamp law before the Senate Agriculture Committee in 1964, one Department official boldly suggested that it would not help those with little or no income. Committee Chairman Allen J. Ellender (D-La.) indignantly dismissed this complaint against the bill, revealing clearly his own legislative intent.

"I know that in my state we had a number of fishermen who were unable to catch fish," retorted Ellender. "Do you expect the government, because they cannot catch fish, to feed them until the fish are there? In other words, this food stamp program is not to be considered a program just simply to feed people because they cannot get work. This is not what it is supposed to be."

SURPLUS SERFS

What the food stamp program was "supposed to be" was a substitute for a free commodity program that had outlived its usefulness—to Southern plantation owners. Surplus commodities—barely enough to live on—were distributed in the winter when work ceased on the Mississippi plantation of Senator James Eastland (D-Miss.) and on the huge Texas ranches. In the spring, when the $3-a-day planting jobs opened up, the food aid ended. The federal government eased the planter's responsibility by keeping his workers alive during the winter, then permitted the counties that administered the program to withdraw that meager support during planting season—forcing the workers to accept near-starvation wages for survival. When the rural serfs were no longer needed, having been slowly replaced by machines, even that support vanished as the government stopped free commodities in favor of food stamps, which the poorest rural people could not afford. As counties throughout the nation changed from commodities to food stamps, participation fell off by 40 percent; more than 1 million persons, including 100,000 in Mississippi, were forced to drop out of the food program. Whispers of "planned starvation" emerged from the economic crisis of 1967, when the combination of production cutbacks in cotton, automated machinery, and the end of free commodities left the Deep South with thousands of blacks who were unneeded—and hungry. The decisions of the white supremacists in Congress, supported by the subservient Department of Agriculture, contributed to that result.

Whitten's decisions are not always understood by the uninitiated. With his wily ability to juggle figures and cloud ideas, Whitten convinces officials unfamiliar with his technique (and lacking intimate knowledge of the facts) that he is quite a reasonable man—especially when the conversation turns to hunger and the food programs. As he tells it, he was a pioneer on the nutrition issue.

In 1950, he fought for funds for a Department of Agriculture cookbook, and he warned the House it had better concern itself with human as well as animal health. To this day, Whitten insists that the Agriculture Department keep the book in print; he sends a free copy to newlyweds in his district.

The subcommittee chairman also denies that he paralyzed Freeman on the hunger issue: "I *helped* the Secretary by making two points with him," Whitten insists. "I told him he had to charge people what they were accustomed to paying for food stamps because that's what the law says. And I pointed out to him that the law forbids selling food stamps and distributing commodities in the same counties." By making these two helpful points, Whitten blocked the most feasible emergency measures.

"Why, I gave him more money for those food programs than he could spend!" said Whitten.

Actually, the hopelessly inadequate $45 million for food programs Whitten "gave" to Freeman was fought, bought, and paid for by the administration and congressional liberals; this was what was left after Whitten and Holland whittled down the original $100 million, three-year authorization won by liberals on the House floor.

Whitten's explanations of food programs may have appeared perfectly reasonable to Freeman, Sargent Shriver, and many members of Congress, but their total impact was to stop any reform that would get food to the hungry. His own strongly held view is that the food programs should serve the farm programs, not vice versa, and his actions over the years have halted any kind of aid the Agriculture Department might have directed toward the poor. In the early 1960s, when the Kennedy Administration was momentarily concerned for the poor of Appalachia, Agriculture found a way to provide housing grants to aid the hardest-core poor; but once Whitten discovered the grant program in operation, he killed all further appropriations for it.

A few years later, a new cotton program provided advance payments to cotton farmers for withdrawing some of their acreage from production. Sharecroppers, who provided most of the cotton labor force, were supposed to receive their "share" of government payments for idle land. With Whitten's inspiration or blessing, Agriculture adopted a regulation permitting the plantation owner to deduct from the sharecropper's government payments the amount he claimed was owed for the sharecropper's rent, farming expenses, etc. Under the feudal system of the plantation, however, the sharecropper *never* had any legal guarantee that he would receive his fair share of profit for the crop he produced. Blacks who declined to turn over their checks were kicked off hundreds of plantations. The Agriculture Department did not halt the practice.

One of Whitten's sharecropper constituents, trying desperately to find food for her family, gave her own intuitive view of her congressman's attitudes: "He's probably with the bossman's side, don't you know. He's with them. No one's with us but ourselves, and no matter how many of us there are, we don't have what they have."

WINE FOR MISSISSIPPI

Although much of the legislation he favors has enriched American agricultural business with government funds, Whitten's stock answer to any proposed liberalization of the Department of Agriculture food programs is that they are "food programs, not welfare programs." He is adamant about suggestions that food programs be moved to the more liberal Department of Health, Education, and Welfare. "Who'll see to it that [funds for food] don't go for frivolity and wine?" he asks.

Whitten's views on welfare, so strongly felt through the Department of Agriculture, are shared by many Americans. Yet when viewed against the background of Tallahatchie County and its social history, these views, and their interpretations through Agriculture programs, take on a different meaning. Since hunger means poverty, and poverty in Mississippi usually means black, any expanded aid to the hungry means one more threat to the socio-economic order in which the black worker has always been held in absolute dependency upon crumbs from the plantation owner.

The 100,000 or more black Mississippi farm workers who suddenly found themselves with nothing to hold onto in the winter of 1967 were little concerned with frivolity and wine. They had lost their sole supply of food, as Mississippi counties switched over from the inadequate but free surplus commodities to a food stamp program the poor could not afford. "No work, no money, and now, no food," was their outcry, and they desperately sought a reduction in the price of stamps at the very moment when Jamie Whitten was starting his annual review of the Department of Agriculture's budget, with its accompanying discourses on the nature of the poor man. He had heard, the chairman said, that "organized groups" sought to make food stamps free to the poor.

"This is one of the things you always run into," he said to Secretary Freeman. "You make stamps available at 30 percent discount; then they want them at 50, then 75. Now, I have heard reports that some of the organized minority groups are insisting they be provided free of charge. When you start giving people something for nothing, just giving them all they want for nothing, I wonder if you don't destroy character more than you might improve nutrition. I think more and more American people are coming to that conclusion."

They built a lot of character in Mississippi that winter, where the disruption caused by the abrupt changeover to food stamps contributed to the kind of wholesale destitution not seen in this country since the Great Depression.

But the chairman did not seem to think his black constituents were learning the character lesson well enough when it came to the school lunch and new school breakfast programs. Out of work and out of money, few Mississippi Negroes could afford to give their children 25 cents a day for a school lunch, and few schools provided the free lunches that the law technically required for the poor. Agriculture officials virtually begged that the special school lunch assistance budget be raised from $2 million to $10 million annually to give meals to an added 360,000 children in poor areas. Whitten expressed concern only about the impact of civil rights sanctions as he slashed the request by two-thirds.

When another project—a requested million dollars for a pilot school breakfast program to help the neediest youngsters—came up, Whitten's patience wore thin. "Do you contemplate having a pilot dinner program—evening meals—called supper where I grew up?" Whitten asked sarcastically.

When agriculture Department officials explained that "a hungry child in the morning is not able to take full advantage of the schooling that is offered," Whitten wanted to know why the government should be supplying what the family should have supplied before the child left home.

"We all recognize that the type of home from which some children come affects them in many, many ways, but there is a problem always as to whether the federal government should start doing everything for the citizens. You may end up with a certain class of people doing nothing to help themselves. To strike a happy medium is always a real problem."

In this case, Whitten struck it by cutting all $6.5 million requested for breakfast funds from the budget.

Each time a group of doctors, team of reporters, or other investigators produced firsthand reports of hunger in the South, Whitten launched his own "investigation" and announced that parental neglect is largely responsible for any problems. In 1968, when the drive for a bigger food program began to gather steam nationally, Whitten sent out the FBI to disprove the evidence of the problem. The FBI men, who are assigned to the House Appropriations Committee, in effect intimidated people who had provided evidence of hunger.

When a private group investigating hunger, the Citizens' Board of Inquiry, reported after a lengthy investigation that "we have found concrete evidence of chronic hunger and malnutrition in every part of the United States where we have held hearings or conducted hearings," even the Pentagon rallied to the defense of Jamie Whitten's system. The Pentagon-financed Institute for Defense Analyses published an attack on the book *Hunger USA*,[1] which contained the Board of Inquiry report. The author of the defense document, Dr. Herbert Pollack, took the position that ignorance was at the root of any hunger problems in the

---

[1]Citizen's Board of Inquiry. *Hunger USA* (Boston: Beacon Press, 1968).

United States—the same position taken by Whitten and his congressional allies.

The Mississippi Congressman demands that the poor, if they are to get any benefits, must prove they are hungry on a case-by-case basis. "The doctors have not submitted any names," he wrote one concerned Northern lady, assuring her that he would be "most sympathetic and helpful in trying to work this matter out."

Time after time, Whitten has requested names and addresses of the poor who complain of ill-treatment in his home state. Yet in Jamie Whitten's home county, the thought of having their names known strikes terror among those who have had dealings with the local officials.

A news team from television's Public Broadcast Laboratory (PBL), interviewing a black housewife in Whitten's home town of Charleston, felt the danger involved in "naming names." As Mrs. Metcalf began to explain why the food stamp and school lunch programs were not helping her family, a task force of sedans and panel trucks began to cruise back and forth on the U.S. highway about fifty yards from her plantation shack. Suddenly the trucks lunged off the highway into the shack's front yard, surrounding the television crew's two station wagons. A rifle or shotgun was mounted in the rear window of each truck.

"You're trespassing. Git!" growled the plantation manager as he pushed his way past the TV reporter and ordered Mrs. Metcalf to get outside the shack if she knew what was good for her.

"You were trespassing when you crossed the Mississippi state line," shouted Deputy Sheriff Buck Shaw as he ordered the PBL crew to clear out.

In an attempt to ensure Mrs. Metcalf's safety from the local "law," the reporter phoned Congressman Whitten in Washington.

"You remember when Martin Luther King went through my town!" the Congressman answered. "You read the *Wall Street Journal?* It said that he went through there and everybody turned out to look at him. And as soon as he left, they just turned over and went back to sleep. I just know, I live down there and I know. Good God, Chicago, Washington, Detroit. Every one of them would give any amount of money if they could go to sleep feeling as safe—both races—as my folks will!"

It wasn't so peaceful about three o'clock that afternoon with those hard-eyed men threatening Mrs. Metcalf, the reporter explained.

"I suspect Deputy Shaw's like I am," Whitten snapped. "They recognized when you crossed that state line you had no good intention in your mind. I'm no kingfish. I just know my people and my people get along. Unfortunately, you folks and the folks up here don't know how to get along. I bet you money if I ran tomorrow, and nobody voted except the colored people, I'd get the majority. I grew up where five or six of my closest neighbors were Negroes. We played together as kids. We swapped vegetables. Why, I grew up hugging my Momma, and my Momma hugging them."

There were as many Negroes as whites at his father's funeral, Whitten asserts—and he keeps on his desk a yellowed 1936 newspaper editorial that praised District Attorney Jamie Whitten for successfully prosecuting the white man who burned some Mississippi Negroes to death.

Against Whitten's statements about how he is respected by Negroes and would get their vote, about how close his relationship and understanding with Negroes has been, about how quiet and peaceful life is in Charleston, another point of view appeared, as one of his black constituents spoke on the same subject—rambling much as Jamie Whitten does. An eloquent, middle-aged woman told Dr. Robert Coles about the plantation owner for whom her husband works, about his wife, about food, and about life in America:

> He [the plantation owner] doesn't want us trying to vote and like that—and first I'd like to feed my kids, before I go trying to vote.
>
> His wife—the boss man's—she'll come over here sometimes and give me some extra grits and once or twice in the year some good bacon. She tells me we get along fine down here and I says "yes" to her. What else would I be saying, I ask you?
>
> But it's no good. The kids aren't eating enough, and you'd have to be wrong in the head, pure crazy to say they are. Sometimes we talk of leaving; but you know it's just no good up there either, we hear. They eat better, but they have bad things up there I hear, rats as big as raccoons I hear, and they bit my sister's kid real bad.
>
> It's no kind of country to be proud of, with all this going on—the colored people still having it so bad, and the kids being sick and there's nothing you can do about it.[2]

AFFECTION, NOT CASH

Whitten's affection for black constituents like this woman does not extend to federal measures to assist their lot in life. Of the 24,081 residents of Tallahatchie County, 18,000 have family incomes less than $3,000 a year, and 15,197 make less than $2,000. Of these thousands legally defined as poor, only 2,367 qualify for public assistance, and 6,710 receive food stamps. Only a few blocks from Whitten's own white frame home, Negroes live in shacks without toilets, running water, electricity—or food.

Whitten and his fellow white Mississippians point with great pride to the economic progress their state has made in recent years. Improved farming methods, conversion of marginal cropland to timber and other uses, and a strong soil bank program have greatly enriched the commercial farmer in Mississippi. Other government programs, including state tax inducements, have promoted wide industrialization, and rural white workers

---

[2]Robert Coles and Harry Hughe, "We Need Help," *New Republic,* March 8, 1969.

have found a new affluence in the hundreds of factories and small shops that have sprung up.

But the new farming has eliminated thousands of jobs for Negro plantation workers while the segregated social system denies them factory jobs. The able-bodied usually head north, leaving the very young, the very old, and the unskilled to cope with "progress." The rural black does not share in the new prosperity of Mississippi, and some Negroes are worse off than at any time since the Depression. Indeed, in many parts of the Deep South the black man is literally being starved out by the new prosperity.

Perhaps the white Southern politician is no more to blame than are whites anywhere. But the white in the South could not afford to see the truth of the Negro's suffering, because to feel that truth would have shattered a whole way of life.

Jamie Whitten truly believes in his own fairness, his idea of good works, and the imagined affection he receives from Negroes back home. For fifty-nine years, he has anesthetized his soul to the human misery and indignity only a few yards from his own home and has refused to believe that the responsibility for that indignity lies on his white shoulders. His belief in the basic laziness, indifference, and unworthiness of the black poor is as strong as his belief in the virtues of a way of life that for three centuries has denied these same black poor any avenues of pursuing ambition, self-respect, or a better future for their children.

That Jamie Whitten should suffer from blindness to human need is one thing. But that he can use this blindness as an excuse to limit the destiny of millions of Americans is another matter, one which should concern anyone who believes in the basic strengths of this country's constitutional guarantees. The checks and balances of a reasonable democratic republic have gone completely awry when a huge bureaucracy and the top officials of an Administration base their actions concerning deepest human need on their fearful perception of what one rather limited man seems to want.

The system of seniority and temerity that gives a man such as Jamie Whitten such awesome power must come under more serious public scrutiny if the American system of government is ever to establish itself on the basis of moral concern about the individual human being.

Congressional Staff:
The Surrogates of Power

☐   Both the committee and personal staffs of Capitol Hill are important forces in the legislative process. Astute senators and congressmen know that their effectiveness in Congress largely depends upon the caliber of their staff. Each member of Congress has a personal staff; and the committee chairmen control staffs that are usually far greater in number than those in congressional and senatorial offices.

Although an embryo congressional staff began to develop in the nineteenth century, the origins of today's professional staff are found in the Legislative Reorganization Act of 1946, which increased the staffs of committees and their members. More important than the actual numbers of professional aides provided by the Act was the fact that Congress, for the first time, officially recognized the need for expert assistance, not only to cope with the increasingly complex problems confronting government but also to counterbalance the growing dominance of a highly expert executive branch.

Since the passage of the Legislative Reorganization Act in 1946 there has been a vast increase in congressional staff to approximately 14,000 aides in 1981. The greatest increment in staff occurred during the period from 1970 to 1980, as subcommittees expanded at an unprecedented rate. Moreover, as committee staffs grew, members who were not committee chairmen, noting how effective chairmen used their staffs to boost their power on Capitol Hill, demanded more personal staff. Over 10,000 professional staffers now serve in the offices of members, and approximately 4,000 are employed by the close to 300 committees and subcommittees of Congress.

To what extent does congressional staff constitute an invisible government, exercising power and responsibility that the Constitution has delegated to the elected members of Congress? While senators and congressmen nominally exert control over their staffs, in actual fact, staffers often control their bosses. The time constraints upon members alone make it impossible for them to exercise more than cursory control of staff, and usually, this increases their dependence upon staff. Members rely upon their aides to set their daily schedules, keep them abreast of important issues, and determine what should be on their legislative agenda. Members often become the surrogates of the staffers, rather than vice versa.

An absorbing account of the role of the staff on Capitol Hill is presented by Eric Redman, who, fresh from college with a Rhodes Scholarship ahead of him, was employed temporarily as a junior aide by Senator Warren Magnuson, at that time chairman of the Commerce Committee. No one could have been more junior staffer than Redman, yet he was able to operate effectively as Magnuson's surrogate in securing the passage of a National Health Service Corps bill by the Senate, and indirectly, by the House.

In this selection Redman describes some of the lessons he learned as a beginner on Capitol Hill. He attempted first to get the National Health Service Corps proposal passed, not as legislation but through the appropriations process. Magnuson was the chairman of the HEW Appropriations Subcommittee, which could earmark money for the doctor service corps that Redman wanted to have included under the umbrella appropriation for the Public Health Service in HEW. The appropriations route was an especially attractive strategy, not only because it would avoid the cumbersome, risky, and slow legislative process, but also because Magnuson had clear jurisdiction over HEW appropriations but not over legislation for the department. Each committee chairman has tight control over legislation falling under his jurisdiction. Redman, even as a beginner, knew that his strategy, if it worked, would be an easy way to give credit to Magnuson for the new program. Above all, as a loyal staffer, Redman did not want his, and by extension, Magnuson's proposal to be "stolen" by other senators and staffers. He wanted to assure that Magnuson would get full credit for the plan, to keep the proposal on Magnuson's turf—at all costs.

48
Eric Redman

BEGINNER'S LESSONS

Confronted with a National Health Service Corps scheme that purported to strengthen the system of private practice, a sufficiently paranoid member of the American Medical Association might have recognized it immediately as the Trojan Horse of socialized medicine. In Senator Magnuson's office, however, the Corps proposal seemed singularly undramatic at first, and we hardly pursued it with the zeal one would expect of conspirators. In fact, we agreed from the first that the NHSC should not be as grand in scale as it might be in philosophy; even [Dr. Abe] Bergman [a consultant to Magnuson] did not want it to begin as a massive new program, for he doubted any single approach could solve the complex "doctor distribution" problem. So we settled for what we hoped would be a small but imaginative experiment: an NHSC in which several dozen Public Health Service doctors would run a handful of health-care projects in a few selected communities scattered throughout the United States. If this limited program proved successful, we reasoned, Senator Magnuson could eventually persuade Congress to expand it.

One reason our plans were so modest was that our initial strategy called for Magnuson to create the NHSC without any new legislation.

Legislation would have been "best," of course, in the sense that legislation alone could give visibility, coherence, and an unambiguous mission to the new Corps. But an NHSC bill, unlike earlier Bergman-inspired legislation, would not fall within the jurisdiction of the Senate Commerce Committee, where Magnuson, as Chairman, could pass virtually any bill he liked. Instead, such a bill would automatically go to the Committee on Labor and Public Welfare, which considers all health legislation in the Senate—and Magnuson was not a member of that Committee. Nor did Magnuson sit on the Senate Armed Services Committee, which might ask to review the bill no matter how carefully we tried to skirt the draft law. So the one thing we knew for certain was that we didn't want to establish the NHSC through new legislation; this reinforced the seeming wisdom of aiming for a small NHSC.

Fortunately, Magnuson could create the Corps without writing a bill—or so we thought. Through the HEW Appropriations Subcommittee, the Senator controlled HEW's funds and the funds of its relevant subdivision, the Public Health Service. Our initial strategy, therefore, was simple: Magnuson would merely add a few million dollars to the HEW Appropriation bill and "earmark" the money (i.e., specify its use, in the bill or in the accompanying Report) for an NHSC-type experiment under Public Health Service auspices. Since the total HEW Appropriations involved approximately $20 billion, and since Congress habitually adds a few hundred million dollars to the President's annual budget request for HEW, a small increase for the NHSC might go unnoticed, or at least cause little controversy.

We knew Magnuson would have no difficulty earmarking the funds; the question was whether HEW would cooperate thereafter. The whole strategy hinged on HEW's willingness to play along: if the Department was inclined to balk, it could refuse to spend the money, on the ground that the Public Health Service law did not explicitly authorize any program like the NHSC. But if, on the other hand, HEW did want to establish the Corps, it could quietly agree with Senator Magnuson that, yes, the law *could* be interpreted broadly as allowing this new experiment.

Obviously, we needed to reach an understanding with the Department of Health, Education and Welfare. This would have been true even with a less covert strategy, however, because in practice hostile Departments can effectively scuttle even the firmest of Congressional directives. Moreover, I had been taught in college (and consequently insisted to Bergman) that a prerequisite of "good" public administration is that the Executive Branch, with all its expertise, participate in designing the programs it will eventually have to administer. Whenever I passed the vast HEW Building at the foot of Capitol Hill, I couldn't help thinking that somewhere within that labyrinth there must be people who understood the "doctor distribution" problem better than Bergman and I did (particularly since all *I* knew was what Bergman had told me).

We anticipated that HEW would want to cooperate. First of all, the Department would be stupid not to "play ball" with Magnuson, the Chairman of the HEW Appropriations Subcommittee. But more important, we thought HEW would like the Corps proposal itself. Top HEW officials were already feuding publicly with the White House, asserting the need for new health programs but checked by fiscal and policy constraints from the President and the Office of Management and Budget (OMB). Dr. Roger O. Egeberg, the Assistant Secretary of HEW for Health and Scientific Affairs (and hence the "nation's number one doctor"), charged openly that the men on Pennsylvania Avenue were "callous," "indifferent," or "insensitive" to America's health-care problems. Egeberg's criticism received widespread coverage in the news, not only as one of the first indications of dissension within the Nixon Administration, but also as evidence that Egeberg himself was not the docile yes-man observers had once thought. Nixon's first choice for the post Egeberg occupied had, after all, been the reform-minded Dr. John M. Knowles, but that nomination had provoked such an outcry from the American Medical Association (AMA) that Nixon had withdrawn it and substituted Egeberg, a seemingly innocuous academic administrator whom the AMA could accept. Nixon's capitulation to the AMA had seemed to indicate that no one in the Administration (least of all Egeberg himself) would challenge the status quo of American medicine— but now Egeberg was proving that judgment premature.

In addition to Egeberg's growing independence, the historical "alliance" between HEW and Congress encouraged us to seek the Department's cooperation in making plans for the NHSC. Throughout the 1950s and early 1960s,[1] Congress had consistently provided more funds for HEW than the President had requested, and the increases had been engineered through more or less open collusion between HEW officials and the Chairmen of the HEW Appropriations Subcommittees in the House and Senate. Magnuson continued this pattern when he became Chairman in 1969, adding a standard $300 million to the Fiscal 1970 HEW Appropriation, but President Nixon promptly vetoed the entire bill. The veto (Nixon's first, and televised live to the nation) meant more work for Magnuson—he and his Subcommittee had to rewrite the whole appropriation during the Christmas holidays—but it stung HEW more severely. Speculation grew that HEW would seek to reforge its traditional alliance with Congress in order to resist Presidential "downgrading" of its programs—a classic textbook response for any out-of-favor Department, and one that HEW particularly had followed in the past.

Under the circumstances, we didn't hesitate to ask HEW's help in creating the National Health Service Corps, nor did the Department's

---

[1]President Eisenhower established HEW in 1953. In the mid-1960s, for a number of reasons (including the Vietnam war), HEW funding remained relatively stable.

initial reaction disappoint us. When we requested technical assistance, for example, in drafting the earmarking provision and in determining how much money to allot the proposed Corps, HEW promptly agreed to send us some of its top talent—a young doctor and a young lawyer from the Department's operating division, the Health Services and Mental Health Administration (HSMHA).

In order to elicit maximum cooperation from the HSMHA doctor and lawyer, Bergman and I carefully staged our first meeting to impress upon them the control Magnuson exercised over their Department's money. We picked as a conference site the cavernous hearing room of the HEW Appropriations Subcommittee in the New Senate Office Building, and in case the significance of the chamber should escape our visitors, we deliberately invited a fifth participant: Harley Dirks, the chief clerk of the Subcommittee and hence Magnuson's top aide in deciding the size and distribution of HEW's funds. Not a subtle show of power, perhaps, but one not easily dismissed.

We needn't have worried. Our doctor and lawyer readily endorsed the NHSC concept; in fact, they insisted, people in HSMHA had long been eager for just such a program. HEW welcomed innovative proposals for better health care, they said, but the White House and the OMB blocked the Department's own initiatives. Conspiring with Congress, however, could bring fast results; perhaps after we had set up the NHSC (an easy matter, they suggested), we could undertake some more substantial tasks together. The only caveat entered in this optimistic discussion was the lawyer's cautious remark, just before leaving, that the legality of our earmarking strategy was unclear; if the PHS lacked authority for patient care, Magnuson could not create that authority simply by giving the agency more money. Perhaps, the lawyer added, specific authorizing legislation might be needed, in which case the earmarking strategy wouldn't work. But this was only a possibility, and the lawyer promised to consult his books and produce a definitive answer.

With the technical details "farmed out" to the HSMHA doctor and lawyer, we began to consider the more rarefied politics of our earmarking strategy. We decided the next step was to visit Dr. Egeberg himself, the unexpected new advocate of innovative health-care programs. And we knew the most important person to include as a member of our delegation was again Harley Dirks.

Dirks is in many ways a legendary man on Capitol Hill. Rumor has it that he was once a shoe salesman in Othello, Washington, a drowsy little farm town in the dry Columbia Basin. A more likely version is that Dirks *owned* a shoe store in Othello, and if he occasionally fitted the customers himself, it was not because he lacked grander dreams. Othello is miles from anywhere, an oasis of sorts in prairielike Eastern Washington, and its isolation—even from Seattle—cannot be adequately expressed in a mileage number on a road map. Othello was so slow, and Dirks so fast, that soon he found himself owning a host of its businesses and one of its banks—or so the story goes—despite the fact that he spent much of his time catching trout, shooting pheasant, and siring offspring. For whatever reason, Dirks eventually felt the urge to move on, and to a man of his imagination that did not mean bundling up the family and heading for Walla Walla. Instead, he worked for Senator Magnuson in the 1962 campaign and then followed him back to Washington, D.C.

Dirks became a "clerk" on the Appropriations Committee at a time when Magnuson handled the funds of HUD, NASA, and the many independent agencies and regulatory commissions. When Magnuson switched to the HEW Appropriations post, Dirks went with him, simply moving his pipe rack to a new office and confronting a new set of figures. At first, his nominal superior was the "Chief Clerk" of the Subcommittee, an irascible Southerner who had served under chairmen now almost forgotten on Capitol Hill. Before long, however, Dirks moved in behind the Chief Clerk's desk (his own had become an unworkable mountain of papers), and within a few months the Chief Clerk stopped coming to work altogether. Dirks redecorated the staid office with oils he had painted, and as a quiet joke he arrayed on his new desk such "authoritative" academic works as *The Power of the Purse* and *The Politics of the Budgetary Process.* He had neither the time nor the need to read books about appropriations; he ran a Subcommittee that appropriated nearly $40 billion each year (an amount second only to the Defense Department's).[2]

Like other Appropriations Committee clerks, Dirks is unknown to the public and to much of the Washington press corps. Tourists do not call at his office (although Senators and Secretaries do), and at appropriations hearings members of the audience sometimes whisper, "Who is that man sitting next to the Chairman?" That Dirks carries his power so judiciously says much about his fierce loyalty to Senator Magnuson, his sole constituent. Magnuson relies on Dirks heavily, not simply because he is loyal, or because a chairman has little choice, but also because Dirks is thorough, alert, and discreet. The only outsider, in fact, who has ever sensed Dirks's true influence was an academic researcher who interviewed him in connection with a study attempting to correlate appropriations figures with Senators' backgrounds; amused, Dirks simply jotted down for his visitor his own prediction of dollar amounts, by program, in an appropriations bill the Senators themselves had not yet even discussed. When the bill finally passed, Dirks's projections corresponded uncannily with the approved figures.

Dirks's anonymity does not extend to the Department of Health, Educa-

---

[2]When trust fund expenditures are included, the HEW appropriation totals some $80 billion, an amount in excess of the regular Defense Department appropriation.

tion and Welfare. Bergman and I witnessed a revealing, if somewhat comic, demonstration of this as we walked with Harley down HEW's long corridors on our way to discuss the earmarking strategy with Dr. Egeberg. From one doorway after another, men and women emerged to intone respectfully, "Good morning, Mr. Dirks," or "Hello, Harley!" and so on down the list of ingratiating pleasantries. Bergman and I felt obscure and incidental, as if we were Secret Service escorts; Dirks, for his part, smiled and waved like a Presidential candidate. It was hard to imagine him ever going back to Othello.

Even Dr. Egeberg, when we arrived, seemed sensitive to Dirks's presence. He welcomed us warmly and ushered us immediately into his inner office, hastily summoning aides and ordering coffee. A huge, bald man in his late sixties, Egeberg sported a jaunty yellow BULLSHIT button on his lapel. Hardly giving us time to sit down (much less to broach the subject of our visit), he launched into an animated monologue, designed (I supposed) to establish his credentials as a critic of the president and presidential health policies.

"I had an appointment to see the President a month or so ago," he began, "because I wanted him to add a hundred and fifty million dollars to our budget for training more doctors. I was sitting outside the door to the Oval Office, waiting, when John Ehrlichman [the President's top aide for domestic affairs] came up and asked, 'This visit doesn't have anything to do with money, does it?' I said, 'Of course it has to do with money—we need a hundred and fifty million dollars to train more doctors.' 'Oh, well,' Ehrlichman said, 'if it has to do with money, we'll have to reprogram this appointment. No one can discuss money matters with the President unless George Shultz [Nixon's fiscal adviser] is here.'

"Now, I've called every single week since," Egeberg concluded, "and I still haven't been able to get the appointment 'reprogrammed.' And the hell of it is, I *know* the President of the AMA can walk in and see Nixon anytime he wants!"

The anecdote suggested Egeberg might cooperate with us; so did his eagerness in turning to Harley to ask why we had come (evidently he hadn't been briefed). Harley, adopting the role of silent sage, nodded to indicate that I should explain our plan. Somewhat nervously (this was the "nation's number one doctor"), I told Egeberg what we hoped to establish: a National Health Service Corps, within the Public Health Service, created solely through an earmarking of funds in the HEW Appropriation. Would Egeberg and the Department help?

Egeberg responded without hesitation. "I've always wanted a program like that," he said, "but I can't come right out and ask for it myself. I've got certain problems down *there,* you know [he motioned toward the White House]. But if *Maggie* proposed it," he went on, in mock conspiratorial tones, "and if he provided the *money* for it, well then I'd *have* to set it up, wouldn't I?

"We need a new mission for the Public Health Service," he continued, after exchanging broad smiles with Dirks, "and in fact, I've got a committee looking at the problem right now. I think the answer has got to be some kind of doctor corps. So let's hear your plan."

The plan we agreed upon, after a brief discussion, was simple. Egeberg's staff would write some questions, based on the HSMHA doctor-lawyer team's research, and give them to Magnuson so that he could "spontaneously" ask Egeberg about an NHSC when the doctor came to testify during the HEW Appropriation hearings in June. Magnuson would describe his idea briefly, then ask Egeberg (for example), "if Congress provided you with three million dollars for this type of program, staffed with Public Health Service doctors, how would you spend it?" Egeberg would then reply, "Well, Mr. Chairman, of course the department has not *asked* for any such program, but if you and the Committee feel so strongly about it that you provide three million dollars, I guess this is what we would have to do. . . . " Then Egeberg would outline the details of the hypothetical Corps, prompted occasionally by carefully prearranged questions from Magnuson. The exchange, printed in the hearing record and in the Report accompanying the appropriation, would serve both to define the "Congressional intent" behind the NHSC (since no legislation would be available for this purpose) and to create the impression that Magnuson had "forced" the new program upon a reluctant but ultimately pliable HEW officialdom. The scheme was so clever that we wondered if Magnuson and Egeberg would be able to keep straight faces while reciting their lines.

After chuckling over the impending "drama" in the hearing room, Egeberg rose and walked us to the door. As we left, I mentioned to him the HSMHA lawyer's warning that the strategy might prove impossible for legal reasons. Egeberg replied that he hoped the lawyer was wrong, and that if not, we could still count on the services of HEW's General Counsel in drafting any legislation we might need. "Let's keep in touch," he added, and bade us goodbye.

I had to admit, as we walked away, that I felt better about our enlisting Egeberg as an ally than I had before the visit. My misgivings had stemmed from my only previous exposure to him, at a press conference in 1969 when HEW announced a partial ban on cyclamate sweeteners, which had just been found to cause cancer in rats. In later weeks, the cyclamate "ban" became the object of Washington humor, but the press conference had been tense (and held on a Saturday for a deliberate reason: the stock market would be closed). "This is going to be ten times worse than when Thalidomide hit," confided a White House aide I knew, and HEW secretary Robert Finch, who had spoken first, gripped the podium tightly; sweat showed all over his face. Yet Dr. Egeberg, speaking next, treated the issue nonchalantly from the first, pointing out that everything—cyclamates, the Pill, cigarettes—had its advantages and disadvantages from a health standpoint. This attitude had surprised the press corps, and reinforced my distasteful image of Egeberg, an image I had picked up during the earlier "Knowles Affair."

Now, however, I found I liked Egeberg. I could even interpret sympathetically his position on cyclamates, something I had judged too quickly in any event. I could see why Magnuson liked Egeberg too, almost alone of the HEW officials he confronted each year (the indecisive Finch had become "Secretary Flinch" in Magnuson's vocabulary). What struck me most about Egeberg was his good nature and his obviously good intentions. Climbing into a cab for a brief ride back to Capitol Hill, I confided all this to Bergman and Harley Dirks.

Harley looked at me and grinned. "Wait and see," he admonished. "You like him because he's barking at the White House, but he's barking because the White House keeps him on a very short leash."

☐   Redman's initial optimism was soon dashed when it became clear that HEW was not going to cooperate with his strategy. He soon found that the Washington power establishment, with the key committee chairmen of Capitol Hill at the apex, was far more complicated and sensitive than he ever could have imagined. Eventually, "Magnuson's" and "Redman's" National Health Service Corps bill was passed by both the House and the Senate, but only after intricate and often frustrating political maneuvering to enlist the aid of the powerful committee chairmen in the Senate and the House who had jurisdiction over the proposal. Just as Magnuson's staff claimed credit for their senator, the staffs of Senator Ralph Yarborough, chairman of the key Committee on Labor and Public Welfare (now called the Labor and Human Resources Committee) and its Health Subcommittee, proclaimed that *their* senator was responsible for the bill. On the House side, the bill was credited to Congressman Paul Rogers of West Palm Beach, Florida, who, as acting chairman of the Health Subcommittee skillfully guided the legislation through numerous obstacles to a floor victory.

Successful congressional careers are built upon good staff work. While staff tends to be more an attribute of power in the Senate than in the House, politically astute congressmen know that they, too, can build their Capitol Hill power and status through a talented and adroit staff.

Congress and the Electoral Connection

☐ Throughout the 1970s public opinion polls consistently revealed that Congress was held in low esteem by the American people. The book *Who Runs Congress?* published by the Ralph Nader Congress Project reflected and at the same time helped to crystallize public disenchantment with Capitol Hill.[1] The book emphasized the need for citizens to take on Congress to prevent a further flagging of the institution. In his introduction, Ralph Nader summarized the contents of the book by stating that "the people have indeed abdicated their power, their money, and their democratic birthright to Congress. As a result, without the participation of the people, Congress has surrendered its enormous authority and resources to special interest groups, waste, insensitivity, ignorance, and bureaucracy."[2] The 1972 theme of the Nader project that Congress was in crisis continues to be accepted by the vast majority of people.

While Ralph Nader and his colleagues feel that the major cause of the demise of Congress is its detachment from the people, Richard Fenno in the following selection adopts a different viewpoint. He feels that people fault the *institution* of Congress, not their individual representatives on Capitol Hill. In fact, he points out that there is a close connection between legislators and constituents, and often, a feeling of affection by voters for their representatives. Fenno feels that we apply different standards in judging individual members of Congress than we do in assessing the institution, being far more lenient in the former than the latter case. The individual is judged for his personality, style, and representativeness, while the institution is judged by its ability to recognize and solve the nation's problems. But, the institution cannot be thought of apart from the members that compose it. It is they who have given it its unique character. It is the individual member who, more often than not, has supported a decentralized and fragmented legislature because of the members' incentive to achieve personal power and status on Capitol Hill.

---

[1]Mark J. Green et al. (editors), *Who Runs Congress?* (New York: Bantam/Grossman, 1972).

[2]Ibid., p. 1.

49

Richard F. Fenno, Jr.

IF, AS RALPH NADER SAYS, CONGRESS IS "THE BROKEN BRANCH," HOW COME WE LOVE OUR CONGRESSMEN SO MUCH?

Off and on during the past two years, I accompanied ten members of the House of Representatives as they traveled around in their home districts. In every one of those districts I heard a common theme, one that I had not expected. Invariably, the representative I was with—young or old, liberal or conservative, Northerner, Southerner, Easterner, or Westerner, Democrat or Republican—was described as "the best congressman in the United States." Having heard it so often, I now accept the description as fact. I am even prepared to believe the same thing (though I cannot claim to have heard it with my own ears) of the members of the Senate. Each of our 435 representatives and 100 senators is, indeed, "the best congressman in the United States." Which is to say that each enjoys a great deal of support and approbation among his or her constituents. Judging by the election returns, this isn't much of an exaggeration. In the recent election, 96 percent of all House incumbents who ran were reelected; and 85 percent of all Senate incumbents who ran were reelected. These convincing figures are close to the average reelection rates of incumbents for the past ten elections. We do, it appears, love our congressmen.

On the other hand, it seems equally clear that we do not love our Congress. Louis Harris reported in 1970 that only one-quarter of the electorate gave Congress a positive rating on its job performance—while nearly two-thirds expressed themselves negatively on the subject. . . . There [is] considerable concern—dramatized recently by the critical Nader project—for the performance of Congress as an institution. On the evidence, we seem to approve of our legislators a good deal more than we do our legislature. And therein hangs something of a puzzle. If our congressmen are so good, how can our Congress be so bad? If it is the individuals that make up the institution, why should there be such a disparity in our judgments? What follows are a few reflections on this puzzle.

A first answer is that we apply different standards of judgment, those that we apply to the individual being less demanding than those we apply to

From Richard F. Fenno, Jr., "If, As Ralph Nader Says, Congress Is 'The Broken Branch,' How Come We Love Our Congressmen So Much?" Originally written as part of an editorial project entitled "The Role of Congress: A Study of the Legislative Branch," © 1972 by Time, Inc., and Richard F. Fenno, Jr. Reprinted by permission.

the institution. For the individual, our standard is one of representativeness—of personal style and policy views. Stylistically, we ask that our legislator display a sense of identity with us so that we, in turn, can identify with him or her—via personal visits to the district, concern for local projects and individual "cases," and media contact of all sorts, for example. On the policy side, we ask only that his general policy stance does not get too frequently out of line with ours. And, if he should become a national leader in some policy area of interest to us, so much the better. These standards are admittedly vague. But because they are locally defined and locally applied, they are consistent and manageable enough so that legislators can devise rules of thumb to meet them. What is more, by their performance they help shape the standards, thereby making them easier to meet. Thus they win constituent recognition as "the best in the United States." And thus they establish the core relationship for a representative democracy.

For the institution, however, our standards emphasize efforts to solve national problems—a far less tractable task than the one we (and he) set for the individual. Given the inevitable existence of unsolved problems, we are destined to be unhappy with congressional performance. The individual legislator knows when he has met our standards of representativeness; he is reelected. But no such definitive measure of legislative success exists. And, precisely because Congress is the most familiar and most human of our national institutions, lacking the distant majesty of the Presidency and the Court, it is the easy and natural target of our criticism. We have met our problem solvers, and they are us.

Furthermore, such standards as we do use for judging the institutional performance of Congress are applied inconsistently. In 1963, when public dissatisfaction was as great as in 1970, Congress was criticized for being obstructionist, dilatory and insufficiently cooperative with regard to the Kennedy programs. Two years later, Congress got its highest performance rating of the decade when it cooperated completely with the executive in rushing the Great Society program into law. But by the late 1960s and early 1970s the standard of judgment had changed radically—from cooperation to counterbalance in Congressional relations with the Executive. Whereas, in 1963, Harris had found "little in the way of public response to the time-honored claim that the Legislative Branch is . . . the guardian against excessive Executive power," by 1968 he found that three-quarters of the electorate wanted Congress to act as the watchdog of the Executive and not to cooperate so readily with it. The easy passage of the Tonkin Resolution reflects the cooperative standards set in the earlier period; its repeal reflects the counterbalancing standards of the recent period. Today we are concerned about Ralph Nader's "broken branch" which, we hear, has lost—and must reclaim from the Executive—its prerogatives in areas such as war-making and spending control. To some degree, then, our judgments on Congress are negative because we change our minds frequently concerning the kind of Congress we want. A Congress whose main job is to cooperate with the Executive would look quite different from one whose main job is to counterbalance the Executive.

Beneath the differences in our standards of judgment, however, lies a deeper dynamic of the political system. Senators and representatives, for their own reasons, spend a good deal more of their time and energy polishing and worrying about their individual performance than they do working at the institution's performance. Though it is, of course, true that their individual activity is related to institutional activity, their first-order concerns are individual, not institutional. Foremost is their desire for reelection. Most members of Congress like their job, want to keep it, and know that there are people back home who want to take it away from them. So they work long and hard at winning reelection. Even those who are safest want election margins large enough to discourage opposition back home and/or to help them float further political ambitions. No matter what other personal goals representatives and senators wish to accomplish—increased influence in Washington and helping to make good public policy are the most common—reelection is a necessary means to those ends.

We cannot criticize these priorities—not in a representative system. If we believe the representative should mirror constituency opinion, we must acknowledge that it requires considerable effort for him to find out what should be mirrored. If we believe a representative should be free to vote his judgment, he will have to cultivate his constituents assiduously before they will trust him with such freedom. Either way we will look favorably on his efforts. We come to love our legislators, in the *second* place, because they so ardently sue for our affections.

As a courtship technique, moreover, they re-enforce our unfavorable judgments about the institution. Every representative with whom I traveled criticized the Congress and portrayed himself, by contrast, as a fighter against its manifest evils. Members run *for* Congress by running *against* Congress. They refurbish their individual reputations as "the best congress-man in the United States" by attacking the collective reputation of the Congress of the United States. Small wonder the voters feel so much more warmly disposed and so much less fickle toward the individuals than toward the institution.

One case in point: the House decision to grant President Nixon a spending ceiling plus authority to cut previously appropriated funds to maintain that ceiling. One-half the representatives I was with blasted the House for being so spineless that it gave away its power of the purse to the President. The other half blasted the House for being so spineless in exercising its power of the purse that the President had been forced to act. Both groups spoke to supportive audiences; and each man enhanced his individual reputation by attacking the institution. Only by raising both questions, however, could one see the whole picture. Once the President forced the issue, how come the House didn't stand up to him and protect its crucial institutional power over the purse strings? On the other hand, if economic experts agreed that a spending ceiling was called for, how come the House didn't enact it and make the necessary budget cuts in the first place? The answer to the first question lies in the proximity of their reelection battles, which re-enforced the tendency of all representatives to think in individualistic rather than institutional terms. The answer to the second question lies in the total absence of institutional machinery whereby the House (or, indeed, Congress) can make overall spending decisions.

Mention of the institutional mechanisms of Congress leads us to a *third* explanation for our prevailing pattern of judgments. When members of Congress think institutionally—as, of course they must—they think in terms of a structure that will be most congenial to the pursuit of their individual concerns—for reelection, for influence, or for policy. Since each individual has been independently designated "the best in the United States," each has an equal status and an equal claim to influence within the structure. For these reasons, the members naturally think in terms of a very fragmented, decentralized institution, providing a maximum of opportunity for individual performance, individual influence, and individual credit.

The 100-member Senate more completely fits this description than the 435-member House. The smaller body permits a more freewheeling and creative individualism. But both chambers tend strongly in this direction, and representatives as well as senators chafe against centralizing mechanisms. Neither body is organized in hierarchical—or even in well-coordinated—patterns of decision-making. Agreements are reached by some fairly subtle forms of mutual adjustment—by negotiation, bargaining, and compromise. And interpersonal relations—of respect, confidence, trust—are crucial building blocks. The members of Congress, in pursuit of their individual desires, have thus created an institution that is internally quite complex. Its structure and processes are, therefore, very difficult to grasp from the outside.

In order to play out some aspects of the original puzzle, however, we must make the effort. And the committee system, the epitome of fragmentation and decentralization, is a good place to start. The performance of Congress as an institution is very largely the performance of its committees. The Nader project's "broken branch" description is mostly a committee-centered description because that is where the countervailing combination of congressional expertise and political skill resides. To strengthen Congress means to strengthen its committees. To love Congress means to love its committees. Certainly when we have not loved our Congress, we have heaped our displeasure upon its committees. The major legislative reorganizations, of 1946 and 1970, were committee-centered reforms—centering on committee jurisdictions, committee democracy, and committee staff support. Other continuing criticisms—of the seniority rule for selecting committee chairmen, for example—have centered on the committees.

Like Congress as a whole, committees must be understood first in terms of what they do for the individual member. To begin with, committees are relatively more important to the individual House member than to the individual senator. The representative's career inside Congress is very closely tied to his committee. For the only way such a large body can function is to divide into highly specialized and independent committees. Policy-making activity funnels through these committees; so does the legislative activity and influence of the individual legislator. While the Senate has a set of committees paralleling those of the House, a committee assignment is nowhere near as constraining for the career of the individual senator. The Senate is more loosely organized, senators sit on many more committees and subcommittees than representatives, and they have easy access to the work of committees of which they are not members. Senators, too, can command and utilize national publicity to gain influence beyond the confines of their committee. Whereas House committees act as funnels for individual activity, Senate committees act as facilitators of individual activity. The difference in functions is considerable—which is why committee chairmen are a good deal more important in the House than in the Senate and why the first modifications of the seniority rule should have come in the House rather than the Senate. My examples will come from the House.

Given the great importance of his committee to the career of the House member, it follows that we will want to know how each committee can affect such careers....

Where a committee's members are especially interested in pyramiding their individual influence, they will act so as to maintain the influence of their committee (and, hence, their personal influence) within the House. They will adopt procedures that enhance the operating independence of the committee. They will work hard to remain relatively independent of the Executive Branch. And they will try to underpin that independence with such resources as specialized expertise, internal cohesion, and the respect of their House colleagues. Ways and Means and Appropriations are committees of this sort. By contrast, where a committee's members are especially interested in getting in on nationally controversial policy action, they will not be much concerned about the independent influence of their committee. They will want to ally themselves closely with any and all groups outside the committee who share their policy views. They want to help enact what they individually regard as good public policy; and if that means ratifying policies shaped elsewhere—in the Executive Branch particularly—so be it. And, since their institutional independence is not a value for them, they make no special effort to acquire such underpinnings as expertise, cohesion, or chamber respect. Education and Labor and Foreign Affairs are committees of this sort.

These two types of committees display quite different strengths in their performance. Those of the first type are especially influential. Ways and Means probably makes a greater independent contribution to policy making than any other House committee. Appropriations probably exerts a more influential overview of executive branch activities than any other House committee. The price they pay, however, is a certain decrease in their responsiveness to noncommittee forces—as complaints about the closed rule on tax bills and executive hearings on appropriations bills will attest. Committees of the second type are especially responsive to noncommittee forces and provide easy conduits for outside influence in policymaking. Education and Labor was probably more receptive to President Johnson's Great Society policies than any other House committee; it successfully passed the largest part of that program. Foreign Affairs has probably remained as thoroughly responsive to Executive Branch policies, in foreign aid for instance, as any House committee. The price they pay, however, is a certain decrease in their influence—as complaints about the rubber-stamp Education and Labor Committee and about the impotent Foreign Affairs Committee will attest. In terms of the earlier discussions of institutional performance standards, our hopes for a cooperative Congress lie more with the latter type of committee; our hopes for a counterbalancing Congress lie more with the former.

So, committees differ. And they differ to an important degree according to the desires of their members. This ought to make us wary of blanket descriptions. Within the House, Foreign Affairs may look like a broken branch, but Ways and Means does not. And, across chambers, Senate Foreign Relations (where member incentives are stronger) is a good deal more potent than House Foreign Affairs. With the two Appropriations committees, the reverse is the case. It is not just that "the broken branch" is an undiscriminating, hence inaccurate, description. It is also that blanket descriptions lead to blanket prescriptions. And it just might be that the wisest course of congressional reform would be to identify existing nodes of committee strength and nourish them rather than to prescribe, as we usually do, reforms in equal dosages for all committees.

One lesson of the analysis should be that member incentives must exist to support any kind of committee activity. Where incentives vary, it may be silly to prescribe the same functions and resources for all committees. The Reorganization Act of 1946 mandated all committees to exercise "continuous watchfulness" over the executive branch—in the absence of any supporting incentive system. We have gotten overview activity only where random individuals have found an incentive for doing so—not by most committees and certainly not continuously. Similarly, I suspect that our current interest in exhorting all committees to acquire more information with which to combat the executive may be misplaced. Information is relatively easy to come by—and some committees have a lot of it. What is hard to come by is the incentive to use it, not to mention the time and the trust necessary to make it useful. I am not suggesting a set of reforms but rather a somewhat different strategy of committee reforms—less wholesale, more retail.

Since the best-known target of wholesale committee reform is the seniority rule, it deserves special comment. If our attacks on the rule have any substance to them, if they are anything other than symbolic, the complaint must be that some or all committee chairmen are not doing a good job. But we can only find out whether this is so by conducting a committee-by-committee examination. Paradoxically, our discussions of the seniority rule tend to steer us away from such a retail examination by mounting very broad, across-the-board kinds of arguments against chairmen as a class—arguments about their old age, their conservatism, their national unrepresentativeness. Such arguments produce great cartoon copy, easy editorial broadsides, and sitting-duck targets for our congressmen on the stump. But we ought not to let the arguments themselves, nor the Pavlovian public reactions induced by our cartoonists, editorial writers, and representatives, pass for good institutional analysis. Rather, they have diverted us from that task.

More crucial to a committee's performance than the selection of its chairman is his working relationship with the other committee members. Does he agree with his members on the functions of the committee? Does he act to facilitate the achievement of their individual concerns? Do they approve of his performance as chairman? Where there is real disagreement between chairman and members, close analysis may lead us to fault the members and not the chairman. If so, we should be focusing our criticisms on the members. If the fault lies with the chairman, a majority of the members have the power to bring him to heel. They need not kill the king; they can constitutionalize the monarchy. While outsiders have been crying "off with his head," the members of several committees have been quietly and effectively constitutionalizing the monarchy. Education and Labor, Post Office, and Interior are recent examples where dissatisfied committee majorities have subjected their chairmen to majority control. Where this has not been done, it is probably due to member satisfaction, member timidity, member disinterest, or member incompetence. And the time we spend railing against the seniority rule might be better spent finding out, for each congressional committee, just which of these is the case. If, as a final possibility, a chairman and his members are united in opposition to the majority part or to the rest of us, the seniority rule is not the problem. More to the point, as I suspect is usually the case, the reasons and the ways individual members get sorted onto the various committees is the critical factor. In sum, I am not saying that the seniority rule is a good thing. I am saying that, for committee performance, it is not a very important thing.

What has all this got to do with the original puzzle—that we love our congressmen so much more than our Congress? We began with a few

explanatory guesses. Our standards of judgment for individual performance are more easily met; the individual member works harder winning
approval for himself than for his institution; and Congress is a complex
institution, difficult for us to understand. The more we try to understand
Congress—as we did briefly with the committee system—the more we are
forced to peel back the institutional layers until we reach the individual
member. At that point, it becomes hard to separate, as we normally do, our
judgments about congressmen and Congress. The more we come to see
institutional performance as influenced by the desires of the individual
member, the more the original puzzle ought to resolve itself. For as the
independence of our judgments decreases, the disparity between them
ought to grow smaller. But if we are to hold this perspective on Congress,
we shall need to understand the close individual-institution relationship—
chamber by chamber, party by party, committee by committee, legislator
by legislator.

This is not a counsel of despair. It is a counsel of sharper focus and a
more discriminating eye. It counsels the mass media, for example to forego
"broken branch" type generalizations about Congress in favor of examining
a committee in depth, or to forego broad criticism of the seniority rule for a
close look at a committee chairman. It counsels the rest of us to focus more
on the individual member and to fix the terms of our dialogue with him
more aggressively. It counsels us to fix terms that will force him to think
more institutionally and which will hold him more accountable for the
performance of the institution. "Who Runs Congress," asks the title of the
Nader report, "the President, Big Business or You?" From the perspective
of this paper, it is none of these. It is the members who run Congress. And
we get pretty much the kind of Congress they want. We shall get a different
kind of Congress when we elect different kinds of congressmen or when we
start applying different standards of judgment to old congressmen. Whether
or not we ought to have a different kind of Congress is still another, much
larger, puzzle.

☐ The previous selection defines one dimension of the relationship
between congressmen and their constituencies. A commonly held assumption about members of Congress is that their primary incentive is to
engage in activities that strengthen their prospects for reelection. David
Mayhew, one proponent of this theory, argues in his book *Congress: The
Electoral Connection* that both the formal and informal organizations of
Congress are oriented principally toward the reelection of its members.
For example, the dispersion of committees, which numbered close to
300 in the 96th Congress (1979–1980), maximizes the opportunities of

committee chairmen to use their power to distribute benefits directly to their districts and states and to take positions on issues that will be appealing to their constituents. Moreover, the weak party structure of Capitol Hill allows individual members to go their own ways in dealing with their diverse constituencies. Unified congressional parties, argues Mayhew, would not allow congressmen the necessary flexibility to advertise, claim credit, and take positions to gain electoral support. In the following selection Mayhew illustrates the kinds of activities congressmen engage in to maximize their electoral support.

50
David Mayhew

CONGRESS:
THE ELECTORAL CONNECTION

Whether they are safe or marginal, cautious or audacious, congressmen must constantly engage in activities related to reelection. There will be differences in emphasis, but all members share the root need to do things — indeed, to do things day in and day out during their terms. The next step here is to present a typology, a short list of the *kinds* of activities congressmen find it electorally useful to engage in. The case will be that there are three basic kinds of activities. It will be important to lay them out with some care, . . .

One activity is *advertising*, defined here as any effort to disseminate one's name among constituents in such a fashion as to create a favorable image but in messages having little or no issue content. A successful congressman builds what amounts to a brand name, which may have a generalized electoral value for other politicians in the same family. The personal qualities to emphasize are experience, knowledge, responsiveness, concern, sincerity, independence, and the like. Just getting one's name across is difficult enough; only about half the electorate, if asked, can supply their House members' names. It helps a congressman to be known. "In the main, recognition carries a positive valence; to be perceived at all is to be perceived favorably." A vital advantage enjoyed by House incumbents is that they are much better known among voters than their November challengers. They are better known because they spend a great deal of

From David R. Mayhew, *Congress: The Electoral Connection,* pp. 49-72. Copyright © 1974 by Yale University. Reprinted by permission of Yale University Press.

time, energy, and money trying to make themselves better known. There are standard routines—frequent visits to the constituency, nonpolitical speeches to home audiences, the sending out of infant care booklets and letters of condolence and congratulation. Of 158 House members questioned . . . 121 said that they regularly sent newsletters to their constituents; 48 wrote separate news or opinion columns for newspapers; 82 regularly reported to their constituencies by radio or television; 89 regularly sent out mail questionnaires. Some routines are less standard. Congressman George E. Shipley (D., Ill.) claims to have met personally about half his constituents (i.e. some 200,000 people). For over twenty years Congressman Charles C. Diggs, Jr. (D., Mich.) has run a radio program featuring himself as a "combination disc jockey-commentator and minister." Congressman Daniel J. Flood (D., Pa.) is "famous for appearing unannounced and often uninvited at wedding anniversaries and other events." Anniversaries and other events aside, congressional advertising is done largely at public expense. Use of the franking privilege has mushroomed in recent years; in early 1973 one estimate predicted that House and Senate members would send out about 476 million pieces of mail in the year 1974, at a public cost of $38.1 million—or about 900,000 pieces per member with a subsidy of $70,000 per member. By far the heaviest mailroom traffic comes in Octobers of even-numbered years. There are some differences between House and Senate members in the ways they go about getting their names across. House members are free to blanket their constituencies with mailings for all boxholders; senators are not. But senators find it easier to appear on national television—for example, in short reaction statements on the nightly news shows. Advertising is a staple congressional activity, and there is no end to it. For each member there are always new voters to be apprised of his worthiness and old voters to be reminded of it.

A second activity may be called *credit claiming,* defined here as acting so as to generate a belief in a relevant political actor (or actors) that one is personally responsible for causing the government, or some unit thereof, to do something that the actor (or actors) considers desirable. The political logic of this, from the congressman's point of view, is that an actor who believes that a member can make pleasing things happen will no doubt wish to keep him in office so that he can make pleasing things happen in the future. The emphasis here is on individual accomplishment (rather than, say, party or governmental accomplishment) and on the congressman as doer (rather than as, say, expounder of constituency views). Credit claiming is highly important to congressmen, with the consequence that much of congressional life is a relentless search for opportunities to engage in it.

Where can credit be found? If there were only one congressman rather than 535, the answer would in principle be simple enough. Credit (or blame) would attach in Downsian fashion to the doing of the government as a whole. But there are 535. Hence it becomes necessary for each congressman to try to peel off pieces of governmental accomplishment for which he can believably generate a sense of responsibility. For the average congressman the staple way of doing this is to traffic in what may be called "particularized benefits." Particularized governmental benefits, as the term will be used here, have two properties: (1) Each benefit is given out to a specific individual, group, or geographical constituency, the recipient unit being of a scale that allows a single congressman to be recognized (by relevant political actors and other congressmen) as the claimant for the benefit (other congressmen being perceived as indifferent or hostile). (2) Each benefit is given out in apparently ad hoc fashion (unlike, say, social security checks) with a congressman apparently having a hand in the allocation. A particularized benefit can normally be regarded as a member of a class. That is, a benefit given out to an individual, group, or constituency can normally be looked upon by congressmen as one of a class of similar benefits given out to sizable numbers of individuals, groups, or constituencies. Hence the impression can arise that a congressman is getting "his share" of whatever it is the government is offering. (The classes may be vaguely defined. Some state legislatures deal in what their members call "local legislation.")

In sheer volume the bulk of particularized benefits come under the heading of "casework"—the thousands of favors congressional offices perform for supplicants in ways that normally do not require legislative action. High school students ask for essay materials, soldiers for emergency leaves, pensioners for location of missing checks, local governments for grant information, and on and on. Each office has skilled professionals who can play the bureaucracy like an organ—pushing the right pedals to produce the desired effects. But many benefits require new legislation, or at least they require important allocative decisions on matters covered by existent legislation. Here the congressman fills the traditional role of supplier of goods to the home district. It is a believable role; when a member claims credit for a benefit on the order of a dam, he may well receive it. Shiny construction projects seem especially useful. . . .

The third activity congressmen engage in may be called *position taking,* defined here as the public enunciation of a judgmental statement on anything likely to be of interest to political actors. The statement may take the form of a roll call vote. The most important classes of judgmental statements are those prescribing American governmental ends (a vote cast against the war; a statement that "the war should be ended immediately") or governmental means (a statement that "the way to end the war is to take it to the United Nations"). The judgments may be implicit rather than explicit, as in: "I will support the president on this matter." But judgments may range far beyond these classes to take in implicit or explicit statements on what almost anybody should do or how he should do it: "The great

Polish scientist Copernicus has been unjustly neglected"; "The way for Israel to achieve peace is to give up the Sinai." The congressman as position taker is a speaker rather than a doer. The electoral requirement is not that he make pleasing things happen but that he make pleasing judgmental statements. The position itself is the political commodity. Especially on matters where governmental responsibility is widely diffused it is not surprising that political actors should fall back on positions as tests of incumbent virtue. For voters ignorant of congressional processes the recourse is an easy one. The following comment [by a Congressman] is highly revealing: "Recently, I went home and began to talk about the——act. I was pleased to have sponsored that bill, but it soon dawned on me that the point wasn't getting through at all. What was getting through was that the act might be a help to people. I changed the emphasis: I didn't mention my role particularly, but stressed my support of the legislation."

The ways in which positions can be registered are numerous and often imaginative. There are floor addresses ranging from weighty orations to mass-produced "nationality day statements." There are speeches before home groups, television appearances, letters, newsletters, press releases, ghostwritten books, *Playboy* articles, even interviews with political scientists. On occasion congressmen generate what amount to petitions; whether or not to sign the 1956 Southern Manifesto defying school desegregation rulings was an important decision for southern members. Outside the roll call process the congressman is usually able to tailor his positions to suit his audiences. A solid consensus in the constituency calls for ringing declarations. . . .

Probably the best position-taking strategy for most congressmen at most times is to be conservative—to cling to their own positions of the past where possible and to reach for new ones with great caution where necessary. Yet in an earlier discussion of strategy the suggestion was made that it might be rational for members in electoral danger to resort to innovation. The form of innovation available is entrepreneurial position taking, its logic being that for a member facing defeat with his old array of positions it makes good sense to gamble on some new ones. It may be that congressional marginals fulfill an important function here as issue pioneers—experimenters who test out new issues and thereby show other politicians which ones are usable. An example of such a pioneer is Senator Warren Magnuson (D., Wash.), who responded to a surprisingly narrow victory in 1962 by reaching for a reputation in the area of consumer affairs. Another example is Senator Ernest Hollings (D., S.C.), a servant of a shaky and racially heterogeneous southern constituency who launched "hunger" as an issue in 1969—at once pointing to a problem and giving it a useful nonracial definition. One of the most successful issue entrepreneurs of recent decades was the late Senator Joseph McCarthy (R., Wis.); it was all there—the close primary in 1946, the fear of defeat in 1952, the desperate casting about for an issue, the famous 1950 dinner at the Colony Restaurant where suggestions were tendered, the decision that "Communism" might just do the trick.

The effect of position taking on electoral behavior is about as hard to measure as the effect of credit claiming. Once again there is a variance problem; congressmen do not differ very much among themselves in the methods they use or the skills they display in attuning themselves to their diverse constituencies. All of them, after all, are professional politicians. . . .

There can be no doubt that congressmen believe positions make a difference. An important consequence of this belief is their custom of watching each other's elections to try to figure out what positions are salable. Nothing is more important in Capitol Hill politics than the shared conviction that election returns have proven a point. . . .

These, then, are the three kinds of electorally oriented activities congressmen engage in—advertising, credit claiming, and position taking. . . .

☐   David Mayhew's thesis, part of which is presented in the preceding selection, is that the Washington activities of congressmen are, with few exceptions, geared toward reelection. In contrast, Richard Fenno argues that the Washington careers of congressmen may or may not be related to reelection. In his early work on Congress, Fenno pointed out that the *incentives* of members of Congress fall generally into three categories: (1) reelection, (2) internal power and influence on Capitol Hill, and (3) good public policy. While the incentives of congressmen cannot always be placed neatly into one of these categories, Fenno's research suggested that the behavior of members *in Congress* tends to be dominated by one of these incentives.[1]

Committee selection, in particular, is made to advance reelection, increase power and status on Capitol Hill, or make a good public policy. For example, such committees as Interior and Insular Affairs in the House serve the reelection incentives of its members by channeling specific benefits, such as water and conservation projects, into their districts. Members seeking influence in the House prefer such committees as Ways and Means and Appropriations, both of which reflect the role of the House in the constitutional system and represent it in the outside world. Congressmen on the Ways and Means and the Appropriations Committees, particularly the chairmen and ranking minority members, can use their positions effectively to bolster their reputations

[1]Richard F. Fenno, Jr., *Congressmen in Committees* (Boston: Little, Brown and Co., 1973).

for power in the House. "Good public policy" committees are those that are used to reflect ideological viewpoints, such as the House Education and Labor Committee, rather than to give particular benefits to constituents or to augment internal influence.

Generally, as congressmen gain seniority, their Washington careers become separated from their constituency activities. If they have built an effective organization within their constituency, they are free to pursue goals on Capitol Hill that are not specifically for the purpose of gaining votes. In the following selection Richard Fenno discusses the linkage between the constituency and Washington activities of congressmen.

51
Richard F. Fenno, Jr.

HOME STYLE
AND WASHINGTON CAREER

... When we speak of constituency careers, we speak primarily of the pursuit of the goal of reelection. When we speak of Washington careers, we speak primarily of the pursuit of the goals of influence in the House and the making of good public policy. Thus the intertwining of careers is, at bottom, an intertwining of member goals.

So long as they are in the expansionist stage of their constituency careers, House members will be especially attentive to their home base. They will pursue the goal of reelection with single-minded intensity and will allocate their resources disproportionately to that end. . . . [F]irst-term members go home more frequently, place a larger proportion of their staff in the district, and more often leave their families at home than do their senior colleagues. Building a reelection constituency at home and providing continuous access to as much of that constituency as possible requires time and energy. Inevitably, these are resources that might otherwise be allocated to efforts in Washington. "The trouble is," said one member near the end of his second term,

> I haven't been a congressman yet. The first two years, I spent all of my time getting myself reelected. That last two years, I spent getting myself a district so that I could get reelected. So I won't be a congressman until next year.

From Richard F. Fenno, Jr., *Home Style: House Members in Their Districts.* Copyright © 1978 by Little, Brown and Company, Inc. Reprinted by permission.

By being "a congressman" he means pursuing goals above and beyond that of reelection (i.e., power in the House and good public policy).

In a House member's first years, the opportunities for gaining inside power and policy influence are limited. Time and energy and staff can be allocated to home without an acute sense of conflict. At rates that vary from congressman to congressman, however, the chances to have some institutional or legislative effect improve. As members stretch to avail themselves of the opportunity, they may begin to experience some allocative strain. It requires time and energy to develop a successful career in Washington just as it does to develop a successful career in the district. Because it may not be possible to allocate these resources to House and home, each to an optimal degree, members may have to make allocative and goal choices.

A four-term congressman with a person-to-person home style described the dilemma of choice:

> I'm beginning to be a little concerned about my political future. I can feel myself getting into what I guess is a natural and inevitable condition—the gradual erosion of my local orientation. I'm not as enthused about tending my constituency relations as I used to be and I'm not paying them the attention I should be. There's a natural tension between being a good representative and taking an interest in government. I'm getting into some heady things in Washington, and I want to make an input into the government. It's making me a poorer representative than I was. I find myself avoiding the personal collisions that arise in the constituency—turning away from that one last handshake, not bothering to go to that one last meeting. I find myself forgetting people's names. And I find myself caring less about it than I used to. Right now, it's just a feeling I have. In eight years I have still to come home less than forty weekends a year. This is my thirty-sixth trip this year. What was it Arthur Rubinstein said? "If I miss one practice, I notice it. If I miss two practices, my teacher notices it. If I miss a week of practice, my audience notices it." I'm at stage one right now—or maybe stage one and stage two. But I'm beginning to feel that I could be defeated before long. And I'm not going to change. I don't want the status. I want to contribute to government.

The onset of a Washington career is altering his personal goals and his established home style. He is worried about the costs of the change; but he is willing to accept some loss of reelection support in exchange for his increased influence in Congress.

This dilemma faces every member of Congress. It is built into the twin requirements that Congress be a representative and a legislative institution. Some members believe they can achieve reelection at home together with influence or policy in Washington without sacrificing either. During Congressman O's first year as a subcommittee chairman, I asked him whether his new position would make it more difficult to tend to district matters. He replied,

> If you mean, am I getting Potomac fever, the answer is, no. If you mean, has the change in my official duties here made me a better congressman, the answer is, yes. If you mean has it taken away from my activity in the constituency, the answer is no.

Congressman *O,* we recall, has been going home less; but he has been increasing the number and the activity of his district staff. Although he speaks confidently of his allocative solution, he is not unaware of potential problems. "My staff operation runs by itself. They don't need me. Maybe I should worry about that. You aren't going back and say I'm ripe for the plucking are you? I don't think I am."

A three-term member responded very positively when I paraphrased the worries of the congressman friend of his who had quoted Arthur Rubinstein:

> You can do your job in Washington and in your district if you know how. My quarrel with [the people like him] of this world is that they don't learn to be good politicians before they get to Congress. They get there because some people are sitting around the table one day and ask them to do it. They're smart, but they don't learn to organize a district. Once you learn to do that, it's much easier to do your job in Washington.

This member, however, has not yet tasted the inside influence of his friend. Moreover, he does not always talk with such assurance. His district is not so well organized that he has reduced his personal attentiveness to it.

> Ralph Krug [the congressman in the adjacent district] tells me I spoil my constituents. He says, "You've been elected twice; you know your district; once a month is enough to come home." But that's not my philosophy. Maybe it will be someday.... My lack of confidence is still a pressure which brings me home. This is my political base. Washington is not my political base. I feel I have to come home to get nourished, to see for myself what's going on. It's my security blanket—coming home.

For now, he feels no competing pulls; but he is not unaware of his friend's dilemma.

Members pose the dilemma with varying degrees of immediacy. No matter how confident members may be of their ability to pursue their Washington and their constituency careers simultaneously, however, they all recognize the potentiality of conflict and worry about coping with it. It is our guess that the conflict between the reelection goal on the one hand and the power or policy goals on the other hand becomes most acute for members as they near the peak of influence internally. For, at this stage of their Washington career, the resource requirements of the Washington job make it nearly impossible to meet established expectations of attentiveness at home. Individuals who want nothing from their Washington careers except the status of being a member of Congress will never pursue any other goal except reelection. For these people, the dilemma of which we speak is minimal. Our concern is with those individuals who find, sooner or later, that they wish to pursue a mix of goals in which reelection must be weighed along with power or policy.

One formula for managing a mix of goals that gives heavy weight to a Washington career is to make one's influence in Washington the center-piece of home style. The member says, in effect, "I can't come home to present myself in person as much as I once did, because I'm so busy tending to the nation's business; but my seniority, my influence, my effectiveness in Washington is of great benefit to you." He asks his supportive constituents to adopt a new set of expectations, one that would put less of a premium on access. Furthermore, he asks these constituents to remain sufficiently intense in their support to discourage challengers—especially those who will promise access. All members do some of this when they explain their Washington activity—especially in connection with "explaining power." And, where possible, they quote from favorable national commentary in their campaign literature. But [very few Congressmen] have made Washington influence the central element of [their] home style.

One difficulty of completely adopting such a home style is that the powerful Washington legislator can actually get pretty far out of touch with his supportive constituents back home. One of the more senior members of [Congress], and a leader of his committee, recounted the case when his preoccupation with an internal legislative impasse affecting Israel caused him to neglect the crucial Jewish element of his primary constituency—a group "who contribute two-thirds of my money." A member of the commit-tee staff had devised an amendment to break the deadlock.

> Peter Tompkins looked at it and said to me, "Why don't we sponsor it?" So we put it forward, and it became known as the Crowder-Tompkins Amendment. I did it because I respected the staff man who suggested it and because I wanted to get something through that was reasonable. Well, a member of the committee called people back home and said, "Crowder is selling out." All hell broke loose. I started getting calls at two and three in the morning from my friends asking me what I was doing. So I went back home and discussed the issue with them. When I walked into the room, it made me feel sad and shocked to feel their hostility. They wanted me to know that they would clobber me if they thought I was selling out. Two hours later, we walked out friends again. I dropped the Crowder-Tompkins Amendment. That's the only little flare up I've ever had with the Jewish community. But it reminded me of their sensitivity to anything that smacks of discrimination.

The congressman survived. But he would not have needed so forceful a reminder of his strongest supporters' concerns were he nearer the begin-ning of his constituency career. But, of course, neither would he have been a committee leader, and neither would the imperatives of a House career bulked so large in his mix of goals.

Another way to manage conflicting reelection and Washington career goals might be to use one's Washington influence to alter support patterns at home. That is, instead of acting—as is the normal case—to reenforce home support, to keep what he had "last time," the congressman might act to displace that old support with compensating new support. He might even accomplish this inadvertently, should his pursuit of power or policy attract, willy-nilly, constituents who welcome his new mix of goals. The very Washington activity that left him out of touch with previously support- ive constituents might put him in touch with newly supportive ones. A newly acquired position of influence in a particular policy area or a new reputation as an effective legislator might produce such a feedback effect....

...[There is] a tendency for successful home styles to harden over time and to place stylistic constraints on the congressman's subsequent behavior. The pursuit of a Washington career helps us explain this constitu- ency phenomenon. That is, to the degree that a congressman pursues power or policy goals in the House, he will have that much less time or energy to devote to the consideration of alternative home styles. His predisposition to "do what we did last time" at home will be further strengthened by his growing preoccupation with Washington matters. Indeed, the speed with which a congressman begins to develop a Washington career will affect the speed with which his home style solidifies....

In all of this speculation about career linkages, we have assumed that most members of Congress develop, over time, a mix of personal goals. We particularly assume that most members will trade off some of their per- sonal commitment to reelection in order to satisfy a personal desire for institutional or policy influence. It is our observation . . . that House mem- bers do, in fact, exhibit varying degrees of commitment to reelection. All want reelection in the abstract, but not all will pay any price to achieve it; nor will all pay the same price. . . .

One senior member contemplated retirement in the face of an adverse redistricting but, because he had the prospect of a committee chairmanship, he decided to run and hope for the best. He wanted reelection because he wanted continued influence; but he was unwilling to put his present influ- ence in jeopardy by pursuing reelection with the same intensity that marked his earlier constituency career. As he put it,

> Ten years ago, I whipped another redistricting. And I did it by neglecting my congressional duties . . . Today I don't have the time, and I'm not going to neglect my duties . . . If I do what is necessary to get reelected and thus become chairman of the committee, I will lose the respect and confidence of my fellow committee members because of being absent from the hearings and, occasionally, the votes.

He did not work hard at reelection, and he won by his narrowest margin ever. But he succeeded in sustaining a mix of personal goals very different from an earlier one. . . .

The congressman's home activities are more difficult and taxing than we have previously recognized. Under the best of circumstances, the tension involved in maintaining constituency contact and achieving legislative competence is considerable. Members cannot be in two places at once, and the growth of a Washington career exacerbates the problem. But, more than that, the demands in both places have grown recently. The legislative workload and the demand for legislative expertise are steadily increasing. So is the problem of maintaining meaningful contact with their several constituencies. Years ago, House members returned home for months at a time to live among their supportive constituencies, soak up the home atmosphere, absorb local problems at first hand. Today, they race home for a day, a weekend, a week at a time. [Few] maintain a family home in their district. [Many] stay with relatives or friends or in barely furnished rooms when they are at home. The citizen demand for access, for communication, and for the establishment of trust is as great as ever. So members go home. But the quality of their contact has suffered. "It's like a one-night stand in a singles bar." It is harder to sustain a genuine two-way communication than it once was. House member worries about the home relationship—great under any circumstances, but greater now—contribute to the strain and frustration of the job. Some cope; but others retire. It may be those members who cannot stand the heat of the home relationship who are getting out of the House kitchen. If so, people prepared to be more attentive to home . . . are likely to replace them.

The interplay between home careers and Washington careers continues even as House members leave Congress. For, in retirement or in defeat, they still face a choice—to return home or to remain in Washington. The subject of postcongressional careers is too vast to be treated here. But students of home politics can find, in these choices, indications of the depth and durability of home attachments in the face of influential Washington careers. It is conventional wisdom in the nation's capital that senators and representatives "get Potomac fever" and that "they don't go back to Pocatello" when their legislative careers end. Having pursued the goals of power and policy in Washington with increasing success, they prefer, it is said, to continue their Washington career in some nonlegislative job rather than to go back home. In such a choice, perhaps, we might find the ultimate displacement of the constituency career with the Washington career.

An examination of the place of residence of 370 individuals who left the House between 1954 and 1974, and who were alive in 1974, sheds considerable doubt on this Washington wisdom. It appears that most House members do, indeed, "go back to Pocatello." Of the 370 former members studied, 253 (68 percent) resided in their home states in 1974; 91 lived in the Washington, D.C., area; and 26 resided someplace else. Of those 344 who chose either Washington or home, therefore, nearly three-quarters chose home. This simple fact underscores the very great strength of the home attachments we have described in this book.

No cross section of living former members will tell us for sure how many members lingered in Washington for a while before eventually returning home. Only a careful tracing of all individual cases, therefore, will give us a full and accurate description of the Washington-home choice. Even so, among the former members most likely to be attracted to Washington—those who left Congress from 1970 to 1974—only 37 percent have chosen to remain there. A cursory glance at all those who have chosen to prolong their Washington careers, however, tells us what we might expect—that they have already had longer congressional careers than those who returned home. Our data also tell us that these members are younger than those who choose to return home. Thus, we speculate, the success of a member's previous career in Congress and the prospect that he or she still has time to capitalize on that success in the Washington community are positive inducements to stay. And these inducements seem unaffected by the manner of his or her leaving Congress—whether by electoral defeat (for renomination or reelection) or retirement. Those who were defeated, however, had shorter congressional careers and were younger than those who had voluntarily retired.

☐   Free competitive elections are essential to the democratic process. James Madison wrote in *Federalist 52,* "As it is essential to liberty that the government in general should have a common interest with the people, so it is particularly essential that [the House] should have an immediate dependence on and an immediate sympathy with the people. Frequent elections are unquestionably the only policy by which this dependence and sympathy can be effectually secured." Free elections support representative government, and electoral politics determines the nature of representation.

Electoral politics is above all highly individualistic in character. Members of Congress have their own organizations to help them win reelection. Advertising, credit-claiming, and position-taking are all done to emphasize the importance of the individual candidate. Members pursuing reelection do not stress their responsibility for the actions of Congress as a whole, or for the course their congressional party may have taken. Often they run *against* Congress, stressing their separateness from the institution in which they serve.

The author of the following selection agrees with David Mayhew that a congressman's primary incentive is reelection. He argues that the dominance of that incentive makes it difficult if not impossible for Congress to govern effectively because it encourages individualism on Capitol Hill rather than responsible collective action to solve pressing national problems. As an institution constantly seeking to serve constituent rather than national interests, Congress has become a decentralized and parochial body that lacks the will to govern. Congressmen, always seeking to take a safe course with their constituents by avoiding controversial position-taking and focusing upon, in David Mayhew's terms, advertising and credit-claiming to win reelection, willingly delegate to the president and the executive branch broad authority to govern.

An example of delegation with a new twist was the so-called Gramm-Rudman Bill that Congress passed in 1986 delegating to the Controller General—technically an agent of Congress—the *executive* authority and responsibility to make budget cuts to reduce the federal deficit by a Congressionally stipulated percentage each year. Congress was apparently unwilling to use and incapable of exercising its constitutional authority to make budget decisions.

Several members of Congress, as "interested and aggrieved parties," challenged the legislation on unconstitutional grounds, alleging a violation of the separation of powers doctrine because of the delegation of *executive* power to an agency of Congress. The Supreme Court in 1986 held that the law was an impermissible delegation of executive authority to an agent of Congress—the Controller General.

Congress has, as the following selection describes, attempted from time to time to strengthen its collective capacity to make decisions. Usually such efforts follow an "imperial presidency" that, in the view of a congressional majority, has gone too far in dominating Capitol Hill. The first major twentieth century effort to increase congressional collective decision-making capabilities came in 1946 with the passage of the Legislative Reorganization Act. Responding to the growth of presidential and executive branch power under Franklin D. Roosevelt, Congress streamlined its committees, increased its professional staff, and sought to increase the powers of its party leaders, in order to strengthen its capacity to govern. Not until the 1970s did Congress once more undertake a major reform effort to cope with the continued anarchy of the legislative process. Again a dominant presidency, this time under Richard M. Nixon, spurred Congress to act. Addressed in the following selection is the question of whether the resurgent Congress of the 1970s and 1980s will once again succumb as in the past to the forces of decentralization.

52

James L. Sundquist

REPRESENTATION AND
THE WILL TO GOVERN

Representative Barbara Jordan, in the introspective days of 1973, admonished a resurgent Congress to "regain the will to govern." Theodore Sorensen, less elegantly, saw the issue as one of "guts." Many others found the Congress similarly deficient. "There is a deeply unheroic streak in Congress that does not covet responsibility nor welcome tests of courage," wrote John W. Gardner, a former cabinet member. Journalist Arlen J. Large similarly diagnosed the congressional ailment as a "failure of nerve," which led it to express opinions but leave final decisions to the president. "Congress is really a body of followers, not leaders," Representative Donald W. Riegle, Jr., Republican (later senator and Democrat) of Michigan, confided to his diary. "Congress usually won't face up to a problem until it has to, before it is forced to." "Unfortunately, it is in the nature of the Congressional animal," agreed Representative Bob Eckhardt, Democrat of Texas, "to be overly concerned with the backwaters of public policy and too little disposed to make hard decisions on mainstream national issues." Congressmen practice "collective avoidance" of important questions, said Representative Michael J. Harrington, Democrat of Massachusetts, on his retirement in 1978. "I'm not sure we really want to participate." And their colleague, Representative Les Aspin, Democrat of Wisconsin, explained the reason: "Since only the most politically secure congressman can afford to offend constituents—and since there are so many ways to offend them—natural survival instincts dictate that a congressman will duck any tough issues that he can. Politically, it is often much safer to let the Executive do the leading."

In this composite view, the long decline of Congress was not just an accident of history. It flowed from the very nature of the congressional animal, a creature compelled to nurture its relationship with the state or district that determines, at two- or six-year intervals, whether it lives or dies. The demands of the constituency are so urgent and incessant as to lead the members of Congress—House members in particular but senators as well—to concentrate on the role of *representative* of their areas, to deal with local and peripheral matters, avoid broader responsibility, and leave basic decisions to the president. If that view is correct, the will to govern,

From James L. Sundquist, *The Decline and Resurgence of Congress.* Copyright © 1981 by The Brookings Institution. Reprinted by permission.

the necessary guts, will not be regained—or acquired in the first place—without radical change in the nature or the behavior, or both, of the members themselves. To the extent that they are oriented toward state, district, and constituency, they would have to be reoriented toward the nation, induced somehow to set aside local demands and interests in order to concentrate on the broad concerns of the whole country. The question is whether legislators elected from narrow constituencies can ever, in the nature of things, alter fundamentally the modes of conduct that have evolved out of the peculiar relationships they bear to their constituencies in the United States.

This question has both quantitative and qualitative aspects. First, the volume and diversity of constituent demands impose an enormous burden on the members' time, distracting them from concentration on fundamental issues of national policy. Second, constituency pressures impel individual legislators to consider broad policy questions from a local rather than a national viewpoint, producing the oft-criticized "parochialism" and "irresponsibility" of the Congress. . . .

FROM REPRESENTATION TO DECLINE—AND RESURGENCE

Through a chain of causation, then, the long decline of the Congress in relation to the president can be traced to its roots in the principle of representation, which is unchangeable—embodied in the Constitution, necessitated by the size and diversity of the United States, and hallowed by tradition. Representation produces individualism and parochialism. Individualism produces fragmentation and dispersion of authority within the Congress. Fragmentation and dispersion vitiate the capacity of the Congress to integrate policy, to lead, and to govern. Parochialism produces irresponsibility, and irresponsibility undermines the will to govern. Deficient in both capacity and will, the Congress lets authority over broad public questions—as distinct from local and peripheral matters—drift to the executive branch. Representative Aspin set out the linkage from representation to irresponsibility to decline in simple terms: it was to take the "safer" course in relation to their constituents that congressmen established the president in his role of leadership; "tough issues" could then be evaded. The purpose was not necessarily always acknowledged, or even understood, but at times it became explicit, as in the Budget and Accounting Act debate of 1919-20, when members openly sought to transfer to the president the political accountability for future budget deficits.

The decline of Congress appears, then, to have been a natural historic trend, flowing from the fundamentals of the political system. As soon as strong presidents willing to assume responsibility became the norm, the Congress was equally willing to let them have an increasing share of the totality of decisionmaking as the scale and range of governmental activity expanded. That responded to the needs of the members, and their wants. It relieved them of responsibility to do things they did not wish to do, things that were politically dangerous to do. Indeed, it gave them the best of both worlds, the right and the opportunity to intervene in the affairs of government when there was political credit to be gained, but the freedom to leave matters to the president when that appeared to be the safer course.

If the decline was natural, even historically inevitable, what then of the resurgence? The constitutional crisis of the Nixon period wrenched the legislators out of their complacency and thrust responsibility on them, whether they liked it or not, in spite of the burgeoning culture of individualism. It produced institutional changes. Some power—over fiscal policy and war, in particular—flowed back. The conflict also generated new attitudes in the Congress—the new assertiveness. But it did nothing to change the structure of incentives that control and motivate congressmen, for it did not alter in any way their relations with their constituencies, did not lessen their representational responsibilities. As time passes and the memory of Nixon and his "usurpations" fades, and congressmen live with presidents they respect and trust, the links in the old causal chain are likely to reappear. The will to govern will again wane. The capabilities that are missing will not be acquired, because the members will not be willing to sacrifice their individual freedom and, in the literal sense, their irresponsibility. Nor, even if they wished, would their inescapable role as representatives permit them to. "No matter how assertive [Congress] is, or how creative and qualified for leadership individual members are," said Senator Edmund Muskie of Maine in 1978, "maybe the institution is not really equipped to act as a strong leader." This from the chairman of the Senate Budget Committee who, perhaps more than any other member of the Congress, was carrying the burden of asserting the restored authority of the legislative branch.

The institutional changes will work to inhibit a new decline, but they are not enough to stop it altogether. The War Powers Resolution does compel the Congress to arrive at a decision to affirm or overrule a presidential course of action that utilizes military force, but legislators who wish to evade responsibility can hide again behind the president's constitutional prerogatives as commander in chief and the superior information and expertise of his advisers—as they did in the long series of postwar crises from Korea to the Gulf of Tonkin. The Congressional Budget and Impoundment Control Act establishes a process, but it does not require the process to reject, or even significantly alter, the president's budget; and the process itself is never out of danger of collapse. Perhaps the most important force for maintaining congressional authority will be the expanded staff, not likely to decline much in numbers (despite the gestures in that direction by the new Republican majority in the Senate) and not likely, either, to abet a congressional relapse into passivity. To a member of Congress, irresponsibility may discourage action, but for the bright and transient young people who make up the bulk of the legislative staff it has the opposite effect. They can act, enjoy power, and perhaps affect history, without having to face either the political consequences in a constituency or administrative accountability in an executive department.

With the Ninety-seventh Congress, party control is divided in a way not known for nearly half a century, since Herbert Hoover's time. Interparty competition will not spill over into conflict between the executive and legislative branches, as in the Nixon-Ford years, but primarily into clashes between the House (when the Democratic majority is able to prevail) and the Senate, with the latter allied with the president, and with the conference committees the main battleground.

The record of the past five decades, however, suggests that the divided Congress of 1981–82 will prove transitory, and the two houses will shortly be restored to the similarity of composition and outlook that has been the normal pattern. When that time comes, the balance of power between the branches will not be static, as it has not been in the past. But in all probability it will fluctuate within a narrower range than in the 1970s. The Congress will not soon again reach as low a point as the nadir of 1972. Nor will it soon again be as assertive as in the crisis years of 1973 and 1974.

A Day in the United States Senate

☐   The environments of the Senate and the House differ rather significantly. Election to the United States Senate means that one has arrived politically. With the exception of the White House, the Senate is the most prestigious body in Washington. Rarely does a senator resign to take another post, as did Maine Senator Edmund Muskie in 1980 to become Secretary of State, considered to be the highest ranking job in the Cabinet. Senators are statesmen in their own right, and they often act as sovereign bodies. They may be involved in international as well as national politics. The six-year term of office and the broad constituencies of senators make them less directly dependent upon the people, and as the framers of the Constitution intended, more capable of independent, deliberative action than members of the House.

Although the Senate is no longer dominated by an inner club of senior members, as described by William S. White in *The Citadel* in 1956, a spirit of collegiality prevails and some past traditions do linger. Norms of hard work, expertise, courtesy, and respect for the institution and its ways continue to characterize those senators who have achieved power and status in the body. A long apprenticeship is no longer required of junior senators before they can make their voice heard on Capitol

Hill, but it still behooves them to respect the informal rules governing the way in which the Senate operates.

In the following selection, Elizabeth Drew, Washington correspondent for *The New Yorker* magazine and a freelance writer on politics, describes a day in the life of Senator John Culver of Iowa. Culver first arrived at Capitol Hill in 1964, when he was elected to the House. He was an influential member of the Democratic Study Group and was a leading proponent of House reform. He ran for the Senate in 1974 and won with 52 percent of the vote. He became an active member of the Senate, leading his Democratic colleagues on a number of issues, including arms control and the SALT treaty. As a member of the Armed Services Committee he developed a reputation for hard work, expertise, and an aggressive stance on reviewing defense expenditures that did not always conform to the hawkish views of the committee. He did not hesitate to fight what he considered to be unwarranted increases in defense expenditures. He was an active chairman of the Research and Development Subcommittee of Armed Services. In another policy sphere, he was a member of the Environment and Public Works Committee and chairman of its Resource Protections Subcommittee, which he used to sponsor the endangered-species legislation for which he was the floor-manager.

While Culver was building his profile in the Senate, he was defeated in 1980 in a state that was shifting to the Republican party. To what extent was the senator's day, described in the following selection and largely devoted to floor-managing his endangered-species bill, helpful to reelection? Was Culver striving for power and status in the Senate and in the broader world of Washington? Was the senator's visibility on Capitol Hill useful to him back home?

A DAY IN THE LIFE OF A
UNITED STATES SENATOR

Wednesday, July 19th: Culver has gone to the White House for the eight-o'clock breakfast meeting on lifting the embargo on the sale of arms to Turkey (he asked the President to what extent the policy of lifting the embargo, in the interests of strengthening NATO, had anticipated a negative reaction in Greece, which could have consequences that would weaken NATO); at nine-thirty, he met on the Senate steps with 4-H Clubs from three counties in Iowa; at nine-forty-five, he met with Charles Stevenson to go over some questions he had on the material, which he had read early this morning, for the press conference on Soviet civil defense; and then he met with George Jacobson and Kathi Korpon on amendments that will come up today on the endangered-species bill.

Now, at ten o'clock, the Senate resumes debate on the bill. S. I. Hayakawa, Republican of California, offers a minor amendment, which Culver accepts, in accordance with his policy of accepting as many as he can in order to build a consensus behind the bill. Representatives of the Fish and Wildlife Service are stationed in the Vice President's Capitol Hill office, off the Senate floor, and amendments that Culver is giving consideration to accepting are sent out to them for their opinion. He turns the floor over to [Senator Malcolm] Wallop [R., Wy.] so that Wallop can engage Hayakawa in a colloquy to establish the legislative history of the amendment. Culver is giving Wallop a larger role than the majority manager usually affords the minority—also in the interest of building a consensus.

Shortly before ten-thirty, Culver leaves the floor to go to the Dirksen Office Building for his press conference on Soviet civil defense. Just before the press conference begins, he goes over again with Charles Stevenson the points he wants to stress. A fair number of newspaper reporters are here, along with reporters from two television networks and one television station in Iowa. Culver enters the room and sits behind a table that has several microphones on it. He is wearing a navy-blue suit, a blue shirt, and a navy-blue tie with small white dots. He reads a statement explaining that "for the past two years I have sought an official but unclassified assessment of Soviet civil defense which could be made available for a better-informed public debate on this issue." The report he has received, and is releasing today, he says, "represents the first comprehensive and authoritative analysis of this crucial topic in unclassified form." He says that "the study indicates that the Soviet civil-defense system, while representing a significant national effort, is by no means sufficiently effective to encourage the Soviets to risk starting a nuclear war."

He continues, "While crediting the Soviet Union with a major, ongoing civil-defense program, this report demonstrates that those efforts are not sufficient to prevent millions of casualties and massive industrial damage in the event of a nuclear war. In short, Soviet programs are not enough to tip the strategic balance against us." He is addressing himself to recent alarms that the Soviets are engaged in a new civil-defense effort of sufficient proportions that the strategic balance might indeed be tipped, and to arguments that therefore the United States should also engage in a new, enlarged civil-defense program. Now, also addressing himself to the arguments of critics of SALT, and pursuing his goal, about which he spoke to me earlier, of achieving more understanding in both the United States and the Soviet Union concerning the consequences of a nuclear exchange, he says, "Despite the widespread claims that Soviet leaders might launch a nuclear attack because they expect to suffer only moderate damage and few casualties—and we hear that suggested today in a number of quarters—the professional judgment of our intelligence community is that they would not be emboldened to expose themselves and their country to a higher risk of nuclear attack. Even under the 'worst case' assumptions of this study, nuclear war would be a disaster for the Soviet Union." He takes questions, and answers earnestly and with a large number of facts. He says that the estimates of each side's losses in a nuclear attack vary with the targeting plan and the warning time—that the Soviet Union could lose well over a hundred million people, but that figure could be cut by more than fifty per cent if it had two to three days' warning. "I guess the bottom line in all this," he says, "is that even in the worst case the casualties would be awesome."

When one of the reporters questions his conclusions, Culver becomes annoyed. "We do have a great deal of speculation. It's rampant," he says, referring to the alarms about the nature of the Soviet threat. His voice rises. "We don't need to panic," he says. "There is no surge planning. Since they can't have high confidence—and that's what this report is about—the Soviet Union would not be emboldened to risk a nuclear war." Culver is getting involved, and he just keeps going, making his argument, ranging into the way he thinks about the whole subject. He may have a bill pending on the Senate floor, but now he gives this his all, takes the opportunity to present his case. He says, "We talk so much about military doctrine—that General So-and-So says this, that General So-and-So says that. Soldiers in every country all the time talk about victory. They're not paid to talk about defeat. They are trained with the can-do spirit, and the can-do spirit can lead to nuclear war—holocaust, believe it or not." The passion has come to the surface again. "The political leadership on both sides believe that nuclear war would be a disaster," he says. "Now, whether the troops have got the message is another question." Addressing himself to his questioner, he continues, "The Soviet civil-defense effort, I beg your pardon, is not the coördinated, effective system that some so-called experts have claimed, according to the judgment of the people who wrote this report." He goes on—as he did with me in his office, as he did with the constituents in Des Moines—about both sides having civil-defense signs in their subways, both sides having pamphlets. He says, "If you just like to embrace rumor and innuendo and fear, fine. Some people make a lifetime career of it."

He then tries to turn to someone else, but the reporter follows up with a question based on a statement by a Soviet general.

"I could probably provide you with some statements by our highest military or some article they've written," Culver replies. "In that context, everyone's talking about, quote, winning a war, unquote."

He goes on for a while, talking about Soviet history. "I'm not minimizing their effort, and it may be comfortable to characterize my position as 'weak on civil defense,'" he says, "but what I want to do is to get objective information before the public."

In answer to a question about whether he thinks that the United States should proceed to spend substantially increased funds on civil defense over the next few years, Culver says, "I think that we're just going to have to carefully look at it and review it." He adds that he thinks this is an area that should be explored in future SALT talks. "It seems to me that before we all pour a lot of money along this line," he says, "why don't we get together and try to agree, in the spirit of the A.B.M. agreement"—in 1972, the United States and the Soviet Union agreed to limit substantially their deployment of anti-ballistic missiles—"and try to find a way to minimize the threat." This is how he argued in opposing construction of a military base on Diego Garcia, and later there were talks on demilitarizing the Indian Ocean; this is how he argued about conventional-arms sales, and later there were talks on that subject. However fruitful the talks may or may not be, Culver considers such efforts worth a try.

Culver concludes the press conference at eleven-fifteen.

In an anteroom, Don Brownlee is waiting with a tape-recording machine, so that Culver can record "actualities" to send out to the Iowa radio stations. As Brownlee holds a microphone, Culver reads two excerpts from his statement. Charles Stevenson tells Culver that he has some questions about provisions that Culver backed which might come up in the House-Senate conference on the military-procurement bill this afternoon—questions about which provisions he might want to trade for what. "We'll have to talk about that more, Charlie," Culver says.

When Culver returns to the Senate floor, an amendment by [Gaylord] Nelson [D., Wis.] is pending. This one would limit projects that could be exempted to those for which "a substantial and irretrievable commitment of resources had been made." Culver speaks in opposition, saying that the amendment "does have some superficial appeal" but could have undesirable results—that it could have the effect of discouraging agencies from confronting the problem until a project was well along. He does an imitation, in a prissy voice, of an imagined, unrealistic statement by a representative of the Fish and Wildlife Service in the course of a discussion over whether a project should proceed. He draws an analogy—perhaps because of what he was dealing with in his press conference—between such discussions and the bargaining over SALT. "This amendment could have the force and effect of accelerating the move toward construction," he says. "This amendment says the only way you can have any hope for receiving an exemption is to get in there and build." He cites Nelson's proposed language—"a substantial and irretrievable commitment of resources." He bellows, "What on earth is that? Is there a lawyer in the house? Substantial to whom? Irretrievable to whom?" He returns to the defense analogy, referring now to the current controversy over whether and what sort of a mobile-missile system should be built. "We may have to dig a hole where the Furbish lousewort lives," he says, and he goes on to say that we should not get into a situation where it would be like saying to the Defense Department, " 'Go ahead and build the damn thing, and if you build it enough to spend thirty million dollars, then we will tell you you should not have done it in the first place.' " Nelson's amendment is defeated by a vote of twenty-five to seventy.

During the roll call, Culver goes over to the Republican side to confer with Scott.

Now [William] Scott [R., Va.] offers an amendment to exempt a project that might prevent the recurrence of a natural disaster, and Culver accepts it. Scott previously referred several times in the debate to a flood in Virginia that took the lives of four people, and yesterday afternoon Culver decided to try to reach agreement with him on an amendment to cover natural disasters. Next, he accepts an amendment by Scott to provide that five rather than all seven members of the interagency committee will constitute a quorum. Culver's hope is that if he accommodates Scott, Scott may reciprocate by withholding some of the several amendments he still has pending. "It's like a negotiating situation," Culver has explained to me. "You have twelve amendments, but there are only three or four you care about." Scott, however, is unpredictable. And though Scott has little influence within the Senate, Culver still has to be concerned that, as the day goes on, the Senate might accept something that Scott proposes or an atmosphere might be created in which some surprise amendment would be adopted. When Senate sessions go on until late in the day or into the evening, matters can get increasingly out of hand: tempers rise, a few drinks may have been consumed, and a certain "what the hell?" attitude can take over. "Late in the day gets to be the silly season," Culver has explained to me. "It gets harder and harder to control what happens."

For that reason, Culver has persuaded Scott to bring up now the amendment that Culver most fears: the one to require a majority vote, rather than a vote of five of the seven members, of the interagency committee in granting an exemption. He is worried that his proposal is vulnerable here. And he is concerned that if the number of votes required to exempt a project should be reduced to a simple majority many more projects might be exempted. Scott was not enthusiastic about offering the amendment at this point, but Culver has talked him into it. The theory behind having Scott bring up the amendment now is that it is better to have such a proposal come up in the morning—a time when many senators are in committee meetings or in their offices and are more distracted than usual from the business that is taking place on the floor. Also, Culver figures that most of his colleagues will assume that at this point, especially after a long day of taking up amendments—and major ones—yesterday, only routine, "housekeeping" amendments are being considered, and that they will pay less attention to the issue, be less eager to join the fray, than they might be later on.

These are the sorts of calculations that managers of bills must make. Culver figures, further, that if an amendment is to be offered on the voting of the new committee he would prefer that it be offered by Scott. And, by a prior arrangement that Culver has made with Nelson, Nelson will ask for a roll-call vote on the amendment. Scott does not want a roll call on it. Culver's idea is to beat the amendment, and beat it good, burying the issue in the Senate once and for all, and also putting him in a position to tell a Senate-House conference on the bill that the proposal was resoundingly defeated in the Senate. "It's a judgment call," Culver has said, explaining to me the considerations behind whether or not to put something to a roll-call vote. Sometimes, as happened when [John] Stennis, as chairman of the Armed Services Committee and floor manager of the military-procurement bill, accepted Culver's amendment on aircraft carriers, a senator will decide not to press for a roll-call vote, to—as Culver puts it—"God, take it and run."

So now Scott calls up his amendment to require that the votes of only four of the seven members of the interagency committee are necessary in order to exempt a project. Culver, speaking in opposition to the amendment, offers some precedents for requiring a "super-majority" vote. Culver wasn't sure there were any precedents, but his staff has been imaginative: he uses the example of jury trials in criminal cases—which require unanimity—and he cites the Senate rule that a filibuster can be cut off only by the votes of sixty members, or three-fifths, of the Senate. Scott's amendment is defeated on a roll-call vote, twenty-three to sixty-nine.

Now Culver accepts a number of other amendments offered by Republicans. He has told me, "You can take a couple of amendments you know you are going to drop in a spittoon on the way to the conference." Nelson had some other amendments, too, but by one-thirty he and the environmentalists backing him have decided to give up.

Off the Senate floor, a Democratic senator talks to me about Culver.

"He's doing a real good job of managing the bill," the senator says. "It's a controversial issue; he's picking his way through the amendments, and working some out, and fighting and defeating others, and establishing his control over the floor. That's very important: others will follow your lead if they feel that you're being sensible and you have control."

This afternoon, Culver—he has skipped lunch again—works to keep that control. He quickly moves against a senator who has asked for more time than was permitted under the unanimous-consent agreement and who wants to offer a non-germane amendment.

While another senator is speaking, Culver leaves the floor briefly; he has received a card of the sort that visitors send in when they want to see senators, this one telling him that a delegation of forty-one Catholics from Dubuque would like to see him. (He has turned down a number of other requests today to meet with people off the Senate floor.) He goes over to the Rotunda of the Capitol and meets with the group for five minutes, explaining to them that he is managing a bill on the Senate floor, and adding, "I figured if I didn't come out to see you, you'd fire me, but if I don't get back in there the Majority Leader will fire me."

When Culver returns to the Senate, Wallop is sitting next to Scott's seat, in the second-to-last row, talking to Scott, and Culver goes back to join them. After he accepted Scott's amendments this morning, Culver told him that he hoped that that would take care of matters and that Scott would offer no further amendments. Scott said then that he wanted to go back to his office and look over his other amendments. This afternoon, he returned to say that he had four more he wanted to offer, and Culver asked Wallop to go back and talk to Scott and see what he could do. Now Culver finds that they haven't got very far; Scott is insisting that either he be allowed to offer four amendments or he will ultimately offer twelve. Culver has asked for a quorum call—a device used from time to time during a debate in order to gain time to get a senator to the floor, or to regroup, or to work out an amendment, or to negotiate—and the clerk calls the roll, slowly. At one point during the negotiations, Culver puts his head in his hands, seeming very weary.

Finally, at five minutes to three, Culver comes back to his desk and asks that the quorum call be ended. He has talked Scott into offering just one more amendment. Now Scott offers one providing that if the National Security Council determines that any interference with a critical military installation on behalf of an endangered species "would have an adverse effect on the security of the United States," it is authorized to notify the interagency committee in writing and that "the committee shall give immediate consideration to such determination." In the preceding negotiations, Culver has succeeded in getting Scott to modify this amendment; in its original form, it would have allowed the National Security Council to grant an automatic exemption, and it would have been invoked to prevent an adverse effect on any installation, not just one deemed essential to the national security. Culver's objections were that anything might be found adverse to an installation and that granting an automatic exemption was contrary to the spirit of the bill.

Now Scott says, "Suppose a bird or some endangered species was in front of an intercontinental ballistic missile. They could not release that missile." He goes on to say that he thinks "any commander worth his salt" would go ahead and fire the missile, but that, under the Endangered Species Act, the commander would then "be subject to a fine of twenty thousand dollars and imprisonment for up to a year."

Culver, who appears to be struggling to keep a straight face, commends Scott, saying that his amendment "is extremely important and is acceptable."

Then, just as the debate is nearing its end, the Senate sets aside the endangered-species bill to take up the Quiet Communities Act of 1978—the noise-control bill that Culver had talked about in Des Moines, and that he must also manage. Culver is waiting for a certain senator to reach the floor to offer an amendment to the endangered-species bill, and he knows that the noise-control bill is noncontroversial and will take little time, so he and [Majority Leader Robert] Byrd have decided to bring it up now. Arrangements of this sort are made from time to time, both to accommodate senators and to move legislation along. After Culver reads a statement explaining the provisions of the noise-control bill, it is adopted by voice vote, and the Senate returns to the endangered-species bill, and the last pending amendment is offered and withdrawn.

Now Wallop and Culver commend each other, and their own staffs, on the work on the bill, a few other senators make brief statements, and the roll is called on final passage.

It is clear that the bill will pass, so during the roll call Culver leaves the floor. Don Brownlee has asked him to meet on a grassy spot in front of the Capitol with Dean Norland, a television correspondent from Cedar Rapids. Norland has to have his film at the airport by four o'clock in order to get it on tonight's news.

It is one of those hot, humid Washington summer afternoons. "Hi, Dean," Culver says to Norland. "Can we do this before your subject melts?"

Norland asks him what this bill will do for Iowa, and makes specific reference to the problem of the Dubuque bridge and the Higgins' eye clam. Culver explains that the bill would require a consultation process. He stands with his hands folded in front of him, and has his somber look; he talks firmly and with composure. There is no sign of how hot and tired he is. The bill, he says, "represents a responsible and rational balance of competing needs, with a strong presumption in favor, whenever there is doubt, of the endangered species." He talks a bit longer, says, "Thank you, Dean, 'preciate it," and then says, "I think I'll go see how my vote is."

On the way back, he glances at his schedule card and notices that he was to meet a constituent for a handshake at three o'clock. He asks

Brownlee, "What happened to that constituent?" Brownlee isn't sure. Culver reads a memorandum Brownlee has given him about phone calls that have come in for him: James Schlesinger, the Secretary of Energy, has called him, and so has Patricia Harris, the Secretary of Housing and Urban Development.

When Culver reaches the Senate floor, the roll call is just about completed, and in a few moments Adlai Stevenson, who is presiding, gives the final tally. "On this vote," he says, "the yeas are ninety-four and the nays are three." Culver allows himself a smile of satisfaction, but quickly suppresses it and accepts the congratulations of his colleagues.

It is now shortly after four, and, after going into the cloakroom to talk with some of his colleagues and unwind for a few minutes, Culver goes to the President's Room, a small room behind the Senate floor, to meet Bill Griffee, an Iowa state representative from Nashua, who has been attempting to obtain funds from the Department of Energy to revitalize an old power-dam system. "What would you like me to do at this stage, Bill?" Culver asks.

Griffee replies, "I would like you to keep track of the people in the Department of Energy." Jim Larew, who has accompanied Griffee here, takes notes. Griffee continues, "It just helps if they know a United States senator is darned interested."

Culver offers to make calls when Griffee thinks it would be helpful, and Griffee asks whether he has any objections if when he talks to the press he says that he has spoken with Senator Culver about this project. Culver says, "No, that's all right," and he adds, "I'm not familiar with all the feelings about the project." Don Brownlee takes a picture of the two men standing together.

It is now four-twenty. Jim Larew gives Culver a memorandum from Mike Naylor, Culver's legislative director, telling him that tomorrow the Administration will announce its position on product-liability insurance for small businesses, and that it will fall short of what Culver has proposed. He suggests that Culver get ready to respond to the Administration's announce-ment, and asks whether, if Culver does not have time to receive a briefing on it this afternoon—he doesn't—Naylor may tell Commerce Department staff members that Culver has asked that Naylor be briefed on the details. Culver writes "Yes" on the memorandum. An aide sends word that today the Agriculture Appropriations Subcommittee has approved one hundred million dollars for Culver's soil-conservation, clean-water program. Brownlee gives him a note saying that a certain part of the military-procurement bill is coming up in conference at four-thirty. Culver decides that if it is important enough one of his colleagues will send word asking him to come.

Now Culver proceeds to the Radio and Television Gallery to talk about the endangered-species bill. This is routine for major figures in a legislative battle. Culver goes into a room containing a set that consists of a mock office. He sits at a desk, with rows of maroon-bound volumes of the *Congressional Record* behind him. There are blue drapes on either side, and Culver pops a cigar that he has been smoking—the cigar is one small way to relieve the tension—on a shelf behind one of the drapes. ABC and CBS are here, and so are several radio reporters.

The first question is "Senator Culver, why did you find it necessary to weaken this act?"

Culver replies carefully—and evenly, under the circumstances—"I don't think we've weakened this act. I think we effected a compromise that would enable it to continue at all. Our subcommittee's hearings indicated that either it would be compromised or it wouldn't be reauthorized at all or it would be emasculated." He explains the bill. This is his best opportunity to explain publicly what it is about. He hasn't had lunch, and he's very tired—he hasn't stopped going all day—but now he states clearly and with energy why the bill was necessary. He draws on his capacity for discipline one more time. He tells how the inflexibility of the existing law had inhibited the Fish and Wildlife Service in carrying it out, and says, "So if you're really concerned about endangered species you've got to be concerned about inflexibility in the law." He stresses the point that through the requirement for five out of seven votes in the committee "the presumption is heavily in favor of the species."

A reporter says that he has had trouble with his tape recorder, and asks Culver if he will explain it all again.

Culver's eyes roll upward, but he coöperates. Then he says, "I hope what we've done is get out ahead of this problem a little bit."

He takes a few more questions, and ends the press conference and retrieves his cigar.

Over coffee in the Senate dining room, Culver talks about the day and goes over some of the messages he has been given. A State Department official is trying to reach him in connection with the proposal to lift the embargo on the sale of arms to Turkey; Howard Metzenbaum is trying to reach him in connection with a torts bill that is pending before the Judiciary Committee. Culver looks at a memorandum about the torts bill. "Doesn't it all just defy belief?" he says to me.

It is now six o'clock. The Senate has taken up the authorization bill for the Department of Housing and Urban Development and is still in session. Later, Culver will go to a fund-raiser for a friend of his who is running for attorney general of Iowa. Tomorrow, he is scheduled to go at eight o'clock to a breakfast seminar on SALT; and then attend a hearing of the Environmental Pollution Subcommittee; and meet with Dr. Norman Borlaug, who is from Iowa, and who received a Nobel Peace Prize for his development of high-yield grain (the "green revolution"); and then meet with Josy Gittler about bills pending before his Juvenile Delinquency Subcommittee; and then have lunch with his two daughters who are in Washington (this weekend, he will go back to McGregor); and then attend the House-Senate conference on the military-procurement bill and also a meeting of the Environment and Public Works Committee on a bill that is part of the President's economic stimulus program (these two meetings will overlap); and meet with a constituent for a handshake; and, of course, go to the Senate floor to vote.

The Contemporary Congress:
A Perspective

☐   The twentieth century has been witness to important but infrequent changes in the way Congress carries out its business. The "Revolt of 1910" deposed a powerful House Speaker and reduced the influence of party leaders, resulting in a decentralized Congress dominated by committee chairmen. Those chairmen, who were soon to be almost universally chosen by the seniority rule under which the most senior committee member of the majority party becomes chairman, ruled the roost on Capitol Hill until the early 1970s.

An influx of new members in both the House and the Senate in the 1970s caused pressures to distribute internal power more evenly. No longer were freshman senators willing to wait years before they could make their "maiden" speeches on the floor and participate meaningfully in the body's decision making. Nor could new House members accept the old way of doing things that largely excluded them from power for many years.

Junior senators began to demand their "rights" within the body, and on the House side rank-and-file Democrats revived their caucus and summarily deposed three of the most senior committee chairmanships as examples to others that their chairmanships too might be in jeopardy if they acted arbitrarily without consulting committee members. Subcommittee chairmen succeeded in passing a "Subcommittee Bill of Rights," which prevented the Standing Committee chairman from arbitrarily and unilaterally controlling subcommittee budgets, staff, and legislative jurisdictions.

Also changing in the 1970s was the external political environment of Congress. New developments included a growing lobbying corps and political action committees, both of which increased special-interest pressures on legislators. Also the media came fully into its own as a powerful force that could sway congressional elections and shape images of personal power on Capitol Hill that so many members eagerly seek.

The author of the following selection looks at the contemporary Congress, observing that in the view of many members its new attributes have taken the joy out of being a congressman.

WHO TOOK THE FUN
OUT OF CONGRESS?

From 1961 to 1986, politics in Washington has ridden a roller coaster of emotions to arrive again at a time of apparent routine. A popular president stares down Pennsylvania Avenue at a fretful and balky Congress, worried about the next election. On the surface, it's a thoroughly familiar scene.

But the 25-year ride from John F. Kennedy's capital to Ronald Reagan's has seen a vast and dramatic change in Washington's political landscape. In conversations with some of the survivors, it is clear that Washington has become a far worse place for them to do the business of governing.

They talk of a governmental city where elected officials are all but buried in growing legislative and executive bureaucracies; where lobbyists promote special interests more effectively than leaders hold out a vision of the national interest; where everyone but the president is subjected to the demeaning pressures of perpetual fund-raising; and where everyone, including the president, can gain more credit by public relations ploys than by substantive policy work.

"Today, it seems as if we just hurtle from one event to another—and without time to judge the consequences of what we've done," says retiring Republican Sen. Charles McC. Mathias Jr. of Maryland. "It just doesn't seem as if there are clear themes anymore."

What these members and former members are describing is the submergence of leadership in a swamp of conflicting pressures. Part of the problem is the times. Many of the current leaders are of the World War II generation, not as spry or as energetic as they once were. They hold the levers of power, but their grip is not strong.

The people who aspire to succeed them are eager, well trained and well educated. But they come from a generation whose formative years enshrined the commandment to "do your own thing." And so far, at least, they seem more adept at promoting their own careers than any larger cause. As newcomers in the 1970s, these juniors overthrew the seniority system and rejected their predecessors' habits of deference. Now many of them find themselves frustrated by the maze of separate power centers they created.

A few years ago, political scientist Morris P. Fiorina set out to define "the Washington establishment" that candidates were running against.

The Industry of Congress, 1960–1985		
	1960s[a]	1980s[a]
Congressional staff	7,091[b]	17,963[c]
House & Senate subcommittee staff	910[b]	3,183[d]
Lawyers	12,564	25,000[d]
Lobbyists	236	7,600[d]
Reporters & photographers[e]	1,522	4,273
Congressional mailings (in millions of pieces)	85.1	540[c]
Costs of official mail (in millions of dollars)	3.836[f]	107.077
Roll call votes (House & Senate)	320	683

[a]Unless otherwise noted, actual years of reference are 1961 and 1985, respectively.
    [b]Year of reference, 1960.
    [c]Year of reference, 1984.
    [d]Estimate.
    [e]Figures reflect only those reporters and photographers/cameramen accredited to House and Senate press galleries.
    [f]Year of reference, 1962.
    Source: Adapted from data compiled by *Washington Post* researcher Lee Kennedy.

"There is a Washington establishment," he wrote. "In fact, it is a hydra with each head only marginally concerned with the others' existence. These establishments are not malevolent, centrally directed conspiracies against the American people. Rather, they are unconsciously evolved and evolving networks of congressmen, bureaucrats and organized subgroups of the citizenry—all seeking to achieve their own goals. Contrary to what is popularly believed, the bureaucrats are not the problem. Congressmen are. The Congress is the key to the Washington establishment. The Congress created the establishment, sustains it, and most likely will continue to sustain and even expand it."

Despite the strictures of two self-proclaimed "outsiders"—Jimmy Carter and Ronald Reagan—staffs and budgets of government have continued to expand—not least on Capitol Hill itself. The network of lobbyists, lawyers, researchers, publicists, campaign consultants and fund-raisers has also grown thicker. The ranks of reporters, photographers and microphone-holders who help set the tone of the city's politics have increased. That is why it is so disturbing to find so many of the veterans of Capitol Hill lamenting the changes they have seen.

Their complaint is not a complaint about the city, nor is it the tired argument that government would be closer to the people if the capital were in Springfield, Mo., or Topeka, Kan. The members deny that they are distant—psychologically or politically—from the folks they represent back home.

But in one sense, staying in touch has become more difficult. Congress adjourned on Sept. 1 in 1960 and on Sept. 27 in 1961. Of late, the legislators count themselves lucky if they are finished before Christmas. But members have been inventive about ways to stay in touch. They are constantly a presence in their districts—via flying visits, television and radio tapes, mailings and scattered home offices—even while they spend more of their year in Washington.

On the surface, the system that political scientist Fiorina described in his book "Congress: Keystone of the Washington Establishment" seems to be working. The main goal of members of Congress, he said, is reelection; and in 1984, 92.8 percent of the members seeking another term were successful. Why then do they complain?

Ex-representative Henry S. Reuss of Wisconsin, who came from Milwaukee in 1955 and retired in 1982, summarizes the indictment:

"While the level of people in Congress today is higher than it's ever been in terms of education and general ability, Congress is not as effective as it was, nor as joyous a place to be as it was 25 years ago. Campaigns that used to cost $15,000 often cost $200,000, even $500,000. And that puts a psychological mortgage on people, even if it doesn't distort their judgment.

"The second reason that things aren't as joyous as [at] an earlier time is that public relations and manipulation of the media are increasingly what people in Congress have to do. A certain amount of that is okay; it's part of the game. But it used to be a member of Congress could genuinely make himself an expert in a field or two and be useful. . . . But now there's an imperative to look like a universal genius, so too much time is spent on public relations and too little on substantive work.

"Third, Congress is overrun with subcommittees and staff, as a result of a revolution that went too far. There was a successful move in the 1970s to come to grips with the Neanderthal rigidity of seniority and committee chairman autocracy. . . . But in the House, we went overboard . . . there is no focusing of responsibility. . . . " These words—coming from a liberal Democrat—echo many of the traditional conservative complaints. Veterans of the last 25 years hand up a four-point indictment:

• Congress has become bogged down in the intricacies of its own process, the diffusion of its own power and the increase of its own workload.

"We've reached the point," says Republican Sen. Robert T. Stafford of Vermont, who came to Congress 25 years ago, "where everyone in the

Senate can institute a filibuster to get his own way on matters that may be important to him but not to the nation. . . . "

That kind of autonomy—or anarchy—didn't always prevail. The old Congress was very much a pyramidal place. Democratic Rep. John D. Dingell of Michigan recalls that when he came in the mid-1950s, House Speaker Sam Rayburn and Senate Majority Leader Lyndon B. Johnson "met every evening in H-128, the 'Board of Education' room, over bourbon and branch water. They talked about what had happened that day, what they wanted to have happen tomorrow, and what they thought was good for the country. . . . You didn't have the kind of divided structure you have here now, with a Senate at war with the House, and both of them at war, on different issues, with the White House."

The old Congress was very much of a southern and western institution. To read the roster of committee chairmen from the 1961 Congressional Directory is to remind oneself of the fact that the Civil War's outcome was not really acknowledged in the Capitol. On the Senate side, the committee chairmen came from 13 states—all south of the Mason-Dixon line or west of the Rockies.

Nor was the House much different. Fourteen of the 20 standing committee chairmen were southerners or westerners. This posed a serious challenge for the new president from Massachusetts, who had to expend a sizable chunk of his skimpy political capital early in [1961] on a 217-212 roll-call vote to "pack" the House Rules Committee. That allowed him to bring some bills to the floor despite the opposition of "Judge" Howard W. Smith of Virginia, its conservative Democratic chairman.

Chairmen like Smith ruled with an iron hand; and while it was hard on young presidents—and junior members of Congress—there was no doubt where the power lay. Many of the veterans, looking back, see that accountability as having vanished somewhere in the reforms of the 1970s and the increase in the scale of government.

The southerners, unsurprisingly, are most sensitive to the change. "The budget we're dealing with is so much bigger," says Sen. John C. Stennis, a Mississippi Democrat who came to the Senate in 1947. "The volume of work is much greater now. . . . In the old days, senators really mastered the subject matter in their areas of specialization, and the presentations they made on the floor showed that mastery. It's just not as thorough now."

George McGovern of South Dakota, a liberal voice from 1963 through 1980, agrees. "The Senate has deteriorated as an institution. It's not as inspiring a place. . . . In the 1960s and early 1970s, we had a lot of senators who could stand up on the floor and debate issues with conviction. . . . They were strong figures."

As for the House, Democrat Morris Udall of Arizona recalls that in the '60s and '70s he was part of the movement to break the seniority system and reduce the power of the committee chairmen. Now chairman of the Interior Committee, he says, "We wanted to democratize the place, and we've done that, but maybe we overshot a bit. . . . I think about 75 percent of the Democrats have subcommittee chairmanships; but if everybody's in charge, nobody's in charge."

In fact, there are 165 different people in the House and Senate who can answer to the proud title "Mr. Chairman," having been given committees or subcommittees of their own. With the spread of power has come a massive increase in staff. In the past quarter-century, the number of congressional employes has jumped 250 percent, to 17,963—a ratio of about 33 of them to each elected official.

• There is insufficient deference to leaders who have earned that respect by their expertise and experience. Edmund S. Muskie of Maine, who in 1980 left the Senate after 21 years to become Secretary of State, recalls watching more senior members of the Senate. "They all seemed to be impressive figures . . . somehow, taller than today's senators. . . . The Senate was a more structured and hierarchical place than it is today, but it was more comfortable, too."

Structure and predictability may be regarded as dispensable. What is lacking, the veterans say, is the sense of responsibility that went with them.

"I don't want to denigrate the abilities of the people there today," says former senator John Sherman Cooper of Kentucky. "These people in the House and Senate are pretty able. But they don't seem to respond to their leaders. There were times, particularly in foreign affairs, when you saw Republicans and Democrats rise to the challenge of resolving great issues, but we don't see that so often now."

The feelings about the House are no different. John B. Anderson of Illinois, who came to the House in 1961 and left in 1980 to run for president, dropping his Republican Party ties in the process, says there has been a revolution. "When I came," he says, "the norm was one of deference to your elders. The seniority system was in full and unbridled control of the place. We ended automatic seniority in 1971 on the Republican side and the Democrats did the same in 1975; and now, my gosh, the place is filled with policy entrepreneurs doing their own thing. You have two freshmen like Phil Gramm and Warren Rudman [senators from Texas and New Hampshire, respectively] just grabbing the reins [with their deficit-control measure] and the establishment falls into line. . . . "

• There are too many rewards—especially in coveted media attention— for the showoffs, and not enough incentives for those who really do the work.

Democratic Rep. Neal Smith of Iowa, a 27-year veteran, says that television-dominated campaigns have produced a different—and inferior— breed of congressmen. "The process of getting here . . . has changed members' attitudes and behavior," he says. "We see people who come here and do nothing, or almost nothing, but public relations. And it pays off. But the more members try to save themselves for the next election, the less and less people are carrying the load here . . . and that's not a good development at all."

• The pressures on members of Congress—especially the campaign finance demands—have grown beyond safe limits.

The average cost of a House candidacy hit $302,000 in 1984 and a Senate bid, $1,087,000. Some are sanguine about these sums, but Richard S. Schweiker, formerly a representative and senator from Pennsylvania and later secretary of Health and Human Services in the first Reagan Cabinet, says, "We've reached the point where a member of Congress has to be either a millionaire or a continual fund-raiser, and that's a tragic commentary on where we're going."

The political obligations that go with financial contributions concern many people, but George McGovern is probably right when he says, "The special interests have always been here. I feel overwhelmed sometimes by the numbers. When you go to a party now, it seems like every third person you meet is working on some kind of [lobbying] campaign. But I've never regarded lobbyists as evil."

Evil or good, the lawyers and lobbyists have certainly become ubiquitous. Between 1960 and today, the number of lawyers in Washington has doubled to 25,000. And the number of lobbyists has grown 365 to 7,600, according to registrations with the clerk of the House.

The other great growth area has been with the media. The number of journalists accredited to Congress has increased from 1,500 to 4,200 in the last quarter-century.

Not only have the numbers multiplied, but the intrusiveness of the media has grown. Frank Cormier, an Associated Press veteran, says, "The adversarial relationship has become more acute. There was a much greater tendency then to be protective of sources in general and politicians in particular. They don't get that kind of coddling now. Reporters saw John Kennedy in the back seat of a limousine with a woman who wasn't his wife, and nothing was said or written. Today, there would be tremendous competitive pressures to report that."

Charles B. Seib, who was managing editor of the old Washington Star, agrees that on topics large and small, reporters have become "much more questioning."

"Today's reporters are much more qualified to do the job the press has to do," Seib says, "but the more you take on yourself, the more responsibilities you have, and I think the press has been a little laggard in meeting them."

If Congress is the heart of the Washington establishment, as Fiorina claims, then Rep. Jim Wright of Texas, the probable Speaker of the House next year, is the man who faces the personal challenge of trying to make it work.

"It's a more participatory and less authoritarian society in which we live and work now," he says of Capitol Hill. "I'm not sure if it is more or less enjoyable. It's busier. There is less time available for the easy, flowing camaraderie that characterized our personal relationships 25 years ago. The House is in session later and longer. The mail volume and the caseload is more voluminous. But when it comes to our work as legislators, persuasion is the coin of the realm. And that's pretty healthy for a democracy."

Wright—or someone else—may grasp the tools of formal leadership, but no Speaker can shut down the publicity tools available to individual members—or curb their impulse to do their own thing.

CHAPTER 9

The Judiciary

An independent judicial system is an important part of constitutional government. The United States Supreme Court was created with this view, and its members were given life tenure and guaranteed compensation to maintain their independence. However, Congress was given power to structure the entire subordinate judicial system, including control over the appellate jurisdiction of the Supreme Court. Regardless of any initial lack of power and various attempts made by and through Congress to curb its power, the Supreme Court today occupies a predominant position in the governmental system. The evolution of the Court, its present powers, and their implications are analyzed in this chapter, along with selected problems in the administration of justice.

Constitutional Background: Judicial Independence and Judicial Review

The Supreme Court and the judicial system play important roles in the intricate separation-of-powers scheme. Through judicial review, both legislative and executive decisions may be overruled by the courts for a number of reasons. To some extent, then, the judiciary acts as a check upon arbitrary action by governmental departments and agencies. The intent of the framers of the Constitution regarding the role of the judiciary, particularly the Supreme Court, in our governmental system is examined in *Federalist 78.*

FEDERALIST 78

We proceed now to an examination of the judiciary department of the proposed government.

In unfolding the defects of the existing confederation, the utility and necessity of a federal judicature have been clearly pointed out. It is the less necessary to recapitulate the considerations there urged; as the propriety of the institution in the abstract is not disputed; the only questions which have been raised being relative to the manner of constituting it, and to its extent. To these points, therefore, our observations shall be confined.

The manner of constituting it seems to embrace these several objects: 1st. The mode of appointing the judges; 2nd. The tenure by which they are to hold their places; 3rd. The partition of the judiciary authority between different courts, and their relations to each other.

First. As to the mode of appointing the judges: This is the same with that of appointing the officers of the union in general, and has been so fully discussed . . . that nothing can be said here which would not be useless repetition.

Second. As to the tenure by which the judges are to hold their places: This chiefly concerns their duration in office; the provisions for their support; the precautions for their responsibility.

According to the plan of the convention, all the judges who may be appointed by the United States are to hold their offices *during good behavior;* which is conformable to the most approved of the state constitutions. . . . The standard of good behavior for the continuance in office of the judicial magistracy is certainly one of the most valuable of the modern improvements in the practice of government. In a monarchy, it is an excellent barrier to the despotism of the prince; in a republic, it is a no less excellent barrier to the encroachments and oppressions of the representative body. And it is the best expedient which can be devised in any government, to secure a steady, upright, and impartial administration of the laws.

Whoever attentively considers the different departments of power must perceive, that, in a government in which they are separated from each other, the judiciary, from the nature of its functions, will always be the least dangerous to the political rights of the constitution; because it will be least in a capacity to annoy or injure them. The executive not only dispenses the honors, but holds the sword of the community. The legislature not only commands the purse, but prescribes the rules by which the duties and rights of every citizen are to be regulated. The judiciary, on the contrary, has no influence over either the sword or the purse; no direction either of the strength or of the wealth of the society; and can take no active resolution whatever. It may truly be said to have neither FORCE NOR WILL, but merely judgment; and must ultimately depend upon the aid of the executive arm for the efficacious exercise even of this faculty.

This simple view of the matter suggests several important consequences: It proves incontestably, that the judiciary is beyond comparison, the weakest of the three departments of power, that it can never attack with success either of the other two; and that all possible care is requisite to enable it to defend itself against their attacks. It equally proves, that, though individual oppression may now and then proceed from the courts of justice, the general liberty of the people can never be endangered from that quarter; I mean so long as the judiciary remains truly distinct from both the legislature and executive. For I agree, that "there is no liberty, if the power of judging be not separated from the legislative and executive powers." It proves, in the last place, that as liberty can have nothing to fear from the judiciary alone, but would have everything to fear from its union with either of the other departments; that, as all the effects of such a union must ensue from a dependence of the former on the latter, notwithstanding a nominal and apparent separation; that as, from the natural feebleness of the judiciary, it is in continual jeopardy of being overpowered, awed or influenced by its coordinate branches; that, as nothing can contribute so much to its firmness and independence as PERMANENCY IN OFFICE, this quality may therefore be justly regarded as an indispensable ingredient in its constitution; and, in a great measure, as the CITADEL of the public justice and the public security.

The complete independence of the courts of justice is peculiarly essential in a limited constitution. By a limited constitution, I understand one which contains certain specified exceptions to the legislative no ex post facto laws, and the like. Limitations of this kind can be preserved in practice no other way than through the medium of the courts of justice, whose duty it must be to declare all acts contrary to the manifest tenor of the constitution void. Without this, all the reservations of particular rights or privileges would amount to nothing.

Some perplexity respecting the right of the courts to pronounce legislative acts void, because contrary to the constitution, has arisen from an imagination that the doctrine would imply a superiority of the judiciary to the legislative power. It is urged that the authority which can declare the acts of another void, must necessarily be superior to the one whose acts may be declared void. As this doctrine is of great importance in all the American constitutions, a brief discussion of the grounds on which it rests cannot be unacceptable.

There is no position which depends on clearer principles than that every act of a delegated authority, contrary to the tenor of the commission under which it is exercised, is void. No legislative act, therefore, contrary to the constitution, can be valid. To deny this would be to affirm, that the deputy is greater than his principal; that the servant is above his master; that the representatives of the people are superior to the people themselves; that men, acting by virtue of powers, may do not only what their powers do not authorize, but what they forbid.

If it be said that that legislative body are themselves the constitutional judges of their powers, and that the construction they put upon them is conclusive upon the other departments, it may be answered, that this cannot be the natural presumption, where it is not to be collected from any particular provisions in the constitution. It is not otherwise to be supposed that the constitution could intend to enable the representatives of the people to substitute their *will* to that of their constituents. It is far more rational to suppose that the courts were designed to be an intermediate body between the people and the legislature, in order, among other things, to keep the latter within the limits assigned to their authority. The interpretation of the laws is the proper and peculiar province of the courts. A constitution is, in fact, and must be, regarded by the judges as a fundamental law. It must therefore belong to them to ascertain its meaning, as well as the meaning of any particular act proceeding from the legislative body. If there should happen to be an irreconcilable variance between the two, that which has the superior obligation and validity ought, of course, to be preferred; in other words, the constitution ought to be preferred to the statute, the intention of the people to the intention of their agents.

Nor does this conclusion by any means suppose a superiority of the judicial to the legislative power. It only supposes that the power of the people is superior to both; and that where the will of the legislature declared in its statutes, stands in opposition to that of the people declared in the constitution, the judges ought to be governed by the latter, rather than the former. They ought to regulate their decisions by the fundamental laws, rather than by those which are not fundamental. . . .

It can be of no weight to say, that the courts, on the pretense of a repugnancy, may substitute their own pleasure to the constitutional intentions of the legislature. This might as well happen in the case of two contradictory statutes; or it might as well happen in every adjudication upon any single statute. The courts must declare the sense of the law; and if they should be disposed to exercise WILL instead of JUDGMENT, the consequence would equally be the substitution of their pleasure to that of the legislative body. The observation, if it proved anything, would prove that there ought to be no judges distinct from the body.

If then the courts of justice are to be considered as the bulwarks of a limited constitution, against legislative encroachments, this consideration will afford a strong argument for the permanent tenure of judicial officers, since nothing will contribute so much as this to that independent spirit in the judges, which must be essential to the faithful performance of so arduous a duty.

This independence of the judges is equally requisite to guard the constitution and the rights of individuals, from the effects of those ill-humors which the arts of designing men, or the influence of particular conjunctures, sometimes disseminate among the people themselves, and which, though they speedily give place to better information, and more deliberate reflection, have a tendency, in the meantime, to occasion danger-ous innovations in the government, and serious oppressions of the minor party in the community. . . . Until the people have, by some solemn and authoritative act, annulled or changed the established form, it is binding upon themselves collectively, as well as individually; and no presumption, or even knowledge of their sentiments, can warrant their representatives in a departure from it, prior to such an act. But it is easy to see, that it would require an uncommon portion of fortitude in the judges to do their duty as faithful guardians of the constitution, where legislative invasions of it had been instigated by the major voice of the community.

But it is not with a view to infractions of the constitution only, that the independence of the judges may be an essential safeguard against the effects of occasional ill-humors in the society. These sometimes extend no farther than to the injury of the private rights of particular classes of citizens, by unjust and partial laws. Here also the firmness of the judicial magistracy is of vast importance in mitigating the severity, and confining the operation of such laws. It not only serves to moderate the immediate mischiefs of those which may have been passed, but it operates as a check upon the legislative body in passing them; who, perceiving that obstacles to the success of an iniquitous intention are to be expected from the scruples of the courts, are in a manner compelled by the very motives of the injustice they mediate, to qualify their attempts. . . .

That inflexible and uniform adherence to the rights of the constitution, and of individuals, which we perceive to be indispensable in the courts of justice, can certainly not be expected from judges who hold their offices by a temporary commission. Periodical appointments, however regulated, or by whomsoever made, would, in some way or other, be fatal to their necessary independence. If the power of making them was committed either to the executive or legislature, there would be danger of an improper compliance to the branch which possessed it; if to both, there would be an unwillingness to hazard the displeasure of either; if to the people, or to persons chosen by them for the special purpose, there would be too great a disposition to consult popularity to justify a reliance that nothing would be consulted but the constitution and the laws.

There is yet a further and a weighty reason for the permanency of judicial offices, which is deducible from the nature of the qualifications they require. It has been frequently remarked, with great propriety, that a voluminous code of laws is one of the inconveniences necessarily connected with the advantages of a free government. To avoid an arbitrary discretion in the courts, it is indispensable that they should be bound down by strict rules and precedents, which serve to define and point out their duty in every particular case that comes before them; and it will readily be conceived, from the variety of controversies which grow out of the folly and wickedness of mankind, that the records of those precedents must unavoidably swell to a very considerable bulk, and must demand long and laborious study to acquire a competent knowledge of them. Hence it is, that there can be but few men in the society, who will have sufficient skill in the laws to qualify them for the stations of judges. And making the proper deductions for the ordinary depravity of human nature, the number must be still smaller, of those who unite the requisite integrity with the requisite knowledge. . . .

☐   From *Federalist 78* students can observe that the intent of the framers of the Constitution, at least as expressed and represented by Hamilton, was to give to the courts the power of judicial review over legislative acts. Students should note that this concept was not explicitly written into the Constitution. Although the cause of this omission is not known, it is reasonable to assume that the framers felt that judicial power implied judicial review. Further, it is possible that the framers did not expressly mention judicial review because they had to rely on the states for adoption of the Constitution; judicial power would extend to the states as well as to the coordinate departments of the national government.

The power of the Supreme Court to invalidate an act of Congress was stated by John Marshall in *Marbury* v. *Madison,* 1 Cranch 137 (1803). At issue was a provision in the Judiciary Act of 1789 which extended the *original jurisdiction* of the Supreme Court by authorizing it to issue writs of mandamus in cases involving public officers of the United States and private persons, a power not conferred upon the Court in the Constitution. Marbury had been appointed a justice of the peace by President John Adams under the Judiciary Act of 1801, passed by the Federalists after Jefferson and the Republican Party won the elections in the fall of 1800 so that President Adams could fill various newly created judicial posts with Federalists before he left office in March, 1801. Marbury was scheduled to receive one of these commissions, but when Jefferson took office on March 4, with Madison as his Secretary of State, it had not been delivered. Marbury filed a suit with the Supreme Court requesting it to exercise its original jurisdiction and issue a writ of mandamus (a writ to compel an administrative officer to perform his duty) to force Madison to deliver the commission, an act which both Jefferson and Madison were opposed to doing. In his decision, Marshall, a prominent Federalist, stated that although Marbury had a legal right to his commission, and although mandamus was the proper remedy, the Supreme Court could not extend its original jurisdiction beyond the limits specified in the Constitution; therefore, that section of the Judiciary Act of 1789 permitting the court to issue such writs to public officers was unconstitutional. Incidentally, the Republicans were so outraged at the last-minute appointments of Adams that there were threats that Marshall would be impeached if he issued a writ of mandamus directing Madison to deliver the commission. This is not to suggest that Marshall let such considerations influence him; however, politically his decision was thought to be a masterpiece of reconciling his position as a Federalist with the political tenor of the times.

56

MARBURY v. MADISON
1 Cranch 137 (1803)

Mr. Chief Justice Marshall delivered the opinion of the Court, saying in part:
... The authority, therefore, given to the Supreme Court, by the [Judiciary Act of 1789] ... establishing the judicial courts of the United States, to issue writs of mandamus to public officers, appears not to be warranted by the Constitution [because it adds to the original jurisdiction of the Court delineated by the framers of the Constitution in Article III; had they wished this power to be conferred upon the Court it would be so stated, in the same manner that the other parts of the Court's original jurisdiction are stated]; ... it becomes necessary to inquire whether a jurisdiction so conferred can be exercised.

The question whether an act repugnant to the Constitution can become the law of the land, is a question deeply interesting to the United States; but, happily, not of an intricacy proportioned to its interest. It seems only necessary to recognize certain principles supposed to have been long and well established, to decide it.

That the people have an original right to establish, for their future government, such principles as, in their opinion, shall most conduce to their own happiness, is the basis on which the whole American fabric has been erected. The exercise of this original right is a very great exertion; nor can it nor ought it to be frequently repeated. The principles, therefore, so established, are deemed fundamental. And as the authority from which they proceed is supreme, and can seldom act, they are designed to be permanent.

This original and supreme will organizes the government, and assigns to different departments their respective powers. It may either stop here, or establish certain limits not to be transcended by those departments.

The government of the United States is of the latter description. The powers of the legislature are defined and limited; and that those limits may not be mistaken, or forgotten, the Constitution is written. To what purpose are powers limited, and to what purpose is that limitation committed to writing, if these limits may, at any time, be passed by those intended to be restrained? The distinction between a government with limited and unlimited powers is abolished, if those limits do not confine the persons on whom they are imposed, and if acts prohibited and acts allowed, are of equal obligation. It is a proposition too plain to be contested, that the Constitution controls any legislative act repugnant to it; or, that the legislature may alter the Constitution by an ordinary act.

Between these alternatives there is no middle ground. The Constitution is either a superior paramount law, unchangeable by ordinary means, or it is on a level with ordinary legislative acts, and, like other acts, is alterable when the legislature shall please to alter it.

If the former part of the alternative be true, then a legislative act contrary to the Constitution, is not law; if the latter part be true, then written constitutions are absurd attempts, on the part of the people, to limit a power in its own nature illimitable.

Certainly all those who have framed written constitutions contemplate them as forming the fundamental and paramount law of the nation, and, consequently, the theory of every such government must be, that an act of the legislature, repugnant to the constitution, is void.

This theory is essentially attached to a written constitution, and is consequently to be considered, by this court, as one of the fundamental principles of our society. It is not, therefore, to be lost sight of in the further consideration of this subject.

If an act of the legislature, repugnant to the Constitution, is void, does it, notwithstanding its invalidity, bind the courts, and oblige them to give it effect? Or, in other words, though it be not law, does it constitute a rule as operative as if it was a law? This would be to overthrow in fact what was established in theory; and would seem, at first view, an absurdity too gross to be insisted on. It shall, however, receive a more attentive consideration.

It is emphatically the province and duty of the judicial department to say what the law is. Those who apply the rule to particular cases, must of necessity expound and interpret that rule. If two laws conflict with each other, the courts must decide on the operation of each.

So if the law be in opposition to the Constitution; if both the law and the Constitution apply to a particular case, so that the court must either decide that case conformably to the law, disregarding the Constitution, or comformably to the Constitution, disregarding the law, the court must determine which of these conflicting rules governs the case. This is of the very essence of judicial duty.

If, then, the courts are to regard the Constitution, and the Constitution is superior to any ordinary act of the legislature, the Constitution, and not such ordinary act, must govern the case to which they both apply.

Those, then, who controvert the principle that the Constitution is to be considered, in court, as a paramount law, are reduced to the necessity of maintaining that courts must close their eyes on the Constitution, and see only the law.

This doctrine would subvert the very foundation of all written constitutions. It would declare that an act which, according to the principles and theory of our government, is entirely void, is yet, in practice, completely obligatory. It would declare that if the legislature shall do what is expressly forbidden, such act, notwithstanding the express prohibition, is in reality effectual. It would be giving to the legislature a practical and real omnipotence, with the same breath which professes to restrict their powers within narrow limits. It is prescribing limits, and declaring that those limits may be passed at pleasure.

That it thus reduces to nothing what we have deemed the greatest improvement on political institutions, a written constitution, would of itself be sufficient, in America, where written constitutions have been viewed with so much reverence, for rejecting the construction. But the peculiar expressions of the Constitution of the United States furnish additional arguments in favor of its rejection.

The judicial power of the United States is extended to all cases arising under the Constitution.

Could it be the intention of those who gave this power, to say that in using it the Constitution should not be looked into? That a case arising under the Constitution should be decided without examining the instrument under which it arises?

This is too extravagant to be maintained.

In some cases, then, the Constitution must be looked into by the judges. And if they can open it at all, what part of it are they forbidden to read or obey?

There are many other parts of the Constitution which serve to illustrate this subject.

It is declared that "no tax or duty shall be laid on articles exported from any State." Suppose a duty on the export of cotton, of tobacco, or of flour; and a suit instituted to recover it. Ought judgment to be rendered in such a case? Ought the judges to close their eyes on the Constitution, and only see the law?

The Constitution declares "that no bill of attainder or ex post facto law shall be passed."

If, however, such a bill should be passed, and a person should be prosecuted under it, must the court condemn to death those victims whom the Constitution endeavors to preserve?

"No person," says the Constitution, "shall be convicted of treason unless on the testimony of two witnesses to the same overt act, or on confession in open court."

Here the language of the Constitution is addressed especially to the courts. It prescribes, directly for them, a rule of evidence not to be departed from. If the legislature should change that rule, and declare one witness, or a confession out of court, sufficient for conviction, must the constitutional principle yield to the legislative act?

From these, and many other selections which might be made, it is apparent that the framers of the Constitution contemplated that instrument as a rule for the government of courts, as well as of the legislature.

Why otherwise does it direct the judges to take an oath to support it? This oath certainly applies in an especial manner to this conduct in their official character. How immoral to impose it on them, if they were to be used as the instruments, and the knowing instruments, for violating what they swear to support!

The oath of office, too, imposed by the legislature, is completely demonstrative of the legislative opinion on this subject. It is in these words: "I do solemnly swear that I will administer justice without respect to persons, and do equal right to the poor and to the rich; and that I will faithfully and impartially discharge all the duties incumbent on me as _____, according to the best of my abilities and understanding, agreeably to the Constitution and laws of the United States."

Why does a judge swear to discharge his duties agreeably to the Constitution of the United States, if that Constitution forms no rule for his government—if it is closed upon him, and cannot be inspected by him?

If such be the real state of things, this is worse than solemn mockery. To prescribe, or to take this oath, becomes equally a crime.

It is also not entirely unworthy of observation, that in declaring what shall be the supreme law of the land, the Constitution itself is first mentioned; and not the laws of the United States generally, but those only which shall be made in pursuance of the Constitution, have that rank.

Thus, the particular phraseology of the Constitution of the United States confirms and strengthens the principle, supposed to be essential to all written constitutions, that a law repugnant to the Constitution is void; and that courts, as well as other departments, are bound by that instrument.

The rule must be discharged.

Powers and Limitations of the Supreme Court

☐   Paul A. Freund, in his book *On Understanding the Supreme Court* (1949), notes that the Supreme Court has a definite political role. He asks:

"Is the law of the Supreme Court a reflection of the notions of 'policy' held by its members? The question recalls the controversy over whether judges 'make' or 'find' the law. A generation or two ago it was thought rather daring to insist that judges make law. Old Jeremiah Smith, who began the teaching of law at Harvard after a career on the New Hampshire Supreme Court, properly deflated the issue. 'Do judges make law?' he repeated. 'Course they do. Made some myself.' Of course Supreme Court Justices decide cases on the basis of their ideas of policy."

To emphasize this point today is to repeat the familiar. The Court makes policy. It would be difficult to conceive how a Court having the power to interpret the Constitution could fail to make policy, i.e., could fail to make rulings that have *general* impact upon the community as a whole. The essential distinction between policy making and adjudication is that the former has a general effect while the latter touches only a specifically designated person or group.

If the Supreme Court has this power of constitutional interpretation, how is it controlled by the other governmental departments and the community? Is it, as some have claimed, completely arbitrary in rendering many of its decisions? Is it potentially a dictatorial body? The Supreme Court and lower courts are limited to the consideration of cases and controversies brought before them by outside parties. Courts cannot initiate law. Moreover, all courts, and the Supreme Court in particular, exercise judicial self-restraint in certain cases to avoid difficult and controversial issues and to avoid outside pressure to limit the powers of the judiciary. The discussion by John P. Roche deals with the background, the nature, and the implications of judicial doctrines of self-restraint.

JUDICIAL SELF-RESTRAINT

Every society, sociological research suggests, has its set of myths which incorporate and symbolize its political, economic, and social aspirations. Thus, as medieval society had the Quest for the Holy Grail and the cult of numerology, we, in our enlightened epoch, have as significant manifestations of our collective hopes the dream of impartial decision-making and the cult of "behavioral science." While in my view these latter two are but different facets of the same fundamental drive, namely, the age-old effort to exorcise human variables from human action, our concern here is with the first of them, the pervasive tendency in the American political and constitutional tradition directed toward taking the politics out of politics, and substituting some set of Platonic guardians for fallible politicians.

While this dream of objectivizing political Truth is in no sense a unique American phenomenon, it is surely true to say that in no other democratic nation has the effort been carried so far and with such persistence. Everywhere one turns in the United States, he finds institutionalized attempts to narrow the political sector and to substitute allegedly "independent" and "impartial" bodies for elected decision-makers. The so-called "independent regulatory commissions" are a classic example of this tendency in the area of administration, but unquestionably the greatest hopes for injecting pure Truth-serum into the body politic have been traditionally reserved for the federal judiciary, and particularly for the Supreme Court. The rationale for this viewpoint is simple: "The people must be protected from themselves, and no institution is better fitted for the role of chaperone than the federal judiciary, dedicated as it is to the supremacy of the rule of law."

Patently central to this function of social chaperonage is the right of the judiciary to review legislative and executive actions and nullify those measures which derogate from eternal principles of truth and justice as incarnated in the Constitution. Some authorities, enraged at what the Supreme Court has found the Constitution to mean, have essayed to demonstrate that the framers did not intend the Court to exercise this function, to have, as they put it, "the last word." I find no merit in this contention; indeed, it seems to me undeniable not only that the authors of the Constitution intended to create a federal government, but also that they

From John P. Roche, "Judicial Self-Restraint," *The American Political Science Review,* 49 (September 1955). Reprinted by permission.

assumed *sub silentio* that the Supreme Court would have the power to review both national and state legislation.

However, since the intention of the framers is essentially irrelevant except to antiquarians and polemicists, it is unnecessary to examine further the matter of origins. The fact is that the United States Supreme Court, and the inferior federal courts under the oversight of the high Court, have enormous policy-making functions. Unlike their British and French counterparts, federal judges are not merely technicians who live in the shadow of a supreme legislature, but are fully equipped to intervene in the process of political decision making. In theory, they are limited by the Constitution and the jurisdiction it confers, but, in practice, it would be a clumsy judge indeed who could not, by a little skillful exegesis, adapt the Constitution to a necessary end. This statement is in no sense intended as a condemnation; on the contrary, it has been this perpetual reinvigoration by reinterpretation, in which the legislature and the executive as well as the courts play a part, that has given the Constitution its survival power. Applying a Constitution which contains at key points inspired ambiguity, the courts have been able to pour the new wine in the old bottle. Note that the point at issue is not the legitimacy or wisdom of judicial legislation; it is simply the enormous scope that this prerogative gives to judges to substitute their views for those of past generations, or, more controversially, for those of a contemporary Congress and President.

Thus it is naive to assert that the Supreme Court is limited by the Constitution, and we must turn elsewhere for the sources of judicial restraint. The great power exercised by the Court has carried with it great risks, so it is not surprising that American political history has been sprinkled with demands that the judiciary be emasculated. The really startling thing is that, with the notable exception of the McCardle incident in 1869, the Supreme Court has emerged intact from each of these encounters. Despite the plenary power that Congress, under Article III of the Constitution, can exercise over the the appellate jurisdiction of the high Court, the national legislature has never taken sustained and effective action against its House of Lords. It is beyond the purview of this analysis to examine the reasons for Congressional inaction; suffice it here to say that the most significant form of judicial limitation has remained self-limitation. This is not to suggest that such a development as statutory codification has not cut down the area of interpretive discretion, for it obviously has. It is rather to maintain that when the justices have held back from assaults on legislative or executive actions, they have done so on the basis of self-established rationalizations. . . .

The remainder of this paper is therefore concerned with two aspects of this auto-limitation: first, the techniques by which it is put into practice; and, second, the conditions under which it is exercised. . . .

TECHNIQUES OF JUDICIAL SELF-RESTRAINT

The major techniques of judicial self-restraint appear to fall under the two familiar rubrics: procedural and substantive. Under the former fall the various techniques by which the Court can avoid coming to grips with substantive issues, while under the latter would fall those methods by which the Court, in a substantive holding, finds that the matter at issue in the litigation is not properly one for judicial settlement. Let us examine these two categories in some detail.

Procedural Self-Restraint

Since the passage of the Judiciary Act of 1925, the Supreme Court has had almost complete control over its business. United States Supreme Court *Rule 38*, which governs the certiorari policy, states, (§ 5) that discretionary review will be granted only "where there are special and important reasons therefor." Professor Fowler Harper has suggested in a series of detailed and persuasive articles on the application of this discretion [*University of Pennsylvania Law Review*, vols. 99–101; 103] that the Court has used it in such a fashion as to duck certain significant but controversial problems. While one must be extremely careful about generalizing in this area, since the reasons for denying certiorari are many and complex, Harper's evidence does suggest that the Court in the period since 1949 has refused to review cases involving important civil liberties problems which on their merits appeared to warrant adjudication. As he states at one point: "It is disconcerting when the Court will review a controversy over a patent on a pin ball machine while one man is deprived of his citizenship and another of his liberty without Supreme Court review of a plausible challenge to the validity of government action." . . .

Furthermore, the Supreme Court can issue certiorari on its own terms. Thus in *Dennis* v. *United States*, appealing the Smith Act convictions of the American communist leadership, the Court accepted the evidential findings of the Second Circuit as final and limited its review to two narrow constitutional issues. This, in effect, burked the basic problem: whether the evidence was sufficient to demonstrate that the Communist Party, U.S.A., was *in fact* clear and present danger to the security of the nation, or whether the communists were merely shouting "Fire!" in an empty theater.

Other related procedural techniques are applicable in some situations. Simple delay can be employed, perhaps in the spirit of the Croatian proverb that "delay is the handmaiden of justice." . . . However, the technique of procedural self-restraint is founded on the essentially simple gadget of refusing jurisdiction, or of procrastinating the acceptance of jurisdiction, and need not concern us further here.

Substantive Self-Restraint

Once a case has come before the Court on its merits, the justices are forced to give some explanation for whatever action they may take. Here self-restraint can take many forms, notably, the doctrine of political questions, the operation of judicial parsimony, and—particularly with respect to the actions of administrative officers of agencies—the theory of judicial inexpertise.

The doctrine of political questions is too familiar to require much elaboration here. Suffice it to say that if the Court feels that a question before it, e.g., the legitimacy of a state government, the validity of a legislative apportionment, or the correctness of executive action in the field of foreign relations, is one that is not properly amenable to judicial settlement, it will refer the plaintiff to the "political" organs of government for any possible relief. The extent to which this doctrine is applied seems to be a direct coefficient of judicial egotism, for the definition of a political question can be expanded or contracted in accordion-like fashion to meet the exigencies of the times. A juridical definition of the term is impossible, for at root the logic that supports it is circular: political questions are matters not soluble by the judicial process; matters not soluble by the judicial process are political questions. As an early dictionary explained, violins are small cellos, and cellos are large violins.

Nor do examples help much in definition. While it is certainly true that the Court cannot mandamus a legislature to apportion a state in equitable fashion, it seems equally true that the Court is without the authority to force state legislators to implement unsegregated public education. Yet in the former instance the Court genuflected to the "political" organs and took no action, while in the latter it struck down segregation as violative of the Constitution.

Judicial parsimony is another major technique of substantive self-restraint. In what is essentially a legal application of Occam's razor, the court has held that it will not apply any more principles to the settlement of a case than are absolutely necessary, e.g., it will not discuss the constitutionality of a law if it can settle the instant case by statutory construction. Furthermore, if an action is found to rest on erroneous statutory construction, the review terminates at that point: the Court will not go on to discuss whether the statute, properly construed, would be constitutional. A variant form of this doctrine, and a most important one, employs the "case of controversy" approach, to wit, the Court, admitting the importance of the issue, inquires as to whether the litigant actually has standing to bring the matter up. . . .

A classic use of parsimony to escape from a dangerous situation occurred in connection with the evacuation of the Nisei from the West Coast in 1942. Gordon Hirabayashi, in an attempt to test the validity of the regulations clamped on the American-Japanese by the military, violated the curfew and refused to report to an evacuation center. He was convicted on both counts by the district court and sentenced to three months for each offense, the sentences to run *concurrently*. When the case came before the Supreme Court, the justices sustained his conviction for violating the *curfew*, but refused to examine the validity of the evacuation order on the ground that it would not make any difference to Hirabayashi anyway; he was in for ninety days no matter what the Court did with evacuation.

A third method of utilizing substantive self-restraint is particularly useful in connection with the activities of executive departments or regulatory agencies, both state and federal. I have entitled it the doctrine of judicial *inexpertise*, for it is founded on the unwillingness of the Court to revise the findings of experts. The earmarks of this form of restraint are great defer- ence to the holdings of the expert agency usually coupled with such a statement as "It is not for the federal courts to supplant the [Texas Rail- road] Commission's judgment even in the face of convincing proof that a different result would have been better." In this tradition, the Court has refused to question *some* exercises of discretion by the National Labor Relations Board, the Federal Trade Commission, and other federal and state agencies. But the emphasis on *some* gives the point away; in other cases, apparently on all fours with those in which it pleads its technical *inexpertise*, the Court feels free to assess evidence de novo and reach independent judgment on the technical issues involved. . . .

In short, with respect to expert agencies, the Court is equipped with both offensive and defensive gambits. If it chooses to intervene, one set of precedents is brought out, while if it decides to hold back, another set of equal validity is invoked. Perhaps the best summary of this point was made by Justice Harlan in 1910, when he stated bluntly that "the Courts have rarely, if ever, felt themselves so restrained by technical rules that they could not find some remedy, consistent with the law, for acts . . . that violated natural justice or were hostile to the fundamental principles devised for the protection of the essential rights of property."

This does not pretend to be an exhaustive analysis of the techniques of judicial self-restraint; on the contrary, others will probably find many which are not given adequate discussion here. The remainder of this paper, however, is devoted to the second area of concern: the conditions under which the Court refrains from acting.

THE CONDITIONS OF JUDICIAL SELF-RESTRAINT

The conditions which lead the Supreme Court to exercise auto-limitation are many and varied. In the great bulk of cases, this restraint is an outgrowth of sound and quasi-automatic legal maxims which defy teleological interpretation. It would take a master of the conspiracy theory of history to assign meaning, for example, to the great majority of certiorari denials; the simple fact is that these cases do not merit review. However, in a small proportion of cases, purpose does appear to enter the picture, sometimes with a vengeance. It is perhaps unjust to the Court to center our attention on this small proportion, but it should be said in extenuation that these cases often involve extremely significant political and social issues. In the broad picture, the refusal to grant certiorari in 1943 to the Minneapolis Trotskyites convicted under the Smith Act is far more meaningful than the similar refusal to grant five hundred petitions to prison "lawyers" who have suddenly discovered the writ of habeas corpus. Likewise, the holding that the legality of Congressional apportionment is a "political question" vitally affects the operation of the whole democratic process.

What we must therefore seek are the conditions under which the Court holds back *in this designated category of cases.* Furthermore, it is important to realize that there are positive consequences of negative action; as Charles Warren has implied, the post-Civil War Court's emphasis on self-restraint was a judicial concomitant of the resurgence of states' rights. Thus self-restraint may, as in wartime, be an outgrowth of judicial caution, or it may be part of a purposeful pattern of abdicating national power to the states.

Ever since the first political scientist discovered Mr. Dooley, the changes have been run on the aphorism that the Supreme Court "follows the election returns," and I see no particular point in ringing my variation on this theme through again. Therefore, referring those who would like a more detailed explanation to earlier analyses, the discussion here will be confined to the bare bones of my hypothesis.

The power of the Supreme Court to invade the decision-making arena, I submit, is a consequence of that fragmentation of political power which is normal in the United States. No cohesive majority, such as normally exists in Britain, would permit a politically irresponsible judiciary to usurp decision-making functions, but, for complex social and institutional reasons, there are few issues in the United States on which cohesive majorities exist. The guerrilla warfare which usually rages between Congress and the President, as well as the internal civil wars which are endemic in both the legislature and the administration, give the judiciary considerable room for maneuver. If, for example, the Court strikes down a controversial decision of the Federal Power Commission, it will be supported by a substantial bloc of congressmen; if it supports the FPC's decision, it will also receive considerable congressional support. But the important point is that *either* way it decides the case, there is no possibility that Congress will exact any vengeance on the Court for its action. A disciplined majority would be necessary to clip the judicial wings, and such a majority does not exist on this issue.

On the other hand, when monolithic majorities do exist on issues, the

Court is likely to resort to judicial self-restraint. A good case here is the current tidal wave of anti-communist legislation and administrative action, the latter particularly with regard to aliens, which the Court has treated most gingerly. About the only issues on which there can be found cohesive majorities are those relating to national defense, and the Court has, as Clinton Rossiter demonstrated in an incisive analysis [*The Supreme Court and the Commander-in-Chief,* Ithaca, 1951], traditionally avoided problems arising in this area irrespective of their constitutional merits. Like the slave who accompanied a Roman consul on his triumph whispering "You too are mortal," the shade of Thad Stevens haunts the Supreme Court chamber to remind the justices what an angry Congress can do.

To state the proposition in this brief compass is to oversimplify it considerably. I have, for instance, ignored the crucial question of how the Court knows when a majority *does* exist, and I recognize that certain aspects of judicial behavior cannot be jammed into my hypothesis without creating essentially spurious epicycles. However, I am not trying to establish a monistic theory of judicial action; group action, like that of individuals, is motivated by many factors, some often contradictory, and my objective is to elucidate what seems to be one tradition of judicial motivation. In short, judicial self-restraint and judicial power seem to be opposite sides of the same coin: it has been by judicious application of the former that the latter has been maintained. A tradition beginning with Marshall's *coup* in *Marbury* v. *Madison* and running through *Mississippi* v. *Johnson* and *Ex Parte Vallandigham* to *Dennis* v. *United States* suggests that the Court's power has been maintained by a wise refusal to employ it in unequal combat.

☐   While the Supreme Court may not enter unequal political combat, as John Roche contends in the previous selection (No. 57), it has made many highly controversial decisions since he wrote his article in 1955. (For example, see selections Nos. 17–19.) One conservative law scholar has gone so far as to state, "In the years since *Brown* v. *Board of Education* (1954) nearly every fundamental change in domestic social policy has been brought about not by the decentralized democratic (or, more accurately, republican) process contemplated by the Constitution, but simply by the Court's decree."[1]

Conservatives, clearly unhappy with the trend in Supreme Court decision making not only during the Warren era (1953 to 1969) but under the Chief Justiceship of Warren Burger (1969–1986), charged that the

[1]Lino A. Graglia, "How the Constitution Disappeared," *Commentary,* February 1986, p. 19.

Court's "loose" constitutional interpretations have been contrary to the wishes of the majority of the people and have made a mockery of the Constitution itself. Responding to their conservative constituencies, Republican presidential candidates Richard M. Nixon in 1968 and Ronald Reagan in 1980 promised to take action to reverse the Supreme Court's alleged liberalism by appointing conservative justices.

Ironically, one of Nixon's appointees, Harry Blackmun, authored the Court's controversial abortion decision in 1973 (see selection No. 18). Another Nixon appointee, Lewis Powell, joined the more liberal justices in the *Bakke* case (see selection No. 15) to allow universities and the colleges to take race into account in their admissions processes, a tacit although far from direct support for the affirmative action programs conservatives so strongly opposed. Nixon found, as had Dwight D. Eisenhower who appointed Earl Warren to be Chief Justice in 1953, that presidents have no control over their appointees once they are on the Court.

For his part in the conservative cause, President Ronald Reagan, while choosing Sandra Day O'Connor as the first woman Supreme Court Justice, tried to make certain beforehand that she would support conservative positions on such issues as abortion. Although able to select only two Supreme Court Justices by the middle of his second term, Reagan had a far greater impact upon the lower federal judiciary which he "stacked" with conservative judges.

Debate over the role of the Supreme Court intensified during Reagan's second term. His Attorney General, Edwin Meese, in a speech given before the American Bar Association, attacked the Supreme Court for interpreting the Constitution according to its own values rather than the intent of the Founding Fathers. In response, Associate Justice William J. Brennan, speaking to a Georgetown University audience, called the Attorney General "arrogant" and "doctrinaire," stating that it is impossible to "gauge accurately the intent of the framers on the application of principle to specific, contemporary questions." Another Supreme Court justice, John Paul Stevens, joined the attack on Meese.

The arguments in the 1980s over the proper role of the Supreme Court recalled the debate in the early days of the Republic between proponents of "strict" construction of the Constitution on the one hand and "loose" construction on the other. No less an intellectual and political giant than Thomas Jefferson favored the former approach, arguing that judges should not interpret the Constitution to reflect their own political values. He particularly opposed Chief Justice John Marshall's "loose" construction of congressional authority under Article I and the implied powers clause, which supported an expansion of national power over the states. Prior to Marshall's historic decisions in *McCulloch* v. *Maryland* (1819) and *Gibbons* v. *Ogden* that flexibly interpreted the

Constitution to support broad congressional powers over the states (see selection No. 9), Alexander Hamilton had provided the rationale for loose construction in *The Federalist*. He suggested that Congress should be able to carry out its enumerated powers by whatever means it considered to be necessary and proper.

An old adage states that where one stands on political issues depends upon whose ox is being gored. Liberal supporters of Franklin D. Roosevelt attacked the conservative Supreme Court during the early New Deal when it was systematically declaring the core of FDR's program to be unconstitutional. After his overwhelming 1936 electoral victory Roosevelt attempted to "pack" the Court by seeking congressional approval of legislation that would give him the authority to appoint one new justice for each justice over seventy years of age. The legislation would have given him at the time the authority to appoint a Supreme Court majority because there were seven septuagenarian justices on the Court. Conservatives attacked Roosevelt's plan, charging that it was an unconstitutional and even un-American attempt to undermine the Supreme Court's independence. They wanted the Court to continue acting as a super-legislature as long as it advocated conservative views. However, when the tables were turned, and the Court became the advocate of "liberal" views during the Warren era, conservatives were quick to attack it for acting as a super-legislature against the will of the majority, which was the same argument liberals had used against the Court in the 1930s.

In the following selection a federal court judge analyzes the contemporary debate over the role of the Supreme Court and gives his own views on how the federal judiciary can and should construe the Constitution.

58
Irving R. Kaufman

WHAT DID THE FOUNDING FATHERS INTEND?

The Constitution of the United States will be 200 years old on Sept. 17, 1987, and a Bicentennial commission—headed by Chief Justice Warren E. Burger (whose birthday felicitously falls on that date)—is under way, formulating plans for "Constitution Day" festivities. The celebratory air notwithstanding, recent discussions of constitutional values seem to reveal more conflict than shared pride. Some examples:

• Last summer, in remarks before the American Bar Association, Attorney General Edwin Meese 3d criticized the Supreme Court's recent decisions reaffirming the First Amendment requirement that government maintain a "strict neutrality" toward religion. The Attorney General castigated the Court for ignoring the "intent of the framers" and stated that the Philadelphia Convention would find the doctrine of "a strict neutrality between religion and nonreligion . . . somewhat bizarre." In an undelivered portion of his text, the Attorney General seemed to question the applicability of the Bill of Rights to state governments.

• In an address last fall, Justice John Paul Stevens responded to the Attorney General's criticisms by stating that "some uncertainty may attend an effort to identify the precise messages" of the framers.

• Speaking at Georgetown University last October, Justice William J. Brennan Jr. rejected the "arrogance cloaked as humility" of those relying on the "facile historicism" inherent in the original-intent theory.

• The Supreme Court has agreed to hear a case in which it will decide whether the right of privacy includes consensual adult homosexual conduct. Critics contend that no right of privacy is mentioned in the Constitution or was envisioned by our Founding Fathers.

In the ongoing debate over original intent, almost all Federal judges hold to the notion that judicial decisions should be based on the text of the Constitution or the structure it creates. Yet, in requiring judges to be guided solely by the expressed views of the framers, current advocates of original intent seem to call for a narrower concept. Jurists who disregard this interpretation, the argument runs, act lawlessly because they are imposing their own moral standards and political preferences on the community.

As a Federal judge, I have found it often difficult to ascertain the

From *The New York Times,* February 23, 1986. Copyright © 1986 by The New York Times Company. Reprinted by permission.

"intent of the framers," and even more problematic to try to dispose of a constitutional question by giving great weight to the intent argument. Indeed, even if it were possible to decide hard cases on the basis of a strict interpretation of original intent, or originalism, that methodology would conflict with a judge's duty to apply the Constitution's underlying principles to changing circumstances. Furthermore, by attempting to erode the base for judicial affirmation of the freedoms guaranteed by the Bill of Rights and the 14th Amendment (no state shall "deprive any person of life, liberty, or property without due process of law; nor deny to any person . . . the equal protection of the laws"), the intent theory threatens some of the greatest achievements of the Federal judiciary.

Ultimately, the debate centers on the nature of judicial review, or the power of courts to act as the ultimate arbiters of constitutional meaning. This responsibility has been acknowledged ever since the celebrated 1803 case of Marbury v. Madison, in which Chief Justice John Marshall struck down a Congressional grant of jurisdiction to the Supreme Court not authorized by Article III of the Constitution. But here again, originalists would accept judicial review only if it adhered to the allegedly neutral principles embalmed in historical intent.

In the course of 36 years on the Federal bench, I have had to make many difficult constitutional interpretations. I have had to determine whether a teacher could wear a black armband as a protest against the Vietnam War; whether newspapers have a nonactionable right to report accusatory statements, and whether a school system might be guilty of de facto segregation. Unfortunately, the framers' intentions are not made sufficiently clear to provide easy answers. A judge must first determine what the intent was (or would have been)—a notoriously formidable task.

An initial problem is the paucity of materials. Both the official minutes of the Philadelphia Convention of 1787 and James Madison's famous notes of the proceedings, published in 1840, tend toward the terse and cursory, especially in relation to the judiciary. The Congressional debates over the proposed Bill of Rights, which became effective in 1791, are scarcely better. Even Justice William Rehnquist, one of the most articulate spokesmen for original intent, admitted in a recent dissent in a case concerning school prayer that the legislative history behind the provision against the establishment of an official religion "does not seem particularly illuminating."

One source deserves special mention. "The Federalist Papers"—the series of essays written by Alexander Hamilton, James Madison and John Jay in 1787 and 1788—have long been esteemed as the earliest constitutional commentary. In 1825, for example, Thomas Jefferson noted that "The Federalist" was regularly appealed to "as evidence of the general opinion of those who framed and of those who accepted the Constitution of the United States."

"The Federalist," however, did not discuss the Bill of Rights or the Civil

War amendments, which were yet to be written. Moreover, the essays were part of a political campaign—the authors wrote them in support of New York's ratification of the Constitution. The essays, therefore, tended to enunciate general democratic theory or rebut anti-Federalist arguments, neither of which offer much help to modern jurists. (In light of the following passage from "The Federalist," No. 14, I believe Madison would be surprised to find his words of 200 years ago deciding today's cases: "Is it not the glory of the people of America that . . . they have not suffered a blind veneration for antiquity . . . to overrule the suggestions of their own good sense . . . ?")

Another problem with original intent is this: Who were the framers? Generally, they are taken to be the delegates to the Philadelphia Convention and the Congressional sponsors of subsequent amendments. All constitutional provisions, however, have been ratified by state conventions or legislatures on behalf of the people they represented. Is the relevant intention, then, that of the drafters, the ratifiers or the general populace?

The elusiveness of the framers' intent leads to another, more telling problem. Originalist doctrine presumes that intent can be discovered by historical sleuthing or psychological rumination. In fact, this is not possible. Judges are constantly required to resolve questions that 18th-century statesmen, no matter how prescient, simply could not or did not foresee and resolve. On most issues, to look for a collective intention held by either drafters or ratifiers is to hunt for a chimera.

A reading of the Constitution highlights this problem. The principles of our great charter are cast in grand, yet cryptic, phrases. Accordingly, judges usually confront what Justice Robert Jackson in the 1940's termed the "majestic generalities" of the Bill of Rights, or the terse commands of "due process of law," or "equal protection" contained in the 14th Amendment. The use of such open-ended provisions would indicate that the framers did not want the Constitution to become a straitjacket on all events for all times. In contrast, when the framers held a clear intention, they did not mince words. Article II, for example, specifies a minimum Presidential age of 35 years instead of merely requiring "maturity" or "adequate age."

The First Amendment is a good example of a vaguer provision. In guaranteeing freedom of the press, some of our forefathers perhaps had specific thoughts on what publications fell within its purview. Some historians believe, in light of Colonial debates, that the main concern of the framers was to prevent governmental licensing of newspapers. If that were all the First Amendment meant today, then many important decisions protecting the press would have to be overruled. One of them would be the landmark *New York Times* v. *Sullivan* ruling of 1964, giving the press added protection in libel cases brought by public figures. Another would be *Near* v. *Minnesota,* a case involving Jay Near, a newspaper publisher who had run afoul of a Minnesota statute outlawing "malicious, scandalous and defamatory" publications. The Supreme Court struck down the statute in 1931, forbidding governmental prior restraints on publication; this ruling was the precursor of the 1971 Pentagon Papers decision.

The Founding Fathers focused not on particularities but on principles, such as the need in a democracy for people to engage in free and robust discourse. James Madison considered a popular government without popular information a "Prologue to a Farce or a Tragedy." Judges, then, must focus on underlying principles when going about their delicate duty of applying the First Amendment's precepts to today's world.

In fact, our nation's first debate over constitutional interpretation centered on grand principles. Angered at John Adams's Federalist Administration, advocates of states' rights in the late 18th century argued that original intent meant that the Constitution, like the Articles of Confederation, should be construed narrowly — as a compact among separate sovereigns. The 1798 Virginia and Kentucky Resolutions, which sought to reserve to the states the power of ultimate constitutional interpretation, were the most extreme expressions of this view. In rejecting this outlook, a nationalistic Supreme Court construed the Constitution more broadly.

The important point here is that neither side of this debate looked to the stated views of the framers to resolve the issue. Because of his leading role at the Philadelphia Convention, Madison's position is especially illuminating. "Whatever veneration might be entertained for the body of men who formed our Constitution," he declaimed on the floor of Congress in 1796, "the sense of that body could never be regarded as the oracular guide in expounding the Constitution."

Yet, I doubt if strict proponents of original intent will be deterred by such considerations. Their goal is not to venerate dead framers but to restrain living judges from imposing their own values. This restraint is most troublesome when it threatens the protection of individual rights against governmental encroachment.

According to current constitutional doctrine, the due process clause of the 14th Amendment incorporates key provisions of the Bill of Rights, which keeps in check only the Federal Government. Unless the due process clause is construed to include the most important parts of the first eight amendments in the Bill of Rights, then the states would be free, in theory, to establish an official church or inflict cruel and unusual punishments. This doctrine is called incorporation.

Aside from the late Justice Hugo Black, few have believed that history alone is a sufficient basis for applying the Bill of Rights to the states. In his Georgetown University address, Justice Brennan noted that the crucial liberties embodied in the Bill of Rights are so central to our national identity that we cannot imagine any definition of "liberty" without them.

In fact, a cramped reading of the Bill of Rights jeopardizes what I regard as the true original intent—the rationale for having a written Constitution at all. The principal reason for a charter was to restrain government. In 1787, the idea of a fundamental law set down in black and white was revolutionary. Hanoverian England in the 18th century did not have a fully written, unified constitution, having long believed in a partially written one, based on ancient custom and grants from the Crown like the Magna Carta. To this day, the British have kept their democracy alive without one. In theory, the "King-in-Parliament" was and is unlimited in sovereign might, and leading political theorists, such as Thomas Hobbes and John Locke, agreed that governments, once established by a social contract, could not then be fettered.

Although not a Bill of Rights, the Magna Carta—King John's concessions to his barons in 1215—was symbolic of the notion that even the Crown was not all-powerful. Moreover, certain judges believed that Parliament, like the king, had to respect the traditions of the common law. This staunch belief in perpetual rights, in turn, was an important spark for the Revolutionary conflagration of 1776.

In gaining independence, Americans formed the bold concept that sovereignty continually resided with the people, who cede power to governments only to achieve certain specific ends. This view dominated the Philadelphia Convention. Instead of merely improving on the Articles of Confederation, as they had been directed to do, the framers devised a government where certain powers—defined and thereby limited—flowed from the people to the Congress, the President and the Federal judiciary.

Alexander Hamilton recognized that the basic tenets of this scheme mandated judicial review. Individual rights, he observed in "The Federalist," No. 78, "can be preserved in practice no other way than through the medium of courts of justice, whose duty it must be to declare all acts contrary to the manifest tenor of the Constitution void." Through a written constitution and judicial enforcement, the framers intended to preserve the inchoate rights they had lost as Englishmen.

The narrow interpretation of original intent is especially unfortunate because I doubt that many of its proponents are in favor of freeing the states from the constraints of the Bill of Rights. In fact, I believe the concern of many modern "intentionalists" is quite specific: outrage over the right-of-privacy cases, especially *Roe* v. *Wade,* the 1973 Supreme Court decision recognizing a woman's right to an abortion. (The right of privacy, of course, is not mentioned in the Constitution.) Whether one agrees with this controversial decision or not, I would submit that concern over the outcome of one difficult case is not sufficient cause to embrace a theory that calls for so many changes in existing law.

Some opponents of strict interpretations of original intent, too, have been guilty of taking an extreme position. Some, for example, have suggested that invoking the framers is only a cloak to hide more modern and malevolent intentions.

This view, however, ignores the threat of abuse of power posed by a life-tenured judiciary. Unless restrained in some fashion, judges are capable of usurping authority better left to the democratic branches. Judicial critics often refer to the 1907 comment of Charles Evans Hughes (who later became Chief Justice of the United States) that "We are under a Constitution, but the Constitution is what the judges say it is."

The power of judges to declare laws unconstitutional does appear at odds with majority rule. Why should a handful of Supreme Court Justices—or any Federal judge—appointed for life, be able to invalidate the will of the people's elected representatives, as expressed in a duly enacted statute? How does one reconcile this power with our commitment to democracy?

As Hamilton foresaw in "The Federalist," No. 78, and Chief Justice Marshall established in *Marbury* v. *Madison,* review of legislation by nonelected judges is, in fact, justified by their mandate to enforce the entirety of the law including, when there is any conflict, the "supreme law of the land": the Constitution. If judicial decisions are based on political notions instead of legal principles, that imprimatur is lost.

One can, therefore, understand why a clear guide to constitutional interpretation is thought necessary. History tells us of grave abuses of power when judges feel unrestrained. Consider, for instance, the infamous Dred Scott decision in 1857. Dred Scott was a slave whose master had taken him into the Louisiana Territory and, under the terms of the Missouri Compromise, was thus made a free man. Scott, however, later was taken to the slave state of Missouri. With the aid of abolitionist lawyers, Scott brought a suit in Federal court to obtain his freedom on the grounds he had been emancipated.

On appeal, the Supreme Court ruled against him. Hoping to settle the slavery issue through judicial fiat instead of political compromise, the High Court decided blacks were not citizens and Congress could not regulate slavery in the territories. After noting the subjugation of blacks at the time of the Constitution's adoption, Chief Justice Roger Taney concluded "they had no rights which the white man was bound to respect."

The opinion was vociferously denounced in the North. "The Court has rushed into politics," raged The New York Tribune, "without other purpose than to subserve the cause of slavery." Instead of healing sectarian strife, the Court's exercise of power most likely hastened the Civil War.

The Justices likewise suffered ultimate defeat when they attempted to halt the advent of the modern welfare state. The Federal judiciary in the early decades of this century regularly invalidated social legislation, such as child labor statutes and minimum wage/maximum hours laws. Claiming that the due process clause embodied economic liberty, judges relied on the rubric of "substantive due process" to impose their own views on the nation.

This period is known as the "Lochner era," after a famous case in which the Supreme Court struck down a New York statute prescribing a 10-hour workday for bakery employees (Lochner was the owner of a bakery who was prosecuted for violating the statute). The Justices believed that the government lacked the authority to interfere with private contractual arrangements. In a powerful dissent, Justice Oliver Wendell Holmes denounced the Court's imputation of laissez-faire capitalism to the Constitution: "The Fourteenth Amendment does not enact Mr. Herbert Spencer's Social Statics." The Lochner era came to a close when the Supreme Court ultimately accepted President Roosevelt's New Deal programs.

These examples indicate the need for judicial impartiality and restraint, but if original intent is an uncertain guide, does some other, more functional approach to interpreting the Constitution exist?

One suggestion is to emphasize the importance of democratic "process." As John Hart Ely, dean of the Stanford Law School forcefully advocates, this approach would direct the courts to make a distinction between "process" (the rules of the game, so to speak) and "substance" (the results of the game). Laws dealing with process include those affecting voting rights or participation in society; the Supreme Court correctly prohibited segregation, for example, because it imposed on blacks the continuing stigma of slavery. Judges, however, would not have the power to review the substantive decisions of elected officials, such as the distribution of welfare benefits.

Basically, such an approach makes courts the guardians of democracy, but a focus on process affords little help when judges decide between difficult and competing values. Judicial formulation of a democratic vision, for example, requires substantive decision-making. The dignities of human liberty enshrined in the Bill of Rights are not merely a means to an end, even so noble an end as democratic governance. For example, we cherish freedom of speech not only because it is necessary for meaningful elections, but also for its own sake.

The truth is that no litmus test exists by which judges can confidently and consistently measure the constitutionality of their decisions. Notwithstanding the clear need for judicial restraint, judges do not constitute what Prof. Raoul Berger, a retired Harvard Law School fellow, has termed an "imperial judiciary." I would argue that the judicial process itself limits the reach of a jurist's arm.

First, judges do not and cannot deliberately contravene specific constitutional rules or clear indications of original intent. No one would seriously argue or expect, for instance, that the Supreme Court could or would twist the Presidential minimum-age provision into a call for "sufficient maturity," so as to forbid the seating of a 36-year-old.

I doubt, in any event, that Federal judges would ever hear such a question. The Constitution limits our power to traditional "cases" and "controversies" capable of judicial resolution. In cases like the hypothetical one regarding the Presidential age, the High Court employs doctrines of standing (proving injury) and "political question" to keep citizens from suing merely out of a desire to have the government run a certain way.

Moreover, the issues properly before a judge are not presented on a tabula rasa. Even the vaguest constitutional provisions have received the judicial gloss of prior decisions. Precedent alone, of course, should not preserve clearly erroneous decisions; the abhorrent "separate but equal" doctrine survived for more than 50 years before the Warren Court struck it down in 1954.

The conventions of our judicial system also limit a jurist's ability to impose his or her own will. One important restraint, often overlooked, is the tradition that appellate judges issue written opinions. That is, we must support our decisions with reasons instead of whims and indicate how our constitutional rulings relate to the document. A written statement is open to the dissent of colleagues, possible review by a higher court and the judgment, sometimes scathing, of legal scholars.

In addition, the facts of a given case play a pivotal role. Facts delineate the reach of a legal decision and remind us of the "cases and controversies" requirement. Our respect for such ground rules reassures the public that, even in the most controversial case, the outcome is not just a political ruling.

Judges are also mindful that the ultimate justification for their power is public acceptance—acceptance not of every decision, but of the role they play. Without popular support, the power of judicial review would have been eviscerated by political forces long ago.

Lacking the power of the purse or the sword, the courts must rely on the elected branches to enforce their decisions. The school desegregation cases would have been a dead letter unless President Eisenhower had been willing to order out the National Guard—in support of a decision authored by a Chief Justice, Earl Warren, whose appointment the President had called "the biggest damned-fool mistake I ever made."

Instead of achieving the purple of philosopher-kings, an unprincipled judiciary would risk becoming modern King Canutes, with the cold tide of political reality and popular opprobrium lapping at their robes.

My revered predecessor on the Court of Appeals, Judge Learned Hand, remarked in a lecture at Harvard in the late 1950's that he would not want to be ruled by "a bevy of Platonic Guardians." The Constitution balances the danger of judicial abuse against the threat of a temporary majority trampling individual rights. The current debate is a continuation of an age-old, and perhaps endless, struggle to reach a balance between our commitments to democracy and to the rule of law.

Although my office forces me to take a very direct part in the ongoing dialogue, all Americans have a stake in what my judicial colleagues and I say about the Constitution. At bottom, the debate is the consequence of our experiment, now two centuries old, in giving our fundamental ideals written expression in a Constitution. And that is cause for celebration.

Judicial Decision Making

☐   The preceding selections should dissuade students from accepting the commonly held assumption that judicial decision making is quasi-scientific, based upon legal principles and precedent, with the judges set apart from the political process. The interpretation of law, whether constitutional or statutory, involves a large amount of discretion. The majority of the Court can always read its opinion into law if it so chooses.

Justice William J. Brennan, Jr., a current member of the Supreme Court, discusses below the general role of the Court and the procedures it follows in decision making.

59
William J. Brennan, Jr.

HOW THE SUPREME COURT
ARRIVES AT DECISIONS

Throughout its history the Supreme Court has been called upon to face many of the dominant social, political, economic and even philosophical issues that confront the nation. But Solicitor General Cox only recently reminded us that this does not mean that the Court is charged with making social, political, economic or philosophical decisions.

Quite the contrary, the Court is not a council of Platonic guardians for deciding our most difficult and emotional questions according to the Justices' own notions of what is just or wise or politic. To the extent that this is a government function at all, it is the function of the people's elected representatives.

The Justices are charged with deciding according to law. Because the

From *The New York Times*, October 12, 1963. Copyright © 1963 by The New York Times Company. Reprinted by permission.

issues arise in the framework of concrete litigation they must be decided on facts embalmed in a record made by some lower court or administrative agency. And while the Justices may and do consult history and the other disciplines as aids to constitutional decisions, the text of the Constitution and relevant precedents dealing with that text are their primary tools.

It is indeed true, as Judge Learned Hand once said, that the judge's authority

> depends upon the assumption that he speaks with the mouth of others: the momentum of his utterances must be greater than any which his personal reputation and character can command; if it is to do the work assigned to it—if it is to stand against the passionate resentments arising out of the interests he must frustrate—he must preserve his authority by cloaking himself in the majesty of an over-shadowing past, but he must discover some composition with the dominant trends of his times.

ANSWERS UNCLEAR

However, we must keep in mind that, while the words of the Constitution are binding, their application to specific problems is not often easy. The Founding Fathers knew better than to pin down their descendants too closely.

Enduring principles rather than petty details were what they sought.

Thus the Constitution does not take the form of a litany of specifics. There are, therefore, very few cases where the constitutional answers are clear, all one way or all the other, and this is also true of the current cases raising conflicts between the individual and governmental power—an area increasingly requiring the Court's attention.

Ultimately, of course, the Court must resolve the conflicts of competing interests in these cases, but all Americans should keep in mind how intense and troubling these conflicts can be.

Where one man claims a right to speak and the other man claims the right to be protected from abusive or dangerously provocative remarks the conflict is inescapable.

Where the police have ample external evidence of a man's guilt, but to be sure of their case put into evidence a confession obtained through coercion, the conflict arises between his right to a fair prosecution and society's right to protection against his depravity.

Where the orthodox Jew wishes to open his shop and do business on the day which non-Jews have chosen, and the Legislature has sanctioned, as a day of rest, the Court cannot escape a difficult problem of reconciling opposed interests.

Finally, the claims of the Negro citizen, to borrow Solicitor General

Cox's words, present a "conflict between the ideal of liberty and equality expressed in the Declaration of Independence, on the one hand, and, on the other hand, a way of life rooted in the customs of many of our people."

SOCIETY IS DISTURBED

If all segments of our society can be made to appreciate that there are such conflicts, and that cases which involve constitutional rights often require difficult choices, if this alone is accomplished, we will have immeasurably enriched our common understanding of the meaning and significance of our freedoms. And we will have a better appreciation of the Court's function and its difficulties.

How conflicts such as these ought to be resolved constantly troubles our whole society. There should be no surprise, then, that how properly to resolve them often produces sharp division within the Court itself. When problems are so fundamental, the claims of the competing interests are often nicely balanced, and close divisions are almost inevitable.

Supreme Court cases are usually one of three kinds: the "original" action brought directly in the Court by one state against another state or states, or between a state or states and the federal government. Only a handful of such cases arise each year, but they are an important handful.

A recent example was the contest between Arizona and California over the waters of the lower basin of the Colorado River. Another was the contest between the federal government and the newest state of Hawaii over the ownership of lands in Hawaii.

The second kind of case seeks review of the decisions of a federal Court of Appeals—there are eleven such courts—or of a decision of a federal District Court—there is a federal District Court in each of the fifty states.

The third kind of case comes from a state court—the Court may review a state court judgment by the highest court of any of the fifty states, if the judgment rests on the decision of a federal question.

When I came to the Court seven years ago the aggregate of the cases in the three classes was 1,600. In the term just completed there were 2,800, an increase of 75 percent in seven years. Obviously, the volume will have doubled before I complete ten years of service.

How is it possible to manage such a huge volume of cases? The answer is that we have the authority to screen them and select for argument and decision only those which, in our judgment, guided by pertinent criteria, raise the most important and far-reaching questions. By that device we select annually around 6 percent—between 150 and 170 cases—for decision.

PETITION AND RESPONSE

That screening process works like this: when nine Justices sit, it takes five to decide a case on the merits. But it takes only the votes of four of the nine to put a case on the argument calendar for argument and decision. Those four votes are hard to come by—only an exceptional case raising a significant federal question commands them.

Each application for review is usually in the form of a short petition, attached to which are any opinions of the lower courts in the case. The adversary may file a response—also, in practice usually short. Both the petition and response identify the federal questions allegedly involved, argue their substantiality, and whether they were properly raised in the lower courts.

Each Justice receives copies of the petition and response and such parts of the record as the parties may submit. Each Justice then, without any consultation at this stage with the others, reaches his own tentative conclusion whether the application should be granted or denied.

The first consultation about the case comes at the Court conference at which the case is listed on the agenda for discussion. We sit in conference almost every Friday during the term. Conferences begin at ten in the morning and often continue until six, except for a half-hour recess for lunch.

Only the Justices are present. There are no law clerks, no stenographers, no secretaries, no pages—just the nine of us. The junior Justice acts as guardian of the door, receiving and delivering any messages that come in or go from the conference.

ORDER OF SEATING

The conference room is a beautifully oak-paneled chamber with one side lined with books from floor to ceiling. Over the mantel of the exquisite marble fireplace at one end hangs the only adornment in the chamber—a portrait of Chief Justice John Marshall. In the middle of the room stands a rectangular table, not too large but large enough for the nine of us comfortably to gather around it.

The Chief Justice sits at the south end and Mr. Justice Black, the senior Associate Justice, at the north end. Along the side to the left of the Chief Justice sit Justices Stewart, Goldberg, White, and Harlan. On the right side sit Justice Clark, myself and Justice Douglas in that order.

We are summoned to conference by a buzzer which rings in our several chambers five minutes before the hour. Upon entering the conference room each of us shakes hands with his colleagues. The handshake tradition originated when Chief Justice Fuller presided many decades ago. It is a symbol that harmony of aims if not of views is the Court's guiding principle.

Each of us has his copy of the agenda of the day's cases before him. The agenda lists the cases applying for review. Each of us before coming to the conference has noted on his copy his tentative view whether or not review should be granted in each case.

The Chief Justice begins the discussion of each case. He then yields to the senior Associate Justice and discussion proceeds down the line in order of seniority until each Justice has spoken.

Voting goes the other way. The junior Justice votes first and voting then proceeds up the line to the Chief Justice, who votes last.

Each of us has a docket containing a sheet for each case with appropriate places for recording the votes. When any case receives four votes for review, that case is transferred to the oral argument list. Applications in which none of us sees merits may be passed over without discussion.

Now how do we process the decisions we agree to review?

There are rare occasions when the question is so clearly controlled by an earlier decision of the Court that a reversal of the lower court judgment is inevitable. In these rare instances we may summarily reverse without oral argument.

EACH SIDE GETS HOUR

The case must very clearly justify summary disposition, however, because our ordinary practice is not to reverse a decision without oral argument. Indeed, oral argument of cases taken for review, whether from the state or federal courts, is the usual practice. We rarely accept submissions of cases on briefs.

Oral argument ordinarily occurs about four months after the application for review is granted. Each party is usually allowed one hour, but in recent years we have limited oral argument to a half-hour in cases thought to involve issues not requiring longer arguments.

Counsel submit their briefs and record in sufficient time for the distribution of one set to each Justice two or three weeks before the oral argument. Most of the members of the present Court follow the practice of reading the briefs before the argument. Some of us often have a bench memorandum prepared before the argument. This memorandum digests the facts and the arguments of both sides, highlighting the matters about which we may want to question counsel at the argument.

Often I have independent research done in advance of argument and incorporate the results in the bench memorandum.

We follow a schedule of two weeks of argument from Monday through Thursday, followed by two weeks of recess for opinion writing and the study of petitions for review. The argued cases are listed on the conference agenda on the Friday following argument. Conference discussion follows the same procedure I have described for the discussions of certiorari petitions.

OPINION ASSIGNED

Of course, it is much more extended. Not infrequently discussion of particular cases may be spread over two or more conferences.

Not until the discussion is completed and a vote taken is the opinion assigned. The assignment is not made at the conference but formally in writing some few days after the conference.

The Chief Justice assigns the opinions in those cases in which he has voted with the majority. The senior Associate Justice voting with the majority assigns the opinions in the other cases. The dissenters agree among themselves who shall write the dissenting opinion. Of course, each Justice is free to write his own opinion, concurring or dissenting.

The writing of an opinion always takes weeks and sometimes months. The most painstaking research and care are involved.

Research, of course, concentrates on relevant legal materials—precedents particularly. But Supreme Court cases often require some familiarity with history, economics, the social and other sciences, and authorities in these areas, too, are consulted when necessary.

When the author of an opinion feels he has an unanswerable document he sends it to a print shop, which we maintain in our building. The printed draft may be revised several times before his proposed opinion is circulated among the other Justices. Copies are sent to each member of the Court, those in the dissent as well as those in the majority.

SOME CHANGE MINDS

Now the author often discovers that his work has only begun. He receives a return, ordinarily in writing, from each Justice who voted with him and sometimes also from the Justices who voted the other way. He learns who will write the dissent if one is to be written. But his particular concern is whether those who voted with him are still of his view and what they have to say about his proposed opinion.

Often some who voted with him at conference will advise that they reserve final judgment pending the circulation of the dissent. It is a common experience that dissents change votes, even enough votes to become the majority.

I have had to convert more than one of my proposed majority opinions into a dissent before the final decision was announced. I have also, however, had the more satisfying experience of rewriting a dissent as a majority opinion for the Court.

Before everyone has finally made up his mind a constant interchange by memoranda, by telephone, at the lunch table continues while we hammer out the final form of the opinion. I had one case during the past term in which I circulated ten printed drafts before one was approved as the Court opinion.

UNIFORM RULE

The point of this procedure is that each Justice, unless he disqualifies himself in a particular case, passes on every piece of business coming to the Court. The Court does not function by means of committees or panels. Each Justice passes on each petition, each time, no matter how drawn, in long hand, by typewriter, or on a press. Our Constitution vests the judicial power in only one Supreme Court. This does not permit Supreme Court action by committees, panels, or sections.

The method that the Justices use in meeting an enormous caseload varies. There is one uniform rule: Judging is not delegated. Each Justice studies each case in sufficient detail to resolve the question for himself. In a very real sense, each decision is an individual decision of every Justice.

The process can be a lonely, troubling experience for fallible human beings conscious that their best may not be adequate to the challenge.

"We are not unaware," the late Justice Jackson said, "that we are not final because we are infallible; we know that we are infallible only because we are final."

One does not forget how much may depend on his decision. He knows that usually more than the litigants may be affected, that the course of vital social, economic and political currents may be directed.

This then is the decisional process in the Supreme Court. It is not without its tensions, of course—indeed, quite agonizing tensions at times.

I would particularly emphasize that, unlike the case of a Congressional or White House decision, Americans demand of their Supreme Court judges that they produce a written opinion, the collective expression of the judges subscribing to it, setting forth the reason which led them to the decision.

These opinions are the exposition, not just to lawyers, legal scholars and other judges, but to our whole society, of the bases upon which a particular result rests—why a problem, looked at as disinterestedly and dispassionately as nine human beings trained in a tradition of the disinterested and dispassionate approach can look at it, is answered as it is.

It is inevitable, however, that Supreme Court decisions—and the Justices themselves—should be caught up in public debate and be the subjects of bitter controversy.

An editorial in *The Washington Post* did not miss the mark by much in saying that this was so because

> one of the primary functions of the Supreme Court is to keep the people of the country from doing what they would like to do—at times

when what they would like to do runs counter to the Constitution. ... The function of the Supreme Court is not to count constituents; it is to interpret a fundamental charter which imposes restraints on constituents. Independence and integrity, not popularity, must be its standards.

FREUND'S VIEW

Certainly controversy over its work has attended the Court throughout its history. As Professor Paul A. Freund of Harvard remarked, this has been true almost since the Court's first decision:

> When the Court held, in 1793, that the state of Georgia could be sued on a contract in the federal courts, the outraged Assembly of that state passed a bill declaring that any federal marshal who should try to collect the judgment would be guilty of a felony and would suffer death, without benefit of clergy, by being hanged. When the Court decided that state criminal convictions could be reviewed in the Supreme Court, Chief Justice Roane of Virginia exploded, calling it a "most monstrous and unexampled decision. It can only be accounted for by that love of power which history informs us infects and corrupts all who possess it, and from which even the eminent and upright judges are not exempt."

But public understanding has not always been lacking in the past. Perhaps it exists today. But surely a more informed knowledge of the decisional process should aid a better understanding.

It is not agreement with the Court's decisions that I urge. Our law is the richer and the wiser because academic and informed lay criticism is part of the stream of development.

CONSENSUS NEEDED

It is only a greater awareness of the nature and limits of the Supreme Court's function that I seek.

The ultimate resolution of questions fundamental to the whole community must be based on a common consensus of understanding of the unique responsibility assigned to the Supreme Court in our society.

The lack of that understanding led Mr. Justice Holmes to say fifty years ago:

> We are very quiet there, but it is the quiet of a storm center, as we all know. Science has taught the world skepticism and has made it legitimate to put everything to the test of proof. Many beautiful and noble reverences are impaired, but in these days no one can complain if any institution, system, or belief is called on to justify its continuance in life. Of course we are not excepted and have not escaped.

PAINFUL ACCUSATION

Doubts are expressed that go to our very being. Not only are we told that when Marshall pronounced an Act of Congress unconstitutional he usurped a power that the Constitution did not give, but we are told that we are the representatives of a class—a tool of the money power.

I get letters, not always anonymous, intimating that we are corrupt. Well, gentlemen, I admit that it makes my heart ache. It is very painful, when one spends all the energies of one's soul in trying to do good work, with no thought but that of solving a problem according to the rules by which one is bound, to know that many see sinister motives and would be glad of evidence that one was consciously bad.

But we must take such things philosophically and try to see what we can learn from hatred and distrust and whether behind them there may not be a germ of inarticulate truth.

The attacks upon the Court are merely an expression of the unrest that seems to wonder vaguely whether law and order pay. When the ignorant are taught to doubt they do not know what they safely may believe. And it seems to me that at this time we need education in the obvious more than investigation of the obscure.

☐   Justice William J. Brennan, Jr., in his discussion of how the Supreme Court arrives at decisions in the preceding selection, points out that inevitably Supreme Court decisions and the justices are the subjects of public debate and often bitter controversy. It is not surprising that when Supreme Court Justices and lower court judges as well follow the early dictum of Chief Justice John Marshall, which he stated in *Marbury* v. *Madison* in 1803, that "It is emphatically the province and duty of the judicial department to say what the law is," they will become the center of political storms stirred up by those who feel the Court has overstepped its bounds.

The Supreme Court under Chief Justice Earl Warren was one of the most controversial in our history precisely because it, like the early Supreme Court under Chief Justice John Marshall, did not hesitate to say what the law is even in the face of stiff political opposition. The stage was set for heavy drama when Earl Warren was appointed Chief Justice by President Eisenhower in 1953. The school desegregation cases were already pending before the Court. The Vinson Court had noted probable jurisdiction of these cases in 1952, and in June of 1953 the cases were redocketed and scheduled for argument in the fall 1953 session of the Court. This meant that Chief Justice Warren, who was seated on October 4, 1953, was almost immediately confronted with one of the most momentous series of cases ever to confront the Supreme Court.

Although the final decision of the Supreme Court in the *Brown* case as well as in the District of Columbia school desegregation case (*Bolling v. Sharpe,* 347 U.S. 497 [1954], was unanimous in 1954, when the cases were initially brought up in 1952 the Court was far from a consensus to overrule the separate but equal doctrine of *Plessy* v. *Ferguson* (1896). From diaries kept by Associate Justice Harold Burton, who served on the Court from 1945 until 1958, it appears that in 1952 Justices Black, Douglas, Burton, and Minton were leaning toward reversal of the *Plessy* decision, while Chief Justice Vinson, and Justices Reed, Frankfurter, Jackson, and Clark were leaning toward affirmance or at least were doubtful as to the propriety of overruling *Plessy.*[1]

After Warren replaced Vinson as Chief Justice, skepticism still remained in the minds of many Justices about what course of action should be taken in the school desegregation cases. The first Supreme Court conference on the matter was held on December 12, 1953, after the first desegregation case was argued on December 7. At that conference Warren unequivocally stated that the Court should overrule de jure segregation in public schools, although he was careful to note that the problem was far from simple, and that the issue should be handled with as much delicacy as possible. At that conference only Justices Douglas and Minton fully agreed with the Chief Justice, although the tenor of the remarks of the other Justices suggested the possibility that they might be willing to go along with Warren. The final unanimity of the Court on the school desegregation cases was a credit to Warren's leadership skills as Chief Justice.

The following selection illustrates both the internal and the external politics of Supreme Court decision making. Dramatic oral argument took place before the Court. Just as the unanimity of the Court in the first *Brown* decision in 1954 was far from assured when the cases were first argued, the nature of the implementing decision in *Brown* II in 1955 was strongly debated before agreement was reached. External politics came into play not only in the acute awareness the Court had of southern resistance to an overturning of the *Plessy* decision, an awareness that apparently misgauged the extent of feelings in the South, but also in the attempt of President Eisenhower to influence Chief Justice Warren by making an ex parte representation to the Chief Justice after a White House dinner party where Warren was seated opposite the lawyer for the segregation states. President Eisenhower, who felt his appointment of Warren would bring a moderating influence to the Court, was apparently very disappointed with the *Brown* decision, and maintained

[1]For a discussion of the background of the *Brown* decision, and the views of the justices as they were revealed in Burton's diaries, see S. Sidney Ulmer, "Earl Warren and the *Brown* Decision," *Journal of Politics,* vol. 33 (1971): 689–702.

coolly distant relations with the Chief Justice after the decision was announced.

60
Earl Warren

INSIDE THE SUPREME COURT

In a matter of hours after first coming to the Supreme Court, I learned more about the important cases that were lumped as the school desegregation cases.

There were five of them, from Kansas, Virginia, South Carolina, Delaware, and the District of Columbia. While the latter was in a somewhat different setting because it did not involve a state law, they all involved the "separate but equal" doctrine as established by the Supreme Court in the case of *Plessy* v. *Ferguson* (1896). That decision declined to prohibit separate railroad accommodations for blacks and whites. It sought to justify racial segregation for almost every movement or gathering so long as "separate but equal" facilities were provided, and it became known as the "Jim Crow" doctrine. The central issue in each of these school cases was,

> Does segregation of children in public schools solely on the basis of race, even though the physical facilities and other "tangible" factors may be equal, deprive the children of the minority group of equal educational opportunities?

The five cases had been argued during the 1952 term before I came to the Court but had not been decided and had been put over for reargument, with a set of specific questions for discussion.

The United States government, through Assistant Attorney General J. Lee Rankin, supported by a brief signed also by Attorney General Herbert Brownell and other Justice Department attorneys, argued as a friend of the Court in favor of the positions maintained by the black students' lawyers. The first case was argued December 7, 1953, and it was easy to understand why the Court felt it necessary to have a full complement of Justices. Resubmission of the case for argument would normally indicate a difference of opinion within the Court. In these circumstances, particularly if any Justice is absent or disqualifies himself, the danger exists of an evenly

---

"Inside the Supreme Court" from *The Memoirs of Earl Warren* by Earl Warren. Copyright © 1977 by Nina E. Warren as Executrix of the Estate of Earl Warren. Reprinted by permission of Doubleday & Company, Inc.

divided, four-to-four Court, which means that the decision of the lower court is affirmed without opinion from the Supreme Court and without any precedential value.

Some of the cases under review had been decided against the black petitioners in the lower courts on the authority of the much eroded "separate but equal" doctrine of *Plessy* v. *Ferguson.*

To have affirmed these cases without decision and with the mere statement that it was being done by an equally divided Court, if such had been the case, would have aborted the judicial process and resulted in public frustration and disrespect for the Court. The Court was thoroughly conscious of the importance of the decision to be arrived at and of the impact it would have on the nation. With this went realization of the necessity for secrecy in our deliberations and for achieving unity, if possible.

We realized that once a person announces he has reached a conclusion, it is more difficult for him to change his thinking, so we decided that we would dispense with our usual custom of formally expressing our individual views at the first conference and would confine ourselves for a time to informal discussion of the briefs, the arguments made at the hearing, and our own independent research on each conference day, reserving our final opinions until the discussions were concluded.

We followed this plan until February, when we felt that we were ready to vote. On the first vote, we unanimously agreed that the "separate but equal" doctrine had no place in public education. The question then arose as to how this view should be written—as a *per curiam* (by the Court), or as a signed, individualized opinion. We decided that it would carry more force if done through a signed opinion, and some Justices thought it should bear the signature of the Chief Justice. I consented to this, and we discussed the importance of secrecy. We agreed that only my law clerks should be involved, and that any writing between my office and those of the other Justices would be delivered to the Justices personally. This practice was followed throughout and it was the only time it was required in my years on the Court. It was not done because of suspicion of anyone, but because of the sensitiveness of the school segregation matter and the prying for inside information that surrounded the cases. We thought we should confine our communications to the fewest possible people as a matter of security. Progress made in conference was discussed informally from time to time, and on occasion I would so inform Mr. Justice Jackson, who was confined to the hospital, recuperating from a heart attack which had incapacitated him for some time. Finally, at our conference on May 15, we agreed to announce our opinion the following Monday, subject to the approval of Mr. Justice Jackson. I went to the hospital early Monday morning, May 17, and showed the Justice a copy of the proposed opinion as it was to be released. He agreed to it, and to my alarm insisted on attending the Court that day in order to demonstrate our solidarity. I said that was unnecessary, but he insisted, and was there at the appointed time.

It was a momentous courtroom event and, unlike many other such events, it has not lost that character to this day.[1]

These five segregation cases all raised the same central issue and four of them are compendiously referred to as *Brown* v. *Board of Education of Topeka* (1954).

In the *Brown* decision, we decided only that the practice of segregating children in public schools solely because of their race was unconstitutional. This left other questions to be answered. For instance, could plaintiffs bring court actions as *class* actions for all who were similarly situated, or should persons actually joining in the action be entitled to relief only for themselves? What court should determine the decree in each case? For what reason could there or could there not be any delay in obeying the Court's mandate, and to what extent? All such questions we continued until the next term, inviting the United States and all states affected by our decision to file briefs and argue if they desired to do so.

These cases, postponed because of the death of Mr. Justice Jackson, which left an eight-man Court, came on for argument from April 11 to 14, 1955, with the newly appointed Mr. Justice Harlan in attendance. At the time of Mr. Justice Jackson's death in October 1954, John Harlan was a recent appointee to the Court of Appeals of the Second Federal Judicial Circuit. President Eisenhower nominated him to the Supreme Court on January 10, 1955, but those were the investigative days of Joe McCarthy, and Harlan was not approved by the Senate until March 17 because of the silly bulldozing he was given as a result of having been a Rhodes scholar, which some right-wingers vaguely associated with Redtinged "internationalism."

Solicitor General Simon Sobeloff, in response to the Court's invitation,

---

[1]When Earl Warren took over as Chief Justice, the Court was quite divided. Justices Black and Douglas usually took a strongly liberal view in their opinions; Justices Jackson and Frankfurter were more conservative; the other Justices fluctuated in between. In addition, there were personality conflicts which provided a certain amount of bristling discord and admittedly had been beyond Chief Justice Vinson's powers to settle.

Some historians have given Warren credit for bringing greater amity and unity to the Court, at least for all-important racial decisions. Other observers, including the Chief Justice himself, have been more modest in their estimate of his harmonizing influence, holding that nothing could unify such differing spirits unless they individually *wanted* to be unified for a particular purpose. Memoranda in the Warren files for his Court years indicate that the Justices themselves gave Warren much credit for his leadership. A note to Warren from Mr. Justice Frankfurter on the day of the *Brown* decision says:

"Dear Chief: This is a day that will live in glory. It's also a great day in the history of the court, and not in the least for the course of deliberation which brought about the result. I congratulate you."

And from Mr. Justice Burton: "To you goes the credit for the character of the opinions which produced the all-important unanimity. Congratulations."

argued for the United States on behalf of the petitioners as a friend of the Court. The attorneys general or their assistants of the states involved in the litigation argued for their states, which included Arkansas, Florida, Maryland, North Carolina, Oklahoma, and Texas. All opposed school desegregation.

The principal arguments on this phase of the case, as well as in the original proceeding, were made by John W. Davis for the states and Thurgood Marshall, now an Associate Justice of the Supreme Court, for the plaintiffs' side. The arguments, for me at least, took a strange course. One might expect, as I did, that the lawyers representing black schoolchildren would appeal to the emotions of the Court based upon their many years of oppression, and that the states would hold to strictly legal matters. More nearly the opposite developed. Thurgood Marshall made no emotional appeal, and argued the legal issues in a rational manner as cold as steel. On the other hand, states' attorney Davis, a great advocate and orator, former Democratic candidate for the presidency of the United States, displayed a great deal of emotion, and on more than one occasion broke down and took a few moments to compose himself.

Again the Court was unanimous in its decision of May 31, 1955, reaffirming its opinion of May 17, 1954, by asserting the fundamental principle that any kind of racial discrimination in public education is unconstitutional, and that all provisions of federal, state, or local law requiring or permitting such discrimination must yield to this principle. Recognizing that because full application of these constitutional principles might require solution of a wide variety of local school desegregation problems, school authorities were given the primary responsibility for elucidating, assessing, and solving such problems. However, we stipulated that courts would ultimately have to consider whether the action of school authorities constituted implementation in good faith of the governing constitutional principles.

We discussed at great length in conference whether the Supreme Court should make the factual determinations in such cases or whether they should be left to the courts below. We decided finally to leave them to the latter, subject, of course, to our review, because they were getting closer to the problems involved, and were in a better position to engage in the fact-finding process. As guidelines for them, we directed that neither local law nor custom should be permitted to interfere with the establishment of an integrated school system, and that the process of achieving it should be carried out "with all deliberate speed"—a phrase which has been much discussed by those who are of the opinion that desegregation has not proceeded with as much celerity as might have been expected.

These people argued that the Supreme Court should merely have directed the school districts to admit Brown and the other plaintiffs to the schools to which they sought admission, in the belief that this would have quickly ended the litigation. This theory, however, overlooks the complexity of our federal system; the time it takes controversial litigation to proceed through the hierarchy of courts to the Supreme Court; the fact that the administration of the public school system is a state and local function so long as it does not contravene constitutional principles; that each state has its own system with different relationships between state and local government; and that the relationship can be changed at will by the state government if there should be a determination to bypass or defeat the decision of the Supreme Court. Evidence that such evasion would occur came immediately in some of the resolutions and laws initiated by certain states. In this, they were encouraged by the so-called Southern Manifesto, signed by over a hundred southern representatives and senators in the Congress of the United States. It urged all such states to defy the Supreme Court decision as being against their way of life and their "good" race relations, and to use "all lawful means" to make the decision ineffective. So reinforcing to southern defiance was this manifesto that the doctrine of "nullification"—first advanced by John C. Calhoun of South Carolina, discredited more than a century before and made forever inapplicable by the Civil War Amendments—was revived by southern governors, legislators, and candidates for public office. The doctrine, in simple terms, argued that states have the right to declare null and void and to set aside in practice any law of the federal government which violates their voluntary compact embodied in the United States Constitution. The doctrine, of course, did not prevail, but the delay and bitterness occasioned by it caused inestimable damage to the extension of equal rights to citizens of every race, color, or creed as mandated by the Fourteenth Amendment.

With courage drawn from this profession of faith in white supremacy by practically every southern member of Congress, together with oft-repeated congressional speeches and statements to the effect that no nine honest men could possibly have come to the conclusion reached by the Court in *Brown* v. *Board of Education,* excited and racist-minded public officials and candidates for office proposed and enacted every obstacle they could devise to thwart the Court's decision. This was aggravated by the fact that no word of support for the decision emanated from the White House. The most that came from high officials in the Administration was to the effect that they could not be blamed for anything done to enforce desegregation in education because it was the Supreme Court, not the Administration, that determined desegregation to be the law, and the executive branch of the government is required to enforce the law as interpreted by the Supreme Court. Bernard Shanley, the personal counsel of the President, in an effort to allay southern animosity against the Administration, was reported in the press to have said in a speech that the *Brown* case had set race relations in the South back by a quarter of a century. The aphorism (dear to the hearts of those who are insensitive to the rights of minority groups) that discrimination cannot be eliminated by laws, but only by the hearts of people, also emanated from the White House.

A few years later, Governor George Wallace was emboldened to stand at the entrance to the University of Alabama and, in the face of the deputy attorney general of the United States, who had read to him the order of a United States district judge directing the university to admit Vivian Malone and James Hood, two black students, shout in defiance, "Segregation in the past, segregation today, segregation forever."

The Court expected some resistance from the South. But I doubt if any of us expected as much as we got. Nor did I believe that the Republican party, which freed the slaves through the Civil War and the Thirteenth Amendment and granted them all the attributes of citizenship through the Fourteenth and Fifteenth Amendments, would develop a southern strategy intended to restrict such rights in order to capture the electors of those states and achieve the presidency. I, for one, thought it would be wonderful if, by the time of the centennial of the Fourteenth Amendment (1968), the principle of desegregation in *Brown* v. *Board of Education* could be a reality throughout the land. And I still believe that much of our racial strife could have been avoided if President Eisenhower had at least observed that our country is dedicated to the principle that "We hold these Truths to be self-evident, that all Men are created equal, that they are endowed by their Creator with certain unalienable Rights, that among these are Life, Liberty and the Pursuit of Happiness . . . "

With his popularity, if Eisenhower had said that black children were still being discriminated against long after the adoption of the Thirteenth, Fourteenth, and Fifteenth Amendments, that the Supreme Court of the land had now declared it unconstitutional to continue such cruel practices, and that it should be the duty of every good citizen to help rectify more than eighty years of wrongdoing by honoring that decision—if he had said something to this effect, I think we would have been relieved of many of the racial problems which have continued to plague us. But he never stated that he thought the decision was right until after he had left the White House.

I have always believed that President Eisenhower resented our decision in *Brown* v. *Board of Education* and its progeny. Influencing this belief, among other things, is an incident that occurred shortly before the opinion was announced. The President had a program for discussing problems with groups of people at occasional White House dinners. When the *Brown* case was under submission, he invited me to one of them. I wondered why I should be invited, because the dinners were political in nature, and I could not participate in such discussions. But one does not often decline an invitation from the President to the White House, and I accepted. I was the ranking guest, and as such sat at the right of the President and within speaking distance of John W. Davis, the counsel for the segregation states.

During the dinner, the President went to considerable lengths to tell me what a great man Mr. Davis was. At the conclusion of the meal, in accordance with custom, we filed out of the dining room to another room where coffee and an after-dinner drink were served. The President, of course, precedes, and on this occasion he took me by the arm, and, as we walked along, speaking of the southern states in the segregation cases, he said, "These are not bad people. All they are concerned about is to see that their sweet little girls are not required to sit alongside some big overgrown Negroes."

Fortunately, by that time, others had filed into the room, so I was not obliged to reply. Shortly thereafter, the *Brown* case was decided, and with it went our cordial relations. While Nina and I were occasionally invited to the White House after the decision for protocol reasons, when some foreign dignitary was being entertained, or were invited to some foreign embassy for a reciprocal honoring of the President, I can recall few conversations that went beyond a polite, "Good evening, Mr. President" and "Good evening, Mr. Chief Justice."

Some southern states, and northern areas as well, have used every conceivable device to thwart the principle of the *Brown* case, and they have been successful in preventing full compliance or even that degree of compliance sufficient to create good will between the races. Because of these drawbacks, some people are of the belief that the Court's decree was a failure, but the fact is that real progress has been made. However, the tragedy of the situation is that because of die-hard segregationist resistance, advances have come about only after torrid litigation or after federal legislation which has emphasized the unfairness of the white supremacy theory to the point that deep bitterness against whites is felt by all minority groups—blacks, Chicanos, Puerto Ricans, Asians, and American Indians. That, too, can be remedied whenever we all realize the importance of the Thirteenth, Fourteenth, and Fifteenth Amendments to the Constitution in granting absolute equality of citizenship to "*Everyone* born or naturalized in the United States. . . ."

Some more recent cases decided by the Supreme Court emphasize that these patterns die very hard. Despite the Court's condemnation of the principle of racial segregation and outlawing of it in public schools in 1954, not until 1962 was the separation of blacks and whites in state courtrooms likewise outlawed. Not until 1964 was a black witness given the right to be examined by counsel in the same spirit of deference accorded to white witnesses. Not until 1968, over one hundred years after the passage of the civil rights statute on which the Court belatedly relied, were blacks determined to have the same rights as whites to live where they choose. Despite an old holding by the Court that systematic exclusion of Negroes from juries is unconstitutional, that problem still persists. And as late as 1969, after I had retired from the Court, Mr. Justice Black was moved to say in the case of *Alexander* v. *Holmes County Board of Education* that " . . . there are many places still in this country where the schools are either 'white' or 'Negro' and not just schools for all children as the Constitution requires." In Justice Black's view, there was "no reason why such a wholesale deprivation of constitutional rights should be tolerated another minute."

An extremely touchy matter that has arisen out of the need to integrate schools is that of busing. Governor George Wallace of Alabama injected it into a presidential campaign, and others from Berkeley to Boston have brought the "busing issue" before the American public. Opponents hold it to be an undesirable principle whereby the courts are determined to wrench children from their neighborhoods and put them on buses for hours every day all over America in order to bring about a proportionate balance of black and white children in the schools. They have even argued that this must be prevented by depriving the courts of their constitutional jurisdiction.

This, however, is a complete distortion of the situation.

The Supreme Court has never held that there must be exact racial balance in the schools or that long-distance busing is desirable. Until recently, it has not recognized busing as a principle, only as a tool for the courts to use where the authorities have been reluctant to carry out the desegregation called for by *Brown* v. *Board of Education.* That decision was aimed at affording all children an equal opportunity for a good education, nothing more.

I believe that most parents would prefer having their children attend a school within walking distance of their home. They recognize, however, that it often becomes necessary or at least desirable to have pupils transported to a more distant school in order to educate them better. Busing is only one means to accomplish proper results when others have failed or been denied. There is much merit in a suggestion of Notre Dame's Father Hesburgh to the effect that busing can properly be used to transport underprivileged children to better schools but not the opposite; he would leave poorer schools to the bulldozer.

Harmony in race relations is not simply or easily achieved. No matter how comprehensive and clear the law is on this subject, there will always be bigots to promote tensions and patterns of resistance. But the vast majority of people must realize by now that racial equality under law is basic to our institutions and that we will not and cannot have peace in our nation until the race issue is properly settled. We have, and should be aware, 34 million members of minority groups whose civil rights have not been but must be fully respected. That calls for a combination of effective law and good will. In the absence of both or either of these elements, we can only expect chaos. If there is one lesson to be learned from our tragic experience in the Civil War and its wake, it is that the question of racial discrimination is never settled until it is settled right.

The Declaration of Independence[1]

IN CONGRESS, JULY 4, 1776

**The unanimous Declaration of the
thirteen united States of America**

When in the Course of human events it becomes necessary for one people to dissolve the political bands which have connected them with another, and to assume among the Powers of the earth, the separate and equal station to which the Laws of Nature and of Nature's God entitle them, a decent respect to the opinions of mankind requires that they should declare the causes which impel them to the separation.

We hold these truths to be self-evident, that all men are created equal, that they are endowed by their Creator with certain unalienable Rights, that among these are Life, Liberty and the pursuit of Happiness. That to secure these rights, Governments are instituted among Men, deriving their just powers from the consent of the governed. That whenever any Form of Government becomes destructive of these ends, it is the Right of the People to alter or to abolish it, and to institute new Government, laying its foundation on such principles and organizing its powers in such form, as to them shall seem most likely to effect their Safety and Happiness. Prudence, indeed, will dictate that Governments long established should not be changed for light and transient causes; and accordingly all experience hath shown, that mankind are more disposed to suffer, while evils are sufferable, than to right themselves by abolishing the forms to which they are accustomed. But when a long train of abuses and usurpations, pursuing invariably the same Object evinces a design to reduce them under absolute Despotism, it is their right, it is their duty, to throw off such Government,

---

[1]This text retains the spelling, capitalization, and punctuation of the original.

and to provide new Guards for their future security.—Such has been the patient sufferance of these Colonies; and such is now the necessity which constrains them to alter their former Systems of Government. The history of the present King of Great Britain is a history of repeated injuries and usurpations, all having in direct object the establishment of an absolute Tyranny over these States. To prove this, let Facts be submitted to a candid world.

He has refused his Assent to Laws, the most wholesome and necessary for the public good.

He has forbidden his Governors to pass Laws of immediate and pressing importance, unless suspended in their operation till his Assent should be obtained; and when so suspended, he has utterly neglected to attend to them.

He has refused to pass other Laws for the accommodation of large districts of people, unless those people would relinquish the right of Representation in the Legislature, a right inestimable to them and formidable to tyrants only.

He has called together legislative bodies at places unusual, uncomfortable, and distant from the depository of their Public Records, for the sole purpose of fatiguing them into compliance with his measures.

He has dissolved Representative Houses repeatedly, for opposing with manly firmness his invasions on the rights of the people.

He has refused for a long time, after such dissolutions, to cause others to be elected; whereby the Legislative Powers, incapable of Annihilation, have returned to the People at large for their exercise; the State remaining in the mean time exposed to all the dangers of invasion from without, and convulsions within.

He has endeavored to prevent the population of these States; for that purpose obstructing the Laws for Naturalization of Foreigners; refusing to pass others to encourage their migration hither, and raising the conditions of new Appropriations of Lands.

He has obstructed the Administration of Justice, by refusing his Assent to Laws for establishing Judiciary Powers.

He has made Judges dependent on his Will alone, for the tenure of their offices, and the amount and payment of their salaries.

He has erected a multitude of New Offices, and sent hither swarms of Officers to harass our People, and eat out their substance.

He has kept among us, in times of peace, Standing Armies without the Consent of our Legislature.

He has affected to render the Military independent of and superior to the Civil Power.

He has combined with others to subject us to a jurisdiction foreign to our constitution, and unacknowledged by our laws; giving his Assent to their acts of pretended Legislation:

For quartering large bodies of armed troops among us:

For protecting them, by a mock Trial, from Punishment for any Murders which they should commit on the Inhabitants of these States:

For cutting off our Trade with all parts of the world:

For imposing taxes on us without our Consent:

For depriving us in many cases, of the benefits of Trial by Jury:

For transporting us beyond Seas to be tried for pretended offenses:

For abolishing the free System of English Laws in a neighboring Province, establishing therein an Arbitrary government, and enlarging its Boundaries so as to render it at once an example and fit instrument for introducing the same absolute rule into these Colonies:

For taking away our Charters, abolishing our most valuable Laws, and altering fundamentally the Forms of our Government:

For suspending our own Legislature, and declaring themselves invested with Power to legislate for us in all cases whatsoever.

He has abdicated Government here, by declaring us out of his Protection and waging War against us.

He has plundered our seas, ravaged our Coasts, burnt our towns, and destroyed the lives of our people.

He is at this time transporting large armies of foreign mercenaries to compleat the works of death, desolation and tyranny, already begun with circumstances of Cruelty & perfidy scarcely paralleled in the most barbarous ages, and totally unworthy the Head of a civilized nation.

He has constrained our fellow Citizens taken Captive on the high Seas to bear Arms against their Country, to become the executioners of their friends and Brethren, or to fall themselves by their Hands.

He has excited domestic insurrections amongst us, and has endeavored to bring on the inhabitants of our frontiers, the merciless Indian Savages, whose known rule of warfare, is an undistinguished destruction of all ages, sexes and conditions.

In every stage of these Oppressions We have Petitioned for Redress in the most humble terms: Our repeated Petitions have been answered only by repeated injury. A Prince, whose character is thus marked by every act which may define a Tyrant, is unfit to be the ruler of a free People.

Nor have We been wanting in attention to our British brethren. We have warned them from time to time of attempts by their legislature to extend an unwarrantable jurisdiction over us. We have reminded them of the circumstances of our emigration and settlement here. We have appealed to their native justice and magnanimity, and we have conjured them by the ties of our common kindred to disavow these usurpations, which, would inevitably interrupt our connections and correspondence. They too have been deaf to the voice of justice and consanguinity. We must, therefore, acquiesce in the necessity, which denounces our Separation, and hold them, as we hold the rest of mankind, Enemies in War, in Peace Friends.

We, therefore, the Representatives of the united States of America, in General Congress, Assembled, appealing to the Supreme Judge of the world for the rectitude of our intentions, do, in the Name, and by Authority of the good People of these Colonies, solemnly publish and declare, That these United Colonies are, and of Right ought to be Free and Independent States; that they are Absolved from all Allegiance to the British Crown, and that all political connection between them and the State of Great Britain, is and ought to be totally dissolved; and that as Free and Independent States, they have full Power to levy War, conclude Peace, contract Alliances, establish Commerce, and to do all other Acts and Things which Independent States may of right do. And for the support of this Declaration, with a firm reliance on the Protection of Divine Providence, we mutually pledge to each other our Lives, our Fortunes and our sacred Honor.

JOHN HANCOCK

New Hampshire

JOSIAH BARTLETT,   MATTHEW THORNTON.
WM. WHIPPLE,

Massachusetts Bay

SAML. ADAMS,   ROBT. TREAT PAINE,
JOHN ADAMS,   ELBRIDGE GERRY.

Rhode Island

STEP. HOPKINS,   WILLIAM ELLERY.

Connecticut

ROGER SHERMAN,   WM. WILLIAMS,
SAM'EL HUNTINGTON,   OLIVER WOLCOTT.

New York

WM. FLOYD,   FRANS. LEWIS,
PHIL. LIVINGSTON,   LEWIS MORRIS.

New Jersey

RICHD. STOCKTON,   JOHN HART,
JNO. WITHERSPOON,   ABRA. CLARK.
FRAS. HOPKINSON,

Pennsylvania

ROBT. MORRIS,   JAS. SMITH,
BENJAMIN RUSH,   GEO. TAYLOR,
BENJA. FRANKLIN,   JAMES WILSON,
JOHN MORTON,   GEO. ROSS.
GEO. CLYMER,

Delaware

CAESAR RODNEY,   THO. M'KEAN.
GEO. READ,

Maryland

SAMUEL CHASE,   THOS. STONE,
WM. PACA,   CHARLES CAROLL
                                    of Carrollton.

Virginia

GEORGE WYTHE,
RICHARD HENRY LEE,
TH. JEFFERSON,
BENJA. HARRISON,

THOS. NELSON, jr.,
FRANCIS LIGHTFOOT
LEE,
CARTER BRAXTON.

North Carolina

WM. HOOPER,
JOSEPH HEWES,

JOHN PENN.

South Carolina

EDWARD RUTLEDGE,
THOS. HEYWARD, Junr.,

THOMAS LYNCH, jnr.,
ARTHUR MIDDLETON.

Georgia

BUTTON GWINNETT,
LYMAN HALL,

GEO. WALTON.

The Constitution
of the United States

We the People of the United States, in Order to form a more perfect Union, establish Justice, insure domestic Tranquility, provide for the common defence, promote the general Welfare, and secure the Blessings of Liberty to ourselves and our Posterity do ordain and establish this CONSTITUTION for the United States of America.

ARTICLE I

Section 1. All legislative Powers herein granted shall be vested in a Congress of the United States, which shall consist of a Senate and House of Representatives.

Section 2. [1] The House of Representatives shall be composed of members chosen every second Year by the People of the several States, and the Electors in each State shall have the Qualifications requisite for Electors of the most numerous Branch of the State Legislature.

[2] No Person shall be a Representative who shall not have attained to the Age of twenty-five Years, and been seven Years a Citizen of the United States, and who shall not, when elected, be an Inhabitant of that State in which he shall be chosen.

[3] [Representatives and direct Taxes[1] shall be apportioned among the several States which may be included within this Union, according to their respective Numbers, which shall be determined by adding to the whole Number of free Persons, including those bound to Service for a Term of Years, and excluding Indians not taxed, three fifths of all other Persons.][2] The actual Enumeration shall be made within three Years after the first

---

[1]The Sixteenth Amendment replaced this with respect to income taxes.
[2]Repealed by the Fourteenth Amendment.

Meeting of the Congress of the United States, and within every subsequent Term of ten years, in such Manner as they shall by Law direct. The Number of Representatives shall not exceed one for every thirty Thousand, but each State shall have at Least one Representative; and until such enumeration shall be made, the State of New Hampshire shall be entitled to choose three, Massachusetts eight, Rhode-Island and Providence Plantations one, Connecticut five, New York six, New Jersey four, Pennsylvania eight, Delaware one, Maryland six, Virginia ten, North Carolina five, South Carolina five, and Georgia three.

[4] When vacancies happen in the Representation from any State, the Executive Authority thereof shall issue Writs of Election to fill such Vacancies.

[5] The House of Representatives shall choose their Speaker and other Officers; and shall have the sole Power of Impeachment.

Section 3. [1] The Senate of the United States shall be composed of two Senators from each State, [chosen by the Legislature][3] thereof, for six Years; and each Senator shall have one Vote.

[2] Immediately after they shall be assembled in Consequence of the first Election, they shall be divided as equally as may be into three Classes. The Seats of the Senators of the first Class shall be vacated at the Expiration of the second Year, of the second Class at the Expiration of the fourth Year, and of the third Class at the Expiration of the sixth Year, so that one-third may be chosen every second Year; [and if Vacancies happen by Resignation, or otherwise, during the Recess of the Legislature of any State, the Executive thereof may make temporary Appointments until the next Meeting of the Legislature, which shall then fill such Vacancies].[4]

[3] No person shall be a Senator who shall not have attained to the Age of thirty Years, and been nine Years a Citizen of the United States, and who shall not, when elected, be an Inhabitant of that State for which he shall be chosen.

[4] The Vice President of the United States shall be President of the Senate, but shall have no Vote, unless they be equally divided.

[5] The Senate shall choose their other Officers, and also a President pro tempore, in the absence of the Vice President, or when he shall exercise the Office of President of the United States.

[6] The Senate shall have the sole Power to try all Impeachments. When sitting for that Purpose, they shall be on Oath or Affirmation. When the President of the United States is tried, the Chief Justice shall preside: And no Person shall be convicted without the Concurrence of two thirds of the Members present.

[7] Judgment in Cases of Impeachment shall not extend further than to

---

[3]Repealed by the Seventeenth Amendment, Section 1.
[4]Changed by the Seventeenth Amendment.

removal from Office, and disqualification to hold and enjoy any Office of honor, Trust or Profit under the United States: but the Party convicted shall nevertheless be liable and subject to Indictment, Trial, Judgment and Punishment according to Law.

Section 4. [1] The Times, Places and Manner of holding Elections for Senators and Representatives, shall be prescribed in each State by the Legislature thereof; but the Congress may at any time by Law make or alter such Regulations, except as to the Places of Choosing Senators.

[2] The Congress shall assemble at least once in every Year, and such Meeting shall [be on the first Monday in December,][5] unless they shall by Law appoint a different Day.

Section 5. [1] Each House shall be the Judge of the Elections, Returns and Qualifications of its own Members, and a Majority of each shall constitute a Quorum to do Business; but a smaller number may adjourn from day to day, and may be authorized to compel the Attendance of absent Members, in such Manner, and under such Penalties as each House may provide.

[2] Each House may determine the Rules of its Proceedings, punish its Members for disorderly Behavior, and, with the Concurrence of two thirds, expel a Member.

[3] Each House shall keep a Journal of its Proceedings, and from time to time publish the same, excepting such Parts as may in their Judgment require Secrecy; and the Yeas and Nays of the Members of either House on any question shall, at the Desire of one fifth of those Present, be entered on the Journal.

[4] Neither House, during the Session of Congress, shall, without the Consent of the other, adjourn for more than three days, nor to any other Place than that in which the two Houses shall be sitting.

Section 6. [1] The Senators and Representatives shall receive a Compensation for their Services, to be ascertained by Law, and paid out of the Treasury of the United States. They shall in all Cases, except Treason, Felony and Breach of the Peace, be privileged from Arrest during their Attendance at the Session of their respective Houses, and in going to and returning from the same; and for any Speech or Debate in either House, they shall not be questioned in any other Place.

[2] No Senator or Representative shall, during the Time for which he was elected, be appointed to any civil Office under the Authority of the United States, which shall have been created, or the Emoluments whereof have been increased during such time; and no Person holding any Office

---

[5]Changed by the Twentieth Amendment, Section 2.

under the United States, shall be a Member of either House during his Continuance in Office.

Section 7. [1] All Bills for raising Revenue shall originate in the House of Representatives; but the Senate may propose or concur with Amendments as on other Bills.

[2] Every Bill which shall have passed the House of Representatives and the Senate, shall, before it become a Law, be presented to the President of the United States; If he approve he shall sign it, but if not he shall return it, with his Objections to that House in which it shall have originated, who shall enter the Objections at large on their Journal, and proceed to reconsider it. If after such Reconsideration two thirds of that House shall agree to pass the Bill, it shall be sent, together with the Objections, to the other House, by which it shall likewise be reconsidered, and if approved by two thirds of that House, it shall become a Law. But in all such Cases the Votes of both Houses shall be determined by Yeas and Nays, and the Names of the Persons voting for and against the Bill shall be entered on the Journal of each House respectively. If any Bill shall not be returned by the President within ten Days (Sundays excepted) after it shall have been presented to him, the Same shall be a Law, in like Manner as if he had signed it, unless the Congress by their Adjournment prevent its Return, in which Case it shall not be a Law.

[3] Every Order, Resolution, or Vote to which the Concurrence of the Senate and House of Representatives may be necessary (except on a question of Adjournment) shall be presented to the President of the United States; and before the Same shall take Effect, shall be approved by him, or being disapproved by him, shall be repassed by two thirds of the Senate and House of Representatives, according to the Rules and Limitations prescribed in the Case of a Bill.

Section 8. [1] The Congress shall have Power To lay and collect Taxes, Duties, Imposts and Excises, to pay the Debts and provide for the common Defense and general Welfare of the United States; but all Duties, Imposts and Excises shall be uniform throughout the United States;

[2] To borrow money on the credit of the United States;

[3] To regulate Commerce with foreign Nations, and among the several States, and with the Indian Tribes;

[4] To establish an uniform Rule of Naturalization, and uniform Laws on the subject of Bankruptcies throughout the United States;

[5] To coin Money, regulate the Value thereof, and of foreign Coin, and fix the Standard of Weights and Measures;

[6] To provide for the Punishment of counterfeiting the Securities and current Coin of the United States;

[7] To establish Post Offices and post Roads;

[8] To promote the Progress of Science and useful Arts, by securing for limited Times to Authors and Inventors the exclusive Right to their respective Writings and Discoveries;

[9] To constitute Tribunals inferior to the supreme Court;

[10] To define and punish Piracies and Felonies committed on the high Seas, and Offences against the Law of Nations;

[11] To declare War, grant Letters of Marque and Reprisal, and make Rules concerning Captures on Land and Water;

[12] To raise and support Armies, but no Appropriation of Money to that Use shall be for a longer Term than two Years;

[13] To provide and maintain a Navy;

[14] To make rules for the Government and Regulation of the land and naval Forces;

[15] To provide for calling forth the Militia to execute the Laws of the Union, suppress Insurrections and repel Invasions;

[16] To provide for organizing, arming, and disciplining the Militia, and for governing such Part of them as may be employed in the Service of the United States, reserving to the States respectively, the Appointment of the Officers, and the Authority of training the Militia according to the discipline prescribed by Congress;

[17] To exercise exclusive Legislation in all Cases whatsoever, over such District (not exceeding ten Miles square) as may, by Cession of particular States, and the acceptance of Congress, become the Seat of the Government of the United States, and to exercise like Authority over all Places purchased by the Consent of the Legislature of the State in which the Same shall be, for the Erection of Forts, Magazines, Arsenals, dock-Yards, and other needful Buildings; — And

[18] To make all Laws which shall be necessary and proper for carrying into Execution the foregoing Powers, and all other Powers vested by this Constitution in the Government of the United States, or in any Department or Officer thereof.

Section 9. [1] The Migration or Importation of such Persons as any of the States now existing shall think proper to admit, shall not be prohibited by the Congress prior to the Year one thousand eight hundred and eight, but a tax or duty may be imposed on such Importation, not exceeding ten dollars for each Person.

[2] The privilege of the Writ of Habeas Corpus shall not be suspended, unless when in Cases of Rebellion or Invasion the public Safety may require it.

[3] No Bill of Attainder or ex post facto Law shall be passed.

[4] No capitation, or other direct, Tax shall be laid, unless in Proportion to the Census or Enumeration herein before directed to be taken.[6]

---

[6]Changed by the Sixteenth Amendment.

[5] No Tax or Duty shall be laid on Articles exported from any State.

[6] No Preference shall be given by any Regulation of Commerce or Revenue to the Ports of one State over those of another: nor shall Vessels bound to, or from, one State, be obliged to enter, clear, or pay Duties in another.

[7] No Money shall be drawn from the Treasury, but in Consequence of Appropriations made by Law; and a regular Statement and Account of the Receipts and Expenditures of all public Money shall be published from time to time.

[8] No Title of Nobility shall be granted by the United States: And no Person holding any Office of Profit or Trust under them, shall, without the Consent of the Congress, accept of any present, Emolument, Office, or Title, of any kind whatever, from any King, Prince, or foreign State.

Section 10. [1] No State shall enter into any Treaty, Alliance, or Confederation; grant Letters of Marque and Reprisal; coin Moncy; emit Bills of Credit; make any Thing but gold and silver Coin a Tender in Payment of Debts; pass any Bill of Attainder, ex post facto Law, or Law impairing the Obligation of Contracts, or grant any Title of Nobility.

[2] No State shall, without the Consent of the Congress, lay any Imposts or Duties on Imports or Exports, except what may be asolutely necessary for executing its inspection Laws: and the net Produce of all Duties and Imposts, laid by any State on Imports or Exports, shall be for the Use of the Treasury of the United States; and all such Laws shall be subject to the Revision and Control of the Congress.

[3] No State shall, without the Consent of Congress, lay any duty of Tonnage, keep Troops, or Ships of War in time of Peace, enter into any Agreement or Compact with another State, or with a foreign Power, or engage in War, unless actually invaded, or in such imminent Danger as will not admit of delay.

ARTICLE II

Section 1. [1] The executive Power shall be vested in a President of the United States of America. He shall hold his Office during the Term of four Years, and, together with the Vice-President, chosen for the same Term, be elected, as follows

[2] Each State shall appoint, in such Manner as the Legislature thereof may direct, a Number of Electors, equal to the whole Number of Senators and Representatives to which the State may be entitled in the Congress; but no Senator or Representative, or Person holding an Office of Trust or Profit under the United States, shall be appointed an Elector.

[The Electors shall meet in their respective States, and vote by Ballot for two persons, of whom one at least shall not be an Inhabitant of the same

State with themselves. And they shall make a List of all the Persons voted for, and of the Number of Votes for each; which List they shall sign and certify, and transmit sealed to the Seat of the Government of the United States, directed to the President of the Senate. The President of the Senate shall, in the Presence of the Senate and House of Representatives, open all the Certificates, and the Votes shall then be counted. The Person having the greatest Number of Votes shall be the President, if such Number be a Majority of the whole Number of Electors appointed; and if there be more than one who have such Majority, and have an equal Number of Votes, then the House of Representatives shall immediately choose by Ballot one of them for President; and if no Person have a Majority, then from the five highest on the List the said House shall in like Manner choose the President. But in choosing the President, the Votes shall be taken by States, the Representation from each State having one Vote; A quorum for this Purpose shall consist of a Member or Members from two-thirds of the States, and a Majority of all the States shall be necessary to a Choice. In every Case, after the Choice of the President, the Person having the greatest Number of Votes of the Electors shall be the Vice-President. But if there should remain two or more who have equal Votes, the Senate shall choose from them by Ballot the Vice-President.][7]

[3] The Congress may determine the Time of choosing the Electors, and the Day on which they shall give their Votes; which Day shall be the same throughout the United States.

[4] No person except a natural born Citizen, or a Citizen of the United States, at the time of the Adoption of this Constitution, shall be eligible to the Office of President; neither shall any Person be eligible to that Office who shall not have attained to the Age of thirty-five Years, and been fourteen Years a Resident within the United States.

[5] In case of the Removal of the President from Office, or of his Death, Resignation, or Inability to discharge the Powers and Duties of the said Office, the same shall devolve on the Vice-President, and the Congress may by Law provide for the Case of Removal, Death, Resignation or Inability, both of the President and Vice-President, declaring what Officer shall then act as President, and such Officer shall act accordingly, until the Disability be removed, or a President shall be elected.[8]

[6] The President shall, at stated Times, receive for his Services, a Compensation, which shall neither be increased nor diminished during the Period for which he shall have been elected, and he shall not receive within that Period any other Emolument from the United States, or any of them.

[7] Before he enter on the Execution of his Office, he shall take the following Oath or Affirmation: — "I do solemnly swear (or affirm) that I will

---

[7]This paragraph was superseded in 1804 by the Twelfth Amendment.

[8]Changed by the Twenty-fifth Amendment.

faithfully execute the Office of President of the United States, and will to the best of my Ability, preserve, protect and defend the Constitution of the United States."

Section 2. [1] The President shall be Commander in Chief of the Army and Navy of the United States, and of the Militia of the several States, when called into the actual Service of the United States; he may require the Opinion in writing, of the principal Officer in each of the executive Departments, upon any subject relating to the Duties of their respective Offices, and he shall have Power to Grant Reprieves and Pardons for Offenses against the United States, except in Cases of Impeachment.

[2] He shall have Power, by and with the Advice and Consent of the Senate, to make Treaties, provided two-thirds of the Senators present concur; and he shall nominate, and by and with the Advice and Consent of the Senate, shall appoint Ambassadors, other public Ministers and Consuls, Judges of the supreme Court, and all other Officers of the United States, whose Appointments are not herein otherwise provided for, and which shall be established by Law: but the Congress may by Law vest the Appointment of such inferior Officers, as they think proper, in the President alone, in the Court of Law, or in the Heads of Departments.

[3] The President shall have Power to fill up all Vacancies that may happen during the Recess of the Senate, by granting Commissions which shall expire at the End of their next Session.

Section 3. He shall from time to time give to the Congress Information of the State of the Union, and recommend to their Consideration such Measures as he shall judge necessary and expedient; he may, on extraordinary Occasions, convene both Houses, or either of them, and in Case of Disagreement between them, with Respect to the Time of Adjournment, he may adjourn them to such Time as he shall think proper; he shall receive Ambassadors and other public Ministers; he shall take Care that the Laws be faithfully executed, and shall Commission all the Officers of the United States.

Section 4. The President, Vice President and all civil Officers of the United States, shall be removed from Office on Impeachment for, and Conviction of, Treason, Bribery, or other high Crimes and Misdemeanors.

ARTICLE III

Section 1. The judicial Power of the United States, shall be vested in one supreme Court, and in such inferior Courts as the Congress may from time to time ordain and establish. The Judges, both of the supreme and inferior Courts, shall hold their Offices during good Behavior, and shall, at stated

Times, receive for their Services a Compensation which shall not be diminished during their Continuance in Office.

Section 2. [1] The judicial Power shall extend to all Cases, in Law and Equity, arising under this Constitution, the Laws of the United States, and Treaties made, or which shall be made, under their Authority;—to all Cases affecting Ambassadors, other public Ministers and Consuls;—to all Cases of admiralty and maritime Jurisdiction;—to Controversies to which the United States shall be a Party;—to Controversies between two or more States;—[between a State and Citizens of another State];[9]—between Citizens of different States;—between Citizens of the same State claiming Lands under Grants of different States, and [between a State, or the Citizens thereof, and foreign States, Citizens or Subjects].[10]

[2] In all Cases affecting Ambassadors, other public Ministers and Consuls, and those in which a State shall be Party, the supreme Court shall have original Jurisdiction. In all the other Cases before mentioned, the supreme Court shall have appellate Jurisdiction, both as to Law and Fact, with such Exceptions, and under such Regulations as the Congress shall make.

[3] The trial of all Crimes, except in Cases of Impeachment, shall be by Jury; and such Trial shall be held in the State where the said Crimes shall have been committed: but when not committed within any State, the Trial shall be at such Place or Places as the Congress may by Law have directed.

Section 3. [1] Treason against the United States, shall consist only in levying War against them, or in adhering to their Enemies, giving them Aid and Comfort. No Person shall be convicted of Treason unless on the Testimony of two Witnesses to the same overt Act, or on Confession in open Court.

[2] The Congress shall have power to declare the Punishment of Treason, but no Attainder of Treason shall work Corruption of Blood, or Forfeiture except during the Life of the Person attained.

ARTICLE IV

Section 1. Full Faith and Credit shall be given in each State to the public Acts, Records, and judicial Proceedings of every other State. And the Congress may by general Laws prescribe the Manner in which such Acts, Records and Proceedings shall be proved, and the Effect thereof.

Section 2. [1] The Citizens of each State shall be entitled to all Privileges and Immunities of Citizens in the several States.

---

[9]Restricted by the Eleventh Amendment.
[10]Restricted by the Eleventh Amendment.

[2] A Person charged in any State with Treason, Felony, or other Crime, who shall flee from Justice, and be found in another State, shall on demand of the executive Authority of the State from which he fled, be delivered up, to be removed to the State having Jurisdiction of the Crime.

[3] [No Person held to Service or Labor in one State, under the Laws thereof, escaping into another, shall, in Consequence of any Law or Regulation therein, be discharged from such Service or Labor, but shall be delivered up on Claim of the Party to whom such Service or Labor may be due.][11]

Section 3. [1] New States may be admitted by the Congress into this Union; but no new State shall be formed or erected within the Jurisdiction of any other State; nor any State be formed by the Junction of two or more States, or parts of States, without the Consent of the Legislatures of the States concerned as well as of the Congress.

[2] The Congress shall have Power to dispose of and make all needful rules and Regulations respecting the Territory or other Property belonging to the United States; and nothing in this Constitution shall be so construed as to Prejudice any Claims of the United States, or of any particular State.

Section 4. The United States shall guarantee to every State in this Union a Republican Form of Government, and shall protect each of them against Invasion; and on Application of the Legislature, or of the Executive (when the Legislature cannot be convened) against domestic Violence.

ARTICLE V

The Congress, whenever two-thirds of both Houses shall deem it necessary, shall propose Amendments to this Constitution, or, on the Application of the Legislatures of two-thirds of the several States, shall call a Convention for proposing Amendments, which, in either Case, shall be valid to all Intents and Purposes, as part of this Constitution, when ratified by the Legislature of three-fourths of the several States, or by Conventions in three-fourths thereof, as the one or the other Mode of Ratification may be proposed by the Congress; Provided that no Amendment which may be made prior to Year One thousand eight hundred and eight shall in any Manner affect the first and fourth Clauses in the Ninth Section of the first Article; and that no State, without its Consent, shall be deprived of its equal Suffrage in the Senate.

---

[11]This paragraph has been superseded by the Thirteenth Amendment.

ARTICLE VI

[1] All Debts contracted and Engagements entered into, before the Adoption of this Constitution, shall be as valid against the United States under this Constitution, as under the Confederation.

[2] This Constitution, and the Laws of the United States which shall be made in Pursuance thereof; and all Treaties made, or which shall be made, under the Authority of the United States, shall be the supreme Law of the Land; and the Judges in every State shall be bound thereby, any Thing in the Constitution or Laws of any State to the Contrary notwithstanding.

[3] The Senators and Representatives before mentioned, and the Members of the several State Legislatures, and all executive and judicial Officers, both of the United States and of the several States, shall be bound by Oath or Affirmation, to support this Constitution; but no religious Test shall ever be required as a Qualification to any Office or public Trust under the United States.

ARTICLE VII

The Ratification of the conventions of nine States, shall be sufficient for the Establishment of this Constitution between the States so ratifying the Same.

DONE   in Convention by the Unanimous Consent of the States present the Seventeenth Day of September in the Year of our Lord one thousand seven hundred and Eighty seven and the Independence of the United States of America the Twelfth. In Witness whereof We have hereunto subscribed our Names,

Gº WASHINGTON
President and deputy from Virginia

Articles in Addition to, and Amendment of, the Constitution of the United States of America, Proposed by Congress, and Ratified by the Legislatures of the Several States, Pursuant to the Fifth Article of the Original Constitution.

ARTICLE I[12]

Congress shall make no law respecting an establishment of religion, or prohibiting the free exercise thereof; or abridging the freedom of speech, or of the press; or the right of the people peaceably to assemble, and to petition the Government for a redress of grievances.

---

[12]The first ten amendments were adopted in 1791.

ARTICLE II

A well regulated Militia, being necessary to the security of a free State, the right of the people to keep and bear Arms, shall not be infringed.

ARTICLE III

No Soldier shall, in time of peace be quartered in any house, without the consent of the Owner, nor in time of war, but in a manner to be prescribed by law.

ARTICLE IV

The right of the people to be secure in their persons, houses, papers, and effects, against unreasonable searches and seizures, shall not be violated, and no Warrants shall issue, but upon probable cause, supported by Oath or affirmation, and particularly describing the place to be searched, and the persons or things to be seized.

ARTICLE V

No person shall be held to answer for a capital, or otherwise infamous crime, unless on a presentment or indictment of a Grand Jury, except in cases arising in the land or naval forces, or in the Militia, when in actual service in time of War or public danger; nor shall any person be subject for the same offence to be twice put in jeopardy of life or limb; nor shall be compelled in any criminal case to be witness against himself, nor be deprived of life, liberty, or property, without due process of law; nor shall private property be taken for public use, without just compensation.

ARTICLE VI

In all criminal prosecutions, the accused shall enjoy the right to a speedy and public trial, by an impartial jury of the State and district wherein the crime shall have been committed, which district shall have been previously ascertained by law, and to be informed of the nature and cause of the accusation; to be confronted with the witnesses against him; to have compulsory process for obtaining witnesses in his favor, and to have the Assistance of Counsel for his defence.

ARTICLE VII

In suits at common law, where the value in controversy shall exceed twenty dollars, the right of trial by jury shall be preserved, and no fact tried by a jury, shall be otherwise reexamined in any Court of the United States, than according to the rules of the common law.

ARTICLE VIII

Excessive bail shall not be required, nor excessive fines imposed, nor cruel and unusual punishments inflicted.

ARTICLE IX

The enumeration in the Constitution, of certain rights, shall not be construed to deny or disparage others retained by the people.

ARTICLE X

The powers not delegated to the United States by the Constitution, nor prohibited by it to the States, are reserved to the States respectively, or to the people.

ARTICLE XI[13]

The Judicial power of the United States shall not be construed to extend to any suit in law or equity, commenced or prosecuted against one of the United States by Citizens of another State, or by Citizens or Subjects of any Foreign State.

ARTICLE XII[14]

The Electors shall meet in their respective states and vote by ballot for President and Vice-President, one of whom, at least, shall not be an inhabitant of the same state with themselves; they shall name in their ballots the person voted for as President, and in distinct ballots the person voted for as Vice-President, and they shall make distinct lists of all persons voted for as President, and of all persons voted for as Vice-President, and of the number of votes for each, which lists they shall sign and certify, and transmit sealed to the seat of the government of the United States, directed to the President of the Senate;—The President of the Senate shall, in

---

[13]Adopted in 1798.
[14]Adopted in 1804.

presence of the Senate and House of Representatives, open all the certificates and the votes shall then be counted; — The person having the greatest number of votes for President, shall be the President, if such number be a majority of the whole number of Electors appointed; and if no person have such majority, then from the persons having the highest numbers not exceeding three on the list of those voted for as President, the House of Representatives shall choose immediately, by ballot, the President. But in choosing the President, the votes shall be taken by states, the representation from each state having one vote; a quorum for this purpose shall consist of a member or members from two-thirds of the states, and a majority of all the states shall be necessary to a choice. [And if the House of Representatives shall not choose a President whenever the right of choice shall devolve upon them, before the fourth day of March next following, then the Vice-President shall act as President, as in the case of the death or other constitutional disability of the President.][15] — The person having the greatest number of votes as Vice-President, shall be the Vice-President, if such number be a majority of the whole number of Electors appointed, and if no person have a majority, then from the two highest numbers on the list, the Senate shall choose the Vice-President; a quorum for the purpose shall consist of two-thirds of the whole number of Senators, and a majority of the whole number shall be necessary to a choice. But no person constitutionally ineligible to the office of President shall be eligible to that of Vice-President of the United States.

ARTICLE XIII[16]

Section 1. Neither slavery nor involuntary servitude, except as a punishment for crime whereof the party shall have been duly convicted, shall exist within the United States, or any place subject to their jurisdiction.

Section 2. Congress shall have power to enforce this article by appropriate legislation.

ARTICLE XIV[17]

Section 1. All persons born or naturalized in the United States, and subject to the jurisdiction thereof, are citizens of the United States and of the State wherein they reside. No state shall make or enforce any law which shall abridge the privileges or immunities of citizens of the United States; nor shall any State deprive any person of life, liberty, or property, without due

---

[15]Superseded by the Twentieth Amendment, Section 3.
[16]Adopted in 1865.
[17]Adopted in 1868.

process of law; nor deny to any person within its jurisdiction the equal protection of the laws.

Section 2. Representatives shall be apportioned among the several States according to their respective numbers, counting the whole number of persons in each State, excluding Indians not taxed. But when the right to vote at any election for the choice of electors for President and Vice-President of the United States, Representatives in Congress, the Executive and Judicial officers of a State, or the members of the Legislature thereof, is denied to any of the male inhabitants of such State, being twenty-one years of age, and citizens of the United States, or in any way abridged, except for participation in rebellion, or other crime, the basis of representation therein shall be reduced in the proportion which the number of such male citizens shall bear to the whole number of male citizens twenty-one years of age in such State.

Section 3. No person shall be a Senator or Representative in Congress, or elector of President and Vice-President, or hold any office, civil or military, under the United States, or under any State, who, having previously taken an oath, as a member of Congress, or as an officer of the United States, or as a member of any State legislature, or as an executive or judicial officer of any State, to support the Constitution of the United States, shall have engaged in insurrection or rebellion against the same, or given aid or comfort to the enemies thereof. But Congress may by a vote of two-thirds of each House, remove such disability.

Section 4. The validity of the public debt of the United States, authorized by law, including debts incurred for payment of pensions and bounties for services in suppressing insurrection or rebellion, shall not be questioned. But neither the United States nor any State shall assume or pay any debt or obligation incurred in aid of insurrection or rebellion against the United States, or any claim for the loss or emancipation of any slave; but all such debts, obligations and claims shall be held illegal and void.

Section 5. The Congress shall have power to enforce, by appropriate legislation, the provisions of this article.

ARTICLE XV[18]

Section 1. The right of citizens of the United States to vote shall not be denied or abridged by the United States or by any State on account of race, color, or previous condition of servitude—

---

[18]Adopted in 1870.

Section 2. The Congress shall have power to enforce this article by appropriate legislation.

ARTICLE XVI[19]

The Congress shall have power to lay and collect taxes on incomes, from whatever source derived, without apportionment among the several States, and without regard to any census or enumeration.

ARTICLE XVII[20]

The Senate of the United States shall be composed of two Senators from each State, elected by the people thereof, for six years; and each Senator shall have one vote. The electors in each State shall have the qualifications requisite for electors of the most numerous branch of the State legislatures.

When vacancies happen in the representation of any State in the Senate, the executive authority of such State shall issue writs of election to fill such vacancies: *Provided,* That the legislature of any State may empower the executive thereof to make temporary appointments until the people fill the vacancies by election as the legislature may direct.

This amendment shall not be so construed as to affect the election or term of any Senator chosen before it becomes valid as part of the Constitution.

ARTICLE XVIII[21]

Section 1. After one year from the ratification of this article the manufacture, sale, or transportation of intoxicating liquors within, the importation thereof into, or the exportation thereof from the United States and all territory subject to the jurisdiction thereof for beverage purposes is hereby prohibited.

Section 2. The Congress and the several States shall have concurrent power to enforce this article by appropriate legislation.

Section 3. This article shall be inoperative unless it shall have been ratified as an amendment to the Constitution by the legislatures of the several States, as provided in the Constitution, within seven years from the date of the submission hereof to the States by the Congress.

---

[19]Adopted in 1913.
[20]Adopted in 1913.
[21]Adopted in 1919. Repealed by Section 1 of the Twenty-first Amendment.

ARTICLE XIX[22]

The right of citizens of the United States to vote shall not be denied or abridged by the United States or by any State on account of sex.

Congress shall have power to enforce this article by appropriate legislation.

ARTICLE XX[23]

Section 1. The terms of the President and Vice-President shall end at noon on the 20th day of January, and the terms of Senators and Representatives at noon on the 3d day of January, of the years in which such terms would have ended if this article had not been ratified; and the terms of their successors shall then begin.

Section 2. The Congress shall assemble at least once in every year, and such meeting shall begin at noon on the 3d day of January, unless they shall by law appoint a different day.

Section 3. If, at the time fixed for the beginning of the term of the President, the president elect shall have died, the Vice-President elect shall become President. If a President shall not have been chosen before the time fixed for the beginning of his term, or if the President elect shall have failed to qualify, then the Vice-President elect shall act as President until a President shall have qualified; and the Congress may by law provide for the case wherein neither a President elect nor a Vice-President elect shall have qualified, declaring who shall then act as President, or the manner in which one who is to act shall be selected, and such person shall act accordingly until a President or Vice-President shall have qualified.

Section 4. The Congress may by law provide for the case of the death of any of the persons from whom the House of Representatives may choose a President whenever the right of choice shall have devolved upon them, and for the case of the death of any of the persons from whom the Senate may choose a Vice-President whenever the right of choice shall have devolved upon them.

Section 5. Sections 1 and 2 shall take effect on the 15th day of October following the ratification of this article.

Section 6. This article shall be inoperative unless it shall have been ratified

---

[22]Adopted in 1920.
[23]Adopted in 1933.

as an amendment to the Constitution by the legislatures of three-fourths of the several States within seven years from the date of its submission.

ARTICLE XXI[24]

Section 1. The eighteenth article of amendment to the Constitution of the United States is hereby repealed.

Section 2. The transportation or importation into any State, Territory, or possession of the United States for delivery or use therein of intoxicating liquors, in violation of the laws thereof, is hereby prohibited.

Section 3. This article shall be inoperative unless it shall have been ratified as an amendment to the Constitution by conventions in the several States, as provided in the Constitution, within seven years from the date of the submission hereof to the States by the Congress.

ARTICLE XXII[25]

Section 1. No person shall be elected to the office of the President more than twice, and no person who has held the office of President, or acted as President, for more than two years of a term to which some other person was elected President shall be elected to the office of the President more than once. But this Article shall not apply to any person holding the office of President when this Article was proposed by the Congress, and shall not prevent any person who may be holding the office of President, or acting as President, during the term within which this Article becomes operative from holding the office of President or acting as President during the remainder of such term.

Section 2. This article shall be inoperative unless it shall have been ratified as an amendment to the Constitution by the legislatures of three-fourths of the several States within seven years from the date of its submission to the States by the Congress.

ARTICLE XXIII[26]

Section 1. The District constituting the seat of Government of the United States shall appoint in such manner as the Congress may direct:
    A number of electors of President and Vice-President equal to the

[24]Adopted in 1933.
[25]Adopted in 1951.
[26]Adopted in 1961.

whole number of Senators and Representatives in Congress to which the District would be entitled if it were a State, but in no event more than the least populous State; they shall be in addition to those appointed by the States, but they shall be considered, for the purposes of the election of President and Vice-President, to be electors appointed by a State; and they shall meet in the District and perform such duties as provided by the twelfth article of amendment.

Section 2. The Congress shall have power to enforce this article by appropriate legislation.

ARTICLE XXIV[27]

Section 1. The right of citizens of the United States to vote in any primary or other election for President or Vice-President, for electors for President or Vice-President, or for Senator or Representative in Congress, shall not be denied or abridged by the United States or any state by reasons of failure to pay any poll tax or other tax.

Section 2. The Congress shall have power to enforce this article by appropriate legislation.

ARTICLE XXV[28]

Section 1. In case of the removal of the President from office or of his death or resignation, the Vice-President shall become President.

Section 2. Whenever there is a vacancy in the office of the Vice-President, the President shall nominate a Vice-President who shall take office upon confirmation by a majority vote of both Houses of Congress.

Section 3. Whenever the President transmits to the President pro tempore of the Senate and the Speaker of the House of Representatives his written declaration that he is unable to discharge the powers and duties of his office, and until he transmits to them a written declaration to the contrary, such powers and duties shall be discharged by the Vice-President as Acting President.

Section 4. Whenever the Vice-President and a majority of either the principal officers of the Executive departments or of such other body as Congress may by law provide transmit to the President pro tempore of the

---

[27]Adopted in 1964.
[28]Adopted in 1967.

Senate and the Speaker of the House of Representatives their written declaration that the President is unable to discharge the powers and duties of his office, the Vice-President shall immediately assume the powers and duties of the office as Acting President.

Thereafter, when the President transmits to the President pro tempore of the Senate and the Speaker of the House of Representatives his written declaration that no inability exists, he shall resume the powers and duties of his office unless the Vice-President and a majority of either the principal officers of the Executive departments or of such other body as Congress may by law provide transmit within four days to the President pro tempore of the Senate and the Speaker of the House of Representatives their written declaration that the President is unable to discharge the powers and duties of his office. Thereupon Congress shall decide the issue, assembling within forty-eight hours for that purpose if not in session. If the Congress, within twenty-one days after receipt of the latter written declaration, or, if Congress is not in session, within twenty-one days after Congress is required to assemble, determines by two-thirds vote of both houses that the President is unable to discharge the powers and duties of his office, the Vice-President shall continue to discharge the same as Acting President; otherwise, the President shall resume the powers and duties of his office.

ARTICLE XXVI[29]

Section 1. The right of citizens of the United States, who are 18 years of age or older, to vote shall not be denied or abridged by the United States or any state on account of age.

Section 2. The Congress shall have power to enforce this article by appropriate legislation.

---

[29]Adopted in 1971.